AF352725

Letter-Writing Manuals and Instruction from Antiquity to the Present

Letter-Writing Manuals and Instruction
from Antiquity to the Present

Historical and Bibliographic Studies

Edited by

Carol Poster and Linda C. Mitchell

The University of South Carolina Press

Published by the University of South Carolina Press
Columbia, South Carolina 29208

uscpress.com

Printed in the United States of America

Library of Congress Cataloging-in-Publication Data

Letter-writing manuals and instruction from antiquity to the present : historical and bibliographic studies / edited by Carol Poster and Linda C. Mitchell.
    p. cm. — (Studies in rhetoric/communication)
  Includes bibliographical references and index.
  ISBN-13: 978-1-57003-651-4 (cloth : alk. paper)
  ISBN-10: 1-57003-651-9 (cloth : alk. paper)
  1. Letter writing—History. 2. Letter writing—Handbooks, manuals, etc. I. Poster, Carol. II. Mitchell, Linda C.
  PN4400.L45 2007
  808.6—dc22

                                                   2006032828

Contents

Series Editor's Preface

Letter-Writing Manuals and Instruction from Antiquity to the Present tells the story of what might be called a latent discipline of epistolary theory and practice, with a more or less continuous history of scholarship and practice from Isocrates to e-mail. *Epistolarity,* as a scholarly field, has been a thriving but in many ways invisible subject of scholarly inquiry, since it has not in the present day been wholeheartedly adopted as part of the central disciplinary knowledge of the reigning academic disciplines in higher education, though it is present in many—rhetoric, literary studies, classics, biblical scholarship, literacy, composition studies, grammar, sociology, history, women's studies, and others. And yet, as the editors and authors of *Letter-Writing Manuals and Instruction* show in this collection of historical, theoretical, and bibliographical essays—the first modern attempt to bring together the scholarship and make it accessible to the disciplines from which it has emerged—there is a rich tradition of scholarship and a potentially rich field for further scholarly inquiry.

The editors conceive of the field that they call *epistolarity,* the study of letter writing, as divided into two main branches—the study of letters themselves they call *epistolography;* the study of letter-writing theory and instruction they term *epistolary theory,* or they use the traditional term *dictamen.* The present collection concerns itself primarily with the history of letter-writing theory and instruction, in manuals (*artes dictandi*), which may be *formularies,* with examples of model letters, or prescriptive guides to letter writing. In addition the authors sometimes venture into epistolography to recover from actual letters the implicit forms that in turn suggest the underlying theory and instruction that made possible their original creation and reception.

Letter-Writing Manuals and Instruction is a comprehensive, authoritative, and groundbreaking work, providing a comprehensive and refounded history of letter-writing instruction. Every chapter provides extensive bibliographic and historical access to the sources, and a series of appendixes brings together a substantial bibliography of letter-writing manuals and interdisciplinary scholarship.

Thomas W. Benson

Preface

This volume demonstrates the timelessness and universality of letter writing. Letter-writing manuals and their predecessors served to instruct individuals not only on the art of letter composition but also, in effect, on personal conduct. Carol Poster and Linda C. Mitchell contend that the study of letter-writing theory, which bridges rhetorical theory and grammatical studies, represents an emerging discipline in need of definition. In this volume they gather the contributions of eleven experts to sketch the contours of epistolary theory and collect the historic and bibliographic materials that form the basis for its study. In the introduction Carol Poster sets the stage by showing that letter writing is both a rich and, paradoxically, neglected field of scholarly inquiry. She provides an historical context and outlines the terminology, definition, and scope of the field.

"Classical Epistolary Theory and the Letters of Isocrates," by Robert G. Sullivan, extends our knowledge of ancient epistolary theory into the Greek classical era by examining the precepts for letter writing laid down by the Attic rhetorician Isocrates.

Because contemporary rhetorical scholarship generally has not addressed ancient epistolary theory, "A Conversation Halved: Epistolary Theory in Graeco-Roman Antiquity," by Carol Poster, provides an overview of the field for rhetoricians and other scholars unfamiliar with the major issues and texts involved in reconstruction of ancient epistolary theory.

"The *Ars dictaminis,* the Formulary, and Medieval Epistolary Practice," by Malcolm Richardson, shows how the epistolary art of the Middle Ages, or *Ars dictaminis,* rose to become a central part of medieval education but by the end of the period suddenly declined in importance.

"If You Can't Join Them, Beat Them; or, When Grammar Met Business Writing (in Fifteenth-Century Oxford)," by Martin Camargo, demonstrates that "turf wars" that were as common in medieval universities as in their modern descendants. Gideon Burton's "From *Ars dictaminis* to *Ars conscribendi epistolis:* Renaissance Letter-Writing Manuals in the Context of Humanism" shows how letter-writing manuals became associated less and less with the notarial arts and more and more with the *ars humanitatis* and the rhetorical pedagogy of the humanists. An established literary tradition was reinvented for use within the humanist program.

"Dictamen in England, 1500–1700," by Lawrence D. Green, details how the arts of letter writing in Renaissance England have their roots in the *medieval ars dictaminis* of Italy and in the emergent humanist interest in familiar letters as a mode of engagement with the larger culture. Throughout the period England remained heavily reliant on Continental ideas and materials, both Latin and vernacular, for formularies for both legal and social contexts, for teaching manuals, and for discussions of letter writing as a teachable art or occupation. The English imported a great many of their dictaminal materials, but they also published over a hundred titles of their own in different subgenres, and the readership was strong enough to support several hundred editions of these titles.

"Letter Writing and Vernacular Literacy in Sixteenth-Century England," by W. Webster Newbold, discusses letter writing in terms of its social, cultural, and educational aspects, focusing on the popular reception of the three earliest English letter-writing manuals. "Humanism and the Humanities: Erasmus's *Opus de conscribendis epistolis* in Sixteenth-Century Schools," by Judith Rice Henderson, unfolds the complex factors, including religious controversy, that produced a gap between humanist theory and pedagogy are traced in adaptations of Erasmus' influential treatise on letter writing by school teachers throughout the sixteenth century.

"Letter-Writing Instruction Manuals in Seventeenth- and Eighteenth-Century England," by Linda C. Mitchell, proceeds chronologically with the following themes: the sensible pedagogy beneath the manuals' sometimes quirky surfaces; the striking resemblances between seventeenth- and eighteenth-century methodologies and current practice; the persistent emphasis on letter writing as a practical skill for the rising classes; the declining emphasis on classical learning —whether knowledge of Latin or of classical rhetoric; and the authors' struggle to determine the proper materials and boundaries for the texts they are writing.

"Vestiges of Letter Writing in Composition Textbooks, 1850–1914," John T. Gage, surveys a large number of composition textbooks published between 1850 and 1914 to determine the extent to which letter writing is taught in such books and the range of approaches to letter writing they use, leading to some speculations about the effects of conventional formalism in a changing educational environment. "Letter Writing in the Late Age of Print: Electronic Mail and the *Ars dictaminis*," by Joyce R. Walker, focuses on the role of electronic mail in the long history of letter writing. The chapter primarily discusses the similarities and differences that can be found between the online guides presently available for e-mail users and past examples of the *ars dictaminis*. Although the differences might seem significant on the surface, one can find many similarities in the issues under consideration in these guides, regardless of the new electronic environment in which e-mail communications take place.

Acknowledgments

Every edited book is a collaboration among editors, contributors, and publisher. Carol Poster would like to thank her coeditor, Linda Mitchell, for her collaborative efforts; Martin Camargo, who introduced her to letter-writing theory when she was his doctoral student at University of Missouri, for instruction by both precept and example; Malcolm Heath for reading a draft of her contribution to this volume; the organizers and participants of the "Pepperdine" conferences on biblical rhetoric (especially Anders Eriksson, Vernon Robbins, Tom Olbright, Duane Watson, Greg Bloomquist, and Manfred Kraus) for introducing her to the massive and valuable contributions of the scholarly disciple of biblical studies to ancient epistolary theory and providing various forums in which she could present her own investigations of the field; the Project on Rhetoric of Inquiry of University of Iowa and the Tanner Humanities Center of University of Utah, for supporting extensive research on ancient rhetoric and epistolary theory; her previous institutional home, Florida State University, for grant support that aided in the production of this volume; and her current institution, the English department of York University.

Linda Mitchell is grateful to Lawrence D. Green (University of Southern California) for supervising her work in nascent form; Robert Cullen, Jameela Lares, Carol Poster, and E. D. Schragg for extensive comments on her essay; Andrea Camacho, Amber Hsu, Sam Khasin, Yvonne Luft, Carol Q. Mitchell, Christopher Mitchell, Jason Mitchell, John Mitchell, Michelle Perry, and Abir Ward for technical and logistical support; and Lou Eastman for organizing and printing the manuscript and for proofreading the final pages. For inspiration she thanks Melinda Flynn; Erma Jackson; martial arts instructors Kwan Jang Nims Ernie Reyes, Tony Thompson, Donna Bernardi, Dave Medina, and Bu Kwan Jang Nim Brian Go; Judith Sipple; and E. Jane Smith. She also thanks the staff of the William Andrews Clark Library, especially Suzanne Tatian, and Reader's Services at the Henry E. Huntington Library for their help in finding materials. Her work has been supported with generous grants from the College of Arts and Humanities at San José State University, the William Cordell Collection at Indiana State University, and the William Andrews Clark Library (UCLA), and her former institutional home Pepperdine University. She also thanks the Department of English and Comparative Literature at San José State University.

Both editors owe thanks to the extremely patient editors and staff at University of South Carolina Press and to all the contributors to the volume.

*Letter–Writing Manuals
and Instruction
from Antiquity to the Present*

Introduction

Carol Poster

If one were to look at the table of contents of any recent general history of rhetoric,[1] one would find no chapters devoted to letter-writing instruction or manuals. Examining recent essay collections that draw from the entire history of rhetoric and writing instruction would prove equally unproductive.[2] A review of scholarship including nonspecialist anthologies of primary texts and well-known period-specific monographs or collections of critical essays would yield only a few points of reference—for example, Murphy's translation of an anonymous medieval treatise reprinted from Murphy (1971) in Bizzell and Herzberg (1990), selections from the medieval *artes dictandi* in Miller, Prosser, and Benson (1973), several essays by medieval scholars, and a few by Renaissance scholars.[3] From this absence of histories of letter-writing instruction in modern scholarship one might assume that, in fact, letter writing was not a skill that was taught widely outside of the Middle Ages, but rather that letters were normally products of unconstrained personal creativity resulting from an untutored and spontaneous overflowing of language or emotion. Such an assumption, however, would be wrong.

Letter-writing instruction has existed in a well-attested tradition from the earliest known literate Western cultures to the present.[4] If people participated in any form of formal verbal composition at all, they were likely to have written letters or to have had letters written for them. A farmer in a small village in Roman Egypt or early modern England might never have given a speech in a legislative assembly or written a play or poem, but he or she well might have composed (whether by dictation or autograph writing) a note to a merchant in a neighboring town concerning the sale or purchase of goods, a familiar letter to a distant family member, or a complaint to an official concerning the theft of sheep. The epistolary tradition included the training of women who wrote family letters and invitations as well as the textbooks on Latinity of the Renaissance humanists, the training of street scribes and stenographers in antiquity as well as the schools of Quintilian and Libanius, the education of junior clerks as well as papal secretaries, and the village grammar schools as well as Oxford and Cambridge.

Even the writing of familiar letters was a learned skill, acquired in classes, from self-teaching manuals, or by imitation of models, while the skills necessary for writing commercial or bureaucratic letters were taught in numerous educational contexts. Just as letters themselves are probably the single-most-common genre of written discourse—even people who write nothing else may write letters (or, in recent decades, e-mail)—so letter-writing instruction often is interwoven even within the most basic of literacy classes. In light of the ubiquity of letters themselves and the broad diffusion of letter-writing instruction throughout literate education, the paucity of scholarly work on the topic requires explanation.

The central problem in studying the history of letter-writing instruction is one of disciplinarity, both historical and contemporary. For a subject to be written about by scholars for audiences outside narrow period or author specialties, it must be part of some disciplinary discourse, rhetoric, literary studies, sociology, women's studies, or some other identifiable field, with its associated conferences, journals, book series, and bibliographies. The history of letter writing in general, and letter-writing theory, specifically, lacks this sort of field definition.

Letter-writing theory exists at the margins of several other disciplines. Rhetoric, which originated as the study of the art of public speaking, has in common with letter-writing theory a focus on verbal practices, but the disciplines differ in several substantial ways:

1. Rhetoric is concerned with spoken language and letter writing with either written composition or the task of taking dictated materials and rewording them to follow elaborate conventions of letter composition (both verbal and visual).
2. Rhetoric discusses public (one-to-many) address, whereas letter-writing theory is concerned with private or semiprivate discourse.
3. Rhetorical theory examines overt argumentative and persuasive devices, but letter-writing theory emphasizes social affiliations (equal or hierarchical), assuming that conviction is based primarily on relationships rather than argument (e.g., presuming that, if one were to ask a favor of a friend, it would be granted not because one had included irrefutable syllogisms in a letter, but because of the friendship).
4. Rhetorical practice was limited in most periods to a small group of elite males; letter writing permeates a broader range of class and gender.

If letter writing was not part of the discipline of rhetoric,[5] it did not belong exclusively to grammar either. Although grammatical studies, which from antiquity through the nineteenth century would have been the discipline including elementary writing instruction, often had some epistolary components, letter writing was taught in many contexts outside the grammatical classroom. Scribal schools, stenography courses, slave schools, law schools, secretarial schools, and business schools all included, in various periods and places, some letter-writing training, and there were also stand-alone courses in letter writing. Outside formal schoolrooms, instruction on letter writing appeared in various forms of self-teaching or self-improvement manuals, including books on etiquette, universal educators, foreign language texts, tradesman's books, job-hunting manuals, typing manuals, and secretarial guides, along with such uniquely contemporary forms as netiquette guides, letter-templates, and model letters for one's personal computer.

The diffusion of letter-writing theory and practice through a variety of social classes and instructional contexts simultaneously makes it both a rich and, paradoxically, neglected field of scholarly inquiry. Insofar as letter-writing theory has been investigated as a subordinate subfield within disciplines such as rhetoric or literacy, it has been distorted radically by the alien disciplinary lenses through which it has been viewed; however, insofar as letter writing has not been included as the object of some disciplinary inquiry, it has almost unstudiable outside quite limited period specializations, for it has lacked all the necessarily preconditions for study—namely, disciplinary terminology and focus, bibliographies, editions of primary sources, venues for publication and presentation of scholarship, and even scholarly community. In a sense, letter-writing theory is a body of materials in search of a discipline. This book, therefore, is an attempt to collect the historic and bibliographic materials that form the basis for the study of epistolary theory. The chapters focus more on summarizing primary works and giving accounts of their historical and geographical distribution than on constructing broad critical theories about the materials.

The reason for the historical and bibliographic nature of the book is simple: this sort of preliminary ground work has not been done for the field. Whereas, for example, scholars interested in classical rhetoric can take Kennedy's work as a starting point, or medieval rhetoricians can rely on Murphy's introduction, or people just entering into the field of rhetoric can use sweeping histories by Kennedy (1980, 1994) or Conley (1990) to gain a sense of its broad historical contours, there is no equivalent work concerning epistolary theory. This book, therefore, sketches out some of the main historical contours of an emerging discipline.

Terminology, Definition, and Scope

One of the greatest difficulties scholars encounter in talking about the history of letter-writing instruction is the lack of standard disciplinary terminology. For this book, we realized that, because the largest single body of published scholarship on letter-writing theory per se is that concerning the medieval period, we should use some of the conventions developed by medieval scholars across our entire range of contributions.[6]

We divide the study of letter writing (or "epistolarity") into two parts: 1. Epistolography: the study of letters themselves. 2. Epistolary theory (or "dictamen"): the study of letter-writing theory and instruction.

This book is primarily concerned with subfield of epistolary theory, overlapping with epistolography only where study of letters results in information about letter formulae, which in turn can help us understand how letter writing was taught or theorized. Letter-writing manuals (*artes dictandi*) are of two types, prescriptive manuals and collections of model letters, which we term "formularies."

Although we would very much like to claim that we have, in a single collection of essays, defined the contours of an emerging discipline, provided a coherent and tightly knit set of essays on every major chronological, geographical, and theoretical subdivision of that discipline, and added at the end a comprehensive bibliography, we actually have done nothing of the sort.

Epistolary theory is indeed an emerging, rather than a fully emerged, area of study. Before any comprehensive treatments of it can be attempted, the field needs a vast amount of preliminary ground work, especially bio-bibliographical and textual. In this book we have assembled a collection of essays each treating in depth some one period of the history of epistolary theory. These essays have a strongly bibliographic orientation—they often focus primarily on sorting through and categorizing huge collections of primary materials that have rarely, if ever, been discussed in modern scholarship. Although we cover selected periods between antiquity and the early twentieth century, our coverage is necessarily incomplete, following, to some degree, the nature of surviving materials and the current state of scholarship.

Outside the specialized field of New Testament studies, ancient epistolary theory is almost absent from modern scholarship. Robert Sullivan begins our classical section with the highly original claim that we may find a coherent body of epistolary theory in Isocrates, dating the origin of the genre much earlier than has previous been suggested. He gives very detailed analyses of Isocrates' works to support the notion that epistolary theory was a well-defined body of knowledge in classical antiquity. Carol Poster, who summarizes later Greek and Latin works on epistolary theory, also sees a body of epistolary theory permeating ancient schooling, beyond what might be supposed from the limited amounts of available ancient evidence and modern scholarship. Malcolm Richardson surveys the field of medieval dictamen, providing an overview both of the current state of scholarship and the remaining work that needs to be done. Letter-writing manuals are placed in their educational context in fifteenth-century Oxford in Martin Camargo's chapter.

Renaissance epistolary theory consists of almost uncharted territory, but, because of the substantial number of available treatises and their importance as continuations of earlier traditions and emergence of new traditions, occupies a substantial portion of this book. Gideon Burton examines philology and letter-writing theory in the European Renaissance in relation to their medieval precursors. Lawrence Green discusses editions of letter-writing treatises in England in a bibliographic essay that shows how charting details of publication can help us understand the ways in which treatises were read and understood. The relationship between epistolarity and the rise of vernacular English literacy is the subject of Webster Newbold's essay. Judith Henderson investigates the actual uses of Erasmus's *Opus de conscribendi epistolis* in sixteenth-century schools, giving a rich description of what happened to this extremely influential treatise in actual practice and application.

Linda Mitchell shows how the early modern letter-writing instruction adds to the Renaissance model by becoming increasingly diverse in types and sites of instruction; she discusses epistolary theory in eloquence handbooks, self-teaching manuals, and grammar books. Our final essay is by John Gage, who surveys the patterns of inclusion and exclusion of letter-writing instruction from late nineteenth- and early twentieth-century composition textbooks. Joyce Walker's essay explores the idea that electronic medium is reviving the long neglected form of the epistolary tradition. The volume concludes with a very substantial collection of bibliographies on epistolary theory. We hope that these bibliographies and historical essays will provide scholars with the basic tools needed to further explore this fascinating group of materials, either insofar as epistolary theory can illuminate work in other disciplines or as part of an emerging discipline of the study of epistolarity.

Notes

1. For example, Conley (1990), Kennedy (1980, 1999), Murphy (1990), and Vickers (1990). The treatment of letter-writing theory in New Testament studies will be discussed in Carol Poster's chapter in this volume.

2. For example, Horner and Leff (1995), with the exception of parts of Martin Camargo's contribution, Murphy (1982), Poulakos (1993), and Vitanza (1994).

3. The best known of these would be the extended section in Murphy (1981) and selected essays in Mack (1994) and Murphy (1983). For an extended bibliography, primarily of works that would only be known to period specialists, see the relevant bibliographies at the end of this book.

4. Although this volume starts with classical antiquity, the tradition of letter-writing instruction began much earlier. The copying of royal letters appears to have been part of Sumerian scribal training (Kramer 1971, 36) and we have substantial evidence for Egyptian scribal training.

5. The relationship between letter-writing theory and rhetoric has been discussed mainly by New Testament scholars (see Sullivan's essay, this volume) and medieval scholars (see Richardson's essay, this volume). Most classical authors—for example, Ps.-Demetrius 229, in Malherbe (1988); Gregory of Nazianzus *Ep.* 51.5–7, in Malherbe (1988); Cicero *Ad Fam.* 9.21.1—contrast oratorical with epistolary style and letter-writing theory occurs in (1) letter-writing manuals (2) grammar texts (the epistolary excursus to Demetrius) (3) an appendix to Julius Victor's *Ars rhetorica;* in no case is it integrated into a rhetoric text. Although *dictamen* sometimes was seen as a subfield of rhetoric in the Middle Ages, it could be considered a separate discipline and in certain places rhetoric was taught as a subfield of *dictamen* (see Richardson's essay).

6. Richardson's essay in this volume discusses medieval terms for the components of the *ars dictaminis.* For development of a coherent set of terms and theoretical

understanding of medieval *dictamen,* two books have been particularly important, Murphy (1981) and Camargo (1991).

Works Cited and Works of Interest

Bizzell, Patricia, and Bruce Herzberg, eds. *The Rhetorical Tradition: Reading from Classical Times to the Present.* Boston: Bedford Books, 1990.

Camargo, Martin. *Ars dictaminis / Ars dictandi.* Typologie des Sources du Moyen Age Occidental. Turnhout: Brepols, 1991.

Cicero, Marcus Tullius. *The Letters to His Friends.* Translated by W. Glynn Williams. 3 vols. Loeb Classical Library. Cambridge, Mass.: Harvard University Press, 1927–1929.

Conley, Thomas M. *Rhetoric in the European Tradition.* New York: Longman, 1990.

Connors, Robert J., Lisa S. Ede, and Andrea Lunsford, eds. *Essays on Classical Rhetoric and Modern Discourse.* Carbondale: Southern Illinois University Press, 1984.

Demetrius. *On Style. Aristotle XXIII.* Translated by Doreen C. Innes and Rhys Roberts. Loeb Classical Library. Cambridge, Mass.: Harvard University Press, 1995.

Enos, Theresa, ed. *Learning from the Histories of Rhetoric: Essays in Honor of Winifred Bryan Horner.* Carbondale: Southern Illinois University Press, 1993.

Horner, Winifred Bryan, and Michael Leff, eds. *Rhetoric and Pedagogy: Its History, Philosophy, and Practice.* Mahwah, N.J.: Lawrence Erlbaum, 1995.

Kennedy, George. *Classical Rhetoric and Its Christian and Secular Tradition from Ancient to Modern Times.* Chapel Hill: University of North Carolina Press, 1980.

———. *A New History of Classical Rhetoric.* Princeton, N.J.: Princeton University Press, 1994.

Kramer, Samuel Noah. *The Sumerians: Their History, Culture, and Character.* Chicago: University of Chicago Press, 1971.

Mack, Peter, ed. *Renaissance Rhetoric.* New York: St. Martin's Press, 1994.

Malherbe, Abraham J. "Ancient Epistolary Theorists." *Ohio Journal of Religious Studies,* 5 (1977): 3–77. Reprint, Atlanta: Scholars Press, 1988.

Miller, Joseph M., Michael J. Prosser, and Thomas W. Benson, eds. *Readings in Medieval Rhetoric.* Bloomington: Indiana University Press, 1973.

Murphy, James Jerome, ed. *Renaissance Eloquence: Studies in the Theory and Practice of Renaissance Rhetoric.* Berkeley: University of California Press, 1983.

———. *Rhetoric in the Middle Ages: A History of Rhetorical Theory from Augustine to the Renaissance.* Berkeley: University of California Press, 1981.

———. *The Rhetorical Tradition and Modern Writing.* New York: Modern Language Association, 1982.

———, ed. *A Short History of Writing Instruction: From Ancient Greece to Twentieth-Century America.* Davis, Calif.: Hermagoras Press, 1990.

———, ed. *Three Medieval Rhetorical Arts.* Berkeley: University of California Press, 1971.

Poulakos, Takis. *Rethinking the History of Rhetoric: Multidisciplinary Essays in the Rhetorical Tradition.* Boulder, Colo.: Westview Press, 1993.

Vickers, Brian. *In Defence of Rhetoric.* Oxford: Clarendon Paperbacks, 1990.

Vitanza, Victor J. *Writing Histories of Rhetoric.* Carbondale: Southern Illinois University Press, 1994.

Classical Epistolary Theory and the Letters of Isocrates

Robert G. Sullivan

Understanding of Greco-Roman epistolary theory and practice has advanced tremendously in recent years.[1] It is not intemperate, I believe, to describe this advancement as revolutionary. Because of the efforts of classicists, biblical scholars, and historians of rhetoric, we probably know more today about Greco-Roman epistolography than at any time since antiquity. Despite these advances, however, our knowledge of ancient theories of letter writing remains handicapped by a central problem. Virtually all of the epistolary treatises considered by modern scholarship were written no earlier than the second century B.C. and most were written considerably later.[2] Because of this, profound complications arise as we attempt to extend our study back to the earliest letters in the Greek tradition. It seems problematic, to say the least, to examine letters written in the fourth century B.C. in the light of theories written hundreds of years later. In addition many of the ancient letters, from which we might wish to infer a theory of composition, come to us under a cloud of suspicion as to their authenticity. One must suspect that Richard Benchley's spectacular debunking of the epistles of Phalaris in the late seventeenth century, Ulrich von Wilamowitz-Moellendorff Wilamovitz's exchange with Friedrich Blass over the authenticity of the Isocratean letters, and the violent controversies over the attribution of the letters of Plato still dampen scholarly enthusiasm for working on the early letters.[3]

This is most unfortunate. Letters were manifestly an important discursive form in classical antiquity and were used for a wide variety of public and private communicative purposes. Many incontestably authentic letters of public importance have survived, as have a far greater number of private communications. Even if many Greek letters cannot be attributed with absolute certainty to their purported authors, the prevalence of the epistolary form demonstrates the importance of the letter as a compositional and rhetorical device in antiquity. It seems clear that any increase in our knowledge of classical epistolary theory will illuminate many facets of ancient literary culture.

This essay extends our knowledge of classical Greek epistolary theory by analyzing the letters of the Attic rhetorician Isocrates. Nine discourses by Isocrates, sometimes called his epistles, have come to us under the generic rubric of "letters," and two discourses, *To Philip* and *Busiris,* usually numbered among the Isocratean "speeches," are explicitly described by Isocrates as letters.[4] These *logoi* share two features that make them rich sources for the study of ancient epistolary theory. First, Isocrates produced many of his discourses as models for the emulation of his students.[5] To the extent that the letters share this aspect, we can suppose that they contain a master's best attempt to produce many features of the genre. Second, Isocrates' works fairly bristle with commentary on the writer's intentions, stylistics, and procedures of composition. It is, for instance, an Isocratean commonplace to apologize for having transgressed a generic boundary of style or content, either by way of self-correction or to illuminate more brightly his motives.[6] These theoretical asides can be observed in many places in the letters.[7] An Isocratean epistolary theory can be reconstructed from these preceptive statements and induced from some particulars of content and style.

The fundamental problem of the Isocratean letters is one of genre, and more particularly of Isocrates' notion of rhetorical genre. I will first consider the letters as they inform and represent epistolary theory of the era. Isocratean statements about letter writing, as well as elements present within the letters that speak to conventions of letter writing, will be collected and analyzed. From this I abstract an Isocratean epistolary theory or, perhaps more properly, the conventions to which he admitted as a letter writer. Second, I consider the letters as contributions to the Isocratean corpus as a whole. By examining them as rhetorical objects, it will become possible to see how letters might function in the complex Isocratean theory of rhetorical intellection.

An Isocratean Theory of Letter Writing

The first question we must answer is whether in Isocrates' mind epistles differed meaningfully from other types of discourse, such as speeches, manifestoes, or other species of prose. An analysis of the author's terminology for letters and letter writing demonstrates that such a distinction was being made. Of the twenty-six uses of *epistellô* or *epistolê* in the corpus (Preuss [1904] 1971, 82), twenty-three are used in the direct sense of "to send a letter" or "letter." Only three uses, all in the forensic *Trapeziticus,* retain the older sense of "command" or "enjoin."[8] Isocrates refers to each of the letters as an *epistolê,* though he also discusses the letter *To Archidamus* (2) and *To Philip* (25) as *logoi, To Philip* as a *biblion* (21), and the letters *To Timotheus* (10) and *To the Rulers of the Mytilenaeans* (1) as *grammata.* These are self consciously written products, in no way are they speeches, and are all pronounced in Isocrates' authorial voice.[10] In every letter, the form of address is familiar, direct, and personal, in the second-person singular.

Furthermore, letters are written communications that are sent from one person to another Isocrates' term for this being either *epistellô* or a variation on *epistolên pempein*.[11] Letter writing seems to have fallen under a degree of suspicion in this era, and in several places this provokes an apology from Isocrates (*To Dionysius* 1; *To Philip (II)* 4; *To Philip* 25–29). For instance, in the letter *To Dionysius* Isocrates not states that, if he were only younger, he would not be writing a letter at all but would sail to Syracuse to speak to Dionysius in person (1). Following this Isocrates lays out an elaborate defense of written discourses against the attacks of Alcidamas and Plato (2–3).[12] Isocrates notes the common prejudice against offering counsel in a written form and preference for face-to-face dialogue. He says that people mistrust written communications, assuming them to be for the purpose of display, and that written arguments, if they are obscure or challenged, lack a dialogical defender.

The Isocratean letters were written to perform a wide variety of functions. Three are letters of patronage: *To Timotheus* is a letter of introduction; *To Antipater* offers a character reference for one of Isocrates' students; *To the Rulers of the Mytilenaeans* asks a favor for an acquaintance. Several letters offer various kinds of counsel or advice. The letters *To Dionysius, To Archidamus,* and the second epistle *To Philip* urge those monarchs to adopt Isocrates' Panhellenic, anti-Persian political agenda, whereas the letter *To Alexander* recommends the young prince to the study of rhetoric, *To the Children of Jason* offers advice on statecraft, and the first epistle *To Philip* upbraids the Macedonian king for rashness in battle. In addition some of the letters speak of having mixed or multiple functions (*To Philip [I]*, 14; *To the Children of Jason*, 4; *To Timotheus*, 10; *To the Rulers of the Mytilenaeans*, 10). These functions may be as public as the political manifesto *To Dionysius,* or as intimately private as the last letter *To Philip (II)* or those *To Antipater,* or *To Alexander.* Other letters, such as those *To the Children of Jason, To Timotheus,* and *To the Rulers of the Mytilenaeans,* obviously combine public and private purposes.

The Isocratean letters exhibit formulae common to ancient letters in at least three elements; salutations, valedictions, and in certain particulars of the letters of patronage.[13] A great number of the Greek letters that have survived in papyri, as well as those transmitted in manuscript form, carry a formulary address, most often in the form Sender (Nominative) To Receiver (Dative) Greetings (*chairein* Infinitive). The Isocratean letters, in one of the two major families (Φ, the so-called vulgate) of manuscripts, retains this formula consistently.[14] The other family, which derives from the more highly considered Urbinas 111 (Γ), uses a simpler To Receiver (Dative) formula. This is complicated somewhat by the fact that Γ gives two salutations to the letter *To Dionysius,* using both formula, in the same hand. It seems fair to assume that Isocrates employed the standard formula, with some proviso that the formula might have been truncated from its full expression.[15]

Closing formulae are not as easily apparent. *To Dionysius, To the Children of Jason,* and *To Archidamus* are proems to longer discourses so we do not have proper endings at all. The epistles *To Philip (II), To Antipater, To Alexander,* and

To the Rulers of the Mytilenaeans, though relatively intimate, have no discernible formulaic features, nor does the more public *To Philip (II),* even though there are obvious epilogues in each of these. The letter *To Timotheus,* however, ends with a formula noted in many other instances of ancient letter writing (Exler, 69–70)—*errôso* (the pluperfect imperative of *rônnumi*—be healthy!) as farewell, followed by an invitation for further communication.

The letters of patronage seem to display some distinct formulaic elements.[16] One element is of interest because it so greatly clashes with our modern sensibilities. The receivers of two letters are asked to inform the clients that Isocrates' intercessions have been the cause of the success of their petition (*To Timotheus,* 10; *To the Rulers of the Mytilenaeans,* 10). Two of the letters ask that the receiver "take a care" for the client, a formula in many other later letters (*epimelein, To Antipater,* 12; *To Timotheus,* 13). We should also note the great pains that Isocrates takes in each of the patronage letters to both define his relationship to his client and conciliate himself with the receiver, evoking a triangular relationship between the sender, receiver, and client.[17]

In addition to exhibiting these formulaic features Isocrates makes several prescriptive statements about the stylistics of letter writing in his epistles. Consistent with his practice throughout the corpus, many of these prescriptive theoretical statements follow upon Isocrates' violation of a stylistic rule, which is then corrected by his demurral, introduced by his signature, the negative imperative *mê thaumazete,* or a verb of fearing, usually some variation of *phobeomai,* and then a description of the principle involved and how Isocrates is justified in having transgressed against it.

The most commonly invoked principle is that letters should be short. How short is appropriate is left unspecified, but at in the first epistle *To Philip* he notes that in no great time, three modern typeset pages, he has come to feel that he has committed an impropriety (*akairian*) as to the length of his letter and, using a nautical metaphor, describes himself drifting from the proportions of a letter into those of a *logos* (13). In the letter *To Antipater* he apologizes to his reader for the length of the letter: "And do not be amazed if I have written a longer than appropriate letter . . ." in terms that are strikingly similar to the sentiment expressed in the letter *To the Rulers of the Mytilenaeans.*[18]

Other principles can be derived from similar apologies for the violation of stylistic conventions. For instance, letters should be written in a personal tone appropriate to a communication between one person and another (*To Dionysius,* 7). Isocrates goes to great lengths to differentiate two of his letters from epideictic displays on stylistic grounds (*To Dionysius,* 6; *To the Children of Jason,* 4). There are specific terms for stylistics that are overly elaborate (*periergoteron To Antipater,* 13) or that might be put too gracefully (*charisteron To Timotheus,* 10), overzealously (*prothumoteron To the Rulers of the Mytilenaeans,* 10), obsequiously (*ochleros To the Rulers of the Mytilenaeans,* 2), or officiously (*presbutikôteron To Antipater,* 2), and so have no place in a letter. In the letter *To*

Timotheus he apologizes for the apparent effects of hasty composition on the style of the letter (*taxeon*, 10). That Isocrates is recommending against speed, per se, is not at all clear, because he asks Timotheus to respond with alacrity (13).

If we were to abstract an Isocratean epistolary theory—or more properly and probably the conventions to which he acceded—it would look something like this:

Letters are written communications sent directly from one person to another.
These communications may perform a wide variety of rhetorical tasks, of both private and public natures.
As written communications, they have all the strengths and weaknesses of other written forms and may clash with sensibilities more attuned to oral discourse.
Letters should be opened with a formulary address of either a long nominative-<dative-> infinitive construction, or a truncated form indicating the receiver in the dative case.
Formulary closings are available and optional.
Letters of patronage have relatively settled ways of introducing clients and asking for the aid of the receiver in reminding the client of his patron's intercession.
Letters have particular symmetries and stylistics: they should be short, personal, and written in a simpler style than other *logoi.* They should not be impertinent, ostentatious, or excessively elaborate.

All in all, this is a theory that would imply a quite familiar product, not at all unlike most ancient private correspondence, or for that matter, modern letters. What such a theory would not produce are the Isocratean letters as we have them—which are long, by turns obsequious and demanding, argumentative, heavily figured, and clearly written with an eye for posterity. That is to say that the Isocratean letters are notable violators of the generic rules under which they were composed. To understand why this is so we must turn to the problem of the Isocratean theory of rhetorical composition and the place the letters serve within it.

The Isocratean Letters as Rhetorical Objects

It should be clear from our discussion that Isocrates thought of the letter as being a distinct compositional form and recognized a theory of letter writing. But to think of them only as letters seems to miss a larger point, that for Isocrates the letters were located within his broader theory of rhetorical composition. The problem of what the Isocratean letters "are," then, is intimately connected with what all of the Isocratean *logoi* "are." This connection between the Isocratean letters and the rest of his corpus becomes more clear when we examine the letters in the order in which they were written and as parts of the whole of his literary career.

Busiris is, by most accounts, the first discourse Isocrates wrote after *Against the Sophists.*[19] In this stage of his career, Isocrates was experimenting in the use of various vehicles for praise and blame. *Busiris* stands roughly in the middle of seven speeches he wrote over a twenty-five-year span that have strong aspects of praise or blame: *Against Callimachus,* ca. 401; *Against Lochites,* ca. 395; *Concerning the Team of Horses,* ca. 395; *Against the Sophists,* ca. 390; *Busiris,* ca. 385; *Helen,* ca. 385, and *Panegyricus,* ca. 377. During this same period Isocrates had also begun to experiment with the use of letters, or epistles, both as generic forms and as a means of public communication. These two experiments, with the actions of praise and reproof, and with the letter, would come together in the composition of *Busiris.*

Most critics categorize *Busiris* as an epideictic and describe it as an encomium.[20] Close examination makes this position difficult to sustain. Although there certainly is an encomium to the mythical Egyptian king in *Busiris, Busiris* is not, strictly speaking, an encomium. The central purpose of the discourse is critical, Isocrates' term is that he intends to admonish the sophist Polycrates for his having published a faulty encomium (*nouthetein,* 3, 50). The conventional form or vehicle by which this criticism is effected is through the medium of a letter (*episteilai,* 2). The discourse begins in direct address to Polycrates, and this personal second-person address continues throughout all sections of the letter, with the exception of the encomium proper, which takes up only nineteen of the discourse's fifty sections. Polycrates is addressed in the second-person singular no fewer than twenty-five times in a relatively short discourse.[21] In addition, Isocrates says, baldly, that this is a letter, written privately to Polycrates so as not to embarrass him (2). That this generosity of spirit is entirely feigned would seem beyond controversy. Isocrates published this letter to bring the greatest possible embarrassment to Polycrates. What Isocrates seem to be playing with is the plastic capacity of the private letter to express public ideas, using the personal "you" to speak to a wide audience.

The letter *To Dionysius,* a fragmentary letter, was written in 367 or 368 (Mathieu and Bremond, vol. 4, 168; Norlin and Van Hook, vol. 3, 71). This letter was written to Dionysius, the tyrant of Syracuse, urging him to unify the Greeks and lead them on a military campaign against Persia. The letter is undeniably authentic, because Isocrates refers to it in *To Philip* (81), written twenty years later. *To Dionysius* continues Isocrates' experiment, begun with *Busiris,* of using personal letters to make public statements. Whereas in *Busiris* the object was literary criticism, here the statement is aimed at a specific political goal. The explicit purpose of *To Dionysius,* its precise generic marker as it were, is particularly clear. The letter is intended to offer concrete advice to the king (*symbouleuein,* 2, 4, 7, 9). Isocrates distances his letter from display speeches that are aimed at the general public. His letter, he says, is directed to Dionysius because only he is capable of immediately putting its principles into effect (5; cf. *To Philip,* 12–13). Isocrates specifies that the time is ripe for Dionysius to take action (*oud' akairôs,* 8; cf. *Panegyricus,* 24; *To Philip,* 35). The practicality of the advice and the mutual advantages to be achieved by following it are also stressed (8; cf. *Panegyricus*, 15–17; *To Philip*, 24).

The discourse that has come down to us as the letter *To The Children of Jason* is, like the letter *To Dionysius* and the letter *To Archidamas*, fragmentary. The letter was sent in 359 or 358 (Mathieu and Bremond, vol 4, 168–170; Norlin and Van Hook, vol. 3, 433). It seems to be, and is generally interpreted, as an introduction to a longer discourse, the body of which has dropped out. The subject of the missing material would seem to be statecraft, in particular the preferability of constitutional monarchy to tyranny as a political system. Although the subject is clear, the form by which the advice would have been offered is not. Most commentators assume that the body of this letter would have consisted of an essay on the advantages of a constitutional monarchy (Jebb 1962, vol. 2, 241–242; Mathieu and Bremond, vol. 4, 168–170; Norlin and Van Hook, vol. 3, 433). I would argue that it is more likely that the missing body of material was a *paraineses*, a compilation of maxims on the topic of statecraft. Isocrates seems to signal this intention in several ways. For instance, Isocrates alludes to his earlier publications on the subject of statecraft, which at this time consisted of the encomiastic *Busiris* and *Evagoras*, and two *paraineseis*, *To Nicocles*, and *Nicocles*, and despairs that his age prevents him from producing a better treatment of the theme in this letter (4). It seems most unlikely, in view of the characters of the recipients of the letter *To the Children of Jason*, that the author would be writing them an encomium. One assumes that Isocrates is referring, then, to his *paraineseis* as being the models that he fears he cannot match. In addition Isocrates makes a telling comparison in this letter between his mode of rhetorical composition and the means by one ought to govern one's life (8–10), saying that in life we should order our actions around sound ethical principles, just as we order our compositions by general theoretical considerations. In *To Nicocles* (9), Isocrates states that the starting point of his *paraineses* will be to lay out the general duties of a king, and does so by means of maxims on that subject. Isocrates speaks quite directly to such a mode of composition in this letter. He warns the readers that they may find within the work many sayings, *eirêmenôn*, which he has often used before (7). *Paraineseis* consist of collections of just such sayings.[22] I think it a fair conjecture to construe Isocrates quite literally in the designation Isocrates makes to his goal for this discourse (*parainoiên* 14). If I am correct in this the complete text of the letter would have probably looked more like *To Nicocles* than *To Philip*.[22]

The letter *To Archidamus* was sent in 356 and is the last in a series of seven discourses that Isocrates wrote either to or for Greek rulers, kings and tyrants, in the sixteen years between 372 and 356 (Mathieu and Bremond, vol. 4, 170–173; Norlin and Van Hook, vol. 3, 471).[23] In a later and similar flurry of letter writing between 350 and 338, he would send another seven discourses to kings.[24] The letter *To Archidamus* was written in Isocrates' eightieth year, ten years after the speech he had written in Archidamas's voice and that bears his name. This letter, like the letters *To Dionysius* and *To the Children of Jason,* is fragmentary, and we seem to have only the *prooimion* to a longer discourse that has not survived. The subject of the letter was to counsel King Archidamas to adopt Isocrates' Panhellenic scheme, uniting the Greek cities into a military alliance and campaign against the Persian Empire (1, 8–14, 19). The letter breaks off at a point where the writer announces that this scheme is both practical and advantageous for Sparta (*dunata kai sympheronta,* 19). The purpose of the letter is quite plain. In it Isocrates counsels Archidamas to assume the military leadership of the Greeks and lead an expedition against Persia (*symbouleuein,* 2, 6, 9).

The date of *To the Rulers of the Mytilenaeans* is somewhat unsure. Van Hook thinks it to have been written in 350 (Norlin and Van Hook, vol. 3, 459). Mathieu and Bremond opt for two ranges either in the period 353 to 352 or ca. 349–348 (vol. 4, 173). It is a short letter from Isocrates to the oligarchs who had recently taken control of Mytilene. Isocrates was in his mid-eighties when he wrote it to gratify the request of his grandsons, who had asked him to intervene on behalf of Agenor, their music teacher.[25] Agenor was at this time in exile from Mytilene and wished to return to Lesbos with his family. The intention of the letter is clearly defined. Isocrates is writing as a supplicant, asking a favor on behalf of his grandchildren (1). He acknowledges that he is seeking a great favor and is willing to describe himself as a petitioner (*deomai* Ep. 1, 9; *ho deomenos,* 9). At the end of the letter he asks that, if his request is granted, Aphareus and his brothers be informed that Isocrates had been the cause of their return. This last element seems to have been a commonplace in letters of petition. We also find it at the close of the letter *To Timotheus* (11), where Isocrates has asked a favor on behalf of a friend. In sum *To the Rulers of the Mytilenaeans* is a letter of petition.

To Philip is generally considered to be one of Isocrates' masterpieces, and by nearly every account, his last great work. The internal evidence of this discourse place it in the year 346 (Mathieu and Bremond, vol. 4, 3–8; Jebb 1962, vol. 2, 167; Norlin, vol. 1, 244). In it he exhorts the king of Macedon to accomplish Isocrates' great Panhellenic scheme, to unify the Greeks and campaign against the Persians. *To Philip* has always been treated as a symbouleutic, or "deliberative" discourse and this is, in fact, Isocrates' explicit intention (*symbouleuein, To Philip,* 9, 14, 16, 18, 55, 57, 82, 83, 88, 89, 94, 136, 152, 154, 155). To treat it as a deliberative "speech," however, seems odd. The epistolary status of *To Philip* is repeatedly emphasized (1, 10–12, 14, 18, 21, 23, 25–29, 81, 84–85, 93–94, 138, 141–143, 155). Isocrates refers to the discourse as a logos, and time and again as one that was sent to Philip directly (*logos,* 1, 11, 16, 17, 18, 23, *pempein,* 15, 17, 18, 21, 23). He also refers to it as a *biblion,* a fairly rare usage, but one that stresses the settled and written nature of the work (21). Isocrates uses the same word in the *Panathenaicus* 251 to refer to the text of his speech, and in two forensic speeches, *Against Callimachus* (19) and *Aeginiticus* (14), *biblion* is used to refer to a legal document. Isocrates emphasizes that his counsel is personal and directed to Philip because the king is an absolute monarch and as the greatest military power of the era only he, in all of Hellas, can act as he wishes, and had sufficient power to effect these recommendations (10–16; cf. *To Dionysius*, 6). Because of this, Isocrates approaches him by means of a letter; if he were trying to influence Athenian public opinion, he says, he would have composed a panegyric (9, 12). *To Philip* is written in second-person singular address throughout, just as are *Busiris* and the nine epistles. *To Philip*, then, is a letter of political counsel.

The letter *To Timotheus* was written soon after *To Philip*, probably in 345 (Mathieu and Bremond, vol. 4, 173–174; Norlin and Van Hook, vol. 3, 447). It is a short letter, only thirteen sections, and is personally addressed by Isocrates to the newly installed ruler of Euxine Heracleia. Timotheus had succeeded his father, a former student of Isocrates' who had made himself notorious for his absolute and cruel behavior. The letter has the immediate object of introducing Timotheus to another of Isocrates' students, the rhetorician Autocrator, and recommending him to the king's service (11). As such, the letter is an early example of a letter of introduction.

The discourse that is confusingly entitled the first letter *To Philip (I)* is the longest of those usually classified as letters, for which Isocrates offers an apology (13). It was written around 343 (Mathieu and Bremond vol. 4, 174–176; Norlin and Van Hook, vol. 3, 447) and was addressed to the Macedonian king soon after he had been wounded in a battle against the Thracians. The letter announces a dual purpose. The first part of the letter, sections 3–13, admonishes Philip for having risked his life in a meaningless battle; the second part, sections 14–23, urges him to adopt a more friendly attitude toward Athens (*parakaleuein* 14).

The authenticity of the letter *To Antipater* (ca. 340) has been challenged by a fair number of scholars on what are essentially stylistic grounds.[26] The letter begins with a description of the dangers that sending a letter entailed (*pempein epistolên* 1). It also contains an apology for its length and tone (13 *periergoteron kai presbutikôteron*; cf. *To Philip [I]* 13). Like *To Timotheus*, it is also interesting as an example of a very early, and private, letter of recommendation (*martyrêsai* 2). It was, perhaps, retained in the Isocratean corpus by Diodotus, Isocrates' literary executor, who is the object of Isocrates' praise in this letter of recommendation.

The short personal letter *To Alexander* was sent ca. 342–340 when Alexander was about fourteen (Mathieu and Bremond, vol. 4, 176–197; Norlin and Van Hook, vol. 3, 342). Isocrates seems to have appended this letter to one that he had sent to Philip and that has not survived. The letter *To Alexander* is an example of a "protreptic discourse" (*protreptikos logos*). In *To Demonicus* 4–5, Isocrates describes a species of discourse, exhortations to education in oratory (*hoi men epi logon parakalousin*). The letter *To Alexander* has precisely this object. In it Isocrates commends Alexander for seeing that though Aristotle's education in argument (eristic) is a useful mental exercise, it is of little practical value for a king. Isocrates exhorts him to pursue the more noble "discipline concerned with discourses" (4 *tên paideian tên peri tous logous*).

Mathieu and Bremond and Van Hook agree that the letter entitled *To Philip (II)* is an authentic letter sent to Philip in 338, soon after the battle of Charoenea (Mathieu and Bremond, vol. 4, 180–183; Norlin and Van Hook, vol. 3, 401). It is the last Isocratean discourse, and was written just before his death in his ninety-eighth year. The letter begins by referring to conversations that Isocrates had held with Antipater regarding the most advantageous policy for Athens to pursue in terms of her relationship with Macedon in the post-war era. These oral discussions seem to have been most explicit and concrete. In this letter Isocrates will, for the last time, press upon Philip the course of action he had recommended to him at least twice before, to unify the Greeks and campaign against Persia. This particular letter, though, offers no new ideas, nor does it invoke anything new to the situation, other than Isocrates realizes that his death is imminent. Isocrates twice announces that his intention in this speech is to exhort and encourage Philip to the course of action he first advanced in the *Panegyricus* (*parakeleuesthai kai protrepein* 3, 4). So, the letter is, strictly speaking, not so much a counsel as an exhortation.

Isocrates' diligence in specifying his purposes allows us to focus on an important aspect of his theory of letter writing. Isocrates makes not one, but two, generic designations for each of these letters. In every epistle he makes a clear statement that he is framing his discourse as a letter, but Isocrates seems equally concerned with specifying the work's rhetorical goal or purpose. They are not just letters; they are letters that offer counsel, admonish, criticize, ask favors, and offer recommendation, encourage, offer general advice, or advertise his rhetorical program. It seems quite clear that the Isocratean letter only takes on a rhetorical form when it fulfills such a specific and particular instrumental goal. Because of this we can say that the Isocratean theory of the letter is joined seamlessly with, if it is not subsumed under, his general theory of rhetorical composition. For Isocrates, the letter was but one of a number of conventional vehicles (as, for instance, the forensic speech, a speech before a deliberative assembly, or any one of a number of ceremonial forms) by which an author could achieve a variety of goals.[27] These goals—"what must be accomplished by the discourse"—are such rhetorical actions as "exhortation," "introduction," "requesting," "praising," "admonishing," and so on (*ti tô logô . . . diaprakteon estin, To the Children of Jason,* 8)

Whether Isocrates is innovating here or reflecting contemporary conventions is difficult to establish. What is quite clear is that his position on the letter anticipates that of such late antique epistolary theorists as the Ps. Libanius and the Ps. Demetrius, who saw letters as empty rhetorical vessels into which authors poured their intentions.

Notes

1. Enormous debts are owed by every student of ancient epistolography to such scholars as Abraham Malherbe (1988), Stanley Stowers (1986), M. Luther Stirewalt (1993), and Heikki Koskenniemi (1956)

2. A good discussion of the dating of the epistolary treatises will be found in the first chapter of Malherbe (1988) and Emilio Suarez de la Torre (1979, 19–46).

3. A very useful synthetic treatment of the issue as a whole, and helpful bibliography, will be found in Stirewalt (1993, 27–42), "Forgery and Greek Epistolography." This essay will offer no new sallies into the now old controversy regarding the Isocratean letters, other than to note that following upon the arguments of Blass, Drerup, Smith, and Mathieu, the burden of proof has shifted decisively to those who would challenge their authenticity. The challenge to some of the letters of Isocrates can be found in Wilamowitz-Moellendorff (1893, 2.268–273) rejecting *To Philip (II), To Antipater,* and *To Archidamus,* and his recapitulation of these arguments in "Unechte Briefe" (1898, 492–498). Wilamowitz-Moellendorff was contradicted forcefully by Friedrich Blass (1962, 2.293–299 and 326–331), and in greater detail in "Unechte Briefe (1899: 33–39). Englebert Drerup (1906, clviii–clxiv) rejects all claims against the authenticity of the letters. His bibliography is by far the most complete to that time, and an invaluable assessment of the major claims and counterclaims. See, however, "Isokrates" *Pauly-Wissowa Real-Encyclopadie* 9, 2146–2227, and in particular at col. 2216, where the author rejects *To Philip (II), To Antipater, To the Children of Jason,* and *To Archidamus,* The arguments of Smith (1940) are compelling in their dismissal of the stylistic and historical grounds of the challengers. Mathieu and Bremond (1928–1964, 163–183) accept all the letters as genuine. More recently the controversy seems to have died down, and the letters are now generally accepted as having been written by Isocrates. See, for example Joan Castellanos i Vila (1969), who approaches the controversy as a historical curiosity.

4. The best text of the Isocratean discourses is Mathieu and Bremond's. All references to the Greek text in this essay are referenced to that edition. The standard English translation is the Loeb edition, edited and translated by George Norlin and LaRue Van Hook (1945). In this study I will use the titles found in the Loeb. The letters are discussed in detail by Van Hook, vol. 3, 366ff; Mathieu, vol. 4, 163–183; G. Mathieu (1924); Drerup, CLVIII–CLXII; R. C. Jebb (1962, 238–258); and Marcel Lebel (1982).

5. See, in the letters, *To Philip* 12 and *To the Rulers of the Mytilenaeans* 12. Elsewhere, *Busiris,* 200, 271; *Antidosis* 12;

6. As he does, for instance at *To Philip (I)* 13; *To Antipater,* 13; *To the Children of Jason* 4; *To Timotheus* 10; *To the Rulers of the Mytilenaeans* 10.

7. Stylistic prescriptions can be observed in the letters *To Dionysius,* 1–3, 5, 6, 7; *To Philip (I)* 13; *To Philip (II)* 1, 4; *To Antipater* 13; *To Alexander* 1 *To the Children of Jason* 4, 7; *To Timotheus* 10; *To the Rulers of the Mytilenaeans* 1, 2, 10; *To Archidamus* 6, 12; *To Philip* 14–16, 28, 155; and *Busiris,* 50.

8. *Trapeziticus* 5, 6, 37. See Stirewalt 1977 (67–87), for a comprehensive treatment of the Greek vocabulary for letters and letter writing.

9. *Epistolê To Dionysius 1, 2;To Philip (I), 13; To Philip (II) 4; To Antipater 13; To Alexander 1; To the Children of Jason 4; To Timotheus 10, 13; To the Rulers of the Mytilenaeans 2, 10; epistellô To Philip 81; Busiris 2; To Dionysius, 3, 5; To the Children of Jason 4; To Timotheus 12, 13.*

10. *gr), graphein; To Philip (II) 1; To Alexander 1; To Timotheus 10; To the Rulers of the Mytilenaeans 2, 10; poiein To Philip (I) 12*

11. *To Dionysius 1, 5; To Philip (I) 12; To Philip (II) 1; To Antipater 1; To Alexander 1; To the Children of Jason 4; To Timotheus 11, 13; To the Rulers of the Mytilenaeans 1*

12. Ep. 1 2–3. Cf. Alcidamas (trans. in Matsen et al. 1990, 38–42). Compare these arguments against writing to those in Plato's *Phaedrus* 274–278. The supposition engendered by these criticisms that letters were held in suspicion by Athenians is not upheld by the report of Nicias's letter at Thucydides 7. 11–15. There letters are considered more honest than messengers because they cannot change their contents in the face of a hostile audience.

13. For general treatments of the formulae of Greek letters, see Exler (1923); "Briefe," *Pauly-Wissowa Real-Encyclopadie* 3 836–843; see also Stowers (1986, 186), "Index of Selected Epistolary Commonplaces."

14. The Isocratean manuscripts are discussed in great detail in Drerup, IV–XLII, CLVIII–CLXIII. Mathieu and Bremond, Vol. 4, 163–166 discuss the manuscripts of the letters.

15. The range of possibilities are this: either G represents the true Isocratean formulae in its truncation, and the vulgate line (and the second G title of *To Dionysius*) are interpolations of scribes seeking to add formulae where none existed, or the vulgate titles are correct but have been discarded by modern editors retaining the more difficult readings—as is queried in Benseler and Blass, *Isocratis Orationes* (1902), XLIX, of the Bekker retention of the longer salutation to the *To Dionysius*, . . . *"nescio an hic quoque delenda sint, sicut in inscriptionibus reliquarum epistularum ex auctoritate G codicis a Bk. factum est."*—or the letters were bald (or had other formulae attached to them) in the original but were edited to include the formulae we have at some subsequent time in antiquity.

16. These are not only consistent with the formulae derived from the sources noted above, but particularly with those compiled in Keyes (1935, 28–44). See also M. Van den Hout (1949, 19–41 and 138–153); C. H. Kim (1972), and M. Strirewalt, (1977). For the persistence of these forms see H. Cotton (1984). For examples see Stowers (1966, 153–165) and D. Brooke, ed., (1929).

17. See, for instance, *To Antipater*, 2, 8–11; *To Timotheus* 1–2, 10, 12–13; 1–2, 3–6.

18. Ep. 4 13 *kai mê thaumasês, mêt' ei makroteran gegrapha tên epistolên . . .* Ep. 8 10 *Mê thaumazete d' ei prothumoteron kai dia makroterôn gegrapha tên epistolên . . .*

19. Blass ([1892] 1962), *Die Attische*, vol. 2, 91, places it in the first year of Isocrates' school, 391; Jebb (1962), vol. 2, 91 in 391 or 390. Van Hook, vol. 3, 101, accepts a range of years from 390 to 385, whereas Mathieu and Bremond (1928–1964), vol. 1, 183–185, argue for a somewhat later date, ca. 385.

20. As do the ancient hypothesists, Mathieu and Bremond (1928–1964), vol. 1, 186–188; Theodore Burgess (1902): 89–264; Drerup (1906), CXXXI–CXXXIV, Takis Poulakos (1988); John Poulakos, (1986): 1–19. Cf. Jebb (1962), vol. 2, 91; Van Hook, vol. 3, 100–101; Mathieu and Bremond (928–1964), vol. 1, 183–185.

21. Isocrates speaks to Polycrates in the second person singular at *Busiris* 2, 4, 5, 6, 6, 7, 9, 14, 32, 33, 38, 42, 42, 44, 44, 46, 47, 47, 48, 48, 50, 50.

22. On the generic features of the Isocratean parainesis, see *To Demonicus*, 4–5; *To Nicocles*, 6–8, 54; *Nicocles*, 10–13.

23. *To Nicocles, Nicocles, To Dionysius, Evagoras, Archidamus, To the Children of Jason*, and this letter.

24. The letter *To the Rulers of the Mytilenaeans, To Philip, To Timotheus, To Philip (I), To Antipater, To Alexander*, and *To Philip (II)*, only interrupted by the *Panathenaicus*)

25. Actually the sons of Aphareus, who he had adopted when his father, the sophist Hippias, had died.

26. Mathieu and Bremond (1928–1964), who accept the letter as being by Isocrates, though with reservations, collect the arguments for and against it at vol. 4, 178–179.

27. Other collections of letters from this era exhibit the same problematic relationship between compositional form and rhetorical purpose. J. A. Goldstein *The Letters of Demosthenes* (1968), in chapters 7 and 8, argues that the purposes of the Demosthenean letters are derived from the seven genera found in Anaximenes's *Rhetorica Ad Alexandrum*.

Works Cited

Alcidamas. *On the Writers of Written Speeches; or, On Sophists*. Translated by Patricia Matson. In *Readings in Classical Rhetoric*. Edited by Patricia Matson, P. Rollinson, and M. Sousa. Carbondale: Southern Illinois University Press, 1990, 38–42.

Blass, Friedrich. *Die attische Beredsamkeit*. 2 vols. Hildesheim: Georg-Olms-Verlag, [1892] 1962.

———. "Briefe" *Pauly-Wissowa Real-Encyclopadie der classischen Altertumswissenschaft* 3 (1894–), 836–43.

———. "Unechte Briefe," *Rheinische Museum* 52 (1899): 33–39.

Brooke, D, ed. *Private Letters Pagan and Christian: An Anthology of Greek and Roman Private Letters from the 5th Century B.C. to the Fifth Century of Our Era*. London: Benn, 1929.

Burgess, Theodore. "Epideictic Literature" *Studies in Classical Philology* 3 (1902): 89–264.

Castellanos i Vila, Joan "Situacio Actual dels Estudias l'Autenticitat i Cronologia de les Cartes d'Isocrates" *ΔΩΡΩΙ ΣΥΝ ΟΛΙΓΩΙ: Homenatage a Josep Alsina*. Barcelona: Ariel, 1969.

Cotton, H. "Greek and Latin Epistolary Formulae: Some Light on Cicero's Letter Writing." *American Journal of Philology* 105 (1984): 409–25.

Exler, F.X.J. *The Form of the Ancient Greek Letter*. Washington, D.C.: Catholic University of America, 1923.

Goldstein, J. A. *The Letters of Demosthenes*. New York: Columbia University Press, 1968.

Isocrates. *Isocrate. Discours*. Edited and translated by Georges Mathieu and Emile Bremond. 4 vols. Paris: Société D'Edition "Les Belles Lettres," 1928–64.

————. *Isocrates.* Edited and translated by George Norlin and LaRue Van Hook. 4 vols. Cambridge, Mass.: Harvard University Press, 1945.

————. *Isocratis Opera Omnia.* Edited by Englebert Drerup. Leipzig: Theodore Weicher, 1906.

————. *Isocratis Orationes.* Edited by Gustave Benseler and Friedrich Blass. Leipzig: Teubner, 1902.

"Isokrates" *Pauly-Wissowa Real-Encyclopadie der classischen Altertumswissenschaft* 9, 2146–2227.

Jebb, Richard C. *Attic Orators from Antiphon to Isaeos.* Reprint, New York: Russell & Russell, 1962.

Keyes, C. W. "The Greek Letter of Introduction." *American Journal of Philology* (1935): 28–44.

Kim, C. H. *Form and Structure of the Familiar Greek Letter of Introduction.* Missoula, Mont.: Scholars Press, 1972.

Koskenniemi, Heikki. "Studien zur Idee und Phaseologie de grieschen Briefs bis 400n. Chr." *Soumalaisen Tiedeakatemian Toimituksia Ser. B* Tom 102, 2, 1956.

Lebel, Marcel "A Propos des Lettres d'Isocrate et des Lettres de Seneque le Philosophe." *Melanges Offert en Homage a Etienne Gareau.* Ottawa: Cahiers de Etudes Anciennes, 1982.

Malherbe, Abraham. *Ancient Epistolary Theorists.* Atlanta: Scholars Press, 1988.

Mathieu, Georges. *Isocrate: Philppe et Lettres a Philippe, a Alexandre, et a Antipatros.* Paris: Edition de Boccard, 1924.

Poulakos, John. "Argument, Practicality, and Eloquence in Isocrates' Helen." *Rhetorica* 4 (1986): 1–19.

Poulakos, Takis. "The Cultural Specification of Isocrates' Epideictic Works at the Political, Social, and Economic Level." PhD diss., University of Miami, 1988.

Preuss, Sigmund. *Index Isocrateus.* Hildesheim: Georg-Olms-Verlag, [1904] 1971.

Smith, Leslie Francis. *The Genuineness of the Ninth and Third Letters of Isocrates.* Lancaster, Pa.: 1940.

Stirewalt, M. Luther. "The Form and Function of the Greek Letter." *The Romans Debate.* Edited by K. Donfried. Minneapolis: Augsburg, 1977.

————. *Studies in Greek Epistolography.* Atlanta: Scholars Press, 1993.

Stowers, Stanley. *Letter Writing in Greco-Roman Antiquity.* Philadelphia: Westminster Press, 1986.

Suarez de la Torre, Emilio. "La Epistolographia Griega." *Estudios Classicos* 23 (1979): 19–46.

Van den Hout, M. "Studies in Early Greek Letter-Writing." *Mnemosyne* 4a Ser B (1949): 19–41, 138–53.

Wilamowitz-Moellendorff, Ulrich von. *Aristotele und Athen.* 2 vols. Berlin: 1893.

————. "Unechte Briefe" *Hermes* 33 (1898): 492–98.

A Conversation Halved

Epistolary Theory in Greco-Roman Antiquity

Carol Poster

Although there is some reason to believe that a coherent, if not necessarily explicit, body of epistolary theory existed in classical Athens, the most substantial body of evidence for ancient epistolarity (i.e., both epistolography and epistolary theory), comes from the postclassical period.[1] In particular, the late materials we have concerning ancient epistolary theory occur in the form of a small amount of direct evidence (letter-writing manuals or precepts for letter writing in other types of handbook) and a large amount of indirect evidence (letters themselves, from which we can, tentatively, derive implicit precepts for or conventions of, letter writing). Because contemporary rhetorical scholarship generally has not addressed ancient epistolary theory, this chapter will provide an overview of the field for rhetoricians and other scholars unfamiliar with the major issues and texts involved in reconstruction of ancient epistolary theory.[2] This discussion will be organized by types of extant sources for ancient epistolary theory, addressing them in the following order:

Letter-writing manuals in the literary tradition:[3] This section will discuss the limited number of extent epistolary manuals that have been preserved by scribal recopying (i.e., those attributed to Demetrius, Ps.-Demetrius,[4] and Libanius, the epistolary appendix to Julius Victor, and relevant comments in other sources).

Letter-Writing Instruction in Grammatical Manuals: This section discusses the elementary epistolary rules taught by grammarians.

Letter-Writing in Rhetorical Instruction: This section discusses the evidence for epistolary training and theory in rhetorical instruction and manuals.

Documentary Educational Papyri: This section discusses the papyri that have bearing on epistolary instruction.

Literary Letters: This section discusses explicit references to epistolary theory in letters that have been preserved in the literary tradition.

Documentary Letters: This section discusses the epistolary conventions found in papyrus letters.

I will not cover sites of epistolary instruction, because doing so would double the length of an already excessively long chapter, and I have discussed them at length elsewhere (Poster 2002).

Although letter-writing manuals are the most direct form of evidence we have for epistolary theory and will occupy the greater part of this chapter, we must be aware that preceptive manuals were, in fact, a relatively minor component of epistolary instruction. The contemporary model, in which students buy textbooks containing theoretical instruction in a field, and may keep them as reference materials, was almost unknown in antiquity. Teachers had notes from which they taught, perhaps in the form of manuals but more probably lecture notes from their own student days, supplemented by collections of model letters.[5] Teachers read models aloud, and students transcribed. Students might also have taken notes on their teacher's summaries of technical precepts. More commonly, however, instruction was dominated by use of models, a method particularly useful because letter-composition tended to be a highly formulaic process, involving copying sections from the appropriate models and making any necessary modifications. Decorum was more highly valued than originality. Commercial and official letters, especially, were often copied with minimal changes from pre-existing formularies.[6] This implies for our understanding of ancient epistolary theory that we must be extremely careful not to let our modern habits of privileging manuals over models influence how we think about ancient epistolary theory and instruction. Instead, we should think of ancient epistolary manuals not as bad attempts at grand and universal theories of discourse, but as brief sketches of how students should select the correct model letters and stylistic registers from which to compose a letter to fit the occasion of writing and relationship between sender and recipient, much like the medieval manuals Malcolm Richardson discusses in chapter 3.

Letter-Writing Manuals in the Literary Tradition

In light of the sheer volume of ancient letters we have preserved in both literary and documentary traditions, we have surprisingly little in the way of letter-writing manuals. There are two extant complete letter-writing manuals—Ps.-Demetrius, *Typoi Epistolikoi*, and Ps.-Libanius, *Epistolimaioi Kharactêres*—and two epistolary excurses in related kinds of treatises—a long section in Demetrius's *De elocutione* and an epistolary appendix to Julius Victor's *Ars rhetorica*. These manuals can be supplemented with very limited *obiter dicta* concerning letters in a few other grammatical treatises, but, even so, our complete extant collection of ancient letter-writing manuals amounts to fewer than thirty pages of Greek and Latin text. All four of these works, with facing English translations, have been collected, along with other miscellaneous fragments on epistolary theory, into a single and extremely useful volume by Abraham Malherbe entitled *Ancient Epistolary Theorists* (1988). For convenience, I use Malherbe's page and line numbering for all authors other than Demetrius, whose work is widely available in several editions and translations using standardized chapter numbers.

In this section, I will describe the four extant epistolary treatises and the tractates on letter writing by Philostratus of Lemnos and Gregory of Nazianzus and then summarize briefly what is mentioned concerning epistolary instruction in grammatical manuals.

Demetrius: *De elocutione*

Although none of the extant epistolary treatises, except Julius Victor's, can be attributed with any confidence to a known author, much less to a reliable date, the earliest of them is probably the epistolary excursus in Demetrius's *On Style*. The treatise itself, bearing the Greek title *Peri hermeneias* (Latin: *De elocutione*; English: *On Style*), has come down to us attributed to Demetrius of Phalerum, a student of Theophrastus and leading Athenian politician, but internal evidence suggests that it could not have been written in Demetrius's lifetime, although it does show the strongly Peripatetic influence one would expect from Demetrius. The actual date and authorship of *On Style* are unknown. Internal evidence of Attic style has led some scholars (e.g., Grube) to argue for early Hellenistic composition (ca. 270 B.C.E.) and others (e.g., Roberts) to support later (first-century C.E.) Atticizing authorship, although the recent consensus (e.g., Schenkveld 2000) tends toward the first-century B.C.E.[7]

The treatment of letter writing in Demetrius begins quite abruptly. In the midst of a section on the nature of the plain style, after brief discussions of vividness (217–218), harsh sounds (219–220), and the use of clarity and familiarity for persuasiveness (221–222), Demetrius introduces letter writing, with the comment, "We next will discuss the style for letters, since that too should be plain" (223). Demetrius begins his account of letter writing by repeating the opinion of Artemon, editor of Aristotle's letters, that a letter should be written in the same style as a dialogue, for letters are conversations halved (223), an opinion found in several other sources. Letters, like conversations and dialogues, are contrasted with orations. Demetrius criticizes Aristotle for a purple patch in a letter, saying, "A man who conversed in that fashion would seem not to conversing, but making an epideictic oration." (225) The style of the letter should be slightly more formal than that of actual conversation, especially when addressed to important men, and consist of complete sentences rather than disjoint exclamations, but "[i]t is absurd to build up periods [in a letter], as if you were writing . . . a speech for the law courts" (229).

The letter, according to Demetrius, "should abound in glimpses of character" and reveal the author's soul (227). Long philosophical or political discourses are inappropriate to the letter; such works are "not in sober truth letters but treatises with the heading 'Dear So-and-So'" (228). Occasional popular maxims are permissible, but, in general, all other forms of ornament and argumentation should be minimized, so a letter remains personal and conversational rather than rhetorical. Demetrius ends his excursus on letter writing with the advice, "In general it may be remarked that, from the point of view of expression, the letter should be a compound of these two styles, the graceful and the plain.—So much with regard to letter writing and the plain style." (235) He then begins a discussion of frigidity, the fault associated with the virtue of plainness.

Demetrius's primary model for epistolarity is the "philophronetic" familiar letter (a term coined by Koskenniemi 1956), one written primarily to maintain a relationship of friendship between the receiver and recipient. Although Demetrius does mention that a slightly heightened style is necessary when writing to "states or royal personages" (234), he does not discuss business and official letters. This indicates that his audience is a Hellenistic aristocracy, something born out by the familiarity with elite literary culture assumed in the rest of the treatise. At this social level, business letters would be written by secretaries or managers (discussed in Poster 2002); only personal letters would be composed in toto by the putative author. Whereas a business letter might be composed by the "author" telling a slave to write to a farm manager for additional wine to be sent to a city house, a familiar letter would be dictated verbatim to a stenographer with an autograph subscription (normally health wish and signature)[8] or written out in its entirety by the elite author, as Julius Victor, discussed below, recommends.

Ps.-Demetrius, *Typoi Epistolikoi*

If Demetrius's *De elocutione* appears to be addressed to an elite audience, concerned with writing familiar letters to peers, and probably able to delegate all but the most important letters to secretaries, Ps.-Demetrius's *Typoi Epistolikoi* (*Letter Types*) may very well be an example of a manual for the secretaries employed in private houses or the upper rungs of imperial or provincial chanceries.

The treatise *Typoi Epistolikoi* is falsely attributed in the manuscript tradition to the Demetrius (presumed to be but not actually Demetrius of Phalerum) who authored *De elocutione*. To avoid having to refer to the author of *De elocutione* as pseudo-Demetrius and the author of *Typoi Epistolikoi* as pseudo-pseudo-Demetrius, it is easier within the context of epistolary theory to call the author of *De elocutione,* "Demetrius" and the author of *Typoi Epistolikoi* "pseudo-Demetrius." The date of *Typoi Epistolikoi* is uncertain. Like many technical treatises, it went through multiple revisions, as different writers and teachers modified it for their own uses, adding or subtracting letter types. Even the author, as he introduces his list of letter types, seems to be aware of their malleability, stating there to be twenty-one kinds of letter types "that we have come across. Perhaps time may produce more than these" (22–24). The work we have seems to date somewhere between the second-century B.C.E. and the third-century C.E., most probably representing a later revised version of an earlier treatise. The treatise itself consists of some six pages of Greek text, beginning with an introduction addressed to one "Heraclides," followed by concise sections on each of twenty-one epistolary types, each section consisting of a very brief (one to three sentence) definition of the type followed by a very short model letter exemplifying the type. These types, although explicitly categories of complete letter, could also function, as Koskenniemi (1956) has pointed out, as models for sections of longer letters.

The treatise opens by claiming, "According to the theory of epistolary types, Heraclides, [letters] can be composed in a great number of styles, but are written in those that always fit the particular circumstances" (Malherbe 1988, 30:1). This statement implies that by the period in which the treatise was written there was some sort of standardized body of epistolary theory, including a categorization of epistolary types, with which readers of the treatise might be expected to have some vague familiarity, in general outline if not specific detail.[9] The fitting of epistolary type to circumstance also appears conventional, and the reader of the treatise appears expected to be aware that such conventions exist and desirous of learning how to employ them correctly.

Like Aristotle's *Rhetoric,* which states that all employ rhetoric but most do so "either at random or with a familiarity arising from habit" (I.i.1), so Ps.-Demetrius argues, "While [letters] ought to be written as skillfully as possible, they are in fact composed indifferently by those who undertake such services for men in public office." (Malherbe 1988, 30:4–6).

The concern of this treatise was not to serve as a basic manual for novices writing short practical or familiar letters, but rather training for secretaries like those addressed in Angel Day's *English Secretorie,* described in following chapters by Lawrence Green and Webster Newbold (i.e., those who made a profession of writing letters and performing related tasks for government or private employers). Ps.-Demetrius promises that this manual will help Heraclides improve his professional skills and obtain renown through them (Malherbe 1988, 30:8–20) and also suggests that advanced age will be of no impediment to using this manual. These statements give significant clues to the intended audience of the manual.

First, Heraclides and the other presumed readers are not slaves or business managers learning to write practical letters, for such careers would hardly be described as splendid (*lampron*).[10] Instead, they are following a career path recommended for impoverished gentlemen as early as Xenophon's *Oeconomicus*—namely, serving as educated secretaries in private houses or government offices.[11] Although these positions were probably open to any who had advanced liberal education, not every educated gentleman or even professional sophist would know the precise conventions of professional letter writing. Even the exact wording of letter salutations was a matter requiring specific knowledge and discrimination and some of the most skilled and famous sophists appointed to the post of *ab epistulis* (imperial secretary) may have lacked the specific epistolary skills necessary for the position.[12] Someone with a good liberal education entering into professional letter writing midcareer might well need precisely this sort of manual; it is perhaps to reassure such readers that Ps.-Demetrius says, "In devising such a mode for treating the subject, I did not at all desire to hinder any class [of people] as being too old" (Malherbe 1988, 30:16–18).

After this brief introduction, Ps.-Demetrius states that there are twenty-one types of letter and lists each one: "friendly, commendatory, blaming, reproachful, consoling, censorious, admonishing, threatening, vituperative, praising, advisory, supplicatory, inquiring, responding, allegorical, accounting, accusing, apologetic, congratulatory, ironic, thankful" (Malherbe 1988, 30:26–30). The first type, the friendly letter, is the one given the longest treatment, possibly because it represents a general category to which all the others are to some degree subordinate.

The friendly letter, according to Ps.-Demetrius, is one that "seems to be written by a friend to a friend" (Malherbe 1988, 32:1–2) but is not restricted to correspondence between actual friends, for those in prominent positions are expected to write in such a manner to other members of the social and bureaucratic elites, even if they are not personally acquainted with them. Underlying Ps.-Demetrius's recommendation of friendly style is a deeply ingrained, and thus unstated, cultural presumption that members of the educated elite, as lovers of the Greek *paideia* (literary culture), form a sort of brotherhood, even without individual acquaintanceship. Especially by the fourth century, both among pagan Hellenes and Christians, shared *paideia*—whether grounded in philosophy, sophistic, initiation into mysteries, or brotherhood in Christ—became a basis for a widespread network of affiliations and alliances underlying the conduct of professional, social, economic, and political activities. People who shared the same cultural heritage of *paideia,* whether personally acquainted or not, owed to each other all the obligations conveyed by the reciprocal notion of friendship. Equally important for understanding the importance of friendship in this discussion of elite professional letter writing is that such educated men as philosophers, grammarians, and sophists, when employed as secretaries, were described as friends (*"philoi"* in Greek, *"amici"* in Latin) rather than as salaried employees, which would have been insulting to well-born males.[13]

The friendly letter uses a characteristically epistolary method of persuasion. In the rhetorical theories of antiquity, which describe the *tria genera causarum,* persuasion is accomplished through argument, even if argument, as Wisse (1989, 13–29) points out, must be taken to include elements of ethos and pathos. In epistolary theory, however, the letter primarily serves to sustain and strengthen a relationship of friendship (or, in petitions, hierarchical obligation) and assumes that, if the relationship is established, particular desiderata mentioned in passing within the letter will be granted because of the obligation of friends to do favors for one another. This indirect persuasion through relationship rather than argument makes both the model letters and letter theory of this manual rather difficult to assimilate to traditional rhetorical models, but nonetheless quite significant as a means of persuasion in antiquity (and, I think, the present as well, insofar as people still tend to behave charitably toward friends). One major consequence of persuasion by relationship is that the letter functions performatively to establish the friendly relationship it proclaims; the more frequently one corresponds with someone, the closer the relationship. The specific content of the letter is less significant than the very fact of its existence. Thus, generalized and formulaic expressions of friendship are quite effective. As long as the letter is obviously of the friendly type, it serves to sustain or build the friendly relationship (whether of personal friendship or friendship within *paideia*). The more clear and immediate recognizable the formulaic expressions of friendship, the more directly and unambiguously the letter fulfills its friendly function.

The performative goals of the letter explain the formulaic and categorical nature of the presentation of the subsequent twenty letter types by Ps.-Demetrius. He clearly explains how each letter type is defined, so that the professional letter writer can easily select the correct type for a given situation. The description of the grateful type, written in what might appear to us almost vapidly general terms, is typical: "I hasten to show by my actions how grateful I am to you for the kindness you showed me in your words. For I know that what I am doing for you is less than I should, for even if I gave my life for you, I should still not be giving adequate thanks for the benefits I have received. If you wish anything that is mine, do not write and request it, but demand a return. For I am in your debt" (21). This example, quoted in it entirety, almost functions as an ancient equivalent of a Hallmark greeting card, a note of thanks written so generally as to be applicable to almost any situation. It can be recopied verbatim, or modified by the addition of particular details. Its utility lies in its provision of phrases that can be reused and its modeling of how a secretary should compose elite familiar correspondence in a tone appropriate to an educated man of *paideia*. The secretary who owned a copy of this manual would not need to work up an admonishing or congratulatory letter *ex nihilo,* but instead could look up the pertinent letter type, and either copy verbatim or embellish the model, and complete his task with some alacrity. This might be especially valuable to the non-native speaker of Greek or to one who spoke fluent *koinê* (popular Greek) but whose command of Atticizing Greek (the elite literary form of postclassical antiquity) was a bit uncertain. Grammatical mistakes or inappropriate diction are less likely when copying than when composing.

Ps.-Libanius, *Epistolimaioi Kharactêres*

Like the *Typoi Epistolikoi,* the *Epistolimaioi Kharactêres* (Epistolary Types) consists of a brief introduction and a list of letter types. The *Epistolimaioi Kharactêres,* which probably dates to the fourth-century C.E., has come down to us in two manuscript traditions, one attributed to the sophist Libanius and one to the Platonist philosopher Proclus. As both attributions are unlikely, I will refer to the author as Ps.-Libanius for convenience. What is most probable is that, as in the case of the *Typoi Epistolikoi,* the treatise evolved gradually at the hands of many authors.

This manual is quite similar to the *Typoi Epistolikoi,* differing mainly in being slightly longer and having more letter types, though the letter type definitions are shorter and less informative than those in the earlier manual. It consists of an introduction, definitions of forty-one letter types, a summary of epistolary theory, and a collection of short model letters illustrating each of the letter types. Ps.-Libanius, while defining and exemplifying letter types in much the same manner as Ps.-Demetrius, differs in not explicitly addressing a secretarial audience. There is no discussion of how to modify letter style when writing to important officials, and the friendly style is defined in terms of actual friendship, with no mention of the possibility of friendly address to equals or inferiors with whom one is not personally acquainted. This, along with the presence of the erotic letter, suggests that the putative (unstated) audience for this manual may well have been members of or aspirants to the elite who either could not afford secretaries or preferred to write some of their own letters. Another possible use of the manual is by writers of fictional letters, either schoolboys (who would write these letters as exercises the preliminary exercise of *prosopopoeia*) or aspiring literati.[14]

Ps.-Libanius begins by stating that "the epistolary style is divided into many parts" (Malherbe 1988, 66:1) and that the person desirous of writing good letters must have learned "what an epistle was, what, generally speaking, custom allowed one to say in it, and into what types it was divided" (66:5–6). This quite matter-of-fact introduction assumes the existence of a relatively familiar and uncontroversial set of epistolary theories and conventions, of which only brief summaries are needed. There is no attempt to convince the reader of the validity of some particular theory or argue that one should follow this model of the conventions of epistolary types rather than competing models. More important, the author presents as completely noncontroversial the notion that writing a good letter depends on deciding on the right type and following the conventions (including those of appropriate subject matter) established for that type.

After giving the common definition of a letter as a "written conversation" addressed to one who is absent, Ps.-Libanius introduces the concept of letter types, cautioning his readers that, although all letters are called *"epistolê"* (letters), they are not all of one style and type (Malherbe 1988, 66:10–14) and then lists the letter types. As shown in the list below, Ps.-Libanius's forty-one types include twelve of the ones found in Ps.-Demetrius and twenty-nine not in Ps.-Demetrius; nine types occur only in Ps.-Demetrius.

Types in Both Manuals

blaming	memptiko/j
censorious	e)pitimhtiko/j
commendatory	sustatiko/j
congratulatory	sugxarhtiko/j
consoling	paramuqhtiko/j
friendly	filiko/j

inquiring	e)rwthmatiko/j
ironic	e)irwniko/j
praising	e)painetiko/j
reproachful	o)neidistiko/j
thankful	a)peuxaristiko/j
threatening	a)peilhtiko/j

Types in Ps.-Demetrius Only

accounting	a)itiologiko/j
accusing	kathgoriko/j
admonishing	nouqethtiko/j
advisory	sumbouleutiko/j (mentioned in Ps.-Libanius' discussion of parainesis but not listed as among the distinct letter types)
allegorical	a)llhgoriko/j
apologetic	a)pologhtiko/j
responding	a)pofantiko/j
supplicatory	a)ciwmatiko/j
vituperative	yektiko/j

Types in Ps.-Libanius Only

angry	sxetliastikh/
commanding	paraggelmatikh/
conciliatory	qerapeutikh/
consulting	a)naqetikh/
contemptuous	paralogistikh/
counteraccusing	a)ntegklhmatike
declaratory	a)pofantikh/
denying	a)parnhtikh/
didactic	didaskalikh/
diplomatic	presbeutikh/
encouraging	paraqarruntikh/
enigmatic	ai)nigmatikh/
erotic	e)rwtikh/
grieving	luphtikh/
insulting	u(bristikh/
maligning	diablhtikh/
mixed	mikth/
mocking	skwptikh/
parainetic	parainetikh/
praying	eu)ktikh/
provoking	parocuntikh/
repenting	metamelhtikh/
replying	a)ntepistaltikh/

reporting	a)ppaggeltikh/
reproving	e)legktikh/
requesting	paraklhtikh/
submissive	metriastikh/
suggestive	u(pomnhstikh/
sympathetic	sumpaqhtikh/

The proliferation of letter types suggests that epistolary theory had become more fully theorized, and probably taught in more advanced stages of the curriculum, by late antiquity in a manner similar to the flourishing of elaborate substructures of *stasis* theory in the later phases of its development described by Heath (1994, 1995).

For Ps.-Demetrius, the friendly style was the first discussed and received the most elaborate treatment; for Ps.-Libanius, the first and most elaborate definition is of the parainetic type. Parainesis is defined as the style "in which we exhort someone to pursue something or to avoid something" and is divided into encouragement and dissuasion. It specifically is exhortation that "does not admit a counter-statement" and that no one would contradict, "were he not mad to begin with," such as exhortation to honor the divine. This differs from the advisory style (*symbouletikos*), which applies to matters where either side could be favored by a rational person—for example, whether to wage war (Malherbe 1988, 68:1–12). Under this definition, parainesis appears similar to the advanced preliminary exercise of "thesis," which argues a general question and overlaps with the teaching of philosophy.[15]

The rest of the letter types, with the singular exception of the praising one, are given very brief, almost circular definitions—namely, "[t]he blaming style (*memptikê*) is that in which we blame (*memphometha*) someone" (Malherbe 1988, 68:12) or "the reproachful style (*oneidistikê*) is that in which we reproach (*oneidizomen*) someone if he forgets how he has benefited by us" (68:29–30).

If a substantial audience for this manual were non-native speakers of Greek, the circularity of these definitions might actually serve to reinforce lessons of grammar, along with the stylistic practice of using various inflections of the same root in the same sentence, something that appears in rhetoric as the *topos* of inflection. Most of these definitions are little more than clarifications of the word distinguishing the type. It may well have been that the manual represents not a self-teaching textbook, but more *an aide de memoire* to be used in classes in which teachers would supplement it with *viva voce* explanations and model letters or be used by students to help them recall matters discussed in class.

The only exception, other than the paranetic type, to the extreme brevity of definition is the praising type. Ps.-Libanius is careful to specify, "The praising style is that in which we praise someone eminent in virtue. We should recognize that praise differs from encomium. For praise is laudatory speech that praises one thing, but an encomium is an encomiastic speech embracing many things in itself. Therefore, the letter that praises one thing is called laudatory, and that which praises many features is called encomiastic" (Malherbe 1988, 70:14–19).

Like the definition of the paranetic type, the definition of praising style is concerned with making a distinction where there is some likelihood of category mistake. In both cases Ps.-Libanius appears to be arguing against some unknown opponent(s) or frequent confusion. The common letter type (parainesis, or praise) seems to be contrasted with the similar but nonidentical oratorical term (advising [*symbouletikos*] or encomium). Ps.-Libanius also provides a mixed style to categorize a letter that fits many of the distinct types.

After listing and defining the letter types, Ps.-Libanius cites the ancients in general, and Philostratus of Lemnos (discussed below) in particular, concerning letter style. According to Ps.-Libanius, the ancients recommended that letters should demonstrate stylistic excellence and a register somewhere between the Atticism of oratory and the informality of ordinary speech. He allows more use of proverbs, philosophic doctrines, history, and ornament than do our other Greek authors, reflecting a growing tendency toward stylistic elaboration in late antiquity, especially in bureaucratic prose (discussed below and in note 18). Ps.-Libanius also emphasizes that a letter should be of whatever length is appropriate to the subject, and "in no way should fullness of treatment be regarded as a fault" (Malherbe 1988, 72:30–32), something in which he also differs from earlier Greek manuals, but is in agreement with the fourth-century Gregory of Nazianzus. This difference, therefore, might represent a chronological evolution, with earlier manuals favoring brevity and later ones allowing flexibility in length depending on subject, but since the fourth-century Latin Julius Victor insists on brevity, the evidence is not unanimous. Unfortunately, there are insufficient precisely datable epistolary manuals in both languages with secure dates to provide conclusive evidence.

Ps.-Libanius's transition to his model letter collection begins with a ten-line comment (Malherbe 1988, 74:1–10) concerning salutation. He recommends the simple form: "So-and-so to So-and-so, greeting," as favored by the ancients, and insists that even the addition of an adverb should be avoided "lest any appearance of flattery and meanness be attached to the letter."[16] His model letters contain neither salutation nor sample subscriptions, but instead consist of brief, formulaic letter bodies, so vague as to be easily recopiable in any situation of the general type being modeled, something that would be make the manual extremely useful for those whose knowledge of the Greek language or whose literacy therein was imperfect. Typical examples are the thanking letter and the letter of denial, which I quote in its entirety:

> The letter of thanks. For many other good gifts I am grateful to your excellent character, but especially for that matter in which you benefited me above all others. (Malherbe 1988, 74:28–30)

The letter of denial. I have done none of those terrible things, most noble sir, which you listen to and accuse me of. So, do not think badly of me. For it is not right to believe a false accusation and an idle rumor that contains nothing sound. For false accusation is the mother of war. (Malherbe 1988, 76:1–4)

Although the *Epistolimaioi Kharactêres* does not resemble the heuristic and argumentative rhetorics of Aristotle or Cicero, it addresses quite effectively the problems facing ancient letter writers. It can be used as a formulary covering most conceivable letter-writing situations. The model letters emphasize not the details of the narrative portion of the letter, which are situation-specific and known, one presumes, to the writer, but instead provide conventionally acceptable phrases for the social interaction of which the letter is part. An etiquette manual as well as an epistolary one, *Epistolimaioi Kharactêres* helps the provincial letter writer or new secretary maintain epistolary relationships without offending either literary or social decorum.

Philostratus of Lemnos

The short tract (Malherbe 1988, 43) on letter writing by Philostratus of Lemnos (third century C.E.) has been preserved for us in the work of his uncle, Flavius Philostratus. Familial fondness was not the only motive for quoting the work; Gregory of Nazianzus and Ps.-Libanius also cite it.

The work itself was the result of one of the numerous rivalries among the prominent sophists of the Roman Empire, who were constantly competing for prestige and patronage. As recounted by Flavius Philostratus, who obviously had strongly partisan views in the matter, the sophist Aspasius who had been appointed to the single most desirable official post available for one of his profession, the office of the imperial *ab epistulis graecae* (imperial secretary, or, literally, letter writer to the Greeks), though a competent orator, was not particularly skilled as a letter writer. Philostratus of Lemnos, who himself probably coveted the position, showed off his own superior qualifications by writing a short work on epistolary style, which, while overtly making general recommendations concerning a desirable middle path in letter writing between overly plain and excessively ornate styles, covertly criticizes Aspasius for being too elaborate and oratorical.

Philostratus of Lemnos begins by listing "those who, next to the ancients," were the best letter writers, naming among the philosophers Dio and Apollonius of Tyana, the latter of whom was the subject of an encomiastic biography by his uncle. Among military commanders, Philostratus of Lemnos recommends "Brutus or the person Brutus employed to write his letters." Marcus Aurelius, a notable patron of Greek literati, is selected as the best writer among the Roman emperors, something born out by his extant correspondence with Fronto. Among rhetoricians, Philostratus of Lemnos prefers the epistolary style of Herodes Atticus, an orator also admired by his uncle,[17] though Herodes is criticized for being overly oratorical and ornate, something inappropriate to the epistolary style. This criticism not only embodies the contrast between rhetorical and epistolary styles that we have seen in the other three Greek works on the topic (Demetrius, Ps.-Demetrius, Ps.-Libanius), but also shows that the ancient quarrel, as it were, between epistolary and rhetorical theory, was not mere quibbling over abstractions, but also represented a very practical rivalry concerning qualifications for quite lucrative appointments. Should appointments to upper-level positions in chanceries depend on speaking or letter-writing skills? It seems likely that Philostratus of Lemnos is arguing that the very oratorical skills that make sophists like Aspasius and Herodes Atticus shine in sophistic displays may be drawbacks in letter writing. This is supported both in Flavius Philostratus, who points out that the best imperial secretaries were not necessarily the best orators and that the most successful sophists did not always do well as letter writers (discussed above in note 12).

The stylistic recommendations Philostratus of Lemnos presents are not particularly original, but they are set forth in a memorable style, consisting of the very well-balanced antithetical periods he cautions against using excessively: "For the epistolary style must in appearance be more Attic than everyday speech, but more ordinary than Atticism, and it must be composed in common usage, and yet not be at variance with the graceful style" (Malherbe 1988, 42:9–11). He suggests that one should avoid literary allusions and use periods sparingly, especially in long letters, to avoid sounding too rhetorical. He recommends clarity as especially important in letters and rounds off his tract with a period: "We shall express ourselves clearly and without vulgarity if we express some of our ordinary thoughts in a novel manner, and some novel thoughts in a familiar manner" (Malherbe 1988, 42:23–25).

Gregory of Nazianzus, Epistle 51

Gregory of Nazianus, a noted theologian, orator, and letter writer, wrote to Nicobolus a short (less than fifty lines) tract on letter writing in the form of a letter (384–390 C.E.). He begins by saying that some people write letters that are too long and some letters that are too terse. Using a metaphor that also appears in Ps.-Libanius's discussion of appropriate length (Malherbe 1988, 72:22–26), he continues, "They both completely miss the mean, just as archers either undershoot or overshoot when they try to hit the target. They miss equally, though for opposite reasons" (58:5–7). After a rather flowery argument, filled with literary references, against fixed rules about the length of letters, he emphasizes that a letter should be of a length suiting the subject.

A letter should avoid overly formal or ornate prose style, but instead be conversational, and "persuasive to the educated and uneducated alike" (Malherbe

1988, 58:21). He recommends that a letter not be entirely without figures, but that "antitheses, parisoses, and isocola" (60:9) should be left to the sophists. He finishes his general advice by quoting a maximum from one of those same sophists, that "the greatest adornment of the eagle was that he did not think he was beautiful" (60:13–14) and that, so too, should a letter appear unstudied. He concludes by suggesting that Nicobolus will learn letter writing by working hard, having natural ability, and hearing skilled teachers.

Julius Victor's Ars rhetorica

Our only Latin epistolary treatise is the appendix (Malherbe 1988, 62–64) to Julius Victor's *Ars rhetorica* (fourth century C.E.). It appears to be in a quite different tradition than our Greek sources, but it is difficult to judge whether it differs because it is within a Latin tradition or because it is an appendix to a rhetorical text as opposed to an independent manual or part of a stylistic treatise. Julius Victor begins his appendix: "Many directives which pertain to oral discourse also apply to letters," a statement almost diametrically opposed to the Greek authors who contrasted the epistolary and oratorical styles. One possible reason for the difference is that in the Latin west, especially, rhetorical training was a path to bureaucratic appointments, including those in chanceries. In the Greek east evolving educational systems in letter writing, stenography, Latin, and law were challenging the supremacy of rhetorical education by the fourth century (discussed in Poster 2002), but in the Latin west, the alternatives seemed to be limited to ending with grammatical education, continuing on to Latin rhetorical education, or moving into the Greek system, something that appears relatively rare. Favorinus, for example, describes himself as being defined by three paradoxes, that he was a Gaul who was a Hellene, a eunuch who had been accused of adultery, and a man who had quarreled with the emperor and lived (Philostratus 8). That being a Gaul who knew Greek culture was grouped, even as the least of the three elements of the tricolon crescendo, with such distinctly rare matters as being a (putatively) sexually active eunuch and surviving the wrath of a Roman emperor (even if the emperor in question was the comparatively mild-tempered and philhellenic Hadrian rather than a notoriously temperamental Nero) implies that very few Gauls, or indeed provincial Romans in the west, were fluent in Greek, something that became even more pronounced by the fourth century.

Rather than the proliferation of letter types we found in Ps.-Demetrius and Ps.-Libanius, in Julius Victor we find only two types, the official and the personal. The official letter, a category that subsumes the business letter, is distinguished by its function and seriousness of tone; according to Julius Victor: "Characteristic of this [official] type are weighty statements, clarity of diction, and special effort at terse expression, as well as all the rules of oratory, with one exception, that we prune away some of its great size and let an appropriate familiar style govern the discourse." (Malherbe 1988, 62:4–7)

Although the recommendations of brevity and plainness are relatively typical, the suggestion that the rules of oratory should govern official letter writing is quite unusual, and is further evidence for close association of Latin epistolarity and rhetoric, in theory as well as in the distinctively rhetorical style of writings issuing from imperial chanceries (especially epistles and rescripts, which are legal advice in epistolary form).[18] The equally distinctive bureaucratic style developed by Greek chanceries, though bearing some stylistic influence from rhetoric, seems to have evolved in a slightly different educational system.

Julius Victor's treatment of familiar letter is considerably less complex than that in the two Greek manuals of letter types. He advocates plain style, clarity, and brevity as the virtues of the letter, something closer to the Peripatetic notions of Demetrius than to the moderate Atticism of the later Greek sources. He allows secret codes among close acquaintances exchanging sensitive information, but otherwise points out that one must be clearer in letters than in conversation, because one cannot ask an absent party to elucidate a point (Malherbe 1988, 62:20–21). Obscure facts, archaisms, and unusual words are to be avoided. He seems to have a strong hierarchical but weak categorical sense of epistolary conventions: "A letter written to a superior should not be droll; to an equal, not cold; to an inferior, not haughty. Let not a letter to a learned person be carelessly written, nor indifferently composed when going to a less learned person; let it not be negligently written if to a close friend, nor less cordial to a non-friend" (Malherbe 1988, 64:1–4).

Unlike Greek epistolary theory, which presumes that all educated men are friends and equals due to their common initiation into *paideia,* the Latin tradition appears to insist more on awareness of hierarchy, something anticipating the elaborations of the *salutatio* grounded in very precise distinctions of social rank in the medieval *ars dictaminis.* Julius Victor suggests, "The openings and conclusions of letters should conform with the degree of friendship [you share with the recipient] or with his rank, and should be written according to customary practice" (Malherbe 1988, 64:8–9).

Although this appears to be reminding the reader of the increasingly complex forms of address and rank that were developing in the late empire and the ongoing elaboration of the subscription, Julius Victor does not actually give us any details concerning these customary practices. The Vindolanda tablets, which preserve for us actual salutations in documentary letters, would suggest that Roman practice included adjectives and adverbs rather than the bare names recommended by the Greek theorists. As a rhetorician, Julius Victor seems to concern himself with the rhetorical part of the letter (the narration and style) rather than the technicalities pertaining exclusively to the epistolary art, other than remarking that one should write in one's own hand to close friends, or at least append an autograph postscript.

A few sentences recommend how to write in specific situations, in a manner that seems almost an unsystematic précis of the elaborate Greek theory of letter types. Julius Victor suggests that congratulations should be profuse and consolations brief, that one should not quarrel in letters, and that "recommendations should be written truthfully or not at all" (Malherbe 1988, 64:12). An occasional Greek phrase, line of poetry, or proverb is desirable, as long as not overused. Personal letters may use conversational expressions, but not official letters. Julius Victor's short appendix ends with the admonition, "In conclusion, be careful to discourse well both in your letters and every other kind of writing."

Letter-Writing Instruction in Grammatical Manuals

Although letter writing was an important professional skill, either on its own or as part of the skill set required of people in most literacy professions (described in Poster 2002), many people who were not professional letter writers needed basic letter-writing skills. Soldiers, farmers, craftspeople, and merchants wrote both personal and business letters regularly. Slaves and women, as well as provincial governors and sophists, had extended correspondences. Basic introductions to letter writing, therefore, were scattered through less-specialized and more elementary texts than the letter-writing treatises discussed above.

Letter writing appears in two major groups of grammatical manuals—those emphasizing syntax and those covering the preliminary exercises (*progymnasmata*) that served as preparation for rhetorical studies. Epistolary form is discussed in the grammatical handbooks of Apollonius Dyscolus and Dionysius Thrax (XII), the latter of whom refers to the dative as the "epistolary case," because salutations were normally in the form "sender [in the nominative] to recipient [in the dative] *chairein* [greetings]" with the name of the more important person first. Among the preliminary exercises, *prosopopoeia* (impersonation) was sometimes done in epistolary form (e.g., in Nicolaus 67.2–8 and Theon VIII.10), and Stirewalt (1993) has suggested that the same may be true of the *chreia*. Lanham (1992) also discusses the presence of letter-writing training in grammatical and progymnasmatic contexts. Because the comments by grammarians about letter writing are quite minimal, it is possible to draw from them only a limited number of conclusions about epistolary theory—namely, that there was a standard form of salutation and that, for more advanced students, it was important to make the material in the letter appropriate to the style of the actual or fictional sender.

Letter Writing in Rhetorical Instruction

As Classen (1993) has pointed out, (a) letter-writing theory is not embedded in ancient rhetorical handbooks but either appended or completely separate and (b) ancient comments about letter style clearly oppose it to oratorical style (e.g., Ps.-Demetrius 229, Gregory of Nazianzus *Ep.* 51.5–7, Cicero *Ad Fam.* 9.21.1). On the other hand, rhetoricians obviously wrote letters and were expected to be eloquent letter writers, and many, including Cicero, Libanius, and numerous rhetorically trained Christians (e.g., Augustine and Jerome), left behind significant collections of eloquent letters. Although epistolary instruction appears not to have been a significant part of the rhetorical curriculum and was not included in the body of rhetorical handbooks, the degree to which it may have been a regular but minor component of oral instruction is uncertain. Libanius, for example, read aloud to his students an eloquent letter he had just received from a friend, as a model for emulation (*Ep.* 128). Libanius, however, was a superb letter writer, and sufficiently admired as such that a manual of epistolary theory was attributed to him, so he may well have been atypically expert in the field. In light of the variability Graeco-Roman schooling, it is likely that this is something that may have varied tremendously by region, language, and teacher.[19]

We also know that many rhetorically trained students had careers that involved considerable amounts of letter writing, especially after Constantius issued a decree in 360 C.E. that candidates for bureaucratic positions have a liberal education and a good prose style (*Theodosian Code* 14.1.1). Many of the recommendations in Cassiodorus's *Variae* mention liberal education as a qualification for administrative positions (see also Pedersen 1976, for ancient professional qualifications). Whether administrators would need supplementary formal training, learned on the job, or relied on dictating contents to secretaries with epistolary training who would add requisite formulae is again unknown. We have isolated instances of all three. Our only significant evidence comes from the sixth-century work of John Lydus, which discusses the training and work of bureaucrats in the Greek east and suggests a combination of specialized training, long apprenticeship, and substantial ghost-writing and editing. Early evidence from Lucian and both Flavius Philostratus (*Lives*) and Philostratus of Lemnos (tractate discussed above) suggests that, although some sophists transferred their skills of oral composition to the epistolary genre quite readily, others were less successful in the endeavor (see note 11).

Perhaps our best conclusion about the relationship between rhetorical and epistolary instruction in antiquity would be that they were not identical and competing areas, which nonetheless, like rhetoric and grammar in Ausonius's Bordeaux,[20] were more likely to be combined in the more remote and impoverished areas that could not support several rival schoolmasters.

Documentary Educational Papyri

Whereas literary sources—namely, works that have been preserved in a tradition of scribal copying—help us understand elite canonical works considered worthy of preservation, the documentary tradition, consisting of papyri[21] written for a single purpose and not recopied, presents us with a much broader spectrum of evidence.[22] The works recovered from the sands of Egypt, the peat bogs of Britain (the Vindolanda tablets), and the ashes of Herculaneum, include personal correspondence, reams of bureaucratic paperwork (including census data, legal records, memos, and tax records), and, most important for our purpose, numerous school or educational papyri, including teachers' and students' books.

The main documentary evidence for letter-writing instruction is in the form of model letters, recopied by students. The writers of these letters appear to belong at an intermediate level of literacy. They possess mechanical literacy, with competent, though not elegant, handwriting, and basic grammatical knowledge, but still exhibit mistakes in spelling and syntax characteristic of student or other relatively inexperienced writers. Major examples include P. Paris 63 (discussed in Wilcken 1927) and P. Bon. 5. The latter consists of several short model letters, written out in both Greek and Latin, which resemble many of the models found in Ps.-Libanius. P. Bon. 5 consists of several short letters, each written to a (fictional) recipient of a small legacy. Each letter takes a slightly different approach, including congratulation, consolation, reproach, and advice. Its major significance for epistolary theory is that it shows that the letter-type approach found in the epistolary handbooks is congruent with actual curricular practice, especially insofar as students practiced writing precisely the sort of formulaic letter types that are modeled in the sample letters of the handbooks.

Students applied their knowledge of epistolary theory and their practice in letter-writing skills in letters home to their families (discussed in Préaux 1929, along with other documentary letters concerning education), though such familiar letters are by no means unique to students specifically studying epistolary skills. It is probable that student letters acted as a sort of progress report to parents (supplementing the progress reports provided by their teachers), in the sense that the degree to which students had mastered verbal skills would be apparent in their letters. Student letters also provide glimpses into the daily practices and circumstances of education. For example, the second-century-C.E. writer of P. Giess. 80 (translated by Hunt and Edgar 1932, 116) requests that someone send pigeons and small fowl "to the teacher of my daughter that he might be diligent with her." Other letters give us a sense of the letter-writing skills of various levels of students. P. Oxy. XVIII.2190 (edited and translated in Rea 1993 and Winter 1997, 245–249) shows the letter style of an advanced student who is pursuing rhetorical education, whereas P. Oxy. I:119 shows the marginally literate style of a quite young boy complaining to his father about not being taken along on a visit to town. Another slightly more fluent (and pleasant) schoolboy, Arion, writes to his father, sending greetings and health wishes to his father, brothers, relatives, and friends (P. Lond. Inv. 1575).

Unlike literary letters, such as those of Cicero, the documentary papyri do not raise questions of editorial changes for publication. Instead, they are letters as people actually wrote them, mistakes included. The autograph nature of many of the school papyri enable scholars to correlate handwriting with verbal skills and curricular focus, something especially useful for reconstructing histories of education (see, especially, Cribiore 1996 for this approach). Although they do not, generally, contain substantial theoretical reflections on letter-writing theory, they provide a standard by which it is possible to judge how much the theoretical models preserved in handbooks were actually followed.

Literary Letters

Literary letters, such as those of Cicero or Seneca, are probably what first come to mind when most rhetoricians think of ancient epistolarity, but contribute little to our knowledge of ancient epistolary theory. Cicero, for example, sometimes comments self-reflexively on the nature of letters in his correspondence (Malherbe 1988, 20–26) but offers no manual of epistolary theory. Although Cicero's are examples of familiar letters often functioning to maintain friendships and making some comments about epistolary decorum, the various *obiter dicta* on letter writing may well be specific to the particular correspondence rather than generalizable to ordinary epistolary theory. Moreover, not only was Cicero atypical (in being a consummately skilled Roman orator familiar with Greek learning), but also the letters preserved were selected and edited for publication and circulation among an elite audience and seem not to have been used as models for more ordinary correspondence. The correspondences of Pliny and Cassiodorus, especially the latter, give a better sense of Latin personal and official writing for practical purposes, whereas Libanius is an excellent example of the Greek manner of using correspondence to maintain networks of social affiliation with practical and political benefits. That a letter-writing manual is attributed to him and his voluminous correspondence collected suggests that he was thought of as an important authority for epistolary theory. The more typical the letters, however, the less likely they are to have been preserved in a literary traditions. Letters home from Egyptian soldiers, tradespeople's orders of merchandise, or farmers' correspondence with stewards or minor officials were not recopied by medieval scribes and preserved for posterity; their survival depends on their preservation as physical artifacts.

Another important type of literary letter is the fictitious one. Whether written as preliminary school exercises or displays of sophistic or literary skill, fictitious letters enjoyed substantial popularity in antiquity. The verse epistles of Ovid (*Heroides*) and the fictitious letters of Alciphron and Aelian were widely read and copied. School exercises of writing letters *in alienis personis* often resulted in particularly convincing student works becoming incorporated in collections of the letters of famous authors such as Plato or Diogenes, giving rise to a large body of pseudo-epigrapha that are not precisely forgeries in the modern sense, any more that would be "Platonic" dialogues by Iris Murdoch or the speeches by various kings in Shakespeare's historical plays (see Stirewalt 1993, 27–42, for more comprehensive discussion of ancient pseudo-epigraphy).

Documentary Letters

Although, except in the limited case of the educational papyri discussed above, documentary papyri rarely shed direct light on epistolary theory, they are nonetheless important for understanding how epistolary instruction was applied across broad social and temporal spans. Many papyrus letters belong to quite distinct types, distinguished both by subject matter and the presence of several clearly identifiable formulae; letters of recommendation and petitions are especially clearly standardized in form, as are types of bureaucratic letter.[23]

Even familiar letters, which we now might think the most personal and least formalized, are extremely conventional. After a standard salutation (Sender to Receiver, Greetings), usually come a fixed health wish, a *"parousia"* or presence formula (wishing the recipient were physically present), and a closing formula, often expressing the wish, especially in late antique Greek letters, that the recipient may remain safe from magic and the evil eye. Although the conventionality of most autograph documentary letters, as well as those composed by scribes, suggests that most literate people has some basic epistolary training, the phenomenon may also be accounted for by either imitation of models or simple osmosis. Most people had heard a variety of letters read aloud and from this would have absorbed some vague sense of the sort of way one should go about writing a letter.

There was a strong sense of generic convention among documentary letter writers, with each type of letter having its own standard features. The opening of a letter, for example, normally takes the form "sender [in nominative] to recipient [in dative] greetings [*charein*]," with minor variations, as discussed by Exler (1923). In petitions, and similar documents to officials, the opening is altered to reflect the relatively greater status of the recipient to, "to recipient [in dative] from sender [in genitive] greetings [*charein*]." Invitations, recommendations, introductions, and petitions display particularly distinct formulaic characteristics, as described by Cotton (1981), Exler (1923), Keyes (1935), Kim (1972, 1975) Kim and White (1974), and White (1972a, 1972b, 1982). This formulaic tendency suggests that letter composition was based on handbooks or models that were followed fairly closely rather than being spontaneous and untutored outpourings of the sender's ideas or concerns.

Another important use of documentary letters for the study of ancient epistolarity is to counteract the tendency to take a limited group of elite ancient writers of quite atypical periods and circumstances and use them to make broad statements about antiquity in general. Democratic Athens and republican Rome were atypical in political system, size, and sophistication. The ancient authors—such as Demosthenes, Plato, Isocrates, Cicero, or Augustine—we now read in our study of rhetoric were not average writers or orators. They are "classics" precisely because they were canonized as representing the best of their period. The documentary papyri, on the other hand, were not selected for recopying on the basis of artistic merit. They consist of obsolete government files, recycled papyri used for wrapping crocodile mummies at Tebtunis, and scraps tossed out in the rubbish heaps of Oxyrhynchus. It is possible to read letters by schoolchildren, farmers, minor bureaucrats, soldiers, and young widows that can illuminate how letter-writing skills became diffused through varied social strata, even if the methods by which this diffusion occurred are not as clear as might be wished.

Conclusion

The general portrait of ancient epistolary theory in modern classical and rhetorical scholarship has been one of a few uninteresting and minimally influential treatises, with little to contribute to our understanding of literacy and rhetorical practices.[24] This portrait, however, is based on an overly simplistic analysis of existing evidence and is fundamentally misleading. [25] Epistolary theory was in fact a quite well-developed and important branch of verbal skills instruction, permeating a far greater portion of ancient society than rhetorical training. Although its utility has been widely acknowledged by New Testament scholars interested in the composition and interpretation of the Pauline Epistles, even pagan letter collections, such as those of Cicero, Libanius, or Cassiodorus have rarely been discussed in light of epistolary theory. For example Harrison's (1994) discussion of Horace's *Epistles* dismisses ancient epistolary theory, with the singular exception of Demetrius, as "jejeune . . . and insignificant" and thus not relevant to the study of ancient literary letters. This seems to me quite as absurd as thinking that composition textbooks are irrelevant to studying the history of prose style. People are not born with full-fledged and unchangeable sets of literary habits. Instead, they gradually develop patterns of oral and written communication by imitating models around them in their homes, peer groups, and schools.

Although rhetoricians are aware that rhetorical theories of a period influence habits of speech and writing, a single-minded focus on "rhetoric," while providing many insights into ancient political and forensic practice, has also blinded us to the far broader range of ancient theoretical materials available concerning verbal arts. Theories of grammar, epistolarity, philosophical protreptic, and the religious sublime competed with and influenced rhetorical theories. A focus on rhetoric as independent of these and all-encompassing not only gives an extremely limited account of ancient arts of discourse, excluding those practiced by nonelites, women, and many others, but even worse, by considering rhetoric in isolation, we deliberately exclude from our consideration some of the materials that are most critical to understanding ancient rhetoric in terms of how it positioned itself in relation or opposition to other disciplines.[27]

Notes

1. Robert Sullivan's essay in this volume has discussed the elements of epistolary theory present in Isocrates. Dionysius of Halicarnassus distinguishes Lysias's works in epistolary style from his panegyric and amatory discourses as well as his forensic and deliberative oratory (Lysias 1). Although this confirms the presence of a distinct epistolary genre within classical sophistic practice, it cannot prove the existence of explicit epistolary theory.

2. Despite the importance of letter writing in ancient education as well as daily life, very few of the standard histories of rhetoric or education include discussions of it: Kennedy (1972) omits it entirely, an oversight only perfunctorily remedied in his *Greek Rhetoric under the Christian Emperors* (1983). D. Clark's only discussion of letter writing is a brief summary of comments by Seneca, Cicero, and Demetrius on epistolary style (1957, 103–106). Both of M. L. Clarke's studies (1971, 1996) of ancient rhetoric ignore letter writing; when he condemns the lack of originality (1996, 140) of the later Latin rhetoricians, he fails to note that Julius Victor is the only author he discusses to have included a substantial treatment of letter writing. Two other works on Roman eloquence and education, Bonner (1977) and Dominik (1997), also ignore the topic. Marrou (1956), Murphy (1983, 1990), and Morgan (1998) omit ancient letter-writing instruction entirely. Harris (1989) does include very useful information on letter writing and literacy, but specific letter-writing instruction is somewhat outside the scope of his work. The major, and extremely welcome, exceptions to this general neglect of ancient epistolary theory in antiquity are within the discipline of New Testament studies (summarized in Reed 1997). This work, however, is concerned primarily with how ancient epistolary theory can contribute to our understanding of the Pauline epistles, rather than addressing more general issues; some studies containing extensive bibliographical discussions include Anderson (1999), Classen (1993), Porter (1993), and Reed (1993).

3. Here, I am making the distinction between "literary texts," in the sense of those that have been handed down to us by a long tradition of scribal copying (e.g., Homer, Plato, Cicero, or Pliny) and "documentary texts" that have been recovered in the form of singular documents not recopied for posterity (e.g., tax records, autograph personal letters, or schoolchildren's handwriting practice).

4. Note that I use the name "Demetrius" to refer to the author of "On Style" and Ps.-Demetrius to refer to the letter-writing manual falsely attributed to the author of "On Style."

5. Papyrological finds that shed light on the use of teachers' and students' classroom texts, models, and worksheets are described by Cribiore (1996) and Morgan (1998). Proclus of Naucratis kept a library for his pupils (Philostratus, "Lives" 21).

6. Several of the letters in Cassiodorus's *Variae* may have been used as formularies. Numerous papyrus formularies have been recovered. See, for example, Collomp (1926), Schwartz (1950), and Turner (1975).

7. For discussion of the dates of Demetrius's "On Style," see Grube (1961), Poster (1996), Roberts (1902), and Schenkeveld (1964, 2000). I should note that I am not entirely convinced by Schenkeveld's (2000) arguments concerning the audience for Demetrius's "On Style." Schenkeveld assumes a rather rigid and uniform three tier model of education, and does not take into account a possibility of advanced grammatical

studies, leading to later philological or philosophical studies, or specialized courses in style associated with varied curricula, which might have been the sites of reception of stand-alone figural treatises (e.g., Tiberius's work on the Demosthenic figures).

8. For ancient epistolary conventions, see especially Exler (1923), Kim and White (1974), Stowers (1986), and White (1986).

9. There have been several specialized studies of papyrus letter genres, notably Cotton (1981), Dion (1982), Keyes (1935), Kim (1972, 1975), Stirewalt (1997, 1993), and White (1972a and 1972b). There are interesting parallels between the use of typology in ancient epistolary and epideictic theories. Ancient theories of epideictic are discussed in Menander Rhetor (1981) and Burgess (1987).

10. For a broader discussion of the letter-writing profession in antiquity, including its relation to stenography, see Poster (2002). Slave training is discussed by Booth (1979) and Forbes (1955). Aubert (1994) discusses business managers. The best discussion of ancient stenography training is Teitler (1984)

11. John Lydus gives the most detailed ancient picture of the internal workings of the early Byzantine bureaucracy; see Bandy (1983) for text, translation, and commentary. Carney (1971) provides a broader analysis of late Roman and early Byzantine bureaucracy, with a translation of John Lydus appended. The imperial chanceries are discussed in some detail by Millar (1977, 69–121 and 203–274). Lucian discusses the not altogether pleasant lot of literati serving as secretaries in private houses ("A Slip of the Tongue in Greeting" and "Salaried Posts in Great Houses").

12. The short tract of Philostratus of Lemnos discussed below is aimed at the apparent deficiencies of Aspasius, a sophist appointed to the position of *ab epistulis graecae.* Philostratus, in his *Lives of the Sophists,* cites several sophists who achieved the post of *ab epistulis:* Celer (574), Alexander (571), Hadrian (590), Antipater (607), and Aspasius (628). Bowersock discusses the Greek sophists holding this position (1969, 44, 50–51, 53–57, 92) and Millar (1977, 83–109, 213–227, 313–340) discusses the roles of secretaries in Roman administration. For more specialized discussions of the *ab epistulis* see Lindsay (1994) and Townend (1961). Lewis (1981) takes the controversial stance that literary skills were not the sole, or even primary, qualifications for the position of *ab epistulis.*

13. For ancient discussions of friendship, see especially Seneca's *De benevolentia* and Cicero's *De amicitia.* Secondary sources useful for friendship in relation to letter writing include Konstan (1997) and White (1992). Brown (1992) discusses friendship, and especially based on shared *paideia,* as a persuasive device.

14. For typical fictions letters in prose, see the letters of Alciphron, Aelian and Philostratus (combined conveniently in a single Loeb volume).

15. Robert Sullivan, in his essay in this volume, discusses Isocrates' paraineses. Typically protreptic philosophical letters would include Aristotle's *Protrepticus,* Plato's *Epistle VII,* and Porphyry's *ad Marcellam.* For a general discussion of philosophical protreptic, see Jordan (1986).

16. One finds, though, far more elaborate use of honorifics, anticipating the flowery medieval practices, in late antique papyrus letters of petition. This is probably due both to the proliferation of legally stipulated honorifics in the late empire and the extreme social distance between most of the subelite petitioners and the officials to whom they wrote. Latin salutation formulas are discussed Lanham (1975) and Latin letter formulae in Abram (1994). Lucian ("A Slip of the Tongue in Greeting") is a useful ancient source.

Swain (1996) discusses in great detail the relationship between correct language and social power and status in antiquity. The very prohibition against elaborate salutations might suggest that at the time the manual was composed, more complex salutations were becoming common and that the author disapproved of this innovation. See discussions of papyrus letters (below) for documentary salutation formulas.

17. Anderson (1986, 1993) discusses Flavius Philostratus, and especially his relationship to Herodes Atticus. Bowersock (1969) gives a more general discussion of the role of Greek sophists in the Roman empire.

18. For discussions of chancery Greek and Latin, see Benner (1975), Fridh (1967), Haverling (1988), McMullen (1962), and Vidén (1984).

19. Marrou's (1956) classic presentation of a fairly uniform "three-tier" model has been questioned by more recent scholars (e.g., Booth 1978 and 1981 and Kaster 1983) and especially by papyrological studies showing a far greater diversity of schools and curricula than found in our elite sources. Professional nonelite training, unfortunately, has received comparably little attention; see Poster (2002) for nonelite letter-writing instruction.

20. The history of rivalries and overlaps between rhetoric and grammar is long and complex, varying with language, period, and specific teacher. Useful secondary studies include Kaster (1988) and Copeland (1991).

21. In this essay I use "papyri" in the generalized sense of preserved ancient handwritten materials, which have come down to us on wood tablets, pottery fragments (ostraca), parchment, and lead tablets, as well as on literal papyrus. Inscriptions on stone are not included.

22. Although many official and legal documents were produced in multiple copies, and sometimes recopied and appended to other such documents, and often even writers of personal letters might make and send multiple copies of a letter due to the unreliability of messengers, this was a somewhat different mechanism than an extended tradition of scribal recopying of a canonical literary work, although in certain cases (imperial decrees and rescripts or letters of major literary figures, or unsuccessful literary works we only have in autograph copies) the distinction is far from absolute. On the physical material of papyrus itself, see Lewis (1974). For editorial problems specific to papyri, see Youtie (1958). For general introductions to papyrology, see Gallo (1986), Pestman (1990), and Turner (1980, 1987). Bagnall (1995), Keenan (1991) and Turner (1975) provide analyses of the major issues concerning use of papyri to support general historical claims.

23. Several scholars in New Testament studies have begun the task of gathering papyrological evidence related to ancient epistolarity but the contours of their project are often defined by theological focus rather than by a general interest in the nature of secular education and careers. Deissmann's work (1910, 1911) was seminal. General collections of documentary papyrus letters accompanied by critical commentary include Kim and White (1974), Stowers (1986), and White (1986). There have been several specialized studies of papyrus letter genres as well, notably Cotton (1981), Dion (1982), Keyes (1935), Kim (1972, 1975), Stirewalt (1997, 1993), and White (1972a and 1972b). Broader studies of papyrus letters in relation to epistolary theory within New Testament scholarship include Doty (1973), Exler (1923), and White (1984). Papyrus letters have also been treated by scholars investigating literacy education, especially Cribiore

(1996), Harris (1989), and Morgan (1998) and several of the essays in Bowman and Woolf (1996), but they do not discuss epistolary theory or instruction per se.

24. Application of ancient epistolary and rhetorical theory and papyrus letters to understanding the Pauline epistles is discussed by R. D. Anderson (1996), Classen (1993), and Porter (1993). The omission of epistolary theory and narrowly oralist emphasis of Kennedy (1984) on New Testament criticism and in the majority of his other works (1963, 1972, 1980, 1994) on ancient rhetoric has been a central factor in the omission of epistolary theory from American scholarship in rhetoric, not only in Speech departments, where an oralist bias might be expected, but also even among historians of (written) composition.

25. Chartier explains a comparable numerical rarity of copies of early modern French letter treatises as follows:

> [T]he editions of letter-writing manuals which have survived doubtless represent only a fraction of those actually published. . . . Of little market value, these flimsy little paperbacked books (including and perhaps especially the letter-writing ones) have ill stood the test of time. This explains why, even though we know that these titles had a wide circulation and were reprinted as often as demand dictated, very few have survived in today's libraries and collections. It would be wrong therefore to conclude from their poor survival rate that they did not enjoy broad circulation. Paradoxically, as the numbers of inventoried copies demonstrate, it is, on the contrary, perhaps a token of their commercial success and the intense use to which they were put. (Chartier 1997, 61.)

26. Work on this chapter was done during two visiting fellowships, first the Project on Rhetoric of Inquiry of University of Iowa and later at the Tanner Humanities Center of the University of Utah. Earlier versions of this chapter were presented at Classical Association of the Pacific Northwest, Portland, Oregon, April 1998, and Research Network Forum, College Conference on Composition and Communication, Phoenix, Arizona, March 1997. I owe thanks for various suggestions and prepublication copies of works-in-progress to David DePew, John Garcia, Malcolm Heath, and Tom Olbricht. All errors and infelicities, naturally, are my own.

Works Cited

Papyri, including Tablets

For papyri, the standard abbreviations are listed in *BASP* Suppl. 7 (= Oates et al. 1992). Editions cited are:

P. Lond. VII = *Greek Papyri in the British Museum, Vol. VII: The Zenon Archive.* Edited by T. C. Skeat. London: British Museum Publications, 1974.

P. Lond. Inv. = H. I. Bell, "Some Private Letters from the Roman Period." *Revue égyptologique* I (1919): 200–203.

P. Oxy. I = *The Oxyrynchus Papyri.* Vol. I, Nos. 1–207. Edited by B. P. Grenfell and A. S. Hunt. London, 1898.

P. Oxy. XVIII = *The Oxyrynchus Papyri.* Vol. XVIII, Nos. 2157–2207. Edited by E. Lobel et al. London, 1941.

P. Paris = *Notices et textes des papyrus du Musée du Louvre et de la Bibliotèque Impéri-ale*. Edited by A. J. Letronne et al. Paris, 1865.

T. Vindol. = *Vindolanda: the Latin Writing Tablets*. Edited by A. K. Bowman and J. D. Thomas. London: Brittania Monograph Series No. 4, 1983.

Primary Sources

For classical works not specifically cited, I use the TLG CD ROM D and for Latin the PHI Latin database. Translations are the ones cited below, occasionally silently modified in cases of inaccuracy or ambiguity. For Libanius, I have retained the more commonly used numbering system of Foerster, which does not correspond to that in Norman's translations, though those reading Norman should note the table of correspondences he provides.

Aelian. *The Letters of Alciphron, Aelian and Philostratus*. Translated by Allen Rogers Benner and Francis H. Fobes. Loeb Classical Library. Cambridge, Mass.: Harvard University Press, 1949.

Aristotle. *The "Art" of Rhetoric*. Translated by J. H. Freese. Loeb Classical Library. Cambridge, Mass.: Harvard University Press, 1982.

Bandy, Anastastius C., Intro., ed., trans., comp., *Ioannes Lydus, On Powers or the Magistracies of the Roman State*. Philadelphia, Pa.: The American Philosophical Society, 1983.

Cassiodorus. *Variae*. Trans, notes, and intro. S. J. B. Barnish. Liverpool: Liverpool University Press, 1992.

Cicero, Marcus Tullius. *Letters to Atticus*. Edited and translated by E. O. Winstedt. 3 vols. Loeb Classical Library. Cambridge, Mass.: Harvard University Press, 1962–84.

———. *The Letters to His Friends*. Translated by W. Glynn Williams. 3 vols. Loeb Classical Library. Cambridge, Mass.: Harvard University Press, 1927–29.

———. *De senectute, De amicitia, De divinatione*. Loeb Classical Library. Cambridge, Mass.: Harvard University Press, 1923.

Chroust, Anton-Hermann. *Aristotle: Protrepticus, A Reconstruction*. South Bend, Ind.: University of Notre Dame Press, 1964.

Dionysus of Halicarnassus, *The Critical Essays*. Translated by Stephen Usher. 2 vols. Loeb Classical Library Cambridge, Mass.: Harvard University Press, 1974.

Hercher, Rudolph, ed. *Epistolographi Graeci*. Amsterdam: A. M. Hakkert, 1965.

Hermogenes. *On Issues*. Translated by Malcolm Heath. Oxford: Oxford University Press, 1995.

Hunt, A. S. and C. C. Edgar. *Select Papyri*. 2 vols. Loeb Classical Library. Cambridge, Mass.: Harvard University Press, 1932.

Isocrates. *Isocrates*. Translated by George Norlan. 3 vols. Loeb Classical Library. Cambridge, Mass.: Harvard University Press, 1956.

Kemp, Alan. "The *Tekhnê Grammatikê* of Dionysius Thrax: English Translation with Introduction and Notes." In *The History of Linguistics in the Classical Period*, edited by Daniel J. Taylor. Amsterdam: John Benjamins, 1987, 169–90.

Libanius. *Autobiography and Selected Letters*. Edited and translated by A. F. Norman. 2 vols. Loeb Classical Library. Cambridge, Mass.: Harvard University Press, 1992.

————. *Imaginary Speeches*. Translated by and notes by D. A. Russell. London: Duckworth, 1996.

————. *Opera*. 12 vols. Edited by R. Foerster. Leipzig: Teubner, 1903–27.

————. *Selected Works*. 3 vols. Intro. and Translated by A. F. Norman. Loeb Classical Library. Cambridge, Mass.: Harvard University Press, 1969.

Lucian. *Lucian*. Translated by A. M. Harmon et al. 8 vols. Loeb Classical Library. Cambridge, Mass.: Harvard University Press, 1913.

Malherbe, Abraham J. *Ancient Epistolary Theorists*. Atlanta: Scholars Press, 1988.

Menander Rhetor. *Menander Rhetor*. Edited, translated, and with commentary by D. A. Russell and N. G. Wilson. Oxford: Oxford University Press, 1981.

Philostratus and Eunapius. *Lives of the Sophists*. Translated by Wilmer C. Wright. Loeb Classical Library. Cambridge, Mass.: Harvard University Press, 1989.

Plato. *Plato IX: Timaeus, Critias, Cleitophon, Menexenus, Epistles*. Translated by R. G. Bury. Loeb Classical Library. Cambridge, Mass.: Harvard University Press, 1989.

Quintilian. *The Insititutio Oratoria of Quintilian*. Translated by H. E. Butler. 4 vols. Loeb Classical Library. Cambridge, Mass.: Harvard University Press 1989.

Roberts, W. Rhys. *Demetrius On Style. The Greek text of Demetrius de Elocutione edited after the Paris Manuscript, with introduction, translation, facsimiles, etc.* Cambridge: Cambridge University Press, 1902. Reprint, New York: Arno Press, 1979.

————. *Demetrius On Style. Introduction, Text, and Translation.* Loeb Classical Library No. 199, Cambridge, Mass.: Harvard University Press 1927; rev. 1932; repr. 1982.

Seneca. *Moral Essays*. 3 vols. Loeb Classical Library. Cambridge, Mass.: Harvard University Press, 1963–65.

Seneca the Elder. *Controversiae and Suasoriae*. Translated by Michael Winterbottom. 2 vols. Loeb Classical Library. Cambridge, Mass.: Harvard University Press, 1974.

Theon. "The 'Progymnasmata' of Theon: A New Text with Translation and Commentary." Translated by James R. Butts. PhD diss., Claremont Graduate School, 1986.

Tiberius. *Tiberii de figuris Demosthenicis*. Edited by G. Ballaira. Rome: Ateneo, 1968.

Weichert, Valentin, ed. *Demetrii et Libanii qui feruntur Typoi Epistolikoi et Epistolimaioi Charakteres*. Leipzig: Teubner, 1910.

Secondary Sources

Abram, Suzanne L. "Latin Letters and their Commonplaces in Late Antiquity and the Middle Ages." PhD diss., Indiana University—Bloomington, 1994.

Anderson, Graham. *Philostratus: Biography and Belles Lettres in the Third Century A.D.* London: Croom Helm, 1986.

————. *The Second Sophistic: A Cultural Phenomenon in the Roman Empire*. London: Routlege, 1993

Anderson, R. Dean. *Ancient Rhetorical Theory and Paul*. The Netherlands: Kok Pharos, 1996.

Aubert, Jean-Jacques. *Business Managers in Ancient Rome*. Leiden: E. J. Brill, 1994.

Bagnall, Roger S. *Egypt in Late Antiquity*. Princeton, N.J.: Princeton University Press, 1993.

————. *Reading Papyri, Writing Ancient History*. London: Routledge, 1995.

Benner, Margareta. *The Emperor Says: Studies in the Rhetorical Style in Edicts of the Early Empire*. Göteburg: Acta Universitatis Gothoburgensis, 1975.

Blank, David L. *Ancient Philosophy and Grammar: The Syntax of Apollonius Dysco-lus.* American Classical Studies 10. Chico, Calif.: Scholars Press, 1982.

Bonner, Stanley. *Education in Ancient Rome: From the Elder Cato to the Younger Pliny.* Berkeley: University of California Press, 1977.

Booth, Alan D. "The Appearance of the Schola Grammatici." *Hermes* 106 (1978): 117–25.

———. "Elementary and Secondary Education in the Roman Empire." *Florilegium* 1 (1981): 1–14.

Bowersock, Glen. W. *Greek Sophists in the Roman Empire.* Oxford: Oxford University Press, 1969.

Bowman, Alan K., and Greg Woolf, eds. *Literacy and Power in the Ancient World.* Cambridge: Cambridge University Press, 1994.

Brown, Peter. *Power and Persuasion in Late Antiquity: Towards a Christian Empire.* Madison: University of Wisconsin Press, 1992.

Burgess, Theodore C. *Epideictic Literature.* New York: Garland, 1987.

Carney, T. F. *Bureaucracy in a Traditional Society: Romano-Byzantine Bureaucracies Viewed from Within.* Lawrence, Kans.: Coronado Press. 1971.

Chartier, Roger. "Secrétaires for the People?" In *Correspondence: Models of Letter-Writing from the Middle Ages to the Nineteenth Century,* edited by Roger Chartier et al. Translated by Christopher Woodall. Princeton, N.J.: Princeton University Press, 1997.

Clark, Donald Lemen. *Rhetoric in Greco-Roman Education.* New York: Columbia University Press, 1957.

Clarke, M. L. *Higher Education in the Ancient World.* Albuquerque: University of New Mexico Press, 1971.

———. *Rhetoric at Rome: A Historical Survey.* 3rd ed. Rev. D. H. Berry. London: Routledge, 1996.

Classen, C. Joachim. "St. Paul's Epistles and Ancient Greek and Roman Rhetoric." In *Rhetoric and the New Testament,* edited by Stanley Porter and Thomas Olbricht. Sheffield: Sheffield Academic Publishers, 1993.

Collomp, Paul. *Recherches sur la Chancellerie et la Diplomatique des Lagides.* Paris: Les Belles Lettres, 1926.

Copeland, Rita. *Rhetoric, Hermeneutics, and Translation in the Middle Ages: Academic Traditions and Vernacular Texts.* Cambridge: Cambridge University Press, 1991.

Cotton, Hannah. *Documentary Letters of Recommendation in Latin from the Roman Empire.* Königstein/Ts.: Hain, 1981.

Cribiore, Raffaella. *Writing, Teachers, and Students in Graeco-Roman Egypt.* American Studies in Papyrology 36. Atlanta: Scholars Press, 1996.

Deissmann, Gustav Adolf. *Light from Ancient Letters.* Translated by Lionel R. M. Strachan. London: Hodder and Stoughton, 1910.

———. *Light from the Ancient East.* London: Hodder and Stoughton, 1911.

Dion, Paul E. "The Aramaic 'Family Letter' and Related Epistolary Forms in Other Oriental Languages and in Hellenistic Greek." *Semeia* 22 (1982): 59–76.

Dominik, William J., ed. *Roman Eloquence: Rhetoric in Society and Literature.* London: Routledge, 1997.

Doty, W. G. *Letters in Primitive Christianity.* Philadelphia: Fortress Press, 1973.

Exler, Francis Xavier. "The Form of the Ancient Greek Letter: A Study in Greek. Epistolography." PhD diss., Catholic University of America, 1922. Washington, D.C.: Catholic University of America, 1923.

Forbes, Clarence A. "The Education and Training of Slaves in Antiquity." *Transactions of the American Philological Association* 86 (1955): 321–60.

Fridh, Åke. *Contributions à la critique et à l'interprétation des Variae de Cassiodore.* Stockholm: Almqvist & Wiksell, 1967.

Gallo, Italo. *Greek and Latin Papyrology.* Translated by M. R. Falivene and J. R. March. London: Institute of Classical Studies, 1986.

Grube, G. M. A. *A Greek Critic: Demetrius on Style. Phoenix.* Suppl. Vol. 4. Toronto: Toronto University Press, 1961.

Harris, William V. *Ancient Literacy.* Cambridge, Mass.: Harvard University Press, 1989.

Harrison, Stephen. "Poetry, Philosophy, and Letter-Writing in Horace, Epistles I." In *Ethics and Rhetoric: Classical Essays for Donald Russell on His Seventy-Fifth Birthday,* edited by Doreen Innes et al. Oxford: Clarendon Press, 1995, 47–63.

Haverling, Gerd. *Studies on Symmachus' Language and Style.* Göteburg: Acta Universitatis Gothoburgensis, 1988.

Heath, Malcolm. "The Substructure of *Stasis*-theory from Hermagoras to Hermogenes." *Classical Quarterly* 44 (1994): 114–29.

Jordan, Mark D. "Ancient Philosophic Protreptic and the Problem of Persuasive Genres." *Rhetorica* 4, no. 4 (1986) 309–32.

Kaster, Robert A. *Guardians of Language: The Grammarian and Society in Late Antiquity.* Berkeley: University of California Press, 1988.

———. "Notes on 'Primary' and 'Secondary' Schools in Late Antiquity." *Transactions of the American Philological Association* 113 (1983): 323–46.

Keenan, J. G. "The 'New Papyrology' and Ancient Social History." *Ancient History Bulletin* 5 (1991): 159–69.

Kennedy, George. *The Art of Persuasion in Greece.* Princeton, N.J.: Princeton University Press, 1963.

———. *The Art of Rhetoric in the Roman World, 300 B.C.E.– A.D. 300.* Princeton, N.J.: Princeton University Press, 1972.

———. *Classical Rhetoric and Its Christian and Secular Tradition from Ancient to Modern Times.* Chapel Hill: University of North Carolina Press, 1980.

———. *Greek Rhetoric under the Christian Emperors.* Princeton, N.J.: Princeton University Press, 1983.

———. *A New History of Classical Rhetoric.* Princeton, N.J.: Princeton University Press, 1994.

———. *New Testament Interpretation through Rhetorical Criticism.* Chapel Hill: University of North Carolina Press, 1984.

Keyes, Clinton. "The Greek Letter of Introduction." *American Journal of Philology* 56 (1935): 28–44.

Kim, Chan-Hie. "Form and Structure of the Familiar Greek Letter of Recommendation." PhD diss., Vanderbilt University, 1970; Missoula, Mont.: Society of Biblical Literature for the Seminar on Paul, 1972.

———. "The Papyrus Invitation." *Journal of Biblical Literature* 94 (1975): 391–402.

Kim, Chan-Hie, and John L. White. *Letters from Papyri: A Study Collection.* Society for Biblical Literature, 1974.

Koskenniemi, Heikki. *Studien zur Idee und Phraseologie des griechischen Briefes bis 400 n. Chr.* Helsinki: Suomalainen Tiedeakatemia, 1956.

Lanham, Carol Dana. "Salutatio Formulas in Latin Letters to 1200: Syntax, Style, and Theory." PhD diss., University of California–Los Angeles, 1973; Munich: Arbeo-Gesellschaft, 1975.

Lewis, Naphtali. "Literati in the service of Roman Emperors: Politics Before Culture." In *Coins, Culture, and History in the Ancient World: Numismatic and Other Studies in Honor of Bluma L. Trell,* edited by Lionel Casson and Martin Price. Detroit: Wayne State University Press, 1981.

———. *Papyrus in Classical Antiquity.* Oxford: Clarendon Press, 1974.

Marrou, H. I. *A History of Education in Antiquity.* Translated by George Lamb. New York: Mentor, 1956.

Millar, Fergus. *The Emperor in the Roman World.* Ithaca, N.Y.: Cornell University Press, 1977.

Morgan, Theresa. *Literate Education in the Hellenistic and Roman Worlds.* Cambridge: Cambridge University Press, 1998.

Murphy, James J., ed. *A Short History of Writing Instruction: From Ancient Greece to Twentieth-Century America.* Davis, Calif.: Hermagoras Press, 1990.

———. *A Synoptic History of Classical Rhetoric.* Davis, Calif.: Hermagoras Press, 1983.

Oates, John F., et al., eds. *Checklist of Editions of Greek and Latin Papyri, Ostraca, and Tablets.* 4th ed. *Bulletin of the American Society of Papyrologists,* Suppl. 7. Atlanta: Scholars Press, 1992.

Pedersen, Fritz Saaby. *Late Roman Professionalism.* Odense: Odense University Press, 1976.

Pestman, P. W. *The New Papyrological Primer.* Leiden: Brill, 1990.

Porter, Stanley, ed. *Handbook of Classical Rhetoric in the Hellenistic Period, 330 B.C.E.–A.D. 400.* Leiden: Brill, 1997.

———. "The Theoretical Justification for the Application of Rhetorical Categories to Pauline Epistolary Literature." In *Rhetoric and the New Testament,* edited by Stanley Porter and Thomas Olbricht. Sheffield: Sheffield Academic Publishers, 1993.

Poster, Carol. "Demetrius." In *The Encyclopedia of Rhetoric,* edited by Theresa. New York: Garland Publishing, 1996, 174–75.

———. "The Economy of Letter-Writing in Graeco-Roman Antiquity." In *Rhetorical Argumentation and the New Testament,* edited by Tom Olbricht, Walter Ubelacker, and Anders Eriksson. Harrisonburg, Pa.: Trinity Press International, 2002, 114–26.

Préaux, Claire. "Lettres privées greques d'Egypte relatives à l'éducation." *Revue Belge de Philologie et d'Histoire* 8 (1929): 757–800.

Rea, John. "A Student's Letter to His Father: P. Oxy. XVIII:2190 Revised." *Zeitschrift für Papyrologie und Epigraphik* 99 (1993): 75–88.

Reed, Jeffrey T. "The Epistle." *Handbook of Classical Rhetoric in the Hellenistic Period, 330 B.C.–A.D. 400.* Leiden: Brill, 1997.

———. "Using Ancient Rhetorical Categories to Interpret Paul's Letters: A Question of Genre." In *Rhetoric and the New Testament,* edited by Stanley Porter and Thomas Olbricht. Sheffield: Sheffield Academic Publishers, 1993.

Schenkeveld, Dirk Marie. "The Intended Public of Demetrius *On Style:* The Place of the Treatise in the Hellenistic Educational System." *Rhetorica* 18, no. 1 (2000): 29–48.

———. *Studies in Demetrius on Style.* Amsterdam, Adold M. Hakkert: 1964. Reprint, Chicago: Argonaut, 1967.

Schwartz, J. "Une formulaire de nomographe." *Journal of Juristic Papyrology* 4 (1950): 209–14.

Stirewalt, Martin Luther. "The Form and Function of the Greek Letter-Essay." In *The Romans Debate,* edited by K. P. Donfried. Minneapolis: Augsberg, 1977, 175–206.

———. *Studies in Ancient Greek Epistolography.* Atlanta: Scholars Press, 1993.

Stowers, Stanley K. *Letter Writing in Greco-Roman Antiquity.* Philadelphia: Westminster Press, 1986.

Sykutris, J. "Proclus "Περὶ Ἐπιστολιμαίου." *Byzantisch-Neugr. Jahrbucher* 7 (1928–29): 108–18.

Teitler, H. C. *Notarii and Exceptores.* Amsterdam: J. C. Gieben, 1985.

Turner, E. G. *Greek Manuscripts of the Ancient World,* 2nd ed. Rev. P. J. Parsons. *Institute of Classical Studies Bulletin Supplement* 46. London, 1987.

———. *Greek Papyri: An Introduction.* Oxford: Clarendon Press, 1980.

———. "Oxyrhynchus and Rome." *Harvard Studies in Classical Philology* 79 (1975): 1–24.

Vidén, Gunhild. *The Roman Chancery Tradition: Studies in the Language of Codex Theodosianus and Cassiodorus' Variae.* Göteborg: Acta Universitatis Gothoburgensis, 1984.

Wisse, Jakob. *Ethos and Pathos from Aristotle to Cicero.* Amsterdam: Hakkert, 1989.

White, John L. "The Form and Function of the Body of the Greek Letter: A Study of the Letter-Body in the Non-Literary Papyri and in Paul the Apostle." PhD diss., Vanderbilt University, 1970; Cambridge, Mass.: Society of Biblical Literature, 1972. Reprint, Missoula, Mont.: Scholars Press, 1972b.

———. *The Form and Structure of the Official Petition: A Study in Greek Epistolography.* Missoula, Mont.: Society of Biblical Literature, 1972a.

———. *Light from Ancient Letters.* Philadelphia: Fortress Press, 1986.

———. "New Testament Epistolary Literature in the Framework of Ancient Epistolography." In *Aufstieg und Niedergang der Römischen Welt* II.25.2. Berlin: W. de Gruyter, 1984, 1730–56.

———, ed. *Studies in Ancient Letter-Writing* (= *Semeia* 22). Chico, Calif.: Scholars Press, 1982.

Winter, Bruce. *Philo and Paul among Sophists.* Cambridge: Cambridge University Press, 1997.

Youtie, Herbert. C. "Textual Criticism of Papyri: Prolegomena." *Institute of Classical Studies Bulletin* Suppl. 6. London, 1958.

The Ars dictaminis, *the Formulary, and Medieval Epistolary Practice*

Malcolm Richardson

At the end of the eleventh century Alberic, a teacher at the celebrated Benedictine monastery of Monte Cassino, created the earliest-preserved Western medieval letter-writing manual. In it he discussed epistolary theories and differentiated the authorized parts of the letter. Alberic of Monte Cassino was a rhetorician by profession and consequently saw letter writing as a subfield of rhetoric, in particular Ciceronian rhetoric. During the next two hundred years epistolary rhetoric was a fundamental part of the curriculum at centers of advanced learning, moving from Monte Cassino to the great school at Bologna, and from Bologna throughout Italy, north to France, Germany, England, and elsewhere, before in the thirteenth century its intellectual center returned again to Italy for a final reflourishing. So deep was the academic interest in letter writing that, two centuries after Alberic's time, rhetoric itself was in some universities taught as a subfield of letter writing.

From an academic perspective, then, the period from approximately the beginning of the twelfth century to end of the fourteenth may be said to be the golden age of European letter-writing manuals, a period in which epistolary manuals became in some prestigious universities not only central textbooks in the formal study of rhetoric, but, because rhetoric was a cornerstone of medieval learning, central textbooks in medieval learning itself. From another perspective, however, medieval letter-writing manuals are simply the dead letter office of western culture, an intellectual cul-de-sac preserving the moribund theories of scholars on whom history has played a sad joke. The manual tradition derived from, coexisted, and mingled with—and eventually was survived by—another, more immediately practical tradition, that of the *formulary*. A formulary is the opposite of a theoretical treatise: it is simply a collection of model letters and documents, usually without commentary. In the end the drab formulary tradition prevailed over the best efforts of the academicians.

Because some readers of this collection may be new to medieval epistolography, this essay first describes medieval letter-writing manuals and traces their history, or rather it outlines as much as is now known about that history. In addition it argues that the much-despised formulary tradition should be recognized as a legitimate contribution to rhetorical history and has in fact a tacit theory of its own. Finally, it makes three personal suggestions for future research.

Basic Sources for the Study of Medieval Epistolary Treatises

At the outset, it is necessary to refer readers to important contemporary studies for more detailed information than can be provided here, and indeed to pay tribute to contemporary scholars who have extracted a history from a mass of far-flung and poorly cataloged manuscripts. Pride of place must go to James J. Murphy's detailed chapter on "The Art of Letter-Writing" in his essential *Rhetoric in the Middle Ages* (1974). Murphy's summaries of letter-writing manuals can scarcely be overvalued, especially because few are easily accessible and his history has become the received version. This can be supplemented by chapter 5 of his *Medieval Rhetoric: A Select Bibliography* (1971) and his edition and translation of *Three Medieval Rhetorical Arts* (1971), the first of which is an anonymous Bolognese letter-writing treatise. A broader view of the medieval epistle is found in Giles Constable's *Letters and Letter-Collections* (1976) in the invaluable Typologie des Sources du Moyen Âge Occidental series from Éditions Brepols. In this same series, Martin Camargo's *Ars Dictaminis / Ars Dictandi* (1991) summarizes a wide range of scholarship on medieval letter-writing theory. Both the Constable and Camargo books are central references, especially for their extensive bibliographic range. Those familiar with the work of Murphy, Camargo, and Constable will see my debt to them in every paragraph of the following essay. Even more recent are the bibliography by Janet Luehring and Richard Utz in the opening number of *Disputatio* (1996), a volume devoted to essays on the late medieval epistle, and a stimulating essay on letter-writing manuals by Alain Boureau (1997). Finally, those wishing to examine original manuscripts (relatively few are published) can now refer to the ongoing censuses of manuscript treatises on medieval and Renaissance letter writing compiled by Emil Polak (1993, 1994) and the extensive descriptive catalog of *ars dictandi* underway by Worstbrock, Klaes, and Lütten (1992). Also useful for finding manuscripts is the massive catalog of humanist manuscripts by the great Renaissance scholar Paul O. Kristeller (1963–1997). Besides the treatise translated by Murphy, a large number are found in the mid-nineteenth-century collection by Ludwig Rockinger (1863; repr. 1961), unfortunately still our largest published collection. The recent edition by Camargo of five late-medieval English treatises (in Latin), *Medieval Rhetorics* (1995), is scrupulously prepared, and has an invaluable introduction tying English manuals to the better-developed European tradition. Other useful editions with translations are those of Boncampagno's *Rota Veneris* (1975) and the *Introductiones dictandi* by Transmundus (1995).

Letter Writing and Medieval Society

The general deterioration of civic life and of the Roman-built road system in the earlier Middle Ages were, paradoxically, practical factors in the development of letter writing and letter-writing theory: literate people with business to transact had to write letters instead of travel. Although local and royal governments were, on the whole, primitive before about the year 1000, the church remained a powerful international force for literacy throughout Europe and cultivated an efficient ecclesiastical postal system from Sicily to Scandinavia at the very time when all other communications systems were decaying or disappearing. The papal chancery in Rome was a highly developed scriptorium from at least the seventh century; it remained in remarkably close epistolary contact with even the church's most remote outposts despite the catastrophic travel conditions in most of Europe (Bresslau 1969, esp. 1:86–352). In addition anyone who physically penned letters of any kind was almost certainly a member of the clergy, a situation that remained constant until at least the twelfth century and the rise of the notary and lawyer—and still true in some parts of the world today (Riché 1976, esp. pp. 22–23, 405–406). The church therefore provided the basic models for epistolary communication when secular literacy revived from its long hibernation.

By the eleventh century, the waves of invasions that had harried western Europe since the late Roman period had abated, leading to a renewal of commerce and active government; this created a need for long-distance communication, and consequently for secular chanceries on the public level and, eventually, private notaries and scribes on the private. Italy especially was, by the twelfth century, undergoing a stimulation of trade and education unparalleled since Roman times, and the Italian cities fostered a literate middle class that quickly saw the advantages of written records. The new University of Bologna, the first European center for the study of law, soon also became the center for epistolary theory. The blending of long-standing papal epistolary formats with legal writing was inevitable, and the letter became the chief format of many official documents today found in quite different form, notably deeds, decrees, and other legal and administrative genres. A market quickly sprang up for literate men who could write the various letter formats correctly, and, at their beginnings as now, the schools and universities responded eagerly to the job market while simultaneously proclaiming their allegiance to eternal values.

Training writers requires textbooks, and apparently the need for adequate textbooks lay behind the first medieval letter-writing manuals. At the period when Alberic of Monte Cassino's first manual appears (1087 is the probable date), the chief reference for the proper creation of letters was still the formulary used by papal and royal chancery clerks, notaries, and the like. It is possible for an administrative formulary like that created around 1400 by the English poet and Privy Seal clerk Thomas Hoccleve (British Library Add. Ms. 24062) to contain models of all the necessary documents (writs, letters, and so forth) a specific administrative office might ever need to fulfill its duties. (A formulary page is reproduced in Tessier 1962, 241.) General formularies, however, are limited by the number of examples they can reasonably expect to contain, for the number of letter-writing purposes will always far outstrip the number of examples that even the most ingenious compiler can provide. Rhetoricians like Alberic, therefore, saw that students needed a theoretical foundation from which they could write any letter on any subject quickly and fluidly, much the same way ancient rhetoricians provided theory and techniques for extemporaneous oral delivery. Because public speaking in the manner of the ancients was foreign to medieval culture outside of the art of preaching (*ars praedicandi*), much energy in rhetorical studies shifted about the year 1100 toward the art of letter writing, thereby matching the academic study of rhetoric with the needs of students and their future employment.

Because the study of letter writing was grounded in the academy, it was of necessity caught up in the profound soul-searching European learning underway in the early twelfth century. On the one side were the partisans of the older ecclesiastical education, and on the other the supporters of the newer schools such as Bologna with strong ties to the world outside the church hierarchy. At the beginning, Alberic of Monte Cassino's treatises (*Breviarium de dictaminie* and *Dictaminum radii*) saw letter writing as part of traditional medieval rhetorical training; his treatises are brief and unadorned because his students would already be immersed in the liberal arts curriculum and could readily place Alberic's theory in the context of the entire field of rhetoric. In the next century, however, the controversy divided rhetoricians and, for example, pitted the followers of Hugh of Bologna (*Rationes dictandi*, 1119) against those of Adelberto Samaritano (*Praecepta dictaminum*, 1111–1118). Adelberto was a secular teacher in Bologna who criticized Alberic for remaining within the older liberal arts tradition and urged the creation of a separate discipline of letter writing; Hugh, a Bolognese canon, defended Alberic and tradition.

The Contents of the Manuals

This is a suitable point at which to summarize the general characteristics of these manuals, because the basic precepts remained the same over several hundred years of manuals. As usefully defined by Camargo (*Ars Dictaminis*, 20–21; Murphy's definitions [*Rhetoric*, 219] differ slightly), the general term for the rhetorical art of letter writing was *ars dictaminis* and a textbook that presented this art was an *ars dictandi* (if brief) or a *summa dictandi* (if including both full theoretical treatment and model letters). Unfortunately, in practice these and similar terms were somewhat confused, so the contents of treatises on letter writing are not always apparent from the titles. Teachers of the *ars dictaminis* (sometimes just called the *dictamen*) were universally known as *dictatores*.

Medieval *artes dictandi* after the early twelfth century agree that a letter may be divided into five parts, clearly modeled after the six parts of a Ciceronian *oratio* (Murphy 1971, 224–225):

1. *Salutatio,* or formal greeting of the receiver;
2. *Captatio benevolentiae,* a section to win the receiver's sympathy, attention, and good will;
3. *Narratio,* the background leading to the request or demand;
4. *Petitio,* the request or demand;
5. *Conclusio,* the formal ending, often involving a blessing and the place and date of the letter, 1942).

Aside from the different parts of the letter, the chief topic of most *artes dictandi* was style, broadly conceived. The most frequent stylistic advice was for brevity, advice scrupulously followed in medieval nonliterary letters. *Dictatores* also supplied long lists of *colores,* usually taken from the *Rhetorica ad Herennium,* and stylistic pointers on variety, alliteration, and other traditional concerns.

Because medieval letters were intended to be read aloud to the recipient rather than silently and in private, manuals often spent much time on elements of Latin style that were designed to make the prose sound pleasing when spoken. Foremost among these stylistic refinements is the *cursus,* the rhythmical equivalent of the classical quantitative *clausulae* and widely practiced in the papal chancery and later in many royal and ducal chanceries. Related to the *cursus* were the *distinctiones,* patterns of rhythmical prose to emphasize the direction of thought (Camargo, *Ars Dictaminis,* 25). Some manuals discussed letters written in poetry, although letter-poems are predictably few.

France and Northern Europe

The definitive moment in dictaminal writings lasted roughly from the time of Alberic of Monte Cassino in the 1080s to approximately 1150 and was Italian, chiefly Bolognese. From the end of the twelfth century to approximately the second quarter of the thirteenth, the intellectual focus shifted to France, especially Orléans. The French remained more tied to traditional rhetorical teaching than the Italians and were less likely to create *artes dictandi* intended to stand alone and apart from the liberal arts curriculum. The prestigious University of Paris showed little interest in the *ars dictaminis* except as a secondary part of rhetoric, though other important schools at Tours and Meung were more receptive. French *dictatores* generally saw letter writing as a subset of medieval (Latin) grammar, closer to what is called composition in U.S. universities. They delved into matters of sentence structure, Latin declensions and cases, word arrangement, amplification, tropes, figures, and proverbs. Nor did they shrink from introducing classical allusions and other rhetorical/literary techniques, a tendency that ran counter to the simplifying emphasis of much Italian teaching. On the other hand, they added little that was genuinely new to theory and were content to follow the Bolognese theoretical models. Their other contributions were to add chapters on the *cursus,* already standard practice in the papal chancery in any case and in emphasizing more than the Italians legal and administrative correspondence (Murphy, *Rhetoric* 226–239; Camargo, *Ars Dictaminis,* 35–37).

Compared to the French, the manuals of the Germans are unimaginative derivatives of the Bolognese treatises. German rhetoricians also favored collections of models (*formelbücher*) covering every possible contingency, with a heavy emphasis on legal and administrative documents. English academics paid even less attention to the *artes dictaminis* outside of Thomas Merke's *De moderno dictamine* (1405), curious for a nation that has the largest surviving body of medieval public records (Camargo, *Medieval Rhetorics;* Murphy, *Rhetoric,* 239–243).

Italy Again, and Decline

The interest in letter writing may be seen as part of a rekindled reliance on the written word that crept northward over western Europe from the eleventh century on. In its most developed form, the *dictamen* is part of the same textualizing impetus that created highly evolved royal administrations and, at the same time, the European legal profession. Letter-writing manuals dealing exclusively with legal and official documents are known as *artes notariae,* though in practice the overlap with the *artes dictandi* is often heavy, as in the German treatises. This tension between the legal and humanistic aspects of the *ars dictaminis* characterizes the final phase of the intellectual history of the manuals, when the intellectual energy again returns to Italy.

By 1200, the Italian *dictatores* at Bologna had won the right to have their own faculty, and by 1221 teachers of the *ars notariae* also had theirs. Unlike most modern rhetoricians, these academicians had became involved in the public life of their city, and the political, rough-and-tumble aspect of their careers influenced the practical bent that the Italian *ars dictaminis* took in the thirteenth century and thereafter, when academic rivalries and controversies took on the qualities of political campaigns. The intellectual product was the *summa dictandi,* in which theory and model letters were united in hefty volumes such as those by Boncompagno. The accomplishments of these *dictatores* might be seen as an extension of the French models of slightly earlier. Although shorn of the literary influence favored by the French, their manuals retained sections on the *cursus.* Contrariwise, the later period produced large numbers of short works on specialized aspects of the letter or on one classification of document, perhaps intended for advanced coursework. Other rhetoricians created volumes consisting largely of models, some wholly fabricated. Compilers/authors such as Pier della Vigna and Thomas of Capua brought out widely circulated works that included not only model letters but also replies to them.

The practical bent of later Italian dictaminal writings suggests the economic value of rhetorical studies at the time—namely, that they were a stepping stone to a career. With a liberal arts curriculum as a basis, students could then proceed to an increasingly lucrative legal or notarial civic position. It is small wonder that the *ars notariae* proved a serious rival and in a sense replaced the *ars dictaminis* as the legal profession grew to absorb so much academic interest at the end of the Middle Ages (Murphy, *Rhetoric* 244–266; Camargo, *Ars Dictaminis,* 39–41).

Theory—which had advanced very little if at all from that of the earlier twelfth century—was gradually edged out of manuals by the models, thereby returning the *ars dictaminis* close to the point where it started two centuries earlier in the formulary tradition. The thirteenth and fourteenth centuries found the *ars dictaminis* at the height of its popularity but at the nadir of it originality, for the serious study of the *ars dictaminis* had been replaced in Italy by the *ars notariae* and in France by the *ars grammatica* (Murphy, *Three Medieval Rhetorical Arts,* xvi–xvii).

Descriptions of Two Manuals, Early and Late

Before completing the story of the *ars dictaminis,* it may be appropriate to describe the content of two medieval letter-writing manuals, one early and one late, each of which represents contemporary tendencies in the creation of epistolary manuals.

The first is an anonymous Bolognese manual from 1135, *Rationes dictandi,* conveniently edited and translated by Murphy in *Three Medieval Rhetorical Arts* (1971). The manual is relatively short (around twenty printed pages, with large type) and contains no complete examples of letters. Organized with true scholastic didacticism, it moves from the definition of all written composition to the definition of a letter, then through the letter's subparts, and finally into issues of the arrangement of parts, variations on the standard arrangements, and the acceptable syntax and grammar, the last part lifted from the late Roman grammarian Priscian.

When examining the parts of the letter, the manual is absorbed with the salutation and the securing of good will (*benevolentiae captatio*). It has nothing to say about the narration except such observations as "some narrations are simple, others complex." The petition is subdivided into nine classifications such as supplicatory, exhortative, or direct. The discussion here is again not very penetrating: "A petition is supplicatory when we entreat by prayers that something be done or not done" (19). The section on the *benevolentiae captatio* is more extended and deals with appropriate ways to flatter the recipient, even briefly suggesting grounds on which the good will might be secured ("fellowship," "fatherly feeling and filial feeling," and so forth). Examples are scarce, however, and the author finally admits that sometimes flattery fits best in the salutation, which is indeed his chief interest in the treatise, taking up about half of it. He carefully examines the order in which the recipient's name is initially presented (first, last, multiple times) and which are the appropriate Latin cases, since Latin cases in the address could be used to infer the social relationship between writer and recipient. He then goes through a number of sample salutations, including "The Pope's Universal Salutation," "The Emperor's Salutations to All Men," "Salutations of Ecclesiastials among Themselves," and on down the social ladder.

One curiosity is that the closer the author's examples get to salutations that would most likely be used by the actual (student) readers, the less space he devotes to theory and the more to examples. The sections on "Salutations of Subjects to their Lords," for example, or "Salutations of Sons to their Parents" are largely devoted to concrete examples. Predictably, the "Salutation of a Pupil to his Teacher" is quite flowery: "To N[ame], by divine grace resplendent in Ciceronian charm, [the pupil], inferior to his devoted learning, expresses the servitude of a sincere heart," and so forth On the other hand, the author is reasonably flexible, noting that salutations can be varied and that different parts of the letter can be mixed and varied according to the needs of the message.

The second example of a manual, one illustrating the logical outcome of the practical tendencies of the later epistolary rhetorics, is Lawrence of Aquilegia's *Practica sive usus dictaminis* (c. 1300?). The "art" of letter writing now becomes a mechanical application of stereotypical phrases according to the recipient's social status. Lawrence provides his readers with tables of ready phrases rather than a theoretical discussion even on the level of *Rationes dictandi*. The reader only had to move his fingers across the tables to what he needed out of one of Lawrence's seven levels and choose phrases that seem to fit—even the connecting verbs and phrases are schematized. As usual, the list of potential receivers runs from the pope down through kings, archdeacons, friends, and finally to heretics and "falsos infidelos." As Murphy drily notes, this "represents a dead end unparalleled in the history of the arts of discourse" (*Rhetoric*, 259–263).

A Model Letter

If Lawrence of Aquilegia is an extreme example, even the earliest manuals contained enough examples of the individual phrases and letter parts so that an appropriate letter could be assembled without too much thought. The following is a typical example of a student-level letter recommended by the manuals:

> To the man of all wisdom by divine grace, Benedictus by grace, Benedictus by name, Benedictus even by deed, N____ offers loyal service and wishes the protection of divine blessings [*salutatio*]. Since I truly know that you are bound to me both by the tie of kinship and by the unity of warm affection, therefore I do not hesitate at all to ask your kindness with confident boldness, and then to seek from you a favor [*captatio benevolentiae*]. I therefore ask humbly, I pray most earnestly, I entreat compassionately, that you sustain me generously

with your gifts from now until the feast of the Resurrection [*petitio*]. For indeed you know how scanty are the gifts of parents, how infrequent, how inadequate [etc.] [*narratio*]. If you do this, you will have the entirety of our fullest affection [*conclusio*]. (translated by Murphy, *Three Medieval Rhetorical Arts*, 16, 23, 19)

This is not, however, an authentic model letter, but a do-it-yourself student begging letter I have pieced together from *Rationes dictandi*. It is all quite easy.

Three Potential Areas for Future Research

Having covered the best-studied epistolary manual traditions in the Middle Ages, I will suggest briefly three potentially rewarding areas of rhetorical study, each dealing with exemplary—that is, model—letters. Although the current sad state of publication of medieval epistolary manuals may make such desiderata seem premature or presumptuous, the ongoing work of Polak, Worstbrock, and Camargo suggests that scholars will soon have accurate lists and editions in greater numbers, and this in turn will lead to increased publication. Here are three personal suggestions for scholarly attention, though I would not claim that these represent the most pressing needs:

The Formulary Tradition

Collections of model letters have an uninterrupted history from the early Middle Ages to now, and, although today they are likely to be electronic, they have retained an undying popularity with the busy, lazy, or dishonest writer. Model letter collections are likely to be treated with contempt and scarcely concealed outrage by rhetoricians, whose profession is, after all, to teach students how to invent letters from scratch. They are also likely to be slighted by academic rhetorician/researchers, whose unstated mission is often to demonstrate the importance of their academic ancestors. The most recent bibliographer of the formulary, Guido van Dievoet, disposes of his subject in five pages, or rather five half-pages, since most of his space is taken up with notes citing chiefly historical and legal studies (1986, 75–79). Georges Tessier, whose topic is a thousand years of French royal documents, presents his bibliography on formularies in two pages (1962, 266–267). Murphy (*Rhetoric*, 199–202) likewise seems relieved to move on to the *academic ars dictaminis*, noting that formularies "are chiefly notarial in nature" and hence, it is implied, out of the range of rhetorical studies. (Because formularies often used real-life letters as examples, however, nineteenth-century European historians like Rockinger and Bresslau produced shelves of imposing volumes of source material and analysis.) So, although the highly academic *ars dictaminis* has been the object of numerous studies despite the general admission that it had no lasting effect on the history of rhetoric, the model letter collections go begging for serious rhetorical analysis, even though the medieval "form letter," in fact, was the basis of untold thousands of private and official letters well into the eighteenth century.

Nevertheless, although few would insist that a formulary is engaging late-night reading, formularies reveal the deep structure of medieval letter writing. They existed before the *dictatores* and survived them by several centuries. The rhetorical formats they exemplified were the basis of epistolary communication for many centuries and were used by many more writers than the Roman *cursus* or Guido Faba's treatises. No one leafing through the pages of Thomas Rymer's *Foedera*, a gigantic collection of diplomatic and historical letters, can fail to notice that most of these are written in a direct and simple style that follows a common logic. Furthermore, like Alberic of Monte Cassino's student readers, experienced readers of formularies would carry in their heads years of theory and practical experience that they could apply to each model letter.

To a rhetorician, the most striking feature of this widely used formulary/notarial style must surely be the manner in which it defines social relations. Deriving from a hierarchical age, it adopts a hierarchical rhetoric. Recipients are addressed either as superiors or inferiors; messages are either demands or petitions. Our assessment of medieval social and epistolary relationships must be filtered through a knotty and unyielding epistolary rhetoric. It is thus something of a relief to read about the medieval messenger who normally read letters aloud to the recipient and supplied the private, humorous, or blunt touches not possible with the formulary rhetoric (Constable 1976, 52–55).

Although there is no space here for me to develop this theme adequately, consider the structural similarity of two highly formulaic letters below:

> King Edward sends friendly greetings to Bishop Wulfwig and Earl Gyrth and all my thegns in Oxfordshire. And I inform you that I have given to Westminster, to Christ and to St. Peter, Launton, with sake and soke, with toll and team and infangenetheof, and in all things as fully and completely as I myself possessed it. And I will not permit that anyone have any authority therein except the abbot and brethren in the monastery. God keep you (Harmer 1989, no. 95, 360)

> Right trusty and well-beloved, we greet you well. Humble suit having been made to use in your behalf for leave to remain or live sometimes during your mayoralty out of our City of London, . . . we are graciously pleased to condescend thereto, and we do accordingly, hereby, give and grant you full license and permission . . . etc. And so we bid you heartily farewell. Given at our court at St. James, [etc.] (adapted from Hall 1908, 1:153)

These two letters illustrate the longevity of the formulary styles: the first was written about 1066, the third by George II's secretaries in 1733.

These are, of course, royal letters, but, lest anyone believe that the formulaic, notarial style had little effect on what ordinary literate people wrote, consider this little missive from the otherwise obscure Thomas Hales to his mother, written in London, probably in the 1430s:

> Right worshipful mother, I commend me to you, desiring to hear of your welfare, the which I pray God keep you there in all, so I pray you of your blessing, the which is better to me than any worldly good. Also, I thank you for the cheeses that you sent to my masters and to me. And I pray you to send me the casket that I had at Winchester. And no more to you at this time, but God have you in his keeping. Amen. Written at London the twenty-eighth day of September. (London, Public Record Office, Ancient Correspondence, SC 1/44, no. 33, unpublished)

A letter-writing style in which man may not gracefully thank his mother for cheeses is clearly primed for the reforms of the Renaissance letter-writing manuals.

Bourgeois Manuals

A second interesting and largely unexplored area of cultural and rhetorical analysis is the bourgeois "customal" book. Toward the end of the Middle Ages, basic literacy became a necessity for increasing numbers of middle-class merchants as international travel and complex, multilevel business transactions became more common. More or less standard business letter forms, such as the basic letter of credit, met the needs of merchants trading in a confused legal and linguistic environment (Postan 1973, 55–57). Beginning in Italy in the thirteenth century and moving north steadily, merchants and other middle-class citizens began writing their own letters and documents, or at least recognized the need for such documents in their lives by hiring scribes or secretaries (Roncière 1988, 252–259). These letters were, on the whole, in the vernacular. By the fifteenth-century bourgeois letter writing was common throughout Europe, resulting in such family collections as the Cely or Paston correspondence, and even more so in collections of model business letters such as in British Library Harley MS 3988.

Although many of these letters were actually inscribed by professionals (lawyers, secretaries, notaries, priests), middle-class citizens sometimes kept guides to correspondence and other useful documents on hand. Although a few vernacular *artes dictaminis* were produced (Camargo, *Ars Dictaminis,* 41), the ordinary citizen sometimes used multipurpose books that provided ready models for reference. In Italy well-to-do families produced what are probably the most well-developed of this type, the *libri di famiglia,* multigenerational, secret books that contained for the eyes of the patriarchs only frank discussions of the family business, including the necessary correspondence (Béc 1967; Jed 1989, 74–120). In England, London merchants assembled commonplace books that sometimes contained model letters and other business documents (Meale 1983), culminating in the publication of the so-called *Arnold's Chronicle* of c. 1503, an early printed ready-reference of bourgeois fact and fancy. Richard Arnold's book, more accurately called by its original name *Customs of London,* contains more than thirty pages of samples of forms such as letters of attorney, license, sale, and exchange (*Customs* 1811, 102–137). Indeed, mastering the form of the notarial letter was an important business objective, for the letter format was widely used for a much wider variety of purposes than today. The eminent medievalist H. G. Richardson noted, for example, "Early deeds are often hardly to be distinguished from letters, and a deed, like a letter, was a message meant not only to be read, but to be read aloud; the same rules, it might well be thought, should govern both" (1942, 331).

These citizen's books not only served as model-letter collections for such letter/documents, but, by placing the letters in the proximity of their carefully chosen poetry, family records, chronicles, and historical documents, also placed them in the broad context of late medieval bourgeois culture. Such books, taken as a whole, therefore evoke a social setting as vivid as those of the "compleat letter-writers" of later centuries. Such texts might illuminate the dying days of the *ars dictaminis* in an increasingly middle-class world and also might help explain the death of this medieval rhetorical art as it faced the changed economic and social environment of the sixteenth century.

Linguistic Analysis

Few rhetoricians are trained in linguistics and in general have overlooked the work of historical linguists who deal with letters and letter collections. During the past twenty years, however, medieval letters have been shown to be an important source for historical linguists, especially because medieval private letters, unlike most medieval texts, have not been through innumerable recensions and consequent scribal tinkering. They are thus as close to firsthand reports of language use as linguists are likely to get for this period. A large-scale application of medieval letters can be found in the *Linguistic Map of Late Medieval England,* a monumental study of English dialects.

Of more interest to rhetoricians, perhaps, is the computer-assisted analysis underway on the so-called Helsinki Corpus, especially that portion of the corpus devoted to letters. Some of the resulting work is reported in a collection called *Sociolinguistics and Language History: Studies Based on the Corpus of Early English Correspondence* (1996), edited by Terttu Nevalainen and Helena Raumolin-Brunberg. Contributors to this volume work from a data base to extract highly suggestive ideas about such issues as social stratification and gender difference, and of course similar analysis can also be used to more accurately determine the date and origin of letter-writing manuals. An analysis of tropes, figures, and formulae might also be of considerable value.

Such work illustrates how different methodologies can be used for a broader, more socially aware analysis of letter-writing manuals than we are now being given. Indeed, except for the work of Ronald Witt and a handful of others, much scholarship on medieval letter-writing manuals seems as doggedly narrow as the manuals themselves.

Conclusion

Medieval letter-writing manuals have not had a good press in modern times and are often disparaged for the aridity of their theory. The heavy emphasis on the social status of the sender and on the correctness of the *Salutatio* have not endeared them to future generations, nor did the *summas* that tended toward formularies prove of much use in the changed political, religious, and social environment of the Renaissance and later. Even their most influential modern student, Murphy, can muster no more enthusiasm for the *ars dictaminis* except to say that it is "a rare example of applied rhetoric" (*Rhetoric,* 268).

It could be argued that the chief long-term effects of the *ars dictaminis* were largely unrelated to their theoretical concerns. The most important effect was, of course, the development of a tradition of letter-writing manuals that has never faltered. A second effect was the reintroduction into European oratory of Ciceronian rhetoric, a by-product of the interaction of the *dictatores* with Italian civic life toward the end of the Middle Ages (Witt). A third effect, also chiefly at the end of the Middle Ages, was fostering the widening circle of literacy, including the literacy of women. dictaminal rules, as stultifying as they may seem to us today, provided a rhetorical framework through which middle-class citizens could more confidently move into true literacy. Formulaic writing has its limits as a means of complex communication, but it enables insecure and inexperienced writers to practice their skills within a comfortably narrow frame (M. Richardson, "The *Dictamen*" [1984] and "Women Commercial Writers" [1996]).

Taken as a whole, then, the *artes dictandi* do not represent a high point in the history of western rhetorical theory. Most of advice dispensed by the *dictatores* was taken as a body from other parts of rhetoric (the *colores*) or existing practice (the *cursus,* "common form"). Perhaps the greatest failure of the manuals, at least from a modern perspective, is the failure to analyze cogently the various parts of the letter. The unwillingness to develop adequate treatments of what should be the heart of the letter, the *narratio* and *petitio* sections, reveals the intellectual derivativeness of the *dictatores* and why their names are all but forgotten.

Works Cited

Béc, Christian. *Les marchands ecrivains: affairs et humanisme a Florence, 1375–1434.* Paris: Mouton, 1967.

Boncampagno da Signa. *Rota Veneris.* Translated by Joseph Purkart. Delmar, N.Y.: Scholars' Facsimile and Reprints, 1975.

Boureau, Alain. "The Letter-Writing Norm, a Mediaeval Invention." In *Correspondence: Models of Letter-Writing from the Middle Ages to the Nineteenth Century,* edited by Roger Chartier, Alain Boureau, and Cécile Dauphin. Translated by Christopher Woodall. Princeton, N.J.: Princeton University Press, 1997.

Bresslau, Harry. *Handbuch der Urkundenlehre für Deutschland und Italien.* 4th ed. 3 vols. Berlin: Walter de Gruyter, 1969.

Camargo, Martin. *Ars Dictaminis / Ars Dictandi.* Typologie des Sources du Moyen Âge, fasc. 60. Turnhout, Belgium: Éditions Brepols, 1991.

———. *Medieval Rhetorics of Latin Prose Composition: Five English Artes Dictandi and their Tradition.* Medieval and Renaissance Texts and Studies, no. 115. Binghamton, N.Y.: Binghamton University Press: 1995.

Constable,Giles. *Letters and Letter-Collections.* Typologie des Sources du Moyen Âge, fasc. 17. Turnhout, Belgium: Éditions Brepols, 1976.

Customs of London; otherwise called Arnold's Chronicle; containing, among divers other Matters, the celebrated poem, The Nut-brown Maid. Edited by F. Douce. London, 1811.

Dievoet, Guido van. *Les Coutumiers, Les Styles, Les Formulaires et Les "Artes Notariae."* Typologie des Sources du Moyen Âge, fasc. 48. Turnhout, Belgium: Éditions Brepols, 1986

Formularies Which Bear on the History of Oxford, c. 1204–1420. Edited by H. E. Salter, W. A. Pantin, and H. G. Richardson. 2 vols. Oxford Historical Society, n.s. 4. Oxford: Clarendon Press, 1942.

Hall, Hubert. *A Formula Book of English Official Historical Documents.* 2 vols. Cambridge: University Press, 1908

Harmer, Florence E. *Anglo-Saxon Writs,* 2nd ed. Stamford, England: Paul Watkins, 1989.

Jed, Stephanie H. *Chaste Thinking: The Rape of Lucretia and the Birth of Humanism.* Bloomington: Indiana University Press, 1989.

Kristeller, Paul O. *Iter Italicum: A Finding List of Uncatalogued or Incompletely Catalogued Humanistic Manuscripts of the Renaissance in Italian and other Libraries.* 7 vols. London: Warburg Institute, 1963–97.

Linguistic Map of Late Mediaeval English. 4 vols. Edited by Angus McIntosh et al. Aberdeen: Aberdeen University Press, 1986.

Luehring, Janet, and Richard J. Utz. "Letter Writing in the Middle Ages (c. 1250–1600): An Introductory Bibliography," *Disputatio* 1 (1996): 191–229.

Meale, Carol S. "The Compiler at Work: John Colyns and BL MS Harley 2252." In *Manuscripts and Readers in Fifteenth Century England: The Literary Implications of Manuscript Study,* edited by Derek Pearsall. Cambridge: D.S. Brewer, 1983, 82–103.

Murphy. James J. *Medieval Rhetoric: A Select Bibliography.* Toronto Medieval Bibliographies. Toronto: University of Toronto Press, 1971.

———. *Rhetoric in the Middle Ages.* Berkeley: University of California Press, 1974.

———, ed. *Three Medieval Rhetorical Arts.* Berkeley: University of California Press, 1971.

Nevalainen, Terttu, and Helena Raumolin-Brunberg, eds. *Sociolinguistics and Language History: Studies Based on the Corpus of Early English Correspondence.* Language and Computers: Studies in Practical Lnguistics, no. 15. Amsterdam/Atlanta: Rodolpi, 1996.

Polak, Emil J. *Medieval and Renaissance Letter Treatises and Form Letters: A Census of Manuscripts Found in Eastern Europe and the Former U.S.S.R.* Davis Medieval Texts and Studies, no. 8. New York: E. J. Brill, 1993.

————. *Medieval and Renaissance Letter Treatises and Form Letters: A Census of Manuscripts Found in part of Western Europe, Japan, and the United States of America.* Davis Medieval Texts and Studies, no. 9. New York: E. J. Brill, 1994.

Postan, M. M. *Medieval Trade and Finance.* Cambridge: Cambridge University Press, 1973.

Richardson, H[enry]. G[erald]. "Letters of the Oxford *Dictatores,*" *Formularies Which Bear on the History of Oxford* (1942), 2:331–450.

Richardson, Malcolm. "The *Dictamen* and Its Influence on Fifteenth-Century English Prose," *Rhetorica* 2 (1984): 207–26.

————. "Women Commercial Writers of Late Medieval England," *Disputatio: A Transdisciplinary Journal of Medieval Studies* 1.1 (1996): 123–46.

Riché, Pierre. *Education and Culture in the Barbarian West, Sixth through Eighth Centuries.* 3rd ed. Translated by John J. Contreni. Columbia: University of South Carolina Press, 1976.

Rockinger, Ludwig. *Briefsteller und formelbücher des eilften bis vierzehnten jahrhunderts.* 2 vols. 1863. Reprint, New York: Burt Franklin, 1961.

Roncière, Charles de la. "Tuscan Notables on the Eve of the Renaissance." In *A History of Private Life,* edited by Philip Ariès and Georges Duby II. Cambridge, Mass.: Harvard University Press, 1988, 157–310.

Tessier, Georges. *Diplomatique Royale Française.* Paris: J. Picard, 1962.

Transmundus. *Introductiones dictandi.* Translated by Anne Dalzell. Toronto: Medieval Institute of Pontifical Studies, 1995.

Witt, Ronald. "Medieval 'Ars Dictaminis' and the Beginnings of Humanism." *Renaissance Quarterly* 35 (1982): 1–35.

Worstbrock, Franz Josef, Monica Klaes, and Jutta Lütten. *Repertorium der Artes Dictandi des Mittelalters: Teil I: Von den Anfängen bis um 1200.* Munich: Wilhelm Fink Verlag, 1992.

If You Can't Join Them, Beat Them;
or, When Grammar Met Business Writing (in Fifteenth-Century Oxford)

Martin Camargo

Like most institutions, medieval universities generally introduced new regulations only when the existing regulations were felt to be ineffective. When university officials took the trouble to revise a statute or to write a new one, more often than not they were reacting either to new circumstances or to a chronic problem that had recently become acute. Sometimes the precipitating action can be guessed at only from the record of the reaction (the new statute), but often it can also be recovered through more direct evidence. Cases in which both sides are heard from provide especially illuminating insights into the "turf wars" that were as common in medieval universities as in their modern descendants.

In early fifteenth-century Oxford, the teaching of writing, including letter writing, seems to have been the focus of one such conflict. The nature and the significance of this particular turf war have been misunderstood because it has been assumed that the university was simply refining a longstanding set of regulations when in fact it was reacting to what was a relatively new challenge to its authority. Although the university had issued statutes regulating writing instruction during the fourteenth century, those statutes applied only to persons teaching in Latin grammar schools. By the 1430s the university felt the need to assert its authority over a different sort of teacher, one whose increasingly coherent professional identity had underscored his independence of the university and his rivalry with the very grammar teachers covered by the fourteenth-century statutes. In other words the issue of institutional hegemony arose as a direct result of discipline formation.

The fourteenth-century statutes at Oxford indicate a grammar curriculum that included as a matter of course more extensive training in Latin composition than was normal anywhere else in England. The earliest statute regulating instruction in composition was issued before 1350 and probably before 1313,[1] and the second was issued before 1380. The relevant passages are almost identical in both statutes. No one, they declare, should lecture in grammar unless licensed to do so by the chancellor, and such license should not be granted unless the would-be teacher "has first been examined concerning the manner of composing in verse and in prose and concerning the authors and the parts [of speech]."[2] My translation of "de modo dictandi" as "concerning the manner of composing in prose" represents a middle road between a narrower and a broader possible meaning: "dictandi" could also refer to "letter writing" or even to "composition" in general, but in England, at least, the pairing of "*versificandi et dictandi*" appears to have become a formula for "composition in verse and in prose" no later than the early thirteenth century, when it appears in the titles of Geoffrey of Vinsauf's *Documentum de modo et arte dictandi et versificandi* and Gervase of Melkley's *De arte versificatoria et modo dictandi*. The point is perhaps a small one, because the most important type of written prose was by far the letter, but I make it as a caution against automatically equating any use of the term *dictare* with the *ars dictaminis*. This distinction is particularly important when speaking of the English grammar schools, in which prose composition was often taught by means of exercises in translating English into Latin and vice versa (the *vulgaria* and *latinitates*) but in which the *ars dictaminis* per se would have been taught only at the most advanced levels of instruction, if at all.[3]

The Oxford grammar schools were among those that clearly did provide instruction in letter writing. Those fourteenth-century statutes that spell out the teaching that the grammarians are to provide explicitly include letter writing. Every two weeks, the grammar teachers "are required to assign (*dare*) verses and letters composed with proper words that are neither bombastic nor a yard long (*non ampullosis aut sexquipedalibus*), and with trim, graceful clauses, with metaphors that are clear and, as much as possible, full of wisdom; which verses and which letters the recipients should write down on parchment on the next feast day, or sooner, and then on the next day, when they come to school, they should recite them to their master from memory and submit them in written form."[4]

There is much that the statutes do not tell us about this instruction. No mention is made of the textbooks to be used or of the relationship between this instruction and the ordinary lectures in grammar required for the baccalaureate. The surviving manuscripts suggest that there was significant expansion in the range of materials used by the grammar masters, as locally compiled rhetorics took their place alongside old standards, as well as newly rediscovered treatises from the twelfth and thirteenth centuries, and were supplemented by "literary" works such as Alan of Lille's *De planctu Naturae*, John of Limoges's *Morale somnium Pharaonis*, and Richard of Bury's *Philobiblon* (Camargo, *"Libri Catoniani"* [1994], 165–187), but the statutes pass over such changes in silence.

What they do make absolutely clear is that the composition teaching that they describe was part of a larger course in Latin grammar that was offered under the supervision of two masters appointed by the university. Very little is known about the grammar teachers whose professional activities were regulated by the fourteenth-century statutes. Some of them may have been nonmasters, others probably held only the specialized M.Gramm., while still others seem to have been full-fledged M.A.s. Among those who had not attained the M.A. were teachers who used their experience at Oxford as a stepping stone to teaching positions elsewhere in England, as well as teachers who maintained grammar schools in Oxford for many years (Lobel 1965, 40–43; Hunt 1959–1960, 163–193; Thomson, "Grammar Masters" [1983], 298–310). The only teachers of Latin composition whose names are associated with surviving copies of materials used in such instruction are a pair of M.A.s—John of Briggis (d. 1407) and Simon Alcock (fl. 1420–1436)—whose grammar teaching probably was confined to the years immediately after each attained the master's degree.[5]

Perhaps because of their largely anonymous and somewhat ambiguous status, the university-supervised grammar teachers have been conflated with another group of teachers about whom considerably more is known and who might be called "business teachers." Although most members of this group—which includes John of Bromley and Thomas Sampson in the fourteenth century and Simon O., William Kingsmill, and David Pencaer in the fifteenth century—also taught the art of composing letters in Latin, that is, the only area in which their instruction overlapped with that of the grammar teachers. Because there is no evidence that John of Bromley or Thomas Sampson ever taught Latin grammar, it is unlikely that either man is to be included among the grammar teachers regulated by the fourteenth-century statutes of the university. Moreover, when the business teachers were unambiguously mentioned, as they finally were in a statute of 1432, it seems clear that the university regarded them as outside competitors who needed to be brought under the university's supervision.

According to the writers of the 1432 statute, students who are studying a discipline (*artem*) for which there are no ordinary lectures should attend the ordinary lectures of the faculty or science (*facultatis seu sciencie*) most closely related to the extracurricular subject that they are studying. The statute writers have a specific group of students in mind:

> Because the arts of writing, composing, and speaking the French language, in which there are no ordinary lectures, are closer to grammar and rhetoric than to the other sciences and faculties, although subordinate (*subalternate*) to them, therefore the university ordains and decrees that all scholars who have been trained sufficiently in grammar alone and who are chiefly studying the art of writing or composing or speaking French, or of composing charters or other such-like scripts, or of holding lay courts, or the English method of pleading, should attend the ordinary lectures of the artists lecturing on grammar or rhetoric, paying fees (*cumulando*) to them as to their own masters. [6]

Moreover, the teachers offering these extracurricular subjects are forbidden to teach at the times when members of the arts faculty hold their ordinary lectures, must have the chancellor's and proctors' permission to teach, must swear to observe all university regulations, must submit to the same supervision as the regent masters of grammar, and must pay an annual fee to the liberal artists in compensation for the damage done to them by their teaching—*in recompensam preiudicii per eorum doctrinam arcistis illati* (Gibson 1931, 240–241).

The subjects enumerated are precisely those that were currently being offered by the business teacher William Kingsmill (Legge 1939, 242–243), and the statute clearly was intended to prevent matriculated students from spending their time and money in his school in Cat Street, enjoying the privileges of the university without even the pretense of studying toward a degree. More puzzling is the timing of this statute. Elements of the "business course" had been taught at Oxford since at least the second quarter of the thirteenth century, and Thomas Sampson was teaching precisely the range of subjects listed half a century before the university took aim at his successors.

What had happened during the first quarter of the fifteenth century to convince university officials that it was time to impose their authority on the business teachers after tolerating their relative autonomy for so many years? Although it is possible to speculate about the immediate cause(s), what is certain is that an important change in the professional identity of the business teachers was an essential precondition for the university's response. The evolution of this professional identity can be traced from the changes in teaching materials and through the careers of the men who developed and used them, principally John of Bromley, Thomas Sampson, and William Kingsmill.

The business training available in Oxford from the early thirteenth century through the first half of the fourteenth century included some of the same skills —notably, accounting and letter writing—as the training regulated by the 1432 statute. That earlier training in "estate management," however, seems never to have coalesced into what could be called a "discipline" or even a "course" (Oschinsky 1971). The first signs of what could more properly be called a "business course" emerged during the second half of the fourteenth century, particularly in the teaching of Thomas Sampson. It was not simply a consistent and coherent set of subjects that marked the "business course" as an emergent discipline, however; that autonomy came only when the course no longer depended for its existence on the abilities of the exceptional teacher who created it. When William Kingsmill was able to assume intact a teaching program that he probably had no hand in developing, the "business course" had achieved what amounted to disciplinary status.

The "professionalization" of the business course thus was characterized by two complementary developments—internal coherence and transferability. Both developments can first be observed in the teaching of a certain John of Bromley, who rented a hall, with a school, at the back of All Saints' Church in Oxford as early as 1356 and continued to do so in 1365 (Emden 1957–1959, 276–277). His name appears in the model accounts of a tract on keeping household accounts, dated 1356 (BL, MS. Harley 4971, fols. 26r–29v), and in the model documents of a treatise on conveyancing that must have been composed around 1363 (BL, MS. Harley 4993, fols. 25r–34r). Versions of both texts occur with Thomas

Sampson's name in place of John of Bromley's, which indicates that Sampson adopted his predecessor's textbooks just as his successors would do in their turn. Nevertheless, because the manuscript containing the only extant copy of John's treatise on conveyancing was written in 1459 or later, it has long been assumed that John of Bromley was, like William Kingsmill, a fifteenth-century appropriator of Sampson's work (Richardson, "Business Training" [1941], 278). So far there is no positive evidence that John of Bromley wrote an *ars dictandi* of his own. His predecessors in the thirteenth century were more likely to use a simple collection of model letters, which might be supplemented by an *ars dictandi* imported from Italy or France. It is quite possible that the use of a "domestic" *ars dictandi* was an innovation introduced by Thomas Sampson, who also seems to have pioneered the use of French in the business course that he inherited or appropriated from John of Bromley.

John of Bromley's textbooks—in particular his *cartuaria,* or treatise on conveyancing—proved to be the nucleus around which Thomas Sampson developed the full business course. Whether he studied with John of Bromley or simply replaced him as the premier business teacher, Sampson probably had begun to teach at Oxford in the late 1360s and no later than the mid-1370s. He continued to revise his lectures up to about 1409, when he may have been eighty or more years old. Like John of Bromley, he was married and lived with his wife, Isabel, outside the city walls of Oxford. During his long career, Sampson continued to teach the core subjects of the business teachers—accountancy, conveyancing, and letter writing—gradually expanding the repertoire to include elementary instruction in the French language and a number of other subjects, among them the rudiments of common-law pleading (Arnold 1937, 193–209; Richardson, "Business Training" [1941], 259–280; Hassell 1991).

Sampson may have been succeeded as the reigning teacher of the business course by a shadowy figure who calls himself "Simon O." and whose surname is expanded to "Oxenford" in one of the seven manuscripts containing texts associated with his teaching (Richardson, "Oxford Teacher" [1939], 436–457). Judging from those manuscripts, Simon taught a much narrower range of subjects than Thomas Sampson did: the only works that can be assigned to him are a treatise on conveyancing extant in four copies, an art of letter writing preserved in Rylands MS. 394, and a second art of letter writing that he either composed himself or adapted for his own use, as reflected in the two copies that survive.[7] Moreover, although much if not most of Sampson's teaching was conducted in French, Simon appears to have restricted himself to Latin. Simon O. may have been one of those rivals about whom Thomas Sampson occasionally complained and may have competed for some of the more advanced students among Sampson's potential clientele. The versions of Simon's works that I have studied so far date from the second decade of the fifteenth century, but he may have begun to teach at Oxford somewhat earlier, at a time when Sampson was still active. Further evidence that he was not Sampson's chosen successor is the fact that he composed his own *artes dictandi* and *cartuaria* rather than adapting Sampson's textbooks.

More clearly following in the footsteps of John of Bromley and Thomas Sampson was William Kingsmill. Like Sampson, Kingsmill provides many details of his biography in his model letters and documents, and some of those details may be verified from other sources (Emden 1957–1959, 1074–1075; Legge 1939, 241–246). Kingsmill spent many years doing the sort of work for which Thomas Sampson trained his pupils. In 1402 and again in 1419 he is recorded as "citizen and scrivener of London," and, even after he moved from London to Oxford around 1420, he continued to refer to himself as "scrivenere." He owned property in Cat Street, where he may have resided with his wife, Joanna, and where he gave instruction in much the same subjects as Sampson had before him. Indeed, just as Sampson appropriated some of John of Bromley's teaching materials, Kingsmill in his turn appropriated those of Sampson, updating their contents, occasionally adding a prologue, and, most important, supplying his name in place of Sampson's in the models. Kingsmill may have continued to teach as late as 1450. He was certainly the dominant business teacher in Oxford when the university issued the 1432 statute.

The teachers just described form a coherent group, whose antecedents have been traced as far back as the second quarter of the thirteenth century. Before the mid–fourteenth century, only one such teacher is not anonymous—John of Oxford, who flourished in the last quarter of the thirteenth century (Richardson, "Oxford Teacher" [1939], 451; Maitland 1911, 2:190–201). But from the 1350s to around 1470, we encounter an unbroken series of named teachers: John of Bromley in the 1350s and 1360s, Thomas Sampson from the 1370s to about 1409, Simon O. in the 1410s, William Kingsmill from about 1420 to about 1450, and—a special case, to be discussed later—David Pencaer from the 1440s to perhaps the 1460s. It seems as if the business course is being handed over by each teacher to his successor, along with the rights to revise all teaching materials.

As those teaching materials were transmitted, revised, and augmented, what could be called "paralegal composition" came to occupy a more central place in them. Paul Brand has documented the growth of formal teaching of common law at Oxford during the second half of the fourteenth century, a phenomenon that is doubtless linked to the increasing prominence of common law in the business course. Among the consequences of this legal emphasis was an ever-sharper distinction between the business teachers and the grammar teachers in the one area in which their instruction overlapped: the teaching of the *ars dictaminis* or art of letter writing. A clear sign that Sampson's and Kingsmill's teaching was most closely aligned with training in common law is the fact that so many of their *artes dictandi* are in French or a combination of French and Latin and that the most elementary level of instruction they provided was in French orthography, grammar, vocabulary, and conversation. By contrast what the university-supervised grammar masters offered was the most advanced level of training in

Latin grammar, including what might be called "general composition," within which letter writing was the chief, but by no means only, genre.

The differences between the two approaches to dictaminal instruction can be indicated with some precision by examining the texts or text types that are paradigmatic for each of the pedagogical contexts. For the "paralegal composition" of the business teachers, the component of their teaching that included the *ars dictaminis*, texts of the type designated *cartuariae* were paradigmatic. These *cartuariae* or treatises on drafting deeds consist mainly of model deeds, testaments, and other legal instruments, arranged by type and often interspersed with comments on procedure headed "Regula" or "Nota." Although Sampson's *artes dictandi* in French, Latin, or both are more interesting to historians of rhetoric, his *cartuariae* were the texts that his students invariably copied and his rivals and successors emulated. Not only are they the largest and the most abundantly preserved texts among the instructional materials employed by Sampson, Kingsmill, and others like them, but they also provide a model for the arts of letter writing composed by those same teachers.

The debt of the business teachers' *artes dictandi* to the *cartuariae* can be seen first of all in the format of those arts of letter writing: rhetorical theory is kept to a minimum, usually being confined to a brief introduction and to even briefer notes on procedure scattered among the model letters that are the main content of the teaching. Almost certainly these brief explanations of general rules and/or indications of special conditions requiring departure from the general rules originated in a teacher's lecture notes or responses to questions from students, as did the similar comments in the *cartuariae* and in the copies of lectures on common law recently studied by Paul Brand (1987). The approach to analyzing a text is also the same in the *artes dictandi* as in the *cartuariae* of the business teachers. When Sampson divides up a letter, he is guided less by the rhetorical macrostructure of three to five parts, derived from the parts of a classical oration, than by the physical layout of a typical letter. Each formulaic component is isolated as a distinct part, with no explicit consideration being given to its function in the structure of an argument. Finally, like the *cartuariae,* the "paralegal" *artes dictandi* vary significantly from one exemplar to the next: no two copies of the "same" work are alike. This variation is partly the inevitable consequence of their heavy reliance on models, in which dates and the names of dignitaries must be changed regularly to preserve currency. Because the need to be current, to incorporate the latest events and the latest developments in the law, is greater in the *cartuariae,* which are more closely linked to the study of common law, than in the *artes dictandi,* the direction of influence seems once again beyond doubt.

If the *artes dictandi* of Sampson and Kingsmill were modeled on their *cartuariae,* those of Thomas Merke, John of Briggis, and Simon Alcock were just as clearly shaped by the "arts of poetry and prose" of Matthew of Vendôme, Gervase of Melkley, and especially Geoffrey of Vinsauf. Such textbooks of general composition are ubiquitous in the manuscripts that preserve the teaching of the

Oxford grammar teachers, who invariably refer their readers to them for more detailed information. Many of their own textbooks consist largely of extracts and paraphrases of particular arts of poetry and prose: for example, more than half of Thomas Merke's *Formula moderni et usitati dictaminis* derives from Geoffrey of Vinsauf's *Poetria Nova* and *Documentum de modo et arte dictandi et versificandi,* sometimes with only minimal changes.

In light of their heavy reliance on Geoffrey of Vinsauf, it is not surprising that the grammar teachers tended to emphasize stylistic devices, in particular methods of amplification, variation, and ornamentation, and clearly favored the "high style." By contrast, the business teachers restricted themselves to explaining briefly the rhythms of the *cursus* and the method of writing per *commata et cola* while promoting their own version of the "plain style." The proportion of theory, especially in the form of definitions, is much higher in the works of the grammar teachers, and their examples tend to be short, usually illustrating the single device under discussion. Rather than models of entire fixed-form texts—letters and/or legal documents—they preferred models of small units of discourse that could be used equally well in a sermon, a history, or a letter. The *artes dictandi* of the business teachers consist almost entirely of model letters, whereas Merke included only one complete model letter in his and John of Briggis none at all.[8] Some of the grammar teachers supplemented their letter-writing treatises with "literary" works by authors such as Alan of Lille, John of Hauville, John of Limoges, and Richard of Bury, almost certainly to provide examples of stylistic virtuosity.

Such stylistic virtuosity, or "florida verborum venustas," took longer to master than the simple formulas taught by the business teachers (Jacob 1933, 264–290). Moreover, the training provided by the business teachers offered a direct path to a career, however modest, which would have attracted students unwilling or unable to invest the time and money needed to complete a more prestigious university degree. The many surviving copies of Thomas Sampson's textbooks attest to the popularity of his courses (Richardson, "Business Training" [1941], 276–280).

A successful competitor for fee-paying students, Sampson was nonetheless tolerated by the university and even—so far as we know—allowed relative autonomy in his teaching. To some extent, this benign neglect must be due to Sampson's ambiguous relationship to the university. There is no record of his having graduated, and he never styled himself "master," but he began one of his earliest treatises on letter writing, "To each and every don and master of the university of Oxford, to the *dictatores* and to my friends, Thomas Sampson scholar of the same university though unworthy."[9] This dedication is unique in Sampson's surviving works and may well reflect his status at the time when he wrote, between 1363 and 1368. Elsewhere Sampson claims to have supplemented his teaching income by writing letters for the university: that he did so on at least one occasion is confirmed by the accounts of University College for 1382–1383

(Richardson, "Business Training" [1941], 262). In other words he may have come to Oxford to study at the university, only to abandon his pursuit of a degree, perhaps to study with John of Bromley, marry Isabel, and settle into a career of freelance business teaching and occasional secretarial work for the university. Although technically independent of the university's regulation in his capacity as business teacher, Sampson was not a complete outsider and thus was not perceived to be a threat.

William Kingsmill appears to have had no such ties to the university: that he nonetheless was able to take over Sampson's course in its entirety seems to have alerted the university's authorities to the course's dangerous autonomy, to the fact that it had acquired the internal coherence and transferability necessary to survive intact the death of its creator. The credentials that Kingsmill brought to the job may have been an additional cause for concern. As a professional scrivener who had practiced for many years in London, the center for training in and practice of common law, he would have had firsthand experience of the paralegal working environment that he was preparing his students to enter. His professional connections with London must have further strengthened the association between common law and the business course as he taught it. Perhaps even more important, Kingsmill may have been able to use his insider's knowledge of London to emphasize the career advantages of studying with him rather than with the less pragmatic and not so well-connected grammar teachers.

Already in the decade before Kingsmill moved from London to Oxford there were signs of uneasiness about students' abandoning grammar and rhetoric to pursue administrative and secretarial careers in London. A particularly interesting witness to this anxiety is Simon O., whose textbooks on letter writing resemble in many respects those of the grammar teachers but whose compilation of a *cartuaria* aligned him with the business teachers. In one of his ornately rhetorical epistolary fictions, Simon employed personification allegory to dramatize the grammar teachers' fear that their pupils would be "seduced" by business writing. A faithful subject of Queen Rhetoric writes to his fellows, recounting Queen Rhetoric's lament that their elder brother has forgotten his upbringing by wickedly abandoning her to attach himself to the evil Queen Exchequer. The honest retainer exhorts his brothers to scorn this deluding Queen Exchequer, with her foul, hairy body and wrinkled face and return to their "primitive nurse" with all honor (Camargo, *Medieval Rhetorics* 1995, 220–221). Himself the author of a *cartuaria*, Simon O. could have been charged with aiding and abetting the very apostasy that this letter pretended to combat.

There was no such ambivalence in Kingsmill's position. More than any of his predecessors, including Thomas Sampson, he was clearly and completely identified as a business teacher. The statute issued by the university in 1432 literally made that identity official by enumerating the constituent parts of Kingsmill's course in full detail and by establishing its relationship to instruction covered by existing statutes. So far I have found no evidence of Kingsmill's response to the university's move to regulate his activities and those of his students. Because he continued to teach in Oxford for quite some time, he must have accommodated the authorities in some way. What looks like evidence of a reaction to the 1432 statute eventually does appear in the works of Kingsmill's younger contemporary and probable successor David Pencaer; judging from the changes introduced by Pencaer, the long-term effects of the statute may have been the opposite of what its framers intended.

The passage that casts light on the statute's effects occurs in a *cartuaria* originally compiled in Oxford in 1441 or 1442. This otherwise typical *cartuaria* is unique in containing an extended treatment of hypozeuxis, zeugma, and hyperbaton, the rhetorical figures (*schemata*) that its author judged to be most characteristic of legal instruments. Both definitions and illustrations are drawn from such standard authorities as Matthew of Vendôme (*Ars versificatoria, Tobias*), Alexander of Villa Dei (*Doctrinale*), the Bible, Horace (*Ars poetica*), Ovid (*Epistolae*), Juvenal (*Satirae*), John Balbus of Genoa (*Catholicon*), and Geoffrey of Vinsauf (*Poetria Nova*). (See the edition and translation in the appendix.) The language and contents of this excursus are clearly those of the Latin grammarians, whereas the surrounding context belongs just as clearly to the business teachers. The excursus, however, is no interpolation: it is linked explicitly to the legalistic discussion that precedes it in the text, and many of the illustrative examples are formulaic phrases from legal documents. Who concocted this unprecedented mixture of registers and what motivated him to do so?

Unlike most of his predecessors, the author of the *cartuaria* in question did not insert his own name at every possible opportunity; however, in a copy of this *cartuaria* made in 1470, the scribe John Water of Thame indicated that he wrote according to the instruction of one David Pencaer, of blessed memory. Water doubtless referred to the clerk David Pencaer, who inhabited Oseney Abbey's tenement in Cat Street in 1428 (Salter, *Survey* [1960], 95), whose name continued to appear in Oxford documents through the 1450s (Salter, [*Cartulary* 1929–1931], 2:143 [July 10, 1451], 3:229 [Michaelmas 1428]; *Registrum* 192 [September 29, 1449], 234 [April 7, 1451], 380 [July 28, 1457]), and who, by Water's testimony, was dead by 1470. According to H. E. Salter, Pencaer became town clerk of Oxford in 1449 or 1450 and was involved in preparing other handbooks for common lawyers, containing among other works copies of Thomas Sampson's treatises on conveyancing.[10] In short, what is known about Pencaer suggests that he was, like William Kingsmill, both a practicing scribe and a teacher of business writing who continued the tradition of reusing the standard textbooks developed by John of Bromley and Thomas Sampson.

Pencaer's inclusion of the excursus on the *schemata* in his own version of the *cartuaria* (Oxford, ca. 1442) might be regarded as no more than a curious anomaly were it not for a second work associated with his name. In the second quarter of the fifteenth century, an Oxford teacher extracted, rearranged, and revised the treatment of amplification and abbreviation from the *Tria sunt*, a general composition textbook indebted to Geoffrey of Vinsauf, to create a "new" work that is preserved independently in four English manuscripts and interpolated into Thomas Merke's *ars dictandi* in a fifth.[11] One of those copies carries the title "Breuis tractatus secundum Penkaer de coloribus rethorice" (MS. Harley 941, fol. 80r). Pencaer's interest in rhetorical style was apparently not limited to the excursus in his tract on drafting deeds. Although his pedagogical activity seems to have been focused on the paralegal composition of the business course, he also composed a textbook that is absolutely indistinguishable from those of the grammar masters associated with the university. Even if Pencaer wrote his manual on the "colores rhetorici" early in his career, perhaps even as a teacher of Latin grammar before he shifted to a career as business teacher and municipal clerk, his *cartuaria* indicates that no more than a decade after the 1432 statute he was offering a hybrid course that incorporated and subordinated the stylistic lore of the advanced grammar course to the more narrowly professional writing of the business course.

The timing of this new development in the business course probably was not coincidental. If the 1432 statute was enforced, the business teachers would have been paying fines to the university to compensate for the loss of revenue caused by their luring away fee-paying students. Prior to the issuing of that statute, there had been relatively little overlap between the advanced grammar course and the business course, but, once the university officially cast the business teachers in the role of usurpers, there was no longer any reason for them to maintain a safe distance. If they were to pay "damages" for what they were teaching already, why should they be concerned about the extent of the actual damage they did? David Pencaer, at least, seems to have seized the opportunity to combine some of the instruction hitherto offered only by the grammarians with the traditional components of his business teaching, perhaps in the hope of drawing even more students away from his rivals. If Pencaer's innovation was a response to new regulations and did increase enrollments in his courses, the university's authorities ended up harming the very grammar masters to whom they had extended statutory protection. Regardless of whether the new statute was the direct cause, the first effort to draw a sharp boundary between the grammar teachers supervised by the university and the business teachers whose status had up to then remained ambiguous and unacknowledged was followed almost immediately by the first clear example of a textbook that straddled that boundary.

Pencaer's bold move, however, did not cause a long-term shift in the balance of power. By 1470 Oxford had ceased to be an important center for the study of common law, on which the business course relied, and the course in paralegal composition developed by the Oxford business teachers appears not to have found a place within or alongside the training in common law offered at the Inns of Court in London. It would be almost too perfectly ironic if Pencaer's weakening the disciplinary identity that had taken nearly a century to emerge hastened the ultimate demise of the business course. Even if other factors prove to have had a more significant impact on what was almost certainly an irreversible trend, the fact remains that Pencaer was the last of his kind. During the last few decades of the fifteenth century, new disciplinary issues came to the fore, as both the business teachers and the university-supervised grammar teachers gradually vanished from the scene, quickly rendering the victory in the turf war between them a moot point.

Translated Extract from David Pencaer's Cartuaria, *Concerning the Rhetorical Figures Most Used in Composing Legal Documents*

[The passage concludes the treatment of "landholding in socage" (*tenere in socagio*), in which the three types of socage (land tenure in exchange for a fixed payment or specified services) are explained and background is provided on the practice of awarding tenure for services.]

For King William the First after the Conquest gave part to the ecclesiastics and the religious so that they would defend the realm with their prayers against its spiritual enemies and would pray to God for the good and prosperity of the realm; he gave part to the shield-bearing knights so that they would defend the realm against its corporeal enemies (and these hold in grand serjeanty when wardship, marriages and feudal reliefs are pending); [and] he gave part to the farmers so that they would defend the realm—by tilling the earth—from hunger and thirst (and these hold either in petty serjeanty, when neither wardship, marriages nor feudal reliefs are pending—which two tenures are held only from the king—or in fee simple through purchase or in fee-farm or in socage) so that in this way the realm would be maintained in prosperity, as it is expressed in verse:

> The clerk, the knight, the rustic with words, sword, mule
> Teaches, threatens, plows: these three realms rule.

And here occurs the figure that is called "each to each." And it happens when the constituents of parallel clauses have been pushed together so that the first members of each set support the first members of the other sets, the second the second, the third the third and so on, as in this example:

> The sky, the land, the sea lifts, nourishes, hides
> Birds, beasts, fishes with air, grain, tides.
> Likewise, when *Tobias* is praised as follows:
> He hates, loves, reproves, approves, curses, worships
> Crimes, the laws, wrong, right, idols, God;
> He sows, promotes, nourishes, destroys, accuses, prevents
> Doctrines, the laws, virtue, schisms, indecency, frauds.

And this figure is contained by hypozeuxis. And hypozeuxis is when each of several clauses is assigned its own verb. And it is called "disjunction" by Tullius, as here:

He covets battle and opens his jaws and whets his claws.

(This was said concerning Scipio, a prince of the Romans.) And:

Charm of manners ingratiates, regality of beauty illuminates, abundance of wealth enriches Penelope.

Whence, in the *Doctrinale:*

Hypozeuxis renders to one person many verbs: "Christ's grace cleanses us, adorns us."

Likewise, when one says in a deed "I have given, relinquished, and in this my present deed ratified" etc. Also, one says "hypozeuxis" from "hypos," "against" and "zeuxis," "zeugma," because it is the opposite of zeugma, or from "hypos," "under" and "zeuxis," "word" or "juncture" or "joining," because it subjoins to each clause its own verb, as in our Creed: "He descended into Hell, on the third day He rose from the dead," etc.

Zeugma, by contrast, is the absence of a word, as in that Epistle of Paul: "Hebrews are they, and I," where the "I" is governed by the "are" through the force of zeugma, because the nature of zeugma is the prudent rendering of one verb to several clauses. Whence the Doctrinale:

Zeugma occurs if in one verb you enclose many.

And it is brought about in three ways, according to Isidore. From the top, when the verb is put at the beginning, as "He reads the lots and Plato" (and then occurs the color adjunction, according to Tullius). From the middle, when the verb is put in between, as in the example above: "Hebrews are they, and I" (and then, according to Tullius, occurs the color conjunction). From the bottom, when the verb is put at the end, as in Horace:

You—what I and the public with me desires—hear.
And in Ovid, in the book of the *Epistles:*
You a husband, you a master, you a brother to me were.

And it can be produced by means of seven signs, as this verse suggests:

And, or, but, than, nor, as, except: these attest zeugma.

That is to say by means of a copulative conjunction, as in "Appolonius writes and I"; by a disjunctive conjunction, as in "My comrade or I shall write"; by an adversative conjunction, as in "Not you have done but I," and again in Scripture: "You are clean, but not all"; by "than," an adverb of comparison, as in "I write better than you"; by "as," an adverb of resemblance, as in "Henry writes as I (do)"; by the disjunctive "nor," as in "Neither my brothers nor I shall do"; and by the conjunction "except," as in "No one will respond except I." And when a verb is placed last and refers to the preceding clauses, then in a zeugmatic construction a verb, an adjective and a relative pronoun should agree with the last inflected word in the required inflections,[12] as in "Ego et tu *legis*" (I and you *read* [2d sing.]), "Tu et ego *lego*" (You and I *read* [1st sing.]); "Vir et mulier est *alba*" (The man and the woman is *white* [fem. nom. sing.]), "Mulier et vir est *albus*" (The woman and the man is *white* [masc. nom. sing.]); "Johannes et Margareta, *quam* ego video, sunt amici mei" (John and Margaret, *whom* I see, are my friends [fem. acc. sing.]).

Zeugma and hypozeuxis are the figures most favored among those who write with distinction and in Holy Scripture. And a figure (*schema*) is a decoration in words, whence this: "*Cima* is the top of a bough, the glory of words is a *schema* and of a family a *stemma*, a division of faith is a *schisma*, *thema* gives you subject matter, *zima* yeast." Whence the following is said in the poem about the story of Appolonius: "And because one rules kingdoms better with eloquence (*facundia*) than with the sword (*ferro*) and more nobly with rhetorical figures (*schema*) than with pedigrees (*stemma*), cleverness (*astus*) is more attractive than arrogance (*fastus*), skill with words (*verbi*) better than skill with blows (*verberis*)."

And a pedigree (*stemma*) is the fame of one's ancestors or the enumeration of one's clan, as in one's father, grandfather, great-grandfather etc. Whence Juvenal in his eighth *Satire:* "What do pedigrees accomplish? What good is it, Ponticus, to be esteemed for a long bloodline and to show off the painted faces of one's ancestors? etc." Here the poet reproves the Pontic poet, who said that virtue comes only from nobility and not nobility from virtue, and he reproves others who are excessively proud of their ancestors' nobility but are of bad character themselves.

Knowledge of these figures is necessary to composers of deeds, as is knowledge of the figure that is called hyperbaton—that is, transference in word order, not in meaning—which is equivalent to transgression, which is divided into transposition and inversion. Transposition is the moderate separation of words that grammatical order joins together, as in "Your—I beseech—reverence." Likewise: "In the year—of the reign of King Henry the Sixth after the Conquest—the twentieth." Inversion is the separation of the preposition from its object, as in "In—this to be the case—attesting." Whence the rhetorician Geoffrey, in his *New Poetics:*

> A dignified weightiness of style is added through the order of words alone, when units grammatically related are separated by their position, so that an inversion of this sort occurs: "rege sub illo" (2 under 3 that 1 king); "tempus ad illud" (2 up to 3 that 1 time); "ea de causa" (2 for 1 this 3 reason); "rebus in illis" (2 in 3 those 1 matters); or a transposed order of this sort: "Dura creavit pestiferam fortuna famem" (1 Harsh 4 fortune 2 produced 3 a pestilent 5 famine); "Letalis egenam gente fames spoliavit humum" (1 Deadly 4 famine 5 robbed 2 the destitute 6 soil 3 of produce). Here words related grammatically are separated by their position in the sentence. Juxtaposition of related words conveys the sense more readily, but their moderate separation sounds better to the ear and wins more approval.[13]

Text: Oxford, Bodleian Library, MS. Lat. misc. e. 93, fols. 13r–14v (s. xv med.)[14]

Nam rex Willelmus primus post conquestum dedit partem ecclesiasticis personis et religiosis vt defenderent regnum precibus suis contra inimicos spirituales et deprecentur Deum pro bono <et> prospero statu regni, dedit partem militibus scutiferis vt defenderent regnum contra inimicos corporales (et isti tenent in magna seriantia vbi dependent wardia, maritagia et releuia), dedit partem agricolis vt defenderent regnum—colendo terram—de fame et siti (et isti aut tenent in parua seriantia, vbi non dependent wardia, mar<i>tagia nec releuia—que due tenure solum tenentur de rege[15]—aut in feodo simplici ex perquisicione aut in feodo firme aut in socagio) vt sic regnum prospere sustentur, secundum quod dicitur metrice:

> Clerus, eques, coridon sermonibus, ense, iumento[16]
> Instruit, instat, arat: hec tria regna regunt.

Et hic accidit scema quod dicitur singula singulis, et fit[17] quando inculcatis determinacionibus prima primis, secunda secundis, tercia terciis et sic de ceteris confirmantur, vt in hoc exemplo:

> Celum, terra, fretum volucres, pecuaria,[18] pisces
>> Tollit, alit, celat aere, farre, lacu.
>> Similiter vbi commendatur *Tobias* sic:
>> Odit, amat, reprobat, <probat>, execratur, adorat
>> Crimina, iura, nephas, phas, similacra, Deum;
>> *   *   *
>
>> Seminat, augit, alit, exterminat, arguit, arcet
>> Dogmata, iura, <decus>, scismata, probra, dolos.
>> [Matthew of Vendôme, *Tobias,* 89–90, 93–94]

Et continetur hoc scema sub ypozeusi. Et est ypozeusis quando singulis clausis suum verbum attribuetur. Et vocatur a Tullio disiunctum [*Rhetorica ad Herennium,* IV.27.37], vt hic:

> Bella cupit laxatque genas et temperat vngues. [Statius, *Thebaid,* II.130]
>> (Hoc dictum erat de Scipione Romanorum principe.[19]) Et:
>> Penolopen morum festiuat gracia, forme
>> Purpura declarat, ditat aceruus opum.
>> [Matthew of Vendôme, *Ars versificatoria,* I.13]
>> Vnde *Doctrinali* [2463–2464]:
>> Reddit ypozeusis persone plurima verba
>> Vni: "Nos mundat, [fol. 13v] nos ornat gracia Christi."

Similiter cum dicitur in carta "Dedi, concessi et hac presenti carta mea confirmaui" etc. Dicitur autem ypozeusis ab "ypos," "contra" et "zeusis," "zeuma," quia contrariatur zeumati, vel ab "ypos," "sub" et "zeusis," "diccio" vel "iunctura" seu "iunccio," quia subiungit vnicuique clause suum verbum, vt in Simbolo nostro: "Descendit[20] ad inferna, tercia die resurrexit a mortuis" etc.

Zeuma vero est defectus verbi, vt in illa Epistola Pauli: "Ebrei sunt, et ego" [2 *Corinthians,* 11.22], vbi le "ego" regitur de le "sunt" ex vi zeumatis, quia natura zeumatis est vnius verbi in clausas diuersas discreta reddicio. Vnde *Doctrinale* [2454]:

Zeuma fit in verbo si plurima clauseris vno.

Et fit tripliciter, secundum Isidorum [*Etymologiae,* I.36.3]. A superiore quando verbum preponitur,[21] vt "legit sortes et Plato" (et tunc color accidit adiunccio, secundum Tullium [*Rhetorica ad Herennium,* IV.27.38]). A medio quando verbum interponitur, vt in premisso exemplo "Ebrei sunt, et ego" (et tunc, secundum Tullium, accidit color coniunccio [*Rhetorica ad Herennium,* IV.27.38]). Ab inferiore quando verbum postponitur, vt in Oracio:

Tu, quid ego et populus mecum desiderat, audi. [*Ars poetica,* 153]
Et in Ouidio, in libro *Epistolarum* [III.52]:
Tu vir, tu dominus, tu michi frater eras.[22]
Et potest fieri per septem notas, vt innuit iste versus:
Et, uel, set, quam, nec, sicut, nisi: zeuma probant hec.

Videlicet per coniunccionem copulatiuam, vt "Appollonius scribit et ego"; per coniunccionem disiunctiuam, vt "Socius meus vel ego scribam"; per coniunccionem aduersatiuam, vt "Non vos fecistis set ego," item in Scriptura: "Vos estis mundi, set non omnes" [*John,* 13.10]; per "quam," aduerbium comparandi, vt "Ego scribo melius quam tu"; per "sicut," aduerbium similitudinis, vt "Henricus scribit sicut ego"; per hanc disiunctiuam "nec," vt "Nec fratres mei nec ego faciam"; et per hanc coniunccionem "nisi," vt "Nullus respondebit nisi ego." Et quando verbum postponitur et refertur ad clausas precedentes, tunc in zeumatica construccione verbum, adiectiuum et relatiuum debent conuenire cum posteriori casuali in accidentibus requisitis, vt "Ego et tu legis," "Tu et ego lego"; "Vir et mulier est alba," "Mulier et vir est albus"; "Johannes et Margareta, quam ego video, sunt amici mei."[23]

Zeuma et ypozeusis sunt [fol. 14r] vsitatissima[24] scemata inter egregie dictantes et <in> Scriptura Sacra. Et est scema ornatus in verbis, vnde illud:

Cima caput virge, verborum gloria scema
Et generis stema, fidei diuisio <s>cisma,
Materiam thema, fermentum[25] dat tibi zima.[26]
Vnde in poetria super historiam Apolonii sic dicitur:
Et quia regna regit melius facundia ferro
Scemaque splend<id>ius quam stema, venustius astus
Quam fastus, melius verbi quam verberis vsus.

Et est stema nobilitas antecessorum vel computacio generis, vt pater, auus, attauus etc. <Vnde> Juuenalis Satira octaua:

Stemata quid faciunt? quid prodest, Pontice, longo
Sanguine censeri pictosque ostendere vultus
Maior<um>? etc.

Hic reprehendit poeta ponticum poetam, qui dixit virtutem solum prouenire ex nobilitate et non nobilitatem ex virtute, et reprehendit alios qui superbiunt de nobilitate antecessorum et male morigerati existunt.

Noticia istorum scematum est requisita ad compositores munimentorum, et eciam illius scematis quod dicitur yperbaton—id est transsumpcio in ordine, non in significacione—cui corespondet transgressio, que diuiditur in traieccionem et peruersionem. Traieccio est moderata diccionum remocio quas ordo construccionis adiungit, vt "Vestram deprecor reuerensiam." Item: "Anno regni regis Henrici sexti post conquestum vicesimo."[27] Peruersio est separacio preposicionis a suo casuali, vt "In cuius rei testimonium." Vnde Gaufridus rhetor, in *Noua poetria* [1051–1060]:

Nobilis accedit grauitas ex ordine solo
Quando que sociat construccio separat ordo,
Vt sit in hac forma peruersio: "rege sub illo,"
"Tempus ad illud," "ea de causa," "rebus in illis";
Aut huius generis traieccio: "Dura creauit
Pestiferam fortuna famem," "Letalis egenam
Gente fames spoliauit humum." Sic ordine distant
[fol. 14v]
Que constructa tamen prope stant. Structura propinqua
Declarat leuius sensum set plus sedet auri
Plusque fauoris habet moderata remocio vocum.
[At this point the treatise returns to its usual contents, supplying next a model "carta feodi simplicis" from "Johannes Bernard de Watele."]

Notes

1. The argument for the earlier date is made by Pollard (1968, 69–92).

2. "nisi prius fuerit examinatus de modo versificandi et dictandi et de auctoribus et partibus" (Gibson 1931, 169).

3. Very few dictaminal treatises appear in the grammatical manuscripts inventoried by Thomson (*Catalogue* [1979]). In separate conversations both Nicholas Orme and Jo Ann Hoeppner Moran informed me that they had found little evidence of letter-writing instruction at the grammar-school level in England, outside Oxford.

4. "Item, tenentur singulis quindenis versus dare, et literas compositas verbis decentibus non ampulosis aut sexquipedalibus, et clausulis succinctis, decoris, metaphoris manifestis et, quantum possint, sententia refertis, quos versus et quas literas debent recipientes in proximo die feriato vel ante in percameno scribere, et deinde sequenti die,

cum ad scolas venerint, magistro suo corde tenus reddere et scripturam suam offerre" (Gibson 1931, 171). The caution against using "verbis . . . ampullosis et sexquipedalibus" might suggest that the statute writers were aware of the stylistic excesses that resulted from too close adherence to Geoffrey of Vinsauf, even though the warning is lifted straight from Horace's *Ars poetica* (line 97).

5. John of Briggis probably composed his *Compilacio de arte dictandi* in the mid 1380s (Camargo, *Medieval Rhetorics* [1995], 93–104). Simon Alcock was M.A. by 1420 and rented a school from Exeter College in 1420–1421 (Emden [1957–1959], 1:18–19). Neither his handbook on *dictamen* nor his handbook on amplifying sermons has received a printed edition.

6. "Item, cum racioni sit consonum, et in antiquioribus statutis implicitum, scolarem quemcumque artem aliquam addiscentem, nulla existente lectura ordinaria in eadem, ipsius facultatis seu sciencie ordinarium exercere debere, cui ars ipsa quam addiscit maxime vicinatur; verum quia artes scribendi et dictandi loquendique Gallicanum ydioma, in quibus nulle ordinarie sunt lecture, magis gramatice et rhetorice quam aliis scienciis aut facultatibus, tanquam eis subalternate, appropinquant, ordinauit igitur vniuersitas et decreuit quod singuli scolares competenter instructi in gramatica solummodo, artem scribendi vel dictandi vel loquendi Gallicum, siue cartas aliave huiusmodi scripta componendi, seu curias laicorum tenendi, aut modum placitandi Anglicanum principaliter addiscentes, ordinarias lecciones arcistarum gramaticam vel rethoricam legencium frequentent, eis tanquam propriis magistris cumulando" (Gibson 1931, 240).

7. For an edition of this last work, see Camargo (*Medieval Rhetorics* [1995], 169–219). W. A. Pantin edits part of the other letter-writing treatise (1929, 326–382).

8. The differences between the two approaches to teaching letter writing are well illustrated in Thomas Merke's *Formula moderni et usitati dictaminis* (ca. 1390), the most popular *ars dictandi* composed by an Oxford grammar teacher, and the *Modus dictandi* (1396) of Thomas Sampson, the most prolific and influential of the Oxford business teachers (Camargo, *Medieval Rhetorics* [1995], 105–147, 148–168).

9. "Universis et singulis Universitatis Oxonie dominis et magistris, dictatoribus eciam et amicis, Thomas Sampson eiusdem Universitatis scolaris quamvis indignus" (BL, MS. Harley 4993, fol. 9r).

10. Salter gives two different dates for the beginning of Pencaer's term as clerk: Pencaer "became Town Clerk in 1449" (*Cartulary* [1929–1931], 3:229 n. 1) versus Pencaer "was town clerk 1450–1454" (*Registrum* [1932], 1:380 n. 3). Murphy (1965, 18) cites Pollard to the effect that Pencaer was "town clerk in Oxford" from 1428 to 1457. For a list of "handbooks for lawyers," including several that Salter links to Pencaer, see *Medieval Oxford* (1936, 95 n.).

11. The five manuscript copies, none of which appears to be complete, are London, British Library, MS. Harley 670, fols. 3r–10r (s. xv med.; Oxford); MS. Harley 941, fols. 80r–90r (s. xv med.; Oxford); MS. Royal 12B.xvii, fols. 1r–43r (s. xv med.; Norfolk?); Oxford, Bodleian Library, MS. Rawlinson D.232, fols. 15r–42r (s. xv med.; Cambridge?; interpolated into a late copy of Thomas Merke's *Formula moderni et usitati dictaminis*); Westminster Abbey, Library of the Dean and Chapter, MS. 20, fols. 21r–37r (s. xv; Westminster?). The *Tria sunt* is better known as the "longer version" of Geoffrey of Vinsauf's *Documentum de modo et arte dictandi et versificandi;* but the attribution to Geoffrey cannot be correct (Camargo, *"Tria Sunt"* [1999], 935–955).

12. Because English has retained few inflections, the point being illustrated here cannot be made in translation. I have translated as literally as possible, italicized the focal words, and indicated the categories of inflection involved (gender, case, number, person).

13. The translation is that of Nims (1967, 54), which I have modified only to accommodate differences in format and variant readings. The fixed word order of English precludes the sorts of inversion and transposition being illustrated: for that reason I have added italicized numbers in the translated examples to indicate the order of the corresponding words in the original Latin.

14. Other copies of the excursus can be found in Dublin, Trinity College, MS. 657, fols. 16v–18v (version of 1451/2?; several interpolations); London, British Library, MS. Harley 5240, fols. 15v–17r (version of 1470); Oxford, Bodleian Library, MS. Lat. misc. d. 69, fols. 10v–11v; and MS. Lat. misc. e. 103, fols. 25v–27r. These additional witnesses have been used to correct the text in MS. Lat. misc. e. 93, which, though apparently the earliest version preserved, contains several obvious errors. Whenever a correction is made in the text, the reading from the base ms. is supplied in a note, with the exception of scribal omissions, which are restored within angle brackets <>. The orthography of the base ms. is retained and abbreviations are expanded silently. Information that is not part of the Latin text—i.e., folio numbers, sources—is enclosed within square brackets []. At the point where the text printed below begins, a later reader of MS. Lat. misc. e. 93 has written "Nota" in the right margin.

15. Apparently, the "due tenure" in question are "magna seriantia" and "parua seriantia."

16. Beside this line a later reader of MS. Lat. misc. e. 93 has drawn a *manicula* (small hand with pointing finger) in the left margin.

17. Ms.: sic

18. Ms.: petuaria

19. In its original context, the line is part of a simile comparing Eteocles to a tigress. Pencaer probably quoted the line from Matthew of Vendôme, *Ars versificatoria,* I.13, who cites it as an example of "ypozeuxis" and attributes it to Statius but does not associate it with Scipio.

20. Ms.: Deuscendit

21. Ms.: proponitur

22. Pencaer probably quoted the line from Matthew of Vendôme, *Ars versificatoria,* I.11, rather than directly from the *Heroides.* Pencaer, however, transposed "dominus" and "vir," whereas Matthew preserved Ovid's word order.

23. From the citation of Isidore up to this point in the text, there is a very close—often verbatim—correspondence with the treatment of zeugma in John Balbus of Genoa's *Catholicon* (cf. London, British Library, MS. Burney 323, fol. 50vb).

24. Ms.: visitatissima

25. Ms.: frermentum

26. These verses probably come from one of the numerous mnemonic poems on homonyms and near-homonyms (*equivoca*) used by grammarians in teaching Latin vocabulary.

27. If, as seems likely, Pencaer used the current regnal year in his example, then this version of the *cartuaria* dates from 1441 or 1442.

Works Cited

Arnold, Ivor D. O. "Thomas Sampson and the *Orthographia Gallica.*" *Medium vum* 6 (1937): 193–209.

Brand, Paul. "Courtroom and Schoolroom: The Education of Lawyers in England Prior to 1400." *Historical Research* 60 (1987): 147–65.

Camargo, Martin. "Beyond the *Libri Catoniani*: Models of Latin Prose Style at Oxford University ca. 1400." *Mediaeval Studies* 56 (1994): 165–87.

———, ed. *Medieval Rhetorics of Prose Composition: Five English* Artes dictandi *and Their Tradition.* Binghamton, N.Y.: Medieval and Renaissance Texts and Studies, 1995.

———. "*Tria Sunt:* The Long and the Short of Geoffrey of Vinsauf's *Documentum de modo et arte dictandi et versificandi.*" *Speculum* 74 (1999): 935–55.

Emden, A. B. *A Biographical Register of the University of Oxford to* A.D. 1500. 3 vols. Oxford: Clarendon Press, 1957–59.

Gibson, Strickland, ed. *Statuta antiqua universitatis oxoniensis.* Oxford: Clarendon Press, 1931.

Hassell, James W., III, "Thomas Sampson's Dictaminal Treatises and the Teaching of French in Medieval England: An Edition and Study." PhD diss., University of Toronto, 1991.

Hunt, R. W. "Oxford Grammar Masters in the Middle Ages." *Oxford Studies Presented to Daniel Callus.* Oxford Historical Society, n.s. 16. Oxford: Clarendon Press, 1964; for 1959–60, 163–93.

Jacob, E. F. "*Florida verborum venustas:* Some Early Examples of Euphuism in England." *Bulletin of the John Rylands Library* 17 (1933): 264–90.

Legge, M. Dominica. "William of Kingsmill: A Fifteenth-Century Teacher of French in Oxford." In *Studies in French Language and Mediaeval Literature Presented to Professor Mildred K. Pope.* Manchester: Manchester University Press, 1939, 241–46.

Lobel, Mary D. "The Grammar-Schools of the Medieval University." In *The Victoria History of the Counties of England: Oxfordshire,* vol. 3. Oxford: Oxford University Press, 1954. Reprint, London, 1965, 1994, 40–43.

Maitland, Frederic W. "A Conveyancer in the Thirteenth Century." In *The Collected Papers of Frederic William Maitland,* edited by H. A. L. Fisher. 3 vols. Cambridge: Cambridge University Press, 1911, 2:190–201.

Murphy, James J. "Rhetoric in Fourteenth-Century Oxford." *Medium Ævum* 34 (1965): 1–20.

Nims, Margaret F., trans. *Poetria Nova of Geoffrey of Vinsauf.* Toronto: Pontifical Institute of Mediaeval Studies, 1967.

Oschinsky, Dorothea. *Walter of Henley and Other Treatises on Estate Management and Accounting.* Oxford: Clarendon Press, 1971.

Pantin, W. A. "A Medieval Treatise on Letter-Writing, with Examples, from the Rylands Latin MS. 394." *Bulletin of the John Rylands Library* 13 (1929): 326–82.

Pollard, Graham. "The Oldest Statute Book of the University." *Bodleian Library Record* 8.2 (1968): 69–92.

Richardson, H. G. "Business Training in Medieval Oxford." *American Historical Review* 46 (1941): 259–80.

————. "An Oxford Teacher of the Fifteenth Century." *Bulletin of the John Rylands Library* 23 (1939): 436–57. Reprint, separately with corrections, 1939.

Salter, H. E., ed. *Cartulary of Oseney Abbey.* 3 vols. Oxford Historical Society 89–91. Oxford: Clarendon Press, 1929–31.

————. *Medieval Oxford.* Oxford Historical Society 100. Oxford: Clarendon Press, 1936.

————, ed. *Registrum Cancellarii Oxoniensis* 1434–69, vol. 1. Oxford Historical Society 93. Oxford: Clarendon Press, 1932.

————. *Survey of Oxford,* vol. 1. Oxford Historical Society, n.s. 14. Edited by W. A. Pantin. Oxford: Clarendon Press, 1960; for 1955–56.

Thomson, David. *A Descriptive Catalogue of Middle English Grammatical Texts.* New York: Garland Press, 1979.

————. "The Oxford Grammar Masters Revisited." *Mediaeval Studies* 45 (1983): 298–310.

From Ars dictaminis *to* Ars conscribendi epistolis

RENAISSANCE LETTER-WRITING MANUALS IN
THE CONTEXT OF HUMANISM

Gideon Burton

Although much continuity exists between the letter-writing manuals of medieval and Renaissance Europe,[1] the changes that are apparent came about as humanists became aware of and tried to imitate the pristine and rhetorically efficacious Latin they saw modeled in ancient literature and especially in the writings of Cicero. By the late thirteenth century, the medieval dictaminal manual had developed a relatively standardized set of guidelines for letter writing (see Martin Camargo, chapter 5, this book), focusing on preserving the decorum necessary in communication between those of differing stations within medieval culture. This social sensitivity resulted in an emphasis on the *salutatio* of a letter, consisting of the appropriate titles for addressees as well as model opening phrases of deference—the *captatio benevolentiae,* or "seizing of good will." Renaissance manuals would continue the practice of providing model phrases. The emphasis on diplomatic protocol would diminish, however, replaced by other concerns that reflected new audiences for letters and the new uses to which they were put in the Renaissance. Those concerns and novel uses for letters came about as classical literature was revived within the context of a rhetorically oriented pedagogy that humanists also adopted from antiquity. In short, letter-writing manuals became associated less and less with the notarial arts and more and more with the *ars humanitatis* and the rhetorical pedagogy of the humanists. An established literary tradition was reinvented for use within the humanist program.

The revival of ancient literature by humanists is a familiar narrative. For the purposes of this study, it is significant to note that among the first classical models to be rediscovered, recopied, and imitated by the early humanists were collections of letters. Petrarch uncovered Cicero's *Epistolae ad Atticum* in 1345 in Verona, and in 1392 Coluccio Salutati would uncover a second collection of Cicero's letters, the *Epistolae ad familiares.*[2] These letters, and not the formularies from the late Middle Ages, served as the models humanists would imitate (on many levels) throughout the fifteenth and sixteenth centuries. For example, Orazio Toscanella, a sixteenth-century Italian humanist, taught students to write Latin by reading, analyzing, and even memorizing Cicero's letters (Grendler 1989, 222–229). In contrast to the largely official correspondence taught in the *ars dictaminis,* Cicero's letters demonstrated that this genre could be flexible, personal, and elegant. Indeed, the letter became a form of expressive literature among humanists, with Petrarch initiating the genre that proved a vital corollary to the Renaissance letter-writing manual, the Renaissance letter collection.[3]

Inspired by their Ciceronian example, humanists perceived the abyss that divided their present society from Cicero's and measured this gap in terms of language. The philological efforts of the humanists were undertaken not simply to enable more accurate readings or translations of the texts they were rediscovering, but especially to make possible the purification of the Latin tongue and the imitation of its most efficacious employment. Put simply, humanists desired to recover a pristine Latin, uninfected by the barbarisms that had crept into it during the Middle Ages. The philological works of Lorenzo Valla, discussed below, represent the ardent effort of the humanists to recover a clear and powerful Latin. Cicero's prose demonstrated the pure Latin they aspired to, and his treatises on rhetoric provided both the methodological and the theoretical underpinnings for that persuasive eloquence to which humanists aspired.[4]

These two driving interests—reanimating a moribund Latin and achieving the eloquence and efficaciousness of rhetoric—account for humanist dissatisfaction with dictaminal manuals, even though these manuals had worked very well for preceding generations: their model sentences were in a Latin the humanists considered inferior, and the lists of stock phrases that filled dictaminal manuals were inconsistent with the principles and methods of classical rhetoric that humanists were learning from Cicero and Quintilian. The new humanist standard was to write letters in Latin that was both pure and eloquent, a standard that can be seen emerging in the letter-writing manuals of the late fifteenth century.

One such letter-writing manual that became popular (and later, notorious) in the Renaissance was Francesco Negro's 1492 *Modus epistolandi.* This simple volume, doomed to earn the disdain of the influential Erasmus for its lackluster Latin and rather limited scope, nevertheless demonstrates the influx of humanist values into the genre. Listing some twenty kinds of letters (varying from the *epistola expurgativa* to the *epistola domestica*), Negro supplied brief rules for each, then a *propositio* (a sentence saying what the letter should cover), followed by an example. The familiar medieval sections on the protocol of addressing the sender properly have been abbreviated and relegated to the back of the book, where one also finds something foreign to the letter manuals of the prior period —a set of brief rules, largely grammatical, intended to improve the elegance of one's literary expression. Some medieval dictamen had included instructions on grammar or on *cursus,* Latin prose rhythm. As this example illustrates, however, grammatical instruction appended to Renaissance letter-writing manuals was pointedly rhetorical in nature—that is to say, such grammatical instruction emphasized not simply what grammar is *correct* but what grammatical choices could prove most *eloquent* or *forceful*. For example, Negro explains, "The adjective is more elegantly positioned before the noun. For example, given the expressions *virtus summa* (the highest virtue), *imperium magnum* (the greatest power), *consilium utile* (a useful plan), these are better said *summa virtus, magnum imperium,* and *utile consilium*" ("Regula iii").

This simple suggestion, that it may sound better to invert the normal position of an adjective to a different position (preceding instead of following the noun), reflects a sensitivity to language and to the minutiae of Latin syntax that is characteristically humanist. Moreover, this emphasis is indicative of the humanists' resistance to medieval Latin (in which the adjective regularly followed its noun) and their conscious, archaizing return to classical usage. Negro's inclusion of rhetorically oriented grammatical directions also reflects the changing relations between the language disciplines of grammar and rhetoric that were taking place in the Renaissance—essentially, grammar's subordination to rhetoric.[5]

To discover why grammatical rules for eloquent expression start being introduced into Renaissance letter-writing manuals in the 1490s one must go back fifty years before Negro's manual to the seminal work of Lorenzo Valla. His *Elegantiae Latinae Linguae,* or *Elegancies of the Latin Language,* though by no means a letter-writing manual, nevertheless had its influence felt across the broad spectrum of humanist writings, for Valla's work epitomized humanist efforts to resuscitate Latin.[6] Appearing to modern eyes as something of a dictionary or thesaurus, the *Elegantiae* explains and distinguishes nuances in Latin vocabulary and grammar, pointing out, as Negro would later do in a much more limited and derivative fashion, what was an elegant use of Latin as opposed to mere grammatical exactitude. "A grammarian might put it this way," says Valla throughout, "but a more refined expression would be this. . . . " For example, in the third book of the *Elegantiae* Valla compares several similar expressions—each grammatically correct—distinguishing their relative superiority on the basis of their eloquence: "*Exeo domo,* vel *e domo,* et, *sum in domo,* vel *domi;* hoc grammaticae est; illud vero latinitatis et elegantiae" (3.15.90). Here the most eloquent expressions appear to be those that take advantage of grammatical nuances available to but not always taken advantage of by Latin writers. *Sum in domo* is an acceptable but elementary way of saying one is at home, employing the inflected verb (*sum*) and a preposition indicating place (*in*). The locative case, however—more rare, but both proper and efficient—can accomplish the same meaning in one word, *domi.* One can see that the *regulae* appended to Negro's manual fall into this same pattern.

More explicit than Negro in applying Valla's program of identifying pure and eloquent Latin to the art of letter writing was a very brief manual by Aegidius Suchtelensis, the *Elegantiarum viginti precepta ad perpulchras conficiendas epistolas* (Augsburg, 1497). This work, whose very name echoes Valla's more famous work, makes visually explicit comparable Latin expressions of which both are grammatical yet one is more eloquent. Aegidius's lists of examples are each twofold, the first list headed by "The simple grammarian says [this as . . .]" (*Simplex grammaticus dicit*); the second, by "This is more eloquently expressed by the orator [as . . .]" (*Hoc orator dicit elegantius*). For example, regarding the eloquence possible via the ablative absolute, Aegidius illustrates in this way:

> The grammarian says:
> "When Rome flourished and Scipio the African reigned, then the republic was well governed and Carthage was completely destroyed. . ."
> The orator says more elegantly:
> "Rome flourishing and Scipio the African reigning, the republic was then well governed. . ." ("Rule seven").[7]

Another author to imitate Lorenzo Valla's philological emphasis in his letter-writing manual was Johann Altenstaig. In his *Opus pro conficiundis epistolis* (1512), after discussing several categories of letters, Altenstaig includes several large sections on Latinity (including a miniature dictionary of barbarisms). There, Altenstaig explicitly contrasts bad and good Latin, using Cicero as his authoritative reference point for good Latin. For example, "*Affectus:* This word is never read in Cicero; however, *affectio* is." Once again echoes of Valla and the humanist drive for pure Latin resound, but in length and breadth far beyond Negro or Aegidius. Altenstaig's manual, like so many in the Renaissance, is a blend of the older dictamen tradition with the emerging linguistic and pedagogical traditions of the humanists. Although it includes a large section on how to address men of various positions appropriately (from the emperor to archbishops to poets), it adds the large section on Latinity and then appends a small manual of Latin grammar and a section on the colors (figures) of rhetoric. Already we see the letter-writing manual moving away from serving the simple function of providing model sentences or form letters appropriate for one's addressee. More and more, letter-writing manuals reflected their position as part of the humanist curriculum that began with mastery of the "elegancies" of pristine, classical Latin, and ended with the eloquence and forcefulness made possible through the theory and practice of rhetoric.

Those manual authors who failed to exemplify these new humanist emphases came to be vilified, even if their works retained aspects of the dictaminal tradition that continued to prove serviceable throughout the fifteenth and sixteenth centuries. For example, Erasmus repeatedly disparaged the *Formulae epistolarum* (Cologne, 1493) of Karolus Mennicken (or "Virulus") for its stilted formulas and lack of stylistic eloquence. In actuality Mennicken's work is not so execrable as Erasmus would have people believe. Indeed, his Latin is not that inferior to that of more respected authors. It is not surprising that the philological and rhetorical judgments of the humanists were colored by their ideological allegiances. Later in the sixteenth century, as polemics over the imitation of Cicero would show, one's stylistic loyalties were as significant, and sometimes more so, than one's national or religious loyalties.[8] Thus, in a time when medieval letter-writing traditions blended readily with humanist innovations in philology and rhetoric, indicting a writer for his "barbarous" language was more a political judgment than it was a linguistic reality. One of the ironies of Erasmus's condemnation of Mennicken is that Erasmus ignores the simple fact that Mennicken's manual was adequate for its audience, at least for many years. It satisfied the rhetorical criterion of decorum: it was fitting for the subject, the genre, and those employing it. The same could be said for letter-writing manuals generally in the Middle Ages. Dictamen manuals were adequate and appropriate to their functions. Humanists put forth lofty reasons for rejecting medieval Latin and letters, but this was exchanging one set of linguistic and generic preferences for another.

It is still important to understand the rhetoric of the humanist desire to revive classical Latin and eloquence as they cast aside the language and methods of their immediate predecessors. For the humanists, eloquence was not merely an aesthetic desideratum; they sought to understand and achieve eloquence because they believed ardently in its civic efficacy (Baron 1966). Those who could wax eloquent would be the ones to affect the policies of princes and popes or to obtain positions of social merit themselves.[9] The literacy to which humanists aspired and to which they directed their students was one dominated by the rhetorical ideal of the orator, whose persuasive eloquence swayed audiences and effected meaningful changes in society (Gray 1963).[10] This ideal permeated humanist writings and educational programs and served as a standard for their textbooks.

Curiously, humanist efforts to reform letter writing were actually hindered by their allegiance to rhetoric, at least in one respect. On the one hand, the ideal of eloquence caused humanist dissatisfaction with the rather stilted formalism of late medieval dictamen manuals. On the other, the humanist emphasis on the orator as an ideal actually kept Renaissance letter-writing manuals from embracing humanist principles of flexibility and eloquence. This irony arose due to the fact that the medieval letter was already patterned on the classical oration. Cicero had already provided a structure for the *ars dictaminis* from at least the eleventh century.[11] The five-part epistolary arrangement that became the "approved format" by the twelfth century was essentially an adaptation of the six parts of an oration described in those Ciceronian and pseudo-Ciceronian rhetorics available to the Middle Ages:

Parts of an Oration Outlined by Cicero		Parts of a Letter From the *ars dictaminis*
		1. salutatio
1. exordium	<	
		2. captatio benevolentiae
2. narratio	—	3. narratio
3. divisio	—	(omitted)

4. confirmatio	—	4. petitio
5. refutatio	—	(omitted)
6. peroratio	—	5. conclusio

As Ronald Witt explains, it had been the tendency from the beginning of the *ars dictaminis* to consider the letter to be merely a written oration. Both Alberic of Montecassino, the probable author of the first *artes dictandi,* and his immediate successors displayed "a similar tendency to speak of letters as speeches" (1982, 9). Indeed, Alberic gave examples for letters out of speeches by Sallust. Humanists were more hesitant to reform a tradition that already embraced a classical genre that they were eager to revive, especially one modeled on the writings of their favorite figure from antiquity, Cicero. Moreover, humanists did not immediately resist the dictaminal tradition, for as Paul Kristeller has argued, the early humanists were in fact the very notaries and secretaries who practiced and taught the *ars dictaminis* (1979, 93). And as Charles Faulhaber has claimed, in the dictaminal authors "are to be sought the forerunners of the Italian humanists" (1978, 109). The classical structure of the medieval letter and the professional ties of humanists to that prior tradition were strongly conservative currents that helped maintain the presence of late medieval dictamen into the Renaissance period.

Attitudes about letter writing would not change until humanists began to observe the sharp distinction between the kinds of letters produced through the formal, oratorical dictaminal tradition and the letters of Cicero himself, newly rediscovered. They found Cicero's letters more powerful and flexible, more subtle, reflective, and personal than medieval letters. Not Cicero the teacher of rhetoric, but Cicero the letter writer gave Petrarch means by which he could utter his inmost thoughts and give form to the sinuosities of his personality for the benefit of the learned men of his generation (Witt 1982, 28). Subsequent to Petrarch, we find the humanist appreciation of Cicero manifest in letter-writing manuals and compilations of letters specifically trying to recapture the virtues of this model. Writing letters in imitation of Cicero became a longstanding tradition of publication. One example is Petri Bunelli and Paolo Manuzio's *Epistolae Ciceroniano stylo scriptae* (1581).[12]

Unfortunately, this rage to imitate Cicero seemed to result in the substitution of one moribund formalism for another. I write "seemed" because the ink that has been spent on the problem of Ciceronianism has tended to eclipse, both in the Renaissance and in contemporary criticism, the efficacious and balanced imitation of this figure in the Renaissance. In essence the problem seems to have been one of extremes. Cicero's style was enthusiastically embraced, for he showed the whole range of linguistic and generic possibilities with the Latin tongue. In their philological fervor, certain people went to extremes in following Cicero, becoming too pedantically careful in their imitation and forgetting the larger principles that governed Cicero's methods of composition. These "Ciceronians" would be lambasted by Erasmus in his *Ciceronianus* (1528) and by others (Scott 1910, reprinted 1991).

More relevant to Renaissance letter-writing manuals than the polemical *Ciceronianus* is Erasmus's *Opus de conscribendis epistolis,* on which Judith Rice Henderson has written in this volume (chapter 9). The principles that shaped Erasmus's letter-writing manual, however, are to be found in his early philological and pedagogical works. Chief among these was *De duplici copia verborum ac rerum* ([1512] 1978), "On the twofold abundance of expression and ideas." There, Erasmus provided a framework for students to learn the subtleties of expression possible in the Latin tongue and acquaint themselves with rhetorical invention, a method of coming up with arguments on any topic based on reference to certain commonplaces (such as comparison, cause and effect, and so forth). The first half of this treatise, focusing on "abundance of expression," echoes Lorenzo Valla's *Elegantiae* in its form and purpose, for it contains brief entries demonstrating how Latin can accommodate the same idea in a variety of ways. Accompanying these catalogs of possible expressions is a set of some twenty methods that Erasmus teaches by which one could achieve the desideratum of "copia," or abundant expression. These are followed by a demonstration in which Erasmus shows off how the methods could be applied to varying a couple of mundane sentences. Curiously, the first of these sentences—for which Erasmus provides 147 variations—is "your letter pleased me greatly."

Such a sentence, and variations upon it, would be typical of the *captatio benevolentiae* section of a letter-writing treatise. Indeed, one finds this very sentence, with twenty-seven variations, in an epistolary manual included as the second tract of Aeneas Sylvius Piccolomini's fifteenth-century rhetorical treatise, the *Artis rhetoricae praecepta.* There the sentence is categorized fittingly under the section "*Exordia circa amorem & beneuolentiam.*" This connection between Erasmus and Piccolomini has led Terence Cave to conclude that Erasmus derived his demonstration of copia from Piccolomini (1979, 105). A more valuable (and accurate) conclusion is that Erasmus, by choosing to vary this sentence, was showing the value of copia for the letter-writing tradition. The sentence he varies would be familiar to any reader from letter-writing manuals, but his variations differ markedly from Piccolomini's. The latter restricts himself to certain kinds of variation, whereas Erasmus's variations represent a familiarity with his own instructions to students in how to generate abundance of expression. For example, Piccolomini relies most heavily on the substitution of synonyms to provide variation, as the following three sentences from his work illustrate. Note the way synonyms are bunched together in a series:

> Ex tuis literis intellexi, cognovi, suspicatus sum, didici, animadverti, iudicavi.
>
> Ex tuis literis doctus, admonitus, adhortatus sum.
>
> Ex tuis literis doctior, prudentior, certior factus sum. (1017)

Erasmus, on the other hand, goes well beyond the rather rudimentary substitution of synonyms, flexing the muscles of the language, as it were, according to its various grammatical and rhetorical possibilities. In the following variations, for example, he shows how one may achieve variation through *enallage,* the substitution of differing but semantically equivalent grammar.

> Epistola tua me vehementer exhilaravit.
> Tua quidem epistola sum vehementer exhilaratus.

The second sentence is nearly identical to the first in terms of the words employed but differs markedly in its form (and therefore its rhetorical effect): "Epistola tua" in the first sentence is the subject, in the nominative case; in the second sentence, "Tua . . . epistola" is in the ablative case, and "your letter" is not the subject but constitutes an expression of means. The verb of the first sentence is perfect and active; in the second, perfect and passive. The rhetorical difference between these two sentences is a matter of emphasis: the first emphasizes the agent (the letter), and the second, the effect on its recipient: "Your letter exhilarated me vehemently" versus "By means of your letter I have indeed been vehemently exhilarated." By plying the possibilities of the language in this way, Erasmus is able to generate nearly 150 sentences, whereas Piccolomini provides only twenty-seven.

De copia bridges the letter-writing manual tradition and the new humanist emphases on classical and elegant Latin, for the methods of variation Erasmus prescribes (found in books 12–32 of *De copia*)[13] prior to varying this stock phrase from a typical letter derive directly from the *Elegantiae* of Lorenzo Valla. Indeed, during his schooling years in Paris Erasmus had made an abridgement of Valla's *Elegantiae* for students he was tutoring (*Paraphrasis seu potius epitome in elegantias Laurentii Vallae* [written 1488, published 1531]), and Erasmus simply applied Valla's emphasis on the grammatical and rhetorical richness of the Latin language to his pedagogical texts, including both *De copia* and *De conscribendis epistolis.*

The pedagogical orientation that Erasmus and his fellow humanists gave to Valla's philology significantly reoriented the letter-writing tradition. Students were not simply to copy prepared examples, but were to find and compose their own variations. The presence of variations, which were always part of letter-writing manuals, does not bring to a reader by itself the capacity to invent and compose his own variations. The entire difference between Piccolomini's manual and Erasmus's *De copia* lies in the fact that the variations Erasmus gives follow extensive detailed instructions on how a student might accomplish this on his own. "One should collect a vast supply . . . from all sides out of good authors," instructs Erasmus, "[and] provide oneself with a varied equipment, and, as Quintilian remarks, heap up riches so that we find we have a wealth of words to hand whenever we require it" (307). Erasmus instructs students how to employ commonplace books in conjunction with their reading of classical authors. These were to be divided into one part devoted to verbal expression, another to the development of subject matter. This is the arrangement of *De copia* itself, and it can be seen, at least in one respect, as a model commonplace book. *De copia* contains lists and lists of locutions and quotations that Erasmus has culled from his wide reading, providing students not just the results of his own search for copia, but a model of how the process is to be done by each student. In contrast Piccolomini's manual presents only the results of such efforts to vary without the accompanying rationale or method for culling further expressive means from one's reading.

Erasmus was certainly not the first to suggest exploring variations of expression in the art of letter writing, but his method is more advanced because of its extensive theoretical underpinnings and its specific instructions. Some of the early letter-writing manuals of the Renaissance, such as Piccolomini's, seem to keep one foot in the medieval dictaminal tradition and one foot in the emerging humanistic tradition. For example, Friedric Nausea appended a letter-writing manual to his poetry writing manual, *In artem poeticen carminumque condendorum primordia; eiusdem Syntagma de conficiendis epistolis* (Venice, 1522). This manual, another disliked by Erasmus, maintains a clear allegiance to the established dictaminal tradition, following religiously the arrangement of medieval dictaminal manuals modeled on the classical oration and providing detailed salutations for each of the various positions of individuals to whom one might write: *Ad pontificem, ad caridinalem* [sic], *ad archiepiscopum, ad episocum, ad abbatem ad monachum,* and so on. But, tellingly, Nausea acknowledges in his introduction that letters admit of such variety that one can hardly give rules for them. This is an important acknowledgment: rather than insist upon relying on established forms or formulas, Nausea concedes their inadequacy for all situations. The humanist principle of *kairos,* if not the humanist methods themselves, thus begins to inform the letter-writing manual in the early Renaissance.

As a first step toward accommodating the infinite variety possible in the writing of letters to which Nausea alludes, other letter-writing manuals would begin to include variations of expression of a sort quite different from the variations presented in standard dictamen manuals. The dictamen manuals included variety of expression only in the limited sense of listing different language to be employed for different addressees. The variety of expression that would come to be exemplified in the humanistically oriented letter-writing manuals included varieties of valid grammatical and rhetorical permutations purposefully intended to stretch the limits of the student to embrace the full range of discursive possibilities. Examples of letter-writing manuals of this sort include those by Piccolomini and by Stephanus Fliscus. The *De componendis epistolis* (Venice, 1534) of Fliscus introduces itself not so much as a manual of writing letters as a set of example synonyms. Each locution is introduced in Italian, which suggests that the manual is intended for Italians attempting to acquire the "elegancies" of the Latin language.[14] Significantly, the synonyms are nowhere oriented to specific addressees nor correlated to specific parts of a letter. Obviously the sort of variety exemplified in this manual is of a different sort than that to be found in dictamen manuals. As is most evident in the works of Erasmus, the goal of variety for humanists was not to present readers with a ready-made language to choose from for parts of a letter, but rather to acquaint them with the flexibility of the Latin language and provide a sample of how the student might generate his own letter. Once again, the seminal *De copia* of Erasmus is the text against which Renaissance letter-writing manuals should be read as they present variety of expression. *De copia's* central principle was the reorientation of variety of expression from menu to methodology: the new goal was not to provide boiler plate language, but to expand the linguistic and rhetorical capabilities of the person doing the varying. In other words the letter-writing manual was moved from the domain of pragmatic business to the pedagogical domain of humanist literary study and development.

The principles and methods of Erasmus's *De copia* are the foundation of his actual treatise on letter writing, the *De conscribendis epistolis* of 1522. Although one finds in this work certain vestiges of the medieval tradition, such as certain remnants of the oration as a model for letters, this manual is thoroughly humanistic in its approach to the art of letter writing. The greatest indicator of this orientation is the pedagogical and theoretical apparatus that accompanies the manual. The manual is rich with example letters, but it is equally potent in its prefatory material, which orients the student toward the same rhetorical principles made clear in *De copia*. The next indicator of its thoroughly humanistic orientation is Erasmus's emphasis on style. Erasmus does not simply provide a plethora of categories and suggested ways of addressing various groups, but instead discusses what kind of style is appropriate for a given purpose. To all of these suggestions Erasmus appends examples, usually his own. These also differ from typical manuals in their length and complexity. He does not chop up the letter into its component parts and then give variations upon a single sentence for each part. Rather, he provides whole letters for a given subgenre. Indeed, *De conscribendis epistolis* does not so much give its readers locutions to employ in their letters as it pushes them to the analysis of given genres for a given rhetorical purpose. This is also consistent with Erasmus's educational doctrines (as described in both his *De ratione studii* and the *De copia*) in which Erasmus directs students how to analyze texts, and then imitate them, on the way to composing independently.[15]

Letters and letter writing were serious concerns for Renaissance humanists. The style in which one composed a letter had real consequences in a world increasingly appreciative of antiquity. Equally important in this period was the development of the letter that could be personal, not just formal, and that could reflect the specific thoughts and concerns of its sender as readily as it could fit itself to its targeted audience. As humanists insisted upon these values, their disdain for the inadequacy of medieval formularies increased, even though such a dismissive attitude ignored the simple fact that such letters succeeded in fulfilling their purposes for centuries. Rather than arriving at a value judgment regarding the *ars conscribendi epistolis* of the humanists against the medieval *ars dictaminis*, it may be more useful to see humanists such as Erasmus as those who introduced more sophisticated expectations for letters and letter writers because of the idealism with which they saw discourse succeeding in antiquity and the idealism they had for transforming their own time and place through linguistic and rhetorical means. In its worst form, the humanists' literary idealism turned into an adoration of Cicero that resulted in the fatuous stylistic extremes of the Ciceronians, qualitatively no better than the worst of medieval formularies. At its best this Renaissance idealism manifested itself in the promotion of a new flexibility and independence for discourse. In any case Renaissance letter-writing manuals altered to reflect humanist principles and pedagogy. Even though remnants of medieval formularies clearly persisted throughout the period, the ideas and ideals of the humanists came to reshape letter writing until it became one of several genres dominated by humanist pedagogy in Latin schools. In this light it is no longer possible to isolate the letter-writing manual, for the new traditions that animated letter writing in the Renaissance had more to do with the spectrum of texts and activities associated with Renaissance humanism than it did with its medieval precedents.

Notes

1. No comprehensive work of scholarship has yet been completed with respect to the Renaissance letter-writing manual. See, however, Henderson's essay in this volume (and Henderson 1983) for Europe and also Green's essay in this volume for Britain.

2. See Sandys (1964) and Reynolds and Wilson (1991).

3. Sixteenth-century examples include Paolo Manuzio's *Epistolarum libri XII* (1556) and Johann Sturm's *Classicorum epistolarum* (1565). See the comprehensive survey by Cecil Clough (1976).

4. For the breadth of Cicero's significance to Renaissance humanists, see Seigel (1968), Lorch (1988), and Green (1994).

5. For the relationship between Renaissance grammar and rhetoric, see Percival (1988) and Grendler (1989, 162–202).

6. Complete manuscripts of the *Elegantiae* from the period number 50, with twenty redactions or epitomes found in other manuscripts. From its first edition in 1471, some 147 printed editions have also been identified through 1598. See Ijsewijn and Tournoy (1969, 1971). If the editions proper of Valla's *Elegantiae* are combined with various epitomes of it, this work saw more than two hundred editions through the sixteenth century.

7. Grammaticus dicit:

work, makes visually explicit comparable Latin expressions of which both are grammatical yet one is more eloquent. Aegidius's lists of examples are each twofold, the first list headed by "The simple grammarian says [this as . . .]" (*Simplex grammaticus dicit*); the second, by "This is more eloquently expressed by the orator [as . . .]" (*Hoc orator dicit elegantius*). For example, regarding the eloquence possible via the ablative absolute, Aegidius illustrates in this way:

> The grammarian says:
> "When Rome flourished and Scipio the African reigned, then the republic was well governed and Carthage was completely destroyed . . ."
> The orator says more elegantly:
> "Rome flourishing and Scipio the African reigning, the republic was then well governed . . ." ("Rule seven").[7]

Another author to imitate Lorenzo Valla's philological emphasis in his letter-writing manual was Johann Altenstaig. In his *Opus pro conficiundis epistolis* (1512), after discussing several categories of letters, Altenstaig includes several large sections on Latinity (including a miniature dictionary of barbarisms). There, Altenstaig explicitly contrasts bad and good Latin, using Cicero as his authoritative reference point for good Latin. For example, "*Affectus:* This word is never read in Cicero; however, *affectio* is." Once again echoes of Valla and the humanist drive for pure Latin resound, but in length and breadth far beyond Negro or Aegidius. Altenstaig's manual, like so many in the Renaissance, is a blend of the older dictamen tradition with the emerging linguistic and pedagogical traditions of the humanists. Although it includes a large section on how to address men of various positions appropriately (from the emperor to archbishops to poets), it adds the large section on Latinity and then appends a small manual of Latin grammar and a section on the colors (figures) of rhetoric. Already we see the letter-writing manual moving away from serving the simple function of providing model sentences or form letters appropriate for one's addressee. More and more, letter-writing manuals reflected their position as part of the humanist curriculum that began with mastery of the "elegancies" of pristine, classical Latin, and ended with the eloquence and forcefulness made possible through the theory and practice of rhetoric.

Those manual authors who failed to exemplify these new humanist emphases came to be vilified, even if their works retained aspects of the dictaminal tradition that continued to prove serviceable throughout the fifteenth and sixteenth centuries. For example, Erasmus repeatedly disparaged the *Formulae epistolarum* (Cologne, 1493) of Karolus Mennicken (or "Virulus") for its stilted formulas and lack of stylistic eloquence. In actuality Mennicken's work is not so execrable as Erasmus would have people believe. Indeed, his Latin is not that inferior to that of more respected authors. It is not surprising that the philological and rhetorical judgments of the humanists were colored by their ideological allegiances. Later in the sixteenth century, as polemics over the imitation of Cicero

Works Cited

Primary Texts

Altenstaig, Johann. *Opus pro conficiundis epistolis.* 1512.

Anonymous. *Certaine Epistles of Tully verbally translated.* London, 1611.

———. *Principia Latine Loquendi, scribendique sive, Selecta quaedam ex Ciceronis epistolis, ad pueros in Latina lingua exercendos, adiecta interpretatione Anglica, & (vbi opus esse visum est) Latina declaratione. . . . A very necessary and profitable entraunce to the speakyng and writyng of the Latin tongue; or, A certain draught taken out of Ciceroes Epistles, for the exercise of children in the Latin speache together with an easy and a familiar construction thereof into Englishe.* Translated by "T. W." 1575

Anonymous of Bologna. *The Principles of Letter-Writing (Rationes dictandi).* Translated by James J. Murphy, *Three Medieval Rhetorical Arts.* Berkeley: University of California Press, 1971. 5–25.

Bunelli, Petri, and Paolo Manuzio. *Epistolae Ciceroniano stylo scriptae.* 1581

Erasmus, Desiderius. *Copia: Foundations of the Abundant Style: De duplici copia verborum ac rerum commentarii duo.* Translated and edited by Betty I. Knott. In *Collected Works of Erasmus: Literary and Educational Writings 2.* Edited by Craig R. Thompson. Vol. 28. Toronto: University of Toronto Press, 1978.

———. *Opus de conscribendis epistolis.* Paris: Opud Simone[m] colineu[m], 1523.

Fliscus, Stephanus. *De componendis epistolis.* Venice, 1534.

Knox, *Elegant Epistles . . . from Cicero.* 1794.

Mennicken, Karolus. *Formulae epistolarum.* Cologne, 1493.

Nausea, Friedric. *In artem poeticen carminumque condendorum primordia; eiusdem Syntagma de conficiendis epistolis.* Venice, 1522.

Negro, Pescennio Francesco. *Modus epistolandi.* Venice, 1492.

Manuzio, Paolo. *Eleganze della lingua toscana e latina.* 1558.

———. *Epistolarum libri XII.* Venice. 1556.

Piccolomini, Aeneas Sylvius. *Artis rhetoricae praecepta. Opera Quae Extant Omnia.* Basle: Henricus Petri, 1551.

Sturm, Johann. *Classicorum epistolarum.* 1565.

Suchtelensis, Aegidius. *Elegantiarum viginti precepta ad perpulchras conficiendas epistolas.* Augsburg, 1497.

Valla, Lorenzo. *Elegantiae linguae Latinae.* 1452.

Secondary Texts

Baron, Hans Baron. *The Crisis of the Early Italian Renaissance: Civic Humanism and Republican Liberty in an Age of Classicism and Tyranny,* rev. ed. Princeton, N.J.: Princeton University Press, 1966.

Burton, Gideon O. "Imitation in Renaissance Culture and Humanist Pedagogy." PhD diss., University of Southern California, 1994.

Camargo, Martin. "A Twelfth-Century Treatise on 'Dictamen' and Metaphor." *Traditio* 47 (1992): 161–214.

Cave, Terence. *The Cornucopian Text.* New York: Oxford University Press, 1979.

Clough, Cecil H. "The Cult of Antiquity: Letters and Letter Collections." In *Cultural Aspects of the Italian Renaissance: Essays in Honour of Paul Oskar Kristeller,* edited by Cecil H. Clough. Manchester: Manchester University Press, 1976, 33–67.

Conley, Thomas. *Rhetoric in the European Tradition.* New York: Longman, 1990.

Faulhaber, Charles. "The *Summa dictaminis* of Guido Faba." In *Medieval Eloquence: Studies in the Theory and Practice of Medieval Rhetoric,* edited by James Murphy. Berkeley: University of California Press, 1978, 85–111.

Grafton, Anthony, and Lisa Jardine. *From Humanism to the Humanities: Education and the Liberal Arts in Fifteenth- and Sixteenth-Century Europe.* Cambridge, Mass.: Harvard University Press, 1986.

Gray, Hanna H. "Renaissance Humanism: The Pursuit of Eloquence." *Journal of the History of Ideas* 24 (1963): 497–514.

Green, Lawrence D. "Canonicity and the Renaissance Cicero." In *Composition in Context: Essays in Honor of Donald C. Stewart,* edited by W. Ross Winterowd and Vincent Gillespie. Carbondale: Southern Illinois University Press, 1994, 17–27.

Grendler, Paul F. *Schooling in Renaissance Italy: Literacy and Learning, 1300–1600.* Baltimore: Johns Hopkins University Press, 1989.

Henderson, Judith Rice. "Erasmus on the Art of Letter-Writing." In *Renaissance Eloquence: Studies in the Theory and Practice of Renaissance Rhetoric,* edited by James J. Murphy. Berkeley: University of California Press, 1983, 331–55.

Ijsewijn, Josef, and G. Tournoy. "Nuovi contributi per l'elenco dei manoscritti e delle edizioni delle Elegantiae di Lorenzo Valla." *Humanistica Lovaniensia* 20 (1971): 1–3.

———. "Un primo censimento dei manoscritti e delle edizioni a stampa degli *Elegantiarum linguae latinae libri sex* di Lorenzo Valla." *Humanistica Lovaniensia* 18 (1969): 25–41.

Kristeller, Paul Oskar. *Renaissance Thought and Its Sources.* Edited by Michael Mooney. New York: Columbia University Press, 1979.

Lorch, Maristella. "Petrarch, Cicero, and the Classical Pagan Tradition." In *Renaissance Humanism: Foundation, Forms, and Legacy.* Vol. 1, *Humanism in Italy,* edited by Albert Rabil, Jr. Philadelphia: University of Pennsylvania Press, 1988, 71–94.

Percival, W. Keith. "Renaissance Grammar." In *Renaissance Humanism: Foundation, Forms, and Legacy.* Vol. 3, *Humanism and the Disciplines,* edited by Albert Rabil, Jr. Philadelphia: University of Pennsylvania Press, 1988, 67–83

Reynolds, L. D., and N. G. Wilson, *Scribes and Scholars: A Guide to the Transmission of Greek and Latin Literature,* 3rd ed. London: Oxford University Press, 1991.

Sandys, John Edwin. *A History of Classical Scholarship.* New York: Hafner, 1964.

Scott, Izora. *Controversies over the Imitation of Cicero in the Renaissance.* 1910. Reprint, Davis, Calif.: Hermagoras Press, 1991.

Seigel, Jerrold. *Rhetoric and Philosophy in Renaissance Humanism: The Union of Eloquence and Wisdom, Petrarch to Valla.* Princeton, N.J.: Princeton University Press, 1968.

Witt, Ronald. "Medieval 'Ars Dictaminis' and the Beginnings of Humanism: a New Construction of the Problem." *Renaissance Quarterly* 35 (1982): 1–35.

Dictamen in England, 1500–1700

Lawrence D. Green

Publication in England on the subject of letter writing took place in a culture of literacy that was more Latin than English, more Continental than native, more oriented toward manuscript than toward print, and heavily reliant upon imported imprints. At the start of the period two major trends are present. The first is an inheritance from the medieval *ars dictaminis* in which the canons of classical rhetoric—as they were interpreted and understood during the medieval period—were adapted and adopted in England for writing letters of a nearly formulaic sort. Letters written in this inherited tradition memorialized existing social and legal relations, at least as much as they conveyed social and legal information. The second trend developed from the study and imitation of Cicero that was at the heart of Renaissance humanism. Although the medieval world knew many of the prescriptions of classical rhetoric, they had lost most of the classical context that gave those prescriptions life. With the rediscovery of Cicero's familiar letters, however, writers such as Petrarch felt they had recovered the human presence of a lost world. Letters written in this second tradition sought to use the resources of rhetoric to create and project the human presence of the writer. Within decades, however, this latter effort would lead to the realization that all such created senses of the human self are to some degree rhetorical fictions, that skilled writers can choose among available fictions and that recipients can participate in such fictions.

The early Tudor period was dominated by imported Latin manuals such as those by Macropedius and Hegendorf. Not until 1573 was either published in England, but after that they were published repeatedly for nearly eighty years. So also, Cicero's Latin letters were imported from the Continent and not printed in England until 1571, but thereafter editions were published repeatedly until the end of the period. The early and continued availability of Cicero's letters as models for practical emulation encouraged the notion of letter writing as humane engagement with the larger culture, and after 1570 this notion was extended beyond learned circles with the publication of English vernacular works translated or derived from Continental models. Some of these latter treatises and manuals offer advice that is closely allied with the inherited rhetorical tradition, and it is these works that have received most scholarly study to date. Yet other books after 1570 are collections of exemplars so rigidly formulaic and tied so closely to particular circumstances that it is difficult if not impossible to discern more general principles of letter writing underlying those exemplars: the exemplar is there to be copied, adapted, or ignored.

By the end of the sixteenth century, exemplars and collections of letters proliferated, and, although many advertised themselves as being for critical use in instruction and emulation by the middle classes, some were valued as much for leisurely amusement through vicarious engagement in other peoples' real or imagined lives. Thus, any effort to survey the wealth of material in letter writing entails some unexpected forays into the reasons why people would choose to write letters and why they would choose to read them. Such an effort was made by Jean Robertson (1942), who tried to organize seventeenth-century English dictamen in terms of a general progression from fictional letter-collections, to fashionable French *academies,* and finally to bourgeois *secretaries.*[1] Those categories are still useful, and the present study builds directly upon them, but in the half century since Robertson's survey, much more work has been done in the larger contexts of Renaissance rhetoric and a great many more bibliographical resources have become available. In particular both the Latin Continental and the Ciceronian materials, which were not a part of her study, continue to be published alongside the *academies,* which were still published alongside the *secretaries* at the end of the period. Thus, what was viewed earlier as a seventeenth-century progression is presented here as a braid of interwoven strands, all of which were already present in the sixteenth century and all of which responded to market forces within the book trade.

Greater bibliographical understanding, however, has also come at a sobering price. We now have a better understanding of how much we may never know. Books were used during this period rather than treasured, and bibliography for this period is a story of lost volumes, missing editions, and ghost titles. For many books, we have only later editions and no firm idea of when they first appeared, or we have unbridgeable gaps between, for instance, the third and ninth editions, with no way to recover the intermediate reading history of a significant title. Conversely, some books were printed only once and, against the background of our uncertainty about the book trade, they can appear to have a contemporary importance that is belied by the lack of any known subsequent printing; no publisher was willing to risk the costs of a second edition. Moreover, print runs were generally small and in the earlier period seemed to average five hundred to a thousand copies at most (with slightly higher runs for schooltexts privileged by patent), so, by any calculation, the number of books printed and imported was insufficient to serve the potential letter-writing public.

Equally sobering is our emerging realization of just how insignificant the London book trade was, both in itself and as compared to manuscript culture. A recent study by Mark Bland (1999) provides a generous estimate of the entire yearly trade in printed texts at the end of the sixteenth century as no more than £24,000 and the net assets of the entire London book trade (from print shops to booksellers) as less than the personal net worth of Southampton, Egerton, Pembroke, or Cecil. None of the paper stock for printing was made in England. Bland compares customs figures for paper imports in 1600, the mechanics of book production, the maximum possible press runs, and allows for wastage and then concludes that the printing houses can account for no more than a quarter of the imported paper. The rest was used for manuscripts, and many London booksellers were dependent upon the scribal work by commercial scriveners to make up for the insufficiencies of the printing houses.[2]

From the beginning, the much larger manuscript culture augmented and perhaps surpassed the print culture in dictaminal materials as students and scriveners copied treatises and letters for emulation. One such manuscript collection of letters and speeches from the years 1545–1579 was clearly intended to provide models and precedents, all arranged under the heads of advice, answers to petitions, orations, and letters commendatory, consolatory, expostulatory, gratulatory, orations, narratory, and supplicatory.[3] Sometime around 1599, John Hoskyns wrote his "Direccions for speech and style," and, while copies of the collection circulated in manuscript, the collection was never published.[4] Late in the seventeenth century, around 1665, Heneage Finch, second Earl of Winchilsea, recorded his "Certain rule & observations for a secretary," and "Superscriptions and addresses of letters."[5] For manuscripts, the survival rate is even worse than for books of a utilitarian or ephemeral nature, and to speak of the materials we now have is to alert ourselves to the materials we may never recover.

Nevertheless, we work with what we have, and the gaps in our understanding also represent directions for archival research. All that is certain is that we will misunderstand dictamen in England if we confine ourselves to the readily available materials of modern reprints, if we fail to pay attention to the dynamics of printing, of commercial competition, of patents and privileges, and the larger changes among the writers and readers of letters. Work needs to be done to determine who had access to what, when they had it, and what difference it made in their practices. This will require work in press runs, book prices, book distribution, importation, and commercial competition. In particular we must determine which printers and booksellers invested in dictaminal materials and how those materials complemented what a modern press would call its "book list," whether the trade seemed more or less attractive to different participants at different times, under the impress of what kinds of material conditions, and at all times how this information related to the larger manuscript culture in which letter writing was always meant to function.[6] Such is not the task of the present essay. In the pages that follow I try to point out the kinds of publications that existed side by side, or that competed with one another, or how one kind of material (or even a particular title) endured even as another rose to challenge it. I have made no effort here to list the numerous collections of the letters of contemporary writers unless the compilers or users of those collections made some overt effort to advertise their use for education or emulation.

Part 1: The Sixteenth Century

Two points immediately stand out from looking at the early history of publication. First is the belatedness of the entire enterprise in England. The second is the extent to which the English were indebted to Continental thinking and movements, even after the English started publishing in serious numbers. In marked contrast with the robust publishing trade on the Continent in dictamen, there was comparatively little publishing in England prior to 1570. From 1570 to 1650, the English averaged sixteen printings each decade, and from 1650 to 1700 they averaged twenty-seven printings each decade. From the beginnings of print in England until 1570, there were a total of just nine printings for almost a century (excluding legal dictamen, which I will treat separately). Prior to 1570, almost all of the printings had immediate Continental origins, and after 1570 this English dependence, even subservience, continued until the end of the period. When the English were Latin, they were international, but, as they became more English, they tried to become French.

The earliest printed work, and one of the first books from Richard Pynson's press, is *Elegantiarum viginti precepta* (1498?), sometimes attributed to Aegidius Suchtelensis). As the title suggests, this short treatise distinguishes between grammatical correctness and elegance, and the elegancies are extended to forms of dictaminal address. It appears once only, and is as much tied to mastering Latin as mastering letters. The second earliest work has much the same focus but has a longer lifespan. Giovanni Sulpizio's (Johannes Sulpitius's) *De componendis & ornandis epistolis* first appeared in Rome in 1491 and was reprinted in London in 1502 in collections of grammatical works by Sulpizio, Donatus, and Mancinelli. The work reappeared in similar collections in 1504, 1505, and 1511, drifting among different printing houses before its final printing in 1514 (except as noted, London is the place of publication for works cited in this essay).

The only other dictaminal work during this early period is Erasmus's *De conscribendi epistolis* (1521), which was pirated in an incomplete draft by the upstart Cambridge printer John Siberch [= Johann Lair of Siegburg]. In 1522 Froben printed the authorized Basel edition, but Erasmus had been working on the text at least as early as 1499, when he sent a copy to his English pupil Lord Mountjoy, and Siberch's unauthorized edition derives from this early draft. It was not an auspicious manner for Cambridge printers to enter the dictaminal book trade, and *De conscribendi epistolis* was never reprinted in England. Siberch's piracy thus gives us Erasmus's treatise as a work in progress rather than as a finished product late in his life, and it is roughly contemporaneous with the fractious energy of *Encomium moriae* and the expansive developments of *De copia verborum ac rerum*. In it Erasmus excoriates both the mindless followers of medieval formularies and the mindless imitators of Ciceronian letters (both excoriations are dropped from the mature and authorized edition; Erasmus had

had enough). For Erasmus a letter is a mutual conversation between absent friends,[7] neither a book nor an oration nor a formula, but instead a mercurial messenger changing shape to make the recipient feel the living presence of the writer (1:349C). These are the very sentiments that Petrarch could have articulated a century earlier.

For the next forty years, the only dictaminal works are reprints of a single legal compendium, *A newe boke of presidentes*. It appeared with a preface by Thomas Phaer in 1543 and went through forty editions before 1641. Not surprisingly, the view of letters here is the very antithesis of what Erasmus has in mind, and these pragmatic letters seek, if anything, to efface the living presence of the writer. In 1561 there appears for the first time a Ciceronian letter, in an English translation by G. Gylby, entitled *An epistle or letter of exhortation by M. T. Cicero to his brother Quintus* [*Epistolae. Quint.* Bk 1, letter 1]. As the title makes clear, the translator's announced intentions were as much ethical as dictaminal.

All in all, this is a meager record for the first century of print in England. Even if we add such works as Thomas Wilson's *Arte of Rhetorique* (1553, etc.), with its illustrative letters by Erasmus and the "Lincolnshire Man," the picture does not change appreciably, and even in these cases Wilson's interests are not really dictaminal. Yet we know there was an active interest in letters and letter writing. The standard grammar-school curriculum included the letters of Cicero for both study and emulation, and the entrance requirements for young boys at Oxford included the ability to compose Latin epistles *ex tempore*. The English humanists themselves maintained active correspondence with Continental writers, and their letters were frequently published throughout the century (on the Continent and later in England) as universally recognized exemplars of eloquence. From these scattered bits of information we can hazard a few conclusions. Prior to 1570, the bulk of English printing interest was restricted to pragmatic letters, either legal or simple utilitarian, and in neither case drawing upon medieval nor developing Renaissance dictaminal theory. Care or concern about the construction of letters was reserved for the well educated, probably more as a matter of international community than local efficacy, and such treatises as they relied upon were neither produced nor printed in England. Thus, the letters of Cicero had to, and did, come from the Continent, as did such dictaminal manuals as circulated in England.

Erasmus was the ambiguous source of one of these manuals. He had complained that some of his earlier notes for *De conscribendi epistolis* had been pirated (again!), misappropriated, and excerpted. These notes were published in Basel (1519) by Adam Petri (rather than by Froben, his usual Basel publisher) and then were reprinted widely on the Continent. Other Continental manuals known to have circulated in England prior to 1570 were Aurelio Lippo Brandolini, *De ratione scribendi libri tres* (Basel 1498); Christoph Hegendorf, *Methodus epistolas conscribendi* (Hagenau 1526); Conrad Celtes, *Methodus conficiendarum epistolarum* (Basel 1537); and Juan Luis Vives, *De conscribendis epistolis* (Basel 1536). In 1549 all five of these treatises were published together in Basel under the collective title [Brandolinus,] *De ratione scribendi,* and in 1565 the Basel reprinting added Georgius Macropedius [= Joris van Langeveldt], *Methodus de conscribendis epistolis* (Antwerp 1543, as *Epistolica studiosis traiectinae scholae tyrunculis nuncupata, quae nihilominus quicquid ad prima rhetorices elementa attinet, brevibus praeceptis plane complectitur*). Copies of these several collections circulated in England.

The first major change in this English dependence on Continental publishing came in 1573, with Middleton's London printing of the Basel 1565 edition of Brandolinus's *De ratione scribendi.* The homegrown market finally was large enough to warrant an independent printing, but several of the manual included were nearly out of date by this time, and there were no more English printings of Brandolinus, Erasmus, Celtes, or Vives. The manuals by Macropedius and Hegendorf, however, continued to have a major impact on English dictamen until late in the next century. The two were bundled together under Macropedius's name and published as *De conscribendi epistolis* nearly every five years until 1637, and after these eleven printings Macropedius had one more of his own, in 1649, in a revised version. Other Continental imports competed with Macropedius at various times, such as Spangenberg, *De conficiendis epistolis liber* (Edinburgh, 1580?), and Verepaeus, *De epistolis latine conscribendis libri v* (London, 1592), but without much success. In general, although English publishing in dictamen finally came into its own after 1570, the strong presence and direct influence of Continental dictamen persisted for another six decades.

Starting with the 1570s there is also the one constant of publishing in dictamen throughout the period: the publication of Cicero's letters for study and emulation. Here, as with the dictaminal manuals, English publishing follows Continental practices. Cicero's *Epistolae ad familiares* with annotations by Manutius were published as early as 1467 in Rome; Denis Lambin edited and annotated this edition for a printing in Venice. It is this edition Bynneman printed in London in 1571, and other London publishers reprinted it seven more times before 1607. This edition had commercial competitors almost the moment it appeared. Christoph Hegendorf (the author of the durable dictaminal manual) had edited the *Epistolarum familiarium libri* xvi with the inevitable commercial claim *iam recens emendati* (Lyon, 1545); Thomas Marsh printed it three times in London during the 1570s (1574, 1577, and 1579). Even when Englishmen participated directly in the enterprise of Ciceronian letters, they still followed the European lead. Alexander Scot produced two major editions of letters, one as part of collected works of Cicero, *Operum . . . eius epistolas ad familiares complectens,* the other an independent *Epistolarum ad Atticum lib. xvi.* Both were published in Lyon in 1608 rather than in England, though both circulated in England.

These editions were meant to advance dictaminal understanding by showing Cicero's mastery of letters in the context of his times. Nevertheless, where the larger editions of Cicero stressed the coherence of his historical context, school texts of Cicero were apt to stress the coherence of developing dictaminal theory, and his letters were reorganized to enhance such understanding. As early as 1575 there appeared such a school text, an English edition and translation of a selection Mathurin Cordier first printed in Geneva in 1566: *Principia latine loquendi scribendique: sive selecta quaedam ex Ciceronis epistolis, ad pueros in latina lingua exercendos . . . a very necessary and profitable entraunce to the speakyng and writing of the latin tongue.* It is not until 1602 that we find at last an English effort that is not merely a reprint of Continental work and is specifically formulated for use by schoolboys: T. Cogan's *Epistolarum familiarium . . . epitome secundum tria genera . . . nuntiatorum, iocosum, & grave . . . . Orationes etiam aliquot faciliores. Ad usum scholarum,* published in Cambridge and London in 1602 by Legat, who did much of the printing for the university. Even such homegrown efforts followed Continental models, however, and the real source of Ciceronian dictamen for the rest of the century was Johann Sturm's pedagogical gathering in *Marci Tullii Ciceronis, epistolarum libri quatuor a J. Sturmio puerilis educationis causa selecti, quibus adjecta est brevis explanatio, ex F. Junii . . . commentarius descripta.* Two versions circulated. The first version, published only in Scotland, was by J. Ray (Edinburgh 1618, Aberdeen 1630, Edinburgh 1634, 1640, Aberdeen 1665, Glasgow 1674, Edinburgh 1675, 1694). The second version, published variously in Cambridge and London, was by Lambin (1625, 1631, 1635, 1637, 1656, 1658, 1669, 1670, 1677, 1685, 1686, 1686, 1696, 1700). To these we may add the homegrown English anthology *Epistolae selectae* designed specifically for use in Westminster grammar school (London 1657, 1689, c. 1690]. The dominance of Cicero in this tradition is all the clearer when we look at the paucity of books by other classical figures. Isocrates's Greek *Epistolae* (with Latin translations by G. Silvanus) appears once only, in 1685, as did *The Epistles of Phalaris,* translated by S. Whately in 1699, though based on a much earlier French translation (Antwerp, 1558).

Throughout the period, Cicero provides a central core of understandings on which to anchor the numerous vernacular variations. Charles Hoole, for example, moves freely between Latin and English models for his schoolboys but still bases his work on Cicero: *Centuria epistolarum anglo-latinarum; . . . A century of epistles, English and latine; selected out of the most used school-authors, viz. Tullie, Plinie, and Textor. By imitating of which, children may readily get a proper style for writing letters* (1660, 1677, 1687, 1700). Where Hoole wants competent letter writers in Latin and English, Edward Leedes instead uses English letter writing as a way to teach both Latin and Latin letter writing in his *English examples* (1676, 1677, 1681, 1685, 1687, Dublin 1697, London 1699), *New English examples* (1685), and *More English examples* (1692, 1699). Each of Leede's compilations includes a section of "Examples of epistles," and each carries the pedagogical subtitle of *English examples to be turned into Latin . . . Forms of epistles, themes, and other exercises for the use of young beginners at Bury Schoole.*

Although the interest in Cicero was largely a phenomenon of the schools, it was not confined to the schools, or even to Latin. In 1576 Abraham Fleming published *A panoplie of epistles; or, A looking glasse for the unlearned. Conteyning a perfecte plattforme of inditing letters of all sorts . . . used of the best and eloquentest rhetoricians that have lived in all ages . . . gathered and translated out of Latine into English.* The volume is less interested in historical context than in good letters themselves and in showing that English letter writers are as accomplished as classical. Cicero is the principal letter writer (153 pages), but there are also letters by Isocrates (86 pages), Pliny and other Romans (72 pages), Manutius and other moderns (98 pages), and then the Englishmen Christopher Haddon and Roger Ascham (25 pages). Later in the seventeenth century, occasional translations of Cicero appeared in singular printings, and, as their titles suggest, they were used for singular purposes. In 1611 William Haine edited and translated book 1 of *Epistolae ad familiares* as *Certain epistles of Tully verbally translated: together with a short treatise, containing an order of instructing youth in grammer, and withall the benefite of verball translation.* In 1620 J. Webbe translated selections as *The familiar epistles of M. T. Cicero Englished and conferred with the French Italian and other translations.* And in 1627 a disciple of Webbe's translated book 1 of *Epistolae ad Atticum* as *Lessons and exercises out of Cicero, after the method of Dr Webbe, lately privileged from his Majesty for 31 years.*

As these last titles make clear, the purposes of dictaminal studies often were bound up with other pedagogical and larger social concerns, in which dictamen played an important but subsidiary role. The extent of how thoroughly bound up these studies could be is seen in John Brinsley's (the elder) *Ludus literarius; or, The grammar schoole* (1612, 1627 in five variants). It is intended to be a complete educational and social program, embracing dictamen as part of that program, and chapter 12 addresses "How to make epistles imitating Tully, short, pithie, sweete Latine and familiar; and to indite letters to our friends in English accordingly." Brinsley returned to this approach in *A consolation for our grammar schooles* (1622, 2nd ed.) with his brief chapter on "Epistles and letters." Such comprehensive approaches in the seventeenth century extended to schooling in Latin as well. In 1628 John Clarke published his schoolbook on *Transitionum formulae,* complete with school exercises, composition themes, and practice declamations and orations. In a separate section he added a lengthy *Tractatus epistolaris, nec non praecipua inveniendorum argumentorum capita, regulae ad elegantiorem orationis structuram dirigentes.* In 1630 he revised the entire work as *Formulae oratoriae,* in which he integrated letter writing even more closely with his entire program, and in this form it was reprinted in 1632, 1637, 1647, 1653, 1659, 1664, 1670, and 1672. It was also reprinted twice on the Continent, appearing in Zurich in 1663 and 1694. In addition to works by pedagogues such as Brinsley and Clarke, who went through numerous printings, there were similar publications that had a more restricted printing history. An anonymous "Schoolmaster in London" known only by the initials "F. B." published a single edition of *Clavis grammatica; or, The ready way to the Latine tongue . . . with necessary observations for epistolizing or writing of letters in English or Latine* (1678). Late in the century, John Hawkins published *The English schoolmaster compleated . . . to which is added, an appendix containing . . . copies of letters, titles of honor suitable for men of all degrees and qualities, etc.* (1692, 1694).

This last title is also in keeping with another dictaminal tradition in England, that of instruction in letter writing that somehow completes or supplements that of the schoolroom, or even supplants it. The tradition starts with the very beginnings of serious dictaminal publication in England. In 1568 William Fulwood published *The enimie of idlenesse: teaching the maner and stile how to endite, compose and write all sorts of epistles and letters.* This was the first vernacular treatise devoted to dictamen, and it was popular enough to be reprinted every five years or so until 1621. It was traditional in that it accepted the same rhetorical rubrics of the Latin treatises (with explicit cross-reference to Wilson and Rainolde), but also supplemented those rubrics with new ones closer to the English domestic experience. The idea was not really original with Fulwood, because even here England still followed the Continental lead. Much of *The enimie of idlenesse* is translated from Jean de la Moyne, *Le stile et manière de composer, dicter, et escrire toute sorte d'epistres, ou lettres missiues, tant par répose que autrement, avec epitome de la poinctuation françoise* (Lyon, 1566), which was in turn based on the earlier *Le prothocolle des secretaires & aultres gens desirants savoir l'art et manière de dictes en bon français toutes lettres missives et epistres en prose* (Antwerp, 1550).

Fulwood's success in the vernacular soon spawned imitators, a number of which appeared only once. In 1578 Walter Darell published "Certeine letters verie necessarie for servingmen" as a separate section of his *A short discourse of the life of servingmen,* that offered a mix of practical advice and entertainment that, despite the title, was presumably above the station of servingmen. The next year appeared a small treatise signed only "H. C." (Henry Cheke?) and entitled *The forrest of fancy,* a miscellany of entertainments with numerous *epistles, of diuerse matter and in diuerse manner.* And in 1584, William Fiston produced a similar *The welspring of wittie conceites: containing, a methode, aswell to speake, as to endight aptly and eloquently of sundrie matters.* None of these was a school text or produced by pedagogues—or was ever heard of again. Like Fulwood's durable *The enimie of idlenesse,* however, all three have Continental origins, and Fiston's is an overt translation from Italian. Much more successful was Angel Day's publication two years later (1586) of *The English secretorie,* which promised both a method and a formulary, with letters both practical and more broadly humanist. It was revised and expanded with a new section on tropes and figures in 1592, thus supplying a nearly complete rhetoric of elegant writing—as opposed to a rhetoric of speaking—for an increasingly literate vernacular society, and in roughly this form it was reissued (1595, 1599, 1607, 1614, 1621, 1625, 1635). At the same time there also appeared John Browne's equally pragmatic and long-lived *The marchants avizo,* which contained the useful section "A briefe forme of all such letters as you shall neede to write thoroughout your whole voyage" (1589, 1590, 1590, 1591, 1607, 1616, 1640). Not all such materials found their way into print, or, at least, not immediately. Some time around 1599, John Hoskyns (or Hoskins) prepared a manuscript on "Direccions for speech and style," which circulated and now survives in several exemplars. Hoskyns's section "For penninge of letters" has its own Continental roots in Justus Lipsius's *Epistolica institutio* (1590), and provided the basis for Thomas Blount's much later discussion of "Instructions for writing and addressing letters" in *The academie of eloquence, containing a compleat English rhetorique, exemplified, . . . together with letters both amorous and moral, upon emergent occasions* (1653, 1654, 1656, 1663, 1664, 1670, 1683). Blount's exemplary letters, however, do not seem indebted to Hoskyns or Lipsius.

Part 2: The Seventeenth Century

By the start of the Jacobean period the publishing of dictaminal materials had become much more dynamic, and it can be misleading to single out particular trends without keeping in mind the interplay of numerous trends. Consider, for example, the activity during the decade 1600–1610. There were three Latin printings of Macropedius and Hegendorf (1600, 1604, 1609); two different Latin editions of Cicero's letters (1602, 1607, plus two editions on the Continent by the Englishman Scot); editions of Fulwood, Day, and Browne (all in 1607); and more legal formularies associated with Phaer (1600, 1604, 1607). This kind of vibrant mix would continue, with variations, for the entire century. But in 1602 another element was added with Nicholas Breton's *A poste with a madde packet of letters.* From the beginnings of humanist dictamen, classical letters had been treasured first for the vivacity they brought to the study of classical rhetoric and culture, and second for the promise of vivacity they offered for contemporary emulation. Enjoyment and emulation, in fact, were two pillars of humanist education, but it was always ambiguous which of the two pillars mattered most. Breton resolved upon enjoyment, and he had both instant success and immediate imitators, but his collections of diverting letters, and the numerous collections that followed, must be seen in the context of the wider world of serious dictaminal publishing that continued unabated throughout the period and that exceeded this diverting material in both number and volume.

The history of Breton's collections is complex, because materials were constantly remixed and repackaged, but they can be thought of as part one, part two, and a compendium of both. The 1602 printing of *A poste with a madde packet of letters* was immediately followed by enlarged editions in 1603, 1605, 1607, 1609, 1620, 1628, and 1630, before being absorbed into the compendium in 1633. *A poste with a packet of madde letters. The second part* appeared almost immediately in 1605—though available earlier—and was reissued in 1606, 1609, 1613, and 1628, before being absorbed into the compendium. The compendium of 1633 had the similar title, *A poste with a packet of mad letters. Newly imprinted,* but included both parts and appeared seven more times before a final printing as late as 1685, with the title *A poast with a packet of letters.*

Breton's imitators soon followed. In 1612 *The prompters packet of private and familiar letters* promised models to be emulated by the less adroit, but veered toward the diversionary; it reappeared two decades later in 1633. In 1613 the hack writer Gervase Markham produced *Hobson's horse-load of letters,* and doubled its size in 1617. He may have also produced the otherwise anonymous *Conceyted letters, newly layde open . . . wherin is knit up together all the perfections or arte of episteling* (1618, 1632, 1638). A gentleman identified only as "J. W." made nearly identical promises about emulation in *A speedie poste, with certain new letters,* in 1625 and 1629, and by 1684 the work was in its twelfth edition. Such works continued to be produced even during the Restoration, as with *A flying post with a packet of choice new letters* by "W. P." (1678, 1680). As late as 1693, Charles Gildon turned for new material to the Italian letters of Ferante Pallavicino in *The post-boy robb'd of his mail; or, The paquet broke open,* followed the next year by *The second volume of The post-boy robb'd of his mail.* Gildon published many hundreds of letters—*with observations upon each letter*—and his collections were still being published in the early eighteenth century.

Alongside the seeming frivolity of these collections of letters, there ran at the same time a much more prosaic streak of manuals that offered help to the unschooled and to those whose needs were not addressed in the schools. In 1615 the unknown "M. R." published *A president for young pen-men; or, The letter-writer,* reprinted in 1620 and 1638. In 1616 Thomas Gainsford published *The secretaries studie: containing new familiar epistles; or, Directions, for the formall, orderly, and iudicious inditing of letters.* Samuel Sheppard expanded Gainsford's treatise in 1652, by including women in the target audience, in *The secretaries studie: containing new familiar epistles. Wherein ladies, gentlemen, and all that are ambitious to write and speak elegantly, and elaborately, in a succinct & facetious strein, are furnished with fit phrases, emphaticall expressions, and various directions, for the most polish'd and judicious way of inditing letters, whether amorous, civill, houshold, politick, chiding, excusing, requesting, gratulatory, or, nuncupatory.* Women clearly had not been served well by the schools, but so also the schools had neglected the emergent professions. George Snell's chapter "The most useful and excellent art of writing letters to persons of all estates" explicitly sought to remedy this inadequacy in *The right teaching of useful knowledg, to fit scholars for som honest prefession; shewing so much skil as anie man needeth (that is not a teacher) in all knowledges, in one schole, in a shorter time in a more plaine waie, and for much less expens than ever hath been used, since of old the arts were so taught in the Greek and Romane empire* (1649). Henry Care, in 1671, catered directly to the neglected women, in *The female secretary; or, Choice new letters. Wherein each degree of women may be accommodated with variety of presidents for the expressing themselves aptly and handsomly on any occasion proper to their sex. With plain, yet more exact and pertinent rules and instructioons for the inditing and directing letters in general, than any extant.* At about the same time Hannah Wolley (later Mrs. Challinor) included a chapter entitled "Some general and choice rules for writing of letters" in *The gentlewomans companion . . . with letters and discourses upon all occasions* (1673, 1675, 1682), and she included a series of model letters in her *A supplement to The queen-like closet; or, A little of everything. Presented to all ingenious ladies and gentlewomen* (1674, 1680, 1684). Her work was followed shortly by the anonymous treatise *The compleat academy, or A nursery of compliments, furnished with the best letters* (1676, 1683), followed in turn by *A new academy; or, The accomplish'd secretary: containing instructions to write epistles* (1699).

Some of the publishing for the middle classes was strictly utilitarian and even commercial in orientation. In the same year as Wolley's help for ladies there appeared Henry Preston's *Brief directions. For true-spelling . . . To which is added. Copies of letters, bills of parcels, bills of exchange, bills of debt, receipt, with pertinent rules as helps thereunto* (1673?). A decade later, J. Hill published *The young secretary's guide; or, A speedy help to learning . . . containing the true method of writing letters upon any subject* that went through numerous editions until the end of the century (1689, 1696, 1697, 1698). At the end of the period were a series of competing manuals, which suggests a change in marketing opportunities. In 1697 appeared *Wit and eloquence; or, The accomplish'd secretary's vade mecum. Containing instructions to write epistles; with many curious examples of letters, and answers, suited to love, business, friendship, and other matters, in a most elegant stile.* And utilitarian manuals even closed out the century, with Thomas Goodman's *The experienc'd secretary; or, Citizen and country-man's companion. In two parts. Part I. Containing the most curious art of inditing familiar letters, in an excellent stile . . . Part II. Containing the nature of writings obligatory . . .* (1699).

A commonplace of the Renaissance was that the English had no culture of their own but that they had borrowed bits and pieces of culture from everyone else; it was a commonplace repeated even by the English themselves. We have already seen the extent of English indebtedness to Continental dictamen from the very beginnings of this period, but in the seventeenth century there emerged a new kind of indebtedness as some English writers looked to France as a source for imported culture. Numerous manuals were imported and translated directly from France, promising no less than to make the English as sophisticated as the French in letter writing, conversation, and social comportment. John Wodroephe presents "Missive phrases" and "Missives," along with advice on conversation, in his *The spared houres of a souldier in his travels. Or the true marrowe of the French tongue,* published first on the Continent in Dort (1623); in the London reprint of 1625, the titlepage drops the soldierly reference and stresses bilingualism in *The marrow of the French Tongve . . . With variety of other helpes to the learner, as phrases, letters missiue, sentences, prouerbs, theames, &c. in both languages* (1625). The more enduring note in this tradition is that of amorous letters and conduct as entrances to the elegant life, a note that is struck with *Cupids messenger or A trusty friend stored with sundry sorts of serious, witty, pleasaunt, amorous, and delightful letters* (1629, 1633, 1635, 1638), an anonymous translation from the French and attributed sometimes to the stylist Antoine de Courtin. The note is heard again almost immediately with *Cupids schoole: wherein, yongmen and maids may learne divers sorts of new, witty, and amorous complements,* by "W. S." (William Smythies?) in 1632 and 1642.

This genre of letter writing for social negotiation sometimes overlaps with other dictaminal genres, with recurrent uses of the title words "academy," "compliment," and "secretary," thus occasionally obscuring the distinctness of this genre, but the principal focus remains on using letters to mediate culture, and usually imported French culture. Thus, *The mirrour of complements* (1634; by Gervase Markham?) includes conversation as well as letters; it reappears in 1635 retitled *The mirrour of complements; or, A pleasant academy,* and then as *The mirrour of complements, or; A manuell of choice . . . ceremonies* (1637, 1650). In France one of the most successful dictaminal writers was Jacques du Bosc (or du Bosque), and John Hainhofer in London traded on du Bosc's popular treatise *l'Honnête femme* (Paris 1632) by translating it as *The secretary of ladies. Or a new collection of letters and answers, composed by modern ladies and gentlewomen, collected by Mounsieur Du Bosque* (1638). So also with the French writer Jean Puget de la Serre, whose *Le secretaire a la mode* (Paris 1625) was translated by J. Massinger as *The secretary in fashion or A compendious and refined way of expression in all manner of letters* (1640, 1654, 1658, 1668, 1673, 1683).

All the elements of this genre are present in 1639 in the pseudonymous collection by "Philomusus" (John Gough?), *Academy of complements; wherein, ladies, gentlewomen, schollers, and strangers, may accommodate their courtly practice with gentile ceremonies, complementall amorous high expressions, and formes of speaking, or writing of letters most in fashion,* that went through at least thirteen printings by 1685. W. Elder redacted "Philomusus" as *Pearls of eloquence; or, The school of complements: wherein ladies, gentlewomen, and schollars, may accommodate their courtly practice with gentile ceremonies, complemental, amourous, and high expressions of speaking, or writing of letters* (1656, 1658, 1685), and in 1653 "Philomusus" was imitated by the equally pseudonymous "Musophilus," *The card of courtship; or, The language of love . . . made up of . . . eloquent and winning letters.* The emphasis on fashionable letters of the elegant salon is made explicit in John Cotgrave's chapter "Wits interpreter or The perfect inditer, or letters a la mode," in his *Wits interpreter, the English Parnassus. Or, a sure guide to those admirable accomplishments that compleat our English gentry, the most acceptable qualifications of discourse, or writing. In which briefly the whole mystery of those pleasing witchcrafts of eloquence and love are made easie* (1655, 1662, 1671, 1671). Such delights could not be reserved for just the gentry, so at the same time there appeared the anonymous *The academy of pleasure. Furnished with all kindes of complemental letters, discourses, and dialogues; with variety of new songs, sonets and witty inventions. Teaching all sorts men, maids, widows, &c. to speak and write wittily, and to bear themselves gracefully, for the attaining of their desired ends: how to discourse and demean themselves at feasts and merry-meetings at home and abroad, in the company of friends and or strangers: how to retort, quibble, jeast or joke, and to return an ingenious answer upon any occasion whatsoever* (1656, 1665).

By the Restoration, letter-writing manuals take a mannerist turn, as with Edward Phillips's *The mysteries of love & eloquence; or, The arts of wooing and complementing; . . . [with] the witchcrafts of [ladies'] perswasive language, in their approaches, or other more secret dispatches . . . [and] set forms of expressions for imitation . . . letters, . . . as also epithets, and fourishing similitudes . . . useful on the sudden occasions of discourse or writing,* with its "Mock letters and drolling letters" and "Wit and language." First published in 1658, it was greatly enlarged in 1685 and had a rebirth in 1699 as *The beau's academy.* An unusual collection, published anonymously, claimed to be a compilation of "Letters for all occasions" by Charles Sackville (Lord Buckhurst), Sir Charles Sedley, and Sir William D'Avenant, and others; *The new academy of complements . . . with variety of courtly and civil complements, eloquent letters of love and friendship* (1669, 1671, 1680, 1681, 1698). With the restoration of Charles II from exile in France came a renewed interest in French culture. Antoine de Courtin's *Nouveau traité de la civilité qui se pratique en France parmi les honnestes gens* (Paris 1671) was immediately translated as *The rules of civility; or, Certain ways of deportment observed in France* (1671, 1673, 1675, 1678, 1685), and it included chapters on both letter writing and polite conversation. But not all such treatises insisted upon their French or gentle affiliations in their focus on the world of wit, and two such treatises close out the century. In 1677 an anonymous chapter entitled "Examples of letters and complements of all sorts, both jocose and serious; fitted for business, as well as recreation and delight" appears in *The wits academy; or, The muses delight. Being the newest academy of complements. Consisting of merry dialogues upon various occasions, composed of mirth, wit, and eloquence. As also divers sorts of letters upon several occasions, both mery and jocose: helpful for the inexpert to imitate, and pleasant to those of better judgment at their own leisure to peruse* (reprinted 1696 and on into the next century). And John Shirley has not only a chapter entitled "Curious letters and answers in the most elegant style, on sundry occasions for pleasure and imitation," but also another on the art of "wheedling" in *The triumph of wit; or, Ingenuity display'd in its perfection; being the newest and most useful academy* (1688, 1692). Abel Boyer closes out the period by combining the earlier seventeenth-century interests of John Wodroephe with the sophistication of the eighteenth century; he offers an extensive "Collection of choice letters upon several subjects" in his *The compleat French-master, for ladies and gentlemen. Being a new method, to learn with ease and delight the French tongue, as it is now spoken in the court of France* (1694, 1699, and on into the next century).

Part 3: Legal Dictamen

Despite all the English adoption and adaptation of Continental dictamen, there had always been a strong native English tradition, present at the very beginning of the period and even stronger at the end. This is the tradition of legal dictamen, and materials for it are found in such profusion that only a selection can be offered here. It is difficult to overestimate the impact of such widespread legal dictamen, ranging from prescriptive manuals to formularies (and usually a combination of both), especially because many of the titles already mentioned here include discrete sections on legal letter writing even though the volumes are not dedicated to legal affairs. Moreover, a great many editions and printings are no longer extant, having disintegrated from use during the period, so even the dates listed below must be understood as merely a sampling of the materials known to have existed.

As early as 1544, there was a compilation of model legal instruments, entitled *A newe boke of presidentes, in maner of a register: wherin is comprehended the very trade of making of all maner euidences and instrumêtes of practise, right cômodyous and necessary for euery man to knowe.* For nearly a century it was the indispensable manual, with forty known printings prior to 1641. The compilation first appeared with a preface by Thomas Phaer (Phayer) that was sometimes omitted in later editions, and it was often coupled with an almanac, thus necessitating a fresh edition every few years. The letters themselves were in both Latin and English, and the compilation was often updated or enlarged. Many of the letters are technical, such as instruments of debenture and the like, but, in light of the enormous range of English life that the legal world sought to regulate, the letters inevitably reached into a great many areas of social negotiation. With high legal stakes sometimes involved, the letters could tell stories of human conflict at least as compelling as those of Breton and his imitators.

The Phaer compilation had its greatest number of printings during the sixteenth century, but in the seventeenth century it continued to hold sway until the start of the civil war. In 1649 it was replaced by a new compilation by the lawyer Sir Richard Hutton, and this new compilation was the principal resource for legal dictamen for the rest of the period. It first appeared as *The young clarks guide; or, An exact collection of choice English presidents, according to the best forms now used* in 1649, 1653 (6th ed.), 1656 (7th ed.), 1659 (10th ed.), 1670 (12th ed.), and 1673; I list the editions in this one representative case to demonstrate how much more material once existed. At the same time, an expanded version appeared, *The young clerks guide in four parts. Or an exact collection of choice English presidents;* sixteen editions in twenty-two printings survive spanning the period 1649 to 1690. Parts of this larger compilation were printed separately, as with *The second part of the young clerks guide* (1652, 1652, 1659, 1670), and then again *The third part of the young clerks guide* (1669). The bibliographical relations among these four parts are complex, because different parts frequently were combined and issued at the same time, but with independent title pages. In general the bulk of Hutton's publication was during the Commonwealth period, and became more sporadic with the Restoration.

Along with these enduring treatises, there were a host of volumes with more restricted circulation. In 1653, for example, William Small published *An exact collection of choice declarations, with pleas, replications, rejoynders, demurrers, assignement of errours: and the entries of judgments thereupon affirmed;* it was not reprinted. In 1655 there appeared the anonymous *The compleat clark, and scriveners guide. Containing exact draughts and presidents of all manner of assurances and instruments now in use: as they were penned and perfected by divers learned judges, eminent lawyers, and great conveyancers, both ancient and modern,* that was revised and reprinted with slight variations in the title in 1664, 1671, 1677, and 1683. The last part of the period saw more occasional printings of specialized treatises, such as the *Liber placitandi. A book of special pleadings* (1674), *The clerks grammer* (1683), and *Regula placitandi; a collection of special rules for pleading* (1691, 1694), all issued anonymously. The range of social interest in the seeming technicalities of legal dictamen, however, is best seen in such works as Thomas Goodman's *The experienc'd secretary; or, Citizen and country-man's companion,* already mentioned above. His treatise contained two parts; the first promised a combination of utility and stylish elegance, whereas the second was legally useful, *Containing the nature of writings obligatory.* It appeared in 1699, and thus closes out this period by showing the extent to which legal letter writing had become a broad affair for the middle classes, combining the familiar with the obligatory, the desire for style and elegance with the reality of mundane necessity.

Notes

1. Jean Robertson, *The Art of Letter Writing: An Essay on the Handbooks Published in England during the Sixteenth and Seventeenth Centuries* (1942, 7, 65).

2. Mark Bland, "The London Book-Trade in 1600 and its Contexts."

3. British Library MS Add. 33271.

4. Several manuscripts survive: British Library [BL] MS Harleian 4604; BL MS Harleian 850 (portions); BL MS Add. 15230; Oxford MS Ashmolean Mus. d. 1.

5. British Library MS Stowe 760 (c. 1665, attribution uncertain).

6. A more complete starting point for such studies is my "Rhetoric, 1500–1700" and Lawrence D. Green and James J. Murphy, *Renaissance Rhetoric Short-Title Catalogue 1460–1700* (Aldershot, U.K.: Ashgate Publishing, 2006).

7. Erasmus quotes Turpilus to this effect. See Erasmus, *On the Writing of Letters / De conscribendi epistolas*, 1:349F.

Bibliography of Dictamen in England, 1500–1700

Many of the editions listed here are available in modern facsimile reprint, microfiche, or microfilm, particularly in the expanding collection produced by University Microfilms. Titles in this last collection are not listed here. Other modern sources are listed in this bibliography after each entry, using the conventions listed below. The internet collections known as *Early English Books Online* (EBBO) and *Eighteenth-Century Collections Online* (ECCO) should also be consulted.

Conventions and Abbreviations

The reprint series *The English Experience* is published simultaneously in Amsterdam and by different publishers in the United States:

Amsterdam: Theatrum Orbis Terrarum B. V., 1967–1979.
New York: Da Capo Press, 1967–1973.
Norwood N.J.: Walter J. Johnson Inc., 1974–1979.
Cited as "English Experience," with volume number.
James J. Murphy, *Renaissance Rhetoric: A Microfiche Collection of Key Texts*, A.D. 1472–1602, *from the Bodleian Library, Oxford*. Elmsford N.Y.: Microforms International, 1986. Cited as *Murphy*.
Speech Association of America, *British and Continental Rhetoric and Elocution*. Sixteen microfilm reels. Ann Arbor, Mich.: University Microfilms, 1953. Cited as *BCRE*.

Works Cited

The Academy of Pleasure. Furnished with all kindes of complemental letters, discourses, and dialogues. London: for John Stafford, and Will. Gilbertson, 1656. Also 1665.

B., F. *Clavis grammatica; or, The ready way to the Latine tongue . . . with necessary observations for epistolizing or writing of letters in English or Latine.* London: for Robert Harford, 1678.

Bland, Mark. "The London Book-Trade in 1600 and Its Contexts." In *A Companion to Shakespeare,* edited by David Kasten. Oxford: Blackwell, 1999, 450–63.

Blount, Thomas. *The academie of eloquence, containing a compleat English rhetorique.* London: for H. Moseley, 1653. Also 1654, 1656, 1663, 1664, 1670, 1683. Menston: Scolar Press, 1971 (facsimile of 1654).

Boyer, Abel. "A collection of choice letters upon several subjects." In *The compleat French-master.* London: for T. Salusbury, 1694. Also 1699. Menston: Scolar Press, 1971 (facsimile of 1694).

Brandolinus, Aurelius Lippus. *De ratione scribendi libri tres* [Basel 1498]. Collected with Vives, Erasmus, Celtes, and Hegendorf (Basel 1549), with Macropedius added in the London edition. London: H. Middleton, 1573. Microfiche, *Murphy,* Basel 1549.

Breton, Nicholas. *A poste with a madde packet of letters.* London: [T. Creede] for J. Smethicke, 1602. Also 1603, [1605?], 1607, 1609, 1620, 1628, 1630. Subsequently included in Breton, *A poste with a packet . . . newly imprinted* (see below).

———. *A poste with a packet of madde letters. The second part.* London: T. Creede for J. Browne, 1605. Also 1606, 1609, 1613, 1628). Subsequently included in Breton, *A poste with a packet . . . newly imprinted* (see below).

———. *A poste with a packet of mad letters. Newly imprinted* [includes both parts]. London: [M. Flesher] for J. Marriot, 1633. Also 1634, 1637, [1650?], 1660, 1669, 1674, 1678, 1685 (as *A poast with a packet of letters*). London, 1879, ed. A. B. Grosart, *Works.* Reprint, New York 1966. Reprint, Hildesheim 1969.

Brinsley, John, the elder. "Epistles and letters." In *A consolation for our grammar schooles.* London: R. Field for T. Man, 1622. New York: Scholars' Facsimiles & Reprints, 1943 (facsimile). Amsterdam and New York: English Experience no. 203, 1969 (facsimile).

———. "How to make epistles imitating Tully, short, pithie, sweete Latine and familiar; and to indite letters to our friends in English accordingly." In *Ludus literarius; or, The grammar school.* London: H. Lownes for T. Man, 1612. Also 1627 (5 variants). Menston: Scolar Press, 1968; English Linguistics no. 62 (facsimile of 1612). Liverpool and London, 1917, ed. E. T. Campagnac (1627 edition).

Browne, John. "A briefe forme of all such letters as you shall neede to write throughout your whole voyage." In *The marchants avizo.* London: R. Field for W. Norton, 1589. Also 1590, 1590, 1591, 1607, 1616, 1640. Boston, 1957, ed. P. McGrath (1589 edition). Amsterdam and New York: English Experience no. 98, 1969 (facsimile of 1607).

C., H. [Henry Cheke?]. *The forrest of fancy. Wherein is conteined very prety apothegmes, and pleasant histories, both in meeter and prose, songes, sonets, epigrams and epistles, of diuerse matter and in diuerse manner.* London: T. Purfoote, 1579.

Care, Henry. *The female secretary; or, Choice new letters. Wherein each degree of women may be accommodated with variety of presidents for the expressing themselves aptly and handsomly on any occasion proper to their sex. With plain, yet more exact and pertinent rules and instructioons for the inditing and directing letters in general, than any extant.* London: T. Ratcliffe and Mary Daniel for H. Million, 1671.

Celtes, Conrad. *Methodus conficiendarum epistolarum* [Basel 1537]. In Brandolinus, *De ratione scribendi.* London: H. Middleton, 1573. Microfiche, *Murphy,* Basel 1549.

Cicero, Marcus Tullius. *Certain epistles of Tully verbally translated: together with a short treatise, containing an order of instructing youth in grammer, and withall the benefite of verball translation.* Edited and translated by W. Haine. London: N. Okes for Soc. Stat., 1611.

———. *An epistle or letter of exhortation by M. T. Cicero to his brother Quintus.* Translated by G. G[ylby]. London: R. Hall, 1561.

———. *Epistolae ad familiares. A D. Lambino emendatae. Eiusdem D. Lambini annotationes.* Revision of *Epistolae familiares* [Rome 1467]. Comm. P. Manutius. London: T. Vautrolier, 1575. Also 1579, 1581, 1584, 1585, 1590, 1591, 1595, 1607.

———. *Epistolae selectae in usum scholae Westmonasteriensis.* London: R. Daniel, 1657. Also 1689, [ca. 1690].

———. *Epistolarum ad T. Pomponium Atticum lib. xvi.* Edited by A. Scot. 5 vols. (no editions published in England). Lyon: J. Pillehote, 1608.

———. *Epistolarum familiarium . . . epitome secundum tria genera . . . nuntiatorum, iocosum, & grave . . . ad usum scholarum.* Edited by T. Cogan. Cambridge: J. Legat [London: S. Waterson], 1602.

———. *Epistolarum familiarium libri xvi* [Lyon 1545]. Edited by C. Hegendorf. London: T. Marsh, 1574. Also 1577, 1579.

———. *Epistolarum libri quatuor* [England]. Edited by J. Sturm. London: F. Kingston, 1625. Also Cambridge 1631, 1635, London 1637, 1656, 1658, 1669, Cambridge 1670, London 1677, 1685, 1686, 1686, 1696, 1700.

———. *Epistolarum libri quatuor* [Scotland]. Edited by J. Sturm. Edinburgh: A. Hart, 1618. Also Aberdeen 1630, Edinburgh 1634, 1640, Aberdeen 1665, Glasgow 1674, Edinburgh 1675, 1694.

———. *Epistolarum selectarum libri tres.* London: for Soc. Stat., 1689.

———. *The familiar epistles of M. T. Cicero Englished and conferred with the French Italian and other translations.* Translated by J. Webbe. London: E. Griffin, [1620].

———. *Lessons and exercises out of Cicero, after the method of Dr Webbe.* London: F. Kingston, 1627. Menston: Scolar Press, 1972; English Linguistics no. 322 (facsimile).

———. *M. Tullii Ciceronis operum . . . ejus epistolas ad familiares complectens.* Edited by A. Scot (no editions published in England). Lyon: J. Pillehote, 1608.

Clarke, John. *Transitionum formulae . . . adiungitur tractatus epistolaris.* Revised as *Formulae oratoriae.* London: T. Harper for R. Milbourne, 1628.

———. *Formulae oratoriae.* Revision of *Transitionum formulae.* London: N. P., 1630. Also 1632, 1637, 1647, 1653, 1659, Zurich 1663, London 1664, 1670, 1672, Zurich 1694. Microfilm, *BCRE* 3:28 (1637 edition).

The Clerks Grammer. London: T. B. for F. Kidgilat, 1683.

The compleat academy; or, A nursery of compliments, furnished with the best letters etc. London: for T. Passenger and W. Whitwood, 1676. Also 1683.

The compleat clark, and scriveners guide. Separate title page *The conveyancers light.* London: T. R. for H. Twyford et al., 1655.

The compleat clark, containing the best forms of all sorts of presidents. Revision of *The compleat clark, and scriveners guide.* London: J. S. for H. Twyford et al., 1664. Also 1671, 1677, 1683.

Conceyted letters, newly layde open . . . wherin is knit up together all the perfections or arte of episteling. Sometimes attributed to Gervase Markham. London: B. Alsop for S. Rand, 1618. Also 1632, 1638.

[Copies of letters and speeches]. 1545–79. Manuscript BL Add. 33271.

Cordier, Mathurin. *Principia Latine loquendi scribendique: sive Selecta quaedam ex Ciceronis epistolis, ad pueros in Latina lingua exercendos . . . a very necessary and profitable entraunce to the speakyng and writing of the Latin tongue* [Geneva 1566]. Translated by "T. W." London: J. Kingston for O. Wilkes, 1575. Menston: Scolar Press, 1968; English Linguistics no. 100 (facsimile).

Cotgrave, John. "Wits interpreter or the perfect inditer, or Letters a la mode." In *Wits interpreter, the English parnassus*. London: for N. Brooke, 1655, 1662, 1671, 1671.

Courtin, Antoine de. "Rules to be observed in writing of letters." In *The rules of civility; or, Certain ways of deportment observed in France. Translated from French*. Translation of *Nouveau traité de la civilité qui se pratique en France parmi les honnestes gens* (anon., Paris 1671). London: for J. Martyn & J. Starkey, 1671. Also 1673, 1675, 1678, 1685.

Cupids messenger or A trusty friend stored with sundry sorts of serious, witty, pleasaunt, amorous, and delightful letters. Sometimes attributed to Antoine de Courtin. London: M. Flesher, 1629. Also [1633], [1635], [1638].

Darell, Walter. "Certeine letters verie necessarie for servingmen." In *A short discourse of the life of servingmen, plainly expressing the way that is best to be followed, and the meanes wherby they may lawfully challenge a name and title in the vocation and fellowship. With certaine letters verie necessarie for servingmen, and other persons to peruse. With diverse pretie inventions in English verse. Hereunto is also annexed a treatise,concerning manners and behaviours*. With Casa, *Galateo*. London: R. Newberrie, 1578.

Day, Angel. *The English secretorie. Wherein is contayned, a perfect method, for the inditing of all manner of epistles and familiar letters*. London: R. Waldegrave, 1586. Menston: Scolar Press, 1967; English Linguistics no. 29 (facsimile). Microfilm, *BCRE* 3:24.

————. *The English secretorie; or, Plaine and direct method of enditing of all manner of epistles or letters . . . now corrected, refined, & amended . . . also a declaration of all tropes, figures, as usually or for ornaments sake are in this method required*. London: T. Orwin for R. Jones, 1592 (with *The second part*, dated 1587). Also 1595, 1599, 1607, 1614, 1621, 1625, [1635]. Gainesville: Scholars' Facsimiles & Reprints, 1967 (facsimile of 1599). Microfiche, *Murphy*, 1595 edition.

du Bosc, Jacques (d. 1660). *The secretary of ladies. Or a new collection of letters and answers, composed by modern ladies and gentlewomen, collected by Mounsieur Du Bosque*. Translated by J. H[ainhofer]. London: T. Cotes for W. Hope, 1638.

Elder, W., Gent. *Pearls of eloquence; or, The school of complements: wherein ladies, gentlewomen, and schollars, may accommodate their courtly practice with gentile ceremonies, complemental, amourous, and high expressions of speaking, or writing of letters*. Excerpted from "Philomusus," *Academy of compliments*. London: for T. Lock, 1656. Also 1658, 1685.

Elegantiarum viginti precepta ad perpulcras conficiendas epistolas. Sometimes attributed to Aegidius Suchtelensis. [London: R. Pynson, 1498?].

Erasmus, Desiderius. *De conscribendi epistolis*. Pirate draft of authorized edition (Basel: Froben, 1522). Cambridge: J. Siberch, 1521. Toronto: University of Toronto Press, 1985. Translated by C. Fantazzi, *Works*, vol. 3.

————. *Conficiendarum epistolarum formula* [Basel 1519]. In Brandolinus, *De ratione scribendi*. London: H. Middleton, 1573. Microfiche, *Murphy*, Basel 1549. Toronto: University of Toronto Press, 1985. Translated by C. Fantazzi, *Works*, vol. 3.

————. *On the Writing of Letters / De conscribendi epistolas*. Translated and annotated by Charles Fantazzi. In *Collected Works of Erasmus*. Vol. 25: *Literary and Educational Writings, 3*, Toronto: University of Toronto Press, 1985.

"Examples of letters and complements of all sorts, both jocose and serious; fitted for business, as well as recreation and delight." In *The wits academy . . . also divers sorts of letters upon several occasions, both mery and jocose: helpful for the inexpert to imitate, and pleasant to those of better judgment at their own leisure to peruse* [formerly attributed to "W. P. Gent."]. London: sold by most booksellers, 1677. Also 1696.

Finch, Heneage. "Formulae literarum collected out of the most quaint authors in diverse languages," and "Certain rule & observations for a secretary, [and] superscriptions and addresses of letters." ca. 1665. Manuscript BL Stowe 760.

Fiston, William. *The welspring of wittie conceites: containing, a methode, aswell to speake, as to endight aptly and eloquently of sundrie matters.* Translated from Italian. London: R. Jones, 1584.

Fleming, Abraham. *A panoplie of epistles; or, A looking glasse for the unlearned. Conteyning a perfecte plattforme of inditing letters of all sorts . . . used of the best and eloquentest rhetoricians that have lived in all ages . . . gathered and translated out of Latine into English.* London: H. Middleton for R. Newberie, 1576. Microfiche, *Murphy.*

Fulwood, William. *The enimie of idlenesse: teaching the maner and stile how to endite, compose and write all sorts of epistles and letters.* London: H. Bynneman for L. Maylard, 1568. Also 1571, 1578, 1582, 1586, 1593, 1598, 1607, 1612, 1621. Potsdam, 1907, ed. P. Wolter, *William Fullwood, "The Enimie of Idlenesse." Der älteste englische Briefsteller* (selections).

Gainsford, Thomas. *The secretaries studie: containing new familiar epistles; or, Directions, for the formall, orderly, and iudicious inditing of letters.* London: T. Creede for R. Jackson, 1616 (expanded by Sheppard 1652). Amsterdam and Norwood, N.J.: English Experience no. 658, 1974 (facsimile).

Gildon, Charles. *The post-boy robb'd of his mail; or, The paquet broke open. Consisting of five hundred letters, to persons of several qualities and conditions. With observations upon each letter.* Based in part on Ferante Pallavicino. London: for J. Dunton, 1692 (anon). New York: Garland, 1972, ed. M. J. Bosse.

————. *The second volume of The post-boy robb'd of his mail; or, The paquet broke open: to which are added several ingenious letters lately sent to the gentlemen concern'd in this frollick: as also copies of those private letters which lately past between — : with observations upon each letter.* London: J. Wilde for J. Dunton, 1693 (anon).

Goodman, Thomas. *The experienc'd secretary; or, Citizen and country-man's companion. In two parts. Part I. Containing the most curious art of inditing familiar letters, in an excellent stile . . . Part II. Containing the nature of writings obligatory . . . .* London: for N. Boddington, 1699.

Green, Lawrence D. "Rhetoric, 1500–1700." In *The Cambridge Bibliography of English Literature,* 3rd ed. Cambridge: Cambridge University Press, forthcoming.

Green, Lawrence D., and James J. Murphy. *Renaissance Rhetoric Short-Title Catalogue, 1460–1700.* Aldershot, U.K.: Ashgate, 2006.

Hawkins, John. *The English schoolmaster compleated . . . to which is added, an appendix containing . . . copies of letters, titles of honor sutable for men of all degrees and qualities, etc.* London: A. & I. Dawks for the Stationers Co., 1692. Also 1694.

Hegendorf, Christopher. *Methodus epistolas conscribendi* [Hagenau 1526]. In Brandolinus, *De ratione scribendi.* London: H. Middleton, 1573. Microfiche, *Murphy,* Basel 1549.

———. *Methodus epistolas conscribendi.* In Macropedius, *Methodus de conscribendis epistolis.* London, 1576. Also 1580, 1581, 1592, 1595, 1600, 1604, 1609, 1614, 1621, 1637.

Hill, John, Gent. *The young secretary's guide; or, A speedy help to learning . . . containing the true method of writing letters upon any subject.* London: for H. Rhodes, 1687. Also 1689, 1696, 1697, 1698, 1699.

Hoole, Charles. *Centuria epistolarum anglo-latinarum; . . . A century of epistles, English and Latine; selected out of the most used school-authors, viz. Tullie, Plinie, and Textor. By imitating of which, children may readily get a proper style for writing letters.* London: W. Wilson for Co. of Stat. 1660. Also 1677, 1687, 1700.

Hoskyns, John. "Direccions for speech and style." [1599?] Manuscripts BL Harl. 4604; BL Harl. 850 (portions); BL Add. 15230; Bodley Ash. Mus. D. 1. Princeton, N.J.: Princeton University Press, 1935, ed. H. H. Hudson, New Haven, Conn.: Yale University Press, 1937, ed. L. B. Osborn. Reprint, Hamden, Conn., 1973.

Hutton, Sir Richard. *The second part of the young clerks guide.* By "Sir R. H." London: T. R. & E. M. for M. Walbanck, 1652. Also 1652, 1659, 1670.

———. *The third part of the young clerks guide.* By "Sir R. H." London: T. Ratcliffe & T. Daniel for A. Isted, 1669.

———. *The young clerks guide; or, An exact collection of choice English presidents.* By "Sir R. H." London: for H. Tuckey, 1649. Also 1653, 1656, 1659, 1670, 1673.

———. *The young clerks guide in four parts. Or an exact collection of choice English presidents.* By "Sir R. H." London, 1650 (4 editions). Also 1651, 1652, 1653, 1655 (twice), 1656 (twice), 1658 (twice), 1659 (twice), 1670, 1673, 1682 (twice), 1689, 1690.

Isocrates. *Epistolae.* Translated by "G. Sylvani." Greek and Latin. London: J. Heptinstall, 1685.

La Serre, Jean Puget de. *The secretary in fashion or A compendious and refined way of expression in all manner of letters.* Translated by John Massinger of *Le secretaire a la mode,* Paris 1625. London: J. Beale & S. Bulkley for G. Emerson, 1640. Also 1654, 1658, 1668, 1673, 1683.

Leedes, Edward. "Examples of epistles." In *English examples to be turned into Latin . . . forms of epistles, themes, and other exercises for the use of young beginners at Bury Schoole.* London: for N. Simmons and T. Simmons, 1676. Also 1677, 1681, 1685, 1687, Dublin 1697, London 1699.

———. "Examples of epistles." In *New English examples to be turned into Latin . . . forms of epistles, themes, and other exercises, for the use of young-beginners at Bury-School.* London: for J. Chamberlain, 1685.

———. "Examples of epistles." In *More English examples to be turned into Latin . . . forms of epistles, themes, and other exercises, for the use of young beginners at Bury School.* London: for J. C., 1692. Also 1699.

"Letters for all occasions." In *The new academy of complements . . . with variety of courtly and civil complements, eloquent letters of love and friendship.* Compilation attributed to Charles Sackville (Lord Buckhurst), Sir Charles Sedley, and Sir William D'Avenant. London: for Samuel Speed, 1669. Also 1671, [1680], 1681, 1698.

Liber placitandi. A book of special pleadings. London: for J. Place, T. Basset, H. Twyford, et al., 1674. Also 1674 (2 variants).

Macropedius, Georgius. *Methodus de conscribendis epistolis* [Antwerp 1543, as *Epistolica studiosis traiectinae scholae tyrunculis nuncupata.*] In Brandolinus, *De ratione scribendi.* London: H. Middleton, 1573. Microfiche, *Murphy,* Basel 1549.

————. *Methodus de conscribendis epistolis* [see previous]. With Hegendorf, *Methodus epistolas conscribendi.* London, 1576. Also 1580, 1581, 1592, 1595, 1600, 1604, 1609, 1614, 1621, 1637, 1649.

Markham, Gervase. *Hobsons horse-load of letters; or, A president for epistles.* By "G. M." London: T. Snodham for R. Hawkins, 1613. Also 1617 (with *The second part*).

The Mirrour of Complements. Sometimes attributed to Gervase Markham. London: [T. Harper, 1634]. Also 1635 (as *The mirrour of complements or: a pleasant academy*), 1637 (as *The mirrour of complements or; a manuell of choice . . . ceremonies*), 1650.

"Musophilus." *The card of courtship; or, The language of love . . . made up of . . . eloquent and winning letters.* London: J. C. for H. Moseley, 1653.

A new academy; or, The accomplish'd secretary: containing instructions to write epistles. London: for Roger Clavill, 1699.

A newe boke of presidentes in maner of a register, wherin is comprehended the very trade of makyng all manner euydence and instruments of practyse. Preface by T. Phaer. London: E. Whitchurche, 1543. 40 editions before 1641. Amsterdam and New York: English Experience no. 569, 1973 (facsimile of 1543).

P., W. *A flying post with a packet of choice new letters and complements containing variety of examples of witty and delightful letters, upon all occasions both of love and business, and is of very great use and help to all such as have a desire to learn to indite, and write letters, after the best and most elegant manner now used in court, city, or country, being both pleasant and profitable. Newly written.* London: for John Williamson, 1678. Also 1680.

Phalaris [Pseudo-Phalaris]. *The Epistles of Phalaris.* Translated by S. Whately. London: F. Leach for the Author, 1699.

Phillips, Edward. "Superscriptions for letters," and "Mock letters and drolling letters." In *The mysteries of love and eloquence; or, The arts of wooing and complementing,* by E. P[hillips]. London: for N. Brooks, 1658. Also 1685, 1699 (as *The beau's academy*). Menston: Scolar Press, 1972; English Linguistics no. 321 (facsimile of 1658).

"Philomusus." *Academy of complements; wherein, ladies, gentlewomen, schollers, and strangers, may accommodate their courtly practice with gentile ceremonies, complementall amorous high expressions, and formes of speaking, or writing of letters most in fashion.* Sometimes attributed to John Gough. London: T. Badger for H. Moseley, 1639. Also 1640, 1640, 1641, 1645, 1646, 1650, 1650, 1654, 1658, 1663, 1664, 1670, 1684, 1685.

Preston, Henry. *Brief directions. For true-spelling . . . . To which is added. Copies of letters, bills of parcels, bills of exchange, bills of debt, receipt, with pertinent rules as helps thereunto.* London: J. R. Rand, [1673?]. Menston: Scolar Press, 1968; English Linguistics no. 85 (facsimile).

The prompters packet of private and familiar letters: fitted (in sundrie formes) to mens seuerall occasions, and according to the qualitie of persons. Not unworthy imitation of the most: but most necessarie for such as want either facultie or facilitie to endight. London: By M. Bradwood for S. Macham, 1612. Also 1633.

R., M. *A president for young pen-men. Or the letter-writer.* London: G. Eld for R. Wilson, 1615. Also 1620, 1638.

Regula placitandi; a collection of special rules for pleading. London: assigns of R. & E. Atkyns for T. Bassett, 1691. Also 1694.

Robertson, Jean. *The Art of Letter Writing: An essay on the handbooks published in England during the sixteenth and seventeenth centuries.* London: University Press of Liverpool, 1942.

S., W. [William Smythies?]. *Cupids schoole: wherein, yongmen and maids may learne divers sorts of new, witty, and amorous complements.* London: E. Purslow for F. Grove, 1632. Also 1642.

Sheppard, Samuel. *The secretaries studie: containing new familiar epistles. wherein ladies, gentlemen, and all that are ambitious to write and speak elegantly, and elaborately, in a succinct & facetious strein, are furnished with fit phrases, emphaticall expressions, and various directions, for the most polish'd and judicious way of inditing letters, whether amorous, civill, houshold, politick, chiding, excusing, requesting, gratulatory, or nuncupatory.* By "S. S. Gent." An expansion of Gainsford 1616. London: for John Harrison, 1652.

Shirley, John. "Curious letters and answers in the most elegant style, on sundry occasions for pleasure and imitation." In *The triumph of wit.* London: for Nicholas Bodington, 1688. Also 1692.

Small, William. *An exact collection of choice declarations, with pleas, replications, rejoynders, demurrers, assignement of errours: and the entries of judgments thereupon affirmed.* London: T. W. and T. R. for J. Place, 1653.

Snell, George. "The most useful and excellent art of writing letters to persons of all estates." In *The right teaching of useful knowledg.* Separate title page, *The teacher of the English school.* London: W. Dugard, 1649.

Spangenberg, Johannes. *De conficiendis epistolis liber.* Edinburgh: [J. Ross, 1580?].

Sulpitius, Joannes. *De componendis & ornandis epistolis* [Rome 1491]. With Donatus and Mancinelli in *Posterior editio sulpitiana in partes tris divisa.* London: Boeidens, 1502. Also 1504; in *Grammatice Sulpitiana,* 1505, 1511, [1514?].

Verepaeus, Simon. *De epistolis latine conscribendis libri v* [Antwerp 1571]. London: R. Field for J. Harrison, 1592.

Vives, Juan Luis. *De conscribendis epistolis* [Basel 1536]. In Brandolinus, *De ratione scribendi.* London: H. Middleton, 1573. Leyden and New York, 1989, trans. C. Fantazzi, *Works.* Microfiche, *Murphy,* Basel 1549

W., J. *A speedie poste, with certain new letters. Now published for the helpe of such as are desirous to learne to write letters.* By "I. W. Gent." London: M. Flesher for W. Sheares, 1625, also 1629, 1684.

Wilson, Thomas, Sir. *The arte of rhetorique for the use of all soche as are studious of eloquence sette forth in Englishe.* [London]: Richard Grafton, 1553 [for 1554]. Also 1560, 1562, 1563, 1567, 1580, 1584, 1585.

Wit and eloquence; or, The accomplish'd secretary's vade mecum. Containing instructions to write epistles; with many curious examples of letters, and answers, suited to love, business, friendship, and other matters, in a most elegant stile. directions for true pointing, or stopping, in writing superscriptions of letters suitable to persons of all qualities and degrees, inscriptons, subscriptions, &c. London: for R. Clavell, 1697.

Wodroephe, John. "Missiue phrases" and "Missiues." In *The spared hovres of a sovldier in his travels. Or the true marrowe of the French tongue.* French and English. Dort: Par Nicolas Vincentz Pour George Waters, 1623.

———. "Missiue Phrases," and "Missiues." In *The marrow of the French tongve.* Rev of *Spared hovres of a sovldier.* French and English. London: [M. Flesher] for Richard Meighen, 1625.

Wolley, Hannah. "Letters." In *A Supplement to The Queen-like Closet.* London: T. R. for Richard Lownds, 1674. Also 1680, 1684.

———. "Some general and choice rules for writing of letters." In *The gentlewomans companion . . . with letters and discourses upon all occasions.* London: A. Maxwell for Dorman Newman, 1673. Also 1675, 1682.

Letter Writing and Vernacular Literacy in Sixteenth-Century England

W. Webster Newbold

Printed letter-writing manuals began to appear in English during the second half of the sixteenth century. Until that time, the English had to rely on handbooks in Latin; imported Continental books, predominantly in French and Italian; or manuscript writing aids, which they had either assembled themselves or had others copy for them. These early printed manuals give us an opportunity to discover how ordinary citizens got help with writing and what branches of letter-writing theory and practice they consulted. Even a cursory look at the texts reveals that the humanist tradition of epistolography was strong, providing the theoretical base for each of the books. Closer examination reveals that elements from the tradition of the *ars dictaminis,* the medieval art of letter writing, are also present in the most popular works. Such a combination suggests that vernacular readers were looking for guidance from both the prestigious Latin humanist culture and the more practical dictaminal tradition.

A description of the contents of English dictamen does not, however, explain its context or etiology. It would seem that those educated enough to write letters could have managed with existing Latin aids. In a literate culture so profoundly influenced by Latin, who would have wanted to buy or read English letter writers? What would have made some of them the best sellers among English rhetoric handbooks? Finally, how did these letter manuals reflect or contribute to the increasing use of the English vernacular for important personal, social, and cultural functions? This chapter attempts to answer these questions by contextualizing letter writing in the society and culture of Renaissance England.

I

The latter third of the sixteenth century saw vernacular books join the collection of Latin, Continental, and native manuscript manuals that aided English writers in the "inditing" of letters. The first three general letter-writing handbooks are William Fulwood's *The Enemy of Idlenes* (1568), Abraham Fleming's *A Panoply of Epistles* (1576), and Angel Day's *The English Secretary* by Angel Day (1586, revised 1592; titles spelled and capitalized following current conventions). When their histories and contents are considered together, they can show us a good deal about how vernacular writers approached their tasks in written communication.

The Enemy of Idleness was not originally prepared by Fulwood, who translated and adapted it from a French work by Jean de la Moyne, *Le stile et maniere de composer, dicter, et escrire toute sorte d'epistre, ou lettres missives, tant par response, que autrement,* printed at Lyons in 1566; this was itself based on another antecedent published at Antwerp in 1550 (Robertson 1942, 14). It enjoyed a substantial publication history, which saw ten editions in all—between 5,000 and 10,000 copies—appear by 1621 at a fairly steady pace (1568, 1571, 1578, 1582, 1586, 1588, 1598, 1607, 1612, 1621). The preliminary materials (sigs. A2R–A6R), consisting of a short dedication, a longer "Epistle," and several brief advertisements to prospective readers ("The Book's Verdict" and "To the Well-Disposed Reader"), all bespeak an interest in providing English readers with teaching in their own language about a necessary and sought-after skill.[1] The dedication is to the "Right Worshipful the Master, Wardens, and Company of the Merchant Tailors of London." Little is known of Fulwood, except that he claimed to be a merchant himself, though it is not known whether he was actually a member of the Merchant Tailors' Company. His preface "To the Well Disposed Reader" explains the book's curious title. Letter writing can not only be invaluable in life's urgent affairs, but also provide a healthy antidote for idleness, "the capital enemy to all exercise and virtue."

The *Enemy of Idleness* is divided into four books, which neatly lay out important characteristics found with varying emphasis in subsequent vernacular works. Book I covers general letter-writing theory, which it ultimately derives from the hugely popular treatise by Erasmus, *De conscribendis epistolis* (1522). Letters are "speech with the absent," terms of ancient reference revived by Erasmus and other humanists to assert the importance of the personal letter, informal in style and content (A7R; Erasmus 20). Letters, however, can also resemble orations and follow the teachings of general Ciceronian rhetorical theory. Erasmus categorized letters under the headings "demonstrative," "deliberative, and "judicial," and echoes of that scheme can be found in chapters in book I such as the one entitled "How to Write under the Demonstrative Gender, in the Praise of Some Bodie" (E7R).

Book II reflects a common feature of contemporary letter-writing books: humanist scholars and men of letters, aware of the new learning, engaging in Ciceronian-style correspondence. Books III and IV, however, provide what must have been a vital center of interest: letters of familiar people in recognizable situations, illustrating life's common activities and concerns in a written vernacular idiom. In book III, fifteen pairs and twelve single letters reflect the personal dynamics of family and business relationships. Book IV, however, offers *Enemy*'s readers something even more interesting: love letters. Five letters in prose and six in verse present lovers writing within the conventional dynamics of unrequited love. All but two of the letters are from the man's perspective.

Enemy, then, would seem to present an attractive and useful pattern for subsequent letter-writing books. Abraham Fleming, however, with his *A Panoply of Epistles,* in 1576, failed to follow suit. The author's prefatory epistle "To the Learned and Unlearned Reader" calls the book "An epitome of precepts whereby the ignorant may learne to indite, according to skill and order, reduced into a Dialogue between the Master and the Scholar" (A1–B). *Panoply* seems to want to appeal to a broad audience, but in fact it offers in English what Latin school texts following humanist originals already provided in the way of letter-writing theory accompanied by sample letters of famous people. Fleming's precepts, which he bases on the popular European school text *Methodus conscribendi epistolas* (1526) by Christoph Hegendorff, are so condensed as to be confusing; nor do they match up well with the examples he provides (Robertson 1942, 17). Fleming does some service in making a broad array of Latin letter texts—from fifty-seven writers in all—available in English, some for the first time. The book, though, was clearly not as marketable as the writer may have hoped, because it appeared in only the single edition of 1576.

In contrast, Day's *The English Secretary* had a long publication history similar to Fulwood's: printings appeared 1586, 1592 (revised and expanded), 1595, 1599, 1607, 1614, 1621, 1625, and 1635. The book's title glances at an important Elizabethan profession, not to be confused with the modern type of secretary, who is usually responsible only for clerical tasks. An Elizabethan secretary would be more akin to an "executive assistant." He would represent his employer through writing, receiving, and composing correspondence that would often be private and sensitive, directly related to the master's reputation and honor. Secretaries thus occupied one of the positions created by the demands of literacy.

Day offers the same mix of theory, practical formulae, and vernacular models that the reading public had found attractive in *The Enemy of Idleness.* Erasmus, through *De conscribendis,* is his principal mentor in preceptive matters, but doubtlessly Day was familiar with the other major contemporary Latin epistolographers.[2] The early chapters of book I cover fairly compendiously the main points of the humanist tradition. A letter is "the messenger or familiar speach of the absent," and, in a near paraphrase of Erasmus, Day declares that, although anyone who can write can write letters ("pregnant wit ensuing by nature"), they are "beautified, adorned, and . . . transmuted" by art (B1R–B1V; signatures are from the 1599 edition). In a similar manner, the first seven chapters deal with the main outline of epistolographical theory. Rather than copy from a single original as his predecessors seem to have done, Day synthesizes the major contemporary authorities into a discussion that exemplifies the state of letter writing at this time: mainly Erasmian and humanistic in theory but still incorporating useful parts of an older tradition. Throughout, Day illustrates the types of letters and the appropriate forms of language with nearly one hundred models, arranged according to Erasmus's classification: "descriptory," "laudatory," "deliberatiue," "amatorie," and so forth, in part I, and "iudiciall," "expostulatorie," "comminatorie," "familiar," and so forth, in part II. Day claims to have composed all of these himself.

From a summary of their contents, it is not immediately apparent how this combination of dictaminal and humanistic elements would have provided guidance in composing. The utility of these works becomes more comprehensible in light of the dictaminal and humanist traditions from which Day originated.[3]

The *ars dictaminis* grew out of medieval practicalities, where letters were public instruments and the few people who could write needed to use familiar linguistic and discourse forms accessible to others. Originality was discouraged; letter writers had to observe social hierarchies and protocols. Forms and formulae were the touchstones of the art. Shorter prepared passages could be inserted into letters whole, and, in some cases, only the merest data such as names and dates would be unique.

The Erasmian humanist tradition owed a debt to the *ars dictaminis* but sought diligently to promote Ciceronian eloquence in letter writing and to that end adapted epistolography to Ciceronian rhetorical theory; the letter becomes an "oration," and correspondence between "absent friends" becomes the forum for eloquence. The essential mode of humanist epistolography was teaching, and it was most fully presented in Erasmus's *De conscribendis*. Rather than emphasize formulae (although they were used), humanist episotolographers offered longer samples for imitation rather than reproduction; style was a priority, and the writer was expected to work toward the pure Latinity of Cicero in any letter.

In these terms, then, we find that all three of our books put their teaching in an essentially Erasmian humanist "envelope" but that two of three, *Enemy* and *Secretary,* include clear elements of the *ars dictaminis* as parallel guidance. Fulwood's translation has been acknowledged to be based on Erasmus's *De conscribendis,* but its first few pages gives us an excellent example of this hybridity. The writer begins on the first page by defining a letter as "nothing else but an Oration written, conteyning the mynde of the Orator or wryter" (A7R), but he then immediately classifies letters in hierarchical, dictaminal terms: "there be three principal sortes [of letters] for some are addressed to our superiours, as to Emperors, kings, princes, etc. Some to our equalles as to Marchants, Burgesses, Citizens, etc. Some to our inferiours as to servants, laborers, etc." (A7V). He continues with three necessary points for most letters: the "salutation [or] recommendation," the "Subscription," and the "Superscripcion" (A8R). The latter two are treated primarily in terms of where they should go on the letter: the subscription should be located "at the right syde in the nether ende of the paper," and the superscription or address must (obviously) appear on the back of the folded document. The writer adds examples of subscriptions and superscriptions, reminding the reader that he should not mention the actual name of a superior, only his title (A8V). Thus, the regarding of a letter as a "written oration," a particularly humanist concept, is intermixed with typically dictaminal concerns about social station and document formatting.

Several pages later, we find a passage on audience: "Before that we take in hand the material instruments wherewith to write an epistle or letter, we haue to consider these pointes following: to wit, the estate, dignitie, or qualitie of hym unto whom we write: whyther he bee a publike person, or a priuat, whyther he be rich or poore, a friend or an enemie: also whyther he bee well known unto us, or but little. . . . But to them whom we know to take plesure to reade letters, we should, and may without danger write amply, properly, and eloquently" (B2V–B3R).

This seems to parallel a passage from chapter 3 of Erasmus's *De conscribendis* on the "dignity" of a letter (15). Erasmus there is primarily interested in style as it reflects the context of a letter—that is, the issue of decorum—but *Enemy* emphasizes the degree of a letter's recipient as the subject of "dignity." Although the last sentence returns to Erasmian themes of the abundant and amplified style, the social hierarchical focus of the *ars dictaminis* is here so intermingled with humanist precepts that it is impossible to make a meaningful separation between the two.

Day's *English Secretary* more overtly and comprehensively relies on Erasmus's treatise as its "rhetorical envelope." Moreover, throughout the initial portion of *Secretary*, Day reaffirms the congruence of letter-writing theory with the general Ciceronian rhetorical tradition. In chapter 3, "Of the habite and parts of an Epistle," he discusses general and special letters; general letters correspond to the familiar kind, applied for general purposes such as "for fashions sake, custome, dutie, curtesie." Special letters resemble orations in that they have "a resolute purpose and intendment seriouslie to discourse upon, to answere, mittigate, or avoid" certain important issues (B3V). These weightier letters follow general rhetorical teaching, "as they fall out to be borrowed in an oration" (C1R). The writer must be familiar with "Inuention," "Disposition," and "Eloquution" as the basis of their composition, and an awareness of the three levels of style, the "Sublime," "Humile," and "Mediocre" is as relevant to letter writing as it is to oratory (C1V). Day stresses elocution or style as more important than invention or disposition (or arrangement) and reminds his readers that he has appended an entire book onto his treatise that contains a listing of what were considered the basic elements of style, the schemes and tropes (C1R). Nevertheless, as a "platform" for arrangement, he describes the general Ciceronian parts of a speech: Exordium; Narratio or Propositio; Confirmatio; Confutatio; and Peroratio (C2R).

In the midst of this humanist-inspired discussion, however, Day has smoothly incorporated elements of letter-writing theory usually associated with the *ars dictaminis*. Chapter 4, treating "Of certaine contents generally incident to all maner of Epistles," gives a short introduction to salutations, farewells, addresses, and signatures as "continually incident" to proper letter writing (C2R). Dictaminal manuals usually provided formulae that writers could copy, and Day does the same in chapters 5 and 6, offering literally scores of usable superscriptions, farewells (valedictions), subscriptions, and directions. These formulae continue to acknowledge the social relationships emphasized in letters since the Middle Ages. As Day admits, they were unknown to the "auncient Romanes," but "these daies and seasons haue induced unto us for euerie estate of calling" the careful application of "a more statlie reuerence" (D1V). The "daies and seasons" he refers to reach back almost a thousand years.

The popular success of these two books, and the lack of it for Fleming's work, suggest that a blend of methods, one prestigious, the other practical, must have been attractive to readers. Certainly they wanted to know how to format a letter, but they were also interested in examples of "high-class" epistolography. The syntheses presented by Fulwood and Day offered them a plausible pattern to guide thinking and writing. That Erasmian humanism and the *ars dictaminis* frequently intermingle is not necessarily news. Indeed, Erasmus himself includes many formulae and passages for copying in his *De conscribendis*. What should be noted is the thoroughgoing combination of humanistic and dictaminal elements in these successful early vernacular books, which suggest a willingness or even eagerness on the part of readers to make use of any and all material that are presented skillfully and attractively packaged to address their interests and needs.

II

The origins, contents, and attractiveness of the three significant letter-writing handbooks discussed above do not exist in a vacuum; instead, they depend on the nature of their readership. In a culture where status and education revolved closely around *Latin* literacy, it might seem puzzling that people would invest time and money in *English* literacy. Whoever these readers and would-be writers were, they made *Enemy* and *Secretary* commercially successful for fifty years, and they allowed *Panoply* to die quickly and unlamented. There are two likely reasons for the differing histories of these texts: Fulwood and Day "market" their books to English readers who were not fully latinized by education or profession, whereas Fleming sought a purely humanist appeal, and readers could not find what they wanted in literacy guidance anywhere else.

All three books under consideration address themselves specifically to readers of the "unlearned sort" in their preliminary notes (Fulwood, A3V)—that is, those who had little or no Latin but could read and write English. In general this group would comprise the middle class of tradespeople, retailers, and especially merchants. From the very beginning, Fulwood repeatedly associates his work with the mercantile class. On the title page, he identifies himself as "William Fulwood Marchant" and the book is dedicated to the "Right Worshipful the Master, Wardens, and Company of the Merchant Tailors of London." In preliminary verses called "The bokes verdict," he writes in the persona of the book itself, "Yf needlesse some do me suppose, / The Marchants answere here I craue," asserting the self-evident need for vernacular letter-writing skill among merchants (A5R). Several of the model letters also reflect interchanges between merchants, factors, and cashiers, and in the family letters a mercantile context is either explicit or implicit.

Merchants, then, and those associated with mercantile trade, would comprise one clearly identified and important subgroup of readers. Merchants, or "merchant adventurers," as those who ventured abroad were called, occupied a special position in Elizabethan society, largely because of the wealth they accumulated from expanding exports in the first half of the century, including the lucrative wool and textile trade with the Continent (Dietz 1986, 117–129). In *Literacy and the Social Order,* David Cressy maintains that there was a high degree of literacy among merchants in the London area especially, somewhere around 95 percent (1980, 120–124); they frequently spoke several foreign languages as well.[4] The uses for written literacy in this occupation is clear: merchants had to keep extensive records of goods, communicate with employees and prospective buyers, and, when they traveled, keep in touch as best they could with their families back home. One of the most poignant samples in *The Enemy of Idleness* is an exchange between a merchant abroad and his lonely wife (P4R).

Day's *English Secretary* also identifies the mercantile context for several sample letters; indeed, he relies openly on the well-known handbook *The Merchant's Avizo,* by John Browne (1589) as a source for a sample letter from a factor to his master (HH1V). His overall intention, however, is more broadly based. Day attempts to portray letter-writing contexts of all kinds, and involving all classes, for the interest of anyone who might be able to write; he may also have hoped that his sample letters, which were, by and large, his own literary creations, would be a *reading* entertainment for his audience.

Fleming, on the other hand, in spite of his appeal "To the Learned and Unlearned Reader," was a failure in terms of number of books sold and people reached; he attracted neither "learned" nor Latin-literate readers, nor did he offer "unlearned" English readers the kinds of sample texts they wanted. His translated humanist letters lacked specific reference to the concerns of the vernacular readership, and the topics the others built on typical middle-class relationships— master to servant, husband to wife, daughter to mother, merchant to factor—are simply absent. Fleming's readers who were interested in letters of famous people could find these in abundance in Latin treatises or in European imports.

It is clear that, even if Day's and Fulwood's readership had a little Latin and a knowledge of French or Italian, as more and more of the middle class did at this time, they would only go to the Latin formularies or imported European works if they could not find what they wanted elsewhere. The record suggests that vernacular readers found what they wanted in these English books. With the publication of *The Enemy of Idleness* and then of *The English Secretary,* middle-class readers were offered theory with practical assistance through models in their first language; these selections featured people like themselves, writing with the same cultural outlook and on familiar topics. Furthermore, there were *love* letters!

Both Fulwood and Day offer their readers "epistles amatory," thus adding a new type of letter to the humanist catalog and securing immediate interest in the marketplace. *Enemy*'s samples appear in both prose and verse; Fulwood found his prose letters in the original *Stile et maniere,* but he may have written his own verse. The first piece is a letter from "Eurialus" to a virgin named Lucrece, offering his love and servitude in the distinctly formal courtly style: "It is not wythoute cause (Lady Lucrece) if all they of this citie haue their eyes fired to behold, regard, loue & praise thee: when of the one part they consider the great vertues wherwith thou art enriched, the good & honest manners which adorne thee: and moreouer haue in admiration thy richesse, and yet more thy nobilitie surpassyng all other" (S1V). A more substantial exchange between a lover and his disdainful mistress follows: he declares his emotional extremity and begs her mercy in loving him; she replies in scornful terms, repudiating his letters and asking him not to send or write again. He then replies, newly rent with feelings of suicidal despair that she did not want him, but encouraged that she actually did write to him. He pleads his case in conventional terms, turning the responsibility for the passion back onto her, who inflamed it within him. Doubly ignited by her refusals, he cannot cease writing to her and begs her acceptance of his devotion and service. Six love letters in verse then follow, in various meters, which repeat in conventional poetic terms the same masculine emotions (the ladies' replies are not given) developed in the prose letters earlier, with the addition of the "false-lover" theme. The verse is pedestrian and may seem tedious to late-twentieth-century ears, yet, in the closing decades of the sixteenth century, the themes and emotions expressed in these passages resonated with many readers. The sexual tension implicit in the male offering of love and the female refusal echoes common themes in comedies, romances, and popular ballads of the time.

Nevertheless, the predictable emotions and unrequited love theme did not please all. Such excesses, along with popular credulity and lewdness, were brilliantly parodied by Shakespeare in *The Winter's Tale,* when Autolycus, disguised as a peddler, attempts to sell broadside ballads at Perdita's sheep shearing: "Here's another ballad, of a fish that appeared upon the coast on Wednesday the fourscore of April, forty thousand fathom above water, and sung this ballad against the hard hearts of maids; it was thought she was a woman, and was turned into a cold fish for she would not exchange flesh with one that loved her" (IV.3.275–781 *Riverside* ed.).

The Winter's Tale was written fifty years after Fulwood's translation first appeared, and in sophisticated circles the courtly, rhetorical love dialogues such as *Enemy*'s had long been the butt of comedy. The book's last printing, however, did not come until 1621, which suggests that some part of popular taste continued to find these kinds of letters attractive.

The English Secretary's section of "Epistles Amatorie" is shorter but in many ways more interesting (T4R–U2V). After a preamble setting out the parameters of his chapter as dealing with "only [letters] such . . . as are modestly tendered from men unto women," Day sets out two exchanges: the first gives the man's entreaty of love, followed by the lady's response, ending with the man's reply; the second gives the man's declaration of love and the lady's reply only (V1R–V2V; the arrangement is confusing, not following the expected sequence). Day explains that, in love as in all other social dealings, writers must observe strict decorum regarding the "place" of the recipient. If a person were to write in "the superlative degree," the object of his love and his letter should also be "such a one, whose birth, education, or other complements, maie sufficientlie answere the greatnesse and efficacie thereof," that is, of the letter's elevated and ornate language (U1V). The letter is too long to quote at length, but it indeed amplifies the lady's excellent qualities. The lady's reply is predictably scornful, chastising his excesses and false pictures of her. But she does write back—after all, this is a letter-writing manual, not real life—claiming she does so to satisfy the messenger, who waited impatiently by. Her terms are ambiguous, neither breaking off all communication nor assenting to anything. His reply again continues the high figurative mode, turning her rebukes to compliments and returning the figures back again to her. Throughout all three letters, the rhetorical poses are what matter; issues of substance, such as "when can we meet?" must be conveyed at other times, in other ways— very probably orally, by messenger.

The second exchange is much more direct, less ornate, and clearly more middle class. The man sends to a woman whom he knows but has not met, declaring his good will and his desire to meet her—she will not be disappointed, he says; the standard declaration of "love" is never made explicitly. He sends a love token with the letter. The woman's reply is surprised, but interested; she is cautious, aware that "of fairest speaches ensueth often the fowlest actions" (V2V). Still, she tells him she is available to meet him if he can arrange a suitably modest occasion, and she returns his love token.

Between these two exchanges, middle-class readers have been offered several points: men and women wishing to see how the "better sort" live and love would find the self-consciously ornate and conventional forms of address and response quite interesting, and possibly even mildly titillating. Those men more practical-minded, needing guidance on how to meet someone without offending them, would find the second exchange helpful; and women who imagine themselves the object of someone's affections could learn from the example reply. In each case readers are invited to imagine themselves in another's shoes. Where "romance" is involved, that exercise has always been strangely attractive. Moreover, Day's (and Fulwood's) readers can imagine this romance as a function of their own writing; such a consideration adds an extra dimension to fictional involvement and puts an edge on anyone's desire to improve communication skills.

The possibility of attaching delight to utility that these two books anticipates developments in "letter-writing manuals" soon to come. In 1602 the first of many installments of Nicholas Breton's *A Post with a Packet of Mad Letters* crosses the thin line from letter-writing aid to epistolary fiction. Breton makes no pretense of teaching letter-writing theory but rather offers a fictional glimpse into a lost letter packet dropped by the post, using this device brilliantly to build epistolary characterizations and make social commentary. Breton builds on a formula first made popular in these two earlier books and possibly, in conjunction with Fulwood and Day, accomplished more for vernacular literacy and rhetorical skill than all the more sedate handbooks combined.

III

The readers who responded enthusiastically to Fulwood and Day represent the leading cadre of those using their vernacular for purposes that in the past had been connected mostly with Latin literacy—if connected to literacy at all. Toward the end of the sixteenth century, upper-middle-class English men and women were increasingly applying reading and writing to religious, educational, and cultural pursuits, frequently seeking vernacular literacy in tandem with the prestige of Latin schooling for their children. In spite of this apparent contradiction, they were the driving force behind the slow supplanting of Latin as the language in which anything important should be written. I will conclude by looking at some of the impetus behind this movement toward vernacular literacy, with full acknowledgement that continuing research will help us construct a more detailed picture of English literacy patterns.

Aside from the commercial demands for vernacular described previously, the major push toward literacy was religious. Difficult for us to grasp from the perspective of current culture is the extreme importance Elizabethans accorded right belief and practice in the Christian religion; if the sixteenth century in Europe teaches later ages anything, it is that people will willingly undergo pain and death for their vision of truth, if that vision is clear and strong enough. All sides in the English controversies—radical Protestant, Anglican, and Roman Catholic —held staunch beliefs, and all used the written and printed vernacular to reach the public with their message. For a growing number of believers, true faith and practice depended on getting back to the texts of the scriptures, seeing them without corruption or worldly influence, and taking individual responsibility for interpreting and acting on them. For this, translations, commentaries, Psalters, and prayer books would need to be made available in the vernacular, for as wide a dissemination as possible. The public religion of the time, devoted to civic order and right relationships between subjects and superiors, was also thought to benefit from literacy in a controlled environment—that is, under strict press censorship. Thus, civil order, as well as personal salvation, depended on every citizen understanding duties to God and the state. Literacy, then, insofar as it involved reading for spiritual and moral benefit, was considered a clear advantage: "good for you, good for your soul, and good for everybody else" (Cressy 1980, 6).

Admittedly, such views on literacy were highly partisan, fought out in a controversy-based and turbulent century. The most vociferous proliteracy forces were the radical Protestants who saw reform in terms of knowing and activating the letter of God's word; conservatives in the established churches, Anglican as well as Roman, were wary of a reading and writing populace and feared the effects of individual interpretations of Scripture (Cressy 1980, 2). Whereas the latter view prevailed in the government and the Church, which attempted to enforce strict censorship of printed materials, the Reformation ethos of personal responsibility supported by personal understanding through reading was gaining ground among the middle classes. This group was, after all, reform minded, even Puritan in approach to religious and social practice. Although literacy that led to license was condemned, reading and writing in the service of God was a high calling indeed.

If certain kinds of reading could get one to heaven, other kinds of reading—and writing—could help one get through the world. One such aspect of literacy grew out of humanist education and Latin-language culture: an appreciation of the writings of famous people, and, in the sixteenth century increasingly, the correspondence of well-known men of letters. Because people relied normally on vernacular literacy does not mean that they did not appreciate and aspire to "cultured literacy," at least in some degree. Certainly, the upper middle classes regarded Latin school education as a path to worldly success and, acting either as guilds or individuals, founded scores of grammar schools throughout the sixteenth century. One of the most famous was the Merchant Tailors' school, established as a showcase Latin grammar school in London in 1561, for which the founders recruited one of the premier humanist educators, Richard Mulcaster, as headmaster (Charlton 1965, 92–94). Certainly these schools also aided the cause of vernacular literacy. Roger Ascham, in *The Schoolmaster* ([1570] 1967) had promoted the double translation method of Latin instruction, in which pupils turned Latin into English and then back to Latin. Somewhat later, the influential educator John Brinsley wrote in *Ludus literarius* ([1612] 1968) that he had developed this method to work especially with letters and that his pupils composed letters in English and Latin along the lines of Cicero's familiar epistles (Y3R). Even if the main goal of these activities was the learning of Latin, writing proficiency in the vernacular—also a very useful commodity—was an almost assured outcome.

Both Latin and vernacular education emphasized an important dimension of sixteenth century literacy skill—ornate language, or *elocutio*.[5] The attainment of an ornate style was much sought after in the sixteenth century, encouraged by prevailing literary fashion as well as educational habit. Moderns find this obsession with ornamentation singular, quaint, and even foolish, yet cultivation of this skill represents an important aspect of early modern literacy and one of the chief reasons people might be attracted to writing manuals. Whereas all three of our texts assume a basic familiarity with *elocutio,* Day's *Secretary* alone brings it to the foreground by not only inserting marginal markers where figures and tropes occur in his letters, but also by including an additional section in his book entitled "Of figvres, tropes, and schemes" (KK1R in 1599 ed.; first appears in 1592). Here he offers readers both definitions and examples for sixteen tropes and seventy-seven schemes: "I haue now for better supplement of the learners knowledge, determined in this place to make a collection of them all, remembering with my selfe, that vnto such as are vnexperienced in their particular applications, they shall be but of verie slender moment in their quotations, without also they may be instructed by example, how, where, and in what tearmes, wordes or cariage, they are vsed" (II4V).

Day confidently asserts that his good will toward readers is verified by his extra pains in making both definitions and examples available, "confessing (as by due proofe I haue found) that no speech to be accounted valuable or of weight, that is not graced with these parts" (II4V). That prospective writers believed this is attested to not only by the literature of the age, but also by the singular emphasis on *elocutio* found in grammar school curricula and in school texts throughout the sixteenth and seventeenth centuries. Writers or prospective writers of the time would be attentive to building their figurative skills, finding in Day's supplement one of the attractions that might not be evident to later readers. The extended popularity of the book certainly encourages this view.

Conclusion

Our examination of these three texts has yielded some important but still preliminary insights into letter writing and vernacular literacy in later Elizabethan times: persons likely to acquire Fulwood's *Enemy of Idleness,* Fleming's *A Panoply of Epistles,* and Day's *The English Secretary* were middle or upper middle class, perhaps merchants, wholesalers, retailers, and others of the commercial class, and their families, who identified this subject as one both interesting and ultimately useful. These readers wanted to identify with the humanist tradition presented in all three books but were disappointed if they failed to find something more—reference to their middle-class life and literacy experience, or practical guidance such as that supplied by dictaminal formulations.

We have an emerging picture, then, of why the two rhetoric handbooks by Fulwood and Day may have had such relative success: their synthesis of dictaminal and humanistic material. We can also guess why Fleming's and so many other vernacular rhetoric texts did not: they all supplied what readers could get elsewhere in better known Latin versions. More research in historical literacy studies of this period is, of course, needed. We need to know, for example, whether actual vernacular letters written at this time showed any influence from these manuals' precepts or formulae. More also needs to be known about manuscript letter-writing aids: Where did they come from? How many existed in comparison with copies of printed manuals? Do they also rely on a mixture of preceptive and formula-based theory and practice? Much work remains ahead to fill in our picture of sixteenth-century letter-writing practices and their relationship to the growth of English literacy, but even a preliminary survey can demonstrate the complexity of the traditions and social contexts within which English Renaissance letter writing evolved.

Notes

1. In an older but still useful study of vernacular letter writers, Katherine Hornbeak (1934, 5) asserts that Fulwood is responsible for the preliminary materials in *Enemy.*

2. Day specifically names his sources in chapter 1 of the 1586 edition: Erasmus, Macropedius, Vives, and Hegendorff (A1V). He may well have found all of these widely used sources conveniently bound together in Aurelius (Lippus) Brandolini's well-known collection *De ratione scribendi libri tres* (1549), printed at London in 1573.

3. For full doctrine on the *ars dictaminis,* see Carmago's and Burton's essay in this volume and James J. Murphy (1974, chapter 5) and Martin Camargo (1995). On Erasmian epistolography, see Green's and Mitchell's essays in this volume and Judith Rice Henderson (1983).

4. Cressy, a social historian, defines literacy as the ability to both read and write and uses the technique of examining court and other legal records to see what percentage of people signed their names to documents in relation to how many signed with marks. He defends this method by pointing out that writing one's name was a skill learned relatively late in schooling (after reading and basic orthography) and that people who could do so probably had enough literacy training to be considered literate. He finds that people considered literate by this standard comprised a surprisingly small percentage of the population throughout the period 1550 to 1700 but that the percentage was far higher in London than almost anywhere else. Overall, he posits that literacy was definitely rising through the general period 1500–1650, though not at a steady pace or with similar progress in all social groupings. From 1550 to 1650, general literacy of men increased 75 percent and women 650 percent, though the absolute percentages remained fairly small: about 30 percent for men and 10 percent for women in late-Tudor, early Stuart times (157–174). These figures may be depressed for *readers,* however, by the fact that, in the sixteenth century, reading was taught separately from writing and was more common.

5. For a useful overview of *elocutio,* see Brian Vickers (1986, chapter 6). Lawrence D. Green very usefully applies a literacy perspective to the learning of *elocutio* in "Rhetorical *Elocutio* in Renaissance Grammar Books" (1997). I am indebted to Professor Green for his invaluable comments on early drafts of this chapter.

Works Cited

Books printed before 1900 are published at London unless otherwise noted. Books before 1640 are cross-listed with STC (A. W. Pollard and G. R. Redgrave, *A Short-Title*

Catalogue of Books Printed in England, Scotland, & Ireland and of English Books Printed Abroad, 1475–1640, 2nd ed. Edited by W. A. Jackson, F. S. Ferguson, and Katharine F. Pantzer, London: Bibliographical Society, 1976–86.

Ascham, Roger. *The Schoolmaster.* 1570. Edited by Lawrence V. Ryan. Ithaca, N.Y.: Cornell University Press, 1967.

Brandolini, Aurelius. *De ratione scribendi libri tres.* Basle, 1549. Reprint, London, 1573. STC 3542.

Breton, Nicholas. *A Post With A Packet of Mad Letters.* 1602. *The Works of Nicholas Breton.* Edited by Ursula Kentish-Wright. Vol 2. London: Cresset, 1929. Facsimile reprint, Grosse Point, Mich.: Scholar, 1968.

Brinsley, John. *Ludus literarius.* 1612. Facsimile reprint, Menston: Scolar, 1968.

Browne, John. *The marchants auizo.* 1589. STC 3908.4.

Camargo, Martin. *Medieval Rhetorics of Prose Composition.* Binghamton, N.Y.: Medieval & Renaissance Texts & Studies, 1995.

Charlton, Kenneth. *Education in Renaissance England.* London: Routledge, 1965.

Cressy, David. *Literacy and the Social Order; Reading and Writing in Tudor and Stuart England.* Cambridge: Cambridge University Press, 1980.

Day, Angel. *The English secretary; or, Methode of writing of epistles. Deuided into two bookes.* 4th ed. 1599. STC 6404. (University Microfilms reel no. 380)

————. *The English secretorie. Wherein is contayned, a perfect method, for the inditing of all manner of epistles.* 1586. STC 6401. Facsimile reprint, Menston: Scolar, 1967.

Dietz, Brian. "Overseas Trade and Metropolitan Growth." In *The Making of the Metropolis of London, 1500–1700*, edited by A. L. Beier and Roger Finlay. Harlow: Longman, 1986, 115–40.

Erasmus, Desidirius. *De conscribendis epistolis.* 1522. Translated by Charles Fantazzi. *Collected Works of Erasmus.* Edited by J. K. Sowards. Vol. 25. Toronto: University of Toronto Press, 1985.

Fleming, Abraham. *A panoplie of epistles, Conteyning a perfecte plattforme of inditing letters of all sorts.* 1576. STC 11049.

Fulwood, William. *The enimie of idlenesse: teaching how to endite, epistles.* 1568. STC 11476. (University Microfilms reel no. 294).

Green, Lawrence D. "Rhetorical *Elocutio* in Renaissance Grammar Books." Presented to the National Commmunication Association Convention, Chicago, November 1997.

Henderson, Judith Rice. "Erasmus on the Art of Letter Writing." In *Renaissance Eloquence,* edited by James J. Murphy. Berkeley: University of California Press, 1983, 331–55.

Hornbeak, Katherine Gee. *The Complete Letter Writer in English, 1568–1800.* Smith College Studies in Modern Languages 15. Northampton, Mass.: Smith College, 1934.

Murphy, James J. *Rhetoric in the Middle Ages.* Berkeley: University of California Press, 1974.

Robertson, Jean. *The Art of Letter Writing.* Liverpool: Liverpool University Press, 1942.

Vickers, Brian. *A Defence of Rhetoric.* New York: Oxford University Press, 1986.

Humanism and the Humanities

ERASMUS'S *OPUS DE CONSCRIBENDIS EPISTOLIS* IN
SIXTEENTH-CENTURY SCHOOLS

Judith Rice Henderson

In the conference on "Rhetoric in the Renaissance" that he organized at the Newberry Library in 1979, James J. Murphy lamented the lack of a comprehensive bibliography and a systematic study of Renaissance rhetorical works, and he guessed that research might uncover "One Thousand neglected Authors." As long as a few figures dominate what are mainly footnotes to studies of other subjects, he suggested, it will be impossible to understand the scope of Renaissance rhetoric and thus its importance to its own time or to ours. Thanks in part to Murphy's own research and his efforts to nourish the next generation of scholars, some of the work he called for has been completed. Our bibliography of rhetoricians is larger and our studies of their texts and contexts more numerous than in 1979. We are now in a better position to assess the importance of rhetoric and to assign a place in history to hundreds of "neglected authors." But what place, and in what kind of history? Since the Newberry Library conference, I have studied at least 150 Renaissance textbooks on letter writing, some of which would add little to a traditional intellectual history. Many are compilations or adaptations of the works of already famous rhetoricians, those few who enlisted support through professional networks for changes to discourse theories and teaching methods that had grown inadequate or at least shopworn. These leaders corresponded with their contemporaries—and sometimes traveled—extensively and from the end of the fifteenth century they made full use of the new technology of printing. Although they owed much to their immediate predecessors, they spurned them and claimed a higher authority from classical texts or from nature or even from God. If the history of rhetoric is a history of ideas, it must be based on their polemics. Their unusually self-conscious analyses established the grounds of debate for their contemporaries. As for Murphy's thousand neglected authors of several thousand extant notebooks, handbooks, and textbooks, most of them are of more interest to the social than to the intellectual historian.

Perhaps, though, the historian of rhetoric should be both. Recent scholarship recognizes that ideas develop in a societal context, and no art is more engaged with society than rhetoric. For instance, Anthony Grafton and Lisa Jardine (1986) have attempted to place the history of ideas in the context of social history by describing the gap between humanist theory and schoolroom practice. They organize *From Humanism to the Humanities* around case studies of such famous scholar-teachers as Guarino, Valla, Poliziano, Agricola, Erasmus, and Ramus, but they also include notes and lectures of students and followers of these masters among their source materials. The rich detail and provocative analysis of their study proves the usefulness of examining minor, along with major, figures. Although they offer little proof that scholasticism was "a system far better adapted to many of the traditional intellectual and practical needs of European society" (xii) than the humanism that opposed it, they rightly challenge the claims made by humanists to progress in education. A weakness of their new historicist/cultural materialist approach is that it encourages conclusions that seem to reflect their own experiences in elitist institutions as much as the circumstances of the Renaissance scholars they study. Coauthoring their book from Princeton and Cambridge, respectively, Grafton and Jardine attribute the gap between humanist ideals and teaching to an Establishment effort to train a docile class of civil servants. They say almost nothing about such intellectual, political, and social upheavals as the Reformation. Investigating more of Murphy's "neglected authors" might suggest alternative explanations for the gap between theory and practice that they identify.

To understand Renaissance rhetoric, we do need to study both the famous and the obscure, as Murphy observes; to explore the gap between ideas and practice in education, as Grafton and Jardine do; to place ideas in their societal contexts, yet be careful not to lose the historical thread that guides us through that maze. I propose as an experiment in this endeavor to study the use that sixteenth-century teachers of letter writing made of Erasmus's *Opus de conscribendis epistolis* (Basle: J. Froben, 1522).[1] This treatise was one of the most influential Renaissance rhetorics by the most famous humanist of northern Europe. In the introduction to the modern critical edition, Jean-Claude Margolin notes more than fifty editions or reprints up to Erasmus's *Opera omnia* of 1540, including three at Basle, six at Strasbourg, seven at Cologne, five at Antwerp, fourteen at Paris, eight at Lyons, three at Venice, one at Verona, two at Cracow, and two at Alcala (ASD 1.2:175). Thereafter, the *Opus* continued to appear at Paris until 1549, at Mainz until 1556, at Lyons until 1558, at Antwerp until 1566, at Cologne until 1567, and at Basle until 1585. In the seventeenth century the *Opus* appeared seven times at Amsterdam and once at each of Copenhagen and Osterode. In the eighteenth century it not only was included in the *Opera omnia* (Leiden: P. Vander Aa, 1703–1706), but twice appeared at Nuremberg (ASD 1.2:173–181).

This publishing history does not reveal the full geographical range of Erasmus's influence, because some nations, including England, imported most of their Latin textbooks. During the third and longest (1509–1514) of his sojourns there, Erasmus helped his friend Dean John Colet plan the curriculum for St. Paul's School in London and completed several textbooks for it. Others, such as the *Opus de conscribendis epistolis,* Erasmus published after his return to the Continent. The curriculum of St. Paul's in turn became the model for other schools. Baldwin has concluded from his thorough study of English education in the Tudor period, "In the treatise *De Ratione Studii* by Erasmus [Paris: J. Bade, 1512] is the fundamental philosophy of the grammar school in England. On these general principles it was organized and by these methods it was taught. What is more, the strategic textbooks in the system were suggested, prepared, or approved by Erasmus" (1944, 1:94; cf. 1:75–184, 2:239–287, et passim).

In almost every copy of the *Opus de conscribendis epistolis* that Margolin saw, he found evidence of its pedagogical use in manuscipt *marginalia,* and in some he observed evidence of censorship (ASD 1.2:173, 176). The *Opus* contains typically Erasmian commentary on abuses of the Church, especially in the section on formulas of greeting, address, and farewell, where Erasmus parodies clerical pretensions. The main target of the censors, though, was the famous model letter that attempts to persuade an unnamed young man to marry rather than to vow celibacy.[2] This letter, the *Encomium matrimonii,* had stirred violent controversy when it first appeared in Erasmus's *Declamationes aliquot* (Louvain: T. Martens, 1518). Erasmus claimed that the letter was innocently written as a declamation—that is, a rhetorical exercise, specifically an *epistola suasoria* arguing a particular case. A version of it appeared in Erasmus's *Libellus de conscribendis epistolis* (Cambridge: J. Siberch, 1521), a pirated early draft of the treatise on letter writing. In the authorized *Opus de conscribendis epistolis* of 1522, Erasmus reinforced the declamatory purpose of the letter by reprinting it with the outline of a palinode or argument on the other side of the question: a dissuasion from marriage.[3] Nevertheless, a French translator of the *Encomium matrimonii* and other works of Erasmus, Louis de Berquin, was burned at the stake in 1529.[4] As religious controversy escalated in Europe from the 1520s on, Erasmus's textbooks, as well as his theological and controversial writings, came under attack from theologians and Church leaders, and they were prohibited selectively by authorities in several jurisdictions. With the promulgation of the Pauline Index in 1559, the papacy forbade all of Erasmus's works.[5] Margolin concludes that a systematic study of the surviving copies of Erasmus's treatise would be a "nouveau l'histoire de l'érasmisme lui-même" (ASD 1.2:177).

With copies of numerous editions now scattered worldwide, the survey suggested by Margolin of the comments and excisions of readers may be nearly impossible, but some idea of the pedagogical uses that contemporaries made of Erasmus's treatise on letter writing, as well as the effects of the Reformation and

Counter-Reformation on teaching, can be obtained from another source: adaptations of the treatise published by teachers of grammar and rhetoric, several of whom Margolin mentions (179, 182–183). At least two schoolmasters produced abridgements, and others excerpted the *Opus de conscribendis epistolis* in lectures subsequently printed or in course materials custom published for their students by a nearby printing house, perhaps in the hope of reaching a wider market. Still other teachers incorporated these adaptations, often without acknowledgement, into their own textbooks. Knowing something of the lives of most of these teachers, we can use them as case studies of the conditions of teaching letter writing in northern European schools of the sixteenth century.

Desiderius Erasmus of Rotterdam, 1466 or 1469–1536

Erasmus opens the section on teaching method in his *Opus de conscribendis epistolis* with a complaint against those who think that a few rules will make them good writers. He regrets having started his work on letter writing "twenty-five years ago" for a man who had wasted his life in princes' courts amassing benefices (CWE 25:22). As we know from other allusions, Erasmus had been supporting himself in Paris in 1498 by tutoring the Englishman Robert Fisher, who took the first draft of Erasmus's manual with him when he left that year for Italy (Margolin, ASD 1.2:158–160; CWE 25:10). Now others, Erasmus says, demand shortcuts to learning because they are lazy and want to get back to the inconsequential occupations in which they have wasted their lives (CWE 25:22–23). Erasmus admits that a good teacher can ease the student's toil, but rules are useless without broad learning, intensive study, and practice from childhood (23). Sloth and greed produce bad students, and also bad teachers (23, 34). Parents and magistrates must be willing to pay schoolteachers a decent salary (23), and schoolteachers must be willing to send lazy students back to their parents, even if they lose their fees (42). Schoolteachers must immerse themselves in the whole of classical literature to find good material for student exercises (23–43).

Erasmus's teaching method, outlined earlier in the *De ratione studii*, involves rhetorical analysis of classical models, notation in commonplace books, and exercises in imitation that draw on the notes for both content and illustrations. Rules of rhetoric are not so much direct guides to writing as they are tools of the literary critic and writer studying models for imitation in classical, biblical, or patristic authors (Henderson, "Erasmian Ciceronians" [1992], 283–284). The exercises based on this reading are designed to teach the Christian how to live in and contribute to the world. In the *Opus de conscribendis epistolis*, Erasmus finds that even Ovid's love letters can offer material for exercises arguing "that the common good must take precedence over private grief" or might provide "a splendid opportunity to attack disreputable pleasure, and also to dwell on the immortal glory to be won by exceptional heroism" (CWE 25:24). Erasmus strongly prefers "what is of social value to what is not." For instance, "Topics taken from the historians come closer to the truth, and so confer more profit" than myths about the birth of Pallas Athena from Jupiter's brain (25). Erasmus devotes many pages (29–38) to describing a fictional *epistola suasoria* in which a young man, Lucius, persuades his former companion in vice, Antonius, to reform and take up the study of letters as he himself has done.[6] As Erasmus outlines the argument, it becomes a humanist paean to learning as a spiritual force to develop the capacity for reason that separates humans from beasts: "Nature created man upright and implanted in him the desire to know in order that he might contemplate God's creation and at the same time meditate upon God as the maker of all things, and upon himself and the whole fabric of the universe" (32). Mere rules of rhetoric demanded by men like Fisher could hardly serve Erasmus's educational goals.

In the chapters that immediately precede and follow those on teaching method in the *Opus de conscribendis epistolis* (CWE 25:12–22, 45–65), Erasmus champions what we would call a broad liberal arts education for the professional by criticizing two kinds of legalism in letter writing. He opens the treatise by objecting to a tendency among his learned contemporaries to expect all letters to be brief, clear, commonplace in diction, and simple in style (12). Classical writers had distinguished the conversational style (*sermo*) of the letter from the formal style (*contentio*) of the oration, but, as Erasmus points out, their own letters are sometimes highly rhetorical (14–15). Erasmus insists that a letter can be on any topic and that its style will depend upon its purpose and the relationship between the correspondents (19–20). Scholars, for instance, may want to use Greek words, make obscure allusions, or even play witty games with each other, as Erasmus did when he wrote Thomas Linacre in carefully disguised trochaic tetrameters (16–18). Erasmus seems to be criticizing here the extreme neoclassicists of his age, those who would accept only Cicero as a model for prose.[7] On the other hand, when, after discussing teaching method, he turns to instructions on the salutation and valediction of the letter, he mocks the obsequious formulas of polite address inherited from medieval etiquette. Such flattery, he says, offends Christian values as much as it violates classical taste (53). To Erasmus, both contemporary Ciceronianism and medieval formulas oversimplify the complexity of good letter writing. Students who read widely in classical literature should be able to avoid either trap. They will develop judgment by analyzing how good authors adapt their writing to each occasion. Then, they will know how to use their classical models appropriately in their own Christian world (Henderson, "Erasmus on the Art of Letter-Writing" [1983]).

The chapters of the *Opus de conscribendis epistolis* that I have described were added sometime before 1509 (Henderson, "Despauterius' *Syntaxis*" [1988], 178–180) to the manual that Erasmus claims to have written in less than three weeks (CWE 25:10) for Fisher in 1498. They are the product of many years of struggle with a problem that few contemporary humanists faced so squarely:

how to reconcile their enthusiastic imitation of newly discovered classical letter collections, especially those of Cicero, with the rhetorical tradition of letter writing they had inherited from medieval *dictatores*. Erasmus's long discussions of epistolary style in the *Opus* do not appear in the first extant draft of his treatise, probably composed between May 1499 and September 1500 (Jolidon, "L'évolution" [1979]) and later pirated as the *Libellus de conscribendis epistolis* (Cambridge: J. Siberch, 1521). That early version, far from being a mere set of rules, is already a substantial rhetoric, but its opening remarks on style and organization (*elocutio* and *dispositio*) are brief. They criticize the flattery of the medieval salutation and instruct the letter writer to imitate the conversational quality and simplicity of the ancients. These are standard observations in humanist treatises of the late fifteenth century. Most of the *Libellus* concerns argument (*inventio*). Erasmus classifies subcategories of letters under the categories of the oration (deliberative, demonstrative, and judicial), gives instructions on the topics or places of argument for each subcategory, and provides examples. The resulting treatise is as inconsistent as other manuals of the day: the letter writer is told to avoid the theatrical grandiloquence of oratorical style while employing the formal argumentation of the oration (Henderson, "Erasmus on the Art of Letter-Writing" [1983], 331–344).

Erasmus's subsequent revision of this early draft seems to have been inspired by the Ciceronian controversy, to which he would make a famous contribution in the *Ciceronianus* (Basle: *in officina Frobeniana*, 1528). He may have learned about the controversy first from reading the correspondence of Angelo Poliziano, published posthumously in *Omnia opera* (Venice: *in aedibus Aldi Romani*, 1498). Poliziano, like Erasmus, advocated immersion in classical literature in opposition to the narrow imitation of one model. He defended the eclecticism of his own style in the opening letter and debated the issue of models in his correspondence with Bartolomeo Scala and Paolo Cortesi. Erasmus praises the style of Poliziano as *incredibilis nitor* in the dedication of his *Adagiorum collectanea* to William Blount, Lord Mountjoy (Paris: J. Philippi, 1500). He uses the same phrase to describe Poliziano's epistolary style in a curious little work on letter writing pirated by an unknown printer from Erasmus's manuscripts in 1519 or 1520: *Brevissima maximeque compendiaria conficiendarum epistolarum formula* (Basel: A. Petri?).[8] This *Formula,* which Erasmus hesitated to acknowledge, cannot have been written before July 1501 because it quotes a definition from a Greek treatise on letter writing, *Epistolimaioi charaktéres,* which was falsely attributed to Libanius in the *editio princeps* of that date (Förster 1927, 21–22). I have argued that it consists of notes that Erasmus made for revision of an early draft of the *Opus* (Henderson, "Enigma" [1989]). The *Formula* principally defends letter writing as a rhetorical art. The authorized *Opus de conscribendis epistolis* is likewise a defense of the rhetorical purpose and form of the letter against neoclassical purists who might render the genre useless by demanding too close an imitation of Cicero.

In the *Opus* of 1522, the brief remarks on style at the opening of the *Libellus* are replaced with chapters attacking both narrow Ciceronianism and medieval barbarism. These chapters prepare the reader for the instruction in epistolary argument, which Erasmus has now greatly expanded from the *Libellus* (CWE 25: 65–254). Erasmus distinguishes letters covering one topic ("unmixed") or many ("mixed"). After a brief discussion of how to maintain coherence in the "mixed" letter by skillful use of transitions, he subdivides "unmixed" letters into categories borrowed from the oration: deliberative, demonstrative, or judicial. Certain letters do not fit under these categories. In the *Libellus,* he calls them "extraordinary." In the *Opus,* he names them "familiar," and adds, almost as an afterthought, a fifth category of letters that dispute, investigate, and teach (CWE 25: 65–72). His detailed description of the types under each category begins with the deliberative letters of persuasion and encouragement, drawing on material published in his edition of the letters of St. Jerome.[9] In these chapters of the *Opus,* Erasmus offers advice about direct and indirect beginnings, style, tone, examples, and arguments that might be applied to all types. For each letter type, Erasmus then specifies the rhetorical topics or places that supply its argument. For instance, to encourage the correspondent, the writer can search the topics of praise, hope, fear, love, hatred, pity, rivalry, expectations of friends or of enemies, and examples. Throughout this classification and description of the rhetoric of letter writing, Erasmus offers as models both ancient and contemporary letters, including some of his own. He quotes some models in full and excerpts or cites others in the extensive collections illustrating each type. No doubt this catalog of epistles grew larger each time Erasmus worked on his treatise until the 1522, authorized, version had become a veritable encyclopedia of both principles and models of letter writing.

Erika Rummel complains that in the *Opus* Erasmus violently attacks his immediate predecessors in letter writing without offering anything essentially new, although, she admits, "he brings a new zeal to the subject" (1989, 310) and seems to be addressing teachers as well as students (304). She is certainly correct to point out that his treatise is a compilation from classical, medieval, and humanist sources, but it does take an independent approach to the problem of reconciling the imitation of classical models of letter writing with the classical tradition of rhetoric, originally the art of the oration, handed down to humanist letter writers by the medieval *dictatores.* Erasmus recalls the classical conception of the letter as conversation between absent friends, and he demands an end to medieval pretension, flattery, and "barbaric" Latinity in epistolary style, as well as to rigidity in the organization of the letter. He insists, however, that when Cicero and other classical orators and writers composed letters they did not entirely lay aside their rhetorical skills. To put the imitation of the ancients to use in the contemporary world, Erasmus insists that his contemporaries study rhetoric and use it to analyze a wide range of models. He sees the letter as a genre "by nature diverse and capable of almost infinite variation" (CWE 25:12). Not only can it be written on any subject (12), but it must be adapted to an immediate occasion and audience (14). The rhetoric that Erasmus recommends focuses especially on the topics of invention, so central to his thought (Sloane 1997, *passim*). He certainly derives more from his predecessors than he graciously acknowledges, but he does reconcile classical letters with classical rhetoric, and the *ars dictaminis* with humanism, in a synthesis that contemporaries found valuable. Moreover, he used the new technology of the printing press, and the professional networks that he built through his own extensive correspondence and travel, to publicize and win support for that synthesis (Jardine, *Erasmus* [1993]).

Erasmus's *Opus de conscribendis epistolis* may have originated as a handbook of rules for an adult, but it grew into an encyclopedia of letter writing addressed more to the serious scholar and teacher than to the pubescent schoolboy. Teachers found it necessary to adapt it for students finishing grammar school and beginning the university arts course. The reception of the *Opus* might be divided into two stages, grammatical and rhetorical. Exercises in analyzing and writing letters were used to teach both grammar and rhetoric in the Renaissance, but interest in Erasmus's treatise came first from grammarians. Long before the authorized edition was published in 1522, one of Erasmus's friends from Louvain, Johannes Despauterius, quoted extensively in his *Syntaxis* (Paris: J. Bade, 1509) from a draft on which Erasmus may have been working in the summer of 1506, just before he went to Italy (Henderson, "Despauterius' *Syntaxis*" [1988], 188–189). Despauterius is a central figure in the history of grammar. His collected grammatical textbooks were used for several centuries, and the *Syntaxis* itself went through many editions. From the third edition (Paris: C. Chevallon, ca. 1516–1517), the section on letter writing was removed. It had been revised and published separately by Despauterius with the title *Ars epistolica* (Paris: J. Bade, 1513). That treatise, too, appeared in many subsequent editions. Another Flemish grammarian, Petrus Pontanus, borrowed Erasmian material from it without acknowledgement for his *Sequunda pars artis grammaticae* (Paris: N. des Pres for D. Roce, 1515). Although Pontanus's treatise was also reprinted, Despauterius had captured the market (Henderson, "Despauterius' *Syntaxis*" [1988], 189–190).

Thereafter, Erasmus's observations on letter writing found their way principally into textbooks of rhetoric. Teachers who did not have access to his manuscripts could draw from some of his published works. Erasmus included epistolary formulas in his *De copia* (Paris: J. Bade, 1512) and rhetorical commentary in his edition of the letters of St. Jerome (Basle: J. Froben, 1515).[10] Johann Froben pirated Erasmus's *Colloquia* in 1518 from a manuscript containing an early version of the *De copia*, Latin formulas, brief dialogues, and a model letter. Erasmus subsequently acknowledged and enlarged the work. Together with the *De copia*, the *Colloquia* offered a rich treasury of phrases and formulas for the varied circumstances of letter writing. The *Brevissima maximeque compendiaria conficiendarum epistolarum formula*, pirated in 1519 or 1520, was immediately popular and remained a bestseller throughout Europe for years after the *Opus de conscribendis epistolis* became available. The title, "a very brief and especially compendious formula for composing letters," was no doubt a factor in its success. According to Alain Jolidon ("Histoire" [1986], 242–243), it was printed at least fifty-four times between 1520 and 1602, and its geographical range included Basle, Erfurt, Leipzig, Mainz, Cologne, Paris, Antwerp, Landshut, Augsburg, Cracow, Strasbourg, Wittenberg, Venice, Lyons, Zurich, London, and Copenhagen. This list does not include the lost first edition postulated by R. A. B. Mynors. One ardent Erasmian, Christoph Hegendorff, seems to have borrowed from this *Formula,* as well as from the *De copia* and the edition of St. Jerome's letters, in his *Ratio epistolarum conscribendarum compendiaria* (Leipzig: Valentin Schumann, 1520). Finally, the earliest surviving draft of Erasmus's treatise, the *Libellus* pirated in 1521, was reprinted twice in 1522 before it was superseded by the authorized version (Halkin, "Le traité"). Drawing upon the *Formula,* the *Opus,* and upon relevant material in Erasmus's other works—not only the *De copia,* the edition of St. Jerome's letters, and the *Colloquia,* but eventually too the *Ecclesiastes sive de ratione concionandi* (Basel: H. Froben and N. Episcopius, 1535)—schoolmasters continued throughout the century to anthologize, abridge, and adapt his instructions on letter writing for use in their own classrooms. Their textbooks illustrate concretely the problems they faced and the solutions they found in meeting student demand for efficient instruction.

Johannes Despauterius Ninivita (Jan de Spouter of Ninove), ca. 1480–1520

The *Syntaxis* is only one of a series of textbooks that Despauterius wrote for his students as a complete course in grammar: *Orthographiae isagoge* (1506), *Ars versificatoria* (1510), *Grammaticae prima pars* (1512), *Rudimenta* (1511 or 1514), *De figuris liber ex Quintiliano, Donato, Diomede, Valla . . . diligenter concinnatus* (1519), and annotations to Torrentinus's commentary on the *Doctrinale* of Alexander de Villa Dei (1518 or 1520). Like Erasmus's *Opus de conscribendis epistolis,* the collected grammar textbooks were frequently reprinted and abridged, making him "le Priscien belge" of the sixteenth century (Lavency 1968–1969, 401–402). Born about 1480 at Ninove in Flanders, he earned his M.A. at the University of Louvain in 1501, taught at the Pedagogy of the Lily and at Beghard College there, moved to the Latin school at Komen (Comines), and then to the Latin school at Sint-Winoksbergen (now Bergues). The last move must have been about 1509, because the *Syntaxis* is addressed to his students at both Komen and Sint-Winoksbergen (Matheeussen 1977, 4–5). In 1514 he returned to Komen, where he died in 1520.[11] Despauterius's quotations from Erasmus in the *Syntaxis* refer to him in superlatives (*peritissimus, doctissimus, eloquentissimus, suavissimus, amoenissimo ingenio et poeta et orator*). Their friendship probably dates from Erasmus's sojourn at Louvain in 1502–1504 (Henderson, "Despauterius' *Syntaxis*" [1988], 184–185). The two humanists had many colleagues in common, for instance, the printer Josse Bade, the patron Georgius Haloinus, and Despauterius's student Maarten van Dorp, whose criticism of the *Moriae encomium* (*The Praise of Folly*) was a product of his close association with the Erasmian workshop in Louvain, as Jardine has shown (*Erasmus* 1993, 180–187).

Despauterius had precedents in Quattrocento humanism for his decision to include instructions on letter writing at the end of his *Syntaxis*. Niccolo Perotti's *Rudimenta grammatices* (completed in 1468) ends with a description of letter writing—actually a commentary on a sample letter. The letter was a standard exercise in composition for students who had learned the basics of Latin grammar, and an appendix on letter writing could accommodate new knowledge about Latin constructions that did not fit comfortably into the still medieval structure of grammar textbooks (Jensen 1988, 513). Like his Italian predecessors, Despauterius is an intellectual heir of Lorenzo Valla, whose *Elegantiarum linguae Latinae libri sex* (circulated from the 1440s) had influenced many letter-writing treatises of the late fifteenth century.[12] Despauterius works to reform Latin grammar by studying closely the actual usage of ancient writers, and he is clearly unwilling to limit his investigation to Cicero. He approaches his subject in a spirit of scientific inquiry and of debate with other humanist grammarians, changing his mind as new evidence emerges (Henderson, "Despauterius' *Syntaxis*" [1988], 190–191).

The draft of Erasmus's *Opus* that Despauterius saw in manuscript before he finished his *Syntaxis* must have been nearly complete. Despauterius refers the reader to Erasmus's manuscript for a description of the types of letters with examples. He mentions briefly Erasmus's advice on teaching method but gives us only a tantalizing glimpse of what Erasmus had written on pedagogy before 1509.[13] What Despauterius finds interesting enough to quote at length from Erasmus's manuscript are his contributions to contemporary debates about reclaiming Latin from medieval "barbarism": that is, the opening chapters on the nature and style of the letter, and the chapters following those on teaching method that deal with forms of address, especially in the salutation and valediction.

Despauterius approves Erasmus's attempt to find a practical *via media* between medieval conventions that offend neoclassical taste and a Ciceronian purism that violates contemporary etiquette. Thus, citing other humanists, Despauterius advises the writer to break with medieval customs of salutation by (1) putting his own name before that of the correspondent, even if the correspondent is of higher rank (194–95), (2) using *salus* only in the singular, that is, *salutem optat*, not *salutes* (198), (3) addressing an individual in the singular rather than the polite plural (202), and (4) avoiding obsequious epithets. He cites Erasmus's parody of the medieval salutation: *Perspicacissimo viro, candelabro aureo septem liberalium artium eradianti, theologorum apici, lucernae doctrina rutilanti, charitate flagranti, necnon mysteriorum divinorum sacrario, utriusque testamenti*

*gazophilacio, atque omnium virtutum heroicarum et ethicarum speculo limpidis-
simo, domino meo domino praeceptori, dominationis vestrae discipulus et indignus servulus* (193) (To the most perspicacious man, golden candlestick shining
with the seven liberal arts, apex of theologians, lamp glowing with doctrine,
blazing with charity, likewise to the secret place of divine mysteries and treasury
of both testaments, and brightest mirror of all heroic and ethical virtues, my lord
lord preceptor, the disciple and unworthy little servant of your lordship [sends
greetings]).[14] He also repeats Erasmus's advice against forms of etiquette that are
merely silly, such as calling a theologian *magister noster* rather than *noster magister,* or doubling the title *dominus* (202), as in the above parody. At the same
time, Despauterius agrees with Erasmus in tolerating wise innovation (196). The
Syntaxis ends with a summary of the opening chapters of Erasmus's treatise,
which target not so much medieval formulas as an equally reductive humanist
neoclassicism that insists a letter be brief, clear, and written in ordinary words
without rhetorical artifice. Such a narrow conception of the genre, Erasmus insists, would exclude many classical and patristic letters (207). Despauterius agrees,
and in annotations to the *Syntaxis,* published in 1510, he compares Erasmus's
position to that of Angelo Poliziano in the first letter of his collected correspondence and in his controversy with Paolo Cortesi over the strict imitation of
Cicero in letter writing (210; cf. Scott [1910] 1991, 16–22).

Petrus Pontanus Caecus Brugensis (Pierre de Ponte, blind man of Bruges), ca. 1475–after 1539

If Despauterius prepared the *Syntaxis* as a school textbook, he or his printer,
Bade, probably had in mind a handbook for adults engaged in professional correspondence when they published a revision of the concluding section on letter
writing as the *Ars epistolica* (1513). Petrus Pontanus returned the *Ars epistolica*
to the schoolroom by borrowing substantial portions of it for the final book *de
certa epistolandi forma* of his *Sequunda pars artis grammaticae* (Paris: N. des
Prez for D. Roce, 1515). Born at Bruges about 1475 and blinded accidentally at
age three, he lived in abbeys at Saint-Omer and Arras before establishing himself
as a teacher at Paris in the early sixteenth century. He married, fathered many
children, and published more than thirty works. Pontanus attacked Despauterius
in print several times between 1514 and 1521, the year following Despauterius's
death, but he never acknowledged his use of either Erasmus or Despauterius in
his book on letter writing.[15] Pontanus's chapter on letter writing abridges, slightly
rearranges, and sometimes expands the *Ars epistolica.* In general he seems more
traditional than either Despauterius or Erasmus. For instance, Pontanus adds
descriptions of those parts of the oration—*exordium, narratio, petitio*—that
Despauterius omits. Of the controversial Erasmian material in Despauterius,
Pontanus quotes some on the nature and style of the letter, but he omits an

attack on the servile epithets inherited from the Middle Ages. I have found no evidence that Pontanus had independent access to Erasmus's manuscript.

Christophorus Hegendorphinus Lipsiensis (Christoph Hegendorff of Leipzig), 1500–1540

Hegendorff (born in Leipzig in 1500) was teaching school and studying divinity in his native city when in 1519 he praised Luther in *Carmen de disputatione Lipsiensi*, a poem on the Leipzig debate on the papal primacy between Luther and Johann Eck.[16] Hegendorff would become an important Lutheran scholar, but his early works show above all an enthusiasm for Erasmus. His *Encomium somni, Encomium sobrietatis*, and *Encomium ebrietatis* of 1519 seem to be inspired by Erasmus's *Moriae encomium*. Like his teacher at Leipzig, Petrus Mosellanus, and Erasmus himself, he wrote colloquies to instruct schoolboys in Latin, *Dialogi pueriles* (Leipzig: V. Schumann, 1520). Two were reprinted the same year with Erasmus's *Colloquia* (Strasbourg: J. Knoblouch). This publication was perhaps Hegendorff's excuse for addressing a complimentary letter to Erasmus in 1520, which we know only through Erasmus's reply (Ep. 1168). Along with one of the earliest Lutheran catechisms, *Christiana studiosae juventutis institutio*, Hegendorff published notes to Erasmus's *Colloquia* (Haguenau: J. Setzer, 1526). Two years later, he produced *scholia* to an edition of Erasmus's *De copia* (Haguenau: J. Setzer, 1528).

Hegendorff's *Ratio epistolarum conscribendarum compendiaria* (Leipzig: V. Schumann, 1520) borrows from Erasmus's *De copia* and from his annotations on the letters of St. Jerome. Hegendorff's chapter on the letter of encouragement is for the most part a direct quotation of the first paragraph of Erasmus's *artis annotatio* on St. Jerome's letter to Heliodorus. Erasmus first describes this letter as an *epistola exhortatoria*. In opposition to Aristotle's identification of encouragement with persuasion, Erasmus distinguishes them here, as also in the *Opus de conscribendis epistolis* (CWE 25:73). Erasmus then names the honorable, useful, praiseworthy, possible, necessary, easy, and pleasant as topics of encouragement, and he suggests that men are most stimulated to act by praise and by fear of shame. Such letters as this, Erasmus goes on to say, are really Christian declamations. While secular rhetors debated trivial questions, Christian writers like St. Jerome applied their method to ethical questions with a twofold purpose: teaching eloquence and encouraging piety.[17] Erasmus thus gives authority to Hegendorff's frequent recommendation of the letters of St. Paul and the Church fathers as Christian models for imitation. In this Hegendorff perhaps goes further than Erasmus,[18] and there are other hints in the *Ratio* of the changing religious climate. Hegendorff's example of the *epistola dehortatoria*, discouraging a friend from sedition by the argument of St. Paul that all are members of one body in Christ, strikes an ominous note. He also emphasizes Christian arguments, not only in the letter of consolation, where we should expect to find them, but even in the letter of request, which he would begin with such *sententia* as "men were created by God to help others."[19] Like Erasmus, he questions whether flattering titles such as *magister noster, dominus,* and even *doctus* are Christian. Hegendorff does not list the usual epithets for the ranks of church and state but instead quotes epithets from Erasmus's *De copia:* "a man both learned and good, or a man learned even as good, a man as learned as good, a man no less good than cultured, a man not less in learning than in character, a man equally as cultured as honest," and so on.[20]

Hegendorff's *Ratio* may also have drawn on Erasmus's *Formula,* the notes on letter writing that had been pirated perhaps as early as 1519 from one of Erasmus's manuscripts (Henderson, "Erasmian Ciceronians" [1992], 279–280). Hegendorff could have seen an early edition of it at the press for which he was preparing his own *Ratio epistolarum conscribendarum compendiaria:* Valentin Schumann published both works in Leipzig in 1520. Like Erasmus in the *Formula,* Hegendorff cites pseudo-Libanius's definition of the letter as private conversation, yet he describes letter writing as an art.[21] Hegendorff's treatise outlines the rhetoric of eleven types of letters: *familiaris, suasoria, dissuasoria, exhortatoria, dehortatoria, petitoria, narratoria, gratulatoria, commendatoria, objurgatoria, consolatoria.* Although he does not suggest, as Erasmus does, that they might be classified as demonstative, deliberative, and judicial, he does share Erasmus's interest in topics of invention. He echoes the *Formula* in applying to the letter of persuasion (*suasoria*) the commonplaces of the deliberative oration described by Quintilian: the honorable, the useful, and the easy. In treating deliberative letters in the *Formula,* Erasmus had sought "to reduce the entire discussion to a brief compass, the honourable, the profitable, the easy, or possible" (CWE 25:265).

The title of Hegendorff's first treatise on letter writing, *Ratio epistolarum conscribendarum compendiaria,* deliberately echoes that of Erasmus's recently published handbook of theology, *Ratio seu methodus compendio perveniendi ad veram theologiam* (Basel 1519), an enlarged version of the *Methodus* that had accompanied his 1516 edition of the New Testament. *Ratio* and *methodus* are the words that humanist teachers used to describe efficient instruction. The interest in method has been traced back to Erasmus's own teachers, the Brethren of the Common Life (Codina Mir 1968). It included the custom we now take for granted of teaching a standardized curriculum, graded for difficulty, through which students could move by examination, but it reached extremes we no longer accept, especially in the "single method" of Petrus Ramus and his followers.[22] In his *Ratio,* or *methodus* for learning theology, Erasmus observes that the process is as important as the content of study: "He hastens enough who never strays from the way. He often doubles both expense and labor who finally arrives at that which he intended with frequent errors and by long, roundabout ways, if nonetheless he succeeds in arriving. Moreover, he who points out a shortcut assists the studious by a two-fold favor, first that he may reach his goal sooner, then that he may attain it with less labor and expense."[23] Hegendorff's *Ratio* for epistolary rhetoric concludes with a letter of Andreas Palaeosphyra Gundelfingius recommending the book in similar words: "for those are seen to do well who show a certain brief method, so to speak, when the journey may be long, laborious, and rough."[24] Palaeosphyra suggests that Hegendorff has provided such a brief method for letter writing, as have Erasmus for theology, [Johann] Reuchlin [*De rudimentis hebraicis,* 1506, and *De accentibus et orthographia linguae hebraicae,* 1518] for Hebrew; [Johannes] Oecolampadius [*Dragmata graecae literaturae,* 1518] and Melanchthon [*Institutiones graecae grammaticae,* 1518] for Greek; and [Johann Maier von] Eck [*Elementarius dialectice,* 1517] for dialectic. Gilbert (1960, 107–108, 233–235) has shown that Erasmus's controversial textbook of theology helped to fuel a growing demand for brief introductory textbooks entitled *ratio, methodus,* or *compendium.* The publisher who by 1520 had pirated Erasmus's notes on letter writing under the title *Brevissima maximeque compendiaria conficiendarum epistolarum formula* was responding to this demand, and so was Hegendorff. At first glance, Erasmus's 1519 promotion of his own textbook of theology as a useful shortcut appears inconsistent with his attack on lazy students and teachers in the authorized *Opus de conscribendis epistolis* only three years later, but perhaps that complaint of 1522 should be read as a bitter reaction to having been misinterpreted on the issue of teaching method. The goal of Erasmus's many theological works was to restore Christianity by making the word of God more accessible to Christians (Halkin, *Erasmus* [1993], 104–106). In the *Ratio,* Erasmus was advocating humanist philology as a shortcut to a postgraduate discipline still dominated by scholasticism (Halkin, *Erasmus* [1993], 128). A shortcut to rhetoric, and therefore to the immersion in literature that was Erasmus's means not only of teaching biblical hermeneutics to the Christian reader, but also of training children in Christian living, must have impressed him as an entirely different matter.

In spite of its claim to facilitate learning, Hegendorff's *Ratio* is not a successful textbook: its style is discursive and awkward. The work of an inexperienced teacher in a local grammar school, it reveals all too clearly the place that instruction in letter writing occupied in the educational system of the early sixteenth century and in the careers of those who wrote the textbooks. The recent B.A. would teach rhetoric in upper grammar school or at the lowest level of the university arts course to fund postgraduate studies of theology, law, or medicine. After he earned his M.A. in 1521, Hegendorff taught literature at the University of Leipzig and studied law. In 1526 he published a much better textbook of letter writing, *Methodus conscribendi epistolas* (Haguenau: J. Setzer). Hegendorff's Lutheranism is still apparent in the *Methodus.* In copying verbatim Erasmus's list of epithets in the *Opus de conscribendis epistolis,* Hegendorff omits those for the clergy: *Beatissime papa. Pontifex maxime. Amplissime pater. Sanctissime praesul. Vigilantissime pastor. Sacratissime pater, venerande, suspiciende, obseruande, integerrime, religosissime pater* (ASD 1.2:289). The *Methodus* is, however, otherwise uncontroversial. Its emphasis is not so much on religious content as on clear and efficient instruction.

This difference may perhaps be attributed to not only Hegendorff's maturity and the aid of Erasmus's recently published *Opus de conscribendis epistolis*, but also the development of the Lutheran Reform itself. In 1524 Luther had appealed to the aldermen of all German cities to found Christian schools. He wished to popularize humanist education among the middle classes so that more Christians could read the Bible for themselves. Convincing skeptical burghers to give their sons an expensive education in Latin and Greek instead of putting them to work in the family business did not prove easy (Wright 1975). They at least demanded efficiency. The leisurely medieval system of education through what was essentially an apprenticeship would no longer do. Even as Hegendorff was writing the *Methodus*, Philipp Melanchthon was organizing a new high school at Nuremberg so that instruction could proceed by easy stages, the student mastering each level before progressing to the next (Richard [1898] 1974, 129–136). Hegendorff admired Melanchthon, whom he praised in the *Dialogi pueriles* as the author of *Institutiones graecae grammaticae* and the editor of Terence (Bierlaire, "Les 'Dialogi pueriles'" [1980], 395–396). In 1521 Melanchthon authorized the publication of his *Loci communes*. This famous compendium of Lutheran theology won immediate recognition as a model textbook, "the main points distributed by order and procedure and contracted into a method," as Melanchthon later explained to King Henry VIII (Gilbert 1960, 108–109). The German Protestant concern with "method" may be reflected in not only the title of Hegendorff's work, but also its clear question-and-answer structure: a favorite Protestant device for religious instruction was the catechism, and Hegendorff's contribution to the genre was published the same year that his *Methodus* appeared in print.

Hegendorff's *Methodus conscribendi epistolas* is as original as one can expect a rhetoric textbook to be—compare the composition textbooks published today for first-year university English classes—but it draws freely upon Erasmus's *Opus* and perhaps also on the *Formula,* as well as other sources in the rhetorical tradition. Hegendorff composes some model letters himself and selects the rest from classical authors. Under each question, he provides brief explanations, often referring the reader to Erasmus for more detail. He omits all theoretical, satirical, and controversial material in the *Opus* and says nothing about teaching method. He selects only a few formulas from the chapters of the *Opus* that discuss greetings and forms of address, the section that had particularly interested grammarians such as Despauterius. Instead, he focuses his attention on Erasmus's classification of letters into demonstrative, deliberative, and judicial, omitting extraordinary or familiar letters. Hegendorff's discussion of each category seems to be inspired by Erasmus, perhaps with other sources. For example, he describes the demonstrative letter as praise or blame of persons, deeds, or things, but, like Erasmus, he says little about praise of deeds. In suggesting that a person may be praised from goods of the mind or of the body or from qualities external to him, such as honor, kinship, friendship, money, country, Hegendorff might be remembering Erasmus's analysis in the *Formula* (CWE 25:262–263) of an epistle in which Pliny praises the philosopher Euphrates using these commonplaces (*Ep.* 1.10). In schematizing the commonplaces to be used in praising regions, cities, buildings, rivers, fields, and mountains, Hegendorff could be recalling Erasmus's chapter on the demonstrative letter in the *Opus.*

Hegendorff's *Methodus* was a bestseller. It was reprinted more than fifty times, at Antwerp, Paris, Strasbourg, Basel, Cracow, Cologne, Lyons, Mainz, and London, often accompanying other treatises: Erasmus's *Formula,* Juan Luis Vives's *De conscribendis epistolis, libellus vere aureus,* Conrad Celtes's *Methodus conficiendarum epistolarum,* Aurelio Brandolini's *De ratione scribendi libri tres,* and Georgius Macropedius's *Epistolica.* The *Methodus* of Hegendorff and the *Epistolica* of Macropedius, published in tandem, were among the leading textbooks of letter writing in English schools (Baldwin 1944, 1:413, 492, 2:71, 258, 265–268). The revised *Short Title Catalogue* records twelve editions (Plett 1985, 78–79). For the English vernacular reader, *A Panoplie of Epistles; or, A looking Glasse for the vnlearned . . . Gathered and translated out of Latine into English,* by Abraham Fleming (1576), includes a translation of Hegendorff's *Methodus* entitled "An Epitome of Precepts" (Baldwin 1944, 2:50).

Johannes Monhemius Erverveldis (Johann Monheim of Elberfeld), 1509–1564

Another German schoolteacher, Johann Monheim of Elberfeld, author of a number of textbooks and theological works, made unacknowledged use of Hegendorff's *Methodus* in his abridgement of Erasmus's *Opus de conscribendis epistolis.* Born in 1509, Monheim matriculated at the *Collegium montanum* at Cologne on October 9, 1526, promoted M.A. in 1529, then taught school at Essen from 1532 and at Cologne from 1536.[25] For his students there, he published *Desiderii Erasmi Roterodami opus de conscribendis epistolis in compendium redactum* (Cologne: H. Alopecius, 1539). Monheim explains, "We have instituted lecturing to our students on the *Opus de conscribendis epistolis* of Desiderius Erasmus. . . . But since I have considered that this is somewhat larger than either can be expounded conveniently in schools or can be understood rightly by youth (for those things which are explained in a prolix and diffuse way are both grasped and retained with much more difficulty than those which are explained briefly and succinctly), we have contracted that work into this method for the utility of studious young men."[26] After further studies, in 1545 Monheim became rector of a newly founded school at Dusseldorf. In 1549 he published an abridgement (*non solum in methodum coactam, verumetiam in multis locis emendatam, ac restitutam*) of Despauterius's *Ars versificatoria* (Louvain: B. de Grave), which went through many editions. In 1551 he expressed his esteem for Erasmus's theology with an abridgement (*in compendium redacta*) of Erasmus's *Dilucida explanatio symboli quod apostolorum dicitur* and with *Christianae religionis rudimenta ex Desiderii Erasmi Roterodami lucubrationibus,* but he seems finally to have abandoned Erasmus's *via media.* In 1560 he came under attack from the Jesuits for writing a catechism based on Calvin's *Institutio.* He died on September 9, 1564, before his enemies had succeeded in obtaining his dismissal.

Monheim faithfully abridges Erasmus's classification, description, and illustration of the types of epistolary argument, but he makes it more consistent, eliminates much that is controversial in Erasmus's *Opus,* and often substitutes material from Hegendorff's *Methodus.* Monheim omits two chapters on the "mixed" letter and tries to rationalize Erasmus's sometimes chaotic discussion of the "unmixed" letter, though he retains the category of extraordinary or familiar letters.[27] His discussion of *exordia* abridges Hegendorff rather than Erasmus. Monheim also prefers Hegendorff's discussion of the letter of reconciliation. From Erasmus's copious illustrations, he selects only a few sample letters. He eliminates the letter satirizing court life (CWE 25:195–197). For Erasmus's notorious praise of marriage and the outlined reply to it, Monheim substitutes Hegendorff's sample letters of persuasion (to study civil law) and dissuasion (from becoming a merchant). Like Hegendorff, Monheim omits the first eleven chapters of the *Opus,* beginning his abridgement with the definition that opens the *Methodus:* "The letter is a conversation between those who are apart."[28] He summarizes Erasmus's prescriptions for greeting and farewell more fully than Hegendorff, and in copying Erasmus's list of epithets he includes those for the clergy, but he omits all the passages in which Erasmus satirizes or parodies medieval formulas. His abridgement of the *Opus de conscribendis epistolis* had a limited success. It was reprinted at least twice (Basel 1541 and Paris 1544).

Georgius Macropedius (Joris van Lanckvelt), 1487–1558

One of the treatises most often published with Hegendorff's *Methodus* in the sixteenth and early seventeenth centuries was the *Epistolica* (Antwerp: J. Hillenius, 1543) of Georgius Macropedius, who devoted a lifetime of hard work to teaching and administration in the schools of the Brethren of the Common Life.[29] Born at Gemert in 1487, Macropedius entered the house of the Brethren at nearby Bois-le-Duc ('s-Hertogenbosch) in 1502, and he probably studied in their school, which claimed Erasmus as an alumnus, though Erasmus had little good to say about his experience there (Bainton, *Erasmus* [1969], 12). Johannes Nemius described Macropedius as self-taught; he seems, at any rate, not to have attended a university. By 1510 he had begun teaching at Bois-le-Duc, and his *Asotus,* the first of the Latin school plays for which he is best known today, was composed there. He was ordained a priest and went on to teach at Liege (ca. 1525–1529) and Utrecht (ca. 1529–1556). Troubled with gout, he returned to Bois-le-Duc and died there in July 1558. He was buried in the church of the

Brethren. In addition to twelve plays, Macropedius published Latin school songs (*carmina scholastica*) and textbooks of grammar, dialectic, and prosody, a calendar with rules of calculation, and liturgical readings from the Epistles and Gospels with grammatical notes. After his death, Johannes Nemius and other humanist scholars sung his praises in *Apotheosis D. Georgii Macropedii extemporali carmine* (Antwerp: *ex officina G. Silvii,* 1565).

Macropedius's *Epistolica* is divided into two parts, the first treating invention, the second, disposition and elocution. Although Macropedius does not acknowledge Erasmus, in the first part he draws on the *Opus de conscribendis epistolis* in prescribing forms of greeting, address, and farewell and in classifying letters. He names five categories, demonstrative, deliberative, judicial, *didascalium* or *dialecticum* (Erasmus's letter of discussion), and *indicativum* (Erasmus's extraordinary or familiar class). Macropedius provides his own sample letters, and he is more rigid in applying rhetorical precepts to letter writing than Erasmus. Although he concedes that the structure of the letter varies with the type of argument, he nevertheless defines for each type except the familiar a formal structure based on the divisions of the oration. This is a procedure that Erasmus had criticized in Francesco Negro's *De modo epistolandi* (Henderson, "Erasmus on the Art of Letter-Writing" [1983], 338–339). Macropedius emphasizes art much more, individual judgment and the demands of decorum much less, than Erasmus.

This is not to suggest that Erasmus completely rejects rhetoric in letter writing. As we have seen, he finds far too limited to encompass either ancient or contemporary practice the classical conception of the letter as conversational in style—that is, clear, brief, colloquial, and seemingly artless. He distinguishes a letter from a book mainly by audience: the letter is written on a particular occasion with a particular correspondent in mind, whereas the book addresses a wider, ideally a learned and sympathetic, audience (CWE 25:14). This distinction by audience permits Erasmus to quote classical definitions and classifications of the letter yet to apply to the genre the categories and topics of the oration. In discussing the letter of persuasion, Erasmus briefly describes forms of argumentation (e.g., dilemma, enumeration, induction, inference, syllogism), though he holds an unidentified colleague responsible for finding this material among his papers and inserting it into his treatise on letter writing (CWE 25:110). In the same section, he outlines the divisions of the oration that in the v had come to be applied to the letter—*exordium, narratio, propositio, divisio, confirmatio*—but warns against using them rigidly (CWE 25:65). In a letter to William Blount, Lord Mountjoy, that accompanied a draft of his treatise on letter writing in 1499 or, more likely in 1509, Erasmus criticized Giammario Filelfo's *Novum epistolarium* for summarizing rules of rhetoric that the student might better read in Cicero or Quintilian. Erasmus seems not to mind that the *De componendis et ornandis epistolis* of Giovanni Sulpizio of Veroli does much the same thing. Perhaps Sulpizio simply does it better (Henderson, "Erasmus on the Art of Letter-Writing" [1983], 337–338). In his chapters on teaching method,

Erasmus assumes, as his contemporaries did, that the letter is an appropriate exercise in rhetoric for the student who is not yet sophisticated enough to write an oration, but he warns frequently against allowing the student to rely on rules and collect formulas before he has carefully thought through the assignment. Erasmus is concerned especially to exercise the young writer's judgment.

Macropedius devotes part of his first book and all his second to aspects of rhetorical theory that the modern reader would find irrelevant to the letter. In the first part he outlines the theory of *status* or *stasis* in the forensic oration.[30] The issues or *staseis* in a case are the conjectural (consideration of the motive and ability of the accused to commit the crime), the legal (controversy over the law itself), and the juridical (justification of the act or mitigation of the crime). In the second part he introduces a long catalog of rhetorical figures with a few observations on organization and style. Because he has previously discussed the divisions of the oration, his remarks on organization here are limited to advice about the order of commonplaces (treat boyhood before adolescence, the good before the expedient) and of arguments (treat alien matters first, then those close to home). He then outlines the principles of style: its purposes (to teach, to delight, to move), its qualities (purity, propriety, clarity, charm, and so on), and its characters (sublime, middle, humble). He observes that letters are written sometimes in the middle but more often in the humble style. The humble style, however, has its own elegance and excludes neither tropes nor schemes. Whatever the classical theory of letter writing, Macropedius conceives the letter unequivocally as an exercise in rhetoric; it is, as he says in the preface to his students at Utrecht, one of the best means of learning to speak and write well.

Other schoolmasters no doubt agreed with Macropedius, for the *Epistolica* went through many editions. Those published in the Low Countries, with rare exceptions, retained the original title, but those published in Germany and England were entitled *Methodus de conscribendis epistolis*. Sebald Mayer (Dillingen, 1561) seems to have been responsible both for the change of title and for including with Macropedius's treatise an *Epitome praeceptionum de paranda copia verborum et rerum, per quaestiones*. Because its author, Johannes Rivius, was not named, English educators assumed that this treatise was also by Macropedius.[31] Some of these editions also include an *epitome* of the section of Erasmus's *Opus de conscribendis epistolis* on kinds of oratorical arguments (ASD 1.2:370–400, CWE 25:110–129) under the title *de nouem speciebus argumentationum Rhetoricarum, rem omnem breuiter explicans*. The material thus collected in one convenient volume proved ideal for schools because the student no longer had to buy three separate textbooks of rhetoric: Erasmus's *De copia*, his *Opus de conscribendis epistolis*, and a treatise of rhetorical figures. Together, Macropedius and Rivius provided an introduction to all these aspects of rhetoric for students of Latin (Baldwin 1944, 1:363, 2:71, 181–182, 194). The vernacular reader in England might find some of Macropedius's instructions in Angel Day's *The English Secretary* (1586) (Baldwin 1944, 2:51). Likewise, John Brinsley in his *Lvdus Litterarivs; or, The Grammar Schoole* (1612) translates "Precepts of Composition or placing the words in Latine, as they are set downe by Macropedius, in the end of his method of making Epistles" (Baldwin 1944, 2:257).

Johannes Nemius (Jan Goverts), fl. 1530s to 1550s

A compatriot of Erasmus and Macropedius, Johannes Nemius seems to have been at the University of Cologne when Monheim published an abridgement of Erasmus's *Opus de conscribendis epistolis*. Nemius was, like Macropedius, a priest and teacher in the Low Countries.[32] He took his Latin name from his birthplace, Bois-le-Duc (*Nemus Ducis* or *Silva Ducis,* in Latin). The dates of his birth and death are unknown, and the details of his career are obscure. In July 1537 he enrolled in the faculty of arts at Cologne and because of his poverty had to pay his fee in installments. He acquired his licentiate in liberal arts in 1541. From the prefaces to his works, we learn that he taught at Cologne, at Liege, and from 1550 to 1552 at Nijmegen. From 1556 to 1559, he administered the *schola principalis* (combined Latin schools) at Amsterdam. More than once he seems to have returned to Bois-le-Duc. He served as rector of the school there in his last years. Nemius wrote Latin poetry, a Latin version of the legend of Tijl Uilenspiegel, and textbooks of grammar and rhetoric. Two of these textbooks adapted Erasmus's works for the school at Nijmegen. The first, dedicated September 1, 1550, was an edition of Erasmus's *Syntaxis,* with annotations by Nemius that drew upon Erasmus's *De copia, Opus de conscribendis epistolis, Adagia,* and annotations on the New Testament. The second was his *Epitome ex opere Desiderii Erasmi Roterodami de conscribendis epistolis* (Antwerp 1552).

The so-called *Epitome* is really a compilation from Despauterius's *Syntaxis,* Macropedius's *Epistolica,* and several of Erasmus's literary and rhetorical works: his *Opus de conscribendis epistolis, Brevissima maximeque compendiaria conficiendarum epistolarum formula, Ecclesiastes, De copia, Colloquia,* and commentary on *Nux,* then attributed to Ovid. Nemius does not name Despauterius or Macropedius as sources, but he freely acknowledges his borrowings from Erasmus's works in the title, preface, and text of his treatise.[33] From the *Colloquia* he excerpts formulas of greeting and farewell, and from *Ecclesiastes,* Erasmus's rhetoric of preaching, he quotes a long passage on consolation. Most often, however, he merely refers the reader to Erasmus's works: to *Ecclesiastes,* books II and III, on the *propositio* of a speech, on commonplaces of praise and persuasion, on St. Paul's technique of exhortation, on amplification, and on *status;* to *De copia* on schemes that produce *enargia,* on *exempla,* and on amplification; to Erasmus's commentary on amplification in *Nux.* Frequently, too, Nemius recommends reading Quintilian and other classical rhetoricians.

Nemius's citations reflect his conviction that most letter writing requires a mastery of rhetoric. He follows Macropedius in imposing the divisions of the oration on demonstrative, deliberative, and judicial letters, in expanding Erasmus's brief remarks on the argument of the demonstrative letter, and in explaining *status* in the judicial letter. Nemius, however, is more faithful to Erasmus's conception of letter writing than Hegendorff, Monheim, or Macropedius had been. By omitting Erasmus's controversial discussion of style and emphasizing rhetorical rules, they had unraveled his complex interweaving of *sermo* and *contentio*, imitation and art, classical models and contemporary customs. Nemius not only preserves Erasmus's synthesis but also clarifies it by distinguishing "familiar" from "artificial" (demonstrative, deliberative, and judicial) letters.

Nemius excerpts chapters from both the *Formula* and the *Opus* in which Erasmus develops this synthesis: first, Erasmus's reply in the *Formula* to those who argue that letter writing is not an art, then the chapters of the *Opus* on structure, clarity, and style (*De ordine epistolari, De perspicuitate epistolae,* and *De stylo et habitu epistolae*), and finally the chapters in the *Formula* on imitation and on exercise. The argument that Nemius compiles from Erasmus might be paraphrased as follows: The most intimate letters to friends do not require artifice. Moreover, regardless of whether a letter is "unmixed" or "mixed" in purpose, its structure should arise naturally from the argument rather than seem to be imposed artificially according to the rules of rhetoric. Yet those who think that rhetoric is not applicable to letter writing are clearly mistaken. Some, for example, make a fetish of clarity. Indeed, clarity is essential when the writer addresses a man who lacks scholarship or good humor or leisure, but learned obscurity, such as Greek phrases and recondite allusions, sometimes serves special purposes in letter writing. The writer must adapt his style to the argument and circumstances of the letter and the personality of his correspondent. He learns to do this by reading and imitating a variety of good models, especially Cicero, Pliny, and Poliziano, and by painstaking and frequent practice in writing.

Nemius compares Erasmus's views on style to those expressed by Poliziano in the first letter of his own correspondence and concludes his excerpt from Erasmus's chapter on imitation in the *Formula* by referring the reader to Poliziano's correspondence with Paolo Cortesi and Erasmus's own *Ciceronianus*. The comparison of Erasmus and Poliziano was probably inspired by Despauterius's *Ars epistolica,* from which Nemius also takes a distinction among three kinds of salutation: *tacita vel subaudita, brevis,* and *absoluta, id est, plena seu perfecta.*[34] It proves, however, that Despauterius was not the only contemporary of Erasmus who interpreted the *Opus de conscribendis epistolis* and the related *Formula* as an answer to the Ciceronians.

Nemius then repeats Erasmus's classification of letters and abridges his discussion of each category, but he chooses to treat the familiar letter first, then the "artificial." His reorganization of Erasmus's treatise reflects the contemporary concern with process in education. The student should begin with those letters that require least artifice and proceed gradually to those that require most, meanwhile learning the rules of rhetoric. Thus, Nemius reviews the species of familiar letters even before he discusses the parts of the letter. He next describes those parts common to all letters, *salutatio, valedictio,* and *superscriptio.* Only after he has concluded his discussion of familiar letters does he describe those parts that are special to "artificial" letters—that is, *exordium, narratio, propositio, confirmatio, confutatio, peroratio.* Nemius may have borrowed this distinction between common and special parts from the *Epistolica,* but, unlike Macropedius, he explicitly limits rhetoric to "artificial" letters. In effect, by reordering Erasmus's classification of letters, he has clarified the argument of the *Opus de conscribendis epistolis.*

In its selection and arrangement of sources, Nemius's *Epitome* is much more original than its title suggests. Unfortunately, its shelf life was limited by the escalating religious controversy of the Reformation and Counter-Reformation. To judge by the adaptations of Erasmus by Despauterius, Pontanus, Macropedius, and Nemius, Erasmus's influence on education in the Low Countries remained strong up to the 1560s, in spite of attacks on his religious works by Louvain theologians. The *Encomium matrimonii,* published separately in 1518 and as a sample letter of persuasion in the *Libellus de conscribendis epistolis* of 1521 and the *Opus de conscribendis epistolis* of 1522, had drawn their fire. The 1546 index of the Louvain theologians condemned some editions of the Bible incorporating Erasmus's work as a New Testament editor and translator, and the 1558 index banned French and Flemish translations of his *Liber de sarcienda ecclesiae concordia.* On the other hand, the 1546 index was headed by a decree of the Emperor Charles V that specified the textbooks approved for use in schools. Among these was the *Syntaxis* of Erasmus. Following this initiative, the theologians of Louvain included in the 1550 and 1558 catalogs a list of approved textbooks, adding to Erasmus's *Syntaxis* his *De copia, De conscribendis epistolis, De civilitate morum puerilium, Apopthegmata,* and *Similia* (Bujanda 1984–2002, 2:42–43, 62–64, 374–375, 378, 399). By implication the textbooks not explicitly named were banned. We have seen, however, that in 1552 Nemius dared to cite *Ecclesiastes* and even the *castiora Colloquia,* though both had previously been condemned by the Sorbonne (Bujanda 1984–2002, 2:46–64).

The lines of religious conflict hardened in the late 1550s. In 1555 the principle that the ruler would decide the state religion was established by the Peace of Augsburg. The same year, Cardinal Caraffa, intransigent opponent of the Reformers, was elected Pope Paul IV. These events ended an era of hope that reform of the Church would restore Christian unity. The Peace of Augsburg officially recognized Lutheranism, the Council of Trent (1545–1563) was in the process of defining the Church's irreconcilable differences with the Reformers, Calvinism was spreading, and power had passed into the hands of a new and less-temperate generation than the one inspired by Erasmus: King Henry VIII and King Francis I had died in 1547, and on October 25, 1555, Emperor Charles V resigned his sovereignty of the Low Countries. Gradually divesting himself of his other responsibilities, he retired to Spain to spend his last days in peace. One of the most effective instruments of the Counter-Reformation, the Society of Jesus, had been founded in 1540. Another, the papal *Index librorum prohibitorum,* had been in preparation since the late 1540s. When it was promulgated by Pope Paul IV in 1559, censorship, attempted with varying success in many states of Europe, ceased to be merely a regional issue (Bujanda 1984–2002, 5:91; Green 1964, 145–146, 158, 177–197).

A Papal Index of 1554/1555 had banned the whole works of many Protestant authors, including Melanchthon, Hegendorff, Rivius, and Johann Sturm, but the publishing industry of Venice had blocked its promulgation (Grendler 1977, 95–96). The Pauline Index, printed and promulgated at Rome in January 1559, proved even more severe, condemning the whole works of about 550 authors and about sixty publishers, anonymous works printed within the past forty years, many editions of the Bible, including all in the vernaculars, and works "not heretical, but . . . judged to be anticlerical, immoral, lascivious, or obscene" (116–117). This was the first index to condemn Erasmus's *Opus de conscribendis epistolis* and *Brevissima maximeque compendiaria conficiendarum epistolarum formula.* The entry on Erasmus reads, "Desiderius Erasmus of Rotterdam with all his commentaries, annotations, scholia, dialogues, letters, censures, translations, books, and writings, even if they contain nothing at all against religion or concerning religion."[35] A wave of book burnings followed: between ten thousand the twelve thousand volumes in Venice on March 18, 1559 alone (Grendler 1977, 120). The Tridentine Index of 1564 moderated the severity of the previous index in the case of a few major authors. Of the works of Erasmus, "it banned six titles: the *Colloquia, Moriae encomium, Lingua, Institutio christiani matrimonii, Epistola . . . de interdicto esu carnium,* and the Tomitano translation of the *Paraphrasis in evangelium Matthaei.* But it also insisted upon expurgation by a Catholic theological faculty of all his other religious works" (146). In general it tried to substitute official expurgation for outright prohibition of books, but the Church lacked the resources for the task. Of Erasmus's works, only two were officially expurgated: the *Adagia* in 1575 and the *Apophthegmata* in either 1577 or 1583 (Grendler and Grendler 1976, 6). Local and private expurgation of books was not permitted for decades, and new names were meanwhile added the list of authors prohibited, for instance, Monheim, Petrus Ramus, and Valentinus Erythraeus in an index promulgated by Sixtus V in 1590. Clandestine defiance of the index was risky. In early September 1570, thousands of volumes confiscated in surprise raids on twenty-five or more bookstores were publicly burned on the Piazza San Marco in Venice. Records of the Italian Inquisition have largely disappeared, but there were certainly raids on booksellers in other cities and on some private libraries. Surviving documents show that Erasmus's works, including such textbooks as the *Opus de conscribendis epistolis,* were among the books seized (Grendler 1977, 116–121, 162–169; Grendler and Grendler 1976, 4–5, 7–9).

Whereas enforcement of the papal index was strict in Italy, elsewhere in Europe it varied. In Bavaria and in the Spanish Low Countries, rigorous enforcement was delayed until after the promulgation of the Tridentine Index, which was reprinted with appendices there (Bujanda 1984–2002, 2:13). Ultimately, public opinion ended the use of Erasmus's textbook on letter writing in the Spanish Low Countries. In Antwerp, Nemius's *Epitome* of the *Opus de conscribendis epistolis* was published again in 1556 and in 1564 or 1565,[36] and Erasmus's *Opus de conscribendis epistolis* in 1566. In August of that year, discontent with Spanish rule and religious repression vented itself in widespread attacks on church images and clergy. This popular reaction only invited more extreme repression. Soon the Duke of Alva was appointed Spanish governor and the long revolt of the Netherlands, led by William of Orange, began (Green 1964, 234–244). Writing of the school at Bois-le-Duc, M. A. Nauwelaerts observes that before the iconoclasm Erasmus was honored and his works were used in the classroom. After the iconoclasm, Erasmus's name wholly lost public sympathy and disappeared from school life. Thereafter, the recently founded Jesuit college at Cologne exercised increasing influence on the school at Bois-le-Duc (*Latijnse School* 1974, 255–259).

Georgius Wibotius Puteolanus (Joris Wybo of Pitthem), ca. 1530–1576

The careers of Georgius Wybotius (or Vibotius) and Hannardus Gamerius illustrate the effects of these religious and political conflicts on teachers in the Low Countries. Neither seems to have used Erasmus's *Opus de conscribendis epistolis* as a direct source for their textbooks of letter writing, but they did make unacknowledged use of its adaptations by Macropedius and Hegendorff. Wibotius was born at Pitthem in West Flanders about 1530 and studied at Louvain. His life was troubled by continuous clashes with the authorities. By 1559 he was a Protestant minister at Antwerp. As a result of the iconoclasm there, the ministers were banished in April 1567, and Wybotius went to Emden. When the forces of the Duke of Alva threatened that city, he joined other refugees from the Netherlands in England by 1568 and died in London in June 1576.[37] It was his earlier work as a schoolmaster, however, that produced his *Compendium rhetorices,* accompanied by an *Artis epistolicae compendiolum* (Antwerp: J. Withagius, 1556). In the preface to his pupils at Menin, he cites Erasmus in defense of his efforts to digest the precepts of rhetoric into a compendium for young students.

Together the *Compendium rhetorices* and *Artis epistolicae compendiolum* treat the same topics as Macropedius's *Epistolica.* Like the *Epistolica,* the *Compendium rhetorices* covers invention, disposition, and elocution, though the section on disposition is brief. That on invention describes the parts of the oration and demonstrative, deliberative, and judicial arguments, including under the last a consideration of *status.* The section on elocution catalogs figures of speech. From this general survey of rhetoric Wybotius has separated the specific rules of letter writing. Having quoted Macropedius's definition of the letter and named its three parts, *salutatio, valedictio, et superscriptio,* Wybotius catalogs and describes the species of letters. His classification—demonstrative, deliberative, judicial, and familiar or *indicativum*—is that of Erasmus as revised by Macropedius. Wybo concludes his *Artis epistolicae compendiolum* by recommending the letters of Erasmus as models.

Hannardus Gamerius Mosaeus (Van Gameren), fl. 1550s to 1570s

On the other side of the religious controversy in the Netherlands is Hannardus Gamerius Mosaeus. Gamerius was born in the Low Countries, perhaps at Nederhemert near Heusden on the Maas River (hence Mosaeus). His birthplace and education, however, have been a source of confusion for biographers.[38] Henry de Vocht (1951–1955, 4:315–317) describes him as a student at the Trilingual College of Louvain during the presidency of John Reynders (1544–1559). He earned his licentiate in medicine but became professor of Greek at the University of Ingolstadt in 1564. There Gamerius, encouraged by Duke Albert of Bavaria, wrote Latin poems, the play *Pornius, tragoedia vere sacra,* and polemics against the Reformation. When the University of Ingolstadt came into the hands of the Jesuits, he returned to the Netherlands. In 1568 he became director of the Latin school at Tongres, and by 1571 he was teaching in the Latin school at Harderwijk in Gelderland. Entering the service of Don Juan of Austria, who was made governor of the Low Countries for Spain in 1576, Gamerius became his apologist. Perhaps Gamerius was a victim of the civil war; the place and date of his death are not known.

Gamerius's textbook of letter writing bears the pretentious title *Authoritates Ciceronis, Plinii et aliorum tam veterum quam recentium scriptorum in conscribendis epistolis observandae, et ad certas quasdam regulas redactae, nunc autem juvandorum studiorum gratia in lucem editae et pulcherrimis exemplis illustratae* (Ingolstadt: A. and S. Weissenhorn, 1566). It implies that his sources are primarily classical "authorities," especially Cicero and Pliny. In fact, he has done little more than edit the treatises of Hegendorff and Francesco Negro. Gamerius must have written the first section of the treatise, a bare outline of rules, with Hegendorff's *Methodus* before him. He does not copy Hegendorff's treatise verbatim, but the differences in the content and form of the two works are negligible except that in this section Gamerius omits examples. The rest of his treatise reproduces Francesco Negro's *De modo epistolandi* (Venice, 1488), except that Gamerius has substituted the names of persons and places in northern Europe for the Italian names in some of Negro's sample letters. Only two letters are his own, those at the beginning and end of the treatise addressed to his patron, Abbot Georgius Neupeck. Gamerius acknowledges Negro, but only as the source of a definition of the letter. Perhaps that citation at the beginning of the material borrowed from Negro would have been considered sufficient by a contemporary reader, and Gamerius's silence about his borrowings from Hegendorff's *Methodus* is perhaps understandable in the context of Counter-Reformation censorship. The theological faculty at Louvain had condemned the seemingly innocuous *Methodus* as early as 1546 in its *Catalogus et declaratio librorum reprobatorum* (Bujanda 1984–2000, 2:148–149), and, as we have seen, Hegendorff's works were on the Papal Indices of 1554/1555 and 1559. Gamerius may have been attempting to provide students and teachers loyal to the Church with an acceptable alternative to Hegendorff's popular textbook. No doubt, too, he was under pressure from his patron to publish. In any case, contemporaries seem not to have objected to what we would consider plagiarism: his treatise was twice reprinted with Andreas Diether's *Thesaurus epistolarum contexendarum* (Cologne: J. Gymnicus, 1577, and Antwerp, 1581).

Valentinus Erythraeus Lindaviensis, 1521–1576

Erasmus's teaching methods exerted a strong influence on reformers in the Protestant cities and states of Germany, such as Philipp Melanchthon and Johann Sturm, but, as I have argued elsewhere, their urgent need to educate Luther's "priesthood of all believers" in humanist rhetoric and dialectic as a basis for both scriptural exegesis and theological debate pushed them into a new variety of Ciceronianism (Henderson, "Erasmian Ciceronians"). Like Erasmus, Melanchthon used the rules of rhetoric to analyze texts for imitation, but he was far more interested than Erasmus in dialectic as a tool of textual analysis, and he tended to narrow Erasmus's reading list of classical authors by distinguishing a hierarchy of imitation: while the student could learn techniques of argument from many writers, for diction he should imitate only writers of the Golden Age of Latin, especially Cicero, Terence, Caesar, and Livy. Cicero should be his special model for both clear argument and pure diction. As rector of the Protestant Gymnasium and Academy of Strasbourg, Johann Sturm prepared a selection from Cicero's letters to be used as the principal text in the graded instruction of the gymnasium. The student learned Latin grammar by exercises designed to tie his language as closely as possible to the purity of the original: parsing, noting words and expressions, changing the case of a noun or the mood, tense, or person of a verb, substituting a synonym, translating from Cicero to the vernacular and back again. After studying some rhetoric and dialectic in the upper grades of the gymnasium, he was allowed finally to analyze his Ciceronian model and imitate it closely by addition, ablation, or alteration—that is, expanding or contracting words or arguments or changing their order. Sturm considered this exercise valuable even for the mature writer.

From about 1550 to 1575, Sturm shared his duties as professor of rhetoric (that is, giving public lectures to university-level students in what eventually became the academy) with his colleague Valentinus Erythraeus (Schindling 1977, 210–212). Born at Lindau in 1521, Erythraeus studied in the Latin school there, then at Strasbourg and Wittenberg before Sturm called him to Strasbourg. He was instructing the fourth class of the gymnasium there in 1547, and in 1565

Sturm addressed him as professor of ethics.[39] He edited, annotated, and enlarged several of Sturm's works, and he published academic orations, textbooks of grammar, rhetoric, and dialectic, and commentaries on Cicero's orations. In 1569, Sturm wrote to a special assembly of his concern that Erythraeus's plan to teach letter writing would be an obstacle to their shared teaching of speaking and the orators (Spitz and Tinsley 1995, 337). In 1573, Erythraeus published his course of lectures, *De ratione legendi, explicandi, et scribendi epistolas, libri tres* (Strasbourg: B. Jobin for N. Wyriot), acknowledging his reliance on Brandolini and Vives,[40] but principally on Erasmus's *Opus de conscribendis epistolis*. His overall description of the genre follows categories of dialectic (e.g., final, efficient, material, formal causes), but his classification of letters—book 1, demonstrative, book 2, deliberative, book 3, judicial and extraordinary or familiar letters—synthesizes Erasmus with letter types listed in two ancient Greek treatises.[41] This emphasis on Greek rhetoric reflects Protestant teaching of the original languages of the Bible, but it makes the textbook cumbersome. Some of the sample letters are in Greek, such as epistles of St. Paul. The Latin examples are primarily from Cicero. As his title suggests—"on the method of reading, explicating, and writing letters"—Erythraeus demonstrates the use of rhetoric and dialectic to analyze models for imitation by the writer. The treatise was reprinted at Strasbourg in 1576, though the previous year Erythraeus had become rector of the gymnasium, formerly at Nuremberg, that had moved to nearby Altdorf. He died in 1576.

Melchior Junius Witebergensis (Melchior Jungk of Wittenberg), 1545–1604

An alumnus of Sturm's curriculum succeeded Erythraeus as professor at Strasbourg. Born at Wittenberg on October 27, 1545, Melchior Junius was sent by his father Melchior Jungk, a schoolmaster and pastor, to Strasbourg in 1559 and remained there, teaching the third and second classes before he took the chair of rhetoric in the academy. He published many textbooks, and in 1581, when Sturm was dismissed, he became acting rector. Junius had a lively interest in what we would call the social sciences, but for him they were moral sciences teaching the "wise and eloquent piety" that was the educational goal of Sturm (Bolgar 1954, 350), as of Erasmus before him. Junius considered history, politics, and economics essential to the good orator, and he exercised the students in declamations on political themes. Both the school statutes and the ten volumes of student orations that he published from 1589 to 1603 show that Junius intensified practice in public speaking at Strasbourg, but he modified rather than revolutionized Sturm's program. When he died on January 23, 1604, the school found it impossible to fill adequately his chair of rhetoric.[42]

Like Erythraeus, Junius taught letter writing; he describes his *Scholae rhetoricae de contexendarum epistolarum ratione* (Strasbourg: L. Zetzner, 1587) as based on lectures presented several years earlier. In his preface he says that the student will find much of this art of letter writing in rhetoric but must also observe some special rules. The division of this textbook into four parts—deliberative, demonstrative, judicial, and familiar or extraordinary letters—and some of the types of letters he treats, though not all, are borrowed from Erasmus. He emulates Erasmus's thorough descriptions of each type and cites hundreds of examples, principally from Cicero and the Greek orators Demosthenes, Aeschines, and Isocrates. He describes his teaching method as imitation: "Having divided all Cicero's letters to friends into certain classes, I have tried to show students of eloquence first what arguments should be employed for proving, for moving, and for winning favor in writing individual letters; then the arrangement and treatment of these; then, the outline having been drawn, as it were, how what is discovered in Cicero should be expressed or represented by imitating in this our time, so that the imitation may be concealed, not open, not servile but free. Some difference may be discovered even in likeness."[43] Junius's *Scholae rhetoricae* is an intelligent, practical, and often original adaptation of Erasmus's art of letter writing to the Protestant curriculum.

Conclusions

By the last quarter of the sixteenth-century, the influence of Erasmus's *Opus de conscribendis epistolis* was giving way to new philosophies and methods of teaching rhetoric. Anton Schindling observes that Junius's teaching of rhetoric at Strasbourg reflects the general rise of political science around 1600 (NDB 10:690). An even more significant influence on the teaching of letter writing in northern Europe at the turn of the sixteenth century was Ramism. The ruthlessly efficient separation of dialectic, rhetoric, and the other arts that Petrus Ramus introduced into the humanist curriculum at Paris is a logical development of the sixteenth-century obsession with method, but Ramus was once a student of Sturm, and the roots of his *analysis* of classical texts and *genesis* (composition) by imitation can be traced back to Erasmus's *De ratione studii.*

The gap between humanist theory and schoolroom practice lamented by Grafton and Jardine is obvious in a survey of adaptations of Erasmus's *Opus de conscribendis epistolis,* and the efforts of a governing elite to stifle originality in their civil servants cannot be ruled out as a cause, but in truth, Erasmus's ideal of immersion in classical literature may never have had much chance of implementation in the classroom. He was simply more capable of absorbing and balancing complexities than most human beings can hope to be. He tried to carve a trail between medieval barbarism and Ciceronianism in grammar, between rules and reading in rhetoric, just as he did between Church tradition and reform in theology, but his *via media* crossed treacherous bogs and shifting sands, and others inevitably sought easier paths, even shortcuts. He sometimes did, and sometimes did not, approve their efforts. The case studies presented here suggest many reasons why teachers of rhetoric who admired Erasmus nevertheless rewrote his textbook of letter writing, substituting a few rules or close imitation of a few texts for the absorption of antiquity that he advocated: the ordinary human laziness of students and teachers about which Erasmus complained; the inexperience of young instructors earning their way through graduate school; the pressure on scholars to publish, perhaps even to pilfer or plagiarize or pirate the works of others, in order not to perish in their bids for pupils or patrons; the reluctance of parents to pay for a thorough education or expensive textbooks for their sons; the students' longing for a fast track to lucrative employment. These factors will strike us as oddly familiar today. Others are products of the age, especially of the Reformation that Erasmus helped to begin: the urgent need of each religious sect to indoctrinate the younger generation in its own theology; censorship and persecution, and sometimes the flight, of scholars as religious conflict split Europe into opposing camps and disrupted social order. Under such conditions, what may surprise us is finally that the humanist ideal of a broad liberal arts education to civilize our society and enlighten our souls should have persisted at all, and that so many teachers, then and now, have spent so much of their lives searching for ways to achieve that vision.

Abbreviations for Frequently Cited Works

ADB   *Allgemeine deutsche Biogaphie.* Hrsg. v. die historische Commission bei der königl. Akademie der Wissenschaften. 44 vols. Leipzig: Duncker und Humblot, 1875–1898.

ASD   Erasmus, Desiderius. *Opera omnia* 1.2 and 1.5. Amsterdam: North-Holland Publishing Co., 1971, 1975.

BB   *Bibliotheca Belgica: Bibliographie Générale des Pays-Bas.* Fondée par Ferdinand van der Haeghen, rééditée sous la direction de Marie-Thérèse Lenger. 6 vols. Brussels: Editions Culture et Civilisation, 1979.

BNB   L'Académie Royale des Sciences, des Lettres et des Beaux-arts de Belgique. *Biographie nationale.* 28 vols. Bruxelles, 1866–1944. Supplement in progress 1957– .

CWE   Erasmus, Desiderius. *Collected Works of Erasmus*

NDB   *Neue deutsche Biographie.*

NNBW   *Nieuw Nederlandsch Biografisch Woordenboek.*

Notes

1. I am grateful to the Social Sciences and Humanities Research Council of Canada and the University of Saskatchewan for support of this study; to the staffs of the Bayerische Staatsbibliothek, Munich; the Bodleian Library and St. John's College Library, Oxford, and the Cambridge University Library for their assistance with my research there; and the Bibliotheek van de Rijksuniversiteit, Ghent, Harvard University Library, and the Stiftsbibliothek Klosterneuburg, Austria, for providing me with photocopies of books in their collections.

2. CWE 25:129–145. See von Richthofen (1975) for an interesting example of early seventeenth-century censorship of a copy of the *Opus.*

3. CWE 146–148. On the debate over the letter, see Margolin (ASD 1972, 1.2: 193–196, 1.5:335–382). Sloane has recently published an enlightening discussion of Erasmus's *Encomium matrimonii* in the tradition of declamations (1997, 80–130), with an appendix surveying the question of marriage as a rhetorical exercise (314–319). Sloane, however, makes the questionable assumption (80) that William Blount, Lord Mountjoy, was the addressee of Erasmus's letter. Margolin rightly observes that Erasmus's belated claim in 1523 to have written the letter at the request of Mountjoy, once his student in rhetoric, is probably a defensive fiction (ASD 1972, 1.5:337).

4. Margolin (ASD 1972, 1.5:354). Thomas Wilson's *The Art of Rhetoric* (London: R. Grafton, 1553) includes an English translation of the *Encomium matrimonii.* Sloane (1997, 123) attributes this translation to Wilson himself, but Margolin suggests (ASD 1972, 1.5:359–360) that Wilson adapted an earlier one by Richard Taverner (London: R. Redman, 1533?). In any case, while Wilson was in exile during the reign of Queen Mary I, he was imprisoned for heresy and tortured by the Roman Inquisition, an experience he bitterly blamed on his textbooks of logic and rhetoric in the preface to the second edition of the *Art,* published after his dramatic escape and return to England (London: J. Kingston, 1560). See Wilson (1982, 11, 95–140).

5. See Bujanda (1984–2002), Grendler (1977), Seidel Menchi (1987).

6. John Lyly's *Euphues: The Anatomy of Wit* is a similar story ending in a similar exercise. See Henderson, "Euphues" (1982).

7. Scott ([1910] 1991) remains a useful overview of the Ciceronian controversy.

8. Jolidon, "L'évolution" (1979, 583 n. 1). Fantazzi has translated and annotated Erasmus's *Formula,* CWE 25:258–267, 26:560–562.

9. Jardine, *Erasmus* (1993, 170). "Persuasion" and "encouragement" are Fantazzi's translations (CWE 25:73) for Erasmus's *suasio* and *exhortatio* (ASD 1.2:315), but Sloane (1997, 132 n. 3) observes that these English words do not quite capture the Latin. *Suasio* suggests the rhetorical exercise *suasoria,* a debate that considers both sides of the question in a particular case, even though it argues for one. Erasmus in the chapter cited sums up a long explanation of the difference between *suasio* and *exhortatio:* "Persuasion teaches by proofs; encouragement goads by incentives" (CWE 25:73).

10. Jardine, *Erasmus* (1993, 169–170), compares passages in the *Opus de conscribendis epistolis* to annotations to Jerome's *Epistolae.* Compare her notes (272–273) for the texts.

11. On his life and works, see studies cited in Henderson, "Despauterius' *Syntaxis*" (1988, 185 n. 17).

12. See, for example, Murphy and Davies (1997) nos. 26 (Brack), 35 (Datus), 67 (Lescherius), 81 (Niavis), 84 (Perger), 85 (Perottus), 110 (Valla), 114 (Wimpheling), 116 (Wimpina).

13. The Stiftsbibliothek Klosterneuburg, Austria, has what may be the only surviving copy of the 1509 edition of Despauterius's *Syntaxis.* See Henderson ("Despauterius' *Syntaxis,*" 1988, 193–210) for the text of his citations from Erasmus, especially 209.

14. This parody is modified somewhat in the authorized version, ASD 1.2:282–283. Translations are mine unless otherwise noted. In citing Latin texts, I have silently expanded abbreviations.

15. See Henderson, "Despauterius' *Syntaxis*" (1988, 189–192) and studies cited 190 n. 26.

16. See Bierlaire's biography of Hegendorff, *Contemporaries* 2 (1986): 171–172, and his articles in the Works Cited.

17. Jardine, *Erasmus* (1993, 272 n. 69). In both the early draft of the *Opus de conscribendis epistolis* published by Siberch in 1521 and the authorized edition of 1522 (CWE 25:97), Erasmus cites St. Jerome's letter to Heliodorus as an example of the letter of encouragement (*epistola exhortatoria*).

18. For example, Erasmus admired St. Jerome's skill in argument, but warned against adopting his formulas of salutation (CWE 25:54)

19. . . . *homines ad alios juvandos a deo creatos* (B4v).

20. . . . *viro tum erudito tum probo vel viro docto pariter ac probo, viro tam docto quam bono, viro non minus probo quam literato, viro non inferiori literis quam moribus, viro aeque literato atque incorrupto.* . . . (D1r). Compare CWE 24:365–368.

21. Hegendorf does return to the original Greek rather than quote Erasmus's Latin translation, and elsewhere he cites Libanius on the humble style. Hegendorff's treatise is peppered with Greek phrases and quotations.

22. See Gilbert (1960), Ong (1958), Bruyère (1984).

23. *Et satis festinat, qui nusquam aberrat a via. Saepe & sumptum duplicat, & laborem, qui crebris erroribus, ac longis ambagibus tandem eo pervenit, quo destinarat, si tamen pervenire contingat. Porro qui compendiariam quoque viam indicat, is gemino beneficio juvat studiosum. Primum ut maturius quo tendit pertingat, deinde ut minori labore, sumptuque quod sequitur assequatur* (LB 5: 75).

24. *Bene enim agere videntur qui, ubi laboriosum, salebris respersum, ac longum iter sit, eundum brevem quandam methodum ostendunt* (D3v). Palaeosphyra (Althamer) was, like Hegendorff, a student at Leipzig in 1520. They were about the same age: Althamer was born at Brenz, a village on the upper Danube, toward the end of the fifteenth century. He was to become a leader of the Lutheran Reform. See Hartmann, ADB 1 (1875), 365–366; Karl Schornbaum, NDB 1 (1953), 219.

25. On Monheim's life and works, see Crecelius, ADB, 22 (1885): 167–168; BB 2:175–179; Margolin (1980, 179).

26. *Instituimus discipuis nostris opus Des. Erasmi de conscribendis epistolis praelegere. . . . Verum ubi consideraui hoc aliquanto maius esse, quam uel ut in scholis commode praelegi, uel a iuuentute recte intelligi queat (multo enim difficilius, tum percipiuntur, tum memoriae inhaerent ea, quae prolixe ac diffuse, quam quae breuiter et succincte proponuntur) illud ad utilitatem studiosae pubis in hanc methodum contraximus* (s5r, p. 281).

27. Erasmus lists letters of both conciliation and reconciliation as deliberative, but he then discusses conciliation under friendship, a species of the deliberative letter, and reconciliation under extraordinary letters. Monheim, following Erasmus's original list, separates the letter of conciliation from the letter of friendship and adds Hegendorff's discussion of the letter of reconciliation under the deliberative category. He then omits Erasmus's discussion of this type under the extraordinary category. Copying Erasmus's list of demonstrative letters, Monheim adds descriptions of deeds, perhaps under the influence of Hegendorff, and omits descriptions of prodigies (*monstrorum*). He does not, however, force Erasmus's later chapter on the demonstrative letter into conformity

with either Erasmus's original list or his own. From Erasmus's list of judicial letters, Monheim omits letters of complaint, defense, and threat (*querela, defensio, comminatio*) because Erasmus did not go on to discuss them in separate chapters. To this list he adds the letter of discussion (*disputatoria*), which Erasmus seems to have appended to his treatise as an afterthought.

28. *Epistola est sermo absentis ad absentem.*

29. In his life and works, see Nauwelaerts, ed., *"Brieven"* (1974, 143–161); Best (1972); Nauwelaerts, *Latijnse School* (1974, 135–143, 189, 224–225, 229–231, 233, 248, 261); Dekker (1974); Giebels (1978), with a useful bibliography of scholarship on Macropedius; Lindeman, "Macropedius' *Rebelles*" (1980) and *Two Comedies* (1983).

30. It is possible that Macropedius knew Erasmus's discussion in *Ecclesiastes* applying *stasis* to Scripure (LB 5:858), but he probably drew primarily on classical sources (e.g., *Rhetorica ad Herennium* I.ix.18–19; Quintilian, *Institutio oratoria* III.vi). Sloane's recent study (1997) shows how important *stasis* is to what he calls "contrarianism," the humanist and particularly Erasmian habit of considering both sides of the case in preparation for an argument.

31. This treatise was originally published as the eighth book of Rivius's *De iis disciplinis, quae de sermone agunt, ut sunt Grammatica, Dialectica, Rhetorica, libri XVIII* (Leipzig, 1539). See Müller, ADB (28:709–713). Rivius (August 1, 1500–January 1, 1553) was, like his friend Melanchthon, a German educational reformer. Dr. Frans P. T. Slits alerted me to a letter by Verepaeus (Nauwelaerts, ed., 1974, 293), in which Rivius is identified as the author of this *Epitome.*

32. Nauwelaerts, "De Geschriften van Joannes Nemius" (1950); Nauwelaerts, ed., "Brieven: Goverts" (1957–1958, 1958–1959); Nauwelaerts, *Latijnse School* (1974, 151–154, 189, 223–224); Heesakkers and Kamerbeek (1984, 60–77).

33. Heesakkers and Kamerbeek observe that Nemius's *Apologia Scholae Principalis* "is remarkable because of its very extensive and extremely precise acknowledgement of sources" (1984, XIII). Nemius was certainly more scrupulous than most of his contemporaries in this regard.

34. *Epitome,* B3v. In the first, the greeting is understood, and only the name of the correspondent with an adjective of good or ill will is stated: *Optime pater, Insolentissime fili.* In the second, the name of the writer is omitted but the greeting is expressed: *Salve ter maxime Christiane.* The third is complete, containing the name of the writer, the name of the correspondent, and the greeting: *Joannes Picus Mirandula Angelo Politianus S.D.*

35. *Desiderius Erasmus Roterodamus cum universis commentariis, annotationibus, scholiis, dialogis, epistolis, censuris, versionibus, libris et scriptis suis, etiam si nil penitus contra religionem vel de religione contineant* (Bujanda 1984–2002, 8:429).

36. By J. Latius, the second printing incorrectly dated 1465.

37. On his life and works, see BB 3 (1964): 478–480, 5 (1979): 876–879; A. A. van Shelven, NNBW 3 (1914): cols. 1494–1497; Pettegree (1987, 187–209).

38. J. Fruytier, NNBW 8 (1930): 582–583, reviews the literature. Compare Felix Nève, BNB 7 (1881), cols. 471–472.

39. On his life and teaching, see Halm, ADB 6 (1877): 335–336; Rott (1938, 106–107n.); Schindling (1977, passim); Spitz and Tinsley (1995, 300–301, 329–331, 337).

40. The treatises of Brandolini, Vives, Hegendorff, and Celtis, together with Erasmus's *Formula,* were published at Basel: J. Oporinus, 1549, and in subsequent editions

at Basel, Cologne, and London). The London edition is available in University Microfilms Early English Books 1475–1640, Reel 1725, STC 3542.

41. Kennedy (1983, 71–72) discusses these treatises: *Typoi epistolikoi,* perhaps Hellenistic, and *Epistolimaioi charaktêres,* the treatise of the late Empire that Erasmus
attributes to Libanius. Erasmus contrasts the letter types of the former treatise to his
own classification of letters (CWE 25:72).

42. For his life and works, see Schindling, NDB 10 (1974): 690, and *Humanistische
Hochschule,* 227–235 et passim; Spitz and Tinsley (1995, 41–42).

43. *Ciceronis ex Epistolis familiaribus omnibus certas in classes distinctis, Eloquen-
tiae Studiosis ostendere conatus sum: primum quaenam in singulis contexendis literis
probantia, moventia, conciliantia argumenta adhibenda; deinde cuiusmodi horum col-
locatio et tractatio instituenda; tum primis quasi lineis ductis, quo pacto, quae apud
Ciceronem inveniuntur, hoc nostro tempore imitando sint exprimenda atque effin-
genda, ita ut tecta, non aperta, non servilis, sed libera fiat imitatio. In ipsa quoque simili-
tudine dissimilitudo aliqua deprehendatur* (dedication, dated Strasbourg July 16, 1587,
to the Dukes of Braunschweig and Luneburg, 3v).

Works Cited

Works by Contemporaries

Erasmus, Desiderius. *Collected Works of Erasmus,* 23–24. Edited by Craig R. Thomp-
son. Toronto: University of Toronto Press, 1978.
————. *Collected Works of Erasmus* 25–26. Edited by J. K. Sowards. Toronto: Univer-
sity of Toronto Press, 1985.
————. *Opera omnia.* Edited by Joannes Clericus. 10 vols. Leiden, 1703–6. Reprint,
Hildesheim: Georg Olms Verlagsbuchhandlung, 1962.
Neue deutsche Biographie. Hrsg. v. der historischen Kommission bei der bayerischen
Akademie der Wissenschaften. In progress. Berlin: Duncker und Humblot, 1953– .
Nieuw Nederlandsch Biografisch Woordenboek. Edited by P. C. Molhuysen, P. J. Blok,
Fr. K. H. Kossmann, et al. 10 vols. Leiden: A. W. Sijthoff's Uitgevers-Maatschappij
N.V., 1911–37.

Primary Sources

Bujanda, J. M. de, directeur. *Index des livres interdits.* 11 vols. Sherbrooke, Québec:
Editions de l'Université de Sherbrooke; Genève: Librairie Droz, 1984–2002.
Despauterius, Johannes. *Ars epistolica . . . ex Dato: Sulpitio: Nigro: Herasmo: Badio:
Bebelio: et ipso Cicerone: caeterisque vere latinis diligenter excerpta multo copiosius
quam post Syntaxin habeatur. Recognita & castigata a Despauterio.* N.p., n.d. St.
John's College, Oxford, c. 3.16 (10).
Erasmus, Desiderius. *Brevissima maximeqve compendiaria conficiendarum epistolarum
formula.* Antwerp: M. Hillenius, July 23, 1521. Cambridge University Library,
Bb*.10.29.
————. *Copia: Foundation of the Abundant Style: De duplici copia verborum ac rerum
commentarii duo.* Translated and annotated Betty I. Knott. CWE 24:284–659.
————. *A Formula for the Composition of Letters: Conficiendarum epistolarum formula.*
Translated by and annotated Charles Fantazzi. CWE 25:258–67; 26:559–62.

————. *Libellus de conscribendis epistolis*. Cambridge: J. Siberch, 1521. University Microfilms Early English Books 1475–1640, Reel 1752, STC 10496.

————. *On the Writing of Letters; De conscribendis epistolis*. Translated and annotated by Charles Fantazzi. CWE 25:12–254; 26:493–559.

Erythraeus, Valentinus. *De ratione legendi, explicandi, et scribendi epistolas, libri tres* Strasbourg: B. Jobin for N. Wyriot, 1573. Bodleian Library, Oxford 8∞. E. 9. Art.

Gamerius, Hannardus. *Authoritates Ciceronis, Plinii et aliorum tam veterum quam recentium scriptorum in conscribendis epistolis observandae, et ad certas quasdam regulas redactae, nunc autem juvandorum studiorum gratia in lucem editae et pulcherrimis exemplis illustratae*. Ingolstadt: Alexander and Samuel Weissenhorn, 1566. Bayerische Staatsbibliothek 8∞. Epist. 307m.

Hegendorphinus, Christophorus. *In Macropedius*, 1580.

————. *Ratio epistolarum conscribendarum compendiaria*. Leipzig: Valentin Schumann, 1520. Bayerische Staatsbibliothek 4 Epist. 220 (14).

Junius, Melchior. *Scholae rhetoricae de contexendarum epistolarum ratione. . . . Typis nunc denuo mandatae, & ab auctore recognitae, exemplisque auctae Epistolarum, Demosthenis, Aeschinis, Isocratis, & quae ad Atticum a Cicerone scriptae*. Strasbourg: L. Zetzner, 1602. Bodleian Library 8∞. I. 13. Art.

Macropedius, Georgius, et al. *Methodus de conscribendis epistolis . . . Secundum veram artis rationem tradita. Eiusdem. Epitome praeceptionum de paranda copia verborum & rerum, per quaestiones: item de nouem speciebus argumentationum Rhetoricarum, rem omnem breuiter explicans. Accessit Christophori Hegendorphini Epistolas conscribendi Methodus. Hac aeditione longe quam antea emendatior*. London: T. Vautrollerius, 1580. University Microfilms Early English Books 1475–1640, Reel 478, STC 17176. Bodleian Library 8∞. A. 15. Art., lacking sig. C (a portion of Macropedius).

————. *Methodus de conscribendis epistolis . . .* London: *Ex officina typographica* Richard Field, 1604. Bodleian Library, Oxford Don. f. 362.

Monhemius, Johannes. *D. Erasmi Roterodami opus de conscribendis epistolis in compendium redactum. In L. Vitruvii Roscii Parmensis de commoda ac perfecta elocutione, deque conficiendis epistolis isagogicon una cum aliis*. Basel: Robert Winter, 1541. Harvard University Library, Cambridge, *IC5.R7355.541d.

Müller, Georg. "Rivius: Johann R." ADB 28:703–13.

Nauwelaerts, M. A., ed. "Le correspondance de Simon Verepaeus (1522–1598)." *Humanistica Lovaniensia* 23 (1974): 271–340.

Nemius, Johannes. *Epitome ex opere D. Erasmi Roterod. de Conscribendis Epistolis: cui quod ad scribendi artem pertinet, accessit ex Ecclesiaste, Copia rerum, castioribus Colloquijs, & alijs Erasmi scriptis. Item ex Rhetorum libris, quos ipse in Opere de Componendis Epistolis subinde consulendos esse, admonuit*. Antwerp: J. Latius, 1556. Bibliotheek van de Rijksuniversiteit te Gent BL 3278 (1).

Pontanus, Petrus. *Sequunda pars artis Grammaticae: vndecim dirempta Libris. de triplici recte loquendi modo: Grammatico. Oratorio. Et poetico Ad illustrissimum virum Anthonium pratanum Inuictissimi Gallorum Regis Francisci primi Cancellarium*. Paris: Denis Roce, 1515. St. John's College Library, Oxford, A.3.7. (3).

Wibotius Puteolanus, Georgius. *Compendium rhetorices. Summam ipsius artis, mira facilitate breuitateque complectens*. Antwerp: Joannes Withagius, 1556. Bibliotheek van de Rijksuniversiteit te Gent BL 737 (1).

Secondary Sources

Bainton, Roland H. *Erasmus of Christendom*. New York: Scribner's, 1969.

Baldwin, T. W. *William Shakspere's Small Latine & Lesse Greeke*. 2 vols. Urbana: University of Illinois Press, 1944.

Best, Thomas W. *Macropedius*. Twayne's World Author Series. New York: Twayne, 1972.

Bierlaire, Franz. "Les 'Dialogi pueriles' de Christophe Hegendorff." *Acta conventus neo-Latini Turonensis: Troisième Congrès Internationale d' Etudes Néo-Latines, Tours, Université François-Rabelais 6–10 Septembre 1976*. Edited by Jean-Claude Margolin. De Pétrarque à Descartes. Paris: Vrin, 1980. 389–401.

———. "Un livre du maître au XVIe siècle: Erasme expliqué par Hegendorf." *Quaerendo* 2 (1972): 200–220.

Bolgar, R. R. *The Classical Heritage and Its Beneficiaries*. Cambridge: Cambridge University Press, 1954.

Bruyère, Nelly. *Methode et dialectique dan l'oeuvre de La Ramée: Renaissance et Age Classique*. De Pétrarque à Descartes 45. Paris: Vrin, 1984.

Codina Mir, Gabriel. *Aux sources de la pédagogie des Jésuites: Le 'Modus Parisiensis.'* Bibliotheca Instituti Historici S. I., 28. Rome 1968.

Dekker, Alfred M. M. "Three Unknown 'Cantilenae Martinianae' by Georgius Macropedius: A Contribution to the Study of the Utrecht *Carmina scholastica*." *Humanistica Lovaniensia* 23 (1974), 188–227; 24 (1975), 346.

Förster, Richard, ed. *Libanii Opera*. Leipzig: Teubner, 1927.

Giebels, Henk. *Georgius Macropedius 1487–1558: Een Biografische Schets*. Bijdragen tot de geschiedenis van Gemert, no. 3. Gemert, 1978.

Gilbert, Neal W. *Renaissance Concepts of Method*. New York: Columbia University Press, 1960.

Grafton, Anthony, and Lisa Jardine. *From Humanism to the Humanities: Education and the Liberal Arts in Fifteenth- and Sixteenth-Century Europe*. Cambridge, Mass.: Harvard University Press, 1986.

Green, V. H. H. *Renaissance and Reformation: A Survey of European History between 1450 and 1660*. 2nd ed. London: Arnold, 1964.

Grendler, Marcella and Paul. "The Survival of Erasmus in Italy." *Erasmus in English* 8 (1976): 2–22.

Grendler, Paul F. *The Roman Inquisition and the Venetian Press, 1540–1605*. Princeton, N.J.: Princeton University Press, 1977.

Halkin, Léon-E. *Erasmus: A Critical Biography*. Translated by John Tonkin. Oxford: Blackwell, 1993.

———. "Le traité d'art epistolaire d'Erasme." *Moreana* 21, no. 82 (June 1984): 25–32.

Heesakkers, Chris L., and Wilhelmina G. Kamerbeek, eds. *Carmina scholastica Amstelodamensia: A Selection of Sixteenth Century School Songs from Amsterdam*. Textus minores 55. Leiden: Brill, 1984.

Henderson, Judith Rice. "Despauterius' *Syntaxis* (1509): The Earliest Publication of Erasmus' *De conscribendis epistolis*." *Humanistica Lovaniensia* 37 (1988): 175–210.

———. "The Enigma of Erasmus' *Conficiendarum epistolarum formula*." *Renaissance and Reformation* n.s. 13 (1989): 313–30.

————. "Erasmian Ciceronians: Reformation Teachers of Letter-Writing." *Rhetorica* 10 (1992): 273–302.

————. "Erasmus on the Art of Letter-Writing." In *Renaissance Eloquence: Studies in the Theory and Practice of Renaissance Rhetoric,* edited by James J. Murphy. Berkeley: University of California Press, 1983, 331–55.

————. "Euphues and his Erasmus." *English Literary Renaissance* 12 (1982): 135–61.

Jardine, Lisa. *Erasmus, Man of Letters: The Construction of Charisma in Print.* Princeton, N.J.: Princeton University Press, 1993.

Jensen, Kristian. "The Latin Grammar of Philipp Melanchthon." In *Acta conventus neo-Latini Guelpherbytani: Proceedings of the Sixth International Congress of Neo-Latin Studies, Wolfenbüttel 12 August to 16 August 1985,* edited by Stella P. Revard, Fidel Rädle, and Mario A. DiCesare. Medieval & Renaissance Texts & Studies 53. Binghamton, N.Y.: 1988, 513–19.

Jolidon, A. "Histoire d'un opuscule d'Erasme: In La *Brevissima maximeque compendiaria conficiendarum epistolarum formula.*" *Acta conventus neo-Latini Sanctandreani: Proceedings of the Fifth International Congress of Neo-Latin Studies, St Andrews 24 August to 1 September 1982,* edited by I. D. McFarlane. Medieval & Renaissance Texts & Studies 38. Binghamton, 1986, 229–43.

————. "L'évolution psychologique et littéraire d'Erasme d'après les variantes du 'De conscribendis epistolis.'" In *Acta conventus neo-Latini Amstelodamensis: Proceedings of the Second International Congress of Neo-Latin Studies, Amsterdam 19–24 August 1973,* edited by P. Tuynman, G. C. Kuiper, and E. Keßler. Munich: Fink, 1979, 566–87.

Kennedy, George A. *Greek Rhetoric under Christian Emperors.* Princeton, N.J.: Princeton University Press, 1983.

Lavency, M. "A propos de la grammaire de Despautère." *Humanités Chrétiennes* 12 (1968–69): 401–8.

Lindeman, Yehudi. "Macropedius' *Rebelles* and Erasmus' Principles of Education," *Renaissance and Reformation,* ns 4 (1980): 127–35.

————, ed. and trans. *Two Comedies: Rebelles and Bassarus* by Georgius Macropedius. Nieuskoop, 1983.

Margolin, Jean-Claude, ed. Introduction. *De conscribendis epistolis* by Erasmus. ASD 1.2: 157–203.

————, ed. Introduction. In *Encomium matrimonii* by Erasmus. ASD 1.5:335–82.

Matheeussen, Constant. "A propos d'une lettre inconnue de Despautère: ses relations avec la ville de Comines et Georges d'Halluin." *Lias* 4 (1977): 1–11.

Murphy, James J., ed. "One Thousand neglected Authors: The Scope and Importance of Renaissance Rhetoric." In *Renaissance Eloquence: Studies in the Theory and Practice of Renaissance Rhetoric,* edited by James J. Murphy. Berkeley: University of California Press, 20–36.

————. *Renaissance Eloquence: Studies in the Theory and Practice of Renaissance Rhetoric.* Berkeley: University of California Press, 1983.

Murphy, James J., and Martin Davies, eds. "Rhetorical Incunabula: A Short-Title Catalogue of Texts Printed to the Year 1500." *Rhetorica* 15, no. 4 (August 1997): 355–470.

Mynors, R. A. B. "Introductory Note" to *A Formula for the Composition of Letters.* CWE 25:256–57; 26:559–60.

Nauwelaerts, M. A., ed. "Brieven van en aan Bossche humanisten en docenten: II. Jan Goverts (Joannes Nemius); IV. Georgius Macropedius (van Lanckvelt)." *Bossche Bijdragen,* 23 (1957–58): 255–74; 24 (1958–59): 143–61.

———. "De Geschriften van Joannes Nemius." *Gulden Passer,* 28 (1950): 104–9.

———. *Latijnse School en Onderwijs te's-Hertogenbosch tot 1629.* Bijdragen tot de Geschiedenis van het Zuiden van Nederland 30. Tilburg: Stichting Zuidelijk Historisch Contact, 1974.

Ong, Walter J., S. J. *Ramus, Method, and the Decay of Dialogue: From the Art of Discourse to the Art of Reason.* Cambridge, Mass.: Harvard University Press, 1958.

Pettegree, Andrew. "The Exile Churches and the Churches 'Under the Cross': Antwerp and Emden During the Dutch Revolt." *Journal of Ecclesiastical History* 38 (1987): 187–209.

Plett, Heinrich F. *Englische Rhetorik und Poetik 1479–1660: Eine systematische Bibliographie.* Forschungsberichte des Landes Nordrhein-Westfalen, Fachgruppe Geisteswissenschaften Nr. 3201. Opladen: Westdeutscher Verlag, 1985.

Richard, James William. *Philip Melanchthon: The Protestant Preceptor of Germany 1497–1560.* Heroes of the Reformation 2. New York: Putnam's Sons, 1898. Reprint, New York: Franklin, 1974.

Rott, Jean, trans. and ed. *Classicae epistolae sive Scholae Argentinenses restitutae* by Jean Sturm. Quatrième centenaire du Gymnase Protestant de Strasbourg. Paris: Droz; Strasbourg: Editions Fides, 1938.

Rummel, Erika. "Erasmus' Manual of Letter-Writing: Tradition and Innovation." *Renaissance and Reformation* ns 13 (1989): 299–312.

Schindling, Anton. *Humanistische Hochschule und freie Reichsstadt: Gymnasium und Akademie in Strassburg 1538–1621.* Veroffentlichungen des Instituts für europäische Geschichte Mainz 77, Abteilung Universalgeschichte. Wiesbaden: Steiner, 1977.

Scott, Izora. *Controversies over the Imitation of Cicero in the Renaissance. With Translations of Letters between Pietro Bembo and Gianfranceso Pico on Imitation and a Translation of Desiderius Erasmus, The Ciceronian (Ciceronianus).* Contributions to Education 35. New York: Teachers College, Columbia University, 1910. Reprint, Davis, Calif.: Hermagoras Press, 1991.

Seidel Menchi, Silvana. *Erasmo in Italia 1520–1580.* Turin: Bollati Boringhieri, 1987.

Sloane, Thomas O. *On the Contrary: The Protocol of Traditional Rhetoric.* Washington, D.C.: Catholic University of America Press, 1997.

Spitz, Lewis W., and Barbara Sher Tinsley. *Johann Sturm on Education: The Reformation and Humanist Learning.* St. Louis: Concordia, 1995.

Vocht, Henry de. *History of the Foundation and the Rise of the Collegium Trilingue Lovaniense 1517–1550.* 4 vols. Louvain: Bibliothèque de l'Université; Publications Universitaire de Louvain, 1951–55.

Von Richthofen, Erich. "A Spanish Inquisitor's Objections to Erasmus." *Erasmus in English* 7 (1975): 4–6.

Wilson, Thomas. *Arte of Rhetorique.* Edited by Thomas J. Derrick. The Renaissance Imagination 1. New York: Garland, 1982.

Wright, William J. "The Impact of the Reformation on Hessian Education." *Church History* 44.2 (June 1975): 182–98.

Letter-Writing Instruction Manuals in Seventeenth- and Eighteenth-Century England

Linda C. Mitchell

Previous scholarship on English letter-writing manuals of the seventeenth and eighteenth centuries has focused primarily on a small number of important texts such as Angel Day's *The English Secretorie* (1607) and Thomas Blount's *The Academy of Eloquence* (1653). This chapter describes significant but forgotten texts, including both conventional works such as John Brinsley's *Ludus literarius* (1612) and other more peculiar books such as Ralph Johnson's *The Scholar's Guide* (1665) and William Mather's *The Young Man's Companion* (1695).[1] Although these texts are not widely known or readily available to scholars, they played an important role in England's evolving system of academic and vocational education. In light of the relatively small number of extant texts and their markedly idiosyncratic nature, a taxonomic approach is of little practical use. I shall instead describe and evaluate each text, proceeding chronologically and highlighting these important themes: the sensible pedagogy beneath the manuals' sometimes quirky surfaces; the striking resemblances between seventeenth- and eighteenth-century methodologies and current practice; the persistent stress on letter writing as a practical skill for the rising classes; the declining emphasis on classical learning—whether knowledge of Latin or of classical rhetoric; the authors' struggle to determine the proper materials and boundaries for the texts they are writing.[2]

Significant but lesser-known letter-writing instruction manuals tell us much about academic, vocational, and social training in seventeenth- and eighteenth-century England.[3] Schoolmasters taught letter writing for a number of reasons. For example, letter-writing assignments could incorporate lessons on Latin and English grammar, spelling, punctuation, rhetoric, and composition. Letter writing also prepared students vocationally. A student might have little interest in composing a theme on liberty, but he could understand the usefulness of learning how to write a letter to an unreasonable landlord or a delinquent customer. Less directly, letter-writing texts also served as behavior manuals from which the writer could learn the appropriate social conventions for his station in life.

Despite their differences and idiosyncrasies, the letter-writing instruction manuals discussed here all demonstrate the value bringing the real world to artificial learning situations, a practice still used in business English classes today.

Grammar books are often overlooked as an important source of letter-writing instruction in seventeenth- and eighteenth-century England. A grammar book might include instruction in any or all of the following: parts of speech, parsing, spelling, translation, handwriting, poetry, "hard-word lists,"[4] universal language, Latin vocabulary, reading skills, Bible stories, prayers, composition, printing, bills and receipts, legal procedures, etiquette, orations, and hymns, as well as letter writing. Grammar books usually began by teaching basic literacy skills because many students of the rising classes did not know the rudiments of letters, sounds, and words before they started to school. Only after teaching foundational material could the schoolmaster begin instruction in composition, especially letter writing. Instruction in letter writing typically appears late in these grammar books—often as a culminating lesson.

In the school text *Ludus literarius* (1612), John Brinsley experiments with letter-writing instruction as a means of teaching grammar, composition, literature, and imitation. He distinguishes between the students who will continue with Latin and the "common man" who needs only English for his apprenticeship. Brinsley teaches sounds, letters, words, and sentences as a foundation for teaching Latin grammar. In the section on composing, he relies on Latin models of letters, such as those from Macropedius and Cicero. He argues that a student becomes a better writer if he has good models of writing to imitate. If a student relied too much on his own "Invention in making Epistles, Theames, Verses, [and] disputing," the results would be "nothing but froth, childishnesses and uncertaintie" (210). He also has students compose letters in English and translate them into Latin as a means of learning Latin grammar. Brinsley describes in *Ludus literarius* that a student can be a good letter writer if he does the following: read Tully's epistles twice a week; translate Latin to English and English to Latin, then summarize the letters in Latin and in English; write an imitation of Tully's epistle in English and then translate it into Latin, as well as write a letter to a friend and change numbers, tenses, persons, places, and times; and finally, the next day, write the answer to the letter from the former day, both in English and in Latin (210). In his sensible text, Brinsley used practical letter-writing instruction to reinforce Latin grammar, English grammar, composition rules, and communication skills.

Brinsley's text was directed at the more affluent student, wherea other textbook authors provided more pragmatic instruction to the rising classes. George Snell's *Right Teaching of Useful Knowledg to Fit Scholars for Som Honest Profession* (1649) targeted an audience that needed what are now called "life skills." In the first chapter, he mentions four types of students he will instruct: those who will not learn English well; those who will speak English only; those who will learn other languages; and those who will teach. His approach is utilitarian in that he intends to prepare students for a vocation. After Snell lays a foundation in grammar, punctuation, and spelling, he presents letter-writing instruction made easy for an average student. He begins with five rules of addressing an audience correctly:

1. The writer should use the proper greeting by being aware of whom he is addressing.
2. The writer should use phrases of respect throughout the letter.
3. The writer should close the letter not too abruptly but with a transition phrase leading to the subscription.
4. The writer should write a subscription that is not too long, yet filled with respect and honor.
5. The "indorsment" should be concise with titles and so forth so that nothing is redundant. (105–106)

These five rules define the protocol for writing the opening, body, conclusion, the signature, and the address. A student learned these rules as he practiced writing business letters, much as students still do today.

Ahead of his time, Snell pushed for reform in preparing students with the utilitarian skills to function successfully in the commercial world. One of the most important skills was communication through writing. According to Snell, anyone who can "attein abilitie to express neatly and cautiously all sorts of affairs in missive letters, is in a readie waie to bee assumed to anie imploiment of highest importance" (106). He claims that society associates written language with competency: "Good dexteritie in the skill of a letter writer makes a Scholar so qualified, verie readie and abel to use curious language, and verie courteous speech, in his common talk" (107). In *Right Teaching of Useful Knowledg*, Snell directs a student to have "unwritten paper bound, and therein under certain common-place-heads, shall write chief forms, and best materials, out of all well-pen'd letters, that shall com to his hands, this wil greatly enrich and make copious his epistolarie speech" (109). This manual contains practical information for every future apprentice: "A scholar well experienced in the art of a good Secretarie, shall bee well prepared for a laudabel doing of all civil duties" (109). Snell also explains the proper way to write, fold, address, and seal a letter. A correspondent must avoid coarseness and pretension, and he should shun inflated, stilted, and pompous prose. Models of letters led the correspondent to a plain, natural style. Shopkeepers learned to write simple, direct letters to order goods, request payment, and return the wrong merchandise. Snell's book set the trend in letter-writing instruction because of its sensible, practical advice.

An innovative school grammar that included letter-writing instruction for the middle class is Ralph Johnson's *The Scholars Guide* (1665). Johnson based his text on classical rhetoric and included composition, poetry, Latin, and elocution. Johnson's grammar text was unusual for the seventeenth century because it was one of the first grammars to offer instruction on themes, orations, poetry, hymns, and epistles. He takes a practical, simplified approach when he defines an "epistle" as a "Discourse wherein we talk with an absent friend, as if we were with him" (16). His text identifies epistles as having four "accidents" or parts: superscription, compellation, subscription, and a date. The style of epistles, according to Johnson, should be "low, short, and pithy" without "affectation, periphrase or garrulity." He advises that all epistles "shun Tautologies, by varying the phrase, when the same sence is repeated." Johnson's grammar book was an attempt at providing a well-rounded education for the rising classes who would not be acquiring the skills elsewhere.

Johnson's explanations are succinct. He defines each term, but he does not follow the Renaissance practice of modeling any of the categories. Instead, he relies on the schoolmaster to explain the kinds of correspondence and provide examples, thus being able to tailor business writing to individual student needs. Following classical rhetorical distinctions, Johnson divided letter writing into demonstrative, deliberative, or judicial genres. Under demonstrative he includes as subgenres narrative, lamentatory, eucharistical, gratulatorie, officious, disputatorie, laudatory, and deprecatorie. Deliberative epistles are either suasorie, hortatorie, petitorie, commendatitious, consolatorie, responsatorie, monitorie, convitiatorie, or conciliatory, while judicial epistles are either criminatorie, defensorie, expostulatorie, exprobratorie, or purgatorie. Johnson was ambitious presenting sophisticated instruction to the middle-class student who perhaps needed no more than a shopkeeper's working knowledge of correspondence. In any case, other text writers avoided this error, and the method of teaching letter writing through such detailed classical rhetoric did not become a practice in texts directed to the middle class.

Some grammarians departed from classical models of letter writing and used innovative, creative approaches. Middle-class students related more readily to model letters about the types of people and situations they recognized. *In English Examples to be Turned into Latin* (1676), Edward Leedes departs from the usual serious examples of letters and plays with colorful names and witty narratives in his models of correspondence. He writes in the preface that he has "ventured to put odd and unusual names upon those that write, as well as those that are wrote to, alluding for the most part somewhat to the matter discoursed of between them." His intent is to "please and allure the young men, that they might with more cheerfulness address themselves to their businesses." He dismisses what critics might say of his methodology: "I am very well pleased, although I be thought to have play'd the fool." For example, to keep a reader's attention, he uses colorful names in model letters, such as "William Walk-abroad to Simon," "Shut-up sendeth greeting," "Francis Forward to Leonard Loth-to't sendeth greeting," "Giles Choose-well to Henry Hug-all sendeth greeting," and "Thomas Tell-troth to Christopher, Come-late sendeth greetings."

Gimmicks aside, Leedes usefully and sensibly stresses audience. The correspondent should think about how a person receiving the letter will interpret and react to the contents: a letter is "a writing that contains the talk or discourse of persons absent" (101). Discourse with an absent person differs fundamentally in that there is no interruption, dialogue, gesture, intonation, facial expression, and such to help him interpret what the writer means. Leedes explains several types of epistles: "Narratory, where we tell of any thing done. Petitory, where we ask some thing. Commendatory, where we recommend any person." Throughout his text, Leedes takes a practical approach: "But in the Examples which we shall set down, we shall content our selves with such confused and trifling matter, as boyes use to talk among themselves; for they are the persons to whom we must accommodate all we write here" (101). Leedes keeps the attention of schoolboys by having them write letters as if they are conversing with someone they know. Instead of boring exercises, boys converse in letters about relevant topics, yet at the same time learn acceptable social and vocational conventions.

Leedes also stresses style. He warns the reader that the model letters he will use to imitate the Latin ones will seem a "little uncouth, and not fitted to the present way of writing in England, for though we write in English words, yet we do it with a design, that boys may thereby learn how to indite their Latin Letters." His first "uncouth" model letter is from John Seaman who "Sendeth greeting" to William Smith:

> Tis now a year well nigh (dear Will) since I saw you, and with what trouble of mind I have born the want of you, you may perhaps guess, if ever you were separated from any one so long that you loved so much. 'Twas the fear of the Pox I know that drove you away from us, and now the spreading of that disease is ceased, why should we still be kept a sunder? I hope that day will come ere long when we shall see one another, (and which was ever a great pleasure to me) play together. Given at Bury the fifteenth of the Kallends of March, in the year of our Lord.

It is puzzling that Leedes directs students to write letters in a simple, plain style in their vocational tasks, but models an inflated, stilted style that would be impractical in any letter-writing practice.

Leedes glosses words, a technique not seen in other grammar texts of the period. In his model letters, he numbers various elements and then provides corresponding words of explanation. And it is sound pedagogy, because the study of spelling, vocabulary, composition, and punctuation is contextualized. The following letter from Thomas Talk-well to Henry Do-little illustrates the number system:

> Tis very unpleasant news, which I heard lately (my dear Harry) that you are about to leave us and the School, and for no other Reason, but that you begin to perceive that if you be 2 a Scholar, you must take pains; it were fine 3 indeed, if when the Master readith and you open your mouth instead of your ears, it should presently be filled with all kind of Eloquence, and you should

speak Orations as learned as those of Tully or Demosthenes. But, my dear
Harry, that can't *4* be; the way *5* up the two headed hill is not so easie, thou
mayest if thou pleasest go home, and whilst thy Father is abroad, *6* bear thy
Mother company; but with a short while thy Age will alter thy judgment, and
7 thou wilt be ashamed of thy employment, and *8* repent of thy laziness and
folly as long as thou livest. Farewel, and if thou canst in time be wise.

[Corresponding Key]

1. res ingrata [missing number in text]
2. learned
3. pulchrum
4. i.e., be done
5. which leadeth up.
6. i.e., fit with thy Mother.
7. it will shame thee
8. [Missing gloss] (103)

In the glossing exercise, Leedes teaches many skills, such as grammar, vocabulary, and spelling. He also maintains that a personal letter is more effective than
a selection from literature because a student learns to how to communicate with
a real person in a real situation.

One of the most marketable and popular letter-writing instruction manuals to
serve both the academic and vocational needs of students is John Hill's *The
Young Secretary's Guide or, a Speedy Help to Learning* (1712), a manual that
could easily serve as the prototype of business English texts today. The ability to
write letters brought some degree of power to anyone who had to conduct legal
or commercial business, and the newly literate population soon recognized Hill's
book as an important reference tool. The text was popular because it addressed
the practical aims of the working-class audience:

Containing the True Method of Writing Letters upon any Subject; whether
concerning Business or otherwise: Fitted to all Capacities, in the most smooth
and obliging Style; with about 200 Examples never before published. As also
Instructions how properly to Entitle, Subscribe, or Direct a Letter to any Person of what Quality soever. Together with full Directions for True Pointing;
and many other notable Things.

Containing an Exact Collection of Acquittances, Bills, Bonds, Wills, Indentures, Deeds of Gift, Letters of Attorney, Assignments, Releases, Warrants of
Attorney, Bills of Sale, Counter Securities, with Notes of Directions, relating
to what is most difficult to be understood in the most legal sence, form and
manner: To which are added the Names of Men and Women, Cities, Counties, Sums of Money, Days, Months, Years of Date, Trade, &c. in Latin, as
they ought to be placed in any Latin Obligation: With an Interest Table to
know the Interest due upon any sum of Money, &c. (Title page)

Hill makes the plausible claim that the manual will help a tradesman save
money:

> I dare presage it will stand those in much stead who want those large Endow-
> ments, when in so many cases, relating to Business and important Affairs,
> they may find Forms and Precedents ready drawn up to their Hands, and save
> themselves the Charge, if not (as in Country Towns and Villages it often hap-
> pens) the tedious fruitless search of a Secretary or Scrivener, that is thorough-
> pac'd, as some term it, or well vers'd in these Matters: nor is it all times
> convenient to make a so great a Discovery of Affairs, that may by this means
> be kept more Private. ("Epistle to the Reader")

This manual proved to be very popular because of the instructions Hill offers on
do-it-yourself legal writing. The self-guide resembles software today that helps
the user write documents, such as wills and grant power of attorney.

Earlier texts such as Angel Day's *The English Secretorie* (1607) and William
Fulwood's *The Enimie of Idlenesse* (1568) offer business letters, but Hill's text
focuses entirely on the workaday world of the rising classes.[5] Hill's book is also
different in that he does not offer model letters of courtship, languishing love, or
marriage matches. In the prefatory verses to *The Young Secretary's Guide,* Hill
promises a correspondent to be able "to move his Quill/In pleasing Strains" and
"chuse out what he will." In all occasions the writer "may see What thought can
form, or he cou'd wish to be." The manual will help the "Tradesman to his Correspondent Write/And the plain country-man his Sense Recite" in good style and
expression (1696 A4). The increasing opportunities for education and the establishment of a postal system helped create a demand for manuals such as Hill's.
The Young Secretary's Guide went through well over twenty-seven editions in
London and at least twenty-four in Boston.

In spite of Hill's promise to demonstrate good writing, the model letters in
The Young Secretary's Guide often have a stilted, inflated style. For example, an
apprentice writes awkwardly, "Most Indulgent Father, These are humbly to sat-
isfie you, That I am not a little pleased with the Trade you have put me to, nor
less with the good usage I find" (1696, 29).[6] Another example is a wordy letter
written to someone in prison:

> Sir,
>
> I Cannot but condole your unhappy Condition; and as I had the happi-
> ness to participate in your Prosperity, so give me leave to share with you by
> sympathy in this your Misfortune, and, as a true Friend, to bear a part as
> much as may be in your Sufferings; and entreat you, however grievous such
> a Restraint may prove to so Nobel and Generous a Soul as your's, that you
> would not afflict your self, but bear with your wonted Patience and Bravery
> of Mind, what cannot at present be helped or redressed, considering such
> Casualties and Chances frequently befal Mankind. (87)[7]

Hill borrows an amusing letter from Day's *English Secretorie* (1607). A friend is trying to console another young friend on the death of his old wife:

> Dear Harry,
>
> You cannot conceive how many Fancies of divers kinds came justling into my Head upon the News that you sate whining and sniveling under the Cypurs-Tree of Mourning. Tis true, you have lost a Wife; and what of that? It has been many a jolly Fellow's kind Misfortune to be rid of such an Incumbrance as well as yours. Ay, but say you, she was a good old Woman: Why so say I too; and therefore it's the happier for her that she's out of this wicked World; nay, and let this farther turn to your comfort, that ten to one her time was come by the course of Nature, and she kindly followed her Teeth that were gone before, as mellowed Fruit drops after the Leaves without the east blast of Wind. Then rouze up, and turn your Lamentations to a jovial song; and instead of Tears, drench your Face in Claret and brisk Canary. But sty, if I mistake not, I have hit upon the string that twangs your Grief: and what is that? You'll say; Why, nothing more than that the Estate expired with your Wife. Truly, that was Loss worth weeping for: but say, it went to her Relations. There are other old Woman [*sic*] as wanton as she, that may be had with Estates to supply the defect; then never stand whining, but look out and make hay whilst the sun shines, snap up some Old Beldam or other, whilst the Reputation of a brisk rich Widower stands by; and so in hopes you will take my Advice, I rest in expectation to see you at the old Place,
>
> Your Friend, and Pot-Companion, P. L. (48)[8]

One may well ask the question of whether we are to consider the borrowed letter from Day more as entertainment than as serious letter-writing instruction. The manual also met the needs of females. Katherine Hornbeak points out in *The Complete Letter Writer in English 1568–1800* (1934) that *The Young Secretary's Guide* is the earliest letter-writing manual in which she has found "recognition of the epistolary needs of maid-servants" (80). She also notes that this manual offers twenty-three model letters for women, "more than any of its predecessors," an indication that women were assuming more economic and social responsibility (81).[9]

Hill also teaches social conventions in *The Young Secretary's Guide* for those who would be writing to "Superiors, Equals, or Inferiors." Tradesmen in particular should understand various "measures taken in Inditing Letters, according to the Terms properly given them by the Learned" (105). Hill promises lessons on "Style and Dialect most New, and Modish, in a most accomplished manner, with the most Accurate Spelling, and Elegant Phrases, Distances, Familiarities." The introductory chapter explains how to achieve "brevity and plainness" in letter writing. Model letters like "A Letter from a serving Man to his Master" and "A Servant Maid's Letter to her Friends" guide the hesitant writer. Even though Hill intends to focus on utilitarian tasks, he cannot resist adding some "Fancy, or

Imagination and form, that may add Lustre to things of this nature." He is influenced by La Serre's *Le Secrétaire à la Mode* (1640) and includes a few of the translated French letters, thus contradicting himself about not using any "out of Date" models. In spite of Hill's slight diversions to fancy, his useful book sold many copies and went through many editions. Hill succeeded in selling the book because he delivered what he promised in the introduction: business letters, legal models, social correspondence, and financial tables. The buyer had a valuable reference book in *The Young Secretary's Guide*.

An encyclopedic text that includes letter-writing instruction directed to the working class is William Mather's *The Young Man's Companion* (1710). The Bedfordshire schoolmaster and Quaker editor compiled an unpretentious self-teaching manual that addressed such diverse topics as grammar, spelling, model letters, winemaking, breast cancer, sore nipples, sick cows, childrearing, bricklaying, and marriage advice. Mather stays with the standard model letters of a scholar to a friend, a son to his parents, an excuse from a son to his father, and a letter of advice from a father to a son (66). His method of letter-writing instruction takes the form of a quick reference guide with models for the writer to imitate. Mather ignored the rule against using postscripts that other letter-writing instruction manuals dictated and used the addendum to add a didactic note. In later editions in the eighteenth century, a few letters from La Serre's *Le Secrétaire à la Mode* were added to Mather's text, eloquent letters that appear out of place with the original material on plumbers, shopkeepers, and carpenters.[10]

The Experience'd Secretary; or, Citizen and Countryman's Companion[11] (1699), attributed to Thomas Goodman, covers a variety of business tasks for a future tradesman. Part one of the manual contains "the most curious Art of Inditing Familiar Letters, in an excellent Stile, relating to Business in Merchandize, Trade, Correspondence, Familiarity, Friendship," while part two contains "the nature of Writings obligatory" (A2). In the 1707 edition the attributed author Goodman claims, "Tradesmen, Farmers, Husbandmen, as [well as] Young Gentlemen, Ladies and others, that can Read and Write, may be furnished as out of a Store-house of valuable Wares" (preface). Authors of these manuals lifted letters freely from other books. Several letters in *The Experience'd Secretary* are similar to those in Hill's *The Young Secretary's Guide*.[12] For example, *The Young Secretary's Guide* lists "A Letter to a Young Man upon the Death of his old Wife," while *The Experience'd Secretary* states, "A Letter to a young Man, upon the Death of his old Wife, from one of his Companions." This letter can even be found earlier in Angel Day's 1607 edition of *English Secretorie* (125–127).

An increased emphasis on communication skills in the early eighteenth century is evidenced in texts, especially grammar books. Charles Gildon's *Grammar of the English Tongue* of 1711 contained only grammar, but, when the author revised it in 1712, he included a section on teaching composition and letter writing. Gildon guides the reader through "an easie and genteel way of conveying our Mind in the shortest and most expressive Terms" (193). He urges, "Business requires no Ornaments, and a plain and succinct Information is all that is requir'd." Gildon insists on plain arguments without embellishment and wordiness: "Letters of Complement must have Gaiety, but no Affectations. Easiness must shine thro' all, and a clean Expression; here is no room for the Luxuriance of Fancy, or the embellishments of longer discourses." According to him, the same may be said of condolence and even of persuasion: The "most poignant and coercive Reasons must be us'd" (194).

A few authors clung to the pedagogy of teaching letter-writing skills with traditional rhetoric. In *The English Grammar* (1712) Michael Maittaire, like Ralph Johnson, uses rhetoric to teach composition skills that include letter-writing instruction. He lists the parts of discourse (exordium, narration, confirmation, confutation, conclusion) and then discusses the techniques of good writing. He defines "epistle" as "written in a less elaborate and more familiar but no less correct style than any of the rest; and there is hardly any performance a writer's genius and parts are so soon discover'd by as this" (233). He does not offer any models of letters, thus letting the schoolmaster teach specific writing skills according to the needs of his class.

The best example of an author of incorporating letter-writing instruction with exercises of grammar, spelling, and punctuation in a school grammar book is Anne Fisher's *A New Grammar* (1757). The exercises in her book also highlight style, manners, and "people skills." Fisher, one of the few women to write a school grammar book in the eighteenth century, emphasizes the need to communicate effectively and appropriately in an increasingly literate world. Setting a trend that survived into the twentieth century, *A New Grammar* tests a student's retention of rules of grammar by including exercises of bad English to correct in model letters. In applying the rules, Fisher stresses both style and grammar: a "Tradesman's Letter should be plain, concise, and to the Purpose" (151–152). It should be "free from stiff, or studied Expressions; always pertinent, and writ in such Words, or Terms, as carry a distinct Meaning with them." The person receiving the letter should not have the "least Hesitation or Doubt about the Meaning of any Words, Part, or Order, contained therein." Fisher requires that all "Orders, Commissions, and material Circumstances of Trade" must be stated clearly and exactly. More important, "nothing should be presumed, understood, or implied in obscure or ambiguous Terms." The writer should also take care to answer all the questions addressed to him in the letter he has received. As for style, letters should be "neat, significant, and as concise as the Nature of the Subject will admit." Fisher suggests the following conversational approach: "write to your Correspondent as you would talk to him, and without any formal uncommon Phrases." She advises that a correspondent must always be "frank and affable without Impertinence, obliging and complaisant without Bombast or Flattery." She warns, "nothing is more rude and unmannerly than to praise People to themselves."

What is significant about Fisher's book is that she is one of the first authors to address both males and females on the importance of letter-writing skills. Previous authors considered their audiences to be male, and they supplied the future tradesmen with examples of letters for their vocations and their social obligations. Fisher is different in that she considers the female as important as the male to be learning letter-writing skills. Young girls, Fisher asserts, have a right to learn how to write business letters and answer letters of social obligations; they should also participate in academic writing exercises to develop her mind. As a female in a male-dominated world, Fisher had met with adversity in getting an education and having her texts published. Even though her husband was publisher, she published one of her first books under a male pseudonym.

Fisher also emphasizes the importance of identifying audience: one should not "affect high or hard Terms," but write to the appropriateness of the person receiving the letter. The untrained correspondent should not attempt to write with "Wit, Humour, or Raillery . . . until [becoming] Master of such good Sense" and "good Breeding." From "Reading and Experience," the writer will learn what is "Pure, Moral, or Polite" and what is "Gross, Immoral, or Impure." Fisher cautions the writer against using wit or satire on improper subjects because one may appear "surprisingly ridiculous," just as today's e-mail users are sometimes cautioned against trying to inject wit and humor into a posting, because the recipient may not understand the tone of the message. So a correspondent observes decorum and addresses the receiver correctly, she includes a protocol chart for addresses ranging from royalty to servants and children. Fisher was ahead of her peers in letter-writing instruction; she approached letter-writing exercises with a broader view of looking at the social, practical, and academic results. And she was one of the first to used grammatically "bad" exercises to teach writing skills.

James Buchanan states in the preface to *The British Grammar* (1762) that students do not receive sufficient letter-writing instruction and are therefore deficient in forming their style.[13] In spite of the difficulty of learning to write letters, Buchanan argues, the exercise of writing helps shape how one expresses ideas: "We have often seen the Writing of Letters recommended, without ever a Word of first forming a young Gentleman's Style; notwithstanding epistolary Correspondence, requires the most concise and purest Vein of Language, and is acknowledged by all Judges to be the most difficult Form of Writing" (xxvii). Part of the problem of letter-writing instruction in many manuals, according to Buchanan, is that authors have provided collections with models of letters for students to copy, "most of which are wretched" (xxvii). If more model letters focused on moral issues, he claims, young scholars would learn about the "ruling Passions and distinguishing Characters of Men," the "Consequences of Actions," "Duties belonging to human Life," the "Rules of private and public Conduct," and the "Corruptions of Mankind, and the Snares and Temptations of the World." Model letters demonstrating values introduce students "to the

Knowledge of Mankind, and prepare them for appearing on the Stage of public Life with Honour and Advantage" (xxviii).

Buchanan appears to have lofty goals, yet he can be practical in his instruction. For examples, he comes up with a technique that was not common in teaching letter-writing instruction:

> The Method I take, and I find it so far effectual to the End proposed, is, having got what I judged the best Book of Letters, I make several young Gentlemen stand up, and one of them read a Letter gracefully; after which I read it to them myself, making Observations on the Sentiment and Style, and asking their Opinions with Respect to both. And if the Letter has an Answer, I ask them before they read it, what Answer they would make to this or that Passage? If their Answer happens to tally with that of the Author, it gives them great Spirits. (xxviii–xxix)

The practice he describes works well because "a deep and lasting Impression is made on their Memories, and their Understanding improved" (xxix). It is also a positive experience because students "imagine themselves treated with Respect, and a Deference paid to their Judgment: For Youth, even the youngest in School, are proud of being treated as rational creatures" (xxix). He convinces students to take letter-writing instruction seriously and to improve their communication skills.

Charles Johnson's *The Complete Art of Writing Letters* (1770) claims to be "Adapted to All Classes and Conditions of Life." As the rest of the title indicates, the text contains letters for all the duties one would expect to perform in life: "Entertaining and Instructive Letters, as Examples for Improvement of Style; With an agreeable Variety of Original Letters on Education, Duty, Courtship, Marriage, Amusement, Business, Friendship, Compliment, Trade, and Modern Fashions." Besides including a "useful" grammar, Johnson also recognizes that correspondence is one of the most frequent writing tasks: "There is scarcely any Species of Composition deserves more to be cultivated, than the Art of Writing Letters, since none is of more various or frequent Use, through the whole Course of human Life" (A2r). As letters are "written on all Subjects" and in "all States of Mind," he argues, "they cannot be properly reduced to settled Rules, or described by any single Characteristic" (A2r). He states, "Letters have no Peculiarity but their Form," and "The Qualities of the Epistolary Style, most frequently required, are Ease and Simplicity, an even Flow of unlaboured Diction, and an Artless Arrangement of obvious Sentiments" (A2r). Johnson, however, astutely observes that once these directions are applied "their Scantiness and Imperfections become evident" (A2r). He points out, "Nothing can be more improper than Ease and Laxity of Expression, when the Importance of the Subject expresses Solicitude, or the Dignity of the Person exacts Reverence" (A2r).

Johnson also stresses appropriateness in tone and content when composing a letter. He agrees "That Letters should be written with strict Conformity to

Nature . . . because, nothing but Conformity to Nature can make any Composition beautiful or just" (A2r). At appropriate times, however, "it is natural to depart from Familiarity of Language upon Occasions not familiar" (A2r). If the writer considers the moment, he will determine "Whatever elevates the Sentiments, will consequently raise the Expression; whatever fills us with Hope or Terror, will produce some Perturbation of Images, and some figurative Distortions of Phrase. Wherever we are studious to please, we are afraid to trusting our first Thoughts, and endeavour to recommend our Opinion by studied Ornaments, Accuracy of Method, and Elegance of Style" (A2r). If letters are for enjoyment, then other elements are taken into consideration. He advises, "Letters that have no other End than the Entertainment of the Correspondent, are more properly regulated by critical Precepts, because the Matter and Style are equally arbitrary, and Rules are more necessary, as there is larger Power of Choice" (A2v). Letters of this sort of entertainment vary in attitude: "some conceive Art graceful, and others think Negligence amiable; some model them by the Sonnet, and will allow them no Means of delighting, but the soft Lapse of calm Mellifluence; others adjust them by the Epigram, and expect pointed Sentences, and forcible Periods" (A2v). Johnson makes no judgment on letter writing for entertainment except to present the two points of view: "The one . . . considers Exemption from Faults as the Height of Excellence, the other looks upon neglect of Excellence as the most disgusting Fault; one avoids Censure, the other aspires to Praise; one is always in Danger of Insipidity, the other continually on the Brink of Affectation" (A2v).

Johnson continues to explain what must happen when letters present no serious subject matter: "When the Subject has no intrinsic Dignity, it must necessarily owe its Attractions to artificial Embellishments, and may catch at all Advantages which the Art of Writing can supply" (A2v). A letter without serious content should nonetheless have a goal: "The Purpose for which Letters are written, when no Intelligence is communicated, or Business transacted, is to preserve in the Minds of the Absent, either love or Esteem" (A2v). Furthermore, "To excite Love, we must impart Pleasure; and to raise Esteem, we must discover Abilities." Johnson provides directions for friendly correspondence:

> Pleasure will generally be given, as Abilities are displayed by Scenes of Imagery, Points of Conceit, unexpected Sallies, and artful compliments. Trifles always require Exuberance of Ornament; the Building which has no Strength, can be valued only for the Grace of its Decorations. The Pebble must be polished with Care, which hopes to be valued as a Diamond; and Words ought surely to be laboured, when they are intended to stand for Things. (A2v)

Unlike other authors, Johnson recognizes the need for correspondence that is sometimes not serious or dignified in content.

After twenty pages of basic instruction on grammar, Johnson lays down his rules for letter writing. Avoiding a too familiar tone, he states, "Letters, like polite

Conversation, are most to be prized when they are the least tinctured with Affectation" (21). Instead, "Ease, Elegance, Perspicuity, and Correctness are the chief Characteristics" most valued (21). He suggests, "to attain these Arts, nothing is so essential as a diligent Perusal of correct and elegant Authors; added to which, the Graces of Conversation is no small Point, which Happiness is only to be found by constant Intercourse with the best and politest Company" (21). Johnson claims that, for the correspondent who meets the requirements of reading quality authors and conversing with polite company, "Nature will presently furnish out the rest" (21). The writer will attain "A Purity of Language, and an easy, happy Style" from his "unwearied Diligence" (21). What is required is the ability to write with the same genuine feelings with which one would speak with a friend: "From Sincerity of Thought, and Elegance of Expression, a Person can never be at a Loss to write a Letter well; There needs no more, than to express himself in the same Terms as he would talk, were the Friend, he is writing to, present at the same Time" (21).

Johnson reminds the writer that natural expressions in a letter please a reader. He tells the writer not to think too much about what he is composing: "Nothing requires less Study than a Letter; whoever aims at great Things, will make but a poor Figure" (22). A writer fails at his task when he attempts to do what he is not capable of doing: "To express far-fetched Conceptions, requires a stiff and formal Language, which is not more unpleasing to the Ear than disgustful to the Heart; that which is most easy is most natural, and nature never fails to please" (22). Johnson recognizes that "every Person is not alike qualified for the same Subjects" (22). Not everyone is necessarily good in both conversation and letter writing: "The Graces of Writing and Conversation are of different Kinds; and though he who excels in one, might have been, with Opportunities and Application, equally successful in the other. . . . He, who shall acquit himself well in Letters, shall be often found as wanting in conversation, as on the other Hand, he, who in Conversation is remarked for his Life and Vivacity, shall be as destitute in literary Accomplishments" (22). One must also consider that "Custom and Application may alter either, and both be alike distinguished for the very same Perfections" (22). After Johnson discusses his letter-writing theory, he then provides practical examples on such aspects as proper addresses to people of various ranks and letters on common, useful subjects of family, friendship, and marriage.

In *The New English Letter-Writer* ([1779?]) George Brown targets sincerity as one of the most important elements of a letter. "Every letter," he states, "should convey some instructive precepts; and while we make use of pleasantry, we should never forget duty" (B1r). Brown recognizes that the writer should have "an accurate knowledge of the subject, and the circumstances of the person to whom we address ourselves" (B2r). Honesty, he explains, should be the key element in a letter: "In all letters let truth be the principal object in view; let no falsehood be inserted, and then there can be no inconsistency. If the letter is to contain an accusation of the conduct of a young person, let it be written in tenderness; for if otherwise, it will never be attended with any beneficial consequences" (B2r). Clarity is another important element in letters: "If on business in the mercantile world, let every thing be so clear, as not to admit of a doubt when you come to settle account. This will prevent many anxieties which often take place in families, and secure a part of the property which is often squandered away in suits of law" (B2r-B2v). And on a personal level, he observes, "In love and courtship, unless sincerity take place, no happiness can be expected: let a love-letter contain the language of the heart, and let that heart contain nothing but what is innocent" (B2v). Brown continues to reinforce the precept that sincerity in writing will make a letter "flow with elegance," and as the writer "improves his own rational faculties," he will "instruct and entertain his correspondents" (B2v). If the writer follows these rules, he will never "write with impropriety," and he need only keep careful watch over his grammar (B2v). With an eye toward correctness Brown has "Adapted [his instruction] to the meanest Capacities," or the lower classes (B3r). In all writing, "Grammar is the art of one human creature speaking to another, so as to be understood" (B3r). Brown claimed his peers should take grammar more seriously.

Thomas Cooke covers a wide range of useful material in *The Universal Letter-Writer; or, New Art of Polite Correspondence* ([1770?]). Cooke advertises on the title page a book that contains model letters on "instructive and entertaining subjects," letters that might "serve As Copies for Inditing Letters on the various Occurrences [*sic*] in Life." He adds other practical topics, such as petitions for "low or middling States of Life, to those in higher Stations." After a Grammar of the English Language, Cooke adds the standard "directions for addressing Persons of all Ranks, either in Writing or Discourse." Other types of correspondence in his text are "Forms of Mortgages, Letters of License, Bonds, Indentures, Wills, Wills and Powers, and Letters of Attorney."

Cooke discusses in "Directions for Writing Letters" that "the different characters of the persons must first be considered" (18). For example, a father writing to a son will use a "gentle authority," whereas a son to a father will "express a filial duty." And, "in friendship the heart will dilate itself with an honest freedom; it will applaud with sincerity, and censure with modest reluctance" (18). When a tradesman sends letters, he must monitor the subject matter and keep the "greatest perspicuity and brevity." Correspondents, in fact, can apply these rules "to all other subjects, and conditions of life, viz. a comprehensive idea of the subject, and an unaffected simplicity, though modesty in expression" (18). If the student observes the directions for writing good letters, he will improve within a few months: "Indeed, an assiduous attention to the study of any art, even the most difficult, will enable the learned to surmount every difficulty, and writing letters to his correspondents becomes equally easy as speaking in company" (18). Cooke in particular stresses the important role grammar plays in good writing: "A careful attendance to the plain and simple rules laid down in the preceding Grammar, will enable him to write in the language of the present times" (18). Moreover, if the correspondent "carefully avoids affectation, his thoughts will be clear, his sentiments judicious, and his language plain, easy, sensible, elegant, and suited to the nature of the subject" (18). Cooke is consistent with other instruction manuals and makes the point that as "letters are the copies of conversations, just consider what you would say to your friend if he was present, and write down the very words you would speak, which will render your epistle unaffected, and intelligible" (18). That concept, however, met with some resistance in texts such as William Milns's *The Well-Bred Scholar* (1794): "The idea of being 'easy' and 'natural,' has occasioned greater errors in the epistolary style than a total disregard, or ignorance of every rule" (34). Authors would continue to debate whether or not to consider a letter as informal discourse well into the nineteenth century.

Another practice in letter-writing manuals was for authors to lift large sections of material from another source and publish it as their own. For example, *The Complete Letter-Writer* (1756), a popular self-teaching manual that went through many editions in the second half of the eighteenth century, contained material from early eighteenth-century manuals and was in turn copied by other authors later in the nineteenth century. The author took most of the second chapter about letter-writing instruction from *The Complete English Tradesman* (attributed to Daniel Defoe 1727), and William Gordon in turn used some of the same material in *Every Young Man's Companion* (1755). Thus, throughout the century, one might read the same model letters in manuals by different authors. The author of *The Complete English Tradesman* provides a letter-writing guide for "almost every Individual, from the Boy at School to the Secretary of State" to avoid the "shame of doing it ill" (preface). Because of its inclusive approach, he asks that the selection not "offend the Delicacy of any Reader, that he will here meet with many Epistles of the lower Class: These could not be omitted without deviating from the grand Point in View, namely, General Utility" (preface). The author asks the reader's apology for including examples for the lower classes, but reminds him that the manual is directed to the tradesman who will write letters to order goods, return unsatisfactory shipments, and appeal for credit.

The author of *The Complete Letter-Writer* illustrates his points on plain style and concise language in model letters. He uses a frequently printed letter from someone who writes with "a rumbling bombast Style" and who "makes a very ridiculous Figure in Trade" (48). The following is a parody of a letter from a young country tradesman to a wholesale dealer in London:

Sir,

The Destinies having so appointed it, and my dark Stars concurring, that I, who by Nature was form'd for better Things, should be put out to a Trade, and the Time of my Servitude being at Length expired, I am now launch'd forth into the great Ocean of Business; I thought fit to acquaint you, that last month I received my Fortune, which, by my Father's will, had been my Due two Years past, at which Time I arrived to Man's Estate, and became Major; whereupon I have taken a House in one of the principal Streets of this Town, where I am enter'd upon my Business, and hereby let you know that I shall have Occasion for the Goods hereafter mentioned, which you may send to me by the Carrier. (1795, 41).

The flowery language in this letter decreases the shopkeeper's credibility. The author explains that the comical letter put his "Correspondent in London into a Fit of Laughing; who instead of sending him directly the Goods he wrote for, sent down into the Country to enquire his Character" (49).

The next example from *The Complete Letter-Writer* comes from another young shopkeeper in the country. The correspondence exemplifies the clarity and succinctness that every business letter should demonstrate:

Sir,

Being obliged, by my late master's Decease, to enter immediately upon Business, and consequently open my Shop without going to Town, to furnish myself with such Goods as at present I want, I have sent you a small Order as under written. I hope you will use me well, and let the goods be of the good Sort, tho' I cannot be at London to look them out myself. I have inclosed a Bill of Exchange for 75 l. on Mess. A— and B—, and Company, payable to you, or to your Order, at one and twenty Days sight: Be pleased to get it accepted; and if the Goods amount to more than that Sum, I shall, when I have your Bill of Parcels, send you the Remainder. I repeat my desire, that you will send me the Goods well sorted, and well chosen, and as cheap as possible, and I may be encouraged to a further Correspondence.

I am your humble Servant,

C. K. (1795, 40–41)

This shopkeeper writes as a "Man that understood what he was doing," thus establishing a voice of authority (50). The writer is following the manual's dictate to be "plain and concise, and to the Purpose." He should use "no quaint Expressions, no Book Phrases, no Flourishes; and yet they must be full and sufficient to express what he means, so as not to be doubtful, much less unintelligible" (52). The manual advises that the writer should also avoid using abbreviations in business letters.

The spread of education made it possible for the rising classes to use letters to conduct business, even propose marriage—acts limited earlier to their superiors. Another example from *The Complete Letter-Writer* shows a young tradesman asking a father for his daughter's hand in marriage: "Sir, I hope the justness of my intensions will excuse the freedom of this letter, whereby I am to acquaint you of the affection and esteem I have for your daughter." (97) Another young tradesman sees an attractive woman at a town meeting and writes a letter to her expressing his desire to make her acquaintance. He apologizes for taking the liberty of looking at her but assures her he has honorable thoughts. In his best writing style, he attempts to convince her that he has a stable economic situation and the ability to maintain a family: "I keep a shop, Madam, in _____ Street; and, though but two years in trade, I have a tolerable custom. I do not doubt but it will increase, and I shall be able to do something for a family" (118–119).

The Complete Letter-Writer forbids "quaint Expressions," "Book Phrases," "Flourishes," and abbreviations (50). In addition, it provides six rules for writing letters, paraphrased here:

Project a good attitude; make the length of the letter fit the occasion; do not use contractions; have a natural tone and attitude.

Do not show disrespect in letters, especially to elders; do not use a postscript because it neglects the person in the body of the letter.

Create an ethos.

Be clear; begin every new paragraph at the same distance from the left hand margin of the papers; use correct punctuation.

Close a letter properly; conclude it with the same address as at first (e.g. Sir; Madam); always subscribe your name in a larger hand than the body part of your letter.

Write letters on quarto, a fine gilt post paper, to superiors; use the proper size paper; never seal your letter with a wafer, unless to an equal or inferior.

Seal the letter and write the superscription (if it be to your superior or equal) in the following manner, viz. Write the word "To" by itself, as nigh the left hand upper angle or corner of your letter, as is convenient: then begin the title or name of the person about an inch lower, and almost in the middle or center of it, according to the length of the person's name, or title; and write the place of his abode in a line by itself at the bottom, in a larger character. (44–45)

These practical rules for writing business letters were important for the tradesman. With them he established his professional ethos; for example, by refraining from the use of contractions, he avoided too familiar a tone.

Several interesting manuals have received little attention. *Every Man His Own Letter-Writing; or, The New and Complete Art of Letter-Writing* [1782?] is unfamiliar to most scholars. The Reverend James Wallace and Charles Townshend provide complete instructions for letter writing. They follow with examples for business letters, personal letters, letters of advice and rebuke, and courtship and marriage letters. They include chapters on an English oratory, the art of being pleasing in conversation, and a compendium of grammar. Another little-discussed manual is David Fordyce's *The New and Complete British Letter-Writer; or, A Young Secretary's Instructor in Polite Modern Letter-Writing* [1790?]). It is puzzling why this manual is often overlooked, because it has just as many instructions and examples as other manuals of the time. Fordyce claims to include nearly four hundred "Original, plain, Easy, Instructive, and Entertaining Letters on the most useful and important subjects" that include business, courtship, marriage, religion and morality. The manual has a concise guide to grammar, "Directions for addressing Persons of all Ranks either in Writing or Discourse," and instructions for a petitioner. The writing advice that Fordyce offers is well stated: "Some persons make use of strained allusions, redundant descriptions, high-sounding word, &c. but use the expressions so improperly, that the reader can either affix no meaning at all to them, or he may affix any meaning he pleases" (A2r). Fordyce focuses on the pedagogical principles in his book, addressing "young writers" who "too often use a stile very unconnected" (A2r). To these writers, he states, "this volume will be found infinitely useful, as it will teach them to make a proper choice of words, and to express them with purity and perspicuity, which are two very essential objects of a learner's attention" (A2r). Fordyce's letter-writing manual in particular reflects the increasing emphasis on business correspondence in commercial world, both locally and abroad.

The list of letter-writing instruction manuals discussed in this essay is by no means complete. Scholars will continue to discover long-forgotten manuals or variations of the more popular ones. What will be of interest to these studies is what the need for letter-writing skills tell us about history. The manuals reflect social, economic, and educational changes that are taking place in the seventeenth and eighteenth centuries.

The significant but forgotten letter-writing instruction manuals played an important role in the teaching of academic, vocational, and social skills in seventeenth- and eighteenth-century England. A survey of these letter-writing instruction manuals indicates that little has changed during the past four hundred years. The same rules that appeared in seventeenth- and eighteenth-century texts appear today in business English books, software programs, and e-mail etiquette guides. Correspondents are still asked to use a sincere tone, be succinct and clear, adopt an unpretentious style, and speak to the recipient as if he is in the room. Letter writing has remained one of the most useful skills taught in classrooms for centuries. Students still learn grammar, composition, vocational skills, and social graces from letter-writing exercises. And letter-writing instruction continues to be one of the pleasant learning activities enjoyed for centuries because a student participates in what seems to be a real-life activity.

Notes

1. Several landmark studies have been done on letter-writing instruction manuals in seventeenth- and eighteenth-century England. One of the most significant is Kathryn Hornbeck's *The Complete Letter Writer in English 1568–1800*. Smith College Studies in Modern Languages, 15 (Northampton, Mass.: Collegiate Press, 1934). In her study, Hornbeck examines the influence of French models of letter writing on those in English. She also looks at handbooks used by the more privileged classes and at the influence

those texts had on the letter-writing practices of the middle classes. Her book follows editions of manuals, even at times pointing out the generous borrowing of one author from another.

2. I presented early versions of this essay at the Rocky Mountain Modern Language Association Conference, Spokane, 1995 and the Renaissance Society of America Conference, Florence, 2000. I am grateful to Robert Cullen, Lawrence D. Green, Jameela Lares, Carol Poster, and E. D. Schragg for their helpful comments on versions of this essay. I wish to thank Reader's services at the William Andrews Clark Library, Los Angeles and at the Huntington Library, San Marino, California, for assistance.

3. Gary Schneider observes, in *The Culture of Epistolarity: Vernacular Letters and Letter Writing in Early Modern England, 1500–1700* (Newark: University of Delaware Press, 2005), that "Letters and letter writing touched almost every facet of early modern life: early modern peoples employed letters in social, political, religious, and literary spheres in order to accomplish numerous practical purposes and to pursue various aesthetic goals" (286). He urges scholars to look at letters for the social interaction that letters and letter-writing manuals can provide. He argues, "[E]ven though the formal and the cultural are interinforming concepts, shifting emphasis onto the cultural allows us to bring into sharper focus the historical circumstances of letter writing" (287).

4. Hard-word lists consisted of words the readers probably did not know. Words more commonly known were not included.

5. William Fulwood's *Enimie of Idelnesse* (1568) is considered the earliest printed English letter writer published (Hornbeck, fn 2, vii).

6. Many of the letters from Hill appear later in Samuel Richardson's *Familiar Letters*. See Letter XL, "From an Apprentice to his Friends, in Praise of his Master and Family."

7. See Richardson, *Familiar Letters*, Letter CXII, "Of Consolation to a Friend in Prison for Debt."

8. See Angel Day's *English Secretorie*, 1607, part I, pp. 125–126, quoted from 26–27, "An example consolatorie, pleasantly written to one, who had buried his olde wife."

9. Jean Robertson notes, in *The Art of Letter Writing: An Essay on the Handbooks Published in England during the Sixteenth and Seventeenth Centuries* (Liverpool: Hodder and Soughton / Liverpool University Press, 1942), that the "only seventeenth-century book given over entirely to explicit instructions for women wishing to write letters is *The Female Secretary* (1671) by Henry Care (60). James Daybell states, in *Early Modern Women's Letter-Writing, 1450–1700* (London: Palgrave, 2001), "that women's letter writing during the later medieval and early modern periods was a very much larger and more socially diversified area of female activity than has generally been assumed, one that extended from royal women . . . through women of the nobility and genry, to members of the middling classes" (3). Janet Gurkin Altman demonstrates how letter writing is an excellent source for the study of eighteenth-century culture. She provides evidence of discursive, commercial, and social conventions of letter writing, as well as some of the changes in these conventions ("Political Ideology in the Letter Manual: France, England, New England, " in John W. Yolton and Leslie Allen Brown, eds., *Studies in Eighteenth-Century Culture*, no. 18 (East Lansing, Mich., 1988), 105–22.

10. William Gordon's *The Young Man's Companion* (1775) is another encyclopedic manual that ranges from letter-writing instruction to measuring, gardening, arithmetic,

geometry and trigonometry. It is "adapted to the lowest capacity," and Gordon makes the standard recommendation of these manuals, that is, to adopt a plain style in letter writing.

11. Possibly written by Thomas Goodman.

12. The American editions of *The Secretary's Guide* in the first half of the eighteenth century are products of the London editions of *The Young secretary's Guide*, according to Hornbeak (95).

13. For a discussion on style in letter-writing manuals, see Schneider's *Culture of Epistolarity*, especially "Letters and Print Culture II," 233ff. He suggests that "the great number of letter-writing, courtesy, and civilizing manuals regarding epistolary composition implies an obsessive concern with style" (283).

Works Cited

Primary

Blount, Thomas. *The Academy of Eloquence.* London, 1653.

Brinsley, John, the Elder. "Epistles and Letters." *In a Consolation for Our Grammar Schooles.* London, 1622.

———."How to make epistles imitating Tully, short, pithie, sweete Latine and familiar; and to indite letters to our friends in English accordingly." In *Ludus literarius; or, The Grammar School.* London, 1612.

Brown, Rev. George, *The New English Letter-Writer; or, Whole Art of General Correspondence.* London: for Alex. Hogg, [1779?].

Buchanan, James. *The British Grammar.* London: A. Millar, 1762.

Care, Henry. *The Female Secretary.* London: for Henry Million, [1671?].

Day, Angel. *The English Secretorie, or; Plaine and direct method of enditing of all manner of epistles or letters.* London: 1607.

Defoe, Daniel. *The Complete English Tradesman.* London: for Charles Rivington, 1727. Attribution uncertain.

Fisher, Anne. *A New Grammar, with Exercises of Bad English.* New Castle: sold by C. Hitch, 1757.

Fordyce, David. *The New and Complete British Letter-Writer; or, Young Secretary's Instructor in Polite Modern Letter-Writing.* London: for C. Cooke, [1790?].

Fuiwood, William. *The Enimie of Idlenesse: Teaching the Maner and Stile How to Endite, Compose and Write all Sorts of Epistles and Letters.* London: 1568.

Gildon, Charles, and John Brightland. *A Grammar of the English Tongue.* London: for John Brightiand, 1712.

Goodman, Thomas. *The Experience'd Secretary; or, Citizen and Country-Man's Companion.* London: for N. Boddington, 1699.

Gordon, William. *Every Young Man's Companion.* London: for J. and J. Rivington, 1755.

Hill, J. *The Young Secretary's Guide, or; A Speedy Help to Learning.* London: for H. Rhodes, 1696, 1712.

Johnson, Charles. *The Complete Art of Writing Letters.* London: for T. Lowndes, 1770.

Johnson, Ralph. *The Scholars Guide.* London: for Tho. Pierrepont, 1665.

Leedes, Edward. *English Examples to be Turned into Latin . . . forms of epistles, themes, and other exercises for the use of young beginners at Bury Schoole.* London, 1676.

Maittaire, Michael. *The English Grammar.* London: by W. B. for H. Clements, 1712.

Mather, William. *The Young Man's Companion.* London: by T. Snowden, 1710.

Milns, William. *The Well-Bred Scholar.* London: S. Gosnell, 1794.

Richardson, Samuel. *Letters Written to and for Particular Friends, on the Most Important Occasions.* London: for C. Rivington, 1741.

Snell, George. *The Right Teaching of Useful Knowledg.* London: for W. Dugard 1649.

Wallace, James, D.D., and Charles Townshend, A.M. *Every Man His Own Letter-Writing; or, The New and Complete Art of Letter-Writing Made Plain and Familiar to Every Capacity.* London: for J. Cooke, [1782?].

Secondary Sources

Daybell, James. Ed. *Early Modern Women's Letter Writing, 1450–1700.* New York: Palgrave, 2001.

Hornbeak, Katherine G. *The Complete Letter Writer in English, 1568–1800.* Smith College Studies in Modern Languages, 15. Northampton, Mass.: Collegiate Press, 1934.

Robertson, Jean. *The Art of Letter Writing: An Essay on the Handbooks Published in England during the Sixteenth and Seventeenth Centuries.* London: Hodder and Stoughton / Liverpool: Liverpool University Press, 1942.

Vestiges of Letter Writing in Composition Textbooks, 1850–1914

John T. Gage

Instruction in how to write letters occurs frequently in composition textbooks during the last half of the nineteenth-century, but its presence by no means signifies agreement about the importance of letter writing or its relation to other modes of writing. Nan Johnson has observed that "nineteenth-century rhetoricians followed Blair's example of designating the epistolary form as a mode of rhetoric, but they generally took a much wider view of this genre" (1991, 211). The "wider view" demonstrated by the present study is no less than complete lack of agreement about the necessary relationship between letter writing and composition pedagogy. Its presence is often perfunctory and anomalous, a vestige of times in which letter writing functioned as a principle means of teaching writing, though efforts were made in this period, more or less successfully, to integrate letter writing into newer approaches to composition pedagogy. Few changes occur in how letter writing itself is taught, though those changes themselves identify areas in which the perfunctory and vestigial presence of letter writing seems to be dealt with by attempts to find a functional role for letter-writing skills.

Using the resources of a data base containing information about the holdings in nineteenth-century rhetoric of the University of Oregon Library, I surveyed 193 composition textbooks (all in English) published between 1850 and 1914.[1] On the basis of this survey, the following essay will discuss (1) the extent to which letter writing is found in composition textbooks over this period, (2) the genres of letter taught in such books, (3) the relationship between the teaching of letter writing and the pedagogical approach of the textbook, and (4) the sorts of writing skills taught through the practice of writing letters. Throughout these discussions I will be concerned with both the most conventional uses of letter writing (i.e., the norm provided by a survey of such a large number of textbooks) and the range of variation found among the books.

Where Is Letter Writing?

Instruction in letter writing went on outside the school writing curriculum during this period, as it does today. The primary resources for the would-be letter

Table 1: *Percentage of 193 composition textbooks surveyed*
in which letter writing is found

10-year period	no. of texts surveyed	no. with letter writing	% with letter writing
1850–1859	11	4	36%
1860–1869	11	2	18%
1870–1879	15	8	53%
1880–1889	23	13	46%
1890–1899	40	16	38%
1900–1909	74	44	59%
1910–1914	19	13	68%
totals	193	100	52%

writer included a number of mass-market letter-writing manuals, and letter writing was frequently included in self-help books such as etiquette manuals, business or typing manuals, and encylopedic reference works. In school, as in the seventeenth and eighteenth centuries, letter writing frequently appears in grammar textbooks as well. The present focus on letter writing in composition textbooks, therefore, is not intended to survey the whole fate of *ars dictaminis* during this era but to look closely at its relation to writing pedagogy.

Of those 193 composition textbooks, 100 books, or 52 percent,[2] were found to contain instruction in the writing of letters, as Table 1 shows. Letter writing, consequently, may be seen as a considerable and consistent feature of composition instruction throughout this period, though clearly a dispensable one, because 48 percent of composition textbooks contain no instruction in letter writing. Table 1 also suggests that in the postbellum era the percentage of textbooks containing letter writing increases, declines somewhat toward the end of the century, and then rises again at the turn of the century. Just after the turn of the century, letter writing is included in composition instruction, more often than not becoming, it seems, less dispensable.

The increase in the percentage of composition textbooks containing letter writing that occurs between 1870 and 1879 coincides with the expansion of public education in America that occurs over this time, the increased attention to literacy skills that is needed to educate populations new to public education. The Morrill Act (1865) opened the way for the founding of land-grant universities with more technical and vocational emphases, resulting in larger college student populations and the founding of composition curricula (see Brereton 1995, 8, and Connors 1997, 9.) Letter writing was among the more mundane "sorts of material [included] in composition textbooks in these years," as Albert Kitzhaber notes, as a "sign of the movement away from a primarily abstract view of rhetoric" (1990, 207) that had dominated earlier approaches. Of all forms of writing, letter writing was practiced by the broadest segment of society, and as such it was considered an appropriate educational practice as education aimed to reach a broader segment of society. Gordon Southworth demonstrates this view in his note "To the Teacher" at the beginning of the letter-writing chapter of his 1887 textbook *Our Language: Its Uses and Structure:*

> As a means of training in purely original composition, letter-writing claims our attention first. Like storytelling it is easy to begin with, and is moreover an art that soon becomes practically useful and even necessary; for everybody that can write, writes letters, and most persons write nothing else.
>
> However much the matter may have been neglected, no argument is needed to show that the ordinary forms and conventions of this the most common of the uses of written speech ought to be made familiar to all those who study language in school. (32)

Southworth is defending a perceived tradition against the possibility of neglect—some find letter writing important pedagogically, whereas others find it insignificant—and doing so on the basis of the need for composition to reach a large number of students.

Different explanations account for the increase in the percentage of composition textbooks that include letter writing at the turn of the century. Among them must be the effects of the widespread practice in America's colleges of requiring a composition course for freshmen, following Harvard's 1885 example. Connors argues that the curriculum for such a course, after a period of "winnowing," is fairly fixed by 1900 (1997, 10–11). In this winnowing process, letter writing seems to win out over other practices. Another factor helping to explain this rise is the introduction of business to the college curriculum and business-writing to composition courses (see Adams 1993, 123–130.) Finally, this is a period in which the theorizing of the composition curriculum intensifies (Connors 1997, 82) and rhetorical forms are superimposed on developmental categories. An example of such a process is the idea of a composition sequence or "series," as discussed by Emerson White in his *Elements of Pedagogy* (1886). Writing in school begins, for White when the student is

> thrown upon his own resources, and begins what may properly be called *original composition.* . . . The essential direction to all pupils is that they do not attempt to write on subjects *of which they know nothing,* the possession of thoughts being necessary to their expression. The seven series of exercises given below will afford much excellent practice. (252)

White then lists his seven exercises (252–253):

1. Letters.
2. Description of known objects.
3. Narratives of personal experience.
4. Descriptions of journeys, real and imaginary.
5. Biographical sketches.
6. Descriptions of current events.
7. The discussion of themes (i.e. "the essay proper").

Letter writing is thus the first in a series of exercises in original composition designed to progress in difficulty, toward the essay. By 1886, at least, letter writing is a basic unit in constructions of pedagogical theory. By 1900 a survey of composition courses offered in normal schools reveals that letter writing is mentioned in descriptions of those courses more often than any other practice except "systematic writing" and "criticism" (Jewett 1927, 71).

The Extent and Kinds of Letters Taught

Among the data I collected about the textbooks in which letter writing appears is the number of pages each devotes to letter-writing instruction, which was compared to the overall length of the book to determine the percentage of the book devoted to letter writing. The result of this analysis, as shown in Table 2, suggests that the percentage of textbooks given over to letter-writing instruction during this entire period is relatively stable, averaging only 6 percent. This may indicate that, even while letter writing is given a somewhat larger role in composition teaching, that role is also perceived as relatively unimportant.

Table 2: Letter-writing textbooks, showing average number of pages devoted to letters, average percentage of text devoted to letters, and average number of genres distinguished

10-year period	average no. of pages devoted to letter writing	average % of whole devoted to letter writing	average no. of letter letter genres distinguished
1850–1859	13	3	8
1860–1869	19	8	4
1870–1879	7	3	3
1880–1889	17	7	4
1890–1899	16	6	4
1900–1909	18	7	4
1910–1914	16	5	4
totals	106	39	31

Individual textbooks can be found that depart from these averages considerably. For instance the textbook included in this survey that devotes the largest percentage of its contents to letter writing is W. Monkhouse's *The Precis Book* (1897) in which seventy-nine pages, or 41 percent of the whole, are taken up by the subject. Although intended for use in the schools, Monkhouse's textbook, subtitled *Lessons in Accuracy of Statement and Precision of Expression,* has a decidedly practical orientation, serving primarily to prepare students for civil service examinations. M. L. Knox's more conventional *Elementary Lessons in English* (1882) devotes fifty-four pages, or 19 percent of the whole, to letter writing. And from an earlier period, Augustus Layres's *Belles-Lettres* (1867), written "to facilitate the art, and abridge the study of composition" (3) devotes thirty-four pages to letter writing, or 14 percent of the whole, as compared to ten pages on description and six on the essay.

At the other extreme, some of the textbooks barely give lip-service to letter writing. A page or two, and less than 1 percent of the whole, is devoted to letter writing, for example, in A. D. Hepburn's *Manual of English Rhetoric* (1875), Adams Sherman Hill's *Principles of Rhetoric* (1878) and *Foundations of Rhetoric* (1892), John McElroy's *Structures of English Prose* (1885), Huber Buehler's *A Modern English Grammar and Composition* (1900), Fred Newton Scott and Joseph Denney's *Elementary English Composition* (1902), and Henry Canby's *English Composition* (1911). In such cases, typically, the letter is mentioned as a means of clarifying or distinguishing a related rhetorical principle: for example, in McElroy to contrast the relationship of the audience in oratory (35) or in Canby to provide examples for analysis of "the masterly use of a specific word" (384). Hill merely cites letters to illustrate the difference between *will* and *shall* (62) and the use of periodic sentences (225).

As an index of pedagogical sophistication in the treatment of letter writing, I also noted whether the textbook distinguishes kinds or genres of letters in its discussion and if so how many genres it distinguishes. Table 2 also indicates that textbooks that contain letter writing distinguish an average of four genres of letter quite uniformly across this era, except at the beginning, in the decade 1850–1860, when there is a tendency (if the four textbooks in the collection from this decade are typical) to divide the subject more discretely. Such regularity, set against the broader changes in the percentages of books in which letter writing appears, suggests that in the treatment of letter writing, genre is a stable issue, governed by convention and not affected by the length of the treatment of letter writing.

This stability suggests that letter writing is taught in the context of composition in a manner vastly oversimplified from the way in which it is presented in letter-writing manuals written for the nonschool market. Table 3 illustrates the numbers of genres treated in five such commercial letter writers, chosen at random.

Nearly all of the genres distinguished in the manuals otherwise appear in one way or another in the composition textbooks, in a wide variety of combinations.[3]

Table 3: *Numbers of genres of letter distinguished in selected mass-market letter-writing manuals*

	Number of letter genres distinguished
Martine's Sensible Letter-Writer (1866)	9
Frost's Original Letter-Writer (1867)	14
Payne's Social Letter Writer for All Occasions (1888)	14
The New Standard Business and Social Letter-Writer (1900)	7
Standard Up-to-Date Practial Letter-Writer (1902)	12

The difference between an average of four genres in the textbooks and an average of eleven in the manuals is not a matter of whether any given genre is appropriate for school. It is rather a function of the simplification in the textbooks of a body of discourse that is subject to considerable analytical differentiation. Table 4 demonstrates this by listing the actual genres distinguished in two of the manuals compared to a sample of three of the composition textbooks that make the average number of genre distinctions. The composition textbooks seem to be adapting a few of the genres from the manuals and omitting other genres of letter altogether, presumably for the sake of simplicity.

This indicates that letter writing is not present in the composition textbooks to accomplish the task of enabling students to write letters in the real world, as the manuals clearly intend. Rather, letter writing is present as a means of practicing composition in a simplified format, as we saw White theorizing above. This use of letter writing is a manifestation of a widespread attitude, expressed, for instance, by John Franklin Genung in his contribution to William Morton Payne's 1895 *English in American Universities, by Professors in the English Departments of Twenty Representative Institutions:*

> Drill must be furnished, but the drill must be wisely directed. And one thing can be done. It can be recognized that such seeming is not the whole truth; that beyond the stiff and labored stage of writing, as also beyond the dashing and accidentally brilliant stage, there is a calm permanence of assured mastery, corresponding to what the runner calls his second wind, wherein the writer can do his best and keep it up. Toward this goal of mastery the drill of writing and exercises in language should be directed; and this not only by setting the student working systematically *through* the crude and rudimentary stage, but by infusing into his task such interest as will give it vitality. (quoted in Brereton, 174)

Letter writing, as an exercise or drill, seems to fit all of the criteria needed for the student to attain "mastery": it is systematic, rudimentary, and potentially vital, but it often seems that the one thing letter-writing lessons in the composition classroom were not intended to accomplish was to enable a student to write

Table 4: *Genres of letters distinguised in selected mass-market manuals and textbooks*

Manuals
Frost's Original Letler-Writer (1867)
    Letters of introduction
    Business letters
    In answer to advertisements
    Recommendations
    Declining to recommend
    Answering applications for character, unfavorably
    Congratulations
    Friendship and relationship
    Love
    Invitation and answer
    Accompanying gifts
    Favor
    Advice
    Excuse
Standard Up-to-Date Practical Letter-Writer (1902)
    Love and friendship
    Accompanying gifts
    Advice
    Apology
    Congratulations
    Condolence
    Favor
    Introduction
    Application
    Business
    Official
    Invitations

Textbooks
Reed and Kellog, *An Elementary English Grammar* (1891)
    Ordering merchanise, answer
    Application
    Invitation and acceptance
    Letter of introduction
    Letter of friendship
Herrick and Damon, *Composition and Rhetoric for Schools* (1900)
    Business letters
    Formal letters in the first person
    Formal letters in the third person
    Informal notes

better letters in the real world. Although real-world situations call for a wide range of types of letters, skills may be mastered within a much narrower range, by using genres (such as letters to imaginary friends or invitations to imaginary events) from which real-world contraints are missing.

A few of the textbooks surveyed, however, include types of letters that go beyond enabling students to master language skills through practice. These are genres that enable students to master something we might call "getting along in the world." Social skills and attitudes are often reflected in genres of letters such as "letters of condolence," which are distinguished in four of the textbooks, or letters of "excuse," which are distinguished in eight of the textbooks. These are categories of letter frequently found in the formularies, but their presence in the composition textbooks suggests an attempt to make letter writing in school a preparation for the awkwardness to be faced in life. Sara Lockwood, in her 1888 *Lessons in English,* for example, introduces letter writing to the teacher typically as an efficient means of "practice" (257), but in her "Five-Minute Exercises" designed for this purpose, she slips in a few assignments, among the typical invitations, congratulations, and thank yous, that put students in ethically charged social situations:

> Write to a school friend who has met with an accident or an affliction.
> Express your sympathy and offer your help. . . .
> Write a note of apology to your teacher, for some thoughtless act.

Writing these letters is more than a sheer exercise in formal convention, requiring the application also of moral judgment. Similarly, moral issues are raised but left to the student to solve by James Robert Boyd in his 1858 *Elements of Rhetoric,* as when he distinguishes the category "Letters of excuse" and uses it to make both a rhetorical point about *kairos* and an ethical point about responsibility:

> In writing these, you must not forget that almost all depends on the time and the manner of making an excuse: it may be too late to be effective; or so mistimed as to aggravate the previous offense. The excuse which would be freely accepted to-day, might be indignantly rejected a month hence. (116)

Other genres of letters seem to have an analogous function with regard to life's more mundane, yet problematic, activities. For example, eight of the textbooks taught letters to the editor of the newspaper as a genre. Fifteen singled out telegrams as a kind of letter. Eleven distinguished letters that respond to advertisements. One textbook distinguished the type of letter that seeks patronage from a sponsor. Two distinguished letters that petition the government. One unique genre of letter occurs in Henry Coppee's *Elements of Rhetoric,* published in 1859: military and naval dispatches. Here is a clear example of letter writing as more than practice to achieve mastery of standard English; something is at stake in the world, possibly one's life.

The treatment of letter-writing genres typically starts from a basic distinction between "familiar" and "formal" letters and in each category perhaps makes a further division: "familiar" into "family" and "friends" and "formal" into "social" and "business." Something like this paradigmatic arrangement occurs in a majority of the textbooks that employ any genre categories at all. It will appear often simply as a distinction among letters of friendship, invitations, and business. Business writing, as taught in the context of composition text-books, is a special case. It occurs, with increasing emphasis throughout the period under study, in 78 percent of the textbooks in which letter writing is present. Its frequent presence in these textbooks suggests that students are assumed to be preparing for careers in business, and in many cases the extensive treatment of business situations, and forms, bears this assumption out; the textbooks are in this way going beyond writing "mastery" for academic reasons and teaching practical, vocational knowledge. Yet, many of the textbooks treat "business" letters in a trivial way, which suggest that, rather than directed at practical ends outside of school, business correspondence is included as a conventional school exercise in formality. This tone is struck early on by Richard Parker in his *Aids to English Composition* (1846; the 1857 edition is used in this study):

> Under the head of Letter Writing, it is intended in this exercise to include all the forms of epistolary correspondence, whether in the shape of billets, notes, formal letters, or ceremonious cards, &c. It is proper to premise, that, whenever a letter is to be written, regard should be had to the usual forms of complimentary address, to the date, the superscription, and the closing. The folding, also, of the letter, should not be disregarded. If it is true that "trifles form the principal distinction between the refined and the unrefined," surely those trifles deserve some sort of consideration. (184)

So, in aiming at refinement in general, Parker, true to his claims, includes an example of business correspondence, as illustrated in fig. 1.

The only "business" being taught or served by such instruction is the business of subservience to convention. Similarly, and more typically, the business letter merely fills a generic niche in J. B. Fletcher and George Carpenter's *Introduction to Theme-Writing* (1893) and serves to set stylistic targets for the student to hit. The authors write:

> The forms of letter writing certainly do not concern us here, and we will confine ourselves strictly to the considerations of the kinds of subject-matter that letters may appropriately contain, and the qualities of style they may show. Letters are, roughly speaking, of two kinds, impersonal and personal. In the impersonal or business letter the writer restrains himself from all extraneous adornment of style, or even any particular display of individuality. Here merit lies in extreme clearness and conciseness.

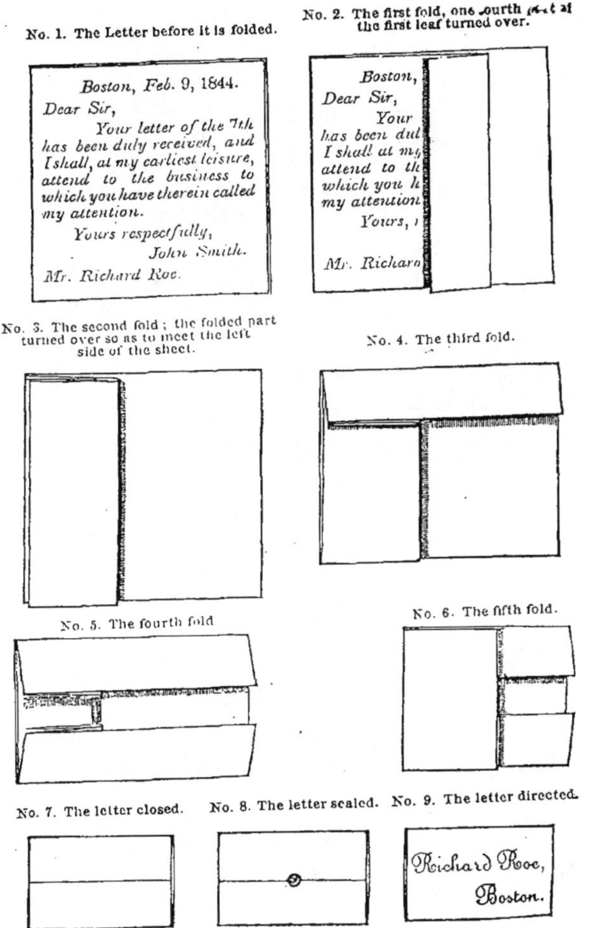

Fig. 1. Illustration of a business letter from Richard Green Parker's
Aide to English Composition (1857)

When taken somewhat more seriously as a practical, vocational emphasis, as for example in Robert Herrick's *New Composition and Rhetoric* (1911), the teaching of business writing still shows considerable remnants of Parker's obsession with external formalisms and Fletcher and Carpenter's use of the genre to inculcate habits of style.

Pedagogical Approaches

To identify trends in the way in which different approaches to composition might correlate to the presence of letter-writing instruction, I assigned to each textbook surveyed one or two of the following classifications: modes, style, grammar, argument, invention, and belles-lettres.[4] Sorting the textbooks according to these classifications yielded the result charted in Table 5, revealing tendencies that are for the most part predictable but worthy nevertheless of some discussion.

First of all, letter writing features heavily in textbooks that are oriented pedagogically toward a "modes" approach, with increasing emphasis placed on letter writing within this approach in the later half of this era. At the same time, as noted above, "modes" themselves are the predominant pedagogical orientation during this time. A textbook appearing between 1890 and 1914 is more likely to teach composition using modes than any other approach, and if it does, it is likely include letter writing. This raises the question of how the modes and letter writing are perceived as being related.

Letter writing is itself often conceived as a mode, along with the conventional quadrivium of narration, description, exposition, and argument. Indeed, because during this era the "modes" are sometimes held to be five, or six, or more in

Table 5: Textbooks compared: those with letter writing and those without, 1850–1915

10-year period	Modes *with* *without*	Style *with* *without*	Grammar *with* *without*	Argument *with* *without*	Invention *with* *without*	Belles lettres *with* *without*
1850–1859	4 1	1 1	1 5	0 0	0 0	0 0
1860–1869	0 3	1 3	1 6	0 2	0 0	1 0
1870–1879	3 1	4 4	3 5	1 0	0 1	1 0
1880–1889	6 1	3 5	10 6	0 1	0 1	1 0
1890–1899	6 3	7 11	8 9	2 5	0 1	2 0
1900–1909	24 12	7 9	21 7	5 10	3 2	6 1
1910–1914	10 5	2 0	5 0	2 2	1 1	1 0
totals	53 26	25 33	49 38	10 21	4 6	14 1

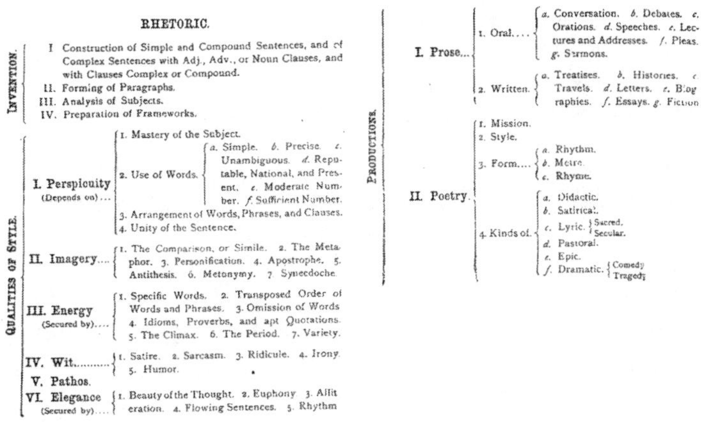

Fig. 2. Schema from Brainerd Kellogg's *A Text-Book on Rhetoric* (1889) showing the conceptual placement of letters in relation to other forms of rhetorical "productions"

number (Kitzhaber 1990, 123, 126), such an extension should not be surprising. Many of the textbooks treat letter writing as a mode without worrying the question of just what a mode is, by simply giving equal representation to letter writing among chapters otherwise devoted to the modal types. In this regard, Southworth's *Our Language: Its Use and Structure* (1897) is typical. A chapter on letter writing simply precedes chapters on narrative and descriptive writing. Treating letter writing as a mode in this way has its origin, perhaps, in rhetorical schemes that treat the issue of kinds of writing separately from issues of style or manner, the most influential of which is Hugh Blair's *Lectures on Rhetoric and Belles-Lettres* (1819) in which the lectures are organized to deal with issues of taste, style, oral genres, written genres (including the epistolary), and poetry. (Johnson 1991, 211–212) A late nineteenth-century reformulation of this pattern can be seen in Brainerd Kellogg's *A Text-Book on Rhetoric* (1889) in which the schema reproduced here as fig. 2 is adduced to organize the contents of his book.

Letters fall naturally into such a configuration without the apparatus of "modes," but insofar as the modes are developed in relation to similar schemata (see Connors 1997, 227–234), letter writing and "narration" have in common a generic relation to the superordinate category "types of prose writing."

Even modally dominated composition textbooks, however, have difficulty placing letter writing into their organization. One way is to merge letter writing into one of the other modes, as in the case of Erle E. Clippinger's *Written and Spoken English* (1914) in which the opening chapters are modal and letter writing is folded into them:

1. Discourse Primarily Descriptive
2. Letters and Narration
3. Discourse Primarily Expository
4. Business Letters and Argumentation

This schema enables Clippinger to embed the informal/formal genres of letters into the modal narration/argumentation distinction. Another, more typical, approach is to lay out the modal pattern and include letter writing in an altogether separate part of the book. This miscellaneous approach is represented by Robert Herrick and Lindsay Todd Damon's *Composition and Rhetoric for Schools* (1900), in which the modes are presented in the final two chapters of the last part of the text, "The Whole Composition," while the letter-writing chapter concludes the first part, "Preliminary Work." This is precisely the opposite arrangement from that of John Hayes Gardiner, George Lyman Kittredge, and Sarah Louise Arnold, in *Manual of Composition and Rhetoric* (1907), in which the first five chapters cover the modes and the rest of the book deals with style, with a final chapter on letter writing.

Thus, letter writing is treated either as a way to practice writing as a sort of warm-up to the real business of writing whole compositions, or as an afterthought, so to speak, after the modes are developed. In a similar and decidedly ambiguous vein, the chapters in Sara Lockwood's *Lessons in English* proceed through figures, diction, sentences, and punctuation, and then turn to whole compositions: chapter 9, "Letter-Writing," and chapter 10, "Composition" (including the standard modes). Lockwood's design is not much different from that of Augustus Layres's 1867 *Belles Lettres,* in which chapters take up topics in the following sequence:

Literary Composition
Style
The Fable
Narration
Oratorical Narration
Fictitious Narration
Descriptions
Letters
Essays

Layres seems to base these distinctions on an eclectic range of theory, from the progymnasmata of classical rhetoric, from Blair's categories, and from Campbell's.

Common to all such arrangements is the ambiguous relation between letter writing and other kinds of prose compositions. In such ways, letter writing can be both a mode and not a mode. It is a kind of whole composition, but it is separated from the real kinds of whole composition that have become commonplace. What seems clear about such books is that both the modes and letter writing have assumed a canonical status without having anything like a theoretical relation, so the textbook writer must invent a way to have them both. Henry Day, in *Rhetorical Praxis* (1879), includes "Epistolary" among his five forms of discourse, on the first page of his textbook, and defines it rather sweepingly as "that form of Discourse in which thought is communicated to an absent mind" (15), though he never again returns to the form in his book as something to be taught or practiced.[5] The ambivalence of all such treatments may be traced at least to Blair himself, for whom "epistolary writing . . . possesses a kind of middle place between the serious and amusing species of composition" (369–370).

Looking back at Table 5, we see that letter writing also predominates in composition textbooks that are oriented around grammar instruction, and those that take a belles-lettristic approach, whereas letter writing has a "mixed" presence in relation to stylistic approaches and is found less frequently in books that emphasize teaching composition through argumentation or invention. Only in the case of the grammar orientation is there any significant change over time in the relation between pedagogical approach and the presence of letter writing. Books that approach writing through grammar are consistently less likely to include letter writing before 1880 and more likely to include it after 1880.[6]

A typical example of the anomalous presence of letter writing in a grammar-oriented textbook is Horace S. Tarbell's *Lessons in Language Book II* (1896). Tarbell explains his book's organization as follows:

> In the part that treats Grammar are included analysis and punctuation; in that which treats Composition are included the conventional forms of epistolary, social, business, and parliamentary writing; and practice in the art of writing, for which abundant material is supplied by exercises in the selection and arrangement of words, in description, narration, reproduction, paraphrase, and essay-writing. (iii)

When one turns from this explanation to the table of contents, however, these subjects are treated in what appears to be a random order. The first fifteen lessons are headed as follows:

The Sentence
Kinds of Sentence
Margins—the Paragraph
Punctuation
Definition—Description
The Noun
Classes of Nouns
Letters
Description
Pronouns
Description
Verbs

Subjects, Predicates, Modifiers
Letter Forms
The Adjective

Tarbell says that his arrangement is "in the order in which the pupil can best study them, and not in the deductive order in which an adult might find most pleasure" (iii), without further discussion of any principle on which "best study" is based. He concludes his book with yet a third schema for these topics, reorganized into a "deductive" outline, with letters appearing under the heading "form" of composition, rather than under "kind" of composition. Behind the orderliness that Tarbell devises to justify the randomness of his presentation lies a deeper randomness.

In the case of textbooks with a style or grammar emphasis letter writing most often provides a means of practicing or of understanding the relevance of a narrow grammatical or stylistic concept. Adams Sherman Hill's *Beginnings of Rhetoric and Composition* (1902), for example, places letter writing into a context that emphasizes it as a site for practicing correctness and "good use."

Part I. Correct and Incorrect Forms of Expression
Chapter 1.   Good English Defined
Chapter 2.   Punctuation
Chapter 3.   Letter writing
Chapter 4.   Nouns
Chapter 5.   Pronouns
Chapter 6.   Verbs
Chapter 7.   Articles
Chapter 8.   Adjectives and Adverbs
Chapter 9.   Prepositions
Chapter 10. Conjunctions

Parts II and III of Hill's text deal with paragraphs, sentences, word choice, and qualities of expression (unity, clarity, force, and ease). Thus, letter writing is the only *form* of composition given lengthy discussion and, because it is the only form of composing students engage in, it is presumably available to them to use as a way to practice any of the book's grammatical or stylistic principles. Lillian G. Kimball adopts a similar plan for her textbook for younger students, *Elementary English: Book One* (1911), briefly treating such matters as singular and plural words, correct usage, contractions, using the dictionary, and punctuation before introducing letter writing at more length. But then, letter-writing exercises are sequenced throughout the rest of the book with other kinds of writing practice to focus on a principle under discussion, for instance:

105. Letter writing
    Write your exposition in the form of a letter to a friend who has asked you for information. Attend carefully to the paragraphing.

In this way, the letter is not taught as a separate mode, but as an occasional means of making a compositional principle come to life. Kimball's is one of the few texts considered in this study in which students revise letters, and that is because letter writing is employed as an occasion for making revision practical:

> 52. Rewriting a letter
>
> After hearing your teacher's criticism, rewrite your letter describing a show window. Improve it all you can. Fold it and place it in an envelope properly addressed. Read your letter aloud in class.

But even with such a functional emphasis, matters of merely formal obligation creep in ("properly addressed . . ." to whom?). Letters lend themselves to the teaching of stylistic principles precisely because they are conventionally stylized in the culture, a fact that Barrett Wendell exploits when he makes his only mention of letter writing in his *English Composition: Eight Lectures Given at the Lowell Institute* (1911).[7] This paragraph occurs in Wendell's discussion of three kinds of "good use":

> Perhaps, however, the most suggestive example of good use—reputable, national, and present—is a fact within the personal experience of every one of us. When we write letters, we begin them with the adjective *dear*. Now, the occasions when we mean by this word to express even the smallest degree of personal affection are so rare that at such moments we often feel called upon to change the word to *dearest*, or *very dear*, or *darling*. There is another form of address in all respects but one decidedly more expressive of what we really mean,—*Friend*. Yet none of us begins a letter "Friend Tompkins." And the only reason why none of us commits this unpardonable sin is that custom, fashion, good use forbids. So, nowadays we are no longer "obedient, Humble Servants," but "Truly" or "Sincerely" or "Faithfully Yours,"—not because either phrase was ever literally true, but simply and solely because, nobody knows why, good use once sanctioned one form, and now sanctions the others. (25)

Wendell is not teaching the use of these forms in letter writing, but the principle of good use through reference to the practice of letter writing everyone in his audience is assumed to have experienced.

What Gets Taught Using Letter Writing

Because letter writing may be taught as a separate category or as an exercise in relation to other kinds of writing, the question of what sorts of skills are addressed through letter writing is my next concern. In this survey, I recorded whether the letter-writing portion of a textbook included the teaching of any of thirteen writing skills, ranging from invention to spelling; a given book may be counted as teaching any number of these skills in any combination. I then

Table 6. Percentage of texts in which various writing skills are taught in letter-writing sections, according to principle pedagogical approach

skills taught in letter-writing section	modes	style	grammar	argument	invention	belles-lettres
arrangement	70	76	67	70	50	64
format	70	72	76	60	25	64
salutations	79	68	86	60	50	50
style/diction	68	44	47	70	25	50
paragraphing	20	4	14	10	50	0
etiquette	23	28	12	30	0	14
audience	25	24	20	10	25	29
spelling	2	0	4	10	0	0
mechanics	20	4	41	30	25	64
handwriting	38	28	31	20	25	14
argument	2	4	0	10	0	7
invention	3	0	2	0	25	14
revision	5	8	2	0	0	14

calculated the percentage of textbooks teaching such a skill according to the dominant pedagogical orientation(s) of the texts (fig. 2).

In this classification of writing skills, "arrangement" means that there was some discussion of the opening, "body," and closing of the letter in relation to its content or purpose (often by means of outlining), as distinguished from "format," meaning the placement on the page of various formal elements of the letter, such as the "heading," the address, the salutation, and so forth. These two similar skills often appear together, but there are cases in which "format" is taught without any concept of the structural integrity of the content of the letter and, more rarely, vice versa. An extreme example of the separation of arrangement from format is the approach taken by some textbooks in which the model format contains no words at all. Fig. 3 shows two such instances of empty forms.[8]

"Salutations," indicates that the textbook teaches various modes of addressing the recipient and of punctuating the salutation, as well as modes of signing off. To be counted as teaching "paragraphing," a text needs to advise students about indenting paragraphs and something about the unity of a paragraph. To be counted as teaching "style" it has to address word choice, tone, voice, usage,

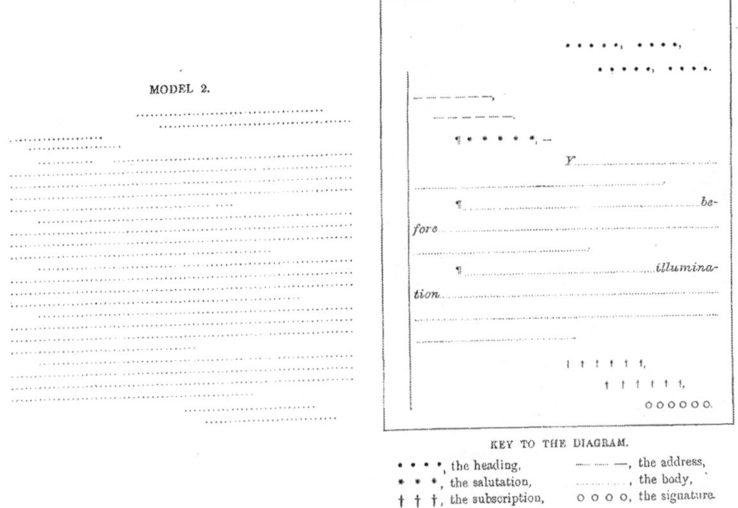

Fig. 3. Empty formats for letter writing. Left: from N. L. Knox's
Elementary Lessons in English (1882). Right: from Fred Newton Scott
and Joseph Villiers Denney's *Elementary English Composition* (1900)

or clarity in some way. To be counted as teaching "etiquette" the book must use letter writing to address issues of courtesy and behavior, such as promptness or the demands of social occasions. "Audience," indicates, that over and above matters of style and etiquette, students are specifically being taught to adjust their letter writing to an audience, either real or make-believe. By "mechanics" is meant punctuation, capitalization, and the like, apart from salutations and closings. What is meant by "spelling" and "handwriting" is self-evident, I presume. "Invention" here means that the textbook undertakes to teach some process by which the student determines appropriate content for the letter, such as observation, a case method, or some sort of analysis. "Argument" indicates that the letter-writing instruction includes advice or instruction on how to make a compelling case for whatever it is the letter argues, and "revision" denotes instances in which the student is asked to revise a letter to make it better, sometimes a canned letter provided for this purpose and, more rarely, a student's own draft.

What of potential significance does the analysis in table 7 show about how letter writing is used? First of all, I believe it shows, once again not surprisingly, that in the teaching of letter-writing convention and standardization predominate. Even when the overall approach of the composition textbook varies, the arrangement, formatting, and opening and closings of letters are taught in a majority of cases. Such consistency is the overwhelming norm, and it predates the era, of course; the categories derive from the medieval dictaminal tradition (see, e.g., Connors 1997, 33). It may even surprise one to note that in some textbooks of every kind, these features are missing from the teaching of letter writing. The room for variation is still considerable, and even in the most conventional kind of composition textbook—that is, in the grammar-driven approach to writing, 24 percent of the texts teach letter writing without teaching format and 14 percent teach letter writing without teaching the conventions of salutation and closing.

In addition to this relative consistency in what skills are taught most often in relation to letter writing, there is some consistency in which skills are taught least often. Although there is a 70 percent chance that any discussion of letter writing in a book featuring modes will present the formatting of a letter, there is only a 25 percent chance that such a discussion will also teach students to consider the specific audience to whom their letter is written. Nor does that chance improve if the textbook takes a different general approach; the odds are about the same for each kind of textbook. Audience awareness, surprisingly, is not a major feature of letter-writing instruction. Even less frequently is letter writing used to teach invention, argument, or revision.

In addition, this analysis reveals that there are certain ways in which different approaches to composition affect how letter writing is taught, although few absolutes pertain here. Notice, for instance, that, whereas paragraphing is never a major consideration of letter-writing instruction, there is considerable variation across pedagogical approaches: A "modes" approach to writing in general is much more likely to include paragraphing than a "style" approach. This is perhaps explained by the concern of "modes" with larger units of discourse and the concern of "style" with smaller. The even greater likelihood of paragraphing appearing in the letter-writing discussion of a textbook featuring "invention," however, is not so easily explained. As another example of not easily explained inconsistency, notice that, although awareness of audience is found fairly uniformly in around 25 percent of all other letter-writing discussions, in textbooks with a dominant "argument" focus that issue is addressed far less often. This is counterintuitive, in light of the presumably more audience-centered nature of argumentative writing. Rather than suggesting how anomalous the argument approach is, this perhaps provides further evidence of how conventional letter-writing instruction is: even in an approach to composition in which audience is expected to be a primary consideration, when letter writing is introduced, that consideration is overwhelmed by the sheer conventionality of letter-writing pedagogy. Indeed, why would only 25 percent of the textbooks address audience awareness in teaching letter writing, when that connection seems to us, as it seemed to George Carpenter in 1904, to be a natural one insofar as it has the potential to make classroom writing serve a real purpose? Carpenter writes in his *Teaching of English in the Elementary and the Secondary School:*

> Not only the matter but also the motives of the earlier exercises are important. The making of a sentence or a paragraph may not be a comprehensible

or an interesting purpose to a young child, but the telling of a story or the writing of a letter will be. Why should one write, but to communicate ideas? A story or a message told in a letter, to be sent, as letters should be, to an absent acquaintance, will seem to the child a reasonable motive for writing. . . . As language always concerns two, him who talks and him who listens, or him who writes and him who reads, its employment in teaching should recognize this natural relationship. (126–127)

And yet, Carpenter's own textbooks surveyed here in which letter writing is found (1893, 1906, 1896), like nearly all the others, fail to encourage students to actually send the letters they write. His own belief in employing the natural connection between reader and writer in letter writing fails him under the pressure of convention. His *Exercises in Rhetoric and English Composition* (1896) introduces letter writing as an exemplar of the principle that "we usually communicate with others most effectively when we make use of the means well known and in good repute among them" (13), a principle that merely enables him to seem to be invoking a natural connection to the audience while his presentation of the requirements of a good letter is based wholly on the usual formal matters: "That it should be legible. . . . That it should begin courteously and appropriately," and so forth (13). If there is any doubt about whether Carpenter's rhetorical allegiance is with an audience-centered or a form-dominated approach, he ends his letter-writing section with the advice that "Letters illustrating typical errors should be written on the black-board" (17).

Table 6 also suggests that, although there is a standard, conventional approach to letter writing, our attention can nevertheless be drawn to significant departures from that approach. According to these percentages, the most typical way in which letter writing is taught will be found in a composition textbook that has a basic "modes," or "style," or "grammar" approach. It will teach the arrangement and format of the letter, the conventions of salutation and closing, it will teach something about style. These characteristics are consistent over time, as can be seen by their presence for example in Parker's, *Aids to English Composition* (1857), employing a predominantly modes approach, Swinton's *New Language Lessons* (1883) employing a predominantly grammar approach, and Hanson's *Two Year's Course in English Composition* (1912), employing a predominantly style approach.

Despite the predominance of this paradigm, textbooks throughout this period employ letter writing for a variety of purposes. For example, Frances Perry's *Introductory Course in Argumentation* (1906) includes examples of letters to illustrate argument; Charles Sears Baldwin's *Composition* (1909) uses letters to teach style and includes exercises focusing on the use of letters for persuasion; Gardiner, Kittredge, and Arnold's *Manual of Composition and Rhetoric* (1907) sets up cases to use letter writing to teach how to construct arguments; Mandel Radford's *Composition and Rhetoric* (1903) uses letter writing to teach the concept of unity; Stratton Brooks's *Composition-Rhetoric* (1903) uses letter writing to teach invention in conjunction with categories of faculty psychology; Huber Buehler's *Modern English Lessons* (1902) uses letters as reading exercises to teach interpretation; John McElroy's *Structure of English Prose* (1885) uses letter writing to distinguish oral and written styles, and compares letters and orations; William Brewster's *English Composition and Style* (1912) uses letters to teach awareness of style and tone by offering positive and negative examples for analysis; John Nichol and W. S. McCormick's *Questions and Exercises on English Composition* (1893) uses letter writing to teach revision through imitation; and Alfred Hitchcock's *Composition and Rhetoric* (1906) also teaches revision through letter writing. William Maxwell's *First Book in English* (1894) uses letter writing to teach punctuation; Luella Clay Carson's *English Composition: Standard Rules and Usage* (1903) emphasizes the courteous aspect of conventional closings; and C. W. Bardeen's *Shorter Course in Rhetoric* (1885) emphasizes promptness in replying to letters, frankness and discretion, and care in the indiscriminate placement of one's signature to avoid being taken in by swindlers.

Although it is also conventional to teach letter writing as a separate mode or to confine it to a separate section, a few textbooks integrate it into a series of sequenced assignments. Examples of this approach include Horace Tarbell's *Lessons in Language* (1896), William Maxwell's *School Composition* (1902), W. F. Webster's *Language, Grammar, and Composition* (1903), Sarah Arnold's *The Mother Tongue: Book I* (1900), Lillian Kimball's *Elementary English* (1911), and Effie McFadden's *McFadden Language Series: Grammar and Composition* (1914). In very rare instances, such as N. L. Knox's *Elementary Lessons in English* (1882), letter writing is the only kind of writing used, in this case as a means of practicing grammatical principles. And, although it is common for the letter-writing section to be "tacked on," as it were, to the end of a textbook in which it does not otherwise feature, or employed early as a "warm-up" for the important forms of writing to follow, as in J. B. Fletcher and George Carpenter's *Introduction to Theme-Writing* (1893),[9] a few textbooks, such as Sara Lockwood's *Lessons in English* (1888), emphasize letter writing an "the most important division of composition work" (257).

Conclusion

The method of surveying a large number of textbooks employed here may be redundant insofar as it demonstrates what is already obvious to the discerning reader of a few of these books, that letter writing is taught conventionally, even perfunctorily. What such a methodology is able to reveal that casual reading does not, however, is that against the highly conventional norm is an incredibly diverse range of variation. Although some textbooks of the era fall decidedly within the norm, the era also produced maverick texts, curiously different approaches, strangely anomalous categories, and valiant but ill-fated attempts by some teachers to find a different way of putting letter writing to use. Such instances of departure from the conventional norm may tell us as much, if not more, about the strengths and limits of the norm than do the typical examples.

Any method underlying letter writing as a mode of teaching writing in the nineteenth century, despite the general appearance of sameness and convention, is in a state of flux.

Convention and innovation, similarity and difference, are of course in a dialectical relation, and we can hardly know one without the other. Letter writing seems to have found a firm niche in nineteenth-century composition textbooks, yet let us not overlook the 48 percent of the textbooks surveyed for this study in which letter writing does not appear. The niche itself and the conventional approaches occupying it are part of this dialectic: one difference across the whole corpus is the decision to include letter writing at all in one's teaching of writing. It is only in the context of that choice that the conventions and innovations appear. Given the choice to include letter writing, certain other choices that seem as if they ought to be available are not often made. I refer to possible alternatives to teaching letter writing by prescription and practice, in the form of recipes for the parts, kinds, and qualities of letters. In 1901 Gertrude Buck objected to the prescriptive approach in general:

> [T]he practical problem, "How can natural conditions of writing be substituted in the schoolroom for artificial?" has found various answers. The first of these was inevitably negative; abolish all writing by rule. Nowhere outside of composition classes does one write to conform with a certain rhetorical law. The condition is absurd. No wonder the student on whom it is imposed writes painfully and pretentiously; no wonder that continued exercises of this sort form "a habit of stringing together empty commonplaces and vapid declamations,—of multiplying words and spreading out the matter thin,—of composing in a stiff, artificial, and frigid manner." No real literature, no genuine writing of any kind, was ever fashioned to the pattern of a rule. Let us, then, cast off the yoke of formal rhetoric, said the progressive teachers of an earlier decade. Let the student only write; the oftener the better. It is by writing that writing is learned. The process itself, if only it be normally conditioned, can work out its own perfection. And the first step toward securing normal conditions is to dispense with hampering rules.
>
> . . . The next movement might easily have been foretold—so logically inevitable was it. After doing away with the artificial motive for writing, that of exemplifying certain rules of discourse, it became necessary to substitute a real motive. The first that suggested itself was naturally that which impels one to write on any "genuine occasion"—the motive of having something to say that another person wishes or needs to hear. The acceptance of this motive as essential to any normal process of communication both initiated and justified the movements in composition teaching that immediately succeeded it; namely

the derivation of subjects for writing from the student's own experience and the direction of his writing toward a definite audience. ([1901] 1995, 242–243)

One finds little evidence in the textbooks themselves that the casting off of rhetorical rules in favor of "normal" conditions for writing was applied to letter writing. Yet, if such a possibility had occurred to an "earlier decade," as Buck presumes, one must wonder why. Furthermore, the conditions that Buck offers as the next step, the substitution of a genuine motive and audience for writing, would seem to apply to letter writing above all other forms, insofar as letters written outside of school are generated in response to real situations and addressed to real individuals. Buck's sense of what ought to be "inevitable" here stands firmly against the grain of convention, such that convention persists in the very form of writing on which a genuinely different approach might have been based: writing letters to be read by real people in response to real situations.

Instead, textbook writers persisted in proffering rules, and letter writing as an art could be said to have suffered in consequence. To some commentators, such as George Dawson, sheer fakery seemed the norm. In an essay published in 1888, Dawson called the popular letter-writing manuals of his time "the refuge for the destitute, the great ready-made clothes-shop for literary aspirants." (237) He takes the stance further:

> It has been asked if the art of letter writing can be taught. Some people think it can; and if anybody has doubts about it, he should get hold of a promising pupil and try to teach him. But you may take my word for it, that if it is not in him, the teacher may as well sit down and try to teach a class to write a second part of "Paradise Lost." If you see anyone biting the tip of his pen, and in the agonies of composition, you may depend that nothing good will come of it. (238)

The middle way suggested by Buck seems to have been doomed in the face of an all-or-nothing conflict between the art of rhetoric by rule and the romantic sense of innate ability appealed to by Dawson.

So, although the momentum provided by the nineteenth-century caused letter writing to persist as a medium of composition instruction well into the twentieth century,[10] by mid-century its pedagogical salience nearly vanishes. This is no doubt because the legacy of letter writing is rule-bound and it comes to stand for what is most artificial about rule-governed writing. It might have formed the basis for a "genuine" writing pedagogy in the twentieth-century, but the nineteenth-century legacy was against this possibility.

Notes

1. In conducting this survey, I was assisted by Brad Hawley. A considerable number of other graduate students, to whom I am also grateful, have contributed to the data base as a whole, which consists of more than a thousand entries. This survey focused

only on school textbooks in which writing is taught. The books chosen for the survey do not include letter-writing manuals produced for a mass market or other kinds of books, for instance etiquette manuals or business handbooks, in which letter writing appears. It also excludes strictly grammar textbooks, but grammar texts were included if they contained a significant writing-instruction component. Because this survey is restricted to the holdings of a single library, its statistical claims are conditional, but insofar as the collection is representative and the sample relatively large, the survey method employed here may be assumed to identify trends.

2. All percentages and averages reported in this study have been rounded off to the nearest whole number.

3. Only one textbook in this study, Alphonso Newcomer's *Practical Course in English Composition* (1893) refers, for example, to the love letter. Newcomer's approach in general stresses personal writing to an unusual degree for the period, and he mentions the love letter only to exemplify the range of letters, from the most personal to the most public aspects of life (225).

4. Classifying the textbooks in this way often involved a weighing of different aspects of the book to get a sense of its predominant pedagogical orientation, and then making a judgment call. Books to which I assigned these descriptors tend to have the following characteristics:

modes the approach features writing whole compositions according to a typology of kinds of essays, usually, but not exclusively "narrative," "descriptive," "expository," "argumentative," etc.

style the approach features a working up from the parts, including qualities of words (diction, usage, formal and familiar registers), sentences, and paragraphs (unity, coherence, emphasis, etc).

grammar the approach features rules of correctness and uses writing to practice knowledge of grammatical principles.

argument the approach features writing on issues, exclusive of using argumentative writing as one of the modes given more or less equal treatment, or teaches writing in relation to logical categories.

invention the approach features the use of observation, conversation, cases, or some other means of encouraging students to explore ideas and basing their compositions on those ideas.

belles-lettres the approach features writing in relation to the reading of literary texts, or teaches predominantly literary genres of writing.

5. Hence, in this study Day's textbook is not counted among those in which letter writing appears, despite his passing mention of the epistolary form.

6. If one looks at strict grammar textbooks themselves, rather than at composition textbooks focusing on grammar, one finds letter writing "tacked on" frequently, throughout the period. The dominance of letter writing in the grammar curriculum before the nineteenth-century (see Linda Mitchell's essay in this volume) is giving way, perhaps because the traditional role of grammar as preparation for the study of rhetoric is also eroding.

7. Because this mention of letters is so brief, and because the practice of letter writing as such is not being taught here, Wendell's textbook is among those in this study counted as not including letter writing.

8. In later editions of Scott and Denney's text, this wordless model is changed to a worded one. Other examples of this sort of thing include Parker's *Aids to English Composition* (1857), Buehler's *Modern English Lessons* (1902), and Carolyn Robbins's *Grammar and Composition* (1907).

9. Fletcher and Carpenter write: "The kinds of composition which we shall consider are Letter-Writing, Translation, Description, Narration, Criticism, Exposition, Argument, and Persuasion. Of these, Description, Narration, Exposition, Argument, and Persuasion are the most important, for they may be considered as constituting, in a large sense, the elements of composition, in as much as nothing can be written in prose or verse that is not either one of them or a combination of two or more of them" (2). Compare this to Lockwood: "Letter-writing is, perhaps, the most important division of composition work, since it is the most practical. After you leave school, you may never be called upon to write a formal essay or a fictitious story; but all through life there will be occasions for writing letters of business or friendship. It is very important, therefore, that you should know what are the requisites of a good letter" (257).

10. In 1929 Roy Ivans Johnson undertook a survey of forty composition textbooks in which he found that they devoted 6 percent of their contents to letter writing, and reported that "practically all the emphasis is laid on *forms* of business correspondence and formal notes," which indicates that not much had changed. In response to his sense that something should change, however, to make letter-writing instruction more effective, he also undertook a statistical analysis of the qualities of actual letters, which he compared to the frequency with which those qualities were mentioned in the textbooks. Finding the textbooks lacking, he appealed to his analysis as having "sufficient particularization . . . to facilitate the determination of proper activities and experiences to be included in a course of instruction designed to improve ability in letter-writing." (*English Expression*, 51, 69) The presumed result: more rules.

Works Cited Other Than Textbooks

Adams, Katherine. *A History of Professional Writing Instruction in American Colleges: Years of Acceptance, Growth, and Doubt.* Dallas: Southern Methodist University Press. 1993.

Blair, Hugh. *Lectures on Rhetoric and Belles-Lettres.* New York, 1819.

Brereton, John C. *The Origins of Composition Studies in the American College, 1875–1925.* Pittsburgh, 1995.

Buck, Gertrude. "Recent Tendencies in the Teaching of English Composition." *Educational Review* 22 (1901). Reprint in Brereton, *The Origins of Composition Studies.*

Connors, Robert J. *Composition-Rhetoric: Background, Theory, and Pedagogy.* Pittsburgh, 1997.

Dawson, George. "Letter-Writing and Famous Letter Writers." *Shakespeare and Other Lectures.* London, 1888, 234–47.

Jewett, Ida A. *English in State Teachers College: A Catalogue Survey.* New York: Columbia University Burueau of Publications, 1927.

Johnson, Nan. *Nineteenth-Century Rhetoric in North America.* Carbondale: Southern Illinois University Press. 1991.

Johnson, Roy Ivan. *English Expression: A Study in Curriculum Building.* Bloomington, 1929.

Kitzhaber, Albert R. *Rhetoric in American Colleges, 1850–1900* Dallas, 1990.

Textbooks Surveyed in This Study

These books are part of a larger data base containing information about the holdings in nineteenth-century rhetoric of the Knight Library at the University of Oregon. Editions used for this survey are those of found in the University of Oregon collection; the earliest edition found in the collection was used for this survey. Abbreviated titles are given in this list, and one author given for multiple-authored textbooks.

Textbooks Surveyed in Which Letter Writing Appears

Arnold, Sarah. *Manual of Rhetoric and Composition.* 1907.

———. *The Mother Tongue II.* 1900.

———. *The Mother Tongue III.* 1902.

Baldwin, Charles. *Composition.* 1909.

Bardeen, C. W. *Shorter Course in Rhetoric.* 1885.

Bartlett, A. L. *Elements of English Grammar.* 1906.

Bates, Arlo. *Talks on Writing English.* 1901.

Blaisdell, Thomas. *Steps in English Composition-Rhetoric.* 1906.

Boyd, James. *Elements of Rhetoric.* 1858.

Brewster, William. *English Composition and Style.* 1912.

Brooks, Stratton. *Composition-Rhetoric.* 1905.

———. *English Composition Book I.* 1911.

Brubaker, A. R. *High School English Book I.* 1910.

———. *High School English Book II.* 1910.

Buehler, Huber. *A Modern English Grammar and Composition.* 1900.

———. *Modern English Lessons.* 1902.

Canby, Henry. *English Composition.* 1911.

Carpenter, George. *Exercises in Rhetoric and English Composition.* 1896.

———. *Introduction to Theme Writing.* 1893.

———. *Rhetoric and English Composition.* 1906.

Carson, Luella Clay. *English.* 1898.

———. *English Composition.* 1903.

———. *English Composition: Standard Rules.* 1903.

———. *Handbook of English Composition.* 1907.

Chittenden, L.A. *Elements of English Composition.* 1890.

Clippinger, Erle. *Composition and Rhetoric.* 1914.

Coppee, Henry. *Elements of Rhetoric.* 1859.

Coppens, Charles. *Practical Introduction to English Rhetoric.* 1880.

Emerson, Henry. *Modern Rhetoric Book II.* 1907.

Hanson, Charles. *English Composition.* 1908.

———. *Two Years' Course in English Composition.* 1912.

Harris, Ada. *Guidebooks to English Book I.* 1907.

———. *Guidebooks to English Book II.* 1907.

Hart, John. *First Lessons in Composition.* 1870.

———. *Manual of Comosition and Rhetoric.* 1878.

Harvey, Thomas. *Elementary Grammar and Composition.* 1869.

Hepburn. A. D. *Manual of English Rhetoric.* 1875.

Herrick, Robert. *Composition and Rhetoric.* 1902.

———. *New Composition and Rhetoric.* 1911.

Hill, Adams S. *Beginnings of Rhetoric and Composition.* 1902.

———. *Foundations of Rhetoric.* 1892.

———. *Principles of Rhetoric.* 1878.

Hill, David. *Elements of Rhetoric and Composition.* 1878.

Hitchcock, Alfred. *Composition and Rhetoric.* 1906.

———. *Enlarged Practice Book.* 1906.

———. *New Practice Book in English Composition.* 1914.

Hyde, Mary. *Practical English Grammar.* 1900.

Kellogg, Brainerd. *Text-book on Rhetoric.* 1882.

Kimball, Lillian. *Elementary English.* 1911.

Knox, M. L. *Elementary Lessons In English.* 1882.

Lamont, Hammond. *English Composition.* 1906.

Layres, Augustus. *Belles-Lettres.* 1867.

Lockwood, Sara. *Composition and Rhetoric.* 1901.

———. *Lessons in English.* 1888.

Lyle, Orum. *Advanced Grammar and Composition.* 1899.

Maxwell, William. *First Book in English.* 1894.

———. *Primary Lessons in English.* 1886.

———. *School Composition.* 1902.

———. *Writing in English.* 1900.

McElroy, John. *Structure of English Prose.* 1885.

McFadden, Effie. *Grammar and Composition.* 1914.

———. *McFadden Language Series Book One.* 1915.

McLean, A. C. *Advanced Steps in English.* 1903.

———. *Steps in English.* 1903.

Meiklejohn, J. *Art of Writing English.* 1900.

Merkley, George. *Modern Rhetoric.* 1902.

Metcalf, Robert. *A Language Series Book Two.* 1910.

Monkhouse, W. *The Precis Book.* 1896.

Newcomer, Alphonse. *Elements of Rhetoric.* 1898.

———. *Practical Course in English Composition.* 1893.

Nichol, John. *English Composition.* 1878.

Park, J. G. *Language Lessons.* 1898.

Parker, Richard. *Aids to English Composition.* 1857.

Patterson, Calvin. *Advanced Grammar.* 1887.

Paul, George F. *Composition Through Life and Literature.* 1906.

Quackenbos, G. P. *Advanced Course of Composition.* 1854.

———. *First Lessons in Composition.* 1884.

Quackenbos, John. *Practical Rhetoric.* 1896.

Raub, Albert. *Practical Rhetoric and Composition.* 1891.

Redford, Mandel. *Composition and Rhetoric.* 1903.

Reed, Alonzo. *An Elementary English Grammar.* 1880.
———. *Graded Lessons in English.* 1896.
———. *Higher Lessons in English.* 1901.
———. *Work in English Grammar.* 1877.
Robbins, Carolyn. *Grammar and Composition.* 1907.
Scott, Fred Newton. *Elementary English Composition.* 1902.
Simons, Emogene. *First Year in English.* 1906.
Smith, Lewis. *Modern Composition and Rhetoric.* 1900.
Southworth, Gordon. *Our Language: Its Uses and Structure.* 1887.
Spalding, Elizabeth. *The Principles of Rhetoric.* 1905.
Swinton, John. *New Language Lessons.* 1883.
———. *Progressive Grammar.* 1876.
Sykes, Frederick. *Elementary English Composition.* 1905.
Tarbell, Horace. *Lessons in English: Second Book.* 1896.
Waddy, Virginia. *Elements of Composition and Rhetoric.* 1889.
Webster, W. F. *Elementary Composition.* 1903.
———. *Language, Grammar, and Composition.* 1903.
Wendell, Barrett. *English Composition: Eight Lectures.* 1891.
Williams, William. *Composition and Rhetoric.* 1893.
Wooley, Edwin. *Handbook of Composition.* 1909.

Textbooks Surveyed in Which Letter-Writing Does Not Appear

Abbott, Edwin. *How to Write Clearly.* 1879.
Anderson, Jessie. *Sixty Composition-Topics.* 1894.
Bain, Alexander. *English Composition and Rhetoric.* 1866.
Baker, George. *Principles of Argumentation.* 1895.
Baldwin, Charles. *College Manual of Rhetoric.* 1905.
———. *How to Write.* 1905.
Bardeen, C.W. *Outlines of Sentence-Making.* 1884.
Baskerville, W. M. *English Grammar.* 1895.
Berkeley, Francis. *College Course in Writing from Models.* 1910.
Blackman, R. D. *Composition and Style.* 1908.
Brookfield, F. *First Book in Composition.* 1856.
Brown, Goold. *Grammar of English Grammars.* 1851.
———. *Institutes of English Grammar.* 1853.
Buck, Gertrude. *Course in Argumentative Writing.* 1899.
Buehler, Huber. *Practical Exercises in English.* 1895.
Canby, Henry. *English Composition.* 1909.
Carpenter, George. *Elements of Rhetoric.* 1899.
———. *English Grammar.* 1906.
———. *Exercises in English.* 1893.
———. *Exposition in Classroom Practice.* 1906.
———. *Principles of English Grammar.* 1898.
———. *Studies in Literature and Style.* 1896.
Clark, Stephen. *First Lessons in English Grammar.* 1856.
———. *Normal Grammar.* 1875.
Coppee, Henry. *Elements of Logic.* 1857.

Covell, L. T. *Digest of English Grammar.* 1866.

Day, Henry. *The Art of Discourse.* 1867.

———. *Rhetorical Praxis.* 1860.

Donnelly, Francis. *Imitation and Analysis.* 1902.

Earle, John. *English Prose.* 1890.

———. *Philology of the English Language.* 1892.

Espenshade, A.H. *Essentials of Composition and Rhetoric.* 1904.

Fernald, James. *Connectives of English Speech.* 1904.

Foster, William T. *Argumentation and Debating.* 1908.

Fowler, Thomas. Logic, *Inductive and Deductive.* 1893.

Gaw, James. *Method of English, Part I.* 1892.

Gay, George. *Drill Book in English.* 1891.

Genung, John. *Handbook of Rhetorical Analysis.* 1888.

———. *Practical Elements of Rhetoric.* 1891.

———. *Working Principles of Rhetoric.* 1900.

Gowdy, Chestine. *English Grammar.* 1901.

Greene, Samual. *English Grammar.* 1856.

Gregory, D. S. *Practical Logic.* 1885.

Grose, Howard. *Specimens of English Composition.* 1909.

Hackett, Fred. *Pure English.* 1884.

Hart, James. *Essentials of Prose Composition.* 1902.

Hartog, Philip. *Writing in English.* 1908.

Harvey, Thomas. *Practical Grammar.* 1878.

Hill, Adams S. *Our English.* 1889.

Hill, David. *The Science of Rhetoric.* 1877.

Hitchcock, Alfred. *Rhetoric and the Study of Literature.* 1913.

Hodgson, William. *Errors in the Use of English.* 1882.

Holbrook, Alfred. *English Grammar.* 1873.

Johnson, Rossiter. *Alphabet of Rhetoric.* 1903.

Kavana, Rose. *Composition and Rhetoric.* 1902.

Kerl, Simon. *Common-School Grammar.* 1864.

Lamont, Hammond. *Specimens on Exposition.* 1894.

Laycock, Craven. *Argumentation and Debate.* 1904.

Lewes, George. *Principles of Success in Literature.* 1891.

Lewis, Frances. *Inductive Lessons in Rhetoric.* 1900.

Linn, James. *Essentials of English Composition.* 1912.

Lounsbury, Thomas. *Standard Usage in English.* 1907.

MacEwan, Elias. *Essentials of Argumentation.* 1898.

Marsh, George. *Lectures in the English Language.* 1859.

Meiklejohn, J. *English Grammar.* 1887.

Murray, Lindley. *English Grammar-Abridgement.* 1866.

———. *Lindley Murray's English Grammar.* 1868.

Nutter, Charles. *Specimens on Prose Composition.* 1906.

Pearson, H. G. *Principles of Composition.* 1897.

Percival, Milton. *Specimens of Exposition and Argument.* 1908.

Perry, Frances. *Introductory Course in Argumentation.* 1906.

———. *Introductory Course in Exposition.* 1908.

Pryde, David. *Studies in Composition.* 1901.

Quackenbos. G.P. *English Grammar.* 1862.

Robinson, A. T. *Applications of Logic.* 1912.

Scott, Fred Newton. *Composition-Literature.* 1902.

———. *Composition-Rhetoric.* 1897.

———. *New Composition and Rhetoric.* 1911.

———. *Paragraph Writing.* 1893.

Sherman, Lucius. *Elements of Literature and Composition.* 1908.

Sidgwick, Alfred. *Process of Argument.* 1893.

Skinner, W. H. *Studies in Literature and Composition.* 1897.

Smith, George. *Longman's English Grammar.* 1901.

Smith, Roswell. *English Grammar on the Productive System.* 1864.

Starkweather, Asher. *Aid to English Grammar.* 1885.

Stebbins, Charles. *Progressive Course in English.* 1908.

Strang, H. I. *Exercises in English.* 1892.

Swinton, William. *School Manual of English Composition.* 1877.

Taylor, Joseph. *Composition in Narration.* 1910.

Tompkins, Arnold. *Science of Discourse.* 1889.

Webster, W. F. *English: Composition and Literature.* 1900.

Whitney, William. *Essentials of English Grammar.* 1877.

Wilson, Mary. *Lessons in Language.* 1889.

Letter Writing in the
Late Age of Print

ELECTRONIC MAIL AND THE *ARS DICTAMINIS*

Joyce R. Walker

In the early 1990s, e-mail exploded onto the letter-writing scene, rescuing the letter from the neglect it had suffered in the preceding decades. As a friend of mine said recently, "Before e-mail, a letter was something you wrote to someone who owed you money—or to your grandmother." As the numbers of individuals and organizations using e-mail grew, pundits and scholars alike applauded e-mail as a reincarnation of the epistolary tradition. Many commentators made even grander claims for e-mail, arguing that it was a revolutionary form of communication with a decorum all its own. E-mail stylists have worked to separate evolving e-mail styles and forms from those of the traditional print letter. For instance, Goode and Johnson called it "a new, different, and still evolving medium" (1991, 61) and stressed its dissimilarity from the traditional letter.

The flurry of e-mail activity over the past decade and a half has been accompanied by a proliferation of netiquette manuals that attempt to explain the ins and outs of e-mail usage for the "newbie," or inexperienced user. Although many of these manuals were written in the mid to late 1990s, it is possible to find updated versions still being produced in 2005, along with manuals to cover style and etiquette issues for e-mail's younger sibling, instant messaging.[1] The focus of these manuals often seems to be differences between electronic messages and other letter-writing forms, and authors often emphasize the importance of establishing conventions to govern activities in these new epistolary environments. In an attempt to chart this new territory, stylists advise users regarding such unfamiliar terms as "spamming," "flaming," "killfiles," and "cybersex," none of which can be found in the letter-writing manuals of the past. What is perhaps not fully understood, however, is that the issues under discussion in these online guides represent only the most current manifestation of an ancient genre, the *ars dictaminis,* designed to instruct letter writers in the task of writing and sending effective letters. Although the advice given by modern stylists on such matters as whether it is more appropriate to use an informal or formal style, how much the relative social positions of the sender and recipient should dictate the letter's tone, and whether changes in the private and public nature of a letter require different methods of composition may have shifted dramatically in the intervening years, these issues play as important a role in present day *artes dictandi* as they did to the medieval *dictatores*.

As a response to the need for letters to suit various rhetorical purposes, letter-writing manuals of different periods have provided rules, guidelines, and models for writing proper and readable prose, as well as philosophies regarding what a letter is supposed to achieve and what each writer's responsibilities are. Careful consideration of the changes that have occurred in letter-writing manuals of different periods can help us to better understand the guidelines that are being set up to govern our electronic communications. Although electronic correspondence forms such as e-mail and instant messaging certainly diverge significantly from the forms and styles used in more traditional letter writing, a look at the manuals that have been used to guide letter writers in the past may give us a clearer picture of the ways these new forms fit into the ongoing tradition of letter writing.

An excellent example of the connections that can be made between present and past letter-writing forms is the discussion of the letter's position at the boundary between written and spoken communication. The informal tone of most e-mail messages is said to be a direct result of this merger between writing and speaking and is one of the important claims made for the unique nature of e-mail and instant messaging communications. An association with the spoken word, however, was also considered one of the primary factors accounting for the extravagant formality that often accompanied the medieval letter. During the medieval period, the letter's prominence was largely due to its importance as a method of communication between political and religious leaders in various, distant locations. Martin Camargo argues that the letter of this time was primarily meant as an accompaniment to an oral message. The medieval letter strictly adhered to a five-part structure: *salutatio, exordium, narratio, argumentio,* and *conclusio.* Camargo sees the fact that this form was grafted from Cicero's structure for the five parts of an oration as evidence of the letter's oral component ("Where's the Brief?" [1996], 4). If, as Camargo points out, the recipient of a letter was sometimes labeled the *auditor,* it makes sense that the language of the letter would be structured so that it might be read impressively in public (5). The physical letter would thus serve as both an ornamentation and a written record of the transaction. The medieval letter had a public quality that required not only strict attention to the proper forms, but a language suitable for formal, public occasions.

Both e-mail messages and official letters of the medieval period can therefore claim an incorporation of aspects of both written and spoken communication, but, whereas medieval letters might be said to privilege orality, using the written letter as a sort of reinforcement, or even as a keepsake to accompany a spoken presentation (11), e-mail and instant messages manage instead to incorporate certain qualities of oral communication into the format of written text. The blending of these qualities results in something quite different from the formality and ornamentation of the medieval letter, and this informality can sometimes cause unique problems. Not only are such messages not read aloud, but they are sometimes not even read thoroughly. One frequently cited online guide reminds users, "Read carefully, especially if you think you disagree with something. People tend to read e-mail messages and postings too quickly, and to fail to understand the real intent behind a message."[2] The informality of the medium and the carelessness that can sometimes result from continue to be a primary concern for e-mail stylists. Careless readings can cause respondents to dash off a quick reply, which is why the flame—defined by Adam Gaffin and Jørg Heitkotter in *EEF's Extended Guide to the Internet* (2005) as a "particularly nasty, personal attack on somebody for something he or she has written"—takes up considerable space in online manuals. Flames can occur as a result of a disagreement over the topic under discussion or even over stylistic or grammatical errors.[3] Whereas some stylists take the more conservative approach of discouraging all flaming (encouraging writers who are flamed to avoid responding), Virginia Shea notes that the flame has its place in the online environment: "Some USENET newsgroups, like alt.flame and alt.tasteless, exist purely for the purpose of sharing rude and offensive writings" (*Netiquette* [1994], 79). The general opinion in online guides, however, is that flames occur because readers lose track of the distinction between the e-mail message as an informal conversation and the e-mail message as a permanent, written document.

Since electronic messages are very often back-and-forth exchanges that take place with much greater rapidity than letter exchanges of the past, writers must also consider the issue of what to include in their messages to make the connection to past messages evident. Multiple online guides for listserves and forums warn their users to be careful to "quote just enough of the [previous] message to allow someone reading your article to know what you are talking about." For example, when one wishes to respond in agreement to a statement that another writer has made, it is bad form to either quote the entire message and then add "me too," or to write only "me too" without any reference to the comment or idea that prompted the response. The informality inherent in a medium that can allow within its parameters the possibility that a correspondent might send a message that simply says, "Yes" or "O.K." is clear. It is this informality that some stylists claim makes electronic correspondence so similar to the qualities of spoken conversation (particularly for instant messaging, which most closely appropriates the give-and-take of spoken conversation).

This similarity means that netiquette stylists must continually strive to find ways to help e-mail writers be effective within the gray area between writing and speaking and find the appropriate tone to create a balance between the two. For example, "Instant Messaging Etiquette, in *PC World,* takes care to explain that even though instant messaging *seems* conversational, its limitations (space, time, lack of visual cues) make it inappropriate as a replacement for serious, face-to-face conversations. As a result, users must remember to keep messages short and switch to another mode (e.g., the telephone) if they find themselves continually "bumping up against the word limit" (Thorsborg 2002, 2).

The general issue of tone in letter writing, however, is one that has received a great deal of attention throughout the history of the *ars dictaminis,* and Camargo's discussion of the medieval letter shows that the distinction between writing and speaking has been blurred at other times in the letter's history. Perhaps one task of present online manuals might be to explore how the medium's purposes and environment create new requirements for writers, which, while different in some ways, share the need for a careful consideration of all facets of each particular communication in order to be effective.

Dictatores during the medieval period also placed great importance on the status of the sender and receiver, which is reflected in the amount of space medieval manual writers gave to the *salutatio,* discussing at length the placement of the names of the sender and receiver and certain additions, which "should be selected so that they point to some aspect of the recipient's renown and good character" (Anonymous of Bologna 1971, 8).[4] The emphasis placed on this portion of the letter seems logical, given that letters at this time were mainly sent between dignitaries who were unable to meet face to face. And as William Wiethoff notes, "The demand for well-trained secretaries to keep official records . . . and to express important policy statements in formal letters" was the reason why "the rhetoric of letter writing" remained so important throughout this period (1991, 268). In other words, the medieval letter was meant to be written and read on official occasions, and the *artes dictandi,* which were written to aid secretaries in their task, might be comparable to twentieth-century business writing manuals such as Robert L. Shurter's, *Effective Letters in Business,* a mid-century textbook for aspiring business writers. Like his predecessors, Shurter also spends substantial time on the various ways in which the heading of a letter can be constructed, elaborating carefully the merits of each form (1954, 24–33).

In the e-mail message, the sender and recipient can also be important. On a purely practical level, the sender and recipient's e-mail addresses must be listed correctly in the "To:" and "From:" headings so a message to be routed correctly through the network. Within the body of the message, however, the *salutatio* is often dispensed with entirely. A simple "hello," or even nothing at all may open the e-mail message. One reason for this is that the issue of sender and recipient becomes extremely complicated when one is sending messages to multiple recipients—the members of a newsgroup or listserv for example. All messages in these situations are sent to all members of the group, who participate because of a shared interest in the topic(s) under discussion. Opening such messages with a traditional twentieth-century "To Whom it May Concern" seems redundant.

On the other hand, the issue of signatures (a line or series of lines at the *end* of an e-mail message identifying the sender) is one that is subject to a great deal of speculation and varying advice in online manuals. Arlene Rinaldi's *Net User Guidelines* stipulates that signatures should always "include your name, position, affiliation, and Internet and/or BITNET addresses and should not exceed more than four lines" (1992). Another source that takes a more satirical stance on the subject (but nevertheless brings the point home) is Emily Postnews, a mock-serious netiquette advice column on the worldwide web. It provides the following facetious guideline: "Dear Verbose: Please try and make your signature as long as you can. It's much more important than your article, of course, so try to have more lines of signature that actual text." The generally approved style for signature files is to keep them as short as possible and to list only pertinent information, yet there are many users who include quotations, epigrams, inspirational messages, text-images (pictures created from an arrangement of text characters) or graphics in their signature files. So, although e-mail may in some ways limit or even eliminate the importance of the salutatio, in other ways it opens new discussions of how a writer might best identify and present him or herself to various readers.[5]

Although some online guides permit a certain amount of artistic ornamentation at the end of an e-mail message, *dicatores* of epistolography in the late twentieth century would be unlikely to approve of the ornate style that often characterized the medieval letter. Charles Fantazzi suggests that the shift away from this ornate style was precipitated by Petrarch's discovery of a manuscript of Cicero's letters. This crucial event gave Petrarch access to specific examples of Cicero's simple style and lack of ornamentation (*De conscribendis epistolis* [1989], 5–6). Previously, dictatores had worked with only Cicero's *De inventione* and the pseudo-Ciceronian *Rhetorica ad Herennium*, both of which had been written with orations, not letters, in mind. At least partially as a result of the use of these sources, medieval author Brunetto Latini, in his *Tresor*, so closely allied the letter to the oration that he finally claimed that any letter that did not contain controversy was unfit for rhetorical treatment (Witt 1982, 19).

Petrarch, using the letters of Cicero as his example, claimed that the true letter's purpose was simply to send information, and in his own letters strove to emulate Cicero's "plain, familiar style" (Fantazzi, *De conscribendis epistolis* [1989], 6). Petrarch's efforts may mark the beginnings of humanism—as Witt claims—a turn in the history of the letter that allowed a form of personal, intimate communication with great artistic potential to emerge. In the medieval period, the distinctions between the letter as a public and private form had been de-emphasized by *dictatores* for whom the private letter was relatively unimportant. Petrarch appears to have been one of the leading forces in bringing the private letter into the spotlight.

This transformation might also be an illustration of how philosophies of letter writing have been affected by the purposes for which letters are written. The shift in focus occurred at a time when the private letter was becoming more diverse in its uses.

As the fifteenth century progressed, official letters sent in the name of a ruling authority increasingly lost importance as a means of carrying on diplomatic relations and political propaganda. There were more embassies, whereas letters and tracts composed by humanists in their own name and written in humanistic Latin became the major vehicle for propaganda (Witt 1982, 33).

Scholars were beginning to use the letter to write to each other, defining points and defending their own theories. As it became easier to send and receive mail, it became necessary, almost imperative, to bring the familiar letter into the fold of the *ars dictaminis*. No one event or public figure prompted this shift; rather, a transformation in the way scholars communicated made the change appear inevitable. The issues discussed by scholars altered as new information became available, while at the same time new uses for the letter altered the issues that required discussion. It was no longer possible to consider the public letter as the only form worthy of discussion in letter-writing manuals—and therefore discussions of the rhetoric of private, familiar letters became common.

The blending of public and private purposes in guides for letter writing is a trend that has continued and perhaps even expanded in their latest electronic reincarnations. The use of e-mail and instant messaging for a great variety of both public and private communications means that online guides must provide writers with information that helps them distinguish between public/formal, public/informal, and more private communications. For example, communication spaces such as *Friendster* (www.friendster.com) are very public environments that nevertheless require a very informal tone—in fact, it is possible to cause misunderstandings with the use of a tone or style that is too formal.[6] Readers can mistake this tone for condescension or a stiffness of manner that is incompatible to the free discussion taking place in these environments. On the other hand, an e-mail message sent through a company's intranet from a subordinate to his or her supervisor must contain a certain level of formality even though it is a more intimate communication. And, although personal letters sent via e-mail can be both informal in tone and private in nature, online guides warn that privacy is unpredictable on the Internet, and as a result, writers must always keep potential public audiences in mind. Rinaldi reminds users, "Never assume that your E-mail can be read by no one except yourself; others may be able to read or access your mail. Never send or keep anything that you would not mind seeing on the evening news" (1992, online). So, although the content of an e-mail letter may be private, the tone and style must be appropriate in many cases for more public distribution. The issues of public versus private, formal versus informal, and ornate versus unadorned have undergone significant transformations in the electronic environment, yet they retain their connection to the purpose of the letter-writing situation. As in the past, changing purposes for the letters that must be written have led to shifts in focus for the *ars dictaminis*. Similar to the shift toward a more careful consideration of the private letter that took place with the new purposes for letter writing occurring at the close of the medieval period, present-day considerations of tone and style must be consistent with the public and private purposes for which e-mail and instant messages are used.

Erasmus's revised version of *De conscribendis epistolis,* a letter-writing guide that was published in 1522, provides evidence of the transition that the study of the letter had undergone, due in part to the work of the humanists in the twelfth through fourteenth centuries. It marks a shift along the public/private continuum that the letter continues to travel in its new electronic environment. Camargo points out that "the boundary between 'public' and 'private' letters was less sharply drawn in the Middle Ages than it is today" (1996, 11), but the work of the humanists served to create a distinction between the two. The letter's use for communications other than those strictly official resulted in two entirely different treatments. Whereas the humanist scholars focused on the letter as a personal communication, and an art form, the rule of the *ars dictaminis* remained unchallenged over the area of the public letter (Witt 1982, 3). *De conscribendis epistolis* may be viewed as Erasmus's attempt to reconcile the two, a practical wish to consider letter writing as an art whose defining characteristic is its flexibility.

Erasmus begins his treatise by claiming that letters must be, above all, flexible: "To expect all letters to conform to a single type, or to teach that they should, as I notice even learned men sometimes do, is in my view at least to impose a narrow and inflexible definition on what is by nature diverse and capable of almost infinite variation" (1985, 12). He goes on to say that "no topic is excluded from the letter form" and that "the mode of expression must never be at variance with the nature of the subject" (12). This comment provides the key to two aspects of this work that are important to the evolution of the letter. First, Erasmus includes in his discussion the three classes of subject approved "by the majority of rhetoricians": persuasive, ecomiastic, and judicial (71), but to these subjects he adds a fourth, which he terms the familiar. In this way he brings the private letter into the same discussion as the public letter. The second issue of importance is the stress he places on the subject matter as opposed to the status of the sender and the receiver as the impetus for determining tone. Whereas the medieval author, writing official letters, focused on the recipient's title and position, and Petrarch initiated a focus on the recipient's character as the main determiner, Erasmus advised the writer to focus on these issues in conjunction with the content of the letter being written: "In my opinion the best form of expression is that which is most appropriate to the context" (12).

Erasmus makes it clear that he does not intend to provide the writer with the perfect letter for every occasion, but his method of enumerating specific types of letters, and of using the subject matter to group all letters, not just official correspondence, into categories, became an accepted method for writing manuals throughout the following centuries. The increased focus on subject matter allowed the familiar letter to take its place in the *artes dictandi,* and this focus, (along with the flexibility it encourages), remains in the online manuals designed for e-mail and instant message users. The intervention of various "communication technologies" over the years, however, actually shifted the focus away from the familiar letter during the early twentieth century, though the process of providing sample letter to guide writers remained popular.

For example, during the seventeenth and eighteenth centuries, manuals often consisted primarily of sample letters, which varied to account for diverse writing situations. *Familiar Letters on Important Occasions,* a guide written by Samuel Richardson, the author of the epistolary novel *Pamela,* might serve as an example of an eighteenth-century version of this type of manual ([1741] 1928).[7] Richardson's text contains a brief introduction followed by a long list of sample letters of various kinds. Unlike Erasmus, Richardson provides his samples for very specific situations, rather than grouping them first into broad categories. His samples, though, do include both business and personal letters, such as "From a Town Tenant to his Landlord excusing Delay of Payment" and "Of Consolation to a Friend in Prison for Debt" (xxxvi). The text contains a preponderance of more personal letters, designed, as the author maintains "[to] direct the forms requisite to be observed on the most important occasions" (xxvii).

During the eighteenth century the familiar letter achieved dominance over the formal, public letter in letter-writing manuals, perhaps through the continual attempts of writers to achieve a style that came as close as possible to a conversation. As a result, the term *Familiar* seems to have come to encompass almost any letter that might be written from one person to another. The primacy of the familiar letter during this period does not, of course, mean that letters of business were not written, any more than the focus of the medieval *ars dictaminis* on the formal letter meant that personal, intimate letters between two people were not written in the Middle Ages. This focus on the familiar letter means rather that the letters that were considered the most worthy of study and comment were letters that maintained the illusion of unstudied ease, whether the writing situation was formal or informal.

In a substantial tome of the nineteenth century, *Gaskell's Compendium of Forms: Social, Educational, Legal and Commercial,* G. A. Gaskell proposes to provide, as his title page claims, a "Complete Encyclopedia of Reference" for "The Young Men and Young Women of the United States." Although this guide covers many practical issues of business and personal writing, the introduction to the section on letter-writing claims: "The great art is to be able to write gracefully and with ease, to suit the style to the correspondence, and while carefully avoiding error, to avoid also the appearance of having studied the letter" (1882, 206).

This demand for naturalness, however arduously produced, remained a goal of the letter writer well into the twentiethth century. The letter, as a form of communication and art, was valued for its flexibility, and for what Claudio Guillén calls "the fictional impulse" (1994, 4). Guillén proposes that it is "in the imaginary impulse connecting the writer with the addressee that we find the particular equivocation of the letter"(7). Once the nature of the letter as a private communication between friends had been reestablished (through Petrarch), the letter moved on, in the eighteenth century, into the realm of fiction.[6] Guillén sees this as a natural progression: "Thus in the epistolary genres the thrust of the language, the progress of the writing itself, have been proven to have irresistibly fictional consequences. In fact, it seems that to compose a letter may lead the writer toward fiction before he even begins to approach literature" (4). The letter's ability to "propel us toward inventiveness" is seen as a great asset in everyday use, as well as an opportunity for creative expression (14). Whereas the introduction of "writing technologies" in the late nineteenth century tended to curtail the exploration of familiar letters in writing in the guides of that period, e-mail guides, with their focus on flexibility and diversity, once again encourage writers toward inventive strategies for communicating ideas.

The widespread use, beginning in the late 1800s, of the typewriter in the business office, is perhaps as good a marker as any of the beginning of the decline in the familiar letter and a subsequent decline in the creativity that letter-writing manuals encouraged (Zuboff 1988, 115). By 1922 Thomas Arkle Clarke, in his letter-writing guide, *When You Write a Letter,* is forced to lament, "Stenography has done a great deal to facilitate and accelerate letter writing, but in many ways it has injured and cheapened the art" (8). Machines such as the typewriter, the Dictaphone and the telephone, according to Clarke, "have taken away from [the letter] its charm and its personal flavor"(6). After discussing the poor quality of many of the letters that he, as a dean of men and professor of rhetoric at the University of Illinois, has received, he goes on to say, "Writing letters is something more than merely putting one word after another upon paper. It is an art, and an art almost universally employed, which is well worth our study" (32).

Clarke follows the structure of presenting samples of various types of letters, but unlike Erasmus or Richardson, he divides his letters into specific categories: The Friendly Letter, Formal Notes, The Business Letter, and Letters of Courtesy. Clarke spends some time within each chapter explaining how the letter writing of his time falls short of what should be considered acceptable. For example, when introducing the subject of the Formal Note, he relates a story about his sister giving a dinner party. He deplores the fact that "less than a third of those invited had replied" and that the notes of those who did reply were written without knowledge of the form or tone proper to the occasion (99).

Clarke may have had good reason to lament the lost value of the familiar letter as an art form requiring care and attention. By the mid–twentieth century, letter-writing manuals had moved once more toward a more narrow focus on letters of business. Consequently, it is possible to find letter-writing texts in which the familiar, personal letter is barely mentioned. The telephone being the quickest way to contact friends and family, guides such as Rosemary Fruehling and Sharon Bouchard's *Art of Writing Effective Letters,* published in 1972, exclude the personal letter from their discussion almost entirely, providing examples only of the type of personal note that might be said to fulfill a specific rhetorical purpose such as responding to an invitation or sending a note of thanks. The guides of the mid–twentieth century often provide a discussion of set structures for letter writing that resemble the prescriptions of the medieval *dictatores* more than they do Erasmus's notion of flexibility, whereas the demand for an "everyday, conversational, easy-to-read style" remains (Fruehling and Bouchard, 1972, vii), closing off even the opportunity for artful ornamentation that medieval letter writing provided.

Fortunately, the explosion in the use of e-mail and instant messaging for business and personal communications has returned the letter's potential for flexibility and creativity to the forefront, and necessitates further exploration of many of the issues that have been under discussion throughout the letter's evolution. In fact, the ever-increasing number of users (more than 2.25 million in North America in 2005)[8] makes it crucial for writers and readers of electronic letters to take up the discussion once more, and netiquette guides appear to be a centralized location for this discussion. These guides include three basic types: Internet how-to manuals, which focus on the actual use of software programs and communication spaces; general Internet guides, which are usually brief documents with pointers about basic rules of netiquette; and more extended guides, which attempt to provide users with basic information, rules of polite behavior, and the philosophy behind various types of electronic communication. Unlike manuals such as *Gaskell's Compendium of Forms,* these guides rarely provide sample messages for readers. Instead they focus on such general issues as style and tone, as well as more specific issues related to the nature of the medium, such as intellectual property, accessing FAQs (frequently asked questions), or the use of brief, descriptive subject lines by which messages can be identified.

Online guides also deal with issues related to the sociology of the Internet, how different communication groups work, and how users interact with one another. Although some guides focus on a particular type of online communication (newsgroups or chat spaces, for example), many guides are divided up into categories, such as e-mail, listservs, newsgroups, instant messaging, and so forth. These groupings differ from former guides in that letters are categorized according to the environment they are being used within rather than the content of the message. Some guides also divide online communications into such categories as "one-to-one" and "one-to-many" interchanges, which also seems to be related more to the kind of communication taking place than the subject matter under discussion (Shea, 1994, 94–96). Whatever their organization, the primary goal of these guides seems to be to help users understand how writing works in various electronic environments. They also remind users of the international nature of the web and stress the importance of understanding the audience for any given communication.

Another important aspect of netiquette guides is their focus on unusual stylistic features. Whereas stylists maintain that spelling and punctuation are very important matters, even in the informal arena of electronic communication, a certain casual playfulness has made its way into e-mail and instant messaging, and netiquette guides approve and reinforce this attitude. For example, the use of abbreviations for certain standard comments—known as emoticons—is allowed and in some guides even encouraged: IMHO (in my humble opinion) and FYI (for your information) are standard abbreviations that Arlene Rinaldi's guide encourages writers to use whenever possible. Eric Gillin's guide for instant message users also encourages their use, but notes that the desire to be "ultra-hip" in using cool acronyms can conflict with the need for clarity. He points out that acronyms that readers do not know—and that consequently must be explained by the writer—do not serve their purpose as finger-and-time-saving devices. Most guides do encourage the use of emoticons to indicate mood. These are text-images that are created to show humor :-) or sarcasm ;-}.[9] The reasoning behind the use of emoticons involves both the informal nature of the medium and the problems that can occur as a result of the blended qualities of written and spoken communications. Netiquette stylists claim that this blending makes humor easily misunderstood, and they advocate the use of emoticons to make meaning clear.

Perhaps the most interesting and complicated issues with which these manuals must deal is the indistinct relationship between the public and private nature of the letter and the formal and informal tone that different letters may require. The flexibility of the letter is stretched far indeed by the purposes of electronic communication, and online manuals must help writers identify how these different purposes affect issues such as style and tone. The blurring of public and private within the electronic environment is increased as a result of the ease with which any reader can "forward" or resend a received message on to another (or multiple other) reader(s), as well as by the number of individuals who might be participating in any given "real-time" conversation online. In her *Netiquette* guide, Virginia Shea (1994) tells the story of two middle managers who accidentally sent their love letters, meant only for each other, to everyone at the company. In addition to situations of inadvertent publicity, users who participate in listservs and bulletin boards must compose their comments and responses keeping in mind that every member of this virtual community might read them. Shea provides sample situations in which a member of a group who is having problems with another user might need to forsake the public forum and send a message privately to that individual, rather than to the group (75). This issue is still of central concern, as is shown by the following comment in an instant messaging guide published by *PC World* in 2002: "If you wouldn't want to see your words on a postcard or a billboard, don't put them in an instant message" (Thorsberg, 2). In fact, the user sending a personal message has no guarantee that the receiver will not decide to publish this message to the group or forward it to another reader, though Shea points out that to do so without the sender's permission is "bad netiquette" (72). As complex as it is, this fusion of public and private is not a new circumstance in the history of letter writing. Letters of a very personal nature, written by public figures to friends and family, have often been published and read by a much wider audience. And as Guillén points out, the illusion of privacy has been used by authors of epistolary novels to create for the books' many readers a sense of intimacy and naturalness (1994, 4–7).

Negotiating levels of formality in electronic correspondence is another matter on which online guides must provide advice. In this area the medieval system of using the status of the sender and receiver to determine tone is no longer very useful. It can be difficult, if not impossible, to construct some messages using either the recipient's status or character as a determiner, because many electronic correspondents never actually meet in the physical world, however close they might become within the confines of a listserv, chat space, or other virtual community. In business-related correspondence it may be important to keep in mind the recipients' position—certainly the e-mail message one might send to a supervisor needs to be more carefully constructed than the message one might dash off to a friend. But even within the realm of business communications the status of the recipient may not be known, or the nature of the communication may require a level of informality that would seem inconsistent with the relative status of the sender and receiver.

Netiquette manuals can no longer make distinctions between the formal and informal by dividing letters between business and personal correspondence, as mid-twentieth-century stylists often did. An e-mail letter sent from one colleague to another within an organization might be extremely casual, lacking even a salutation and signature, and containing only a few lines. On the other hand, an e-mail message inquiring about a product or service offered online might be very formal—in keeping with the type of letter advocated by mid-twentieth-century manuals. That electronic communications permit and even seem to encourage such wide swings between formal and informal communications does seem unique. Every e-mail letter in an "In" box has the same appearance until it is opened, but once inside the message the tone may vary widely. The history of the letter's evolution, however, shows us that there is room along the continuum of public/private and formal/informal communications for negotiation between calls for decorum and the trend toward informality.

Netiquette guides can help writers by giving them terms and definitions for unfamiliar aspects of electronic communication; they can give practical advice regarding extraneous features (signature files or hyperlink) that may interfere with communication; they can discuss issues of tone and style and the changes that different online environments require; and they can attempt to ease the difficulties inherent in navigating a space that falls between the boundaries of written and spoken communication. In light of the wide variety of possible purposes for electronic communications, it may not be practical to attempt guides that give sample messages in the manner of Samuel Richardson or G. A. Gaskell. In fact, few online guides make any attempt to give "templates" for writers to follow. Netiquette guides, however, do attempt to give writers a better understanding of the environment within which they are operating. In their discussions regarding tone and style and the changes that different online environments require these guides can accentuate the new and unique qualities of electronic writing while maintaining a connection to the long tradition of letter-writing guides that have sought to serve the letter writer and make the act of letter writing more pleasurable. A greater awareness of this tradition can only be a benefit, both to netiquette stylists as they seek to provide information and to users who will better understand the heritage of their electronic communications.

Notes

1. Examples of instant message guides include Eric Gillin's, "The Instant Messenger Handbook," which can be found at http://www.blacktable.com/imhandbook.htm.

2. One verion of this guide, titled "Roberts Rules of Internet Order," can be found at http://www.cs.ut.ee/~jaanus/inet/netikett1.txt (accessed August 11, 2006).

3. The issue of spelling is a controversial on the Internet. "Spelling flames" have their own category in some online guides. A guide posted via the Oxford University Libraries Automation service, written by Chuq Von Rospach, calls these flames "a plague" that causes "everyone on the net to turn into a 6th grade English teacher and pick apart each other's postings for a few weeks."

4. A more detailed description of this particular *Ars dictandi* can be found in Richardson's article, "The Ars Dictaminis, the Formulary, and Medieval Epistolary Practice," in this volume.

5. The Eudora e-mail program includes a function that allows writers to keep several alternating signature files and to turn the signature file off with a simple command. This reflects the idea that signature files can and must be shaped to appeal to different audiences. For more personal communications a writer might choose a more extravagant, artistic, or humorous signature, while reserving a strictly informative signature for more formal communications.

6. The friendster web site (www.friendster.com) is one of several new sites where individuals can set up and use multiple communication tools, including instant messaging, chat spaces, and blogs.

7. The eighteenth century was a period of great popularity for the epistolary novel. See Frank G. Black (1940).

8. An online firm, World Intenet Stats (http://www.internetworldstats.com/stats.htm) offers updated statistics for Internet users worldwide. Additionally, the Pew Internet and American Life Project web site (http://www.pewinternet.org/PPF/p/1083/pipcomments.asp) offers the results of myriad research projects designed to explore Americans' use of the Internet.

9. For further explanation and listings of emoticons, see the netiquette web page developed by IBM (http://www.ntepath.net/~gwicker/email.htm) or the one developed by The Electronic Frontier Foundation (http://www.eff.org/papers/eegtti/eeg_52.html#SEC53).

Works Cited

Anonymous of Bologna. "The Principle of Letter-Writing." Translated by James J. Murphy. *Three Medieval Rhetorical Arts*. Berkeley: University of California Press, 1971.

Black, Frank G. *The Epistolary Novel in the Late Eighteenth Century: A Descriptive and Bibliographical Study.* Eugene: University of Oregon Press, 1940.

Camargo, Martin. "Where's the Brief? The *Ars Dictaminis* and Reading/Writing Between the Lines." *Disputatio: An International Transdisciplinary Journal of the Late Middle Ages* 1 (1996): 1–18.

Clark, Thomas Arkel. *When You Write a Letter: Some Suggestions as to Why, When, and How It Should Be Done.* Chicago: B. H. Sanford, 1921.

Erasmus, Desiderius. *Collected Works of Erasmus.* Translated by Charles Fantazzi. Edited by J. K. Sowards. Vol. 25. Toronto: University of Toronto Press, 1985.

Fantazzi, Charles. Introduction. *De conscribendis epistolis.* By J. L. Vives. Translated by Charles Fantazzi. Leiden: E. J. Brill, 1989.

Fruehling, Rosemary T., and Sharon Bouchard. *The Art of Writing Effective Letters.* New York: McGraw Hill, 1972.

Gaffin, Adam and Jörg Heitkötter. "EFF's (Extended) Guide to the Internet: A Round Trip through Global Networks, Life in Cyberspace, and Everything. . ." September 1994. http://www.utia.cas.cz/EFF/eeg_toc.html (accessed August 1, 2005).

Gaskell, G.A. *Gaskell's Compendium of Forms.* 19th ed. St. Louis: R. S. Peale & Co., 1882.

Gillin, Eric. "The Instant Messanger Handbook." *Black Table.* http://www.blacktable.com/imhandbook.htm (accessed August 8, 2005).

Goode, Joanne, and Maggie Johnson. "Putting out the Flames: The Etiquette and Law of E-mail." *Online, Inc.* 15, no. 6 (November 1991): 61–65.

Guillén, Claudio. "On the Edge of Literariness: The Writing of Letters." *Comparative Literature Studies* 3, no. 1 (1994): 1–24.

Richardson, Samuel. *Familiar Letters on Important Occasions.* 1741. Reprint, London: Routledge, 1928.

Rinaldi, Arlene H. "The Net User Guidelines and Netiquette." September 3, 1992. Computer User services. Florida Atlantic University. http://www.fau.edu/netiquette/net/ (accessed August 1, 2005).

Shea, Virginia. *Netiquette.* San Francisco: Albion Books, 1994.

Shurter, Robert L. *Effective Letters in Business.* 2nd ed. New York: McGraw-Hill, 1954.

Thorsburg, Frank. Instant Messaging Etiquette. *PC World.* http://www.pcworld.com (accessed May 30, 2002).

Von Rospach, Chuq. "A Primer on How to Work with the Usenet Community Newsgroups." Oxford University Libraries Automation service World Wide Web Server. September 23 1996. http://www.utia.cas.cz/EFF/eeg_toc.html (accessed August 1, 2005).

Wiethoff, William E. "Common Law Reflections of a Forensic 'Urge' in the Art of Letter-Writing." *Southern Communication Journal* 56:4 (1991): 268–78.

Witt, Ronald. "Medieval 'Ars Dictaminis' and the Beginnings of Humanism: A New Construction of the Problem." *Renaissance Quarterly* 35(1982): 1–35.

Zuboff, Shoshana. *In the Age of the Smart Machine: The Future of Work and Power.* New York: HarperCollins, 1988.

Appendix A

SELECT BIBLIOGRAPHY OF ANCIENT LETTER-WRITING
COLLECTIONS AND EPISTOLARY THEORY

Suzanne Abram

This bibliography is introductory rather than comprehensive. It treats letter collections
and epistolary theory of the ancient world, defined as the period ending with the sixth
century of the common era. Letters culled from papyri are not included, nor is the
extensive scholarship centering on Bible letters. Obscure single letters and letters that
are preserved in ancient histories are also generally omitted. The focus is on works that
are readily available in research libraries.

For popular classical writers such as Cicero, Horace, Ovid, and Pliny, the number
of scholarly articles is now truly great. This bibliography, of necessity, cites only a very
small part of what exists.

Primary Sources

Bibliographies and Indices

Beschorner, Andreas. "Griechische Briefbücher Berühmter Männer: Eine Bibliographie." In *Der griechische Briefroman: Gattungstypologie und Textanalyse,* edited by
Niklas Holzberg, 169–90. Tübingen: Gunter Narr Verlag, 1994.

Cavallo, Guglielmo, Paolo Fideli, and Andrea Giardina. *Lo Spazio Letterario di Rome
Antica.* Vol. 5: *Cronologia e Bibliografia della Letteratura Latina.* Rome: Salerno
Editrice, 1989.

Hester, James D. *A Select Critical Bibliography on Pauline Epistolography and Related
Literature.* Redlands, Calif.: University of Redlands, 1976.

Migne, J.-P. "Index alphabeticus eorum omnium epistolae inscribuntur." *Indices generales simul et speciales Patrologiae Latinae Tomus Quartus.* Patrologia Latina. Vol.
221. Paris, 1890, 187–342.

———. "Index epistolarum circa moralem et philosophiam." *Indices generales simul et
speciales Patrologiae Latinae Tomus Quartus.* Patrologia Latina. Vol. 221. Paris,
1890, 119–24.

———. "Index epistolarum dogmaticarum et polemicarum." *Indices generales simul et
speciales Patrologiae Latinae Tomus Quartus.* Patrologia Latina. Vol. 221. Paris,
1890, 113–18.

———. "Index epistolarum de diversis argumentis." *Indices generales simul et speciales
Patrologiae Latinae Tomus Quartus.* Patrologia Latina. Vol. 221. Paris, 1890,
131–88.

————. "Index epistolarum quae de iure canonico, rebus liturgicis, caeremoniis vel ritibus." *Indices generales simul et speciales Patrologiae Latinae Tomus Quartus.* Patrologia Latina. Vol. 221. Paris, 1890, 123–30.

————. "Index generalis alphabeticus scriptorum quorum epistolae, quaecunque sint genere vel numero, in Patrologiae cursu recensentur." *Indices generales simul et speciales Patrologiae Latinae Tomus Quartus.* Patrologia Latina. Vol. 221. Paris, 1890, 91–112.

————. "Index omnium quibus epistolae inscriptae fuerunt, juxta regionum ordinem alphabeticum." *Indices generales simul et speciales Patrologiae Latinae Tomus Quartus.* Patrologia Latina. Vol. 221. Paris, 1890, 343–428.

Naldini, Mario, Clara Burini, Giovanna Andrubali Pintiti, Maria Carla Spadoni Cerroni, and Freancesca Silliti, eds. *Epistolari cristiani secc. I–V: repertorio bibliografico.* 3 vols. Rome: Benedictina editrice, 1990.

Richardson, Ernest C. "Bibliographical Synopsis." Ante-Nicene Fathers. Edited by Alexander Roberts and James Donaldson. Vol. 10. New York: Christian Literature Publishing, 1887. Reprint, Peabody, Mass.: Hendrickson Publishers, 1994, 1–133.

Anthologies

Brooke, Dorothy [Dorothy Lamb Nicholson]. *Private Letters Pagan and Christian.* New York: Dutton, 1930.

Cugusi, Paolo. *Epistolographi Latini Minores.* 2 vols. Aug. Taurinorum: Io. Bapt. Paraviae, 1970.

Hercher, Rudolf. *Epistolographi Graeci.* Paris: F. Didot, 1873. Reprint, Amsterdam: A. M. Hakkert, 1965.

Hofmann, Michael. Antike Briefe. Munich: E. Heimeran, 1935.

Hooper, Finley and Matthew Schwartz. *Roman Letters: History from A Personal Point of View.* Detroit: Wayne State University Press, 1991.

Kytzler, Bernhard. *Erotische Briefe der griechischen Antike: Aristaenetos, Alkiphron, Ailianos, Philostratos, Theophylaktos Simokattes.* Munich: Winkler, 1967.

Rüdiger, Horst. *Briefe des Altertums.* Zurich: Artemis-Verlag, 1965. Reprint, 1983 as *Und bleibe mein Freund.*

Sherk, Robert K. *Roman Documents from the Greek East: Senatus Consulta and Epistulae to the Age of Augustus.* Baltimore: Johns Hopkins UniversityPress, 1969.

Welles, C[harles] Bradford. *Royal Correspondence in the Hellenistic Period: A Study in Greek Epigraphy.* New Haven, Conn.: Yale University Press, 1934. Reprint, Rome: L'Erma di Bretschneider, 1966.

Editions and Translations of Letter Collections

Aelian. The Letters of Alciphron, Aelian and Philostratus. Translated by Allen Rogers Benner and Francis H. Fobes. Loeb Classical Library. London: William Heinemann; Cambridge, Mass.: Harvard University Press, 1949, 343–83.

[Aeschines].* *Aeschinis quae feruntur epistulae.* Edited by Engelbert Drerup. Leipzig: Sumptibus Dieterichii [Theodori Weideri], 1904.

---

*Many of the letters of this age are anonymous or falsely attributed. Where a letter has been falsely attributed, I have enclosed the supposed author's name in square brackets.

————. *Discours.* Tome II. Edited and translated by Victor Martin and Guy de Budé. Paris: Les Belles Lettres, 1928.

Alciphron. *Epistulae.* Edited by M. A. Schepers. Stuttgart: Teubner, 1969.

————. *The Letters of Alciphron, Aelian and Philostratus.* Translated by Allen Rogers Benner and Francis H. Fobes. Loeb Classical Library. London: William Heinemann; Cambridge, Mass.: Harvard University Press, 1949. 1–342.

————. *Lettere di parassiti e di cortigiane.* Edited by Elisa Avezzù and Oddone Longo. Venice: Marsilio, 1985.

Alexander of Alexandria. "Epistles on the Arian Heresy." Ante-Nicene Fathers. Edited by Alexander Roberts and James Donaldson. Vol. 6. New York: Christian Literature Publishing, 1886. Reprint, Peabody, Mass.: Hendrickson Publishers, 1994, 291–302.

[Alexander the Great]. "Epistola Alexandri ad Aristotelem." Edited by W. W. Boer. PhD diss., Leiden, 1953.

————. *Epistola Alexandri ad Aristotelem de miraculis Indiae.* Edited by Michael Feldbusch. Meisenheim am Glan: Hain, 1976.

Ambrose. *Epistulae et acta.* Edited by Otto Faller and Michaela Zelzer. Corpus scriptorum ecclesiasticorum latinorum 82.1–3. Vienna: Hoelder-Pichler-Tempsky, 1968–90.

————. *Saint Ambrose: Letters.* Translated by Mary Melchior Beyenka. Fathers of the Church 26. New York: Fathers of the Church, 1954.

————. *The Principal Works of St. Ambrose.* Translated by H. De Romestin, E. De Romestin, and H. T. F. Duckworth. Nicene and Post-Nicene Fathers, Second Series. Edited by Philip Schaff and Henry Wace. Vol. 10. New York: Christian Literature Publishing, 1896. Reprint, Peabody, Mass.: Hendrickson Publishers, 1994, 411–73.

[Anarcharsis]. *Anacarsi Scita: Lettere.* Translated by G. Morel. Palermo: Sellerio, 1991.

————. *Die Briefe des Anacharsis.* Edited and translated by F. H. Reuters. Berlin, 1963.

————. "Epistles." Translated by Anne M. McGuire. In *The Cynic Epistles,* edited by Abraham J. Malherbe. Missoula, Mont.: Scholars Press, 1977, 35–51.

Apollonius of Tyana. *Apollonio Tianeo: Epistole e frammenti.* Translated by Ferdinando Lo Cascio. Palermo: Istituto siciliano di studi bizantini e neoellenici, 1984.

————. *Apollonius de Tyane: Sa vie, ses voyages, ses prodiges par Philostrate, et ses lettres.* Translated by A. Chassang. Paris, 1862.

————. *Flavii Philostrati opera, accedunt Apollonii epistolae, Eusebius adversus Hieroclem, Philostrati junioris imagines, Callistrati descriptiones.* Edited by C. L. Kayser. 2 vols. Leipzig: Teubner, 1870–71.

————. *The Letters of Apollonius of Tyana: A Critical Text with Prolegomema, Translation, and Commentary.* Edited by Robert J. Penella. Leiden: Brill, 1979.

————. *Philostratus, The Life of Apollonius of Tyana, The Epistles of Apollonius and the Treatise of Eusebius.* Vol. 2. Edited and translated by F. C. Conybeare. Loeb Classical Library. London: William Heinemann; Cambridge, Mass.: Harvard University Press, 1912, 408–81.

Aristaenetus. *Aristaeneti epistularum libri II.* Edited by Otto Mazal. Stuttgart: Teubner, 1971.

————. *Aristaietos: Erotische Briefe.* Translated by Albin Lesky. Zurich:, Artemis-Verlag, 1951.

————. *Lettres d'amour.* Edited and translated by Jean-Rene Vieillefond. Paris: Les Belles Lettres, 1992.

Aristotle. *Aristoteles pseudepigraphus.* Edited by Valentin Rose. Leipzig, 1863. Reprint, Hildesheim: G. Olms, 1971, 585–97.

———. *Aristotelis qui ferebantur librorum fragmenta.* Edited by Valentin Rose. Leipzig: Teubner, 1886. 411–21.

———. *Aristotelis privatorum scriptorum fragmenta.* Edited by M. Plezia. Leipzig: Teubner, 1977.

Athanasius. *The Armenian Version of the Letters of Athanasius to Bishop Serapion Concerning the Holy Spirit.* Translated by George A. Egan. Salt Lake City: University of Utah Press, 1968.

———. *Letters Concerning the Holy Spirit.* Edited and translated by C. R. B. Shapland. London: Epworth Press, 1951.

———. *Lettres à Sérapion sur la divinité du Saint-Esprit.* Translated by Joseph Lebon. Sources chrétiennes 15. Paris: Éditions du Cerf, 1947.

———. *Life of Antony and the Letter to Marcellinus.* Translated by Robert C. Gregg. New York: Paulist Press, 1980.

———. *The Monastic Letters of Saint Athanasius the Great.* Translated by L. W. Barnard. Oxford: SLG, 1994.

———. *Select Writings and Letters of Athanasius, Bishop of Alexandria.* Edited and translated by Archibald Robertson. Nicene and Post-Nicene Fathers, Second Series. Edited by Philip Schaff and Henry Wace. Vol. 4. New York: Christian Literature Publishing, 1892. Reprint, Peabody, Mass.: Hendrickson Publishers, 1994.

Augustine. *Ces frères que tu m'as donnés: Lettres de saint Augustin.* Translated by Soeur Douceline. Paris: Le Centurion, 1983.

———. *Epistulae.* Edited by Al[ois] Goldbacher. Corpus scriptorum ecclesiasticorum latinorum 34.1, 34.2, 44, 57, 58. Vienna: F. Tempsky, 1895–1923.

———. *Letters.* Translated by Robert B. Eno. Fathers of the Church 81. Washington, D.C.: Catholic University of America Press, 1989.

———. *The Letters of St. Augustin.* Translated by J. G. Cunningham. Nicene and Post-Nicene Fathers, First Series. Edited by Philip Schaff. Vol. 1. New York: Christian Literature Publishing, 1886. Reprint, Peabody, Mass.: Hendrickson Publishers, 1994.

———. *Letters of Saint Augustine.* Translated by John Leinenweber. Ligouri, Mo.: Triumph Books, 1992.

———. *Saint Augustine: Letters.* Translated by Wilfrid Parsons. Fathers of the Church 12, 18, 20, 30, 32. New York: Fathers of the Church, 1951–56.

———. *Select Letters.* Translated by J. H. Baxter. Loeb Classical Library. London: William Heinemann; Cambridge, Mass.: Harvard University Press, 1930.

Ausonius. *Ausonius.* Translated by Hugh G. Evelyn White. Vol. 2. Loeb Classical Library. London: William Heinemann; Cambridge, Mass.: Harvard University Press, 1921.

———. *D. Magni Ausonii Opuscula.* Edited by K. Schenkl. Monumenta Germaniae Historica, Auctores Antiquissimi 2. Berlin: Weidmann, 1883.

———. *Decimi Magni Ausonii Burdigalensis Opuscula.* Edited by R. Peiper. Leipzig: Teubner, 1886. 2d ed rev. by Sextus Prete. Leipzig: Teubner, 1978.

———. *Epistole.* Edited by Luca Mondin. Venice: Cardo, 1995.

———. *Opere di Decimo Magno Ausonio.* Edited by A Pastorino. Turin: Unione tipografico-editrice torinese, 1971.

———. "The Text of the Letters of Decimus Magnus Ausonius." Edited by James Francis Coleman. PhD diss., Fordham University, 1970.

————. *The Works of Ausonius*. Edited by R. P. H. Green. Oxford: Clarendon, 1991.

[Barnabas]. "Epistle." In *Apostolic Fathers*. Edited and translated by Kirsopp Lake. Vol. 1. Loeb Classical Library. London: William Heinemann; Cambridge, Mass.: Harvard University Press, 1912, 335–409.

————. "Epistle." Ante-Nicene Fathers. Edited by Alexander Roberts and James Donaldson. Vol. 1. New York: Christian Literature Publishing, 1885. Reprint, Peabody, Mass.: Hendrickson Publishers, 1994. 133–50.

Basil the Great. *The Fathers Speak: St. Basil the Great, St. Gregory of Nazianzus, St. Gregory of Nyssa*. Translated by Georges A. Barrois. Crestwood, N.Y.: St. Vladimir's Seminary Press, 1986.

————. "Letters." Translated by Blomfield Jackson. Nicene and Post-Nicene Fathers, Second Series. Edited by Philip Schaff and Henry Wace. Vol. 8. New York: Christian Literature Publishing, 1895. Reprint, Peabody, Mass.: Hendrickson Publishers, 1994, 109–327.

————. *Letters*. Translated by Agnes Clare Way. 2 vols. Fathers of the Church 13, 28. Washington, D.C.: Catholic University of America Press, 1951–55.

————. *Saint Basil: The Letters*. Edited and translated by Roy J. Deferrari. 4 vols. Loeb Classical Library. London: William Heinemann; Cambridge, Mass.: Harvard University Press, 1926–34.

Brutus. *Marci Bruti Epistolae Graecae*. Edited by M. Westermann. Leipzig, 1855.

————. *Marco Giunio Bruto: Epistole greche*. Edited and translated by L. Torraca. Naples: Libreria scientifica editrice, 1959.

Chion. *Chion of Heraclea: A Novel in Letters*. Edited and translated by Ingemar Düring. Göteborg: Wettergren & Kerbers, 1951. Reprint, New York: Arno Press, 1979.

Cicero. *Cicero's Letters to Atticus*. Translated by D. R. Shackleton Bailey. 7 vols. Cambridge: Cambridge University Press, 1965–70.

————. *Correspondance*. Edited and translated by Léopold Albert Constans and Jean Bayet. 11 vols. Paris: Les Belles Lettres, 1934–96.

————. *Epistulae ad Familiares*. Edited by D. R. Shackleton Bailey. 2 vols. Cambridge: Cambridge University Press, 1977.

————. *Epistulae ad Quintum Fratrem et M. Brutum*. Edited by D. R. Shackleton Bailey. Cambridge: Cambridge University Press, 1980.

————. *Letters to Atticus*. Edited and translated by E. O. Winstedt. 3 vols. Loeb Classical Library. London: William Heinemann; Cambridge, Mass.: Harvard University Press, 1962–84.

————. *The Letters to His Friends*. Translated by W. Glynn Williams. 3 vols. Loeb Classical Library. London: William Heinemann; Cambridge, Mass.: Harvard University Press, 1927–29.

————. *M. Tulli Ciceronis Epistulae Vol. 1: Epistulae ad Familiares*. Edited by Ludovicus [Louis] Claude Purser. Oxford: Clarendon, 1901.

————. *M. Tulli Ciceronis Epistulae Vol. 1: Epistulae ad Familiares*. Edited by W. S. Watt. Oxford: Clarendon, 1982.

————. *M. Tulli Ciceronis Epistulae Vol. 2: Epistulae ad Atticum*. Edited by D. R. Shackleton Bailey. Oxford: Clarendon, 1961.

————. *M. Tulli Ciceronis Epistulae Vol. 3: Epistulae ad Quintum fratrem, Epistulae ad M. Brutum, Fragmenta epistularum*. Edited by W. S. Watt. Oxford: Clarendon, 1958.

[Clement of Rome]. "Epistles to the Corinthians." *Apostolic Fathers.* Vol. 1. Edited and translated by Kirsopp Lake. Loeb Classical Library. London: William Heinemann; Cambridge, Mass.: Harvard University Press, 1912, 1–164.

———. *The Epistles of St. Clement of Rome and St. Ignatius of Antioch.* Translated by James A. Kleist. Westminster, Md.: The Newman Bookshop, 1946.

———. "Epistle to the Corinthians." Ante-Nicene Fathers. Edited by Alexander Roberts and James Donaldson. Vol. 1. New York: Christian Literature Publishing, 1885. Reprint, Peabody, Mass.: Hendrickson Publishers, 1994, 1–22.

———. "The Epistles of Clement, Completed From a Manuscript Recently Discovered." Ante-Nicene Fathers. Edited by Alexander Roberts and James Donaldson. Vol. 9. New York: Christian Literature Publishing, 1896. Reprint, Peabody, Mass.: Hendrickson Publishers, 1994, 227–58.

[Collectio Avellana]. *Epistulae imperatorum pontificum aliorum inde ab a. CCCLXVII usque ad a. DLIII datae Avellana quae dicitur collectio.* Edited by Otto Günther. Corpus scriptorum ecclesiasticorum latinorum 35.1–2. Vienna: F. Tempsky, 1895–98.

[Crates]. "Cynic Epistles (Selections)." Translated by Leif E. Vaage. *Ascetic Behavior in Greco-Roman Antiquity.* Edited by Vincent L. Wimbush. Minneapolis: Fortress Press, 1990.

———. "Epistles." Translated by Ronald Hock. In *The Cynic Epistles,* edited by Abraham J. Malherbe. Missoula, Mont.: Scholars Press, 1977, 53–89.

———. *Die Kynikerbriefe.* Edited by Eike Müseler. 2 vols. Paderborn: F. Schöningh, 1994.

———. *Socratis et Socraticorum reliquae.* Edited by Gabriele Giannantoni. 4 vols. Naples: Bibliopolis, 1990.

Cyril of Alexandria. *A Collection of Unpublished Syriac Letters of Cyril of Alexandria.* Edited and translated by R. Y. Ebied and Lionel R. Wickham. 2 vols. Corpus scriptorum christianorum, scriptores syri 359–60 (157–58). Louvain: Secrétariat du Corpus SCO, 1975.

———. *The Festal Letters of Saint Cyril of Alexandria: The Manuscript Tradition, Text, and Translation.* Edited and translated by William Harris Burns. 2 vols. PhD diss., University of Southampton, 1988.

———. *Lettres festales.* Edited and translated by Pierre Evieux, W. H. Burns, and Louis Arragon. 3 vols. Sources chrétiennes 372, 392, and 434. Paris: Éditions du Cerf, 1991–98.

———. *Select Letters.* Edited and translated by Lionel R. Wickham. Oxford: Clarendon, 1983.

———. *St. Cyril of Alexandria: Letters.* Translated by John I. McEnerney. 2 vols. Fathers of the Church 76–77. Washington, D.C.: Catholic University of America Press, 1987.

Cyprian. "The Epistles of Cyprian." Ante-Nicene Fathers. Edited by Alexander Roberts and James Donaldson. Vol. 5. New York: Christian Literature Publishing, 1886. Reprint, Peabody, Mass.: Hendrickson Publishers, 1994, 275–420.

———. *Letters.* Translated by Rose Bernard Donna. Fathers of the Church 51. Washington, D.C.: Catholic University of America Press, 1964.

———. *The Letters of St. Cyprian of Carthage.* Translated by G. W. Clarke. 4 vols. Ancient Christian Writers 43, 44, 46, 47. New York: Newman Press, 1984–89.

————. *Opera omnia*. Edited by Guilelmus [Wilhelm] Hartel. Corpus scriptorum ecclesiasticorum latinorum 3.2. Vienna, 1871.

Demosthenes. *Demosthenes. Vol. VII: Funeral Speech, Erotic Essays, Exordia, and Letters*. Translated by N. W. DeWitt and N. J. DeWitt. Loeb Classical Library. London: William Heinemann; Cambridge, Mass.: Harvard University Press, 1949.

————. *Lettres et fragments*. Edited and translated by Robert Clavaud. Paris: Les Belles Lettres, 1987.

[Diogenes]. "Cynic Epistles (Selections)." Translated by Leif E. Vaage. *Ascetic Behavior in Greco-Roman Antiquity*. Edited by Vincent L. Wimbush. Minneapolis: Fortress Press, 1990.

————. "Epistles." Translated by Benjamin Fiore. In *The Cynic Epistles*, edited by Abraham J. Malherbe. Missoula, Mont.: Scholars Press, 1977, 91–183.

————. *Die Kynikerbriefe*. Edited by Eike Müseler. 2 vols. Paderborn: F. Schöningh, 1994.

Dionysius of Corinth. "Fragments from a Letter to the Roman Church." Ante-Nicene Fathers. Edited by Alexander Roberts and James Donaldson. Vol. 8. New York: Christian Literature Publishing, 1886. Reprint, Peabody, Mass.: Hendrickson Publishers, 1994, 765.

Epicurus. *Epicuri Ethica et Epistulae*. Edited by Carolus [Carlo] Diano. Firenze: in aedibus Sansonianis [Sansoni], 1974.

————. *Epicurus: The Extant Remains*. Translated by Cyril Bailey. Oxford: Clarendon, 1926.

————. *The Philosophy of Epicurus: Letters, Doctrines, and Parallel Passages from Lucretius*. Translated by George K. Strodach. Evanston, Ill.: Northwestern University Press, 1963.

Epistle to Diognetus. "Epistle to Diognetus." Translated by Kirsopp Lake. *Apostolic Fathers*. Vol. 2. Loeb Classical Library. London: William Heinemann; Cambridge, Mass.: Harvard University Press, 1913, 347–79.

————. "Epistle to Diognetus." Ante-Nicene Fathers. Vol. 1. Edited by Alexander Roberts and James Donaldson. New York: Christian Literature Publishing, 1885. Reprint, Peabody, Mass.: Hendrickson Publishers, 1994, 23–30.

Epistula Didonis ad Aeneam. *Anthologia Latina* 83. Edited by Franciscus Buecheler and Alexander Riese. Vol 1.1. Leipzig, 1894. Reprint, Amsterdam: A. M. Hakkert, 1964, 113–19.

————. *Anthologia Latina* 71. Edited by D. R. Shackleton Bailey. Stuttgart: Teubner, 1982.

————. *Epistula Didonis ad Aeneam*. Edited and translated by G. Solimano. Genova: Darficlet, 1988.

————. *Poetae Latini minores*. Edited by Ae. Baehrens. Vol. 4. Leipzig: Teubner, 1882, 271–77.

Epistolae Arelatenses genuinae. Edited by W. Gundlach. Monumentae Germania Historica Epistolarum Tomus III. Berlin: Weidmann, 1892, 1–83.

Euripides. *Die Briefe des Euripides*. Edited and translated by H.-U. Güsswein. Meisenheim am Glan: Hain, 1975.

Faustus of Riez. *Opera*. Edited by Augustus [August] Engelbrecht. Corpus scriptorum ecclesiasticorum latinorum 21. Vienna: F. Tempsky, 1891.

Firmus of Caesarea. *Lettres*. Edited and translated by Marie-Ange Calvet-Sebasti and Pierre-Louis Gatier. Sources chrétiennes 350. Paris: Les Éditions du Cerf, 1989.

Fronto. *The Correspondence of Marcus Cornelius Fronto with Marcus Aurelius Antoninus, Lucius Verus, Antoninus Pius, and Various Friends.* Edited and translated by C. R. Haines. 2 vols. Loeb Classical Library. London: W. Heinemann; Cambridge, Mass.: Harvard University Press, 1919–20.

———. *M. Cornelii Frontonis Epistulae.* Edited by Michael Petrus Josephus van den Hout. Leiden: E. J. Brill, 1954. Reprint, New York: Arno Press, 1975. Reprint, Leipzig: Teubner, 1988.

———. *Opere di Marco Cornelio Frontone.* Edited by Felicita Portalupi. Turin: Unione tipografico-editrice torinese, 1974.

Gelasius I. "Epistulae theodericianae variae." Edited by Th. Mommsen. Monumenta Germaniae Historica, Auctores Antiquissimi 12. Berlin: Weidmann, 1894.

———. *Lettre contre les Lupercales et dix huit messes du Sacramentaire léonien.* Edited and translated by Gilbert Pomarès. Sources chrétiennes 65. Paris: Éditions du Cerf, 1959.

Gregory Nazianzen. *The Fathers Speak: St. Basil the Great, St. Gregory of Nazianzus, St. Gregory of Nyssa.* Translated by Georges A. Barrois. Crestwood, N.Y.: St. Vladimir's Seminary Press, 1986.

———. "Letters." Edited and translated by Charles Gordon Browne and James Edward Swallow. Nicene and Post-Nicene Fathers, Second Series. Edited by Philip Schaff and Henry Wace. Vol. 7. New York: Christian Literature Publishing, 1894. Reprint, Peabody, Mass.: Hendrickson Publishers, 1994, 437–82.

———. *Lettres théologiques.* Edited and translated by Paul Gallay, with the collaboration of Maurice Jourion. Sources chrétiennes 208. Paris: Les Éditions du Cerf, 1974.

Gregory of Nyssa. *Briefe.* Edited by Dörte Teske. Stuttgart: W. Engelmann, 1997.

———. *The Fathers Speak: St. Basil the Great, St. Gregory of Nazianzus, St. Gregory of Nyssa.* Translated by Georges A. Barrois. Crestwood, N.Y.: St. Vladimir's Seminary Press, 1986.

———. *Gregorii Nysseni epistulae.* Edited by Georgius [Georgio] Pasquali. Leiden: Brill, 1952. Reprint, 1998.

———. "Letters." Translated by H. C. Ogle, William Moore, and Henry Austin Wilson. Nicene and Post-Nicene Fathers, Second Series. Edited by Philip Schaff and Henry Wace. Vol. 5. New York: Christian Literature Publishing, 1893. Reprint, Peabody, Mass.: Hendrickson Publishers, 1994, 527–48.

———. *Lettres.* Edited and translated by Pierre Maraval. Sources chrétiennes 363. Paris: Les Éditions du Cerf, 1990.

———. *Opere di Gregorio di Nissa.* Edited by Claudio Moreschini. Turin: Union tipigrafico-editrice torinese, 1992.

[Heraclitus]. *The Cynic Epistles.* Edited by Abraham J. Malherbe. Missoula, Mont.: Scholars Press, 1977, 185–215.

———. "Epistole pseudo eraclitee." *Eraclito: Testimonianze e frammenti.* Translated by Emilio Bodrero. Turin: Fratelli Bocca, 1910. Reprint, Rome: G. Bretschneider, 1978, 179–202.

———. *First-Century Cynicism in the Epistles of Heraclitus.* Edited and translated by Harold W. Attridge. Missoula, Mont.: Scholars Press, 1976.

———. "Heracliti quae feruntur epistolae." In *Heracliti Ephesii reliquiae,* edited by I. Bywater. Oxford, 1877, 70–79.

————. "Lettere pseudo-eraclitee." *Eraclito: Testimonianze e imitazioni*. Translated by Rodolfo Mondolfo and Leonardo Tarán. Firenze: La Nuova Italia, 1972, 279–359.

[Hippocrates]. "Die Briefe des Hippokrates." Translated by Anton Fingerle. In *Die Werke des Hippokrates*, edited by Richard Kapferer. Stuttgart: Hippokrates-Verlag, 1938.

————. *Hippocrates: Pseudepigraphic Writings: Letters, Embassy, Speech from the Altar, Decree*. Edited and translated by Wesley D. Smith. Leiden: Brill, 1990.

————. "Lettres, décret et harangues." Translated by Emile Littré. *Oeuvres complètes d'Hippocrate*. Vol. 9. Paris, 1861. Reprint, Amsterdam: A. M. Hakkert, 1962, 312–429.

Horace. *Les épitres littéraires d'Horace*. Namur: Wesmael-Charlier, 1958.

————. *Horace: Epistles, Book I*. Edited by O. A. W. Dilke. London: Methuen, 1954. Reprint, 1963.

————. *Q. Horati Flacci opera*. Edited by Fridericus [Friedrich] Klingner. Leipzig: Teubner, 1970.

————. *Q. Horatii Flacci opera*. Edited by D. R. Shackleton Bailey. Stuttgart: Teubner, 1985.

————. *Q. Horatii Flacci opera*. Edited by E. C. Wickham. Oxford: Clarendon, 1901. Rev. ed. H. W. Garrod, 1912.

————. *Q. Horatius Flaccus: Briefe*. Edited by A. Kiesling and R. Heinze. Berlin: Weidmann, 1898. Reprint, 1957.

————. *Q. Horatius Flaccus: Episteln*. Edited by G. Krüger, C. Nauck, and P. Hoppe. Leipzig: Teubner, 1920.

————. *Satires, Epistles and Ars Poetica*. Translated by H. Rushton Fairclough. Loeb Classical Library. London: William Heinemann; Cambridge, Mass.: Harvard University Press, 1926.

Ignatius of Antioch. *Epistles. Apostolic Fathers*. Translated by Kirsopp Lake. Vol. 1. Loeb Classical Library. London: William Heinemann; Cambridge, Mass.: Harvard University Press, 1912, 165–278.

————. *The Epistles of St. Clement of Rome and St. Ignatius of Antioch*. Translated by James A. Kleist. Westminster, Md.: Newman Bookshop, 1946.

————. *Epistles*. Ante-Nicene Fathers. Edited by Alexander Roberts and James Donaldson. Vol. 1. New York: Christian Literature Publishing, 1885. Reprint, Peabody, Mass.: Hendrickson Publishers, 1994, 45–126.

————. *Lettres*. Edited and translated by Thomas Camelot. Sources chrétiennes 10. Paris: Éditions du Cerf, 1958.

Innocent I. *La lettre du pape Innocent Ier à Décentius de Gubbio, 19 mars 416*. Edited by Robert Cabié. Louvain: Publications universitaires de Louvain, 1973.

Isidore of Pelusium. *Lettres*. Edited by and trans. Pierre Evieux. Sources chrétiennes 422. Paris: Éditions du Cerf, 1997.

————. *Quarante-neuf lettres de Saint Isidore de Péluse: édition critique de l'ancienne version latine contenue dans deux manuscrits du Concile d'Ephèse*. Edited by René Aigrain. Paris: Picard, 1911.

Isocrates. "Epistole." Edited and translated by Mario Marzi. *Opere di Isocrate*. Vol. 2. Turin: Unione tipografico-editrice torinese, 1991, 450–507.

————. "The Letters of Isocrates." *Isocrates*. Translated by L. van Hook. Vol. 3. Loeb Classical Library. London: William Heinemann; Cambridge, Mass.: Harvard University Press, 1945, 365–485.

———. "Lettres." *Isocrate.* Edited and translated by Georges Mathieu and Émile Brémond. Vol. 4. Paris: Les Belles Lettres, 1962, 161–223.

Jerome. *Epistulae.* Edited by Isidorus [Isidor] Hilberg. Corpus scriptorum ecclesiasticorum latinorum 54–56. Vienna: F. Tempsky, 1910–18.

———. *Letters and Select Works.* Translated by W. H. Fremantle, G. Lewis, and W. G. Martley. Nicene and Post-Nicene Fathers, Second Series. Edited by Philip Schaff and Henry Wace. Vol. 6. New York: Christian Literature Publishing, 1893. Reprint, Peabody, Mass.: Hendrickson Publishers, 1994, 1–295.

———. *The Letters of Saint Jerome.* Translated by Charles Christopher Mierow. Ancient Christian Writers 33. Westminster, Md.: Newman Press, 1963.

———. *Lettres.* Edited and translated by Jérôme Labourt. 8 vols. Paris: Les Belles Lettres, 1949–63.

———. *Lettres spirituelles de Saint Jérôme.* Translated by Denys Gorce. 2 vols. Paris: Libraire Lecoffre, 1932–34.

———. *Select Letters.* Translated by F. A. Wright. Loeb Classical Library. London: William Heinemann; Cambridge, Mass.: Harvard University Press, 1933.

John Chrysostom. *A Théodore.* Edited and translated by Jean Dumortier. Sources chrétiennes 117. Paris: Les Éditions du Cerf, 1966.

———. *Lettre d'exil à Olympias et à tous les fidèles (Quod nemo laeditur).* Edited and translated by Anne Marie Malingrey. Sources chrétiennes 103. Paris: Les Éditions du Cerf, 1964.

———. *Lettres à Olympias.* Translated by Anne-Marie Malingrey. Sources chrétiennes 13. Paris: Éditions du Cerf, 1947.

———. *Select Homilies and Letters.* Translated by W. R. W. Stephens. Nicene and Post-Nicene Fathers, First Series. Edited by Philip Schaff. Vol. 9. New York: Christian Literature Publishing, 1889. Reprint, Peabody, Mass.: Hendrickson Publishers, 1994.

Julian the Apostate. *L'epistolario di Giuliano Imperatore.* Edited and translated by Matilde Caltabiano. Naples: D'Auria, 1991.

———. *A Few Notes on Julian and a Translation of His Public Letters.* Edited by Edward James Chinnock. London: D. Nutt, 1901.

———. *Oeuvres completes.* Edited by Joseph Bidez. Vol. 2. 2nd ed. Paris: Les Belles Lettres, 1960.

———. *The Works of the Emperor Julian.* Translated by Wilmer Cave Wright. 2 vols. Loeb Classical Library. London: William Heinemann; Cambridge, Mass.: Harvard University Press, 1913–23.

Leo I (Leo the Great). *Epistolae. Patrologia Latina* 54. Edited by J.-P. Migne. Paris, 1881. 551–1218.

———. *Epistula ad Demetriadem de vera humilitate: A Critical Text with Introduction and Commentary.* Translated by Mary Kathryn Clare Krabbe. Washington, D.C.: Catholic University of America Press, 1965.

———. *Epistulae contra Eutychis haeresim.* Edited by Carlos da Silva Tarouca and Francesco Di Capua. 2 vols. Rome: Apud aedes Pont. Universitatis Gregorianae, 1934.

———. *Lettere dogmatiche.* Edited and translated by Giulio Trettel. Rome: Città Nuova, 1993.

———. *Letters.* Translated by Edmund Hunt. The Fathers of the Church 34. New York: Fathers of the Church, 1957.

————. *Omilie, Lettere.* Edited by Tommaso Mariucci. Turin: Unione tipografico-editrice torinese, 1969.

————. *Select Letters and Sermons.* Translated by Charles Lett Feltoe. Nicene and Post-Nicene Fathers, Second Series. Edited by Philip Schaff and Henry Wace. Vol. 12. New York: Christian Literature Publishing, 1895. Reprint, Peabody, Mass.: Hendrickson Publishers, 1994, 1–114.

————. *Studien zum Priszillianismus: die Forschung, die Quellen, der Fünfzehnte Brief Papst Leos des Grossen.* Edited by Benedikt Vollmann. Erzabtei St. Ottilien: Eos Verlag, 1965.

————. *Tomus ad Flavianum episc. Constantinopolitanum (Epistula XXVII) additis testimoniis patrum et eiusdem S. Leonis M. epistula ad Leonem I imp. (Epistula CLXV).* Edited by Carlos da Silva Tarouca. Rome: Gregoriana, 1932.

Libanius. *Autobiography and Selected Letters.* Edited and translated by A. F. Norman. 2 vols. Loeb Classical Library. London: William Heinemann; Cambridge, Mass.: Harvard University Press, 1992.

————. *Briefe.* Edited and translated by Georgios Fatouros and Tilman Krischer. Munich: Heimeran-Verlag, 1980.

————. *Libanii opera: Epistulae.* Edited by Richardus [Richard] Foerster. Vols. 10–11. Leipzig: Teubner, 1922–27. Reprint, Hildesheim: Georg Olms-Verlag, 1963.

————. *Themistius in Libanius' Brieven: Critische Uitgave van 52 Brieven.* Edited by Herman F. Bouchery. Antwerpen: De Sikkel, 1936.

Malchion of Antioch. "Epistles." Ante-Nicene Fathers. Vol. 6. Edited by Alexander Roberts and James Donaldson. New York: Christian Literature Publishing, 1886. Reprint, Peabody, Mass.: Hendrickson Publishers, 1994, 168–72.

Origen. "Letters." Ante-Nicene Fathers. Edited by Alexander Roberts and James Donaldson. Vol. 4. New York: Christian Literature Publishing, 1885. Reprint, Peabody, Mass.: Hendrickson Publishers, 1994, 385–94.

Ovid. *Ovid: Tristia, Ex ponto.* Edited and translated by Arthur Leslie Wheeler. Loeb Classical Library. London: William Heinemann; Cambridge, Mass.: Harvard University Press, 1924. 2nd ed. rev. by G. P. Goold, 1988.

————. *Epistulae ex Ponto.* Edited by J. A. Richmond. Leipzig: Teubner, 1990.

————. *Heroides and Amores.* Translated by Grant Showerman. Loeb Classical Library. London: William Heinemann; Cambridge, Mass.: Harvard University Press, 1914.

————. *Ovide: Pontiques.* Edited and translated by Jacques André. Paris: Les Belles Lettres, 1977.

————. *Ovide: Héroïdes.* Edited and translated by H. Bornecque and M. Prévost. Paris: Les Belles Lettres, 1928.

————. *P. Ovidii Nasonis Epistulae Heroidum.* Edited by Henricus [Heinrich] Dörrie. Berlin: Walter de Gruyter, 1971.

————. *P. Ovidi Nasonis Tristium libri quinque, Ibis, Ex Ponto libri quattuor, Halieutica, Fragmenta.* Edited by S. G. Owen. Oxford: Clarendon, 1915.

————. *Sorrows of an Exile: Tristia.* Translated by A. D. Melville. Oxford: Clarendon, 1992.

Pachomius, et al. *Pachomian Koinonia.* Vol. 3. Translated by Armand Veilleux. Kalamazoo, Mich.: Cistercian Publications, 1982.

Patrick. *Confession, Lettre à Coroticus.* Edited and translated by R. P. C. Hanson and Cécile Blanc. Sources chrétiennes 249. Paris: Éditions du Cerf, 1978.

———. *Confession of St. Patrick and Letter to Coroticus.* Translated by John Skinner. New York: Image, 1998.

———. *Liber epistolarum Sancti Patricii episcopi = The Book of Letters of Saint Patrick the Bishop.* Edited and translated by David R. Howlett. Blackrock Co. Dublin: Four Courts Press, 1994.

———. *Patrick, the Pilgrim Apostle of Ireland: St. Patrick's Confessio and Epistola.* Edited by Déaglán De Paor. Dublin: Veritas, 1998.

Paulinus of Nola. *Ausonius.* Translated by Hugh G. Evelyn White. Vol. 2. Loeb Classical Library. London: William Heinemann; Cambridge, Mass.: Harvard University Press, 1921.

———. *Epistole ad Agostino.* Edited and translated by Teresa Piscitelli Carpino. Naples: Libr. Ed. Redenzione, 1989.

———. *Epistulae.* Edited by Guilelmus de [Wilhelm von] Hartel. Corpus scriptorum ecclesiasticorum latinorum 29. Vienna: F. Tempsky, 1894.

———. *Letters of Paulinus of Nola.* Translated by P. G. Walsh. Ancient Christian Writers 35–36. New York: Newman Press, 1966–67.

Phalaris. *Epistolographi Graeci.* Edited by Rudolf Hercher. Paris: F. Didot, 1873. Reprint, Amsterdam: A. M. Hakkert, 1965, 409–59.

———. *Phalaridis epistolae.* Edited by Gottfried Heinrich Schaefer. Leipzig: apud Gerhardum Fleischerum, 1823.

Phileas of Thmuis. "Epistles." Ante-Nicene Fathers. Edited by Alexander Roberts and James Donaldson. Vol. 6. New York: Christian Literature Publishing, 1886. Reprint, Peabody, Mass.: Hendrickson Publishers, 1994, 161–64.

Philostratus. *Flavii Philostrati opera.* Edited by C. L. Kayser. 2 vols. Leipzig: Teubner, 1870–71. Reprint, Hildesheim: Georg Olms Verlag, 1964.

———. *The Letters of Alciphron, Aelian and Philostratus.* Translated by Allen Rogers Benner and Francis H. Fobes. Loeb Classical Library. London: William Heinemann; Cambridge, Mass.: Harvard University Press, 1949, 387–545.

Plato. *Die echten Briefe Platos.* Edited and translated by Ernst Howald. Zurich: Artemis-Verlag, 1951.

———. *Letters.* Translated by L. A. Post. In *Plato: The Collected Dialogues,* edited by Edith Hamilton and Huntingdon Cairns. Princeton, N.J.: Princeton University Press, 1961, 1560–1606.

———. *Lettres.* Edited and translated by J. Souilhé. *Platon: Oeuvres complètes.* Vol. 13.1. Paris: Les Belles Lettres, 1926.

———. *Platon: Briefe.* Edited and translated by Willi Neumann. Munich: Heimeran, 1967.

———. *Platonis epistulae.* Edited by J. Moore-Blunt. Leipzig: Teubner, 1985.

———. *Platonis opera: Epistulae.* Edited by Ioannes [John] Burnet. Vol. 5. Oxford: Clarendon, 1907.

Pliny. *Correspondence with Trajan from Bythinia (Epistles X).* Translated by Wynne Williams. Warminster: Aris and Phillips, 1990.

———. *Epistulae = Briefe.* Edited by Curt Loehning. Munich: Deutscher Taschenbuch Verlag, 1984.

———. *Epistularum libri decem.* Translated by Helmut Kasten. Munich: Heimeran, 1968. Reprint, as *Briefe.* Berlin: Akademie-Verlag, 1982.

————. *Epistularum libri decem*. Edited by R. A. B. Mynors. Oxford: Clarendon, 1963.

————. *Lettere, libro decimo, il Panegirico di Traiano*. Edited by Giovanni Bellardi. Bologna: N. Zanichelli, 1964.

————. *Letters and Panegyricus*. Edited and translated by Betty Radice. 2 vols. Loeb Classical Library. London: William Heinemann; Cambridge, Mass.: Harvard University Press, 1969.

————. *Pline le Jeune*. Edited and translated by Anne-Marie Guillemin and Marcel Durry. 4 vols. Paris: Les Belles Lettres, 1927–47.

————. *Pliny: Letters*. Translated by William Melmoth and rev. by W. M. L. Hutchison. 2 vols. Loeb Classical Library. London: William Heinemann; Cambridge, Mass.: Harvard University Press, 1915.

————. *Pliny: A Selection of His Letters*. Translated by Clarence Greig. Cambridge: Cambridge University Press, 1978.

Plutarch. "Consolation à Apollonios." *Plutarque: Oeuvres morales*. Vol. 2. Edited and translated by Jean Defradas, Jean Hani, and Robert Klaerr. Paris: Les Belles Lettres, 1985, 1–89.

————. "Consolation à sa femme." *Plutarque: Oeuvres morales*. Vol. 8. Edited and translated by Jean Hani. Paris: Les Belles Lettres, 1980, 173–98.

————. "Consolation to His Wife." *Plutarch's Moralia*. Vol. 7. Edited and translated by Phillip H. De Lacy and Benedict Einarson. Loeb Classical Library. London: William Heinemann; Cambridge, Mass.: Harvard University Press, 1959, 573–605.

————. "A Letter of Consolation to Apollonius." *Plutarch's Moralia*. Vol. 2. Edited and translated by Frank Cole Babbitt. Loeb Classical Library. London: William Heinemann; New York: G. P. Putnam's Sons, 1928, 105–211.

————. "Two Consolatory Letters of Plutarch: Touching the Death of a Friend's Son and of His Own Daughter." Chelsea: Ashendene Press, 1909.

Polycarp of Smyrna. *The Didache, the Epistle of Barnabas, the Epistles and the Martyrdom of St. Polycarp, the Fragments of Papias, the Epistle to Diognetus*. Translated by James A. Kleist. Ancient Christian Writers 6. Westminster, Md.: Newman Press, 1948.

————. "The Epistle of Polycarp to the Philippians." Translated by Kirsopp Lake. *Apostolic Fathers*. Vol. 1. Loeb Classical Library. London: William Heinemann; Cambridge, Mass.: Harvard University Press, 1912, 279–301.

————. "Epistle to the Philippians." Ante-Nicene Fathers. Edited by Alexander Roberts and James Donaldson. Vol. 1. New York: Christian Literature Publishing, 1885. Reprint, Peabody, Mass.: Hendrickson Publishers, 1994, 31–36.

————. *Lettres*. Edited and translated by Thomas Camelot. Sources chrétiennes 10. Paris: Éditions du Cerf, 1958.

[Pontius Pilate]. "The Letter of Pontius Pilate." Ante-Nicene Fathers. Edited by Alexander Roberts and James Donaldson. Vol. 8. New York: Christian Literature Publishing, 1886. Reprint, Peabody, Mass.: Hendrickson Publishers, 1994, 459.

————. "Letter to Claudius." Ante-Nicene Fathers. Edited by Alexander Roberts and James Donaldson. Vol. 8. New York: Christian Literature Publishing, 1886. Reprint, Peabody, Mass.: Hendrickson Publishers, 1994, 454, 480–81.

Pythagoras and the Pythagoreans. *Die Briefe des Pythagoras und der Pythagoreer*. Edited and translated by Alfons Städele. Meisenheim am Glan: Anton Hain, 1980.

————. "Lettres de Pythagoriciennes." *Femmes pythagoriciennes: Fragments et lettres de Théano, Périctioné, Phintys, Mélissa et Myia*. Translated by Mario Meunier. Paris: L'Artisan du livre, 1932, 77–118.

————. *The Pythagorean Texts of the Hellenistic Period*. Edited by H. Thesleff. Abo: Abo Akademi, 1965.

[Sallust]. *Sallust*. Edited and translated by J. C. Rolfe. Loeb Classical Library. London: William Heinemann; Cambridge, Mass.: Harvard University Press, 1921.

————. *Pseudo-Salluste: Lettres à César, Invectives*. Edited and translated by A. Ernout. Paris: Les Belles Lettres, 1962.

Seneca. *Ad Lucilium Epistulae Morales*. Translated by Richard M. Gummere. Loeb Classical Library. 3 vols. London: William Heinemann; Cambridge, Mass.: Harvard University Press, 1917–25.

————. *Dialogues and Letters*. Edited and translated by C. D. N. Costa. London: Penguin, 1997.

————. *Epistulae morales ad Lucilium*. Edited by A. Beltrami. 2 vols. Rome: Istituto Poligrafico, 1931. Reprint, 1949.

————. *Epistulae morales ad Lucilium*. Edited and translated by F. Préchac and H. Noblot. 5 vols. Paris: Les Belles Lettres, 1945–64.

————. *Epistulae morales ad Lucilium*. Edited by L. D. Reynolds. 2 vols. Oxford: Clarendon, 1965.

[Seneca]. *Epistolae Senecae ad Paulum et Pauli ad Senecam*. Edited by Claude W. Barlow. Horn: Austria, Ferdinand Berger for the American Academy in Rome, 1938.

————. *Epistolario apocrifo di Seneca e san Paolo*. Edited by Laura Bocciolini Palagi. Firenze: Nardini, 1985.

Sidonius Apollinaris. *Gai Sollii Apollinaris Sidonii Epistulae et carmina*. Edited by Ch. Lütjohann. Monumenta Germaniae Historica, Auctores Antiquissimi 8. Berlin: Weidmann, 1887.

————. *Gai Sollii Apollinaris Sidonii Epistulae et carmina*. Edited by P. Mohr. Leipzig: Teubner, 1895.

————. *The Letters of Sidonius*. Translated by O. M. Dalton. 2 vols. Oxford: Clarendon, 1915.

————. *Poems and Letters*. Translated by W. B. Anderson. 2 vols. Loeb Classical Library. London: William Heinemann; Cambridge, Mass.: Harvard University Press, 1936–65.

————. *Poèmes, Lettres*. Edited and translated by A. Loyen. 3 vols. Paris: Les Belles Lettres, 1960–70.

[Socrates and the Socratics]. "Die Briefe des Sokrates und der Sokratiker." Edited and translated by Liselotte Köhler. PhD diss., Zurich, 1925. Leipzig: Dieterich'sche Verlag, 1928.

————. "Epistles." Translated by Stanley K. Stowers. In *The Cynic Epistles*, edited by Abraham J. Malherbe. Missoula, Mont.: Scholars Press, 1977, 217–307.

————. "Le epistole pseudosocratiche." Translated by Gabriele Giannantoni. *Socrate: Tutte le testimonianze*. Bari: Laterza, 1971.

————. *Socratis et Socraticorum reliquae*. Edited by Gabriele Giannantoni. 4 vols. Naples: Bibliopolis, 1990.

————. *Speusippo: Frammenti*. Edited by Margherita Isnardi Parente. Naples: Bibliopolis, 1980.

————. "Speusipps Brief an König Philipp." Edited by E. Bickermann and J. Sykutris. *Philologisch-historische Klasse* 80.3 (1928).

Sulpicius Severus. *Sulpicii Severi Libri qui supersunt.* Edited by Carolus [Karl] Halm. Corpus scriptorum ecclesiasticorum latinorum 1. Vienna: apud C. Geroldi filium, 1866.

————. "Letters" and "Doubtful Letters." Translated by Alexander Roberts. Nicene and Post-Nicene Fathers, Second Series. Edited by Philip Schaff and Henry Wace. Vol. 11. New York: Christian Literature Publishing, 1894. Reprint, Peabody, Mass.: Hendrickson Publishers, 1994, 18–23; 55–70.

————. "Three Letters on St. Martin." *The Western Fathers.* Edited and translated by F. R. Hoare. London: Sheed & Ward, 1954. Reprint, New York: Harper, 1965.

Symmachus. *Lettres.* Edited and translated by Jean Pierre Callu. 3 vols. Paris: Les Belles Lettres, 1972–95.

————. *Prefect and Emperor: The Relationes of Symmachus,* A.D. 384. Edited and translated by R. H. Barrow. Oxford: Clarendon, 1973.

————. *Q. Aurelii Symmachi quae supersunt.* Edited by Otto Seeck. Monumenta Germaniae Historica, Auctores Antiquissimi 6.1. Berlin: Weidmann, 1883.

————. *Relationes.* Edited by W. Meyer. Leipzig: Teubner, 1872.

Synesius. *Epistolographi graeci.* Edited by Rudolf Hercher. Paris: F. Didot, 1873. Reprint, Amsterdam: A. M. Hakkert, 1965.

————. *The Letters of Synesius of Cyrene.* Translated by Augustine FitzGerald. London: Oxford University Press, 1926.

————. *Opere di Sinesio di Cirene: Epistole, Operette, Inni.* Edited by Antonio Garzya. Turin: Unione tipografico-editrice torinese, 1989.

Themistocles. *Le Lettere di Temistocle.* Edited by Guido Cortassa and E. Culasso Gastaldi. 2 vols. Padova: Editrice Programma, 1990.

————. *The Letters of Themistokles.* Edited and translated by Norman A. Doenges. New York: Arno Press, 1981.

Theodoret of Cyrus. *Correspondance.* Edited and translated by Yvan Azéma. Sources chrétiennes 40, 98, 111, 429. Paris: Les Éditions du Cerf, 1955–98.

————. "Letters." Translated by Blomfield Jackson. Nicene and Post-Nicene Fathers, Second Series. Edited by Philip Schaff and Henry Wace. Vol. 3. New York: Christian Literature Publishing, 1892. Reprint, Peabody, Mass.: Hendrickson Publishers, 1994, 250–348.

Xenophon. *Epistolographi Graeci.* Edited by Rudolf Hercher. Paris: F. Didot, 1873. Reprint, Amsterdam: A. M. Hakkert, 1965, 788–91.

Ancient Epistolary Theory

Primary Sources

Demetrius. *Aristotle, The Poetics; "Longinus," On the Sublime; Demetrius, On Style.* Edited and translated by W. Rhys Roberts. Loeb Classical Library. London: William Heinemann; Cambridge, Mass.: Harvard University Press, 1932, 255–487.

————. *De elocutione [On Style].* In *Ancient Epistolary Theorists,* edited by Abraham J. Malherbe. Atlanta: Scholars Press, 1988, 16–19.

————. *The Greek and Roman Critics.* Edited and translated by G. M. A. Grube. London: Methuen, 1965.

[Demetrius]. "Typoi Epistolikoi." In *Ancient Epistolary Theorists,* edited by Abraham J. Malherbe. Atlanta: Scholars Press, 1988, 30–41.

———. "Typoi Epistolikoi." *Demetrii et Libanii qui feruntur Typoi Epistolikoi et Epistolimaioi Charakteres.* Edited by Valentin Weichert. Leipzig: Teubner, 1910.

Julius Victor. "*Ars Rhetorica 27.*" In *Ancient Epistolary Theorists,* edited by Abraham J. Malherbe. Atlanta: Scholars Press, 1988, 62–65.

———. *C. Iulii Victoris ars rhetorica.* Edited by R. Giomini and S. Celentano. Leipzig: Teubner, 1980.

———. *C. Iulii Victoris ars rhetorica.* In *Rhetores Latini Minores,* edited by Carolus [Karl] Halm. Leipzig: Teubner, 1863. Reprint, Dubuque, Iowa: William C. Brown Reprint Library, n.d., 371–448.

[Libanius]. *Epistolimaioi charakteres.* In *Ancient Epistolary Theorists,* edited by Abraham J. Malherbe. Atlanta: Scholars Press, 1988, 68–81.

———. "Epistolimaioi Charakteres." In *Demetrii et Libanii qui feruntur Typoi Epistolikoi et Epistolimaioi Charakteres,* edited by Valentin Weichert. Leipzig: Teubner, 1910, 13–34.

———. "Libanii qui feruntur characteres epistolici." In *Libanii opera,* edited by Richardus [Richard] Foerster. Vol. 9. Leipzig: Teubner, 1927. Reprint, Hildesheim: Georg Olms Verlag, 1963, vol. 9.

Papyrus Bononiensis 5. Edited by Orsolina Montevecchi. Milan: Vita e Pensiero, 1953.

———.*Ancient Epistolary Theorists.* Edited by Abraham J. Malherbe and translated by Benjamin Fiore. Atlanta: Scholars Press, 1988, 44–57.

Philostratus of Lemnos. "De epistulis [On Letters]." *Ancient Epistolary Theorists.* Edited and translated by Abraham J. Malherbe. *Ancient Epistolary Theorists.* Atlanta: Scholars Press, 1988.

———. *Flavii Philostrati opera.* Edited by C. L. Kayser. Vol. 2. Leipzig: Teubner, 1871.

Secondary Sources

Studies of Major Individual Writers

Aeschines

Houthuys, F. "Over de zoogenaamde Brieven van Aischynes." PhD diss., Louvain 1947.

Kirschnek, A. "Über die Aischines Namen tragenden Briefe." *Jahresbericht kaiserlich kgl. Staats-Obergymnasium Arnau* 1891–92, 1–24.

Puiggali, J. "La lettre X du Pseudo-Eschine." *Prudentia* 20 (1988): 28–42.

Salomone, S. "Sull'epistolario dello Ps. Eschine." *Maia* 37 (1985): 231–36.

Schwegler, Karl. *De Aeschinis quae feruntur epistolis.* Giessen: Christ und Herr, 1913.

Stöcker, C. "Der 10 Aischines-Brief: Eine Kimon-Novelle." *Mnemosyne* 33 (1980): 307–12.

Alciphron

Ureña, Jesús. "La carta ficticia griega: los nombres de personajes y el uso del encabezamiento en Alcifrón, Aristéneto y Teofilacto." *Emerita* 61 (1993): 267–98.

Ussher, R. G. "Love Letter: Novel: Alciphron and 'Chion.'" *Hermathena* 143 (1987): 99–106.

[Alexander the Great]

Burstein, S. M. "SEG 33.802 and the Alexander Romance." *Zeitschrift für Papyrologie und Epigraphik* 77 (1989): 275–76.

Gunderson, Lloyd L. *Alexander's Letter to Aristotle about India*. Meisenheim am Glan: Hain, 1980.

Hamilton, J. R. "Alexander and His So-Called Father." *Classical Quarterly* 47 (1953): 151–57.

Merkelbach, R. "Der Brief des Dareios im Getty-Museum und Alexanders Wortwechsel mit Parmenion." *Zeitschrift für Papyrologie und Epigraphik* 77 (1989): 277–80.

————. "Pap. Hamb. 129." *Griechische Papyri der Hamburger Staats- und Universitätsbibliothek*. Hamburg: J. J. Augustin, 1954. 51–74.

————. "Pseudo-Kallisthenes und ein Briefroman über Alexander." *Aegyptus* 27 (1947): 144–58.

————. *Die Quellen des griechischen Alexanderromans*. Munich: C. H. Beck, 1954.

Pieraccioni, D. "1285. Lettere del ciclo di Alessandro." In *Pubblicazioni della Società Italiana per la ricerca dei Papiri greci e latini in Egitto*, edited by M. Norsa and V. Bartoletti. Florence, 1951, 166–90.

Ambrose

Adams, Mariam Annuncita. *The Latinity of the Letters of Saint Ambrose*. Washington, D.C.: Catholic University of America, 1927.

Campliani, Alberto. *Le lettere festali di Atanasio di Alessandria: studio storico-critico*. Rome: C.I.M., 1989.

Klein, R. *Der Streit um den Victoriaaltar: Die Dritte Relatio des Symmachus und die Briefe 17, 18, und 57 des Mailänder Bischofs Ambrosius*. Darmstadt: Wissenschaftliche Buchgesellschaft, 1972.

Savon, Hervé. "Saint Ambroise a-t-il imité le recueil de lettres de Pline le Jeune?" *Revue des études augustiniennes* 41 (1995): 3–17.

Anacharsis

Garzya, Antonio. "On a neglected Manuscript of Anacharsis' Epistles." *Eranos* 59 (1961): 81–83.

Mühl, M. "Der 2. und 9. Anacharsisbrief und Isokrates." *L'antiquité classique* 40 (1971): 111–20.

Nachov, I. M. "Die Anacharsis-Briefe und das Problem der Einheit der antiken Welt." In *Miszellen zur Wissenschaftsgeschichte der Altertumskunde*, edited by Horst Gericke. Halle (Saale): Martin-Luther-Universität Halle-Wittenberg, 1980, 17–28.

Praechter, K. "Die Berner Handschrift des Anacharsisbriefe." *Philologus* 58 (1899): 252–57.

————. "Der fünfte Anacharsisbrief." *Hermes* 56 (1921): 422–31.

Reuters, F. H. "Die Briefe des Anacharsis." *Das Altertum* 11 (1965): 36–40.

Apollonius of Tyana

Dzielska, Maria. *Apollonius of Tyana in Legend and History*. Translated by P. Piehkowski. Rome: L'Erma di Bretschneider, 1986.

Jones, C. P. "A martyria for Apollonius of Tyana." *Chiron* 12 (1982): 137–44.

Lo Cascio, Ferdinando. *Sulla autenticità delle epistole di Apollonio Tianeo*. Palermo: n.p., 1978.

Norden, Eduard. "Zu Apollonius von Tyana. 1. Die Briefe." *Agnostos Theos*. Leipzig: Teubner, 1913, 337–42.

Penella, R. J. "Anacharsis in a Letter of Apollonius of Tyana." *Classical Quarterly* 82 (1988): 570–72.

Petzke, Gerd. "Die Briefe des Apollonius." *Die Traditionen über Apollonius von Tyana und das Neue Testament*. Leiden: Brill, 1970, 40–45.

Taggert, B. L. "Apollonius' Letters: Apollonius of Tyana: His Biographers and Critics." PhD diss., Tufts University 1972, 79–83.

Wilamowitz-Moellendorff, Ulrich von. "Lesefrüchte." *Hermes* 60 (1925): 280–316.

Aristaenetus

Ureña, Jesús. "La carta ficticia griega: los nombres de personajes y el uso del encabezamiento en Alcifrón, Aristéneto y Teofilacto." *Emerita* 61 (1993): 267–98.

Aristotle

Heitz, E. "Die Briefe des Aristoteles." *Die verlorenen Schriften des Aristotles*. Leipzig: Teubner, 1865, 280–89.

Plezia, M. "De Aristotelis epistulis observationes criticae." *Eos* 45 (1951): 77–85.

Praechter, K. "Zu Ps.-Aristoteles epist. 6." *Philologus* 85 (1930): 97–100.

Athanasius

Brakke, David Bernhard. "St. Athanasius and Ascetic Christians in Egypt." PhD diss., Yale University, 1992.

Augustine

de Bruyne, D. "Les anciennes collections et la chronologie des lettres de Saint Augustin." *Revue bénédictine* 43 (1931): 284–95.

———. "Notes sur les lettres de saint Augustin." *Revue d'histoire ecclésiastique* 23 (1927): 523–30.

Courcelle, Peter. "Les lacunes de la correspondance entre saint Augustin et Paulin de Nole." *Revue des études anciennes* 53 (1951): 253–300.

———. "Sur la correspondance entre saint Augustin et saint Paulin de Nole." *Bulletin de la Société nationale des Antiquaires de France* (1950–51): 204.

Keenan, Mary E. "Classical Writers in the *Letters* of Augustine." *Classical Journal* 32 (1936): 35–37.

———. *The Life and Times of Saint Augustine as Revealed in His Letters*. Washington, D.C.: Catholic University Press, 1935.

Ausonius

Isbell, Harold. "Decimus Magnus Ausonius: The Poet and His World." In *Latin Literature of the Fourth Century*, edited by J. W. Binns. London: Routledge and Kegan Paul, 1974, 22–57.

Mondin, Luca. "Per la storia dell'epistolografia latina tardoantica: le lettere di Ausonio." In *Miscellanea di studi in occasione del 500 anniversario di fondazione dell'Istituto*. Rome: Carucci, 1990, 107–49.

Basil

Cavallin, A. *Studien zu den Briefen des Hl. Basilius*. Lund: Gleerup, 1944.

Fedwick, Paul J., ed. *Basil of Caesarea: Christian, Humanist, Ascetic*. Toronto: Pontifical Institute of Mediaeval Studies, 1981.

Gregg, Robert C. *Consolation Philosophy: Greek and Christian Paideia in Basil and the Two Categories.* Cambridge, Mass.: Philadelphia Patristic Foundation, 1975.

Pouchet, Robert. *Basile le Grand et son univers d'amis d'après sa correspondance: une stratégie de communion.* Rome: Inst. Patristicum Augustinianum, 1992.

Way, Agnes C. *The Language and the Style of the Letters of St. Basil.* Washington, D.C.: Catholic University Press of America, 1927.

Brutus

Ament, Ernest Joseph. "The Vatican Manuscripts of 'The Greek Letters of Brutus.'" PhD diss., St. Louis University, 1958.

Hercher, Rudolf. "Zu den Briefen des Brutus." *Philologus* 9 (1854): 592.

Meucci, P. L. "Le lettere greche di Bruto." *Studi italiani di filologia classica* 19 (1942): 47–102.

Przychocki, Gustaw. "Ciceroniana. 4. De M. Bruti epistulis." *Eos* 23 (1918): 22–24.

Rühl, F. "Die griechischen Briefe des Brutus." *Rheinisches Museum* 70 (1915): 315–25.

Smith, R. E. "The Greek Letters of M. Junius Brutus." *Classical Quarterly* 30 (1936): 194–203.

Chion

Billault, A. "Les Lettres de Chion d'Héraclée." *Revue des études grecques* 90 (1977): 29–37.

Howe, H. M. "The Authenticity of the Letters of Chio of Heraclea." *Transactions and Proceedings of the American Philological Association* 73 (1942): 29–30.

Konstan, David, and P. Mitsis. "Chion of Heraclea: A Philosophical Novel in Letters." In *The Poetics of Therapy,* edited by Martha C. Nussbaum. Edmonton: Academic Printing, 1990. 257–79.

Lana, I. "La lotta al tiranno nell'epistolario apocrifo di Chione di Eraclea." *Il pensiero politico* 7 (1974): 265–75.

Sabatucci, A. "Alcune note sulle epistole di Chione." *Studi italiani di filologica classica* 14 (1906): 374–414.

Ussher, R. G. "Love Letter, Novel: Alciphron and 'Chion.'" *Hermathena* 143 (1987): 99–106.

Zucchelli, B. "A proposito dell'epistolario di Chione d'Eraclea." *Paideia* 41 (1986): 13–24.

Cicero

Abbott, Frank Frost. "Colloquial Latin in the Letters to Cicero." PhD diss., Yale University, 1891.

Austin, L. "The Caerellia of Cicero's Correspondence." *Classical Journal* 41 (1946): 305–9.

Bailey, D. R. S. "Expectatio Corfiniensis." *Journal of Roman Studies* 46 (1956): 57–64.

Baldson, J. P. V. D. "The Commentariolum Petitionis." *Classical Quarterly* 13 (1963): 242–50.

Bornecque, H. *La prose métrique dans la correspondance de Cicéron.* Paris: E. Bouillon, 1898.

Brunt, P. A. "Cicero, Ad Atticum xiv.5.1." *Classical Review* n.s. 11 (1961): 199–200.

Carcopino, Jérôme. *Les secrets de la correspondance de Cicéron.* Paris: L'Artisan du livre, 1947. Translated by E. O. Lorimer as *Cicero, The Secrets of His Correspondence.* 2

vols. New Haven, Conn.: Yale University Press, 1951. Reprint, New York: Greenwood Press, 1969.

Cavarzere, Alberto. "La corrispondenza di Celio e la precettistica di Cicerone." *Quaderni di retorica e poetica* 1 (1985): 25–32.

———. *Marco Celio Rufo, Lettere (Cic. fam. l. VIII).* Brescia: Paideia, 1983.

Cotton, Hannah. "Greek and Latin Epistolary Formulae: Some Light on Cicero's Letter Writing." *American Journal of Philology* 105 (1984): 409–25.

———. "Mirificium genus commendationis: Cicero and the Latin Letter of Recommendation." *American Journal of Philology* 106 (1985): 328–34.

Demmel, M. "Cicero and Paetus (ad fam. IX 15–26)." PhD diss., Cologne, 1962.

Fallu, E. "Les rationes du proconsul Cicéron: Un exemple de style administratif et d'interprétation historique dans la correspondance de Cicéron." In *Aufstieg und Niedergang der Römischen Welt* I.3. Berlin: W. de Gruyter, 1973, 209–38.

Grant, W. L. "Cicero, Ad fam. viii, 8, 9." *Classical Review* 61 (1947): 10–11.

Hutchinson, G. O. *Cicero's Correspondence.* Oxford: Clarendon, 1998.

Innes, D. C. "Cicero, Ad Atticum i.14.4." *Classical Review* n.s. 16 (1966): 145–46.

Jacobs, J. P. "Cornelius Dolabella in den Korrespondenz Ciceros." PhD diss., Cologne, 1982.

Jaeger, Wolfgang. *Briefanalysen: Zum Zusammenhang von Realitätserfahrung und Sprache in Briefen Ciceros.* Frankfurt am Main: Lang, 1986.

Jocelyn, H. D. "Cicero, Ad Atticum i.18.1." *Classical Review* n.s. 16 (1966): 149–50.

Keim, Charles Z. "Lambinus and the Greek in the Text of Cicero's 'Letters to Atticus.'" PhD diss., University of Pittsburgh 1938.

Koskenniemi, Heikki. "Cicero über die Briefarten (Genera epistularum)." *Arctos* 1 (1954): 97–102.

Marshall, A. J. "Cicero, Ad Quintum fratrem ii, 10, 1." *Classical Review* n.s. 18 (1968): 16–17.

McCall, John Frederick. "The Syntax of Cicero's Greek in His Letters." PhD diss., SUNY—Albany, 1980.

Monsuez, R. "Le style épistolaire de Cicéron et la langue de la conversation." *Annales publiées par la Faculté des Lettres de Toulouse* 1 (1952): 67–80; 2 (1953): 97–120.

———. "Le style épistolaire de Cicéron: la réflexion et le choix." *Annales publiées par la Faculté des Lettres de Toulouse* 3 (1954): 41–77.

Schmidt, Otto Eduard. "Zu Ciceros Briefwechsel mit M. Brutus." *Jahrbücher für classische Philologie* 8 (1883): 559–67.

Schneider, Wolfgang Christian. *Vom Handeln der Römer: Kommunikation und Interaktion der politischen Führungsschicht vor Ausbruch des Bürgerkriegs im Briefwechsel mit Cicero.* Hildesheim: Olms, 1998.

Schwaiger, U. "Untersuchungen zu Ciceros Briefwechsel mit Marcus Junius Brutus." PhD diss., Innsbruck, 1979.

Shackleton Bailey, D. R. *Onomasticon to Cicero's Letters.* Stuttgart: Teubner, 1995.

Springer, Karl. "Supplementum Tullianum: Sunagwg: epistularum quae ad Ciceronianas annorum 68/49 spectant." PhD diss., Berlin, 1926.

Trisoglio, F. *La lettera ciceroniana come specchio di umanità.* Turin: Giappichelli, 1985.

———. "La lettera di raccomandazione nell'epistolario ciceroniano." *Latomus* 43 (1984): 751–75.

————. "La quotidianità dei rapporti sociali in Cicerone epistolografo." *Civiltà classica e cristiana* 5 (1984): 95–143.

Tuomi, Raimo. *Studien zur Textform der Briefe Ciceros.* Turku: Turun Yliopisto, 1975.

Watt, W. S. "Cicero. Ad Atticum 4.3." *Classical Quarterly* 43 (1949): 9–21.

————. "Cicero. Ad Atticum v.12.2." *Classical Review* n.s. 13 (1963): 129–31.

————. "Notes on Cicero, Ad Atticum 1 and 2." *Classical Quarterly* 12 (1962): 252–62.

Wiseman, T. P. "Two Friends of Clodius in Cicero's Letters." *Classical Quarterly* 18 (1968): 297–302.

Wistrand, Magnus. *Cicero Imperator: Studies in Cicero's Correspondence 51–47 B.C.* Göteborg: Acta Universitatis Gothoburgensis, 1979.

Cyprian

Taisne, A.-M. "Saint Cyprien et saint Jérôme, chantres du Paradis." *Bulletin de l'Association Guillaume Budé* 1992: 47–61.

Cyril of Alexandria

Burns, William Harris. "The Festal Letters of Saint Cyril of Alexandria: The Manuscript Tradition, Text and Translation." Vol. 2. PhD diss., University of Southampton, 1988.

Demetrius

Brinkmann, A. "Zu Dionysios' Brief an Pompeius und Demetrios περ̀ ρμηνὲα" *Rheinisches Museum* 49 (1914): 255–66.

Bruggiser, Philippe. "L'appellation δεσπότῆς μου της ψυχῆς dans la lettre P. Strasb. III 286." *Museum Helveticum* 46 (1989): 231–36.

Schenkeveld, D. M. *Studies in Demetrius on Style.* Amsterdam: A. M. Hakkert, 1964.

[Demetrius]

Brinkmann, L. "Der älteste Briefsteller." *Rheinisches Museum* 64 (1909): 310–17.

Demosthenes

Bickerman, Elias. "Lettres de Démosthène." *Revue de philologie* 3d ser. 11 (1937).

Bracchesi, L. "Un interpretazione della III epistola demostenica." *Rendiconti della Classe di Scienze morali, storiche e filologiche dell'Accademia nazionale dei Lincei* 21 (1966): 35–45.

Drerup, Engelbert. *Vorläufiger Bericht über eine Studienreise zur Erforschung der Demosthenesüberlieferung.* Sitzungsberichte der kgl. bayerischen Akademie der Wissenschaften 1902. Munich, n.p., 1903, 287–323.

Eitrem, S., and L. Amundsen. "Demosthenes' Epistola II." *Eranos* 54 (1956): 101–8.

Goldstein, Jonathan A. *The Letters of Demosthenes.* New York: Columbia University Press, 1968.

Jackson, D. F., and G. O. Rowe. "Demosthenes 1915–1965. The Letters." *Lustrum* 14 (1969): 79–81.

Milazzo, A. M. "Le epistole di Giovanni Crisostomo ad Innocenzo I e le epistole 1–4 di Demostene." *Orpheus* 3 (1982): 200–223.

Neupert, Albert. *De Demosthenicarum quae feruntur epistularum fide et auctoritate.* Leipzig: G. Schmidt, 1885.

Packman, Z. M. "Demosthenes' Second Epistle." *Bulletin of the American Society of Papyrologists* 10 (1973): 31–41.

Sachsenweger, Horst. *De Demosthenis epistulis.* Weidae Thuringorum: Thomas et Hubert, 1935.

Diogenes

Emeljanow, V. E. "The Letters of Diogenes." PhD diss., Stanford University, 1967.

Nihard, R. "Les lettres de Diogène à Monime et la confrontation des τόποι." *Revue de philologie* 38 (1914): 259–77.

Sicherl, Martin. "Bemerkungen zum Text der Kynikerbriefe." *Illinois Classical Studies* 18 (1993): 263–77.

Tsirimpas, D. A. "Kritika eis Diogenous epistolas." *Aqhna* 57 (1953): 69–77.

Euripides

Jouan, F. and D. Auger. "Sur le corpus des 'Lettres d'Euripide.'" *Mélanges Edouard Delebecque.* Aix-en-Provence: Publications Université de Provence, 1983, 183–98.

Tudeer, Lauri Oscar Theodor. *Some Remarks on the Letters of Euripides.* Helsinki: Suomalainen Tiedeakatemien, 1921.

Faustus of Riez

Prioco, Salvatore. "La lettera di Fausto di Riez a Magno Felice." In *Herrschaft, Kirche, Kulture: Beiträge zur Geschichte des Mittelalters: Festschrift für Friedrich Prinz zu seinem 65. Geburtstag,* edited by G. Jenal. Stuttgart: Hiersemann, 1993, 281–95.

Fronto

Cawley, E. M. "The Literary Theory and Style of Marcus Cornelius Fronto." PhD diss., Tufts University, 1971.

Champlin, E. "The Chronology of Fronto." *Journal of Roman Studies* 64 (1974): 136–59.

Cugusi, Paolo. "L'epistolario frontoniano." *Evoluzione e forme dell'epistolografia latina nella tarda repubblica e nei primi due secoli dell'Impero.* Rome: Herder, 1983.

Eck, Werner C. "P. Aelius Apollonides, ab epistulis Graecis, und ein Brief des Cornelius Fronto." *Zeitschrift für Papyrologie und Epigraphik* 91 (1992): 236–42.

Hanslik, R. "Die Anordnung der Briefsammlung Frontos." *Comm. Vindob.* 1 (1935): 21–47.

Levi, Mario Attilio. *Ricerche su Frontone.* Rome: Accademia nazionale dei Lincei, 1994.

Pflaum, H. G. "Les correspondants de l'orateur M. Cornelius Fronto de Cirta." In *Hommages à Jean Bayet,* edited by Marcel Renard. Brussels: Latomus, 1964, 544–60.

Portalupi, Felicità. "La presenza di Orazio nell'épistolario frontoniano." *Civiltà classica e cristiana* 12 (1991): 97–108.

Selvatico, G. P. "Lo scambio epistolare tra Frontone e M. Aurelio: Esercitazioni retoriche e cultura letteraria." *Memorie dell'Accademia delle Scienze di Torino* V.5 (1981): 225–301.

Gregory Nazianzen

Guignet, M. *Les procédés épistolaires de Saint Gregoire de Nazianze.* Paris: A. Picard, 1911.

Przychocki, Gustaw. *De Gregorii Nazianzeni epistolis quaestiones selectae.* Cracow: Sumptibus Academiae Litterarum, 1912.

Ruether, Rosemary Radford. *Gregory of Nazianzus: Rhetor and Philosopher.* Oxford: Clarendon, 1969.

Heraclitus

Kassel, R. "Der siebente pseudoheraklitische Brief auf Pergament und Papyrus." *Zeitschrift für Papyrologie und Epigraphik* 14 (1974): 128–32.

Kindstrand, J. F. "The Cynics and Heraclitus." *Eranos* 82 (1984): 149–78.

Malherbe, Abraham J. "Pseudo Heraclitus, Epistle 4: The Divinization of the Wise Man." *Jahrbuch für Antike und Christentum* 21 (1978): 42–64.

Strugnell, J., and H. W. Attridge. "The Epistles of Heraclitus and the Jewish Pseudepigrapha: A Warning." *Harvard Theological Review* 64 (1971): 411–13.

Hippocrates

Pohlenz, M. "Zu den Hippokratischen Briefen." *Hermes* 52 (1917): 348–53.

Sakalis, D. T. "Beiträge zu den pseudo-hippokratischen Briefen." In *Formes de pensée dans la collection hippocratique,* edited by F. Lasserre and P. Mudry. Actes du IVe Colloque International Hippocratique (Lausanne, 21–26 septembre 1981). Genève: Droz, 1983. 499–514.

Horace

Bösing, L. *Griechen und Römer im Augustusbrief des Horaz.* Konstanz: Universitätsverlag, 1972.

Brink, C. O. "Prolegomena to the Literary Epistles." *Horace on Poetry.* Cambridge: Cambridge University Press, 1963.

Cameron, A. "Horace, Epistles ii.2.87ff." *Classical Review* n.s. 15 (1965): 11–13.

Courbaud, E. *Horace: Sa vie et sa pensée à l'époque des épitres.* Paris: Hachette, 1914.

Cupaiuolo, F. *L'Epistola di Orazio ai Pisoni.* Naples: Rondinella, 1941.

Gagliardi, D. *Un'arte di vivere: Saggio sul I libro delle "Epistole" oraziane.* Rome: Ateneo, 1988.

Garn, E. "Odenelemente im 1. Epistelbuch des Horaz." PhD diss., Freiburg, 1954.

Grimal, P. *Essai sur l' "Art Poetique" d'Horace.* Paris: Societé d'édition d'enseignement superieur, 1968.

Haight, E. H. "Epistula Item Quaevis Non Magna Poema Est: A Fresh Approach to Horace's First Book of Epistles." *Studies in Philology* 45 (1948): 525–40.

———. "Lyre and Whetstone: Horatius Redivivus." *Classical Philology* 41 (1946): 135–42.

Heller, J. L. "Horace, Epist. I, 1, 47–54." *American Journal of Philology* 85 (1964): 297–303.

Hirth, Hans Joachim. *Horaz, der Dichter der Briefe: rus und urbs, die Valenz der Briefform am Beispiel der ersten Epistel an Maecenas.* Hildesheim: Olms-Weidmann, 1985.

Kettner, G. *Die "Episteln" des Horaz.* Berlin: Weidmann, 1900.

Kilpatrick, R. S. *The Poetry of Criticism: Horace, Epistles II and Ars Poetica.* Edmonton: University of Alberta Press, 1990.

———. *The Poetry of Friendship: Horace, Epistles I.* Edmonton: University of Alberta Press, 1986.

Klingner, Friedrich. *Horazens Briefe an die Pisonen.* Leipzig: Hirzel, 1937.

McGann, M. J. "Horace, Epistles ii.2.87ff: Another View." *Classical Review* n.s. 16 (1966): 266–67.

———. "The Sixteenth Epistle of Horace." *Classical Quarterly* 10 (1960): 205–12.

———. *Studies in Horace's First Book of Epistles.* Bruxelles: Latomus, 1969.

Nisbet, R. G. M. "Notes on Horace, Epistles I." *Classical Quarterly* 9 (1959): 73–76.

Ott, W. *Metrische Analysen zur "Ars Poetica" des Horaz.* Göppingen, Kümmerle, 1970.

Pasoli, E. *Le epistole letterarie di Orazio.* Bologna: Pàtron, 1964.

Perret, J. "The Book of Epistles." In *Horace.* Translated by Bertha Humez. New York: New York University Press, 1964, 101–23.

Peterson, R. G. "The Unity of Horace Epistle 1.7." *Classical Journal* 63 (1968): 309–14.

Schrijvers, P. H. *Horatius: Ars Poetica.* Amsterdam: Athenaeum, 1980.

Stégen, G. *Essai sur la composition de cinq épitres d'Horace (I, 1, 2, 3, 11 & 15).* Namur: Wesmael-Charlier, 1960.

———. *L'unité et la clarté des "Epitres" d'Horace: Étude sur sept pièces du premier livre (4, 6, 7, 9, 13, 14, 16).* Namur: Wesmael-Charlier, 1963.

Steidle, W. *Studien zur "Ars poetica" des Horaz: Interpretation des auf Dichtkunst und Gedicht Bezüglichen Hauptteiles (verse 1–294).* Würzburg: Triltsch, 1939.

Isocrates

Gaines, R. N. "Isocrates: Ep. 6.8." *Hermes* 118 (1990): 165–70.

Jebb, R. C. *The Attic Orators from Antiphon to Isaeos.* Vol. 2. London: Macmillan, 1876. 238–56.

Smith, L. F. "The Genuineness of the Ninth and Third Letters of Isocrates." PhD diss., Columbia University, Lancaster, Pa.., 1940.

Wilamowitz-Moellendorff, Ulrich von. "Die Briefe des Isokrates." *Aristoteles und Athen.* Vol. 2. Berlin: Weidmann, 1893, 391–99.

———. "Unechte Briefe." *Hermes* 33 (1898): 492–98.

Jerome

Arns, Paulo Evaristo. *La technique du livre d'après saint Jérôme.* Paris: E. de Boccard, 1953.

Cavallera, Ferdinand. *Saint Jérôme: Sa vie et son oeuvre.* 2 vols. Louvain: "Spicilegium Sacrum Lovaniense" Bureaux, 1922.

Gilliam, J. F. "Pro Caelio in St. Jerome's Letters." *Harvard Theological Review* 46 (1953): 103–7.

Hritzu, J. N. *Style of the Letters of St. Jerome.* Washington, D.C.: Catholic University of America Press, 1939.

Hulley, Karl Kelchner. "Light Cast by Saint Jerome on Certain Paleographical Points." *Harvard Studies in Classical Philology* 54 (1943): 83–92.

Lawler, Thomas C. "Jerome's First Letter to Damasus." In *KYRIAKON: Festschrift Johannes Quasten,* edited by Patrick Granfield and Josef A. Jungmann. Vol. 2. Munster Westfalen: Verlag Aschendorff, 1970, 548–52.

Levy, Harry L. "Claudian's In Rufinium and an Epistle of St. Jerome." *American Journal of Philology* 69 (1948): 62–68.

John Chrysostom
Milazzo, A. M. "Le epistole di Giovanni Crisostomo ad Innocenzo I e le epistole 1–4 di Demostene." *Orpheus* 3 (1982): 200–223.

Julian
Boer, William den. "Two Letters from the Corpus Iulianeum." *Vigiliae Christianae* 16 (1962): 179–97.
Bradbury, Scott. "The Date of Julian's Letter to Themistius." *Greek, Roman, and Byzantine Studies* 28 (1987): 235–51.

Julius Victor
Celentano, Maria Silvana. "Un galateo dell conversazione nell'Ars rhetorica di Giulio Vittore." *Vichiana* 3d ser. 1 (1990): 245–53.

Libanius
Bruggisser, Philippe. "Libanios, Symmaque et son père Avianus: culture littéraire dans les cercles païens tardifs." *Ancient Society* 21 (1990): 17–31.
Foerster, Richardus [Richard]. "Prolegomena ad Epistulas." *Libanii opera*. Vol. 9. Leipzig: Teubner, 1927. Reprint, Hildesheim: Georg Olms Verlag, 1963.
López Eire, Antonio. "Una carta muy larga de Libanio: Lib. Ep. 636 F." *De Homero a Libanio: Estudios actuales sobre textos griegos*. Edited by Juan Antonio López Férez. Madrid: Edited by clásicas, 1995.
———. "Las citas homéricas en las Epístolas de Libanio." *Habis* 24 (1993): 159–77.

[Libanius]
Hinck, H. "Die epistolimaioi charakteres des Pseudo-Libanius." *Neue Jahrbücher für Philologie und Paedagogik* 99 (1869): 537–62.

Ovid
Agostino, V. d.' "Introduzione all lettura delle Eroide ovidiane." *Rivista di studi classici* 3 (1955): 107–20.
Anderson, James Nesbitt. *On the Sources of Ovid's Heroides I, III, VII, X, XII*. Berlin: Calvary & Co., 1896.
Anderson, W. S. "The Heroides." In *Ovid*, edited by J. W. Binns. London: Routledge & Kegan Paul, 1973, 49–83.
Baca, A. R. "Ovid's Claim to Originality and *Heroides* 1." *Transactions of the American Philological Association* 100 (1969): 1–10.
———. "Ovid's Epistle from Sappho to Phaon: *Heroides* 15." *Transactions of the American Philological Association* 102 (1971): 29–38.
———. "The Themes of *Querela* and *Lacrimae* in Ovid's *Heroides*." *Emerita* 39 (1971): 195–201.
Barchiesi, A. "Narratività e convenzione nelle 'Heroides.'" *Materiale e discussioni per l'analisi dei testi classici* 19 (1987): 63–90.
———. "Ovidio, 'Heroides' 7,115." *Rivista di filologia e d'istruzione classica* 118 (1990): 408–17.
Bernhardt, U. *Die Funktion der Kataloge in Ovids Exilpoesie*. Hildesheim: Olms-Weidmann, 1986.
Bettini, M. "'Heroides' 8, 47 e i gradi di parentela in Ovidio." *Rivista filologia e d'istruzione classica* 118 (1990): 418–29.

Bradley, E. M. "Ovid *Heroides* V: Reality and Illusion." *Classical Journal* 64 (1969): 158–62.

Bretzigheimer, G. "Exul ludens: Zur Rolle von relegans und relegatus in Ovids *Tristien*." *Gymnasium* 98 (1991): 39–76.

Casali, Sergio. "Strategies of Tension (Ovid, Heroides 4)." *Proceedings of the Cambridge Philological Society* 41 (1995): 1–15.

———. "Tragic Irony in Ovid, Heroides 9 and 11." *Classical Quarterly* 45 (1995): 505–11.

Clark, S. B. "The Authorship and the Date of the Double Letters in Ovid's Heroides." *Harvard Studies in Classical Philology* 19 (1908): 121–55.

Claasen, Jo-M. "Ovid's Wavering Identity: Personification and Depersonalisation in the Exilic Poems." *Latomus* 49 (1990): 102–16.

Courtney, E. "Ovidian and Non-Ovidian Heroides." *Bulletin of the Institute of Classical Studies* 12 (1965): 63–66.

Cunningham, M. P. "The Novelty of Ovid's *Heroides*." *Classical Philology* 44 (1949): 100–106.

Davis, Peter J. "Rewriting Euripides: Ovid, Heroides 4." *Scholia* 4 (1995): 41–55.

Dickinson, R. J. "The *Tristia:* Poetry in Exile." In *Ovid,* edited by J. W. Binns. London: Routledge & Kegan Paul, 1973, 154–90.

Dörrie, Heinrich. "Die dichterische Absicht Ovids in der Epistulae Heroidum." *Antike und Abendland* 13 (1967): 41–55.

———. *P. Ovidius Naso: Der Brief der Sappho an Phaon.* Munich: Beck, 1975.

———. *Untersuchungen zur Überlieferungsgeschichte von Ovids epistulae Heroidum.* 3 vols. Göttingen: Vandenhoeck & Ruprecht, 1960–72.

Flaherty, Shiela M. "The Rhetoric of Female Self-Destruction: A Study in Homer, Euripides, and Ovid." PhD diss., Yale University, 1994.

Focardi, G. "Difesa, preghiera, ironia nel II libro dei "Tristia" di Ovidio." *Studi italiani di filologia classica* 47 (1975): 86–129.

Haley, L. "The Feminine Complex in the *Heroides*." *Classical Journal* 20 (1924–25): 15–25.

Hansen, Gustaf Charles. "A Stylistic Analysis of Ovid's Elegiac Poetry with a View Towards Determining the Authorship of 'Heroides' 16–21." PhD diss., University of Toronto 1993.

Hintermeier, Cornelia M. *Die Briefpaare in Ovids Heroides.* Stuttgart: F. Steiner, 1993.

Housman, A. E. "Ovid's *Heroides*." In *The Classical Papers of A. E. Housman.* 3 vols. Edited by James Diggle and Francis Richard David Goodyear. Cambridge: Cambridge University Press, 1972, 380–421.

Jacobson, Howard. *Ovid's Heroides.* Princeton, N.J. Princeton University Press, 1974.

Kennedy, D. C. "The Epistolary Mode and the First of Ovid's *Heroides*." *Classical Quarterly* 34 (1984): 413–22.

Kenney, E. J. "Love and Legalism: Ovid *Heroides* 20 and 21." *Arion* 9 (1970): 388–414.

———. "Two Disputed Passages in the *Heroides*." *Classical Quarterly* 29 (1979): 394–431.

Kirfel, E.-A. *Untersuchungen zur Briefform der Heroides Ovids.* Bern: Haupt, 1969.

Knox, P. "Ovid's Medea and the Authenticity of *Heroides* 12." *Harvard Studies in Classical Philology* 90 (1986): 207–23.

Kraus, W. "Die Briefpaare in Ovids Heroides." *Wiener Studien* 65 (1950): 54–77.

Lindheim, Sara Helaine. "Voices of Desire: The Ventriloquized Letters of Ovid's Heroides." PhD diss., Brown University, 1995.

Marg, W. "Ovid, Heroides 10, 95/6." *Hermes* 88 (1960): 505–6.

Merchant, W. P. H. "Ovid, *Heroides* 16.177." *Classical Review* n.s. 17 (1967): 262–63.

Merone, Emilio. *Studi sulle Eroidi di Ovidio.* Naples: Editrice Intercontinentalia, 1964.

Nagle, Betty R. *The Poetics of Exile: Program and Polemic in the Tristia and Epistulae ex Ponto of Ovid.* Bruxelles: Latomus, 1980.

Nisbet, R. G. M. "Great and Lesser Bear (Ovid, *Tristia* 4.3)." *Journal of Roman Studies* 72 (1982): 49–56.

Peters, Wilhelm. *Observationes ad P. Ovidii Nasonis Heroidum epistulas.* Leipzig: Teubner, 1882.

Reeve, M. D. "Notes on Ovid's *Heroides*." *Classical Quarterly* 29 (1973): 117–30.

Rittenbaum, Ann Haigler. "The Process of Grieving in Ovid's Heroides." PhD diss., Washington University, 1997.

Schawaller, Doris. "Semantische Wortspiele in Ovids Metamorphosen und Heroides." *Grazer Beiträge* 14 (1987): 199–214.

Spoth, Friedrich. *Ovids Heroides als Elegien.* Munich: Beck, 1992.

Steinmetz, P. "Die literarische Form der Epistulae Heroidum Ovids." *Gymnasium* 94 (1987): 128–45.

Tarrant, R. J. "The Authenticity of the Letter of Sappho to Phaon (Heroides XV)." *Harvard Studies in Classical Philology* 85 (1981): 133–53.

———. "Ovid. *Heroides. Epistula Sapphus.*" In *Texts and Transmission: A Survey of the Latin Classics,* edited by L. D. Reynolds. Oxford: Clarendon, 1983, 268–73.

Vessey, D. W. T. C. "Notes on Ovid, *Heroides* 9." *Classical Quarterly* 19 (1969): 349–61.

Winniczuk, L. "Ovid's Elegie und epistolographische Theorie." *Publius Ovidius Naso.* Bucuresti: Editura Academiei Republicii Populare Romine, 1957. 39–70.

Winsor, E. J. "A Study in the Sources and Rhetoric of Chaucer's Legend of Good Women and Ovid's Heroides." PhD diss., Yale University, 1963.

Paulinus of Nola

Courcelle, Pierre. "Sur la correspondance entre saint Augustin et saint Paulin de Nole." *Bulletin de la Société nationale des Antiquaires de France* (1950–51): 204.

Erdt, W. *Christentum und heidnisch-antike Bildung bei Paulin von Nola.* Meisenheim: Anton Hain, 1976.

Frend, W. H. C. "The Two Worlds of Paulinus of Nola." In *Latin Literature of the Fourth Century,* edited by J. W. Binns. London: Routledge and Kegan Paul, 1974, 100–133.

Trout, Dennis E. *Paulinus of Nola: Life, Letters, and Poems.* Berkeley: University of California Press, 1999.

Patrick

Conneely, Daniel, et al. *St. Patrick's Letters: A Study of Their Theological Dimensions.* Maynooth: An Sagart, 1993.

272 Appendix A

[Phalaris]

Bruno, O. "L'epistola 92 dello Pseudo-Falaride e i Nostoi di Stesicoro." *Helikon* 7 (1967): 323–56.

Russell, D. A. "The Ass in the Lion's Skin: Thoughts on the *Letters of Phalaris*." *Journal of Hellenic Studies* 108 (1988): 94–106.

Tudeer, Lauri O. Th. *The Epistles of Phalaris: Preliminary Investigations of the Manuscripts*. Helsinki: Suomalainen Tiedeakatemien, 1931.

Plato

Bluck, R. S. "Notes on Plato's Seventh Letter." *Classical Review* 60 (1946): 7–8.

Bowra, C. M. "Plato's Epigram on Dion's Death." *American Journal of Philology* 59 (1938): 394–404.

Dornseiff, F. "Platons Buch 'Briefe.'" *Hermes* 69 (1934): 223–26.

Edelstein, L. *Plato's Seventh Letter*. Leiden: Brill, 1966.

Pliny

André, J.-M. "Pensée et philosophie dans les lettres de Pline le Jeune." *Revue des études latines* 53 (1975): 225–47.

Aubrion, E. "La 'Correspondance' de Pline le Jeune: problèmes et orientations actuelles de la recherche." *Aufstieg und Niedergang der Römischen Welt* II.33.1. Berlin: W. de Gruyter, 1989. 304–74.

Bütler, Hans-Peter. *Die geistige Welt des jüngeren Plinius: Studien zur Thematik seiner Briefe*. Heidelberg: C. Winter, 1970.

Cameron, Alan. "The Fate of Pliny's Letters in the Late Empire." *Classical Quarterly* 15 (1965): 289–98.

Cugusi, Paolo. "L'epistolario pliniano." *Evoluzione e forme dell'epistolografia latina nella tarfa repubblica e nei primi due secoli dell'Impero, con cenni sulla epistolografia preciceroniana*. Rome: Herder, 1983. 207–39.

Förtsch, Reinhard. *Archäologischen Kommentar zu den Villenbriefen des jüngeren Plinius*. Mainz am Rhein: P. von Zabern, 1993.

Gazich, Roberto. "Retorica dell'ostensione nelle lettere di Plinio." In *Letteratura dell'Italia settentrionale*, edited by Pier Vincenzo Cova et al. Milan: Vita e Pensiero, 1992, 141–95.

Grant, R. M. "Pliny and the Christians." *Harvard Theological Review* 41 (1948): 273–74.

Hengst, D. den. "Plinius' literaire ambities." *Lampas* 24 (1991): 19–29.

Illias-Zarifopol, Christina Ioana. "Portrait of a Pragmatic Hero: Narrative Strategies of Self-Presentation in Pliny's Letters." PhD diss., Indiana University, 1994.

Jal, Paul. "Pline épistolier: ecrivain superficiel? Quelques remarques." *Revue des études latines* 71 (1993): 212–27.

Lehmann-Hartleren, K. *Plinio il Giovane: Lettere scelte con commento archeologico*. Firenze: Sansoni, 1936.

Lilja, S. "On the Nature of Pliny's Letters." *Arctos* 6 (1970): 60–79.

Lowe, E. A., and E. K. Rand. *A Sixth-Century Fragment of the Letters of Pliny the Younger*. Washington, D.C.: Carnegie Institution of Washington, 1922.

Ludolph, Matthias. *Epistolographie und Selbstdarstellung: Untersuchungen zu den "Paradebriefen" Plinius des Jüngeren*. Tübingen: Narr, 1997.

Marcone, Arnaldo. "Due epistolari a confronto: Corpus pliniano e corpus simmachiano." In *Studi di storia e storiografia antiche per Emilio Gabba.* Como: New Press, 1988, 143–54.

Melzani, Graziano. "Elementi della lingua d'uso nelle lettere di Plinio il Giovane." In *Letteratura dell'Italia settentrionale,* edited by Pier Vincenzo Cova et al. Milan: Vita e Pensiero, 1992, 197–244.

Merwald, G. "Die Buchkomposition des jüngeren Plinius ('Epistulae' I–IX)." PhD diss., Erlangen-Nürnberg, 1964.

Miller, C. L. "The Younger Pliny's Dolphin Story (Epistulae IX 33): An Analysis." *Classical World* 60 (1966): 6–8.

Paardt, Rudi Th. van der. "Plinius als verslaggever?" *Lampas* 24 (1991): 54–65.

Picone, Giusto. *L'eloquenza di Plinio: teoria e prassi.* Palermo: Palumbro, 1978.

Radice, Betty. "A Fresh Approach to Pliny's Letters." *Greece and Rome* 9 (1962): 160–69.

Rusca, Luigi. *Plinio il giovane attraverso le sue lettere.* Como: P. Cairoli, 1971.

Sherwin-White, A. N. *The Letters of Pliny: A Historical and Social Commentary.* Oxford: Clarendon, 1966.

———. "Pliny, the Man and His Letters." *Greece and Rome* 16 (1969): 76–90.

Shipp, G. P. "Latin Idiom and Pliny Ep. iv.2.2." *Classical Philology* 39 (1944): 117–18.

Sullivan, F. A. "Pliny Epistulae 6.16 and 20 and Modern Volcanology." *Classical Philology* 63 (1968): 196–200.

Vidman, Ladislav. *Étude sur la correspondance de Pline le jeune avec Trajan.* Prague: Nakladatelství Ceskoslovenskí Akademie Ved, 1960. Reprint, Rome: L'Erma di Bretschneider, 1972.

Zucker, F. "Untersuchungen zur Charakter der Briefsammlung des jüngeren Plinius." PhD diss., Vienna, 1962.

[Sallust]

Dihle, A. "Zu den Epistulae ad Caesarem senem." *Museum Helveticum* 11 (1954): 125–30.

Nisbet, R. G. M. "The Invective in Ciceronem and Epistula Secunda of Pseudo-Sallust." *Journal of Roman Studies* 48 (1958): 30–32.

Seyfarth, W. "Sallusts Briefe an Caesar: Versuch eines Beweises ihrer Echtheit im Hinblick auf die Widersprüchlichkeit der Gesellschaft ihrer Zeit." *Klio* 40 (1962): 128–41.

Seneca

Abel, K. "Das Problem der Faktizität der Senecanischen Korrispondenz." *Hermes* 109 (1981): 472–99.

Bourgery, A. "Les lettres à Lucilius sont-elles des vraies lettres?" *Revue de philologie* 35 (1911): 40–55.

Cancik, Hildegard. *Untersuchungen zu Senecas Epistulae morales.* Hildesheim: Georg Olms, 1967.

Coleman, R. "The Artful Moralist: A Study of Seneca's Epistolary Style." *Classical Quarterly* 24 (1974): 276–89.

Hachmann, Erwin. *Die Führung des Lesers in Senecas Epistulae morales.* Münster: Aschendorff, 1995.

Hijmans, B. L. *Inlaboratus et facilis: Aspects of Structure in Some Letters of Seneca.* Leiden: Brill, 1976.

Lana, I. *Analisi delle "Lettere a Lucilio" di Seneca.* Turin: Giappichelli, 1988.

Maurach, Gregor. *Der Bau von Senecas Epistulae morales.* Heidelberg: C. Winter, 1970.

Mazzoli, Giancarlo. "Effetti di cornice nell'epistolario di Seneca a Lucilio." In *Seneca e la cultura,* edited by Aldo Setaioli. Naples: Ed. Scientifiche Italiane, 1991, 67–87.

———. "Le 'Epistulae Morales ad Lucilium': Valore letterario e filosofico." *Aufstieg und Niedergang der Römischen Welt* II.36.3. Berlin: W. de Gruyter, 1989. 1823–77.

Motto, Anna Lydia, and John R. Clark. "The Artistry of Seneca's Epistle 62." *Athenaeum* 69 (1991): 583–88.

———. "Epistle 56: Seneca's Ironic Art." *Classical Philology* 65 (1970): 102–5.

Rosati, G. "Seneca sulla lettera filosofica: Un genere letterario nel commino verso la sagezza." *Maia* n.s. 33 (1981): 3–15.

Schindler, W. "Speculum animi oder das absolute Gespräch." *Der altsprachliche Unterricht* 32 (1989): 4–21.

Wilson, M. "Seneca's Epistles to Lucilius: A Revaluation." *Ramus* 16 (1987): 102–21.

[Seneca]

Cid Luna, Perfecto. "El texto de la correspondencia atribuida a Séneca y S. Pablo en el ms. Oxomensis 153." In *Homenatge a Josep Alsina.* Vol. 2. Edited by Esther Artigas. Tarragona: Diputació de Tarragona: 1992, 167–73.

Sidonius Apollinaris

Bailey, D. R. S. "Notes, Critical and Interpretative, on the Letters of Sidonius Apollinaris." *Phoenix* 36 (1976): 344–57.

Harries, J. D. "Sidonius Apollinaris, Rome and the Barbarians: A Climate of Treason?" In *Fifth-Century Rome: A Crisis of Identity?* Edited by John Drinkwater and Hugh Elton. Cambridge: Cambridge University Press, 1992, 298–308.

Hirschberg, Theo. "Zu Apollinaris Sidonius: Epist. 4,3,6." *Hermes* 120 (1992): 124–27.

Sivan, H. S. "Sidonius Apollinaris, Theoderic II and Gothic-Roman Politics from Avitus to Anthemius." *Hermes* 117 (1989): 85–94.

Socrates and the Socratics

Fiore, Benjamin. *The Function of Personal Example in the Socratic and Pastoral Epistles.* Rome: Biblical Institute Press, 1986.

Hock, R. F. "Simon the Shoemaker as an Ideal Cynic." *Greek, Roman and Byzantine Studies* 17 (1976): 41–53.

Markle, M. M., III. "Support of Athenian Intellectuals for Philip: A Study of Isocrates' *Philippus* and Speusippus' *Letter to Philip.*" *Journal of Hellenic Studies* 96 (1976): 80–99.

Sykutris, J. *Die Briefe des Sokrates und der Sokratiker.* Paderborn: F. Schöningh, 1933.

Sulpicius Severus

Lepelley, Claude. "Trois documents méconnus sur l'histoire sociale et religieuse de l'Afrique romaine tardive retrouvés parmi les spuria le Sulpice Sévère." *Antiquités africaines* 25 (1989): 235–62.

Symmachus

Bonney, Robert. "A New Friend for Symmachus?" *Historia* 24 (1975): 357–74.

Bruggisser, Philippe. *Symmaque, ou, Le rituel epistolaire de l'amité litteraire recherches sur le premier livre de la correspondance.* Fribourg: Éditions universitaires, 1993.

Croke, Brian. "The Editing of Symmachus' Letters to Eugenius and Arbogast." *Latomus* 35 (1976): 533–49.

Kaster, Robert A. "The Echo of a Chaste Obscenity: Verg. E. vi.26 and Symm. Ep. vi.22.1." *American Journal of Philology* 104 (1983): 395–97.

Klein, R. *Der Streit um den Victoriaaltar: Die Dritte Relatio des Symmachus und die Briefe 17, 18, und 57 des Mailänder Bischofs Ambrosius.* Darmstadt: Wissenschaftliche Buchgesellschaft, 1972.

Knecht, D. "Symmaque 3,6,6 (à Rusticus Iulianus)." *Latomus* 45 (1986): 180.

———. "Symmaque 4,50 (à Florentinus)." *Latomus* 45 (1986): 180–81.

———. "Symmaque 5,40 (à Nesterius)." *Latomus* 45 (1986): 181–82.

Kovach, Edith M. A. "A Study of the Manuscripts of the Florilegium of the Letters of Symmachus." PhD diss., University of Michigan, 1950.

Marcone, Arnaldo. *Commento storico al libro IV dell'epistolario di Q. Aurelio Simmaco.* Pisa: Giardini, 1987.

———. *Commento storico al libro VI dell'epistolario di Q. Aurelio Simmaco.* Pisa: Giardini, 1983.

———. "Due epistolari a confronto: Corpus pliniano e corpus simmachiano." *Studi di storia e storiografia antiche per Emilio Gabba.* Como: New Press, 1988. 143–54.

Matthews, John F. "The Letters of Symmachus." In *Latin Literature of the Fourth Century,* edited by J. W. Binns. London: Routledge & Kegan Paul, 1974, 58–99.

McGeachy, John Alexander, Jr. "Quintus Aurelius Symmachus and the Senatorial Aristocracy of the West." PhD diss., University of Chicago, 1942.

Pellizzari, Andrea. *Commento storico al libro III dell'Epistolato di Q. Aurelio Simmaco.* Pisa: Istituti editoriali e poligrafici internazionali, 1998.

Roda, Sergio. *Commento storico al libro IX dell'epistolario di Q. Aurelio Simmaco.* Pisa: Giardini, 1981.

———. "Polifunzionalità della lettera commendaticia: Teoria e prassi nell'epistolario simmachianio." In *Colloque genevois sur Symmaque à l'occasion du mille-six-centième anniversaire du conflit de l'autel de la Victoire,* edited by F. Paschoud. Paris: Les Belles Lettres, 1986, 177–207.

Tiberga, Paola Rivolta. *Commento storico al libro V dell'epistolario di Q. Aurelio Simmaco.* Pisa: Giardini, 1992.

Synesius

Long, Jacqueline. "Dating an Ill-fated Journey: Synesius, Ep. 5." *Transactions of the American Philological Association* 122 (1992): 351–80.

Roques, Denis. *Études sur la correspondance de Synésios de Cyrène.* Bruxelles: Latomus, 1989.

Simeon, Xaver. *Untersuchungen zu den Briefen des Bischofs Synesios von Kyrene.* Paderborn: F. Schöningh, 1933.

Theodoret of Cyrus

Tompkins, Ian George. "Problems of Dating and Pertinence in Some Letters of Theodoret of Cyrrhus." *Byzantion* 65 (1995): 176–95.

Wagner, M. Monica. "A Chapter in Byzantine Epistolography: The Letters of Theodoret of Cyrus." *Dumbarton Oaks Papers* 4 (1948): 119–82.

Themistocles

Acosta Esteban, M. "Las epístolas de Themístocles: Dos autores." *Habis* 6 (1975): 35–51.

Doenges, Norman A. "The Letters of Themistocles: A Survey." PhD diss., Princeton University, 1954.

Jackson, J. "The Text of the Epistles of Themistocles." *Classical Quarterly* 19 (1925): 167–76; 20 (1926): 27–35.

Lenardon, Robert J. "The Epistles of Themistocles: A Hero's Justification." In *The Saga of Themistocles*. London: Thames & Hudson, 1978, 154–93.

Penwill, J. L. "The Letters of Themistocles: An Epistolary Novel?" *Antichthon* 12 (1978): 83–103.

Podlecki, Anthony J. *The Life of Themistocles: A Critical Survey of the Literary and Archaeological Evidence.* Montreal: McGill-Queen's University Press, 1975. 129–33.

General Secondary Sources

Ambaglio, Delfino. *La dedica delle opere letterarie antiche fino all'età dei Flavi.* Como: Editizone New Press, 1983.

Andresen, C. "Zum Formula frühchristlicher Gemeindebriefe." *Zeitschrift für die Neutestamentliche Wissenschaft und die Kunde der älteren Kirche* 56 (1965): 233–59.

Andrzeyewski, R. "La structure de la lettre de recommendation antique à la lumière des principes de la rhétorique." Polish text. *Roczniki hum. (Lublin* University *cath.)* 20 (1972): 17–24.

———. "Nova et vetera quae in epistulis latinis IV p. Chr. n. saeculo apparent." Polish text. *Eos* 57 (1967–68): 245–50.

Aujac, G. "La lettre à teneur scientifique à l'époque alexandrine." *Bulletin de la Société toulousaine d'Études classiques* 179–80 (1979–80): 79–102.

Babl, Johann. *De epistularum latinarum formulis.* Bamberg: W. Gärtner, 1893.

Bakir, Abd el-Mohsen. *Egyptian Epistolography from the Eighteenth to the Twenty-First Dynasty.* Le Caire: Institut francais d'archéologie orientale, 1970.

Baldwin, Charles Elbert. "The Form and Function of the Aspazomai Formula: A Study in Greek Epistolography." M.A. thesis, Vanderbilt University, 1973.

Bardt, C[arl]. *Römische Charakterköpfe in Briefen.* Leipzig: Teubner, 1921.

Barnes, Timothy D. "A Correspondent of Iamblichus." *Greek, Roman and Byzantine Studies* 19 (1978): 99–106.

del Barrio Vega, M. L. "Algúnos problemas de la epistolografía griega: Es posiblé una clasificación epistolar?" *Minerva* 5 (1991): 123–37.

Bastiaensen, A. A. R. *Le cérémonial épistolaire des chrétiens latins: Origine de premiers développements.* Graecitas et latinitas christianorum primaeva, Supplementa 2. Nijmegen: Dekker & Van de Vegt, 1964.

Berger, K. "Apostelbrief und apostolische Rede: Zum Formular frühchristlicher Briefe." *Zeitschrift für die Neutestamentliche Wissenschaft und die Kunde der älteren Kirche* 65 (1974): 190–231.

————. "Hellenistische Gattungen im Neuen Testament." In *Aufstieg und Niedergang der römischen Welt* II.25.2. Berlin: W. de Gruyter, 1984, 1326–63.

Bernardi Perini, G. "Alle origini della lettera familiare." *Quaderni di retorica e poetica* 1 (1985): 17–24.

Betz, H. D. "The Literary Composition of Paul's Letter to the Galatians." *Der Apostel Paul und die sokratische Tradition.* Tübingen: Mohr, 1972.

Biedenkopf-Ziehner, A. *Untersuchungen zum koptischen Briefformular unter Berücksichtigung ägyptischer und griechischer Parallelen.* Würzburg: Zauzich, 1983.

————. "Fluarein, eine Verletzung gebotener Höflichkeit im Brief?" *Enchoria* 13 (1985): 7–12.

Bradford, Gamaliel. A Naturalist of Souls: Studies in Psychography. Boston: Houghton-Mifflin, 1926.

Browning, Robert. "Oratory and Epistolography." In *The Cambridge History of Classical Literature,* edited by E. J. Kennedy and W. V. Clausen. Vol. 2. Cambridge: Cambridge University Press, 1982, 755–61.

Buzón, R. P. "Die Briefe der Ptolemäerzeit: Ihre Struktur und ihre Form." PhD diss., Heidelberg, 1980.

Calderini, Aristide. "Pensiero e sentimento nelle lettere private greche dei papiri." In *Studi della scuola papirologica,* 2.2–28.

Calvet-Sebasti, Marie Ange. "L'Iliade et l'Odyssée dans la littérature epistolaire." *Orpheus* 13 (1992): 220–44.

Castillo, C. "La epístola como género literario: De la antigüedad a la edad media latina." *Estudios Clásicos* 18 (1974): 427–42.

Celentano, Maria Silvana. "L'epistola laconica: dalla concisione exemplare all'esiguità iperbolica." In *Retorica della comunicazione nelle letterature classiche,* edited by Adriano Pennacini. Bologna: Pitagora, 1990, 109–29.

Christ, W., Wilhelm Schmid, and O. Stählin. [Pseudepigraphen Brieflitteratur.] *Geschichte der griechischen Litteratur.* Vol. 2.1. Munich: C. H. Becksche, 1920, 482–85.

Citroni, Mario. *Poesia e lettori in Rome antica: forma della comunicazione letteraria.* Rome: Editorial Laterza, 1995.

Cobet, C. G. "De locis nonnullis apud Graecos epistolarum scriptores." *Mnemosyne* n.s. 10 (1882): 42–66.

Cotton, Hannah. *Documentary Letters of Recommendation in Latin from the Roman Empire.* Königstein/Ts.: Hain, 1981.

Cugusi, Paolo. "Aspetti letterari della tarda epistolografia greco-latina." *Annali della Facultà di Lettere, Filosofia e Magistero della Università di Cagliari* n.s. 6 (1985): 115–39.

————. "Epistolographi." In *Dizionario degli Scrittori greci e latini,* edited by Francesco Della Corte. Vol. 2. Milan: Marzorati editore, 1987, 821–53.

————. "L'epistolografia: modelli e tipologie di comunicazione." In *Lo spazio letterario di Rome antica,* edited by Guglielmo Cavallo, Paolo Fedeli and Andrea Giardina. Vol. 2: *La circolazione del testo.* Rome: Salerno Editrice, 1989, 379–419.

————. *Evoluzione e forme dell'epistolografia latina nella tarda repubblica e nei primi due secoli dell'impero.* Rome: Herder, 1983.

————. "Studi sull'epistolografia: I. L'età preciceroniana." *Annali della Facultà di Lettere, Filosofia e Magistero della Università di Cagliari* 33 (1970): 5–112.

————. "Studi sull'epistolografia: II. Le età ciceroniana e augustea." *Annali della Facultà di Lettere, Filosofia e Magistero della Università di Cagliari* 35 (1972): 5–167.

Dahl, N. A. "Letter." *Interpreter's Dictionary of the Bible, Supplement.* 1976. 538–41.

Deissmann, [Gustav] Adolf. *Bible Studies.* Edinburgh: T. & T. Clark, 1901.

————. *Light from the Ancient East.* London: Hodder & Stoughton, 1911.

————. *Light from Ancient Letters.* Translated by Lionel R. M. Strachan. London: Hodder and Stoughton, 1910.

Dekkers, E. "Les autographes des Pères latins." *Colligere fragmenta: Festschrift Alban Dold zum 70. Geburtstag am 7.7.1952.* Beuron in Hohenzollern: Beuroner Kunstverlag, 1952.

Deroux, C. "La lettre poetique de Catulle à Horace." *Didactica classica Gandensia* 20 (1980): 149–66.

Dihle, A. "Antike Höflichkeit und christliche Demut." *Studi italiani di filologia classica* 26 (1952): 169–90.

Dinneen, Lucilla. *Titles of Address in Christian Greek Epistolography to 527 A.D.* Washington, D.C.: Catholic University of America, 1929.

Dörrie, Heinrich. *Der heroische Brief: Bestandsaufnahme, Geschichte, Kritik einer humanistisch-barocken Literaturgattung.* Berlin: W. de Gruyter, 1968.

Doty, W. G. "The Classification of Epistolary Literature." *Catholic Biblical Quarterly* 31 (1969): 183–99.

————. "The Epistle in Late Hellenism and Early Christianity: Developments, Influences, and Literary Form." PhD diss., Drew University, 1966.

————. *Letters in Primitive Christianity.* Philadelphia: Fortress Press, 1973.

Drewniewska, B. "De formula salutationis quam Romani ab initio litterarum scribere soliti sunt." Polish text. *Meander* 21 (1966): 424–43.

Engelbrecht, August. *Das Titelwesen bei den spätlateinischen Epistolographen.* Vienna: R. Brzezowsky & Söhne, 1893.

Exler, Francis Xavier. "The Form of the Ancient Greek Letter: A Study in Greek Epistolography." PhD diss., Catholic University of America, 1922; Washington, D.C.: Catholic University of America, 1923.

Farid, Farouk. "Paniskos: Christian or Pagan?" *Museum Philologum Londiniense* 2 (1977): 109–17.

Fernández Galiano, M. "Los problemas de autenticidad de la literatura griega." *Revista de la Universidad de Madrid* 1 (1952): 213–38.

Fiore, Benjamin. *The Function of Personal Example in the Socratic and Pastoral Epistles.* Rome: Biblical Institute Press, 1986.

Fritsch, A. "Res cottidianae: Locutiones ac loci IV: Sermo epistularis." *Vox Latina* 22 (1986): 21–27.

Fritz, Kurt von. *Pseudepigrapha: I: Pseudopythagorica: Lettres de Platon: Littérature pseudépigraphique juive.* Vandoeuvres-Genève: Fondation Hardt pour l'étude de l'antiquité classique, 1971.

Funaioli, G. "L'epistola in Grecia e a Rome." In *Enciclopedia Italiana.* Vol. 14. 1932, 104–6.

Garzya, Antonio. "L'epistolografia letteraria tardo-antica." In *Il mandarino e il quotidiano: Saggi sulla letteratura tardo-antica e bizantina.* Naples: Bibliopolis, 1983, 115–48.

Gerhard, G. A. "Untersuchungen zur Geschichte des griechischen Briefes I." *Philologus* 64 (1905): 27–65.

Gerlo, A. "De ars epistolica en het opus De conscribendis epistolis van Erasmus." *Hermeneus* 42 (1970): 108–18.

Gorce, Denys. *Les voyages, l'hospitalité et le port des lettres dans le monde chrétien des IVe et Ve siècles.* Paris: A. Picard, 1925.

Grabar'-Passek, M. E., ed. *Antichnaia epistolografiia: ocherki.* Moscow: Nauka, 1967.

Gregg, Robert C. *Consolation Philosophy: Greek and Christian Paideia in Basil and the Two Gregories.* Cambridge, Mass.: Philadelphia Patristic Foundation, 1975.

Hagendahl, Harald. "Die Bedeutung der Stenographie für die spätlateinischen christliche Literatur." *Jahrbuch für Antike und Christentum* 14 (1971): 24–38.

Hercher, Rudolf. "Zu den griechischen Epistolographen." *Hermes* 4 (1870): 427–29.

Hout, Michael Petrus Joseph van den "Studies in Early Greek Letter-Writing." *Mnemosyne* 2 (1949): 19–41, 138–53.

Huit, C. "Les épistolographes grecs." *Revue des études grecques* 2 (1889): 149–63.

Janson, Tore. *Latin Prose Prefaces.* Stockholm: Almqvist & Wiksell, 1964.

Jegher-Bucher, Verena. *Der Galaterbrief auf dem Hintergrund antiker Epistolographie und Rhetorik: Ein anderes Paulusbild.* Zurich: Theologischer Verlag, 1991.

Joxe, Friedrich. "Le Christianisme et l'évolution des sentiments familiaux dans les lettres privées sur papyrus." *Acta antiqua academiae scientarum Hungaricae* 7 (1959): 411–20.

Karlsson, G. "Formelhaftes in Paulusbriefen?" *Eranos* 54 (1956): 138–41.

Kassel, Rudolf. *Untersuchungen zur griechischen und römischen Konsolationsliteratur.* Munich: Beck, 1958. 46–47.

Kennedy, George A. *A New History of Classical Rhetoric.* Princeton, N.J.: Princeton University Press, 1994.

Keyes, Clinton. "The Greek Letter of Introduction." *American Journal of Philology* 56 (1935): 28–44.

Kim, Chan-Hie. "Form and Structure of the Familiar Greek Letter of Recommendation." PhD diss., Vanderbilt University, 1970; Missoula, Mont.: Society of Biblical Literature for the Seminar on Paul, 1972.

———. "The Papyrus Invitation." *Journal of Biblical Literature* 94 (1975): 391–402.

Koskenniemi, Heikki. *Studien zur Idee und Phraseologie des griechischen Briefes bis 400 n. Chr.* Helsinki: Suomalainen Tiedeakatemia, 1956.

Kovel'man, A. B. "The Private Letter in Graeco-Roman Egypt as a Literary Genre." Russian text. *Vestnik Drevnei Istorii* 174 (1985): 134–54.

———. *Rhetoric in the Shadow of the Pyramids.* Russian text. Moskva: Nauka, 1988.

Krautter, K. "Acsi ore ad os. . . . Eine mittelalterliche Theorie des Briefes und ihr antiker Hintergrund." *Antike und Abendland* 28 (1982): 155–68.

Lanham, Carol Dana. "Salutatio formulas in Latin Letters to 1200: Syntax, Style, and Theory." PhD diss., University of California—Los Angeles, 1973; Munich: Arbeo-Gesellschaft, 1975.

Lausberg, Marion. "Cicero—Seneca—Plinius: zur Geschichte des römischen Prosabriefs." *Anregung* 37 (1991): 82–100.

Lebek, W. D. "Neues über Epistolographie und Grammatikunterricht (Inscr. Pomp., Haus des M. Fabius Rufus Nr. 9/11; CIL II 1635,4)." *Zeitschrift für Papyrologie und Epigraphik* 60 (1985): 53–61.

Lebel, M. "A propos des lettres d'Isocrate et des lettres de Sénèque le philosophe." *Cahiers des études anciennes* 14 (1982): 75–89.

Littlewood, A. R. "An Icon of the Soul: The Byzantine Letter." *Visible Language* 10 (1976): 197–226.

Luck, G. "Brief und Epistel in der Antike." *Das Altertum* 7 (1961): 77–84.

Luppino, A. "Una redazione inedita di caratteri epistolari." *Annali della Facoltà di Lettere e Filosofia della Università di Napoli* 7 (1957): 145–50.

Luppino, A., ed. "Epistularum characteres qui feruntur eorumque exempla." *Rendiconti della Accademia di Archeologia, Lettere e Belle Arti (Napoli)* n.s. 34 (1959): 41–62.

Lyonnet, S. "De arte litteras exarandi apud antiquos." *Verbum Domini* 34 (1956): 3–11.

Malherbe, Abraham J. "Ancient Epistolary Theorists." *Ohio Journal of Religious Studies* 5 (1977): 3–77. Reprint, Atlanta: Scholars Press, 1988.

———. "Exhortation in First Thessalonians." *Novum Testamentum* 25 (1983): 238–56.

———. *Moral Exhortation: A Greco-Roman Sourcebook.* Philadelphia: Westminster Press, 1986.

Malunowicz, L. "Epistulae consolatoriae Graecae." Polish text. *Eos* 54 (1964): 245–64.

Marcos Casquero, M. A. "Epistolografía romana." *Helmantica* 34 (1983): 377–406.

Mathisen, Ralph Whitney. "Epistolography, Literary Circles and Family Ties in Late Roman Gaul." *Transactions of the American Philological Association* 111 (1981): 95–109.

Mazzoli, Giancarlo. "La prosa filosofica, scientifica, epistolare." In *La prosa latina,* edited by Franco Montanari. Rome: La Nuova Italia Scientifica, 1991, 145–228.

McGuire, M. "Letters and Letter Carriers in Christian Antiquity." *Classical World* 53 (1960): 148–53, 184–85, 199–200.

Miller, T. A. "Antichnye teorii epistoljarnogo stilja." In *Antichnaia epistolografiia: ocherki,* edited by M. E. Grabar'-Passek. Moscow: Nauka, 1967, 5–25.

———. "Letters of Plato and Isocrates." Russian text. In *Antichnaia epistolografiia: ocherki,* edited by M. E. Grabar'-Passek. Moscow: Nauka, 1967, 85–86.

———. "Pseudo-historical Epistolography." Russian text. In *Antichnaia epistolografiia: ocherki,* edited by M. E. Grabar'-Passek. Moscow: Nauka, 1967, 192–225.

Minn, H. R. "Iterum Paulus!" *Prudentia* 9 (1977): 35–40.

Moriya, Akio. "Aramaic Epistolography: The Hermopolis Letters and Related Material in the Persian Period." PhD diss., Hebrew Union College, 1995.

Müller, W. G. "Der Brief als Spiegel der Seele: Zur Geschichte eines Topos der Epistolartheorie von der Antike bis zu Samuel Richardson." *Antike und Abendland* 26 (1980): 138–57.

Muñoz Martín, María Nieves. "La epistolografía latina: Análisis de la carta latina en prosa." Granada: University of Granada, 1985.

———. *Téoria epistolar y concepción de la carta en Rome.* Granada: University of Granada, 1985.

Murphy-O'Connor, Jerome. *Paul et l'art epistolaire: contexte et structure littéraire.* Paris: Éditions du Cerf, 1994.

Novacovich, D. "Fabularni oblici u antichkoi epistolografii." *Latina et Graeca* 20 (1982): 69–121.

———. "Invention in ancient epistolary literature." Serbo-Croatian text. *Latina et Graeca* 20 (1982): 69–121.

O'Brien, Mary Bridget. "Titles of Address in Christian Latin Epistolography to 543 A.D." PhD diss., Catholic University of America, 1930.

O'Callaghan, J. "El nombre de Dios en las cartas cristianas." *Humanidades* 12 (1960): 193–96.

———. "Lettere cristiane dai papiri greci del v secolo." *Aegyptus* 41 (1961): 26–36.

———. "Trato de los cristianos en su correspondencia privada." *Estudios Eclesiásticos* 34 (1960): 391–402.

———. "El trato de padre en la correspondencia cristiana de siglo v." *Boletín de la Asociación Española de Orientalistas* 1 (1965): 151–53.

Olson, S. N. "Confidence Expressions in Paul: Epistolary Conventions and the Purpose of 2 Corinthians." PhD diss., Yale University, 1976.

Olsson, B. *Papyrusbriefe aus der frühesten Römerzeit.* Uppsala: Almqvist & Wiksells, 1925.

Pennacini, A. "Situazione e struttura dell'epistola familiare nella teoria classica." *Quaderni di retorica e poetica* 1 (1985): 11–15.

Peter, Hermann. *Der Brief in der Römischen Litteratur.* Leipzig: Teubner, 1901.

Piernavieja, P. "Epistolografía latina." *Estudios Clásicos* 22 (1978): 361–74.

Plantera, A. "Osservazioni sulla commendatizie latine da Cicerone a Frontone." *Annali della Facoltà di Magistero dell'Università di Cagliari* 2 (1977–78): 5–36.

Rabe, H. "Aus Rhetoren-Handschriften." *Rheinisches Museum* 64 (1909).

Richards, Ernest Randolph. "The Role of the Secretary in Greco-Roman Antiquity and Its Implications for the Letters of Paul." PhD diss., Southwestern Baptist Theological Seminary, 1988.

Riposati, Benedetto. *Testi di epistolografia poetica latina.* [Milan]: Edizioni Pleion, 1962.

Roberts, C. H. "A Footnote to the Civil War of A.D. 324." *Journal of Egyptian Archaeology* 31 (1945): 113.

Roberts, William. *History of Letter-Writing from the Earliest Period to the Fifth Century.* London: William Pickering, 1843.

Roller, Otto. *Das Formular der paulinischen Briefe: Ein Beitrag zur Lehre vom antike Briefe.* Stuttgart: W. Kohlhammer, 1933.

Romankówna, M. "The Epistolary Art." Polish text. *Filomata* (1961–62): 495–504.

Rosenmeyer, P. A. "The Epistolary Novel." In *Greek Fiction: The Greek Novel in Context,* edited by J. R. Morgan and Richard Stoneman. London: Routledge, 1994, 146–65.

Salonius, Aarne Henrik. *Zur Sprache der griechischen Papyrusbriefe.* Helsingfors: [Akademische buchhandlung], 1927.

Scarpat, G. "L'epistolografia." *Introduzione allo studio della cultura classica.* Vol. 1. Milan: Marzorati, 1972. 473–512.

Schadewaldt, W. "Der Brief bei den Griechen: Ein Instrument des Humanen." In *Studia Humanitatis: Ernesto Grassi zum 70 Geburtstag,* Edited by Eginhard Hora and Eckhard Kessler. Munich: W. Fink, 1973, 31–42.

Schneider, J. "Brief." *Reallexicon für Antike und Christentum* 2 (1954): 564–85.

Schnider, Frans and Werner Stenger. *Studien zum neutestamentlichen Briefformular.* Leiden: Brill, 1987.

Schubert, Paul. *The Form and Function of the Pauline Thanksgiving.* Berlin: A. Töpelmann, 1939.

Schuman, V. B. "An Archive in the Old Style." *Bulletin of the American Society of Papyrologists* 9 (1972): 71–84.

Sicherl, Martin. "Epistolographen-Handschriften kretischer Kopisten." In *Scritture, libri e testi nelle aree provinciali di Bisanzio: atti del seminario di Erice (18–25 settembre 1988).* Vol. 1. Edited by Guglielmo Cavallo, Giuseppe De Gregorio, and Marilena Maniaci. Spoleto: Centro Italiano di Studi sull'Alto Medioevo, 1991, 99–124.

Sinanoglu, S. "Yunan edebiyatinda mektup." *Tercüme* 16 (1964): 1–37.

———. "Rome edebiyatinda mektup." *Tercüme* 16 (1964): 38–49.

Smetanin, V. A. *Epistolografija.* Russian text. Sverdlovsk, 1970.

Soverini, Paolo. *Tra retorica e politica in età imperiale: Studi su Plinio il Giovane, Frontone e la "Historia Augusta."* Bologna: Clueb, 1988.

Stirewalt, Martin Luther. "The Form and Function of the Greek Letter-Essay." In *The Romans Debate,* edited by K. P. Donfried. Minneapolis: Augsberg, 1977, 175–206.

———. "The Letter in Greek Literature." PhD diss., Duke University, 1945.

———. *Studies in Ancient Greek Epistolography.* Atlanta: Scholars Press, 1993.

Stowers, Stanley K. *Letter Writing in Greco-Roman Antiquity.* Philadelphia: Westminster Press, 1986.

———. *The Diatribe and Paul's Letter to the Romans.* Chico, Calif.: Scholars Press, 1981.

Suárez de la Torre, Emilio. "*Ars epistolica:* La preceptiva epistolográfica y sus relacions con la retórica." In *Estudios de drama y retórica en Grecia y Rome,* edited by G. Morocho Gayo. Universidad de León, 1987, 177–204.

———. "La epistolografía griega." *Estudios Clásicos* 23 (1979): 19–46.

Susemihl, Franz. "Brieffälschungen." In *Geschichte der griechischen Litteratur in der Alexandrinerzeit.* Vol. 2. Leipzig: Teubner, 1892, 579–601.

Sykutris, J. "Epistolographie." *Paulys Real-Encyclopädie der classischen Altertumswissenshaft.* Supplementband 5 (1931): 185–220.

Tachau, P. "Einst und Jetzt im Neuen Testament: Beobachtungen zu einer urchristlichen Briefliteratur und zu seiner Vorgeschichte." PhD diss., Göttingen, 1968.

Thompson, Glen Louis. "The Earliest Papal Correspondence." PhD diss., Columbia University, 1990.

Thraede, Klaus. "Flügel (Flug) der Seele, II (Briefmotiv)." *Reallexikon für Antike und Christentum* 1969 Lief. 57, 65–67.

———. *Grundzüge griechisch-römischer Brieftopik.* Munich: C. H. Becksche, 1970.

———. "Untersuchungen zum Ursprung und zur Geschichte der christlichen Poesie II." *Jahrbuch für Antike und Christentum* 5 (1962): 125–57.

Tibletti, Giuseppe. *Le lettere private nei papiri greci del III e IV secolo d.C.: Tra paganesimo e cristianesimo.* Milan: Vita e Pensiero, 1979.

Torres Prieto, Juana Maria. "La mujer en la epistolografia griega cristiana, s. iv–v: Tipologia y praxis social." PhD diss., University of Salamanca, 1989.

Ureña, Jesús. "La carta ficticia griega: los nombres de personajes y el uso del encabezamiento en Alcifrón, Aristéneto y Teofilacto." *Emerita* 61 (1993): 267–98.

Vanhove, A. "De brieven in het eerste boek van Diogenes Laertios' compilatie." *Revue belge de philologie et d'histoire* 23 (1944): 5–23.

Vetschera, Rudolph. *Zur griechischen Paranese.* Smichow: Druck von Rohlicek und Sievers in Prag., 1912.

Weber, F. "La lettre d'amitié dans l'antiquité gréco-latine." *Revue des études grecques* 86 (1973): 260–63.

Wehofer, Thomas Maria. *Untersuchungen zur altchristlichen Epistolographie.* Vienna: C. Gerold's Sohn, 1901.

Weima, Jeffrey A. D. *neglected Endings: The Significance of the Pauline Letter Closings.* Sheffield: JSOT Press, 1994.

Weische, Alfons. "Plinius d. J. und Cicero: Untersuchungen zur römischen Epistolographie in Republik und Kaiserzeit." In *Aufstieg und Niedergang der Römischen Welt* II.33.1. Berlin: W. de Gruyter, 1989, 375–86.

Westermann, Anton. *De epistolarum scriptoribus Graecis commentationes.* 8 vols. Leipzig: A. Edelmanni, 1851–58.

White, Carolinne. *The Correspondence (394–419) Between Jerome and Augustine of Hippo.* Lewiston, N.Y.: Edwin Mellen Press, 1990.

White, John L. "The Form and Function of the Body of the Greek Letter: A Study of the Letter-Body in the Non-Literary Papyri and in Paul the Apostle." PhD diss., Vanderbilt University, 1970; Cambridge, Mass.: Society of Biblical Literature, 1972. Reprint, Missoula, Mont.: Scholars Press, 1972.

———. *The Form and Structure of the Official Petition: A Study in Greek Epistolography.* Missoula, Mont.: Society of Biblical Literature, 1972.

———. *Light from Ancient Letters.* Philadelphia: Fortress Press, 1986.

———. "New Testament Epistolary Literature in the Framework of Ancient Epistolography." In *Aufstieg und Niedergang der Römischen Welt* II.25.2. Berlin: W. de Gruyter, 1984, 1730–56.

Whitehead, John David. "Early Aramaic Epistolography: The Arsames Correspondence." PhD diss., University of Chicago, 1974.

Winniczuk, L. *Epistolografia. Lacinskie podreczniki epistolograficzne.* Bibl. Maeandra Warszawa, 1953.

Wright, F. W. "Oaths in the Greek Epistolographers." *American Journal of Philology* 56 (1935): 28–44.

Zilliacus, Henrik. "Anredeformen." *Reallexikon für Antike und Christentum Suppl.-Lief.* 3 (1985): 465 and 4 (1986): 497.

———. *Zur Sprache griechischer Familienbriefe des III Jahrhunderts n. Chr. (P. Mich. 214–221).* Commentationes humanarum litterarum XIII.3. Helsingfors, 1943.

Appendix B

A Bibliography of Medieval Latin Dictamen

Carol Poster and Richard Utz

This is intended as an introductory, rather than comprehensive, bibliography of medieval Latin dictamen. It includes bibliographies, editions, translations, and secondary scholarship. The materials chosen are those readily accessible in major research libraries; manuscripts, incunabula, and other sources only available in rare book collections are listed only if reproduced in facsimile editions. For the purposes of this bibliography, the medieval period is defined as the Latin west from the sixth through fifteenth centuries. Although the entries are divided categorically, the reader should be aware that many works could fit under multiple rubrics.

Bibliographies and Manuscript Catalogs

Haseldine, Judith. "Epistolography." In *Medieval Latin: An Introduction and Bibliographic Guide,* edited by F. A. C. Mantello and A. G. Rigg. Washington D.C.: Catholic University of America Press, 1996.

Faulhaber, Charles. "Retóricas clásicas y medievales en bibliotecas castellanas." *Ábaco* 4 (1973): 151–300.

Luehring, Janet and Richard Utz. "Letter-Writing in the Late Middle Ages (c. 1250–1600): An Introductory Bibliography of Critical Studies." *Disputatio* 1 (1996): 191–229.

Murphy, James Jerome. "The Medieval Arts of Discourse: An Introductory Bibliography." *Speech Monographs* 29 (1962): 71–78.

———. *Medieval Rhetoric: A Select Bibliography.* 2nd ed. Toronto: University of Toronto Press, 1988.

Murphy, James J. and Martin Camargo. "The Middle Ages." In *The Present State of Scholarship in Historical and Contemporary Rhetoric,* rev. ed. Edited by Winifred Horner. Columbia: University of Missouri Press, 1990, 45–83.

Murphy, James J., and Martin Davies. "Rhetorical Incunabula: A Short-Title Catalogue of Texts Printed to the Year 1500." *Rhetorica* 15, no. 4 (1997): 355–474.

Polak, Emil J. *Medieval and Renaissance Letter Treatises and Form Letters: A Census of Manuscripts Found in Eastern Europe and the Former U.S.S.R.* Davis Medieval Texts and Studies, 8. Leiden: Brill, 1993.

———. *Medieval and Renaissance Letter Treatises and Form Letters: A Census of Manuscripts Found in Part of Western Europe, Japan, and the United States of America.* Leiden: Brill, 1994.

Reinsma, Luke. "The Middle Ages." In *Historical Rhetoric: An Annotated Bibliography of Selected Sources,* edited by Winifred Horner. Boston: G. K. Hall, 1980, 43–108.

Thompson, David. *A Descriptive Catalogue of Middle English Grammatical Texts.* New York: Garland, 1979.

Worstbrock, Franz Josef, Monica Klaes, and Jutta Lütten. *Repertorium der Artes Dictandi des Mittelalters, Teil 1: Von den Anfängen bis um 1200.* Munich: Fink, 1992.

Primary Sources: Editions and Translations

Adalbertus Samaritanus. *Praecepta dictaminum.* Edited by Josef Schmale. Weimar: H. Bohlaus Nachfolger, 1961.

Alessio, Gian Carlo, Edited by *Bene Florentini Candelabrum.* Padua: Antenore, 1983.

Baldwinus. *Baldwini Liber Dictaminum.* Edited by S. Durzsa. Bologna: Università degli studi di Bologna, 1970.

Banker, James R. "Giovanni di Bonandrea's 'Ars dictaminis' Treatise and the Doctrine of Invention in the Italian Rhetorical Tradition of the Thirteenth and Early Fourteenth Centuries." PhD diss., University of Rochester, 1972.

Boncompagno da Signa. *Rota Veneris: A facsimile reproduction of the Strassburg Incunabulum with intro., trans., and notes by Josef Purkart.* Delmar, N.Y.: Scholars' Facsimiles & Reprints, 1975.

Bonandree, Iohannis. *Brevis introductio ad dictamen.* Galatina: Congedo, 1993.

Camargo, Martin, ed. Introduction. In *Medieval Rhetorics of Prose Composition: Five English Artes Dictandi and Their Tradition.* Binghamton. N.Y.: Medieval and Renaissance Texts and Studies, 1995, vol. 115.

Davis, Hugh, H. "'De rithmus' of Alberic of Monte Cassino: A Critical Edition." *Medieval Studies* 28 (1966): 198–277.

Faral, Edmond. *Les arts poétiques du XIIe et du XIIIe siècles: Recherches et documents sur la technique littéraire du moyen âge.* Bibliothèque de l'Ecole des Hautes Etudes. Paris: Champion, 1924, 1962.

Fava, Guido. *Dictamina rhetorica. Epistole.* Bologna: Forni, 1971.

Gaudenzi, Augusto, ed. "Guidonis Fabe *Summa dictaminis.*" *Il Propugnatore* n.s. 3, pt. 1 (1890).

Geoffrey of Vinsauf. *Documentum de modo et arte dictandi et verificandi (Instruction in the Method and Art of Speaking and Versifying).* Translated by Roger P. Parr. Medieval Philosophical Texts in Translation, no. 17. Milwaukee: Marquette University Press, 1971.

Groll, Peter-Christian. "Das 'Enchiridion de prosis et de rithmis' des Alberich von Montecassino und die Anonymi 'ars dictandi.'" PhD diss., Freiburg im Breisgau, 1963.

Jacques de Dinant. *A Textual Study of Jacques de Dinant's "Summa dictaminis."* Edited by Emil J. Polak. Etudes de philologie et d'histoire, 28. Geneva: Droz, 1975.

Juan Gil de Zamora. *Dictaminis Epithalium.* Edited by Charles Faulhaber. Biblioteca degli Studi Mediolatini et Volgari, n.s. 2. Pisa: Pacini, 1978.

Kronbichler, Walter, ed. *Die Summa de arte prosandi des Konrad von Mure.* Zurich: Fretz und Wasmuth, 1968.

Heller, Emmy. "Die *Ars Dictandi* des Thomas von Capua." *Sitzungsberichte der Heidelberger Akademie der Wissenschaften, Philolosophisch-historische Klasse*. Vol. 4. Heidelberg: C. Winter Universitätsverlag, 1929.

Lawler, Traugott, ed. and trans. *The Parisiana Poetria of John of Garland*. Yale Studies in English, 182. New Haven, Conn.: Yale University Press, 1974.

Licitra, Vincenzo. "La *Summa de art dictandi* di Maestro Goffredo." *Studi Medievali* ser. 3, 7 (1966): 865–913.

Mari, Giovanni. "Poetria magisti Johannis Anglici de arte prosayca metrica et rithmica." *Romanische Forschungen* 13 (1902): 883–965.

Miller, Joseph, Michael H. Prosser, and Thomas W. Benson, eds. *Readings in Medieval Rhetoric*. Bloomington: Indiana University Press, 1973. [See esp. Alberic of Monte Cassino.]

Murphy, James Jerome, eds. *Three Medieval Rhetorical Arts*. Berkeley: University of California Press, 1971.

Pantin, William Abel, ed. *A Medieval Treatise on Letter-Writing, With Examples, from the Rylands Latin ms. 394. The Bulletin of the John Rylands Library* 13:2 (1929). Reprint, Manchester: Manchester University Press, 1929.

Pini, Virgilio, ed. "*La Summa de vitiis et virtutibus* di Guido di Faba." *Quadrivium* 1 (1956): 41–152.

Rockinger, Ludwig. *Ueber Formelbücher vom dreizehnten bis zum sechzehnten Jahrhundert als rechtsgeschichtliche Quellen*. Munich: C. Kaiser, 1855.

Rockinger, Ludwig. *Briefsteller und formelbücher des eilften* [sic] *bis vierzehnten Jahrhunderts*. Munich: Franz, 1863. Reprint, New York: Franklin, 1961.

Thurot, Charles. *Notices et Extraits de Divers Manuscrits Latins pour servir à l'Histoire des Doctrines Grammaticales au Moyen Age*. Notices et extraits des Manuscrits de la Bibliothèque Impériale, no. 22 vol 2. Paris: Imprimerie Impériale, 1868. Reprint, *Extraits de divers manuscrits pour servir à l'histoire des doctrines grammaticales au Moyen-Age*. Frankfurt am Main: Minerva, 1964.

Transmundus. *Introductiones dictandi*. Edited, translated, and annotated by Ann Dalzell. Studies and Texts vol. 123. Toronto: Pontifical Institute of Medieval Studies, 1995.

Valois, Noël. *De arte scribendi epistolas apud Gallicos medii aevi scriptores rhetoresque* Paris: Picard, 1880. Reprint, New York, B. Franklin, 1964.

Ventura da Bergamo. "Dictamen as a Developed Genre: The *Brevis doctrina* of Ventura da Bergama." Edited by David Thomson and James J. Murphy. *Studi Medievali* 3rd ser. 23:1 (1982): 361–86.

Voltolina, Giuliette. *Un trattato medievale di "ars dictandi": Le "V tabule salutationum" di Boncompagno da Signa*. Frosinone, Italy: Edizioni Casamari, 1990.

Secondary Sources

Studies of Major Individual Dictatores

Alberic of Montecassino

Licitra, Vincenzo. "Il mito di Alberico di Montecassino iniziatore dell'*Ars dictaminis*." *Studi medievali* 18 (1977): 609–27.

Murphy, James Jerome. "Alberic of Monte Cassino: Father of the Medieval *Ars Dictaminis*." *American Benedictine Studues* 22 (1971): 129–46.

Sitzmann, Marion. O.S.B. "The Dictaminal Theories of Alberic of Monte Cassino, Hugh of Bologna, an Anonymous Writer from Orleans, and Lawrence of Aquileja." PhD diss., Southern Illinois University, 1971.

Boncompagno

Purkart, Josef. "Spurious Love Letters in the Manuscripts of Boncompagno's *Rota Veneris*." *Manuscripta* 28:1 (1984): 45–55.

Tunberg, Terence O. "What is Boncompagno's 'Newest Rhetoric'?" *Traditio* 42 (1986): 299–334.

Voltolina, Giulietta. "La scambio epistolare nella società mediovale attraverso l'opera inedita di un magister dell'università di Bologna: Boncompagno da Signa." *Rivista di Cultura Classica et Medioevale* 30:1 (1988): 45–55.

Witt, Ronald. "Boncompagno and the Defense of Rhetoric." *Medieval and Renaissance Studies* 16 (1986): 1–31.

Bernard de Meung

Auer, Leopold. "Eine bisher unbekannte Handschrift des Briefstellers Bernhards von Meung." *Deutsches Archiv für Erforschung des Mittelalters* 26 (1970): 230–40.

Camargo, Martin. "The English Manuscripts of Bernard of Meung's *Flores Dictaminum*." *Viator* 12 (1981): 197–219.

Meisenzahl, Johannes. "Die Bedeutung Bernhards von Meung für das mittelalterliche Notariats- und Schulwesen." PhD diss., Würzburg, 1960.

Vulliez, Charles. "L'évêque au miroir de l'*ars dictaminis*. L'exemple de la *maior compilatio* de Bernard de Meung." *Revue d'Histoire de L'Eglise de France* 70 (1984): 277–304.

———. "Un nouveau manuscrit 'parisien' de la *Summa dictaminis* de Bernard de Meung et sa place dans la tradition manuscrite du texte." *Revue d'histoire des textes* 7 (1977): 133–51.

Brunetto Latini

Alessio, Gian Carlo. "Brunetto Latini e Cicerone (e i Dettatori)." *Italia Medioevale e umanistica* 22 (1979): 123–69.

Davis, Charles T. "Brunetto Latini and Dante." *Studi Medievali* ser. 3, 8 (1967): 421–50.

East, James R. "Brunetto Latini's Rhetoric of Letter-Writing." *Quarterly Journal of Speech* 54 (1968): 241–46.

Witt, Ronald. "Brunetto Latini and the Italian Tradition of *Ars Dictaminis*." *Stanford Italian Review* 3 (1983): 5–24.

Geoffrey of Vinsauf

Camargo, Martin. "Toward a Comprehensive Art of Written Discourse: Geoffrey of Vinsauf and the *Ars dictaminis*." *Rhetorica* 6 (1988): 167–94.

———. "Tria sunt: the long and the short of Geoffrey of Vinsauf's *Documentum de modo e arte dictandi et versifcandi*. *Speculum* 74 (1999): 935–55.

Giovanni di Bonandrea

Banker, James R. "Giovanni di Bonandrea and Civic Values in the Context of the Italian Rhetorical Tradition." *Manuscripta* 18 (1974): 3–20.

Guido Faba

Castellani, Arrigo. "Le formule volgari di Guido Faba." *Studi di Filologia Italiana* 13 (1955): 5–78.

Faulhaber, Charles B. "The *Summa Dictaminis* of Guido Faba." In *Medieval Eloquence: Studies in Theory and Practice of Medieval Rhetoric,* edited by James J. Murphy. Berkeley; Los Angeles: University of California Press, 1978, 85–111.

Kantorowicz, Ernest H. "An 'Autobiography' of Guido de Faba." *Medieval and Renaissance Studies* 1 (1941–43): 253–80. Reprint, in his *Selected Studies.* Locust Valley, N.Y.: J. J. Augustin, 1965: 194–212.

Monaci, Ernesto. "Su la 'Gemma purpurea' e altri scritti volgari di Guido Faba o Fava, maestro di grammatica in Bologna nella pima meta del secolo XIII." *Rendiconti della Reale Accademia dei Lincei* 4:2 (1888): 299–405.

Vecchi, G. "Le arenge di Guido Faba e l'eloquenza d'arte civile e politica duecentesca." *Quadrivium* 4 (1960): 61–90.

Hugh of Bologna

Sitzmann, Marion. O.S.B. "The Dictaminal Theories of Alberic of Monte Cassino, Hugh of Bologna, an Anonymous Writer from Orleans, and Lawrence of Aquileja." PhD diss., Southern Illinois University, 1971.

Lawrence of Aquilegia

Jensen, K. "The Works of Lawrence of Aquileia with a List of Manuscripts." *Manuscripta* 17 (1973): 147–58.

Sitzmann, Marion. O.S.B. "Lawrence of Aquileja and the Origins of the Business Letter." *American Benedictine Review* 28 (1977): 180–85.

————. "The Dictaminal Theories of Alberic of Monte Cassino, Hugh of Bologna, an Anonymous Writer from Orleans, and Lawrence of Aquileja." PhD diss., Southern Illinois University, 1971.

Dictamen in Educational Context

Bonaventure, Brother F.S.C. "The Teaching of Latin in Later Medieval England." *Mediaeval Studies* 23 (1961): 1–20.

Cobban, A. B. *The Medieval Universities: Their Development and Organization.* London: Methuen, 1975.

Gehl, Paul F. "From Monastic Rhetoric to *Ars Dictaminis:* Traditionalism and Innovation in the Schools of Twelfth Century Italy." *American Benedictine Review* 34 (1983): 33–47.

Hajnal, I. *L'enseignement de l'écriture aux universités médiévales.* 2nd ed. Budapest: Académie des Sciences de Hongrie, 1959.

Haskins, Charles H. "The Life of Medieval Students as Illustrated by their Letters." *American Historical Review* 3 (1897–98): 203–29. Revised and expanded in Haskins's *Studies in Mediaeval Culture.* New York: Frederick Ungar, 1929: 1–35. Reprint, 1965.

Hunt, R. W. "Oxford Grammar Masters in the Middle Ages." In *Oxford Studies Presented to Daniel Callus.* OHS, n.s. Vol. 16. Oxford: Clarendon Press for the Oxford Historical Society, 1964, 163–93.

Lanham, Carol Dana. "Freshman Composition in the Early Middle Ages: Epistolography and Rhetoric before the Ars Dictaminis." *Viator* 23 (1992): 115–34.

Legge, M. Dominica. "William of Kingsmill: A Fifteenth Century Teacher of French in Oxford." In *Studies in French Language and Mediaeval Literature Presented to Professor Mildred K. Pope*. Manchester: Manchester University Press, 1939, 241–46.

McMahon, Clara P. *Education in Fifteenth-Century England*. Johns Hopkins University Studies in Education, 35. Baltimore: Johns Hopkins University Press, 1947.

Moran, Jo Ann Hoeppner. *The Growth of English Schooling 1340–1548: Learning, Literacy, and Laicization in Pre-Reformation York Diocese*. Princeton, N.J.: Princeton University Press, 1985.

Murphy, James Jerome. "Rhetoric in Fourteenth-Century Oxford." *Medium vum* 34 (1965): 1–20.

Paetow, Louis J. *The Arts Course at Medieval Universities with Special Reference to Grammar and Rhetoric*. University Studies of the University of Illinois, nos. 3, 7. Champaign: University of Illinois Press, 1910. Reprint, Dubuque, Iowa: William C. Brown Reprint Library, 1962.

Richardson, Henry Gerald. "An Oxford Teacher of the Fifteenth-Century." *Bulletin of the John Rylands Library* 23 (1939): 437–57.

———. "Business Training in Medieval Oxford." *American Historical Review* 46 (1941): 259–80.

———. "The Oxford Law School under John." *Law Quarterly Review* 57 (1941): 319–38.

———. "Letters of the Oxford *Dictatores*." In *Formularies Which Bear on the History of Oxford c. 1204–1420*, edited by H. E. Salter, W. A. Pantin, and H. G. Richardson. *OHS*. n.s. Vol. 5. Oxford: Clarendon Press for the Oxford Historical Society, 1942, 329–450.

Riché, Pierre. *Education and Culture in the Barbarian West from the Sixth through the Eigth Centuries*. 3rd ed. Translated by John C. Contreni. Columbia: University of South Carolina Press, 1978.

Salter, H. E., W. A. Pantin, and H. G. Richardson, eds. *Formularies Which Bear on the History of Oxford c. 1204–1420*. *OHS*. n.s. Vols. 4; 5. Oxford: Clarendon Press for the Oxford Historical Society, 1942.

Samaran, C. "Une *Summa grammatica* de XIIIe siècle avec gloses provençales." *Bulletin du Cange* 31 (1961): 157–224.

Thompson, David. "The Oxford Grammar Masters Revisited." *Mediaeval Studies* 45 (1983): 298–310.

Wieruszowski, Hélène. "Arezzo as a Center of Learning and Letters in the Thirteenth Century." *Traditio* 9 (1953): 321–91.

———. "Rhetoric and the Classics in Italian Education of the Thirteenth Century." *Studia Gratiana* 11 (1967): 169–208.

Cursus

Capua, Francesco di. *Appunti sul "cursus," o ritmo prosaico, nelle opere latine di Dante Alighieri*. Castellamare: di Martino, 1919. Reprint, in Capua, *Scritti minori*. Vol. I, 564–85.

———. "Lo stile della Curia Romana e il 'cursus' nelle epistole di Pier della Vigna e nei documenti della cancelleria sveva." *Giornale Italiano di Filologia* 2 (1944): 97–116. Reprint, in Capua, *Scritti minori*. Vol. I, 500–523.

———. "Per la storia del latino letterario medievale e del 'cursus.'" *Giornale Italiano di Filologia* 4 (1951): 97–113. Reprint, in Capua, *Scritti minori*. Vol. I, 524–62.

Denholm-Young, Noel. "The Cursus in England." *Collected Papers of N. Denholm-Young*. Cardiff: University of Wales, 1961. 42–73; originally published in *Oxford Essays in Medieval History Presented to Herbert Edward Salter*, edited by F. M. Powicke. Oxford: Clarendon Press, 1934, 68–103.

Erdmann, Carl. "'Leonitas.' Zur mittelalterlichen Lehre von Kursus, Rhythmus und Reim." *Corona quernea. Festgabe Karl Strecker zum 80. Geburtstage dargebracht.* Schriften des Reichsinstituts für Ältere Deutsche Geschichtskunde (Monumenta Germaniae historica) 6. Leipzig: K.W. Hiersemann, 1941. Reprint, Stuttgart: A. Hiersemann, 1962.

Janson, Tore. *Prose Rhythm in Medieval Latin from the 9th to the 13th Century.* Acta Universitatis Stockholmiensis, Studia Latina Stockholmiensia, no. 20. Stockholm: Almqvist & Wiskell International, 1975.

Kuhn, Sherman M. "Cursus in Old English: Rhetorical Ornament or Linguistic Phenomenon?" *Speculum* 47 (1972): 188–206.

Marigo, Aristide. "Il 'cursus' nella prosa latina dalle orignini cristiane ai tempi di Dante." *Atti e Memorie della R. Accademia di Scienze Lettere ed Arti in Padova* n.s. 47 (1930/1931): 321–56.

———. "Il 'cursus' nel *De Vulgari Eloquentia* di Dante." *Atti e Memorie* n.s. 48 (1931/32): 85–112.

Parodi, Ernesto Giacomo. "Intorno al testo delle epistole di Dante e al cursus." *Bolletino della Società Dantesca Italiana* n.s. 19 (1912): 249–75.

———. "Osservazioni sul 'cursus' nelle opere latine e volgari del Boccaccio." *Miscellanea Storica della Valdelsa* 21 (1913): 232–45.

Plezia, Marian. "L'Origine de la théorie du 'Cursus' rhythmique au XIIe siècle." *Archivum Latinitatis Medii Aevi* 39 (1974): 5–22.

Smedick, Lois K. "*Cursus* in Middle English: *A talkyng of þe loue of God* Re-considered." *Mediaeval Studies* 37 (1975): 387–406.

Witt, Ronald. "On Bene of Florence's Conception of French and Roman *Cursus*." *Rhetorica* 3 (1985): 77–98.

Dictamen and Literature

Camargo, Martin.. *The Middle English Verse Love Epistle.* Tübingen: M. Niemeyer, 1991.

———. "Where's the Brief: The *Ars Dictaminis* and the Reading/Writing Between the Lines." *Disputatio* 1 (1996): 1–18.

Classen, Albrecht. "Female Explorations of Literacy: Epistolary Challenges to the Literary Canon in the Late Middel Ages." *Disputatio* 1 (1996): 89–122.

Donavin, Georgiana. "Locating a Public Forum for the Personal Letter in Malory's *Morte Darthur.*" *Disputatio* 1 (1996): 19–36.

Lawton, David A. "Gaytyge's Sermon, *Dictamen,* and Middle English Alliterative Verse." *Modern Philology* 76 (1979): 329–43.

Murphy, James Jerome. "Literary Implications of Instruction in the Verbal Arts in Fourteenth-Century England." *Leeds Studies in English* n.s. 1 (1967): 119–35.

Peirone, Luigi. "Dante, i trovatori e le *artes dictaminis.*" *Giornale Italiano di Filologia* 16 (1963): 193–98.

Women and Dictamen

Cherewatuk, Karen and Ulrike Wiethaus, eds. *Dear Sister: Medieval Women and the Epistolary Genre.* Philadelphia: University of Pennsylvania Press, 1993.

Classen, Albrecht. "Female Epistolary Literature from Antiquity to the Present: An Introduction." *Studia Neophilologica* 60 (1988): 3–13.

———. "From *Nonnenbuch* to Epistolary: Elsabeth Stagel as a Late Medieval Woman Writer." In *Medieval German Literature: Proceedings from the 23rd International Congress on Medieval Studies, Kalamazoo, Michigan, May 5–8, 1988,* edited by Albrecht Classen. Göppingen: Kümmerle Verlag, 1989, 147–70.

Goldsmith, Elizabeth C. "Authority, Authenticity, and the Publication of Letters by Women." *Writing the Female Voice: Essays on Epistolary Literature.* Boston: Northeastern University Press, 1989, 46–59.

Margolis, Nadia. "'The Cry of the Chameleon': Evolving Voices in the Epistles of Christine de Pisan." *Disputatio* 1 (1996): 37–70.

Stoudt, Debra L. "The Production and Preservation of Letters by Fourteenth Century Dominican Nuns." *Mediaeval Studies* 53 (1991): 309–26.

General

Alessio, Gian Carlo. "Il De componendis epistolis di Noccolò Perottie l'epistolografia umanistica." *Res public litterarum* 9 (1988): 9–18.

———. "Il De componendis epistolis di Niccolò Perottie l'epistolografìa umanistica." *Res Publica Litterarum* 11 (1988): 91.

———. "L'ars dictaminis nel Quattrocentro italiano: eclissi o persistenza?" *Rhetorica* 19, no. 2 (2001): 155–74.

———. "L'Ars dictaminis nelle scuole dell'Italia meridionale (secoli XI–XIII)." In *Luoghi e Metodi di Insegnamento nell' Italia Medioevale (secoli XII–XIV).* Galatina: Congedo, 1989, 291–308.

Alessio, Gian Carlo, ed. "Il commento di Jacques di Dinant alla Rhetorica ad Herennium." *Studi Medievali* 3, no. 35 (1994): 853–94.

Andrews, Richard. "A Note on the Text of Antonio da Tempo's *Summa artis rithmici vulgaris dictaminis.*" *Italian Studies* 25 (1970): 30–39.

Baerwald, Hermann. *Zur Charakteristik und Kritik mittelalterlicher Formelbücher. Nach Handschriften der Wiener Hofbibliothek.* Vienna: Tendler, 1858.

Baldwin, Charles Sears. *Medieval Rhetoric and Poetic (to 1400) Interpreted from Representative Works.* New York: Macmillan, 1928. Reprint, Gloucester, Mass.: Peter Smith, 1959; St. Clair Shores, Mich.: Scholarly Press, 1976.

Banker, James R. "The *Ars dictaminis* and Rhetorical Textbooks at the Bolognese University of the Fourteenth Century." *Medievalia et Humanistica* n.s. 5 (1974): 153–68.

Barré, Louis Carolus. "Un Recueil épistolaire compose à Saint-Denis sur la croisad (1270–1271)." *Comptes rendus des séances-Académie des inscriptions & belles-lettres* (1966): 555–67.

Barrette, Paul, and Spurgeon Baldwin, trans. *Brunetto Latini: "The Book of the Treasure." ("Li Livres dou Tresor").* New York: Garland, 1993.

Benson, Robert L. "Protohumanism and Narrative Technique in Early Thirteenth-Century Italian 'Ars Dictaminis.'" In *Boccaccio: Secoli di vita. Atti del Congresso*

Internazionale alla University of California-Los Angeles, 17–19 Ottobre 1975, a cura di M. Cottino-Jones e E. F. Tuttle. AA.VV., 4. UCLA, Center of Medieval and Renaissance Studies. Ravenna: Longo, 1979, 31–50.

Bertalot, Ludwig. "Humanistische Vorlesungsankündigungen in Deutschland im 15 Jahrhundert." In *Studien zum italienischen und deutschen Humanismus*. Bd. I, edited by P. O. Kristeller. Rome: Storia e Letteratura, 1975, 235–36.

Bertolucci Pizzorusso, Valeria. "Un trattato di *Ars dictandi* dedicato ad Alfonso X." *Studi Mediolatini e Volgari* 15–16 (1968): 9–88.

Beyer, Heinz-Jürgen. "Die Frühphase der *Ars Dictandi*." *Studi medievali* 18 (1977): 19–43.

Binotti, Lucia. "A 15th-Century Spanish Version of Guarino Veronese's Epistle on Latin." *Romance Philology* 48 (1995): 242–54.

Bittner, Franz, ed. "Eine Bamberger Ars Dictaminis." *Historischer Verein fur die Pege der Geschichte des ehema-ligen Furstbistums Bamberg* 100 (1964): 145–71.

Bloch, H. "Monte Cassino's Teachers and Library in the High Middle Ages." Vol. 19 of *La scuola nell'occidente latino dell'alto medioevo*. Spoleto: Settimane di studio de Centro Italiano de studi sull'alto medioevo, 1972.

Boswell, Grant. "*Captatio Benevolentiae*: A Note on the Relationship of Prayer and Meditation Treatises to the *Ars Dictaminis*." *Disputatio* 1 (1996): 147–52.

Branca, Vittore. "Ciceronianesimo e anticiceronianesimo nell'esperienza epistolografica umanistica a Venezia." *Ciceroniana* 10 (1998): 119–31.

Brodsky, Pavel. "Meznáamy rukopis Mistra Pavlovych epiötol." *Casopis Národního muzearada historická* 151 (1982): 29.

Büngel, Werner. *Der Brief. Ein kulturgeschichtliches Dokument*. Berlin: Ganymend, 1939.

Burdach, Konrad, and Gustav Bebermeyer, eds. *Schlesischböhmische Briefmuster aus der Wende des vierzehnten Jahrhunderts*. Berlin: Weidmann, 1926.

Bütow, Adolf. "Die Entwicklung der mittelalterlichen Briefsteller des 12. Jahrhunderts, mit besonderer Berücksichtigung der Theorien der ars dictandi." PhD diss., Greifswald, 1908.

Camargo, Martin. *Ars dictaminis / Ars dictandi*. Typologie des Sources du Moyen Age Occidental. Turnhout: Brepols, 1991.

———. "Between Grammar and Rhetoric: Composition Teaching at Oxford and Bologna in the Late Middle Ages." In *Rhetoric and Pedagogy: Its History, Philosophy, and Practice*, edited by Winifred Bryan Horner and Michael Leff. Mahwah, N.J.: Lawrence Erlbaum Associates, 1995.

———. "The *Libellus de arte dictandi rhetorice* Attributed to Peter of Blois." *Speculum* 59 (1984): 16–41.

———. "The Middle English Love Letter and Its Rhetorical Background." PhD diss., University of Illinois, 1978.

———. "Rhetoric." In *The Seven Liberal Arts in the Middle Ages*. Edited by David L. Wegner. Bloomington: Indiana University Press, 1983, 96–124.

———. "The Structure of Medieval Society According to the *Dictatores* of the Twelfth Century." In *Law, Church, and Society: Essays in Honor of Stephen Kuttner*, edited by Kenneth Pennington and Robert Sommerville. Philadelphia: University of Pennsylvania Press, 1977.

———. "A Twelfth-Century Treatise on *Dictamen* and Metaphor." *Traditio* 47 (1992): 161–213.

———. "The Waning of Medieval Ars Dictaminis." *Rhetorica* 19, no. 2 (2001): 135–40.

Chartier, Roger, Alain Boureau, and Cecile Dauphin. *Correspondence: Models of Letter-Writing from the Middle Ages to the Nineteenth Century.* Translated by Christopher Woodall. Princeton, N.J.: Princeton University Press, 1997.

Cheney, C. R. *Notaries' Public in England in the Thirteenth and Fourteenth Centuries.* Oxford: Clarendon Press, 1972.

Clough, Cecil H. "The Cult of Antiquity: Letters and Letter Collections." In *Cultural Aspects of the Italian Renaissance: Essays in Honour of Paul Oskar Kristeller,* edited by Cecil H. Clough. Manchester: Manchester University Press, 1976, 33–67.

Constable, Giles. *Letters and Letter-Collections.* Typologie des sources du Moyen Age occidental, 17. Turnhout: Brepols, 1976.

Cremaschi, Giovanni. "Bartolino da Lodi, Professore di Grammatica e di Retorica nello studio di Bologna agli inizi del Quattrocento." *Aevum* 26 (1952): 309–48.

Curtius, Ernest R. *European Literature and the Latin Middle Ages.* Translated by Willard R. Trask. Princeton, N.J.: Princeton University Press, 1967.

D'Alfonso, Rossella. "Fra retorica e teologia: il sistema dei generi letterari nel basso medioevo." *Lingua e stile* 17 (1982): 269–93.

Dalzell, Ann. "The *Forma dictandi* Attibuted to Albert of Morra and Related Texts." *Mediaeval Studies* 39 (1977): 440–65.

Darmé, E. "Signatures des actes notariés." PhD diss., Universite de Toulouse, 1909.

Daunou, Pierre-Claude François. "Recueil de Formules Epistolaires." *Histoire littéraire de la France* 14 (1865): 377–81.

DeBlasi, Nicola. "La lettera mercantile tra formulario appreso e lingua d'uso." *Quaderni di retorica e poetica* 1 (1985): 39–47.

Delisle, L. "Le Formulaire de Clairmarais." *Journal des Savants* (1899): 172–95.

Denholm-Young, Noel. "Richard de Bury and the *Liber Epistolaris.*" *Collected Papers,* 1–41. Revised and extended version of "Richard de Bury (1287–1345)." *Transactions of the Royal Historical Society* 20 (1937): 135–68.

Diener, Hermann. "Ein Formularbuch aus der Kanzlei der Päpste Eugen IV und Nicolaus V." *QFiAB* 42/43 (1963): 370–411.

East, J. R. "Book Three of Brunetto Latini's Tresor: An English Translation and Assessment of Its Contribution to Rhetorical Theory." PhD diss., Stanford University, 1960.

Ernout, A. "Dictare 'Dicter,' allem. Dichten." *Revue des Etudes latines,* 29e année 1951. Paris: Société d'édition "Les Belles Lettres," 1952, 155–61.

Everitt, Charles. "Eloquence as Profession and Art: The Use of the Ars Dictaminis in the Letters of Gilbert Stone and his Contemporaries, 1300–c. 1450." PhD diss., University of Oxford, 1985.

Faulhaber, Charles B. "Las retóricas hispanolatinas medievales siglos XII–XV." *Repertorio de Historia de las ciencias Eclesiásticas en España* 7 (1979): 11–64.

———. *Latin Rhetorical Theory in Thirteenth and Fourteenth Century Castile.* Berkeley: University of California Press, 1972, esp. 103–21; 144–47.

————. "Pedro de Blois. Fuente del *Dictaminis epithalamium,* de Juan Gil de Zamora." *Archivo Ibero-Americano* 33 (1973): 251–68.

Fisher, John H., Malcolm Richardson, and Jane Fisher. *An Anthology of Chancery English.* Knoxville: University of Tennessee Press, 1984.

Frenz, Th. "Das Eindringen humanistischer Schriftformen in die Urkunden und Akten der päpstlichen Kurie im 15. Jahrhundert." *ADipl* 19 (1973): 319–21; 20 (1974): 416–20.

Gabrielli, Annibale. "Le epistole di Cola di Rienzo e l'epistolografia medievale." *Archivio della R. Società romana di storia patria* 11 (1888): 381–479.

Gaiter, Luigi, ed. *Il Tesoro. Volgarizzato da Bono Giamboni, I.* Bologna: Romegnoli, 1878.

Harth, Helene. "Poggio Bracciolini und die Brieftheorie des 15. Jahrhunderts. Zur Gattungsform des Humanistischen Briefs." In *Der Brief im Zeitalter der Renaissance,* edited by Franz Josef Wortsbrock. Deutsche Forschungsgemeinschaft. Mitteilung der Kommission für Humanismusforschung, IX. Weinheim: Verlag Chemie, 1983, 81–99.

Haskins, Charles H. "The Early *Artes dictandi* in Italy." In *Studies in Mediaeval Culture.* Oxford: Clarendon Press, 1929. Reprint, New York: Ungar, 1965, 170–92.

————. "Orleanese Formularies in a Manuscript at Tarragona." *Speculum* 5 (1930): 411–20.

Heathcote, Sheila J. "The Letter Collections Attributed to the Master Transmundus, Papal Notary and Monk of Clarivaux in the Late Twelfth Century. *Analecta Cisterciensia* 21 (1965): 35–109; 167–238.

Henderson, Judith Rice. "The Composition of Erasmus's Opus de conscribendis epistolis: Evidence for the Growth of a Mind." In *Acta Conventus Neo-Latini Torontonensis,* edited by Alexander Dalzell, Charles Fantazzi, and Richard J. Schoeck. Binghamton, N.Y.: Medieval & Renaissance Texts & Studies, 1991, 147–54.

————. "Despauterius' Syntaxis (1509): The Earliest Publication of Erasmus's De conscribendis epistolis." *Humanistica Lovaniensia* 37 (1988): 175–210.

————. "The Enigma of Erasmus's Conciendarum epistolarum formula." *Renaissance and Reformation* 13 (1989): 313–30.

————. "Erasmian Ciceronians: Reformation Teachers of Letter-Writing." *Rhetorica* 10 (1992): 273–302.

————. "Erasmus on the Art of Letter-Writing." *Renaissance Eloquence* 18: 336.

————. "On Reading the Rhetoric of the Renaissance Letter." In *Renaissance-Rhetorik/Renaissance Rhetoric,* edited by Heinrich F. Plett. Berlin: Walter de Gruyter, 1993, 143–62.

————. "Valla's Elegantiae and the Humanist Attack on the Ars Dictaminis." *Rhetorica* 19, no. 2 (2001): 249–68.

Herr, Alfred. "Ein deutscher Briefsteller aus dem Jahre 1484." *Neue Jahrbücher für Pädagogik* 40 (1917): 353.

Hill, Sidney R., Jr. "*Dictamen:* That Bastard of Literature and Law." *Central States Speech Journal* 24 (1973): 17–24.

Jacob, E. F. "Florida Verborum Venustas." *Bulletin of the John Rylands Library* 17 (1933): 264–90.

Joachimsohn, P. "Aus der Vorgeschichte des *Formulare und deutsch Rhetorica.*" *Zeitschrift deutsches Altertum* 37 (1893): 24–121.

Jordan, E. "Notes sur le Formulaire de Richard de Pofi." In *Etudes d'histoire du moyen âge dédiées à Gabriel Monod,* edited by Ernest Larisse. Paris: L. Cerf, 1896, 329–41.

Kalbfuss, Hermann. "Eine Bologneser Ars dictandi des XII. Jahrhunderts." *Quellen und Forschungen aus italienischen Archives und Bibliothteken* 16, no. 2 (1914): 1–35.

Kaltenbrunner, F. "Römische Studien III: Die Briefsammlung des Berardus de Neapoli." *Mitteilungen des Instituts für österreichische Geschichtsforschung* 7 (1886): 21–118, 555–635.

Kane, Peter E. "'Dictamen': The Medieval Rhetoric of Letter-Writing." *Central States Speech Journal* 21 (1970): 224–30.

Kelly, Douglas Douglas. *The Arts of Poetry and Prose. Typologie des Sources du Moyen Age Occidental.* Fasc. 59. Turnhout: Brepols, 1991.

Klais, Monika. "Die 'Summa' des Magister Bernardus: Zu Überlieferung und Textgeschichte einer zentralen Ars dictandi des 12. Jahrhunderts." *Frühmittelalterliche Studien* 24 (1990): 198–234.

Kolberg, Dr. "Ein preussisches Formelbuch des 15. Jahrhunderts." *Zeitschrift für die Geschichte und Altertumskunde Ermland* 9 (1887): 273–328.

Koller, Heinrich. "Zwei Pariser Briefsammlungen." *Mitteilungen des Instituts für österreichische Geschichtsforschung* 59 (1951): 299–327.

Kristeller, Paul O. "Matteo de'Libri, Bolognese Notary of the Thirteenth Century and His *Artes dictaminis.*" *Miscellanea Giovanni Galbiati.* Fontes Ambrosiani, 26. Vol. 2. Milan: Hoepli, 1951, 283–320.

———. "Un'ars dictaminis di Giovanni del Virgilio." *Italia mediovale e umanistica* 4 (1961): 181–200.

Langlois, Charles-Victor. "Formulaires de lettres du XIIe, du XIIIe et du XIVe siècle." *Notices et extraits* 34 (1891): 1–32, 305–32; 34 (1895): 1–18; 19–29; 35 (1897): 409–35, 793–830.

———. "Questions d'Histoire Littéraire: Maître Bernard." *Bibliothèque de l'Ecole des Chartes* 54 (1893): 225–50.

Lanham, Carol D. *Salutatio Formulas in Latin Letters to 1200: Syntax, Style, and Theory.* Municher Beiträge zur Mediävistik und Renaissance-Forschung, no. 22. Munich: Arbeo-Gesellschaft, 1975.

Latini, Brunetto. *La Rettorica, testo critico.* Edited by F. Maggini. Florence: Le Monnier, 1968.

Leclercq, Jean. "Le Genre épistolaire au Moyen Age." *Revue du Moyen Age latin* 2 (1946): 63–70.

Le Saulnier de Saint-Jouan, H. G. *Pons le Provençal, maître en dictamen (XIIIe siècle).* Paris: Thèse Ecole des Chartres, dactyl, 1957.

Lindholm, Gudrun. Studien zum mittellateinischen Prosarhythmus: Seine Entwicklung und sein Abklingen in der Briefliteratur Italiens. (Studia Latina Stockholmiensa, 10. Stockholm: Almqvist & Wiksell, 1963.

Lulvès, Jean. *Die Summa cancellariae des Johann von Neumarkt. Eine Hand-schrifte-nuntersuchung über die Formularbücher aus der Kanzlei Kaiser Karls IV.* Berlin, 1891. Reprint, Leipzig: St. Benno-Verlag, 1964.

Mazur, Zygmunt. "Henryka z Brzegu O.P. list dedykacyjny do królowej Jadwigi." In *Zródloznawstwo I studia historyczne,* edited by Kazimierz Bobowski. Wroclaw: Wydawnictwo Uniwersytetu Wroclawskiego, 1989, 391–98.

Meersseman, Gilles Gerard. "La Raccolta dell umanista ammingo Giovanni de Veris De arte epistolandi." *Italia Medioevale e Umanistica* 15 (1972): 215–81.

———. "L'Epistoaire de Jean van den Veren et le début de l'humanisme en Flandre." *Humanistica Lovaniensia* 19 (1970): 119–200.

Melli, Elio. "I 'salut' e liespistolograpfia medievale." *Convivium* 30 (1962): 385–98.

Murphy, James Jerome. "Caxton's Two Choices: 'Modern' and 'Medieval' Rhetoric in Traversagni's *Nova Rhetorica* and the Anonymous *Court of Sapience*. *Medievalia et Humanistica* n.s. 3 (1972): 241–55.

———. "A Fifteenth-Century Treatise on Prose Style." *Newberry Library Bulletin* 6 (1966): 205–10.

———. *Rhetoric in the Middle Ages: A History of Rhetorical Theory from Saint Augustine to the Renaissance.* Berkeley: University of California Press, 1974.

Murphy, James Jerome. ed. *Medieval Eloquence: Studies in the Theory and Practice of Medieval Rhetoric.* Berkeley: University of California Press, 1978.

Murphy, James Jerome, and M. Davies, eds., "Rhetorical Incunabula: A Short-Title Catalogue of Texts Printed to the Year 1500," *Rhetorica* 15 (1997): 35.

Öberg, Jan. "Über zwei spätmittelalterliche Formularsammlungen aus dem Bistum Linköping." *Classica et medievalia Dissertationes* 9 (1973): 563–85.

Olivar, M. "Notes entorn la inclüencia de l'*Ars dictandi* sobre la prosa catalana de cancilleria de finals del segle XIV." *Estudis Universitaris Catalans* 22 (1936): 631–53.

Orlandelli, Gianfranco. "Genesi dell' ars notariae nel secolo XIII." *Studi Medievali* 3, no. 6 (1965): 329–66.

———. "'Studio' e scuola di notariato." *Atti of the "Convegno per le celebrazioni accursiane tenutosi a Bologna dal 21 al 26 ottobre 1963,* 73–95.

Pantin, W. A. "English Monastic Letter-Books." In *Historical Essays in Honor of James Tait,* edited by J. G. Edwards, V. H. Galbraith, and E. F. Jacob. Manchester: Printed for subscribers, 1933, 201–22.

———. "A Medieval Treatise on Letter Writing with Examples." *Bulletin of the John Rylands Library* 12 (1929): 326–82.

Patt, William D. "The Early 'Ars Dictaminis' as Response to a Changing Society." *Viator* 9 (1978): 133–35.

Petzsch, G. "Über Technik und Stil der mittelhochdeutschen Privatbriefe des 14. und 15. Jahrhunderts." PhD diss., Greifswald, 1913.

Pivec, Karl. "Studien und Forschungen zur Ausgabe des Codex Udalrici," part 1: "Eine Bamberger Diktatoren-schule aus der Zeit Heinrichs IV," part 2: "Der Codex Udalrici unddie Kanzlei Heinrichs V." *Mitteilungen des Institut fur Osterreichische Geschichtsforschung* 45 (1931): 409ff.; 46 (1932): 257ff.

Pizzorusso Bertolucci, Valeria. "Un trattato di *ars dictandi* dedicato ad Alfonso X." *Studi mediolatini e volgari* 15–16 (1968): 9–88.

Plezia, Marian. "Quattuor stili modernorum: Ein Kapitel mittellateinischer Stillehre." In *Orbis mediaevalis: Festgabe für Anton Blaschka,* edited by Horst Gericke, Manfred Lemmer, and Walter Zöllner. Weimar: Böhlau, 1970, 192–210.

Polak, Emil J. "Dictamen." In *Dictionary of the Middle Ages,* edited by Joseph R. Strayer. Vol. 4. New York: Charles Scribner, 1984, 173–77.

———. "Latin Epistolography of the Middle Ages and Renaissance: Manuscript Evidence in Poland." *Eos* 73 (1985): 349–62.

————. *Medieval and Renaissance Letter Treatises and Form Letters: A Census of Manuscripts Found in Part of Western Europe, Japan, and the United States of America.* Davis Medieval Texts and Studies 9. New York: E. J. Brill, 1994.

Quadlbauer, Franz. *Die antike Theorie der Genera dicendi im lateinischen Mittelalter.* Vienna: Böhlau, 1962.

Quondam, Amedeo. "Dal 'Formulario' al 'Formulario': Cento anni di 'Libri de lettere.'" In *Le "carte messaggiere." Retorica e modelli di comunicazione epistolare: per un indice dei libri di lettere del Cinquecento.* Rome: Bulzoni, 1981, 12–156.

Richardson, Malcolm. "The *Dictamen* and Its Influence on Fifteenth-Century English Prose." *Rhetorica* 2 (1984): 207–26.

————. "The Fading Influence of the Medieval Ars Dictaminis in England After 1400." *Rhetorica* 19, no. 2 (2001): 225–48.

————. "Henry V, the English Chancery, and Chancery English." *Speculum* 55 (1980): 726–50.

————. "Letters of the Oxford Dictatores." In *Formularies Which Bear on the History of Oxford, c. 1204–1420,* edited by H. E. Salter, W. A. Pantin, and Malcolm Richardson. 2 vols. Oxford Historical Society 4. Oxford: Clarendon Press, 1942, 331–450.

————. "Women, Commerce, and Rhetoric in Medieval England." In *Listening to their Voices: The Rhetorical Activities of Historical Women,* edited by Molly Meijer Wertheimer. Columbia: University of South Carolina Press, 1997.

Robinson, I. S. "The 'colores rhetorici' in the Investiture Contest." *Traditio* 32 (1976): 209–38.

Rochholz, E. L. "Aus einem Briefsteller von 1492." *Germania* 1 (1886): 207–10.

Rockinger, Ludwig. *Ueber Briefsteller und Formelbücher in Deutschland während des Mittelalters.* Vortrag in der öffentlichen Sitzung der K. Akademie der wissenschaften am 26. märz 1861 zur vorfeier ihres 102. Stiftungstages, gehalten von Dr. Ludwig Rockinger. Munich, 1861.

Rummel, Erika. "Erasmus's Manual of Letter-Writing: Tradition and Innovation." *Renaissance and Reformation* 13 (1989): 299–312.

Rupp, Stephen. "Rhetoric and Patronage in Alfonso Alvarez de Villasandino." *Revista Canadiense de Estudios Hispanicos* 15 (1990): 49–64.

Sabbadini, R. *Epistolario di Guarin veronese.* Venice, 1915.

Schalk, Fritz. "Zur Entwicklung der Artes in Frankreich und Italien." In *Artes liberales von der Antiken Bildung zur Wissenschaft des Mittelalters,* edited by Josef Koch. Leiden: Brill, 1959, 137–48.

Schaller, Hans Martin. "Zur Entstehung der sogenannten Briefsammlung des Petrus de Vinea." *Deutsches Archiv* 12 (1956): 114–59.

Schiaffini, Alfredo. *Tradizione e poesia nella prosa d'arte italiana dalla latinità medievale al Boccaccio.* Rome: Edizioni di Storia e Letteratura, 1969.

Schmale, Franz-Josef. "Die Bologneser Schule der *Ars dictaminis.*" *Deutsches Archiv für die Erforschung des Mittelalters* 13 (1957): 16–34.

Schmücker-Breloer, Maritta. "Gattungsgeschichte und Gattungswandel des altrussischen Briefes." In *Gattung und Genealogie der slavisch-orthodoxen Literaturen des Mittelalters (Dritte Berliner Fachtagung 1988),* edited by Klaus-Dieter Seemann. Veröffentlichung der Abteilung für slavische Sprachen und Literaturen des

Osteuropa-Instituts (Slavisches Seminar) an der Freien Universität Berlin, 72. Wiesbaden: Harrassowitz, 1992, 189–213.

Seigel, Jerrold. *Rhetoric and Philosophy in Humanism: The Union of Eloquence and Wisdom, Petrarch to Valla.* Princeton, N.J.: Princeton University Press, 1968.

Shoeck, R. J. "On Rhetoric in Fourteenth-Century Oxford." *Mediaeval Studies* 30 (1968): 214–25.

Sonkowsky, Robert P. "A Fifteenth-Century Rhetorical Opusculum." In *Classical Mediaeval and Renaissance Studies in Honor of Berthold Louis Ullman,* edited by Charles Henderson Jr. Rome: Edizioni di storia e letteratura, 1964, 259–81.

Stobbe, Otto. "Summa Curiae Regis. Ein Formelbuch aus der Zeit König Rudolf's I und Albrecht's I." *Archiv für Kunde österreichischer Geschichtsquellen* 14. (1855): 305–85.

Sundby, Thor. *Della Vita e delle Opere di Brunetto Latini.* Translated by Rodolfo Renier Florence: Le Monnier, 1884.

Taylor, John. "Letters and Letter Collections in England, 1300–1420." *Nottingham Medieval Studies* 24 (1980): 57–70. Rev. as "Letters and Letter Collections." In *English Historical Literature in the Fourteenth Century.* Oxford: Clarendon Press, 1987, 217–35.

Thomas, M. "De l'origine et de la conception de l'acte sous signatures privées." PhD diss., University of Rennes, 1920.

Triska, Josef. "Prague Rhetoric and the *Epistolare Dictamen* (1278) of Henricus de Isernia." *Rhetorica* 3 (1985): 183–200.

Turcan-Verkerk, A. M. "Lettres d'étudiants de la fin du XIIIe siècle: les saisons du dictamen à Orleans en 1289 d'après les manuscripts B aricano, Borgh.200 et Paris, Bibl. de l'Arsenal 854." *Mélanges de l'Ecole Française de Rome: Moyen Age-Temps Modernes* 105 (1993): 651–714.

Van Dievoet, G. *Les Coutumiers, les styles, les formulaires et les artes notariae.* Typologie des Sources du Moyen Age Occidental. Fasc. 48. Turnhout: Brepols, 1986.

Vecchi, G. *Il Magistero delle "artes latine" a Bologna nel medioevo.* Bologna: Patron, 1958.

Ventura, Iolanda. "L Iconogra a letteraria di Brunetto Latini." *Studi Medievali* 3, no. 38 (1997): 499–528.

Vilaplana, D. Asuncion. "De arte dictandi. Notas en torno a la obra de Juan de Sicilia." In *Estudios de historia medieval en homenaje a Luis Fernadez Suárez.* Valladolid: Universidad de Valladolid, 1991, 523–34.

Voights, Linda E. "A Letter From a Middle English Dictaminal Formulary in Harvard Law Library MS 43." *Speculum* 56, no. 3 (1981): 575–81.

Voltolina, Giulietta. "Da Alberico di Montecassino a Boncompagno da Signa: la tappe più significative dell'ars dictandi in Italia nei secolo XI, XII e XIII." *Rivista Cistercense* 4, no. 3 (1987): 277–87.

———. "La salutatio nel modo religioso medioevale da un'opera inedita della fina del XII secolo." *Benedictina* 35, no. 2 (1988): 555–65.

Vulliez, Charles. "L'apprentissage de la redaction des documents diplomatiques à travers l'ars dictaminis français (et spécialement ligérien) du XIIe siècle." In *Cancellaria e Cultura nel Medio evo.* Citta del Vaticano, 1990.

————. "L'ars dictaminis, survivances et déclin, dans la moitié nord de l'espace français dans le Moyen Age tardif (mil. XIIIe–mil.Xve siècles)." *Rhetorica* 19, no. 2 (2001): 141–54.

Ward, John O. "Rhetorical Theory and the Rise and Decline of Dictamen in the Middle Ages and Early Renaissance." *Rhetorica* 19, no. 2 (2001): 175–224.

Wertis, Sandra Karaus. "The Commentary of Bartolinus de Benincasa de Canulo on the *Rhetorica ad Herennium*." *Viator* 10 (1979): 283–310.

Wieruszowski, Hélène. "Beiträge zur politischen Geschichte Italiens im späten 13. Jahrhundert (aus munizipalen "Artes dictaminis')." *Quellen und Forschungen aus italienischen Archiven und Bibliotheken* 38 (1958): 176–204. Reprint, *Politics and Culture in Medieval Spain and Italy*. Rome: Edizioni di Storia e letteratura, 1971, 279–308.

————. "Mino da Colle di Val d'Elsa: rimatore e dettatore al tempo di Dante." In *Politics and Culture in Medieval Spain and Italy*. Rome: Storia e Letteratura, 1971.

————. "Twelfth Century 'Ars Dictaminis' in the Barberini Collection of the Vatican Library." *Traditio* 18 (1962): 382–93.

Winniczuk, L. *Epistolografia*. Lacinskie podereczniki epistolograficzne w Polsce w XV–XVI. Biblioteka Meandra, 19. Wieku: Warszawa, 1953.

————. "The Latin Manuals of Epistolography in Poland in the Fifteenth and Sixteenth Centuries." In *Acta Conventus Neo-Latini Sanctandreani: Proceedings of the Fifth International Congress of Neo-Latin Studies,* edited by I. D. McFarlane. Binghamton, N.Y.: Medieval and Renaissance Texts and Studies, 1986.

Witt, Ronald G. *"In the Footsteps of the Ancients:" The Origins of Humanism from Lovato to Bruni*. Leiden: Brill, 2000.

————. "Medieval *Ars Dictaminis* and the Beginnings of Humanism: A New Construction of the Problem." *Renaissance Quarterly* 35 (1982): 1–35.

Worstbrock, Franz-Josef. "Die Anfänge der mittelalterlichen *Ars dictandi*." *Frühmittelalterliche Studien* 23 (1989): 1–42.

————. "Zu Galfrids *Summa de arte dictandi*." *Deutsches Archiv für die Erforschung des Mittelalters* 23 (1967): 549–52.

Wutke, Konrad. *Über schlesische Formelbücher des Mittelalters*. Darstellungen und Quellen zur schlesischen Geschichte. Vol 26. Breslau: F. Hurt, 1919.

Zaccagnini, Guido. "Giovanni di Bonandrea dettatore e rimatore e altri grammatici e dottori in arte dello studio Bolognese." *Studi e memorie per la storia dell'Università di Bologna* 5 (1920): 147–204.

————. "Lettere ed orazioni di grammatici dei secc. XIII e XIV." *Archivum Romanicum* 7 (1923): 517–34.

Zatschek, H. *Studien zur mittelalterlichen Urkundenlehre*. Brünn: Rohrer, 1929.

Appendix C

BIBLIOGRAPHY OF DICTAMEN IN ENGLAND, 1500–1700

Lawrence D. Green

This is a selection of materials available in modern reprint, facsimile, or microform. The continuing series from University Microfilms should also be consulted, as should the internet collections known as *Early English Books Online* (EBBO) and *Eighteenth-Century Collections Online* (ECCO).

Conventions and Abbreviations

The reprint series *The English Experience* is published simultaneously in Amsterdam and by different publishers in the United States:
Amsterdam: Theatrum Orbis Terrarum B.V., 1967–79;
New York: Da Capo Press, 1967–73;
Norwood, N.J.: Walter J. Johnson Inc., 1974–79.

Cited as "English Experience" with Volume Number

James J. Murphy, *Renaissance Rhetoric: A Microfiche Collection of Key Texts*, A.D. *1472–1602, from the Bodleian Library, Oxford.* Elmsford, N.Y.: Microforms International, 1986. Cited as *Murphy.*
Speech Association of America, *British and Continental Rhetoric and Elocution.* Sixteen microfilm reels. Ann Arbor: University Microfilms, 1953. Cited as *BCRE.*

Bibliographies

Blount, Thomas. *The academie of eloquence, containing a compleat English rhetorique.* London: for H. Moseley, 1653. Also 1654, 1656, 1663, 1664, 1670, 1683. Menston: Scolar Press, 1971 (facsimile of 1654).
Boyer, Abel. "A collection of choice letters upon several subjects." In *The compleat French-master.* London: for T. Salusbury, 1694. Also 1699. Menston: Scolar Press, 1971 (facsimile of 1694).
Brandolinus, Aurelius Lippus. *De ratione scribendi libri tres* [Basel 1498]. Collected with Vives, Erasmus, Celtes, and Hegendorf (Basel 1549), with Macropedius added in the London edition. London: H. Middleton, 1573.

Microfiche, *Murphy,* Basel 1549.

————. *A poste with a packet of mad letters. newly imprinted* [includes both parts]. London: [M. Flesher] for J. Marriot, 1633. Also 1634, 1637, [1650?], 1660, 1669,

1674, 1678, 1685 (as *A poast with a packet of letters*). London, 1879, ed. A.B. Grosart, *Works*. Reprint, New York 1966. Reprint, Hildesheim 1969.

Brinsley, John, the elder. "Epistles and letters." In *A consolation for our grammar schooles*. London: R. Field for T. Man, 1622. New York: Scholars' Facsimiles & Reprints, 1943 (facsimile). Amsterdam and New York: English Experience no. 203, 1969 (facsimile).

————. "How to make epistles imitating Tully, short, pithie, sweete Latine and famil-iar; and to indite letters to our friends in English accordingly." In *Ludus literarius; or, The grammar school*. London: H. Lownes for T. Man, 1612. Also 1627 (5 vari-ants). Menston: Scolar Press, 1968; English Linguistics no. 62 (facsimile of 1612). Liverpool and London, 1917, ed. E.T. Campagnac (1627 edition).

Browne, John. "A briefe forme of all such letters as you shall neede to write thorough-out your whole voyage." In *The marchants avizo*. London: R. Field for W. Norton, 1589. Also 1590, 1590, 1591, 1607, 1616, 1640. Boston, 1957, ed P. McGrath (1589 edition). Amsterdam and New York: English Experience no. 98, 1969 (fac-simile of 1607).

Celtes, Conrad. *Formulae oratoriae*. Revision of *Transitionum formulae*. London: N. P., 1630. Also 1632, 1637, 1647, 1653, 1659, Zurich 1663, London 1664, 1670, 1672, Zurich 1694. Microfilm, *BCRE* 3:28 (1637 edition).

————. *Lessons and exercises out of Cicero, after the method of Dr Webbe*. Lon-don: F. Kingston, 1627. Menston: Scolar Press, 1972; English Linguistics no. 322 (facsimile).

————. *Methodus conficiendarum epistolarum* [Basel 1537]. In Brandolinus, *De ratione scribendi*. London: H. Middleton, 1573. Microfiche, *Murphy*, Basel 1549.

Cordier, Mathurin. *Principia Latine loquendi scribendique: sive selecta quaedam ex Ciceronis epistolis, ad pueros in Latina lingua exercendos . . . a very necessary and profitable entraunce to the speakyng and writing of the Latin tongue* [Geneva 1566]. Translated by "T.W." London: J. Kingston for O. Wilkes, 1575. Menston: Scolar Press, 1968; English Linguistics no. 100 (facsimile).

Day, Angel. *The English secretorie. Wherein is contayned, a perfect method, for the inditing of all manner of epistles and familiar letters*. London: R. Waldegrave, 1586. Menston: Scolar Press, 1967; English Linguistics no. 29 (facsimile). Microfilm, *BCRE* 3:24.

————. *The English secretorie; or, Plaine and direct method of enditing of all manner of epistles or letters. . . . now corrected, refined, & amended . . . also a declaration of all tropes, figures, as usually or for ornaments sake are in this method required.* London: T. Orwin for R. Jones, 1592 (with *The second part*, dated 1587). Also 1595, 1599, 1607, 1614, 1621, 1625, [1635]. Gainesville, Fla.: Scholars' Facsimiles & Reprints, 1967 (facsimile of 1599). Microfiche, *Murphy*, 1595 edition.

Erasmus, Desiderius. *De conscribendi epistolis*. Pirate draft of authorised edition (Basel: Froben, 1522). Cambridge: J. Siberch, 1521. Toronto: University of Toronto Press, 1985. Translated by C. Fantazzi, *Works*, vol 3.

————. *Conficiendarum epistolarum formula* [Basel 1519]. In Brandolinus, *De ratione scribendi*. London: H. Middleton, 1573. Microfiche, *Murphy*, Basel 1549. Toronto: University of Toronto Press, 1985. Translated by C. Fantazzi, *Works*, vol 3.

Fleming, Abraham. *A panoplie of epistles; or, A looking glasse for the unlearned. Con-teyning a perfecte plattforme of inditing letters of all sorts . . . used of the best and eloquentest rhetoricians that have lived in all ages . . . gathered and translated out of Latine into English*. London: H. Middleton for R. Newberie, 1576. Microfiche, *Murphy*.

Fulwood, William. *The enimie of idlenesse: teaching the maner and stile how to endite, compose and write all sorts of epistles and letters*. London: H. Bynneman for L. Maylard, 1568. Also 1571, 1578, 1582, 1586, 1593, 1598, 1607, 1612, 1621. Potsdam, 1907, ed. P. Wolter, *William Fullwood, "The Enimie of Idlenesse." Der älteste englische Briefsteller* (selections).

Gainsford, Thomas. *The secretaries studie: containing new familiar epistles; or, directions, for the formall, orderly, and iudicious inditing of letters*. London: T. Creede for R. Jackson, 1616 (expanded by Sheppard 1652). Amsterdam and Norwood, N.J.: English Experience no. 658, 1974 (facsimile).

Gildon, Charles. *The post-boy robb'd of his mail; or, The paquet broke open. Consisting of five hundred letters, to persons of several qualities and conditions. With observations upon each letter*. Based in part on Ferante Pallavicino. London: for J. Dunton, 1692 (anon). New York: Garland, 1972, ed. M. J. Bosse.

Hegendorf, Christopher. *Methodus epistolas conscribendi* [Hagenau 1526]. In Brandolinus, *De ratione scribendi*. London: H. Middleton, 1573. Microfiche, *Murphy*, Basel 1549.

Hoskyns, John. "Direccions for speech and style." [1599?] Manuscripts BL Harl. 4604; BL Harl. 850 (portions); BL Add. 15230; Bodley Ash. Mus. D. 1. Princeton, N.J. Princeton University Press, 1935, ed. H.H. Hudson. New Haven, Conn.: Yale University Press, 1937, ed. L.B. Osborn. Reprint, Hamden, Conn.: 1973.

Macropedius, Georgius. *Methodus de conscribendis epistolis* [Antwerp 1543, as *Epistolica studiosis traiectinae scholae tyrunculis nuncupatA*. In Brandolinus, *De ratione scribendi*. London: H. Middleton, 1573. Microfiche.

Murphy, Basel 1549. *A newe boke of presidentes in maner of a register, wherin is comprehended the very trade of makyng all manner euydence and instruments of practyse*. Preface by T. Phaer. London: E. Whitchurche, 1543. 40 editions before 1641. Amsterdam and New York: English Experience no. 569, 1973 (facsimile of 1543).

Phillips, Edward. "Superscriptions for letters," and "Mock letters and drolling letters." In *The mysteries of love and eloquence; or, The arts of wooing and complementing*, by E. P[hillips]. London: for N. Brooks, 1658. Also 1685, 1699 (as *The beau's academy*). Menston: Scolar Press, 1972; English Linguistics no. 321 (facsimile of 1658).

Preston, Henry. *Brief directions. For true-spelling.* . . . *To which is added. Copies of letters, bills of parcels, bills of exchange, bills of debt, receipt, with pertinent rules as helps thereunto*. London: J. R. Rand, [1673?]. Menston: Scolar Press, 1968; English Linguistics no. 85 (facsimile).

Vives, Juan Luis. *De conscribendis epistolis* [Basel 1536]. In Brandolinus, *De ratione scribendi*. London: H. Middleton, 1573. Leyden and New York, 1989, trans. C. Fantazzi, *Works*.

Secondary Sources

Alessio, Gian Carlo. "Il *De componendis epistolis* di Niccolò Perotti e l'epistolografia umanistica." *Res publica litterarum* 11 (1988): 9–18.

Bautier, R.-H. "Les notaires et secrétaires du roi des origines au milieu du XVI siècle." In *Notaires et secrétaires du roi sous les règnes de Louis XI, Charles VIII et Louis XII*, edited by André Apeyre and Remy Scheurer. Vol. 1. Paris: Bibliothèque nationale, 1978.

Clough, C. H. "The Cult of Antiquity: Letters and Letter Collections." In *Cultural Aspects of the Italian Renaissance: Essays in Honour of Paul Oskar Kristeller,* edited by C. H. Clough. Manchester: Zambelli, 1976, 33–67.

Dunn, E.Catherine. "Lipsius and the Art of Letter Writing." *Studies in the Renaissance* 3 (1956): 145–56.

Fumaroli, Marc. *L'Age de l'Eloquence. Rhétorique et "res literaria" de la Renaissance au seuil de l'époque classique.* Genève: Libraire Droz, 1980.

Flachmann, Michael. "The First Epistolary Novel: *The Image of Idleness* (1555): Text, Introduction, and Notes." *Studies in Philology* 87 (1990): 1–74.

Garin, E., ed. *Il pensiero pedagogico dell' umanesimo.* Firenze: Sansoni, 1958. [esp. 306–503]

Gerlo, Alois. "The *Opus de Conscribendis Epistolis* of Erasmus and the tradition of the *Ars Epistolica.*" In *Classical Influences on European Culture,* edited by R. R. Bolgar. Cambridge: Cambridge University Press, 1971, 103–14.

Grendler, Paul. *Schooling in Renaissance Italy: Literacy and Learning, 1300–1600.* Baltimore: Johns Hopkins University Press, 1989.

Halkin, L.-E. "Le traité d'art épistolaire d'Erasme." *Moreana* 82 (1984): 25–30. Reprint, *Erasme. Sa pensée et son comportement.* Vol. 11. London: Variorum Reprints, 1988, 25–30.

Henderson, J. R. "Erasmus on the Art of Letter-Writing." In *Renaissance Eloquence: Studies in the Theory and Practice of Renaissance Rhetoric,* edited by J. J. Murphy. Berkeley: University of California Press, 1983, 331–55.

Hornbeak, Katherine G. *The Complete Letter Writer in English, 1568–1800.* Smith College Studies in Modern Languages, 15. Northampton: Collegiate Press, 1934.

Hunt, A. Jonathan. "Two teachers at the Volterran grammar school and a manuscript of Politian's Latin Letters." *Rinascimento* 31 (1991): 39–90.

Kristeller, Paul O. *Iter Italicum: A Finding List of Uncatalogued or Incompletely Catalogued Humanistic Manuscripts of the Renaissance in Italian and Other Libraries.* 7 vols. London: Warburg Institute, 1963–97.

Müller, Johannes. *Quellenschriften und Geschichte des deutschsprachigen Unterrichts bis zur Mitte des 16. Jahrhunderts.* Gotha: E. F. Thienemann, 1882.

Neveux, Jean B. "Un 'parfait Secrétaire' du XVIIe siècle: *Der Teutsche Secretarius* (1655)." *Etudes Germaniques* 19 (1964): 511–20.

Nuttall, G. F. "Cross-reference Table between LB and *Opus Epistolarum.*" *Erasmus in English* 3 (1971): 18–23.

Pigman III, G. W. "Barzizza's Studies of Cicero." *Rinascimento* 21 (1981): 123–63.

Polak, Emil J. *Medieval and Renaissance Letter Treatises and Form Letters: A Census of Manuscripts found in Eastern Europe and the Former U.S.S.R.* Davis Medieval Texts and Studies, no. 8. New York: E. J. Brill, 1993.

Robertson, Jean. *The Art of Letter Writing: An Essay on the Handbooks Published in England during the Sixteenth and Seventeenth Centuries.* Liverpool: Liverpool University Press; London: Hodder & Stoughton, 1942.

Viala, Alain. "La Genèse des formes epistolaires en français et leurs sources latines et européennes: Essai de chronologie distinctive (XVIe–XVIIe s.)." *Revue de Litterature Comparée* 218, no. 2 (1981): 168–83.

Wolter, Paul. *William Fulwood,* "The Enimie of Idlenesse": Der älteste englische Briefsteller. PhD diss., Rostock, 1907.

Appendix D

SELECT BIBLIOGRAPHY OF CRITICAL STUDIES
ON RENAISSANCE DICTAMEN

Carol Poster

Because several chapters in this volume, especially those by Green and Henderson, contain extensive bibliographical discussions, this bibliography of critical studies concerning Renaissance dictamen is relatively brief and intended only as an introduction and overview of the field. For reasons dictated by the chronological coverage of the medieval and early modern bibliographies in this volume, "Renaissance" is interpreted as covering ca. 1500–1700. The number of secondary works devoted exclusively to Renaissance dicatmen is quite small, and thus several sources of more general scope are included that discuss the topic only briefly.

Bibliographies, Miscellanies, and Manuscript Catalogs

Abbott, Don Paul. "The Renaissance." *The Present State of Scholarship in Historical and Contemporary Rhetoric*. Rev. ed. Winifred Horner. Columbia: University of Missouri Press, 1990.

Basso, J. Le *Genre épistolaire en langue italienne (1583–1662). Répertoire chronologique et analytique*. Nancy: Presses Universitaires de Nancy, 1990.

Hoock, J., and P. Jeannin. *Ars Mercatoria. Handbücher und Traktate für den Gebrauch des Kaufmanns. Manuels et traités à l'usage des marchands. 1470–1820*. Paderborn: Ferdinand Schöning, 1989.

Luehring, Janet, and Richard Utz. "Letter-Writing in the Late Middle Ages (c. 1250–1600): An Introductory Bibliography of Critical Studies." *Disputatio* 1 (1996): 191–229.

Murphy, James Jerome. "One Thousand neglected Authors: The Scope and Importance of Renaissance Rhetoric." In *Renaissance Eloquence: Studies in the Theory and Practice of Renaissance Rhetoric*, edited by James J. Murphy. Berkeley: University of California Press, 1983, 20–36.

———. *Renaissance Rhetoric: A Short-Title Catalogue of Works on Rhetorical Theory from the Beginning of Printing to* A.D. *1700, with Special Attention to the Holdings of the Bodleian Library, Oxford*. New York: Garland, 1981.

Murphy, James J., and Martin Davies, eds. "Rhetorical Incunabula: A Short-Title Catalogue of Texts Printed to the Year 1500." *Rhetorica* 15, no. 4 (August 1997).

Plett, Heinrich F. *Englische Rhetorik und Poetik 1479–1660: Eine systematische Bibliographie*. Forschungsberichte des Landes Nordrhein-Westfalen, Fachgruppe Geisteswissenschaften Nr. 3201. Opladen: Westdeutscher Verlag, 1985.

Polak, Emil J. *Medieval and Renaissance Letter Treatises and Form Letters: A Census of Manuscripts Found in Eastern Europe and the Former U.S.S.R.* Davis Medieval Texts and Studies, 8. Leiden: Brill, 1993.

————. *Medieval and Renaissance Letter Treatises and Form Letters: A Census of Manuscripts Found in Part of Western Europe, Japan, and the United States of America.* Leiden: Brill, 1994.

Critical Studies

Individual Figures

Puget de La Serre

Chupeau, J. "Puget de La Serre et l'esthétique épistolaire: les avatars du 'Secrétaire de la Cour.'" *Cahiers de l'Association Internationale des Études Françaises* 39 (1987): 111–26.

Ernouf, Baron. "Puget de La Serre. Sa vie et ses oeuvres." *Revue contemporaine* 2nd series, 51 (1866): 681–712.

Erasmus

Fantazzi, Charles. "The Evolution of Erasmus' Epistolary Style." *Renaissance and Reformation* 13:3 (1989): 261

Gerlo, Alois. "The *Opus de Conscribendis Epistolis* of Erasmus and the Tradition of the *Ars Epistolica.*" In *Classical Influences on European Culture,* edited by R. R. Bolgar. Cambridge: Cambridge University Press, 1971, 103–14.

Halkin, Léon.-E. "Le traité d'art épistolaire d'Erasme." *Moreana* 82 (1984): 25–32. Reprint, *Erasme. Sa pensée et son comportement.* Vol. 11. London: Variorum Reprints, 1988. 25–32.

Henderson, Judith Rice. "Despauterius' Syntaxis (1509): The Earliest Publication of Erasmus' De conscribendis epistolis." *Humanistica Lovaniensia* 37 (1988): 175–210.

————. "The Enigma of Erasmus' Conficiendarum epistolarum formula." *Renaissance and Reformation* n.s. 13 (1989): 313–30.

————. "Erasmus on the Art of Letter-Writing." In *Renaissance Eloquence: Studies in the Theory and Practice of Renaissance Rhetoric,* edited by James J. Murphy. Berkeley: University of California Press, 1983, 331–55.

————. "Euphues and his Erasmus." *English Literary Renaissance* 12 (1982): 35–161.

Jardine, Lisa. *Erasmus, Man of Letters: The Construction of Charisma in Print.* Princeton, N.J.: Princeton University Press, 1993.

Jolidon, A. "Histoire d'un opuscule d'Erasme: La Brevissima maximeque compendiaria conficiendarum epistolarum formula." In *Acta conventus neo-Latini Sanctandreani: Proceedings of the Fifth International Congress of Neo-Latin Studies, St Andrews 24 August to 1 September 1982,* edited by I. D. McFarlane. Medieval & Renaissance Texts & Studies 38. Binghamton, N.Y.: 1986, 229–43.

————. "L'évolution psychologique et littéraire d'Erasme d'après les variantes du 'De conscribendis epistolis.'" In *Acta conventus neo-Latini Amstelodamensis: Proceedings of the Second International Congress of Neo-Latin Studies, Amsterdam 19–24 August 1973,* edited by P. Tuynman, G. C. Kuiper, and E. Keßler. Munich: Wilhelm Fink Verlag, 1979, 566–87.

Nuttall, G. F. "Cross-reference Table between LB and *Opus Epistolarum.*" *Erasmus in English* 3 (1971): 18–23.

Rummel, Erika. "Erasmus' Manual of Letter-writing: Tradition and Innovation." *Renaissance and Reformation* n.s. 13 (1989): 299–312.

Fulwood

Wolter, Paul. "William Fulwood, "The Enimie of Idlenesse": Der älteste englische Briefsteller." PhD diss., Rostock, 1907.

Hegendorf

Bierlaire, Franz. "Les 'Dialogi pueriles' de Christophe Hegendorff." In *Acta conventus neo-Latini Turonensis: Troisième* Congrès Internationale d'Etudes Néo-Latines, Tours, Université François-Rabelais 6–10 Septembre 1976, edited by Jean-Claude Margolin. De Pétrarque à Descartes. Paris: Librairie Philosophique J. Vrin, 1980, 389–401.

———. "Un livre du maître au XVIe siècle: Erasme expliqué par Hegendorf." *Quaerendo* 2 (1972): 200–220.

Lipsius

Dunn, E. Catherine. "Lipsius and the Art of Letter Writing." *Studies in the Renaissance* 3 (1956): 145–56.

Lipsius, Justus. *Epistolica institutio. English & Latin.* In *Principles of Letter-Writing: A Bilingual Text of Justi Lipsii Epistolica Institution,* edited and translated by R.V. Young and M. Thomas Hester. Carbondale: Southern Illinois University Press, 1996.

Macropedius

Best, Thomas W. *Macropedius.* Twayne's World Author Series. New York: Twayne Publishers, 1972.

Lindeman, Yehudi. "Macropedius' Rebelles and Erasmus' Principles of Education." *Renaissance and Reformation,* n.s. 4 (1980), 127–35.

Melancthon

Jensen, Kristian. "The Latin Grammar of Philipp Melanchthon." In *Acta conventus neo-Latini Guelpherbytani: Proceedings of the Sixth International Congress of Neo-Latin Studies, Wolfenbüttel 12 August to 16 August 1985,* edited by Stella P. Revard, Fidel Rädle, Mario A. DiCesare. Medieval & Renaissance Texts & Studies 53. Binghamton, N.Y.: 1988, 513–19.

Richard, James William. *Philip Melanchthon: The Protestant Preceptor of Germany 1497–1560. Heroes of the Reformation 2.* New York: G. P. Putnam's Sons, 1898. Reprint, New York: Burt Franklin Reprints, 1974.

Niccolò Perotti

Alessio, Gian Carlo. "Il *De componendis epistolis* di Niccolò Perotti e l'epistolografia umanistica." *Res publica litterarum* 11 (1988): 9–18.

Ramus

Bruyère, Nelly. *Methode et dialectique dan l'oeuvre de la Ramée: Renaissance et age classique. De Pétrarque à Descartes 45.* Paris: Librairie Philosophique J. Vrin, 1984.

Ong, Walter J., S. J. *Ramus, Method, and the Decay of Dialogue: From the Art of Discourse to the Art of Reason.* Cambridge, Mass.: Harvard University Press, 1958.

Individual Nations/Languages

England

Charlton, Kenneth. *Education in Renaissance England.* London: Routledge, 1965.

Clark, Donald Lemen. *John Milton at St. Paul's School: A Study of Ancient Rhetoric in English Renaissance Education.* New York: Columbia University Press, 1948.

———. *Rhetoric and Poetry in the Renaissance: A Study of Rhetorical Terms in English Renaissance Literary Criticism.* New York: Columbia University Press, 1922.

Cressy, David. *Literacy and the Social Order: Reading and Writing in Tudor and Stuart England.* Cambridge: Cambridge University Press, 1980.

Graham, Kenneth J. E. *The Performance of Conviction: Plainness and Rhetoric in the Early English Renaissance.* Ithaca, N.Y.: Cornell University Press, 1994.

Hornbeak, Katherine G. *The Complete Letter Writer in English, 1568–1800.* Smith College Studies in Modern Languages, 15. Northampton, Mass.: Collegiate Press, 1934.

Howell, Wilbur S. *Logic and Rhetoric in England, 1500–1700.* Princeton, N.J.: Princeton University Press, 1956.

Robertson, Jean. *The Art of Letter Writing: An Essay on the Handbooks Published in England during the Sixteenth and Seventeenth Centuries.* Liverpool: Liverpool University Press; London: Hodder & Stoughton, 1942.

Watson, Foster. *The English Grammar Schools to 1660: Their Curriculum and Practice.* 1908. Reprint, London: Frank Cass, 1968.

France

Altman, J. Gurkin. "The Letter Book as a Literary Institution 1539–1789: Towards a Cultural History of Published Correspondences in France." *Yale French Studies* 71 (1986): 17–62.

Basso, J. "Les traductions en français de la littérature épistolaire italienne aux XVIe et XVIIe siècle." *Revue d'Histoire Littéraire de la France* (November–December 1978): 906–18.

Bautier, R. -H. "Les notaires et secrétaires du roi des origines au milieu du XVI siècle." In *Notaires et secrétaires du roi sous les règnes de Louis XI, Charles VIII et Louis XII,* edited by André Apeyre and Remy Scheurer. Vol. 1. Paris: Bibliothèque nationale, 1978.

Bossis, M., and C. A. Porter, ed. *L'Epistolarité à travers les siècles. Geste de communications et/ou d'écriture.* Centre Culturel International de Cerisy-la-Salle. Stuttgart: Franz Steiner Verlag, 1990, 106–15.

Gueudet, G. "Les premiers manuels français d'art épistolaire." In *Mélanges sur la littérature de la Renaissance à la mémoire de V.-L. Saulnier.* Geneva: Librairie Droz, 1984, 87–98.

Matheeussen, Constant. "A propos d'une lettre inconnue de Despautère: ses relations avec la ville de Comines et Georges d'Halluin." *Lias* 4 (1977): 1–11.

Meerhof, Kees. *Rhétorique et poétique au XVIe siècle en France: Du Bellay, Ramus, et les autres.* Leiden: Brill, 1986.

Rott, Jean, trans. and ed. *Classicae epistolae sive Scholae Argentinenses restitutae by*

Jean Sturm. Quatrième centenaire du Gymnase Protestant de Strasbourg. Paris: Librairie E. Droz; Strasbourg: Editions Fides, 1938.

Schindling, Anton. *Humanistische Hochschule und freie Reichsstadt: Gymnasium und Akademie in Strassburg 1538–1621*. Veroffentlichungen des Instituts für europäische Geschichte Mainz 77, Abteilung Universalgeschichte. Wiesbaden: Franz Steiner Verlag, 1977.

Sullivan, Marie Saint Francis. Étienne du Tronchet: auteur forézien du XVIe siècle. Étudebiographique et littéraire. Washington, D.C.: Catholic University of America Press, 1932.

Viala, Alain. "La Genèse des formes epistolaires en français et leurs sources latines et européennes: Essai de chronologie distinctive (XVIe–XVIIe s.)." *Revue de Litterature Comparée*. 218, no. 2 (1981): 168–83.

Germany

Neveux, Jean B. "Un 'parfait Secrétaire' du XVIIe siècle: *Der Teutsche Secretarius* (1655)." *Etudes Germaniques* 19 (1964): 511–20.

Italy

Grendler, Paul F. *Schooling in Renaissance Italy: Literacy and Learning 1300–1600*. Baltimore: Johns Hopkins University Press, 1989.

Hunt, A. Jonathan. "Two Teachers at the Volterran Grammar School and a Manuscript of Politian's Latin Letters." *Rinascimento* 31 (1991): 39–90.

Spain

Briesemeister, Dietrich. "Rhetorik und Humanismus in Spanien." In *Renaissance Rhetoric,* edited by Heinrich F. Plett. Berlin: Walter de Gruyter, 1993, 92–106.

General

Abott, Don Paul. "Rhetoric and Writing in Renaissance Europe and England." In *A Short History of Writing Instruction From Ancient Greece to Twentieth-Century America,* edited by James J. Murphy. Davis, Calif.: Hermagoras Press, 1990, 95–120.

Baldwin, Charles Sears. *Renaissance Literary Theory and Practice: Classicism in the Rhetoric and Poetic of Italy, France, and England, 1400–1600*. Edited and introduced by D. L. Clark. New York: Columbia University Press, 1939.

Bray, B. *L'Art de la lettre amoreuse des manuels aux romans (1550–1700)*. Paris: Mouton, 1967.

Burton, Gideon O. "Imitation in Renaissance Culture and Humanist Pedagogy." PhD diss., University of Southern California, 1994.

Chartier, Roger. *The Culture of Print: Power and the Use of Print in Early Modern Europe*. Translated by Lydia G. Cochrane. Cambridge: Polity, 1989.

Chartier, Roger, Alain Boureau, and Cecile Dauphin. *Correspondence: Models of Letter-writing from the Middle Ages to the Nineteenth Century*. Translated by Christopher Woodall. Princeton, N.J.: Princeton University Press, 1997.

Classen, C. J. "Cicero Inter Germanos Redivivus, II." *Humanistica Lovaniensia* 39 (1990): 156–76.

Clough, C. H. "The Cult of Antiquity: Letters and Letter Collections." In *Cultural*

Aspects of the Italian Renaissance: Essays in Honour of Paul Oskar Kristeller, edited by C. H. Clough. Manchester: Zambelli, 1976, 33–67.

Codina Mir, Gabriel, S. I. *Aux sources de la pédagogie des Jésuites: Le 'Modus Parisiensis.'* Bibliotheca Instituti Historici S. I., 28. Rome, 1968.

Crane, William Garrett. *Wit and Rhetoric in the Renaissance: The Formal Basis of Elizabethan Prose Style.* New York: Columbia University Press, 1937.

Fumaroli, Marc. "Genèse de l'épistolographie classique: rhétorique humaniste de la lettre, de Pétrarque à Juste Lipse." *Revue d'Histoire Littéraire de la France* (November–December 1978): 886–98.

———. *L'âge de l'éloquence: Rhétorique et "res literaria" de la Renaissance au seuil de l'époque classique.* Geneva: Librarie Droz, 1980.

Garin, E., ed. *Il pensiero pedagogico dell' umanesimo.* Firenze: Sansoni, 1958. [esp. 306–503]

Grafton, Anthony, and Lisa Jardine. *From Humanism to the Humanities: Education and the Liberal Arts in Fifteenth- and Sixteenth-Century Europe.* Cambridge, Mass.: Harvard University Press, 1986.

Gray, Hanna H. "Renaissance Humanism: The Pursuit of Eloquence." *Journal of the History of Ideas* 24 (1963): 497–514.

Green, Lawrence D. "Canonicity and the Renaissance Cicero." In *Composition in Context: Essays in Honor of Donald C. Stewart*, edited by W. Ross Winterowd and Vincent Gillespie. Carbondale: Southern Illinois University Press, 1994, 17–27.

Henderson, Judith Rice. "Erasmian Ciceronians: Reformation Teachers of Letter-Writing." *Rhetorica* 10, no. 3 (1992): 273–302.

———. "On Reading the Rhetoric of the Renaissance Letter." In *Renaissance Rhetoric*, edited by Heinrich Plett. Berlin: Walter de Gruyter, 1993, 143–62.

Howell, Wilbur S. *Poetics, Rhetoric, and Logic: Studies in the Basic Disciplines of Criticism.* Ithaca, N.Y.: Cornell University Press, 19975.

Kristeller, Paul Oskar. *Renaissance Thought and Its Sources.* Edited by Michael Mooney. New York: Columbia University Press, 1979.

Lavency, M. "A propos de la grammaire de Despautère." *Humanités Chrétiennes* 12 (1968–69): 401–8.

Lechner, Joan Marie. *Renaissance Concepts of the Commonplaces: An Historical Investigation of the General and Universal Ideas Used in All Argumentation and Persuasion, with Special Emphasis on the Educational and Literary Tradition of the Sixteenth and Seventeenth Centuries.* New York, Pageant Press, 1962.

Lukács, Ladislaus, S.J. *Monumenta Paedagogica Societatis Iesu.* Romee: Apud Monumenta Historica Societais Iesu, 1965.

Mack, Peter, ed. *Renaissance Rhetoric.* New York: St. Martin's Press, 1994.

Müller, Johannes. *Quellenschriften und Geschichte des deutschsprachigen Unterrichts bis zur Mitte des 16. Jahrhunderts.* Gotha: E. F. Thienemann, 1882.

Murphy, James J., ed. *Renaissance Eloquence: Studies in the Theory and Practice of Renaissance Rhetoric.* Berkeley: University of California Press, 1983.

Nauwelaerts, M. A., ed. "Brieven van en aan Bossche humanisten en docenten: II. Jan Goverts (Joannes Nemius); IV. Georgius Macropedius (van Lanckvelt)." *Bossche Bijdragen,* 23 (1957–58): 255–74; 24 (1958–59): 143–61.

————. "De Geschriften van Joannes Nemius." *Gulden Passer* 28 (1950): 104–9.

————. *Latijnse School en Onderwijs te's-Hertogenbosch tot 1629. Bijdragen tot de Geschiedenis van het Zuiden van Nederland 30.* Tilburg: Stichting Zuidelijk Historisch Contact, 1974.

Patterson, Annabel M. *Hermogenes and the Renaissance: Seven Ideas of Style.* Princeton, N.J.: Princeton University Press, 1970.

Pigman III, G. W. "Barzizza's Studies of Cicero." *Rinascimento* 21 (1981): 123–63.

Plett, Heinrich, ed. *Renaissance Rhetoric.* Berlin: Walter de Gruyter, 1993.

Rummel, Erika. *The Scholastic and Humanist Debate in the Renaissance and Reformation.* Cambridge, Mass.: Harvard University Press, 1995.

Scott, Izora. *Controversies over the Imitation of Cicero in the Renaissance. With Translations of Letters between Pietro Bembo and Gianfranceso Pico on Imitation and a Translation of Desiderius Erasmus, The Ciceronian (Ciceronianus). Contributions to Education 35.* New York: Teachers College, Columbia University, 1910. Reprint, Davis, Calif.: Hermagoras Press, 1991.

Seigel, Jerrold. *Rhetoric and Philosophy in Renaissance Humanism: The Union of Eloquence and Wisdom, Petrarch to Valla.* Princeton, N.J.: Princeton University Press, 1968.

Sonino, Lee A. *A Handbook to Sixteenth Century Rhetoric.* New York: Barnes and Noble, 1968.

Spitz, Lewis W., and Barbara Sher Tinsley. *Johann Sturm on Education: The Reformation and Humanist Learning.* St. Louis: Concordia Publishing House, 1995.

Trunz, Eric. "Der duetsche Späthumanismus um 1600 als Standeskultur." In *Deutsche Barockforschung,* edited by Richard Alewyn. Köln and Berlin: Kiepenheuer and Witsch, 1966, 147–81.

Vickers, Brian. *A Defence of Rhetoric.* New York: Oxford University Press, 1986.

Witt, Ronald. "Medieval 'Ars Dictaminis' and the Beginnings of Humanism: a New Construction of the Problem." *Renaissance Quarterly* 35 (1982): 1–35.

Woodward, William H. *Studies in Education during the Age of the Renaissance 1400–1600.* 1908. Reprint, Cambridge: Cambridge University Press, 1924.

Appendix E

Bibliography of Dictamen in England, 1700–1800

Linda C. Mitchell

Primary Sources

The Accomplish'd Letter-Writer; or, The Young Gentlemen and Ladies' Polite Guide to an Epistolary Correspondence. Newcastle Upon Tyne: T. Saint: for W. Charnley, 1778.

The Accomplished Letter-Writer; or, a Universal Correspondent. London: for T. Caslon, 1779.

The Art of Letter-Writing, Divided into Two Parts. The first, containing rules and directions for writing letters on all sorts of subjects . . . The second, a collection of letters on the most interesting occasions in life. London: for T. Osborne, 1762.

The Best Young Man's Companion. Glasgow: for the booksellers, 1772.

The British Letter-Writer; or, Letter-Writer's Complete Instructor. London: for J. Cooke, [1765?].

Brown, George, Rev. *The New English Letter-Writer; or, Whole Art of General Correspondence.* London: for Alex. Hogg, [1779?].

Buchanan, James. *The British Grammar.* London: A. Millar, 1762.

Campbell, John. *The Polite Correspondence.* London: for J. Hodges, 1754. Limerick 1756. [Also *Polite Epistolary Correspondence,* compiled by John Campbell, 1754.]

The Compleat Academy of Complements. London: for E. Tracy; and T. Ballard, 1705.

The Compleat Academy of Complements; or, Lover's Magazine. London: by and for J. Willis et al., 1729.

The Complete Art of Writing Love Letters. London: by W. Franklin, for R. Richards, [1795?].

The Complete Letter-Writer Containing Familiar Letters on the Most Common Occasions in Life. London: for the Booksellers, 1798.

The Complete Letter-Writer; or, Polite English Secretary. London: for S. Crowder and H. Woodgate, 1756.

Cooke, Thomas. *The Universal Letter-Writer.* London: for J. Cooke, [1770?].

Correspondent, a Selection of Letters from the Best Authors. 2 vols. London: for T. Cadell et al., 1796.

Defoe, Daniel. *The Compleat English Tradesman.* London: for Charles Rivington, 1727. Attribution uncertain.

The Delightful New Academy of Compliments. Newcastle: sold by Thomas G[ent], [1765?].

Dilworth, W. H. *The Complete Letter-Writer; or, Young Secretary's Instructor.* Glasgow: for Peter Tait, 1783.

Dixon, Henry. *The English Instructor; or, the Art of Spelling Improved.* London: for J. Hazard et al., 1736.

Du Bois, Dorothea. *The Lady's Polite Secretary; or, New Female Letter Writer.* London: for S. Hooper, [1775?].

Fenning, D., and J. Malham. *The Young Man's New Universal Companion.* London: for S. Crowder, 1788.

Fisher, Anne. *A New Grammar, with Exercises of Bad English.* New Castle: sold by C. Hitch, 1757.

Fleetwood, William. *The Relative Duties of Parents and Children, Husbands and Wives, Masters and Servants.* London: for John Hooke, 1705.

Fordyce, David. *The New and Complete British Letter-Writer; or, Young Secretary's Instructor in Polite Modern Letter-Writing.* London: for C. Cooke, [1790?].

Garretson, John. *English Exercises for School-Boys to Translate into Latin.* London: for Tho. Cockerill, [1691], 1719.

G. F., Gent. *The Compleat Secretary.* London: by W. O., 1704. Also as *The Secretary's Guide.*

Gignoux, John, and Philip Bellie. *Epistolary Correspondence Made Pleasant and Familiar.* London: for Edward Dilly, 1759.

Gildon, Charles, and John Brightland. *A Grammar of the English Tongue.* London: for John Brightland, 1712.

[G. L.]. *The Amorous Gallant's Tongue Tipt with Golden Expressions.* London: for F. Coles, T. Vere & I. Wright, 1710.

Goodman, Thomas. *The Experience'd Secretary; or, Citizen and Country-Man's Companion.* London: for N. Boddington, 1707.

Gordon, William. *Every Young Man's Companion.* London: for J. and J. Rivington, 1755.

Guilhermin, Mary. *A Series of Letters for the Use of Young Ladies and Gentlemen in French and English.* London: for J. Dixwell, 1766.

Hallifax, Charles. *Familiar Letters on Various Subjects of Business and Amusement.* London: for R. Baldwin, 1754.

Hill, J. *The Young Secretary's Guide or, a Speedy Help to Learning.* London: for H. Rhodes, 1712.

Johnson, Charles. *The Complete Art of Writing Letters.* London: for T. Lowndes, 1770.

Johnson, S[amuel]. *A Compleat Introduction to the Art of Writing Letters Universally Adapted to all Classes and Conditions of Life.* London: for Henry Dell, 1760.

The Ladies Complete Letter-Writer. London: for T. Lownds, 1763.

The Letter-Writer's Complete Instructor. Glasgow: for James Knox, 1768.

The Letter-Writer's Instructor; or, The Art of Writing Letters Elegantly. Dublin: for Caleb Jenkin and John Beatty, 1776.

Lettres Choises sur Toutes Sortes de Sujets . . . or a Collection of Familiar Letters in French and English. London: for B. Law, 1777.

Maittaire, Michael. *The English Grammar.* London: by W. B. for H. Clements, 1712.

Mather, William. *The Young Man's Companion.* London: by T. Snowden, 1710.

Milns, William. *The Well-Bred Scholar.* London: S. Gosnell, 1794.

A New Academy of Complements; or, The Lover's Secretary [sic]. London: for C. Bates and A. Bettesworth, 1715.

The New Complete Letter Writer; or, The Art of Correspondence. Glasgow: by J. and M. Robertson, 1799.

Newbery, John. *Letters on the Most Common, as Well as Important, Occasions in Life.* London: for J. Newbery, 1756.

The Polite Epistolary Correspondence; or, Rational Amusement. [Compiled by John Campbell.] London: for H. Serjeant, 1759.

Richardson, Samuel. *Letters Written to and for Particular Friends, on the Most Important Occasions.* London: for C. Rivington, 1741.

Rule, John. *L'Ecrivain Anglois & Françoise, ou le Correspondent Général.* London: by Joseph Johnson and Bejamin Davenport, 1766.

Scougal, Henry. *The Compleat English Secretary, and Newest Academy of Complements.* London: by and for Brown, and T. Norris, 1714. Also listed as *A New Academy of Compliments [sic]; or, The Compleat English Secretary.* London for R. Ware et al., 1748.

Seymour, George. *The Instructive Letter Writer.* London: for G. Kearsley, 1763.

Strong, Nathaniel. *England's Perfect School Master . . . letters, acquittances, bills of exchange, bills of parcels, bills of debt, bonds.* London: by J. R. for Benjamin Billingsley, 1704.

Tavernier, John. *The Entertaining Correspondent; or, Newest and Most Compleat Polite Letter Writer.* Berwick, England: by R. Taylor, 1759.

The Tutor or Epistolary Guide. London: F. Newbery, 1772.

Wallace, James, D.D., and Charles Townshend, A.M. *Every Man His Own Letter-Writing; or, The New and Complete Art of Letter-Writing Made Plain and Familiar to Every Capacity.* London: for J. Cooke, [1782?].

Wit's cabinet: A Companion for Gentlemen and Ladies. London: by T. Norris, 1703.

Young, E. *The Compleat English Scholar.* London: for Ben Alsop, 1707.

The Young Secretary's Guide Completed. London: for H. Tracey, 1721. [not verified to be by J. Hill]

The Young Secretary's Polite Guide to an Epistolary Correspondence in Business, Friendship, Love, and Marriage. Newcastleupon Tyne: by T. Saint for W. Charnley et al., 1778.

Secondary Sources

Altman, Janet Gurkin. *Epistolarity: Approaches to a Form.* Columbus: Ohio State University Press, 1982.

———. "Political Ideology in the Letter Manual: France, England, New England." In *Studies in Eighteenth-Century Culture*, no. 18, edited by John W. Yolton and Leslie Allen Brown. East Lansing, Mich., 1988, 105–22.

Anderson, Howard, Philip B. Daghlian, and Irvin Ehrenpreis, eds. *The Familiar Letter in the Eighteenth Century.* Lawrence: University of Kansas Press, 1966.

Backscheider, Paula R. *Daniel Defoe: His Life.* Baltimore: Johns Hopkins University Press, 1989.

Bannet, Eve Tavor. "Empire and Occasional Conformity: David Fordyce's Complete British Letter Writer," *Huntington Library Quarterly* 66 (2003): 55–79.

Barker-Benfield, G. J. *The Culture of Sensibility: Sex and Society in Eighteenth-Century Britain*. Chicago: University of Chicago Press, 1992.

Barton, David, and Nigel Hall, eds. *Letter Writing as a Social Practice*. Philadelphia: John Benjamins, 1999.

Beale, Philip. *A History of the Post in England from the Romans to the Stuarts*. Aldershot: Ashgate, 1998.

Benstock, Shari. "From Letters to Literature: La Carte Postale and the Epistolary Genre," *Genre* 18 (Fall 1985): 257–95.

Chartier, Roger, Alain Boueau, and Cécile Dauphin, ed. *Correspondence: Models of Letter-Writing from the Middle Ages to the Nineteenth century*. Cambridge: Polity Press, 1997.

Cohen, Murray. *Sensible Words: Linguistic Practice in England, 1640–1785*. Baltimore: Johns Hopkins University Press, 1977.

Cressy, David. *Literacy and the Social Order: Reading and Writing in Tudor and Stuart England*. Cambridge: Cambridge University Press, 1980.

Dawson, William James. *The Great English Letter Writers*. New York: Harper, 1908.

Day, Robert A. *Told in Letters: Epistolary Fiction before Richardson*. Ann Arbor: University of Michigan Press, 1966.

Daybell, James, ed. *Early Modern Women's Letter Writing, 1450–1700*. New York: Palgrave, 2001.

Defoe, Daniel. *The Compleat English Gentleman*. Edited and introduced by Karl D. Buelbring. London: David Nutt, 1890.

Dobson, Austin. *Samuel Richardson: English Men of Letters*. New York: Macmillan, 1902.

Downs, Brian W. Richardson. *The Republic of Letters*. London: Routledge, 1928. Reprint, London: Cass, 1969.

Earle, Rebecca, ed. *Epistolary Selves: Letter and Letter-Writers, 1600–1945*. Brookfield: Ashgate, 1999.

Gilroy, Amanda, and W. M. Verhoeven, eds. *Epistolary Histories: Letters, Fiction, Culture*. Charlottesville: University Press of Virginia, 2000.

Hansche, Maude Bingham. *The Formative Period of English Familiar Letter-Writers and Their Contribution to the English Essay*. Philadelphia: 1902. Reprint, New York: Haskell, 1965.

Hornbeak, Katherine G. *The Complete Letter Writer in English, 1568–1800*. Smith College Studies in Modern Languages, 15. Northampton, Mass.: Collegiate Press, 1934.

————. "Richardson's Familiar Letters and the Domestic Conduct Books; Richardson's Aesop." *Smith College Studies in Modern Languages* 19, no. 2 (1938): 1–50.

How, James. *Epistolary Spaces: English Letter Writing from the Foundation of the Post Office to Richardson's Clarissa*. Aldershot: Ashgate, 2003.

Howell, Wilbur Samuel. *Eighteenth-Century British Logic and Rhetoric*. Princeton, N.J.: Princeton University Press, 1971.

Hughes, Helen Sard. "English Epistolary Fiction before Pamela." In *Manly Anniversary Studies*. Chicago: University of Chicago Press, 1928, 256–69.

Irving, William Henry. *The Providence of Wit in the English Letter Writers*. Durham, N.C.: Duke University Press, 1955.

Kay, Carol. Political *Constructions: Defoe, Richardson, and Sterne in Relation to Hobbes, Hume, and Burke*. Ithaca, N.Y.: Cornell University Press, 1988.

Keymer, Tom. *Richardson's Clarissa and the Eighteenth-Century Reader.* Cambridge: Cambridge University Press, 1992.

Langford, Paul. *A Polite and Commercial People: England 1727–1783.* Oxford: Oxford University Press, 1994.

Locker, Kitty. "'This Will Never Do': Model Dunning Letters, 1592–1873," In *Studies in the History of Business Writing,* edited by George H. Douglas and Herbert W. Hildebrandt. Champaign, Ill.: Association for Business Communication, 1985, 179–200.

Lockwood, Laura E., and Amy R. Kelly, eds. *Specimens of Letter Writing.* New York: H. Holt, 1911.

London, William. *A Catalogue of the Most Vendible Books in England (1657, 1658, 1660).* London: Gregg Press, 1965.

McKeon, Michael. *The Origins of the English Novel, 1600–1740.* Baltimore: Johns Hopkins University Press, 1987.

Michael, Ian. Grammatical Categories and the Tradition to 1800. Cambridge: Cambridge University Press, 1987.

———. *The Teaching of English: from the Sixteenth Century to 1870.* Cambridge: Cambridge University Press, 1987.

Mitchell, Linda C. "Entertainment and Instruction: Women's Roles in the English Epistolary Tradition," *Huntington Library Quarterly* 66 (Spring 2003): 332–47.

———. *Grammar Wars: Language as Cultural Battlefield in Seventeenth- and Eighteenth-Century England.* Burlington, Vt.: Ashgate, 2001.

Mitchell, Linda C., and Susan Green, eds. *The Cultural History of Letter Writing.* Berkeley: University of California Press, 2007.

Mullan, John. *Sentiment and Sociability: The Language of Feeling in the Eighteenth Century.* 1988. Reprinted, with corrections, Oxford: Clarendon Press, 1990.

Murphy, James J., ed. *Three Medieval Rhetorical Arts.* Berkeley: University of California Press, 1971.

O'Day, Rosemary. *Education and Society, 1500–1800: The Social Foundations of Education in Early Modern Britain.* New York: Longman, 1982.

Potkay, Adam. *The Fate of Eloquence in the Age of Hume.* Ithaca, N.Y.: Cornell University Press, 1994.

Redford, Bruce. *The Converse of the Pen: Acts of Intimacy in the Eighteenth-Century Familiar Letter.* Chicago: University of Chicago Press, 1986.

Robertson, Jean. *The Art of Letter Writing: An Essay on the Handbooks Published in England during the Sixteenth and Seventeenth Centuries.* London: Hodder & Stoughton/Liverpool: Liverpool University Press, 1942.

Robinson, Howard. *The British Post Office: A History.* Princeton, N.J.: Princeton University Press, 1948.

Schneider, Gary. *The Culture of Epistolarity: Vernacular Letters and Letter Writing in Early Modern England, 1500–1700.* Newark: University of Delaware Press, 2005.

Searle, Thomas. *The English Letter-Writer . . . Designed for the Study of the Art of Letter Writing.* Dresden: Walther, 1828.

Seton, George. *Gossip about Letters and Letter-Writers.* Edinburgh: Edmonston and Douglas, 1870.

Thomson, Clara Linklater. *Samuel Richardson: A Biographical Study.* London: Horace Marshall, 1900. Reprint, Folcroft, Pa.: Folcroft Press, 1969.

Appendix F

BIBLIOGRAPHY OF NINETEENTH-CENTURY
LETTER-WRITING MANUALS

Deirdre M. Mahoney

This bibliography includes primary sources and secondary scholarship. The letter-writing sources presented here represent only a sampling of those published in America during the nineteenth-century. Some of the instruction manuals trace to England and France and were published in numerous editions, often under various titles. Many were self-published. Most of the manuals and periodicals presented within this bibliography are accessible through academic libraries as monographs and/or microforms. Although every effort has been made to list sources categorically, the presented texts do not always lend themselves to definitive categorization. In some cases the boundaries of categorization are blurred; therefore, a category has been chosen based upon a text's prevalent features.

Primary Sources

Comprehensive Letter Writers

American Fashionable Letter Writer, Original and Selected, Containing a Variety of Letters on Business, Love, Courtship, Marriage, Relationship, Friendship, Etc. with Forms of Complimentary Cards. Troy, N.Y.: Merriam Moore, 1850.

The American Letter-Writer, and Mirror of Polite Behaviour: A Useful Guide in the Art of Letter Writing, with Rules of Conduct for Both Sexes. Philadelphia: Fisher & Brothers, 1851

American Letter Writer, the Art of Polite Correspondence, Containing a Variety of Plain and Elegant Letters to Which Are Prefixed Directions for Letter Writing and Rules for Composition. Brookfield, Mass.: E. Merriam, 1830.

The American Letter-Writer; or, New Art of Polite Correspondence: Containing a Course of Interesting and Original Letters of Friendship, Trade, Merchandize, and Other Important and Interesting Subjects. Hartford, Conn.: B. & J. Russell, 1814.

The American Parlor Letter Writer; or, The Art of Polite Correspondence Containing a Variety of Plain and Elegant Letters . . . and Rules for Composition. Springfield: John M. Wood, 1847.

The American Polite Letter Writer. Containing Upwards of Seventy Letters, on Various Subjects, Written in a Concise and Familiar Style. Philadelphia: M. Kelly, 1839.

The Art of Good Behaviour, and Letter Writer on Love Courtship, and Marriage: A Complete Guide for Ladies and Gentlemen, Particularly Those Who Have Not

Enjoyed the Advantages of Fashionable Life . . . Including the Necessary Preparations and Arrangements for the Marriage Ceremony. New York: C. P. Huetis, 1848.

The Belle-Lettres Letter Writer: Containing a Great Variety of Letters, Original and Selected, on the Subjects of Friendship, Love, Courtship, Marriage, Business, Relationship, Cards of Invitation, Etc . . . for the Use of Ladies and Gentlemen. Cincinnati: J. A. & U. P. James, 1853.

Calloway, Frances Bennett. *Charm and Courtesy in Letter-Writing.* New York: Dodd, Mead and Co., 1895.

Carroll, George D. *The Art of Correspondence and Usages of Polite Society.* New York: Dempsey & Carroll, 1880.

Chesterfield's Art of Letter-Writing Simplified. Being a Guide to Friendly, Affectionate, Polite and Business Correspondence, Containing a Large Collection of the Most Valuable Information Relative to the Art of Letter Writing, with Clear and Complete Instructions How to Begin and End Correspondence, Rules for Punctuation and Spelling, &C. To Which Is Appended the Most Complete Rules of Etiquette and the Usage of Society: Containing the Most Approved Rules for Correct Deportment in Fashionable Life, with Hints to Gentlemen and Ladies on Irregular and Vulgar Habits, Also, the Etiquette of Love and Courtship, Marriage Etiquette, &c. New York: Dick & Fitzgerald, 1857.

Chiu, Kwong Ki. *Manual of Correspondence and Social Usages. Containing Instruction and Examples in All Branches of Letter Writing, Forms of Business-papers . . . to Which Are Added Sections on Punctuation and the Use of Capitals; with Some Pages on Grammar and Spelling, and a Chapter on the Chinese Method of Reckoning Time.* San Francisco: Wing Fung, 1885.

The Classical Letter-Writer: Consisting of Epistolary Selections; Designed to Improve Young Ladies and Gentlemen in the Art of Letter Writing. Philadelphia: Key & Biddle, 1833.

The Columbian Letter-Writer; or, Young Lady and Gentleman's Guide, to Epistolary Correspondence: Containing a Choice Selection of Letters upon Advice, Business, Industry, Trade, Love, Courtship, Marriage, Friendship, Education, Morality, Religion. Alexandria: S. Snowden, 1811.

The Complete Letter Writer, or the Art of Correspondence. Containing Letters on the Following Subjects, Viz. Business, Friendship, Politeness, Affections, Love, Courtship, Marriage, Religion, &C. Adapted to the Use of Both Sexes, and Made Familiar to Every Capacity. By Writers Eminent for Perspicuity and Elegance of Expression. Trenton: James Oram, 1811.

Cooke, Thomas. *The New and Complete Letter Writer; or, New Art of Polite Correspondence: Containing a Course of Interesting Original Letters on the Most Important, Instructive, and Entertaining Subjects.* Poughkeepsie: Bowman, Parsons & Potter, 1806.

Dearborn, Nathaniel. *American Text Book for Letters.* Boston: N. Dearborn, 1846.

Dewitt's Handy Letter-Writer. Containing in the Most Plain and Simple Language, Full Directions and Explanations for Writing Every Kind of Letter . . . with a Large Number of Ready Prepared Letters on All Subjects. And an Extensive Compendium of Elegant Poetical Quotations. New York: C. T. Dewitt, 1877.

Dick, William B. *Dick's Common Sense Letter-Writer: Containing Three Hundred and Sixty Sensible Social and Business Letters.* New York: Dick & Fitzgerald, 1889.

Dilworth, W. H. *The Complete Letter Writer; or, Young Secretary's Instructor: Containing a Great Variety of Letters on Friendship, Duty, Love, Marriage, Amusement, Business &C.: To Which Are Prefixed, Plain Instructions for Writing Letters on All Occasions.* Baltimore: William Warner, 1819.

The Fashionable Letter Writer; or, Art of Polite Correspondence. Containing a Variety of Plain and Elegant Letters on Business, Love, Courtship, Marriage, Relationship, Friendship, &C, Adapted to General Use: with Forms of Complimentary Cards and a New and Easy English Grammar Peculiarly Applicable to Writing Letters with Accuracy. New York: George Long, 1818.

Harkavy, A. *American Letter Writer, English and Yiddish.* New York: J. Katzenelenbogen, 1899.

Holbrook, Alfred. *Manual for Training in Letter Writing and Rhetoric.* Lebanon, Ohio: C. K. Hamilton & co., 1895.

How to Write Letters. Everybody's Friend. Samples of Every Conceivable Kind of Letters. New York: Tousey & Small, 1878.

The Improved Letter Writer; or, The Art of Polite Correspondence, Containing a Variety of Plain and Elegant Letters . . . with Forms of Complimentary Cards and Directions for Letter Writing. To Which Are Added Forms of Mortgages, Deeds, Bonds, Powers of Attorney, &c. Baltimore: Fisher & Denison, 1866.

The Letter Writer: Containing a Great Variety of Letters on the Following Subjects: Relationship-business-love-courtship-and Marriage-friendship and Miscellaneous Letters: Selected from Judicious and Eminent Writers. Charlestown, Mass.: G. Davidson, 1827.

The Letter Writer: Containing a Great Variety of Letters on the Following Subjects: Relationship, Business, Love, Courtship, and Marriage, Friendship, and Miscellaneous Letters, Law Forms &C. &C. Selected from Judicious and Eminent Writers. Boston: Charles Gaylord, 1832.

The Letter Writer's Own Book, or the Art of Polite Correspondence. Philadelphia: J. B. Perry, 1843.

Letter-Writing Made Easy. Showing Plainly How to Write Letters upon Almost Every Imaginable Subject. New York: F. A. Brady, 1859.

Magee's London Letter Writer: Being the Complete Art of Fashionable Correspondence Composed in a Plain and Elegant Style Containing Business Letters; Juvenile and Parental Letters; Youth to Maturity; Business, Love, Courtship and Marriage; Friendship and Consolation, Relationship. Philadelphia, 1810.

Martine's Sensible Letter-Writer. Being a Comprehensive and Complete Guide and Assistant for Those Who Desire to Carry on Epistolary Correspondence; Containing a Large Collection of Model Letters on the Simplest Matters of Life, Adapted to All Ages and Conditions. New York: Dick & Fitzgerald, c. 1850.

McMahon, Ella. *Hints on Letter Writing. For the Use of Academies and for Self-instruction. Adapted from the French of the Author of "Golden Sands."* New York: Benziger Brothers, 1885.

The Modern Letter-Writer; on Love, Courtship, Marriage, and Business: Being a Complete Guide . . . with Hints on Courtship, Maxims on Making Love, Poetical

Quotations, and Remarks on Popping the Question . . . with Forms and Rules of Etiquette for Every Condition of Life. Boston: A. J. Wright, 1847.

The New Complete Letter Writer; or, The Art of Correspondence. Containing Letters on the Following Subjects: Business, Friendship, Love and Marriage . . . Composed by Writers Eminent for Perspicuity and Elegance of Expression. To Which Are Added Moral

Maxims and Reflections, by the Late Duke De La Rochefoucault. Albany, N.Y.: Charles R. & George Webster, 1802.

North's Book of Love Letters. New York, c. 1863. Advertised for 50 cents in *How to Conduct a Debate,* published by Dick & Fitzgerald, New York.

O'Neil, J. W. *New Standard Letter-Writer for the People: Containing Copious and Accurate Directions for Conducting Epistolary Correspondence; with Numerous Specimens of Letters, Adapted to Every Age and Situation.* Philadelphia: C. Desilver, 1860.

Raub, Albert N. *Punctuation and Letter Writing: Containing, Also, the Rules for the Use of Capital Letters.* Philadelphia: Raub & Co., 1887.

Shields, Sarah Annie (Frost). *Frost's Original Letter Writer. A Complete Collection of Original Letters and Notes upon Every Imaginable Subject of Everyday Life.* New York: Dick & Fitzgerald, 1867.

The Standard Letter Writer for Ladies and Gentlemen Containing a Complete Collection of Business Letters; Letters of Introduction . . . Social Letters . . . Rules for Conducting Public Debates and Meetings. New York: M. J. Ivers, 1893.

Turner, R. *The Parlour Letter-Writer, and Secretary's Assistant: Consisting of Original Letters on Every Occurrence in Life, Written in a Concise and Familiar Style, and Adapted to Both Sexes. To Which Are Added, Complimentary Cards, Wills, Bonds, &c.* Philadelphia: Desilver Jr. & Thomas, 1834.

The Universal Letter-Writer; or, Whole Art of Polite Correspondence: Containing a Great Variety of Plain, Easy, Entertaining and Familiar Original Letters Adapted to Every Age and Situation in Life, but More Particularly on Business, Education, and Love. New edition. Corrected and enlarged. Philadelphia: Matthew Carey, 1808.

Wandle, Jennie Taylor. *The Art of Letter-Writing, a Manual of Polite Correspondence, Containing the Correct Forms for All Letters of a Commercial, Social or Ceremonial Nature, with Copious Explanatory Chapters on Arrangement, Punctuation, Grammatical Forms, Etc., Etc., Etc.* New York: A. L. Burt, 1889.

Webster's Practical Letter-Writer, Containing General Directions for Writing; Also Model Letters . . . Together with Bible Quotations, Choice Prose Sentiments . . . Also a Copious Dictionary of Synonyms, All the Latin, French, Spanish and Italian Words and Phrases Usually Met With; A Full List of Abbreviations. New York: H. J. Wehman, 1897.

Westlake, James Willis. *How to Write Letters: A Manual of Correspondence, Showing the Correct Structure, Composition, Punctuation, Formalities and Uses of the Various Kinds of Letters, Notes, and Cards.* Philadelphia: Sower/Potts, 1876.

The Writers' Handbook, a Guide to the Art of Composition Embracing a General Treatise on Composition, and Style; Instruction in English Composition, with Exercises for Paraphrasing; and an Elaborate Letter-Writer's Vade Mecum, in Which

Are Numerous Rules and Suggestions Relating to the Epistolary Art. Philadelphia: J. B. Lippincott & Co., 1888.

Letter-Writing Instruction, Commercial

The Complete American Letter-Writer and Best Companion for the Young Man of Business. Containing Letters on Trade and Merchandise, Expressly Calculated for the Youth of the United States; Also, Several Forms of Precedents Used in Transaction of Business in America: To Which Are Added, Familiar Letters on Interesting Subjects. New York: Richard Scott, 1807.

Foster, Benjamin Franklin. *The Clerk's Guide; or, Commercial Correspondence; and an Appendix, Containing Advice to Young Tradesmen, &c.* Boston: Parkins & Marvin, 1837.

Gaskell, George A. *Gaskell's Compendium of Forms, Educational, Social and Commercial, Embracing a Complete Self-teaching Course in Penmanship and Bookkeeping, and Aid to English Composition.* St. Louis: R. S. Peale & Co., 1882.

Hill, Thomas E. *Hills Manual of Social and Business Forms: Guide to Correct Writing.* Chicago: Hill Standard Book Co., 1889.

Hill, Thomas E. *The New Revised Hill's Manual.* Chicago: W. B. Conkey, 1898.

Power, O. M. *Twenty Lessons in Letter Writing and Business Forms. For Private Schools and Study.* Chicago: Powers & Lyons, 1899.

Wards Letter Writing: Business Forms for Schools and Academies. New York: American Book Co., 1885.

Letter-Writing Instruction for Children

Aiken, Lucy. *Juvenile Correspondence; or, Letters Designed as Examples of the Epistolary Style, for Children of Both Sexes.* Listed as being "From the Second London Edition." Boston: Cummings and Hillard, 1822.

Bingham, Caleb. *Juvenile Letters: Being a Correspondence between Children from Eight to Fifteen Years of Age.* Boston: Printed by David Carlisle for Caleb Bingam, 1803. Early American Imprints. Second series. No. 3830.

Classical English Letter-Writers; or, Epistolary Selections; Designed to Improve Young Persons in the Art of Letter-Writing, and in the Principles of Virtue and Piety. Philadelphia: C. Richardson, 1816.

Dewey, Julia M. *Lessons on Manners. Arranged for Grammar Schools, High Schools, and Academies.* New York: Hinds and Noble, 1899.

Farrar, Eliza. *The Youth's Letter-Writer; or, The Epistolary Art Made Plain and Easy to Beginners, through the Example of Henry Moreton.* New York: R. Bartlett & S. Raynor, 1834.

Hardie, James. *The Epistolary Guide, Containing Models of Juvenile Letters, on Familiar Subjects, with Topics for the Exercise of Youth.* New York: S. Marks, 1817.

The Little Writer: Designed as an Aid to Children in Acquiring an Easy and Familiar Epistolary Style. Boston: J. Dowe, 1836.

Points of Etiquette. Designed as a Text Book for the Young. New York: William H. Sadlier, 1879.

Richards, *Cornelia Holroyd Bradley. At Home and Abroad; or, How to Behave.* New York: Evans and Brittan, 1853.

Letter-Writing Instruction, Gender Specific

Beadle's Dime Ladies' Letter-Writer; or, How to Write; When to Write; What to Write! A Complete Manual of Correspondence! Together with Dictionary of Poetic Quotations; Proverbs from Shakespeare; Dictionary of French, Spanish, and Italian Phrases, Etc., Etc., Etc. New York: Beadle & Co., 1868.

"Blunders in Behavior Corrected." *Godey's Lady's Book and Magazine* 60 (May 1860): 413–15. Reprinted from *Blunders in Behaviour Corrected: A Concise Code of Deportment for Both Sexes.* London: Groombridge & Sons, 1855.

Dick, William B., ed. *Dick's Society Letter-Writer for Ladies, Containing More than Five Hundred Entirely Original Letters and Notes, with Appropriate Answers.* New York: Dick & Fitzgerald, 1884.

"Editor's Table." *Godey's Lady's Book and Magazine* 68 (April 1864): 397.

"Editor's Table." *Godey's Lady's Book and Magazine* (December 1859): 557.

"The Escrutoire." *Lady's Book* 2 (March 1831): 121–24.

The Gentlemen's Perfect Letter Writer; or, Hints and Helps to Letter Writing. New York: A. Cogswell, 1877.

"Writing Letters." *Godey's Lady's Book and Magazine* 82 (April 1871): 484–85.

The Young Lady's Book of Classical Letters Consisting of Epistolary Selections: Designed to Improve Young Ladies and Gentlemen in the Art of Letter Writing. Philadelphia: Desilver, Thomas & Co., 1836.

The Young Man's Book of Classical Letters, Consisting of Epistolary Selections; Designed to Improve Young Ladies and Gentlemen in the Act of Letter-Writing. Philadelphia: Grigg & Elliot, 1841.

The Young Woman's Companion & Instructor, in Grammar, Writing, Arithmetic, Geography, Drawing, Book-Keeping, Chronology, History, Letter-Writing, Cooking, Carving, Pickling, Preserving, Brewing, Wine Making &C. Manchester, 1806. Available in the History of Women series, reel 110.

Letter-Writing Instruction in Etiquette-Related Books

Alcott, William A. *Gift Book for Young Ladies; or, Familiar Letters on Their Acquaintances, Male and Female, Employments, Friendships, & c.* Buffalo: Geo. H. Derby and Co., 1852.

Beadle's Dime Book of Practical Etiquette for Ladies and Gentlemen: Being a Guide to True Gentility and Good-Breeding, and a Complete Directory to the Usages and Observances of Society. By a Committee of Three. New York: Irwin P. Beadle and Co., 1859.

Etiquette for Gentlemen; or, Short Rules and Reflections for Conduct in Society. Philadelphia: Lindsay and Blakiston, 1839.

Farrar, Eliza Ware. *The Young Lady's Friend.* Boston: American Stationers' Co., 1836. New York: Arno Press, 1974.

Hale, Sarah. *Manners; or, Happy Homes and Good Society All the Year Round.* Boston: J. E. Tilton, 1868. New York: Arno Press, 1972.

Hall, Florence Howe. *The Correct Thing Is Good Society.* Boston: Estes & Lauriat, c. 1888.

———. *Social Customs.* Boston: Dana Estes and Co., 1887.

Hartley, Cecil B. *The Gentlemen's Book of Etiquette, and Manual of Politeness; Being a Complete Guide for a Gentleman's Conduct in All His Relations toward Society.* Boston: C. W. Cottrell, 1860.

Hartley, Florence. *The Ladies' Book of Etiquette and Manual of Etiquette. A Complete Hand Book for the Use of the Lady in Polite Society.* Boston: G. W. Cottrell, 1860.

Laws of Etiquette, or Short Rules and Reflections for Conduct in Society. Philadelphia: Lea & Blanchard, 1841.

Leslie, Eliza. *Miss Leslie's Behavior Book: A Guide and Manual for Ladies.* Philadelphia: T. B. Peterson & Brothers, 1856. New York: Arno Press, 1972.

Sherwood, Mary Elizabeth Wilson. *Manners and Social Usages.* New York: Harper & Brothers, 1897. New York: Arno Press, 1975.

Thornwell, Emily. *The Lady's Guide to Perfect Gentility, in Manners, Dress and Conversation, in the Family, in Company, at the Piano Forte, the Table, in the Street, and in Gentlemen's Society.* New York: Derby & Jackson, 1858.

Todd, John. *The Daughter at School.* Northampton, Mass.: Hopkins, Bridgman, and Co., 1854.

Wells, Richard A. *Manners, Culture and Dress of the Best American Society: Including Social, Commercial and Legal Forms, Letter Writing, Invitations, &C, Also Valuable Suggestions on Self Culture and Home Training.* Springfield, Mass.: King, Richardson, 1894.

Willis, Henry P. *Etiquette, and the Usages of Society: Containing the Most Approved Rules for Correct Deportment in Fashionable Life, Together with Hints to Gentlemen and Ladies on Irregular and Vulgar Habits.* New York: Dick & Fitzgerald, 1860.

Secondary Sources

Arresty, Esther. *The Best Behavior: The Course of Good Manners, from Antiquity to the Present, as Seen through Courtesy and Etiquette Books.* New York: Simon and Schuster, 1970.

Beachamp, Virginia Walcott, ed. *A Private War: Letters and Diaries of Madge Preston 1862–1867.* New Brunswick, N.J.: Rutgers University Press, 1987.

Carson, Gerald. *The Polite Americans: A Wide Angle View of Our More or Less Good Manners over 300 Years.* New York: William Morrow, 1966.

Chartier, Roger, Alain Boureau, and Cécile Dauphin. *Correspondence: Models of Letter-Writing from the Middle-Ages to the Nineteenth Century.* Translated by Christopher Woodall. Princeton, N.J.: Princeton University Press, 1997.

Davidson, Cathy N. *The Book of Love: Writers and Their Love Letters.* New York, Pocket Books, 1992.

Decker, William Merrill. *Epistolary Practices: Letter Writing in America before Telecommunication.* Chapel Hill: University of North Carolina Press, 1998.

Halttunen, Karen. "Sentimental Culture and the Problem of Etiquette." In *Confidence Men and Painted Women: A Study of Middle-Class Culture in America, 1830–1870.* New Haven, Conn.: Yale University Press, 1982.

Hampsten. Elizabeth. *Read This Only to Yourself: The Private Writings of Midwestern Women, 1880–1910.* Bloomington: Indiana University Press, 1982.

Johnson, Nan. *Nineteenth Century Rhetoric in North America.* Carbondale: Southern Illinois University Press, 1991.

Kasson, John F. *Rudeness and Civility: Manners in Nineteenth-Century Urban America.* New York: Hill and Wang, 1990.

Kenyon, Olga. *800 Years of Women's Letters.* New York: Penguin, 1992.

Lystra, Karen. *Searching the Heart: Women, Men, and Romantic Love in Nineteenth-Century America.* New York: Oxford University Press, 1989.

Mahoney, Deirdre Marie. "Burn as Soon as Read: Love and Negotiation in the Correspondence of Isabel Mantz and John Dice Johnson." Ph.D. diss., University of Arizona, 1995.

Miller, Susan. *Assuming the Positions: Cultural Pedagogy and the Politics of Commonplace Writing.* Pittsburgh: University of Pittsburgh Press, 1998.

Rose, Jane E. "Conduct Books for Women, 1830–1860: A Rationale for Women's Conduct and Domestic Role in America." In *Nineteenth-Century Women Learn to Write,* edited by Catherine Hobbs. Charlottesville: University Press of Virginia, 1995, 37–58.

Rothman, Ellen K. *Hands and Hearts: A History of Courtship in America.* Cambridge, Mass.: Harvard University Press, 1987.

Schultz, Lucille M. "Letter-Writing Instruction in 19th-Century Schools in the United States." In *Letter Writing as a Social Practice.* Edited by David Barton and Nigel Hall. Amsterdam: John Benjamins, 2000, 109–30.

Bibliographies

Bobbitt, Mary Reed. *A Bibliography of Etiquette Books Published in America before 1900.* New York: New York Public Library, 1947.

Carré, Jacques. *The Crisis of Courtesy: Studies in the Conduct-Book in Britain, 1600–1900.* Edited by Jacques Carré. Leiden: E. J. Brill, 1994.

Heltzel, Virgil B. *A Check List of Courtesy Books in the Newberry Library.* Chicago: Newberry Library, 1942.

Mehaffey, Karen Rae. *Victorian American Women, 1840–1880: An Annotated Bibliography.* New York: Garland, 1992.

Newton, Sarah E. *Learning to Behave: A Guide to American Conduct Books before 1900.* Westport, Conn.: Greenwood Press, 1994.

Schlesinger, Arthur M. *Learning How to Behave: A Historical Study of American Etiquette Books.* New York: Cooper Square Publishers, 1968.

Weiss, Harry B. *American Letter Writers: 1698–1943.* New York: New York Public Library, 1945.

Appendix G

BIBLIOGRAPHY OF TWENTIETH-CENTURY
LETTER-WRITING MANUALS

Deirdre M. Mahoney

This bibliography includes primary sources and secondary scholarship. Primary letter-writing texts proliferated during the twentieth century as Americans continued to demonstrate a collective desire to compose "Cultivated" and "Correct" letters on the job and in their private and public lives. The compilation of sources listed here represents an introductory rather than comprehensive bibliographic record and includes a brief listing of software formularies introduced to the marketplace in the last few years of the twentieth century. Many of the sources remain readily accessible through city, county, and academic libraries, as well as retail booksellers.

Primary Sources

Commercial Letter-Writing Instruction

Baugh, L. Sue, Maridell Fryar, and David A. Thomas. *How to Write First-Class Business Correspondence: The Handbook for Business Writing.* Lincolnwood, Ill.: NTC Publishing Group, 1995.

Bertelson, Catherine L. and Charles L. Guatney. "Taking the Pain out of Business Letter Writing." *Balance Sheet* 70 (1989): 7–9.

Bond, Alan J. *Over 300 Successful Business Letters for All Occasions.* Hauppauge, N.Y.: Barrons Educational, 1998.

Booher, Dianna Daniels. *Letter Perfect: A Handbook of Model Letters for the Busy Executive.* Lexington, Mass.: Lexington Books, 1988.

Braun, Carl F. *Letter Writing in Action: A Group of Letters to an Industrial Organization.* Alhambra, Calif.: C. F. Braun, 1947.

Brusaw, Charles T., Gerald J. Alred, and Walter E. Oliu. *The Business Writer's Handbook.* 5th ed. New York: St. Martin's, 1997.

Cay, Vernon. *Supreme Letter Writer: A Guide to Social and Business Correspondence with Forms of Addressing Important Personages.* New York: G. Sully and Co., 1928.

Clapp, John Mantle. *Personal Letters in Business: A Guide to Correct Usage.* New York: The Ronald Press Co., 1935.

Cross, Wilbur. *Action Letters for Small Business Owners.* New York: Wiley, 1991.

Crowther, Mary Owens. *How to Write Letters: A Complete Guide to Correct Business and Personal Correspondence.* Garden City, N.Y.: Doubleday, Page, 1922.

Davidson, Emil Bayard. *The Master Letter Writer: The Science of Successful Letter Writing, Including Three Hundred Master Business Letters.* Rev. 3rd ed. New York: Harper & Brothers, 1930.

DeVries, Mary A. *The Elements of Correspondence: How to Express Yourself Clearly, Persuasively, and Eloquently in Your Personal and Business Writing.* New York: Macmillan, 1994.

———. *Internationally Yours: Writing and Communicating Successfully in Today's Global Marketplace.* Boston: Houghton Mifflin, 1994.

Drach, Harvey E. *American Business Writing.* New York: American Book Co., 1959.

Ellenbogen, Abraham. *Letter Perfect: A Business Person's Guide to More Effective Correspondence.* Rev. and updated ed. of *The Collier Quick and Easy Guide to Business Letter Writing.* New York: Collier Books, 1978.

Frailey, L. E. *Handbook of Business Letters.* Rev. ed. Englewood Cliffs, N.J.: Prentice-Hall, 1965.

Fruehling, Rosemary T., and N. B. Oldham. *Write to the Point! Letters, Memos, and Reports That Get Results.* New York: McGraw-Hill, 1988.

Hager, Hubert Adonley, Marie M. Stewart, and E. Lillian Hutchinson. *Business Letter Writing.* New York: Gregg Publishing Division, McGraw-Hill, 1953.

Holberg, Andrea, ed. *Forms of Address: A Guide for Business and Social Use.* Houston: Rice University Press, in association with the Houston Protocol Alliance, 1994.

Keithley, Erwin M., Marie E. Flatley, and Philip J. Schreiner. *Manual of Style for Business Letters, Memos & Reports.* 4th ed. Cincinnati: South-Western Publishing Co., 1989.

Lewis, Leslie Llewellyn, and Marilyn French. *Correspondence Manual and Transcribers' Handbook.* Chicago: Dartnell Corp., 1960.

Meyer, Harold E. *Lifetime Encyclopedia of Letters.* Revised and expanded. Paramus, N.J.: Prentice Hall, 1992.

Riebel, John P. *How to Write Reports, Papers, Theses, Articles.* New York: Arco, 1972.

Romen, Kenneth, and Joel Raphaelson. *Writing That Works: How to Write Memos, Letters, Reports, Speeches, Resumes, and Other Papers That Say What You Mean, and Get Things Done.* New York: Harper and Row, 1981.

Rosenthal, Irving, and Harry W. Rudman, eds. *Business Letter Writing Made Simple.* Rev. ed. Garden City, N.Y.: Doubleday, 1968.

Seglin, Jeffrey L. *The AMA Handbook of Business Letters.* New York: American Management Association, 1989.

———. *The Banker's Handbook of Letters and Letter Writing: A Complete Collection of Time-Saving Letters That Work.* Chicago: Probus, 1992.

Shidle, Norman Glass. *The Art of Successful Communication: Business and Personal Achievement through Written Communication.* New York: McGraw-Hill, 1965.

Shurter, Robert L. *Effective Letters in Business.* 2nd ed. New York: McGraw-Hill, 1954.

Taylor, John Renford, and Elise Durham Bigger. *The President's Letter Book.* Englewood Cliffs, N.J.: Prentice-Hall, 1987.

Thomsett, Michael C. *The Little Black Book of Business Letters.* New York: American Management Association, 1988.

Vernon, Cay. *Supreme Letter Writer: A Guide to Social and Business Correspondence with Forms of Addressing Important Personages.* New York: G. Sully and Co., 1928.

Watson, Lillian. *Standard Book of Letter Writing and Correct Social Forms*. Englewood Cliffs, N.J.: Prentice-Hall, 1958.

Webster's Guide to Business Correspondence. Springfield, Mass.: Merriam-Webster, 1988.

Wilkinson, Clyde Winfield, Peter B. Clarke, and Dorothy C. Wilkinson. *Communicating through Letters and Reports*. 8th ed. Homewood, Ill.: R. D. Irwin, 1983.

"Writing Effective Business Letters." *Pest Control Technology* 18 (1990): 44–47.

Letter-Writing Instruction in Genealogy Studies

Forbes, Jill. "The Pleasures of Genealogical Letter Writing." *Families* 34 (1995): 108.

"Genealogical Letter Writing Etiquette." *Idaho Genealogical Society Quarterly* 39 (1996): 21–22.

"Research Tips: How to Get Better Results from Your Letter Writing." *Tracer* 12 (1991): 40–52.

Letter-Writing Instruction for Children and Young Adults

Bailly, Sharon. *Pass It On! All about Notes, from Secret Codes and Special Inks to Fancy Folds and Dead Man's Drops*. Brookfield, Conn.: Millbrook Press, 1995.

Barnes, Emile. *A Little Book of Manners*. Eugene, Oreg.: Harvest House, 1998.

Center, Stella S., and L. B. Saul. *A Book of Letters for Young People*. New York: Century Co., 1924.

Harding, Maude Burbank. *The Children's Own Book of Letters and Stories*. Boston: Marshall Jones Co., 1926.

Holyoke, Nancy. *Oops! The Manners Guide for Girls*. American Girl Library. Middleton, Wisconsin: Pleasant Co., 1997.

Jacobson, Helen, and Florence Mischel. *The First Book of Letter Writing*. New York: Franklin Watts, 1957.

Leedy, Loreen. *Messages in the Mailbox: How to Write a Letter*. New York: Holiday House, 1991.

Tchudi, Susan, and Steven Tchudi. *The Young Writer's Handbook*. New York: Scribner's, 1984.

Sales and Marketing Letter-Writing Instruction

Collier, Robert. *The Robert Collier Letter Book*. Englewood Cliffs, N.J.: Prentice-Hall, 1950.

Gilleland, Karen, and Margaret Coel. *450 Best Sales Letters for Every Selling Situation*. Englewood Cliffs, N.J.: Prentice Hall, 1991.

Hemmings, Robert L. "Think Before You Write." *Fund Raising Management* 20 (1990): 23–25.

Hodgson, Richard S. *The Dartnell Direct Mail and Mail Order Handbook*. 3rd. ed. Chicago: Dartnell Corporation, 1980.

Keller, Thomas K. "Direct Mail/Copywriting; Lamentations and Letter Writing." *Fund Raising Management* 27 (1997): 24–27.

Lewis, Hershell Gordon. *Direct Marketing Strategies and Tactics*. Chicago: Dartnell Co., 1992.

———. "What's Wrong with This Letter? Tips for Writing a Sale Letter That Really Sings." *Executive Female* 20 (1997): 27–29.

"Lost Art of Letter Writing." *Folio: The Magazine for Magazine Management* 23 (1994): 41–44.

Ramundo, Michael. *The Complete Customer Service Model Letter & Memo Book.* Englewood Cliffs, N.J.: Prentice Hall, 1995.

Wachtel, George. "How to Write an Effective Sales Letter." *Bank Marketing* 28 (1996): 109–16.

———. "How to Write an Effective Sales Letter, Part II." *Bank Marketing* 28 (1996): 17–29.

Software Formularies

Business Resource Kit. CD-ROM. New York: Macmillan Digital Publishing, 1997.

Lifetime Encyclopedia of Letters. CD-ROM. Santa Monica, Calif.: Streetwise Software, 1997.

2001 Sales and Marketing Letters. CD-ROM. Austin, Tex.: Model Office, 1998.

Foreign Language Letter-Writing Instruction

Cheron, Jeanne, and Eunice Mogan Schenck. *A Handbook of French Correspondence.* New York: Oxford University Press, 1924.

Elkus, Sarah. *Simple Letters for Foreign Born Adults.* New York: C. Scribner's Sons, 1933.

Encyclopedia of Business Letters in Four Languages. Diccionario de cartas comerciales en cuatro idiomas. Lexique des lettres commerciales en quatre langues. Lexikon der Geschaftsbriefe in vier Sprachen. New York: Arco, 1972.

Fuentes, Ventura, and Alfred Elias. *Manual de correspondencia: With Exercises, Notes, and Vocabulary.* New York: Macmillan Co., 1920.

Glinert, Lewis, ed. *Mamme Dear: A Turn-of-the-Century Collection of Model Yiddish Letters.* Northvale, N.J.: Jason Aronson, 1997.

Gordon, Ian. *Practical Letter-Writing, with Exercises and Worked Examples.* London: Heinemann, 1967.

Jackson, Mary H. *Guide to Correspondence in Spanish: A Practical Guide to Social and Commercial Correspondence.* Rev. ed. Lincolnwood, Ill.: Passport Books, 1986.

Oudot, Simone. *Guide to Correspondence in French: A Practical Guide to Social and Commercial Correspondence.* Lincolnwood, Ill.: Passport Books, 1985.

Pomier, Natalie, ed. *French Correspondence.* New York: Oxford University Press, 1997.

Watts, Francoise. "The Art of French Business Letter Writing: Our Modern Form of 'Preciosite.'" *Foreign Language Annals* 26 (1993): 180.

Job Search Letter-Writing Instruction

Farr, J. Michael. *The Quick Resume and Cover Letter Book.* Indianapolis: JIST Works, 1994.

Frank, William S. *200 Letters for Job Hunters.* Rev. ed. Berkeley: Ten Speed Press, 1993.

Hansen, Katherine, and Randall S. Hansen. *Dynamic Cover Letters: How to Sell Yourself to an Employer by Writing a Letter That Will Get Your Resume Read, Get You an Interview, and Get You a Job!* Rev. ed. Berkeley: Ten Speed Press, 1995.

McKinney Anne, ed. *Resumes and Cover Letters That Have Worked.* Fayetteville, N.C.: Prep Publishing, 1996.

Savino, Carl S., and Ronald L. Krannich. *Resumes and Job Search Letters for Transitional Military Personnel.* Manassas Park, Va.: Impact Publications, 1997.

Showalter, English. *The MLA Guide to the Job Search.* New York: Modern Language Association, 1996.

Yate, Martin. *Cover Letters That Knock 'Em Dead.* Holbrook, Mass.: Adams Publishing, 1995.

Love-Letter Writing Instruction

Book of Love Letters and How to Write Them for Ladies and Gentlemen. Containing Complete Instructions Relative to Writing Letters on Love Courtship and Marriage. New York: Wehman Brothers, 1900.

Holtcamp, Brian, and Paula Hilton. *When Romeo Wrote Juliet: Your Inspirational Guide to the Art of Writing Love Letters.* Sunnyvale, Calif.: Stylus, 1994.

Lovric, Michelle. *How to Write Love Letters.* New York: Marlowe and Co., 1995.

Movesian, Ara John. *Pearls of Love: How to Write Love Letters and Love Poems.* Fresno, Calif.: Electric Press, 1993.

Rosenberg, Henrietta. *How to Write Love Letters.* New York: Stravon, 1943.

Secretarial Letter-Writing Instruction

Center, Stella Stewart. *A Course in Secretarial Correspondence.* New York: Columbia University, 1921.

DeVries, Mary A. *The Prentice Hall Complete Book of Model Letters, Memos, and Forms for Secretaries.* Englewood Cliffs, N.J.: Prentice Hall, 1993.

Doris, Lillian, and Besse May Miller. *Complete Secretary's Handbook.* 4th ed. rev. by Mary A. De Vries. Englewood Cliffs, N.J.: Prentice-Hall, 1977.

Merriam-Webster, Inc. *Merriam-Webster's Secretarial Handbook.* Springfield, Mass.: Merriam Webster, 1993.

Taintor, Sarah Augusta. *The Secretary's Handbook: A Manual of Correct Usage.* New York: Mcmillan Co., 1930.

Whalen, Doris H. *The Secretary's Handbook.* 3rd ed. New York: Harcourt Brace Jovanovich, 1978.

Noncommercial Letter-Writing Instruction

Baker, Josephine. *The Art of Social Letter Writing.* Chicago: Correct English Publishing Co., 1909.

Baugh, Sue L. *Handbook for Practical Letter Writing.* Lincolnwood, Ill.: National Textbook Co., 1991.

Brown, Charles W. *Brown's Complete Letter-Writer for Ladies and Gentlemen; Contains Full Directions for Business Correspondence, Commercial Forms, Wills, Notes, Drafts . . . , Etc.* Chicago: Henneberry, 1901.

Carr, Edwin Hamlin. *Putnam's Phrase Book: An Aid to Social Letter Writing and to Ready and Effective Conversation.* New York: G. P. Putnam's Sons, 1919.

Case, Carleton Britton. *Social Letters and Etiquette of Correspondence.* Chicago: Shrewesbury, 1924.

Chambers, Alfred B. *The New Standard Business and Social Letter-Writer; Business, Family and Social Correspondence, Refined Love-Letters, Marriage Proposals, Acceptances and Refusals, Etiquette, Synonyms, Legal Forms, Etc.* Chicago: Laird & Lee, 1921.

Cody, Shervin. *Success in Letter Writing, Business and Social.* Chicago: A. C. McClurg & Co., 1906.

Cramp, Helen. *Letter Writing, Business and Social: A Manual on the Craft of Letter Writing with Instructions and Specimen Letters.* Philadelphia: J. C. Winston Co., 1914.

Crane & Co. Paper Makers. Retail-store pamphlet. Dolton, Mass.: Crane & Co., Inc., 1997.

De Lancey, Caroline. *A Desk Book on Correct Social Correspondence and the Etiquette of Social Stationery.* New York: Crane & Pike Co., 1922.

Eaton, Crane & Pike Co. *A Desk Book on the Etiquette of Letter Writing, and Social Correspondence in General.* New York: Eaton, Crane & Pike Company, 1927.

Gavit, Helen. *The Etiquette of Correspondence: Being Illustrations and Suggestions as to the Proper Form in Present Usage of Social, Club, Diplomatic, Military, and Business Letters, with Information on Heraldic Devices, Monograms, and Engraved Addresses.* New York: A. Wessels, 1900.

Isaacs, Florence. *Just a Note to Say . . . : The Perfect Words for Every Occasion.* New York: Clarkson Potter, 1996.

Lucas, Edward V. *The Second Post: A Companion to "The Gentlest Art."* New York: Macmillan, 1910.

McCarthy, Margaret. *Letter Writing Made Easy!* Vol 2. Santa Monica, Calif.: Santa Monica Press, 1998.

Meade, Marianne. *How to Write Good Social Letters, a Modern Guide to Good Form.* Cleveland: World Syndicate Publishing Co., 1938.

Post, Emily. *The Letters We Write.* Holyoke, Mass.: White & Wyckoff, 1935.

Sheff, Alexander L. *How to Write Letters for All Occasions.* New York: New Home Library, 1942.

Strong, Edward Jefferson. *Standard Up-to-Date Practical Letter Writer: A Comprehensive and Practical Guide to Correspondence, Showing the Structure, Composition, Formalities and Uses of the Various Kinds of Letters, Notes, and Cards.* Chicago: Charles C. Thompson Co., 1912.

Thornburgh, Laura. [pseud.] *The Etiquette of Letter Writing.* New York: Barse & Hopkins, 1924.

Tietz, Robert, and Elaine Tietz. *Complete Book of Effective Personal Letters.* Englewood Cliffs, N.J.: Prentice Hall, 1984.

Van de Water, Virginia. *Present Day Etiquette, Including Social Forms.* New York: A. L. Burt, 1924.

Watson, Lillian Eichler. *Lillian Eichler Watson's Standard Book of Letter Writing.* New York: Prentice-Hall, 1948.

Westlake, James Willis. *How to Write Letters: A Manual of Correspondence, Showing the Correct Structure, Composition, Punctuation, Formalities and Uses of the Various Kinds of Letters, Notes, and Cards.* Philadelphia: C. Sower Co., 1901.

Williams, Jennifer, ed. *The Pleasures of Staying in Touch: Writing Memorable Letters.* New York: Hearst Books, 1998.

Miscellaneous

Aspen Reference Group. *The Aspen Guide to Effective Health Care Correspondence.* Gaithersburg, Md.: Aspen Publishers, 1993.

Chernow, Fred B., and Carol Chernow. *Elementary Principal's Model Letter Kit: With Reproducible Illustrations to Enhance Your Messages!* West Nyack, N.Y.: Parker, 1988.

Cowper, D. M., and S. W. Lenton. "Letter Writing to Parents Following Paediatric Outpatient Consultation: A Survey of Parent and GP Views." *Child: Care, Health and Development* 22 (1996): 303–10.

Frantzich, Stephen E. *Write Your Congressman: Constituent Communications and Representation.* New York: Praeger, 1986.

Gould, Alan. "Letter-Writing." *Quadrant* 34 (1990): 18–21.

Hitchner, Kenneth W., Anne Tifft-Hitchner, and E. Andre Apostol. *School Counselor's Letter Book.* West Nyack, N.Y.: Center for Applied Research in Education, 1991.

Holt, Lucius Hudson, ed. *Military Correspondence, Reports and Orders.* Poughkeepsie: Clinton Press, 1920.

Lawler, Rick. *How to Write World Leaders.* Sacramento, Calif.: MinRef Press, 1990.

"Letter Writing." *Practising Administrator* 14 (1992): 23–27.

Mamchak, P. Susan, and Steven R. Mamchak. *Encyclopedia of School Letters.* West Nyack, N.Y.: Parker Publishing, 1979.

Patriotic Publishers. *What to Write and What Not to Write to Him.* New York: Patriotic Publishers, 1943.

Reeder, Allen G. *Letter Writing in Wartime, "How and What to Write About."* New York: Books, Inc., 1943.

United States Veterans Administration. *Feelings, the Way to Better Letter Writing.* Washington, D.C.: Veterans Administration, Office of Assistant Administrator for Personnel, 1978.

Letter-Writing Instruction Presented in Etiquette and Conduct-Related Books

Baldridge, Letitia. *Letitia Baldridge's Complete Guide to Executive Manners.* New York: Rawson Associates, 1985.

Cole, Hariette. *How to Be: Contemporary Etiquette for African Americans.* New York: Simon and Schuster, 1999.

Diescher, Victor H. *The Book of Good Manners: A Guide to Polite Usage for All Social Functions.* New York: Social Culture Publications, 1923.

Eichler, Lillian. *The New Book of Etiquette.* New York: Doubleday, 1924.

Feinberg, Steven L, ed. *Crane's Blue Book of Stationery: The Styles and Etiquette of Letters, Notes and Invitations.* New York: Doubleday, 1989.

———. *Crane's Wedding Blue Book: The Styles and Etiquette of Announcements, Invitations and Other Correspondence.* New York: Simon and Schuster, 1993.

Ford, Charlotte. *Etiquette: Charlotte Ford's Guide to Modern Manners.* New York: Clarkson N. Potter, Inc., 1988.

Glassman, Audrey. *Can I Fax a Thank You Note and Other Modern Dilemmas.* New York: Berkley Publishers Group, 1998.

Lane, Harriet. *The Book of Culture.* New York: Social Culture Publications, 1922.

Martin, Judith. *Miss Manners' Basic Training: Communication.* New York: Crown Publishers, 1997.

———. *Miss Manners' Guide for the Turn-of-the-Millennium.* New York: Pharos Books, 1989.

Mitchell, Mary, with John Corr. *The Complete Idiot's Guide to Etiquette.* New York: Alpha Books, 1996.

Post, Peggy. *Emily Post's Etiquette.* 16th ed. New York: HarperCollins, 1997.

Roosevelt, Eleanor. *Book of Common Etiquette.* New York: Macmillan, 1962.

Sangster, Margaret E. *Winsome Womanhood.* New York: Fleming H. Revell Co., 1900.

Stoddard, Alexandra. *Gift of a Letter.* New York: Avon, 1990.

Tuckerman, Nancy, and Nancy Dunnan. *The Amy Vanderbilt Complete Book of Etiquette.* Rewritten and updated. New York: Doubleday, 1995.

Wilson, Margery. *Charm.* Revised and enlarged. New York: Frederick A. Stokes Co., 1934.

Secondary Sources

Decker, William Merrill. *Epistolary Practices: Letter Writing in America before Telecommunication.* Chapel Hill: University of North Carolina Press, 1998.

"401 Great Letters for Windows." *Accounting Technology* 11 (1995): 53–54.

Lown, Naomi, and Barbara Britton. "Engaging Families through the Letter Writing Technique." *Journal of Strategic and Systemic Therapies* 10 (1991): 43–48.

Offner, Rose. *Letters from the Soul: Unsent Letters and Stories for Spiritual Growth.* Salt Lake City: Gibbs Smith Publisher, 1997.

Perpager Rasmussen, Peder, and Karl Tomm. "Guided Letter Writing: A Long Brief Therapy Method Whereby Clients Carry Out Their Own Treatment." *Journal of Strategic and Systemic Therapies* 11 (1992): 1–18.

Saintsbury, George. *A Letter Book, Selected with an Introduction on the History and Art of Letter-Writing.* 4th ed. London: G. Bell and Sons; New York: Harcourt, Brace, 1922.

United States Postal Service. *All about Letters.* Washington, D.C., 1979.

Letter-Writing Pedagogical

Anderson, Linda Syverson. "Letters That Make a Difference." *Teaching Pre-K–8* 23 (May): 44–45.

Bright, George W., George D. Hunsberger, and George D. Labercane. "Electronic Letter Writing between Children and Pre-service Teachers: Results, Reflections, and Recommendations." *Computers in the Schools* 5 (1998): 285, passim.

Burns, M. Susan., and Renee Casbergue. "Parent-Child Interaction in a Letter-writing Context." *Journal of Reading Behavior* 24 (1992): 289–312.

Chin, Susan Ho. "Instructional Note. The ABC Approach to Teaching Letter Writing." *Teaching English in the Two-Year College* 21 (1994): 306–8.

Cody, Shervin. *Teaching Letter Writing as a Composition Art: A Teacher's Manual for "Interesting Letters."* New York: Gregg Publishing, 1934.

Dye, Charity. *Letters and Letter Writing as Means to the Study and Practice of English Composition.* Indianapolis: Bobbs-Merrill Co., 1903.

Flack, Jerry. "Letter Writing: A Great Way to Explore Whole Language." *Teaching Pre-K–8* 25 (1995): 42–45.

Frye, Bob. "Bringing Life to Writers and Writing to Life. Artful Compositions, Corder's 'Laws of Composition,' and the Weekly Letter: Two Approaches to Teaching Invention and Arrangement in Freshman Composition." *Journal of Teaching Writing* 8 (1989): 1–14.

Goheen, Craig. "All It Takes Is a Three-Paragraph Letter." *Quarterly of the National Writing Project* 14 (1992): 17–18.

Greene, Jennifer E. *The Nature and Development of Letter Writing in Hispanic and Anglo Children Using a School-based Postal System.* Montebello, Calif.: Montebello Unified School District, 1983.

Linse, Caroline T. *The Treasured Mailbox: How to Use Authentic Correspondence with Children, K-6.* Portsmouth, N.H.: Heinemann, 1997.

"The Middle View/Letter Writing: Link from Individuals to the Community." *English Journal* 80 (1991): 29.

Otfinoski, Steve, and Steven Otfinoski. *Putting It in Writing. Schoolastic Guides.* New York: Schoolastic, 1994.

Vetter, R. "Discourses across Literacies: Personal Letter Writing in a Tuvaluan Context." *Language and Education* 5 (1991): 125–46.

Bibliographies

Hodges, Deborah Robertson. *Etiquette: An Annotated Bibliography of Literature Published in English in the United States, 1900 through 1987.* Jefferson, N.C.: McFarland & Co., 1989.

Weiss, Harry B. *American Letter Writers: 1698–1943.* New York: New York Public Library, 1945.

Contributors

SUZANNE ABRAM earned her doctorate in comparative literature from Indiana University. She also holds degrees in law, Latin, philosophy, and English. She has taught at Indiana University Southeast and at Auburn University, and she writes in the areas of late antiquity, medieval epistolography, and legal theory.

GIDEON BURTON is assistant professor of English at Brigham Young University. He received his PhD from University of Southern California. He has presented numerous papers on Renaissance rhetoric at conferences in North America and Europe.

MARTIN CAMARGO is professor and chair of English at the University of Illinois at Urbana-Champaign. The recipient of fellowships from the American Council of Learned Societies, the National Endowment for the Humanities, the Fulbright Foundation, and the Alexander von Humboldt Foundation, he has published several books and numerous articles dealing with medieval English literature and medieval rhetoric. His current projects include a history of writing instruction in medieval Oxford and a critical edition and translation of the rhetorical treatise *Tria sunt*.

JOHN T. GAGE is the author of *In the Arresting Eye: The Rhetoric of Imagism,* and *The Shape of Reason: Argumentative Writing in College,* as well as numerous articles on classical rhetoric, composition theory, and modern poetry. At the University of Oregon, he has been English department head and director of composition and now serves as director of the Center for Teaching Writing.

LAWRENCE D. GREEN is professor of English at the University of Southern California. He received his PhD from the University of California, Berkeley. He has published widely on the history of rhetoric, both in Europe and in the United States, focusing on the Renaissance reception of Greek and Latin rhetoric and philosophy. His books include *John Rainolds's Oxford Lectures on Aristotle's "Rhetoric,"* and the *Renaissance Rhetoric Short-Title Catalogue 1460–1700* (with James F. Murphy). He is president of the International Society for the History of Rhetoric.

JUDITH RICE HENDERSON, professor of English at the University of Saskatchewan, recently completed a term as associate dean of arts and science. She has published numerous articles on Renaissance epistolography. She founded the Canadian Society for the Study of Rhetoric and has served as president of the International Society for the History of Rhetoric (1995–1997) and the Canadian Society for Renaissance Studies (1998–2000).

DEIRDRE M. MAHONEY is an instructor at Northwestern Michigan College. Her work on letter writing grows out of her doctoral dissertation, "'Burn as Soon as Read': Love and Negotiation in the Correspondence of Isabel Mantz and John Dice Johnson," a study that examines antebellum courtship rituals and literacy practices for women. She has presented her scholarship at numerous national and local conferences and has published articles on the history of composition and basic writing.

LINDA C. MITCHELL, professor of English at San José State University, is author of *Grammar Wars: Language as Cultural Battleground in 17th and 18th Century England* and coeditor with Susan Green of *The Cultural History of Letter Writing.* She has published articles in the *Huntington Library Quarterly, International Journal of Lexicography, Handbook of World Englishes,* and *Studies in Early Modern Philosophy.*

W. WEBSTER NEWBOLD is associate professor of English at Ball State University, in Muncie, Indiana, where he teaches the history of rhetoric and literacy in the graduate program, along with technological applications in teaching. He received his M.A. and PhD from the Shakespeare Institute, University of Birmingham, and has published a critical edition of Thomas Wright's *The Passions of the Mind* (1604).

CAROL POSTER, English Department, York University, has published widely on ancient rhetoric and philosophy.

MALCOLM RICHARDSON is Dr. J. F. Taylor Professor of English at Louisiana State University, where he has taught since 1986. His most recent book is *The English Chancery Under Henry V* (1999), which continues his research interest writing and culture in late medieval England.

ROBERT G. SULLIVAN, PhD, University of Maryland, is associate professor in the Department of Speech Communication at Ithaca College. He has published widely on the Greco-Roman rhetorical tradition and on the contemporary problems of propaganda and communication ethics.

RICHARD UTZ is professor of English at the University of Northern Iowa. His publications include *Literarischer Nominalismus im Spaetmittelalter* (1990), *Literary Nominalism and the Rereading of Late Medieval Texts* (1995), *Nominalism and Literary Discourse* (1997), *Medievalism in the Modern World* (1998), *Chaucer and the Discourse of German Philology* (2002), and *Speculum Sermonis* (2005).

JOYCE R. WALKER received her PhD in 2003 from the Center for Writing Studies at the University of Illinois. She is currently assistant professor at the University of South Florida St. Petersburg. Her dissertation project, "Standing at the End of a Road: Death and the Construction of Cyborg Relationships," won the Hugh Burns Best Dissertation Award at the Computers & Writing Conference in 2004. Currently she is working on two edited collections, *Digital Tools in Composition Studies,* with Ollie Oviedo and Byron Hawk, and *Digital Contexts: Studies of Online Research and Citation,* with James Purdy, Doug Eyman, and Colleen Reilly.